KT-170-478

PERSONAL INJURY DAMAGES IN SCOTLAND

By The Same Author

Divorce in the Sheriff Court (5th ed., 1997)
Style Writs for the Sheriff Court (2nd ed., 1994)

PERSONAL INJURY DAMAGES IN SCOTLAND

An exposition of the law governing the calculation of damages in personal injury cases

by

S. A. Bennett, LLB
Advocate

Barnstoneworth Press
1999

First published, 1999

ISBN 0 9534152 0 1

Published by S. A. Bennett, Advocate, Advocates' Library, Parliament House, Edinburgh EH1 1RF under the name 'Barnstoneworth Press'.

ACKNOWLEDGEMENTS

The Ogden Tables in Appendix I and the Life Tables in Appendix II are Crown copyright items and are reproduced with the kind permission of the Controller of Her Majesty's Stationery Office.

The PNBA Tables in Appendix I are reproduced with the kind permission of the Professional Negligence Bar Association, London.

The Guidelines for the Assessment of General Damages in Personal Injury Cases in Appendix VII are reproduced with the kind permission of the Judicial Studies Board, London and Blackstone Press Limited, London.

I am indebted to the Lord Clyde for taking the time and trouble to write the Foreword for this book. I am also grateful to Matthew Clarke, Q.C. and my sister Inga for their assistance and support. Elizabeth Thompson kindly prepared the Tables of Cases and Statutes.

Edinburgh — Siggi Bennett

FOREWORD

by

The Right Honourable The Lord Clyde, P.C.,
Lord of Appeal in Ordinary

The last few decades of the development of the law have seen a growing sophistication in the assessment of damages for personal injury. There is now available not only an accumulation of precedent but also summaries and guidelines to assist in the difficult task of identifying the proper figure for reasonable compensation for pain and suffering. Until relatively recently there has been little detailed analysis to help in the assessment of claims for pecuniary loss. But the use of elaborate tables now enables some more exact precision in the difficult task of calculating future continuing losses. The broad axe which was once considered sufficient to achieve a rough approximation has now been honed to a sharper tool whereby claims for damages for personal injury can be evaluated with greater accuracy.

All this contributes to secure not only that awards are fair as between pursuers and defenders, but also between pursuers and pursuers in comparable cases. Moreover the recognition in particular of standard techniques for calculating economic heads of claim should enable disputes on quantification to be minimised, the cost of litigation to be reduced, and settlements to be facilitated. But as the quantity and intricacy of the source material grows it is all the more important to have it readily accessible in a convenient form.

Mr Bennett is to be congratulated for his compilation of the material and his presentation of the current state of the law and practice in an area which continues to develop on both sides of the Border. A work such as the present which combines commentary on the subject with a substantial corpus of source material should constitute a valuable aid to the practitioner. I wish it well.

Clyde

CONTENTS

Acknowledgements v
Foreword vii
Table of Cases xxv
Table of Statutes xxxvii
Table of Rules of the Court of Session xxxix
Table of Ordinary Cause Rules xxxix

I. REMEDIES

1. **LUMP SUM AWARDS** 3
Final decrees for damages 3
Orders for interim payment of damages 12

2. **CONSENT ORDERS FOR PERIODICAL PAYMENTS** 16

3. **PROVISIONAL DAMAGES FOR PERSONAL INJURIES** 22
Awards of provisional damages 22
Further awards of damages 25

4. **INTEREST ON DAMAGES** 26

II. HEADS OF CLAIM FOR PERSONAL INJURIES

5. **SOLATIUM** 31

6. **LOSS OF EARNINGS AND PENSION RIGHTS** 36
Loss of earnings 36
Loss of pension rights 46

7. **OUTLAYS AND EXPENSES** 49

8. **INJURED PERSON'S SERVICES** 56
Necessary services 56
Personal services 61

III. HEADS OF CLAIM FOR DEATH OF RELATIVE

9. LOSS OF SOCIETY 67

10. LOSS OF SUPPORT 73

11. FUNERAL EXPENSES 80

12. DECEASED PERSON'S SERVICES 83

APPENDICES

Appendix I: **Tables of Multipliers** 89
A. Ogden Tables 89
Explanatory Notes, with Appendices A, B and C 89
1, Multipliers for Pecuniary Loss for Life (Males) (Historic Mortality) 108
2. Multipliers for Pecuniary Loss for Life (Females) (H M) 110
3. Multipliers for Loss of Earnings to Pension Age 65 (Males) (H M) 112
4. Multipliers for Loss of Earnings to Pension Age 65 (Females) (H M) 113
5. Multipliers for Loss of Earnings to Pension Age 60 (Males) (H M) 114
6. Multipliers for Loss of Earnings to Pension Age 60 (Females) (H M) 115
7. Multipliers for Loss of Pension Commencing Age 65 (Males) (H M) 116
8. Multipliers for Loss of Pension Commencing Age 65 (Females) (H M) 118
9. Multipliers for Loss of Pension Commencing Age 60 (Males) (H M) 120
10. Multipliers for Loss of Pension Commencing Age 60 (Females) (H M) 122
11. Multipliers for Pecuniary Loss for Life (Males) (Projected Mortality) 124
12. Multipliers for Pecuniary Loss for Life (Females) (P M) 126
13. Multipliers for Loss of Earnings to Pension Age 65 (Males) (P M) 128
14. Multipliers for Loss of Earnings to Pension Age 65 (Females) (P M) 129

15. Multipliers for Loss of Earnings to Pension Age 60 (Males) (P M) 130
16. Multipliers for Loss of Earnings to Pension Age 60 (Females) (P M) 131
17. Multipliers for Loss of Pension Commencing Age 65 (Males) (P M) 132
18. Multipliers for Loss of Pension Commencing Age 65 (Females) (P M) 134
19. Multipliers for Loss of Pension Commencing Age 60 (Males) (P M) 136
20. Multipliers for Loss of Pension Commencing Age 60 (Females) (P M) 138
21. Discounting Factors for Term Certain 140
22. Multipliers for Pecuniary Loss for Term Certain 141

Actuarial Formulae and Basis 142

B. PNBA Tables 143

Explanatory Notes 143

1. Multipliers for Future Single Payments 145
2. Multipliers for Annual Payments for Fixed Periods 147
3. Periodic Multipliers 149

Appendix II: **Life Tables** 163

Appendix III: **Model Structured Settlement** 166

Appendix IV: **Specimen Schedule of Damages (Recovery of Benefits)** 171

Appendix V: **Reported Cases Involving Pecuniary Claims** . 172

A. Personal Injury Cases 172

B. Death Cases 283

C. Index of Multipliers Selected 308

1. Loss of Future Earnings 308
2. Loss of Pension Rights 309
3. Future Outlays and Expenses 310
4. Future Necessary Services 310
5. Future Inability to Render Personal Services 310
6. Loss of Support 310
7. Loss of Deceased's Services 311

D. Index of Lump Sum Awards for Loss of Future Earnings 312

E. Index of Awards for Services 314

Appendix VI: **Recovery of Benefits Legislation** 317
- **A. The Social Security (Recovery of Benefits) Act 1997** 317
- **B. The Social Security (Recovery of Benefits) Regulations 1997** 339

Appendix VII: **Judicial Studies Board Guidelines** 349
- **Introduction** 349
- **1. Injuries Involving Paralysis** 352
  - (a) Quadriplegia 352
  - (b) Paraplegia 352
- **2. Head Injuries** 353
  - *(A) Brain Damage* 353
    - (a) Very Severe Brain Damage 353
    - (b) Moderately Severe Brain Damage 353
    - (c) Moderate Brain Damage 354
    - (d) Minor Brain Damage 355
  - *(B) Minor Head Injury* 355
  - *(C) Epilepsy* 356
    - (a) Established Grand Mal 356
    - (b) Established Petit Mal 356
    - (c) Other Epileptic Incidents 356
- **3. Psychiatric Damage** 357
  - *(A) Psychiatric Damage Generally* 357
    - (a) Severe Psychiatric Damage 357
    - (b) Moderately Severe Psychiatric Damage 358
    - (c) Moderate Psychiatric Damage 358
    - (d) Minor Psychiatric Damage 358
  - *(B) Post Traumatic Stress Disorder* 358
    - (a) Severe 359
    - (b) Moderately Severe 359
    - (c) Moderate 359
    - (d) Minor 359
- **4. Injuries Affecting the Senses** 360
  - *(A) Injuries Affecting Sight* 360
    - (a) Total Blindness and Deafness 360
    - (b) Total Blindness 360
    - (c) Loss of Sight in One Eye with Reduced Vision in the Remaining Eye . 360
    - (d) Total Loss of One Eye 360
    - (e) Complete Loss of Sight in One Eye .. 360
    - (f) Serious but Incomplete Loss of Vision in One Eye or Constant Double Vision 360
    - (g) Minor but Permanent Impairment of Vision in One Eye 361

(h) Minor Eye Injuries 361
(i) Transient Eye Injuries 361
(B) Deafness 361
(a) Total Deafness and Loss of Speech 362
(b) Total Deafness 362
(c) Total Loss of Hearing in One Ear 362
(d) Partial Hearing Loss/Tinnitus 362
(i) Severe Tinnitus/Hearing Loss 362
(ii) Moderate Tinnitus/Hearing Loss 362
(iii) Mild Tinnitus with Some Hearing Loss 363
(iv) Slight or Occasional Tinnitus with Slight Hearing Loss 363
(C) Impairment of Taste and Smell 363
(a) Total Loss of Taste and Smell 363
(b) Total Loss of Smell and Significant Loss of Taste 363
(c) Loss of Smell 363
(d) Loss of Taste 363
5. Injuries to Internal Organs 364
(A) Chest Injuries 364
(a) Total Removal of One Lung and/or Serious Heart Damage with Serious and Prolonged Pain and Suffering and Permanent Significant Scarring . 364
(b) Traumatic Injury to Chest, Lungs and/or Heart Causing Permanent Damage, Impairment of Function, Physical Disability and Reduction of Life Expectancy 364
(c) Damage to Chest and Lung Causing Some Continuing Disability 364
(d) Relatively Simple Injury Causing Some Permanent Damage to Tissue but no Significant Long Term Effect on Lung Function 365
(e) Toxic Fume/Smoke Inhalation, Leaving Some Residual Damage, not Serious Enough Permanently to Interfere with Lung Function 365
(f) Injuries Leading to Collapsed Lungs from which Full and Uncomplicated Recovery Made 365
(g) Fractures of Ribs, Causing Serious Pain and Disability over a Period of Weeks only . 365

(B) Lung Disease 365
(a) For Young Person with Serious Disability with Probability of Progressive Worsening Leading to Premature Death 365
(b) Mesothelioma, Lung Cancer or Asbestosis Causing Severe Impairment both of Function and of Quality of Life 365
(c) Disease Causing Significant and Worsening Lung Function and Impairment of Breathing, Prolonged and Frequent Coughing, Sleep Disturbance and Restriction of Physical Activity and Employment .. 366
(d) Breathing Difficulties (Short of Disabling Breathlessness) Requiring Inhaler Use, Lack of Tolerance of Smoky Environment, Significant Pleural Thickening and Uncertain Prognosis but Already Significant Effect on Social and Working Life ... 366
(e) Bronchitis and Wheezing; Pleural Plaques or Thickening not Causing Significant Symptoms; Little or no Serious or Permanent Effect on Working or Social Life; Varying Levels of Anxiety about the Future .. 366
(f) Some Slight Breathlessness with no effect on Working Life and Likelihood of Substantial and Permanent Recovery within a Few Years of Exposure or Aggravation of Existing Condition... 366
(g) Provisional Awards for Cases Otherwise within (f), or the Least Serious Cases within (e) where the Provisional Award Excludes any Risk of Malignancy or of Asbestosis 366
(h) Temporary Aggravation of Bronchitis or Other Chest Problems Resolving within Very Few Months............................. 366
(C) Asthma 367
(a) Severe and Permanently Disabling Asthma, Prolonged and Regular Coughing, Disturbance of Sleep, Severe Impairment of Physical Activity

and Enjoyment of Life and Gross Restriction of any Employment Prospects 367
(b) Chronic Asthma Causing Breathing Difficulties, Need for Inhaler Use and Restriction of Employment Prospects, with Uncertain Prognosis 367
(c) Bronchitic Wheezing, Affecting Working or Social Life, with the Likelihood of Substantial Recovery within a Few Years of Exposure 367
(d) Restrictive Airways Dysfunction Syndrome 367
(e) Mild Asthma, Bronchitis, Colds and Chest Problems Resolving in a Few Months 367
(D) Digestive System 367
(a) Severe Damage with Continuing Pain and Discomfort 367
(b) Serious Non-Penetrating Injury Causing Long Standing or Permanent Complications 368
(c) Penetrating Stab Wounds or Industrial Laceration or Serious Seat Belt Pressure Cases 368
(E) Reproductive System 368
Male:
(a) Impotence 368
(i) Total Impotence and Loss of Sexual Function and Sterility in Young Man 368
(ii) Impotence Likely to be Permanent in Middle Aged Man with Young Children 368
(b) Sterility (Surgical, Chemical and Disease Cases or Traumatic Injuries, often Aggravated by Scarring) 368
(i) Most Serious Cases 368
(ii) Bottom of Range: Much Older Man 368
(c) Uncomplicated Infertility Cases without Aggravating Features in Young Man Without Children 369
(d) Similar Case to (c) but Involving Family Man Who Might Have Intended to Have More Children 369

(e) Cases where Infertility Amounting to Little More than an "Insult" 369

Female:

(a) Infertility with Associated Depression and Anxiety, Pain and Scarring 369

(b) Infertility without Medical Complication and where Injured Person has Children Already (Including where Significant Psychological Damage) 369

(c) Infertility where Injured Person would not have had Children Anyway 369

(d) Failed Sterilisation Leading to Unwanted Pregnancy where no Serious Psychological Impact or Depression 369

(F) Kidney 370

(a) Serious and Permanent Damage or Loss of Both Kidneys 370

(b) Where Significant Risk of Future Urinary Tract Infection or Other Total Loss of Natural Kidney Function 370

(c) Loss of One Kidney with no Damage to the Other 370

(G) Bowels 370

(a) Total Loss of Natural Function and Dependence on Colostomy 370

(b) Severe Abdominal Injury Causing Impairment of Function and often Necessitating Temporary Colostomy (Leaving Disfiguring Scars) and/or Restriction on Employment and on Diet 370

(c) Penetrating Injuries Causing Some Permanent Damage but with Eventual Return to Natural Function and Control 370

(H) Bladder 370

(a) Complete Loss of Function and Control 371

(b) Impairment of Control with Some Pain and Incontinence 371

(c) Where Almost Complete Recovery but Some Fairly Long Term Interference with Natural Function 371

(I) Spleen 371
(a) Loss of Spleen where Continuing Risk of Internal Infection and Disorders Due to Damage to Immune System 371
(b) Where above Risks not Present or are Minimal 371
(J) Hernia 372
(a) Continuing Pain and/or Limitation on Physical Activities, Sport or Employment..................................... 372
(b) Direct (where no Pre-Existing Weakness) Inguinal Hernia, with Some Risk of Recurrence 372
(c) Uncomplicated Indirect Inguinal Hernia with no other Associated Abdominal Injury or Damage 372
6. **Orthopaedic Injuries** 373
(A) Neck Injuries 373
(a) Severe 373
(i) Neck Injury Associated with Incomplete Paraplegia or Resulting in Permanent Spastic Quadriparesis or where Injured Person has Little or no Movement in Neck and Suffers Severe Intractable Headaches 373
(ii) Injuries of Considerable Severity 373
(iii) Injuries Causing Severe Damage to Soft Tissues and/or Ruptured Tendons Resulting in Significant Permanent Disability 374
(iv) Injuries Causing Severe Immediate Symptoms and Maybe Requiring Spinal Fusion, Leaving Markedly Impaired Function or Vulnerability to Further Trauma and Some Limitation of Activities........... 374
(b) Moderate 374
(i) Cases Involving Whiplash or Wrenching Type of Injury and More Severe Disc Lesion Resulting in Cervical Spondylosis, Serious Limitation of Movement, Permanent or Recurring Pain, Stiffness or

Discomfort and Possible Need for Further Surgery or Increased Vulnerability to Further Trauma 374
(ii) Injuries Exacerbating or Accelerating Pre-Existing Unrelated Condition with Complete Recovery from Effects of Injury within a Few Years and Moderate Whiplash Injuries where Period of Recovery Fairly Protracted and where Remaining Increased Vulnerability to Further Trauma 374
(c) Minor 375
(B) Back Injuries 375
(a) Severe 375
(i) Cases of the Most Severe Injury not Involving Paralysis but Very Serious Consequences Such as Impotence or Double Incontinence 375
(ii) Cases with Special Features Including Impaired Bladder and Bowel Function, Severe Sexual Difficulties and Unsightly Scarring and Possibility of Further Surgery 375
(iii) Cases of Disc Lesions or Fractures of Discs or of Vertebral Bodies with Remaining Disabilities such as Continuing Severe Pain and Discomfort, Impaired Sexual Function, Depression, Personality Change, Alcoholism, Unemployability and Risk of Arthritis 375
(b) Moderate 376
(i) Cases where Residual Disability of Less Severity than Above such as Crush Fracture of Lumbar Vertebra with Substantial Risk of Osteoarthritis and Constant Pain and Discomfort with Impairment of Sexual Function, Traumatic Spondylolisthesis with Continuous Pain and Probability of Spinal Fusion or Prolapsed Intervertebral Disc with Substantial Acceleration of Back Degeneration .. 376
(ii) Many Frequently Encountered Injuries such as Disturbance of Ligaments and

Muscles Giving Rise to Back Ache, Soft Tissue Injuries Resulting in Exacerbation of Existing Back Condition or Prolapsed Discs Necessitating Laminectomy Or Resulting in Repeated Relapses 376
(iii) Strains, Sprains, Disc Prolapses and Soft Tissue Injuries Resulting in Full Recovery or Minor Continuing Disability Or Resulting in Acceleration or Exacerbation of Pre-Existing Unrelated Condition for Fairly Brief Period 376
(c) Minor 376
(C) Injuries to the Pelvis and Hips 377
(a) Severe 377
(i) Extensive Fractures of Pelvis Involving e.g. Dislocation of Low Back Joint and Ruptured Bladder or Hip Injury Resulting in Spondylolisthesis of Low Back Joint with Intolerable Pain and Necessitating Spinal Fusion with Substantial Residual Disabilities such as Complicated Arthrodesis with Resulting Lack of Bladder and Bowel Control, Sexual Dysfunction or Hip Deformity Making Use of Caliper Essential 377
(ii) Injuries Slightly Less Severe with Particular Distinguishing Features e.g. Fracture Dislocation of Pelvis Involving both Ischial and Pubic Rami and Resulting in Impotence or Traumatic Myositis Ossificans with Formation Of Ectopic Bone Around Hip 377
(iii) Injuries such as Fracture of Acetabulum Leading to Degenerative Changes and Leg Instability Requiring Osteotomy and Likelihood of Future Hip Replacement, Fracture of Arthritic Femur or Hip Necessitating Hip Replacement or Fracture Resulting in only Partially Successful Hip Replacement so Clear Risk of

Need for Revision Surgery 377
(b) Moderate 378
(c) Injuries of Limited Severity 378
(d) Minor Injuries 378
(D) Shoulder Injuries 378
(a) Serious 378
(b) Moderate 379
(c) Minor 379
(d) Fracture of Clavicle 379
(E) Amputation of Arms 379
(a) Loss of Both Arms 379
(b) Loss of One Arm 379
(i) Arm Amputated at Shoulder 380
(ii) Above Elbow Amputation 380
(iii) Below Elbow Amputation 380
(F) Other Arm Injuries 380
(a) Severe Injuries 380
(b) Injuries Resulting in Permanent and Substantial Disablement 380
(c) Less Severe Injury 380
(d) Simple Fractures of Forearm 381
(G) Injuries to the Elbow 381
(a) Severely Disabling Injury 381
(b) Less Severe Injuries 381
(c) Below Elbow Amputation 381
(H) Wrist Injuries 381
(a) Injuries Resulting in Complete Loss of Function in Wrist 381
(b) Injuries Resulting in Significant Permanent Disability with Some Useful Movement Remaining 381
(c) Less Severe Injuries 381
(d) Where Recovery Complete 382
(e) Uncomplicated Colles Fracture 382
(I) Hand Injuries 382
(a) Total Effective Loss of Both Hands .. 382
(b) Serious Damage to Both Hands 382
(c) Total or Effective Loss of One Hand 382
(d) Amputation of index, middle and/or ring fingers 383
(e) Serious Hand Injuries 383
(f) Severe Fractures to Fingers 383
(g) Total Loss of Index Finger 383
(h) Partial Loss of Index Finger 383
(i) Fracture of Index Finger 383

(j) Total Loss of Middle Finger 384
(k) Serious Injury to Ring or Middle Fingers 384
(l) Loss of Terminal Phalanx of Ring or Middle Fingers 384
(m) Amputation of Little Finger 384
(n) Loss of Part of Little Finger where Remaining Tip is Sensitive 384
(o) Amputation of Ring and Little Fingers 384
(p) Amputation of Terminal Phalanges of Index and Middle Fingers with Further Injury to Fourth Finger 384
(q) Fracture of One Finger 384
(r) Loss of Thumb 384
(s) Very Serious Injury to Thumb 384
(t) Serious Injury to Thumb 385
(u) Moderate Injury to Thumb 385
(v) Severe Dislocation of Thumb 385
(w) Minor Injuries to Thumb 385
(x) Trivial Injuries to Thumb 385
(y) Vibration White Finger 385
(i) Most serious 387
(ii) Serious 387
(iii) Moderate 387
(iv) Minor 387
(J) Work Related Upper Limb Disorders 387
(a) Continuing Bilateral Disability with Surgery and Loss of Employment 388
(b) Continuing Symptoms but Fluctuating and Unilateral 388
(c) Symptoms Resolving over Two Years 388
(d) Complete Recovery within a Short Period 388
(K) Leg Injuries 388
(a) Amputations 388
(i) Total Loss of Both Legs 388
(ii) Below Knee Amputation of Both Legs 388
(iii) Above Knee Amputation of One Leg 389
(iv) Below Knee Amputation of One Leg 389
(b) Severe Leg Injuries 389
(i) Most Serious Injuries Short of Amputation 389

(ii) Very Serious Injuries 390
(iii) Serious Injuries 390
(iv) Moderate Injuries 390
(c) Less Serious Leg Injuries 390
(i) Fractures from which an Incomplete Recovery Made 390
(ii) Simple Fracture of Femur with no Damage to Articular Surface 390
(iii) Simple Fractures and Soft Tissue Injuries 390
(L) Knee Injuries 390
(a) Severe Injuries 392
(i) Serious Knee Injury where Disruption of Joint, Gross Ligamentous Damage, Lengthy Treatment, Considerable Pain and Loss of Function and Arthrodesis 392
(ii) Leg Fracture Extending into Knee Joint Causing Pain, Permanent Limiting Movement or Impairing Agility and Rendering Injured Person Prone to Osteoarthritis and Risk Of Arthrodesis 392
(iii) Less Severe Injuries and/or Injuries which Result in Less Severe Disability, maybe with Continuing Symptoms of Pain and Discomfort and Limitation of Movement or Instability or Deformity with Risk of Degenerative Changes . 392
(b) Moderate Injuries 392
(i) Injuries Involving Dislocation, Torn Cartilage or Meniscus or which Accelerate Symptoms from a Pre-existing Condition but which Additionally Result in Minor Disability, Wasting, Weakness or other Mild Future Disability 392
(ii) Less Serious Injuries and Lacerations, Twisting or Bruising Injuries 392
(M) Ankle Injuries 393
(a) Very Severe Injuries 393
(b) Severe Injuries 393
(c) Moderate Injuries 394
(d) Modest Injuries 394

(N) Achilles Tendon 394
(a) Most Serious 394
(b) Serious 394
(c) Moderate 395
(d) Minor 395
(O) Foot Injuries 395
(a) Amputation of Both Feet 395
(b) Amputation of One Foot 395
(c) Very Severe Injuries 395
(d) Severe Injuries 395
(e) Serious Injuries 396
(f) Moderate Injuries 396
(g) Modest Injuries 396
(P) Toe Injuries 396
(a) Amputation of All Toes 396
(b) Amputation of Great Toe 397
(c) Severe Toe Injuries 397
(d) Serious Toe Injuries 397
(e) Moderate Toe Injuries 397
7. **Facial Injuries** 399
(A) Skeletal Injuries 399
(a) Le Fort Fractures of Frontal Facial Bones 399
(b) Multiple Fractures of Facial Bones .. 399
(c) Fracture of Nose 399
(i) Serious Fractures Requiring a Number of Operations and Resulting in Permanent Damage to Airways and/or Facial Deformity 399
(ii) Displaced Fracture where Recovery Complete after Surgery
(iii) Displaced Fracture Requiring only Manipulation 400
(iv) Simple Undisplaced Fracture with Full Recovery 400
(d) Fractures of Cheekbones 400
(i) Serious Fractures Requiring Surgery but with Lasting Consequences e.g. Paraesthesia or Disfigurement 400
(ii) Simple Fracture Requiring Some Reconstructive Surgery with Complete Recovery with Minimal or no Cosmetic Effects 400
(iii) Simple Fracture Requiring no Surgery and with Complete Recovery 400

(e) Fractures of Jaws 400
(i) Very Serious Multiple Fractures with Prolonged Treatment and Permanent Consequences, Including Severe Pain, Restriction in Eating, Paraesthesia and/or Risk of Arthritis 400
(ii) Serious Fracture with Permanent Consequences e.g. in Opening Mouth or with Eating or where Paraesthesia .. 400
(iii) Simple Fracture Requiring Immobilisation with Complete Recovery 401
(f) Damage to Teeth 401
(i) Loss of or Serious Damage to Several Front Teeth 401
(ii) Loss of Two Front Teeth 401
(iii) Loss of One Front Tooth 401
(iv) Loss of or Damage to Back Teeth..... 401
(B) Facial Disfigurement 401
Female:
(i) Very Severe Facial Scarring 401
(ii) Less Severe Facial Scarring 402
(iii) Significant Scarring 402
(iv) Less Significant Scarring 402
Male:
(i) Very Severe Facial Scars 402
(ii) Severe Facial Scarring 402
(iii) Significant but not Severe Scars 403
(iv) Relatively Minor Scarring 403
(v) Trivial Scarring 403
8. Scarring to Other Parts of the Body 404
9. Damage to Hair 405
(a) Damage Caused by e.g. Permanent Waving or Tinting Causing Loss of Hair Leading to Distress, Depression, Embarrassment and Loss of Confidence, Inhibiting Social Life ... 405
(b) Less Serious Damage where Symptoms are Fewer or Minor 405

Index 407

TABLE OF CASES

A page number in **bold type** indicates that a digest of the case is printed on that page.

Aitken *v.* Midlothian District Council (No. 2), 1990 S.L.T 41 .... **220**
Alexander *v.* J. Smart & Co. Ltd, 1973 S.L.T. (Notes) 22 .... **289**
Allan *v.* Barclay (1864) 2 M. 873 36
Allan *v.* Scott, 1972 S.C. 59 34
Allen *v.* Waters & Co [1935] 1 K.B. 200 53
Almond *v.* Leeds Western Health Authority (1990) 1 Med. L.R. 370 .... 51, 53
Anderson *v.* Brown, 1983 S.L.T. 655 .... 45, **188**
Anderson *v.* Davis [1993] P.I.Q.R. Q87 .... 5, 39
Anderson *v.* Forth Valley Health Board, 1998 S.L.T. 588 52
Anderson *v.* Gerrard, 1994 S.L.T. 1326 .... 40, **257**
Anderson *v.* Thames Case Ltd, 1987 S.L.T. 564 .... **204**
Anderson's Tutor *v.* J. Wallace and Sons, 1989 S.L.T. 150 .... 44, **215**
Anthony *v.* Brabbs, 1998 G.W.D. 28-1437 37
Arafa *v.* Potter [1994] P.I.Q.R. Q73 .... 5, 34
Armstrong *v.* Grampian Health Board, 1994 S.L.T. 380 .... **257**
Arnott *v.* Bristol-Myers Co Ltd, 1998 S.L.T. 110 .... 37, 40
Auty *v.* National Coal Board [1985] 1 W.L.R. 784 .... 47, 48, 98

Baillie *v.* Grahamston Iron Co. Ltd, 1988 S.L.T. 429 .... **209**
Baird *v.* Sellars, 1993 S.L.T. 856 .... **245**
Baker *v.* Willoughby [1970] A.C. 467 6
Balfour *v.* Baird & Sons, 1959 S.C. 64 4
Ballantyne *v.* John Young & Co (Kelvinhaugh) Ltd, 1996 S.L.T. 358 .... **270**
Ballantyne *v.* Tesco Stores Ltd, 1993 S.L.T. 678 .... **239**
Banbury *v.* Bank of Montreal [1918] A.C. 626 3
Barclay *v.* J. & W. Henderson Ltd, 1980 S.L.T. (Notes) 71 .... **181**
Barker *v.* Murdoch, 1979 S.L.T. 145 34
Barrett *v.* Strathclyde Fire Brigade, 1984 S.L.T. 325 .... 45, **191**
Beggs *v.* Motherwell Bridge Fabricators Ltd, 1997 S.C.L.R. 1019 .... 31, 77, 78, 86, **306**
Bennett *v.* Dexion Ltd, 1976 S.L.T. (Notes) 69 .... **176**
Bern's Executor *v.* Montrose Asylum (1893) 20 R. 859 32
Bews *v.* Scottish Hydro Electric plc, 1992 S.L.T. 749 77
Bhatia *v.* Tribax Ltd, 1993 G.W.D. 35-2257 .... 75, 76, 78, 82, 85, 86
Bhatia *v.* Tribax Ltd, 1994 S.L.T. 1201 .... 27, 28, 85
Binnie *v.* Kwik-Fit (GB) Ltd, 1994 S.L.T. 742 .... **256**
Bird *v.* British Beef Co Ltd, 1988 S.L.T. 801 .... 45, **209**
Birkett *v.* Hayes [1982] 1 W.L.R. 816 27
Black *v.* The North British Railway Company, 1908 S.C. 444 5
Blackhall *v.* MacInnes, 1997 S.L.T. 649 .... **275**
Blair *v.* F.J.C. Lilley (Marine) Ltd, 1981 S.L.T. 90 .... 41, 46, **183**
Blamire *v.* South Cumbria Health Authority [1993] P.I.Q.R. Q1 43
Bonar *v.* Trafalgar House Offshore Fabrication Ltd, 1996 S.L.T. 548 .... 23, 24, **271**
Boots the Chemist Ltd *v.* G A Estates Ltd, 1993 S.L.T. 136 27
Bowers *v.* Strathclyde Regional Council, 1981 S.L.T. 122 .... 34, 41, **184**

Boyle *v.* Rennies of Dunfermline Ltd, 1975 S.L.T. (Notes) 13 13
Brayson *v.* Wilmot-Breedon [1976] C.L.Y. 682 41
Breslin *v.* Britoil plc, 1992 S.L.T. 414 .... **235**
Brien *v.* British Telecommunications plc, 1994 S.L.T. 629 .... **256**
Bristow *v.* Judd [1993] P.I.Q.R. Q117 54
British Transport Commission *v.* Gourley [1956] A.C. 185 .... 5, 6, 39, 40, 52
Brodie *v.* British Railways Board, 1986 S.L.T 208 .... **198**
Brogan's Tutors *v.* Glasgow District Council, 1978 S.L.T (Notes) 47 .... 44, **178**
Brown *v.* Ferguson, 1990 S.L.T. 274 .... 63, 64, 76, 78, 85, **301**
Brown *v.* Glasgow Corporation, 1973 S.L.T. (Notes) 45 .... **174**
Bruce *v.* Ailsa Vacuum Extraction Ltd, 1987 S.L.T. 464 .... **203**
Bruce *v.* British Transport Hotels Ltd, 1981 S.L.T. (Notes) 77 .... **184**
Buchanan *v.* Lanarkshire Health Board, 1993 S.L.T. 456 .... **240**
Buckley *v.* Melville Dundas and Whitson Ltd, 1979 S.L.T. (Notes) 102 .... 41, **180**
Burns *v.* Edman [1970] 1 All E. R. 886 37
Burns *v.* Harper Collins Ltd, 1997 S.L.T. 607 .... **274**
Bush *v.* Greater Glasgow Health Board, 1995 G.W.D. 25-1333 .... 6, 7
Bush *v.* Phillips (1989) C.L.Y. 1065 33
Butler *v.* Adam Lynn Ltd, 1965 S.C. 137 34
Byrnes *v.* Fife Health Board, 1979 S.C. 415 .... **180**

Calder *v.* Lummus Crest Ltd, 1989 S.L.T. 689 .... **215**
Cameron *v.* Kidd, 1973 S.L.T. (Notes) 74 .... **289**
Campbell *v.* Campbell & Isherwood Ltd, 1993 S.L.T. 1095 .... **241**
Campbell *v.* City of Glasgow District Council, 1991 S.L.T. 616 .... 45, 58, **229**
Campbell *v.* D.B. Marshall (Newbridge) Ltd, 1991 S.L.T. 837 .... **231**
Campbell *v.* F. & F. Moffat (Transport) Ltd, 1992 S.L.T. 962 38
Campbell *v.* Gillespie, 1996 S.L.T. 503 .... 64, 76, 77, 79, 85, 86, **305**
Cantwell, Petitioner, Lord Milligan, July 28, 1998, unreported 47
Cartledge *v.* Clydeside Steel Fabrications Ltd, 1977 S.L.T. (Notes) 69 .... **177**
Cassel *v.* Riverside Health Authority [1992] P.I.Q.R. Q168 44
Cavanagh *v.* BP Chemicals Ltd, 1995 S.L.T. 1287 .... **264**
Caven *v.* McEwan, 1985 S.L.T. 83 .... **195**
Chan Wai Tong *v.* Li Ping Sum [1985] 1 A.C. 446 .... 34, 39, 44
Chapman *v.* South of Scotland Electricity Board, 1983 S.L.T. 456 .... 44, **189**
Cherry *v.* Strathclyde Regional Council, 1994 S.L.T. 494 .... 50, 59, 60, **247**
Clark *v.* J.M.J. Contractors Ltd, 1982 S.L.T. 299 .... 76, **295**
Clark *v.* Scottish Power plc, 1994 S.L.T. 924 .... **259**
Clark *v.* Sutherland, 1993 S.C. 320 .... 28, 40, 60, **236**
Clarke *v.* McFadyen, 1990 S.L.T. 277 .... **221**
Cleland *v.* Campbell, 1998 S.L.T. 642 14
Clews *v.* B.A. Chemicals Ltd, 1988 S.L.T. 29 .... **208**
Clues *v.* Western S.M.T. Co. Ltd, 1977 S.L.T. (Notes) 51 .... **177**
Cohen *v.* Shaw, 1992 S.L.T. 1022 .... 67, 73, 80, 83
Cole *v.* Weir Pumps Ltd, 1995 S.L.T. 12 .... **264**
Collins *v.* Gates Rubber Co. Ltd, 1992 S.L.T. 622 .... **235**
Comber *v.* Greater Glasgow Health Board, 1992 S.L.T. 22 .... **235**
Comerford *v.* P.S.C. Equipment Ltd, 1981 S.L.T. (Notes) 52 .... **185**
Connolly *v.* Camden and Islington Area Health Authority [1981] 3 All E.R. 250 44
Convery *v.* Kirkwood, 1985 S.L.T. 483 .... **195**
Cook *v.* J L Kier & Co Ltd [1970] 2 All E. R. 513 33
Cook *v.* National Coal Board, 1978 S.L.T. (Notes) 19 .... **178**
Cookson *v.* Knowles [1979] A.C. 556 .... 78, 79
Cooper *v.* Firth Brown [1963] 1 W.L.R. 418 40
Corbett *v.* Barking Health Authority [1991] 2 Q.B. 408 .... 61, 64, 78, 79, 86

Coull *v.* Lothian Regional Council, 1994 S.L.T. 377 .... **255**
Cowan *v.* Greig, 1969 S.L.T. (Notes) 34 .... 77, **286**
Cowie *v.* Atlantic Drilling Co Ltd, 1995 S.C. 288 14
Croke *v.* Wiseman [1981] 3 All E.R. 852 44
Cruikshank *v.* Shiels, 1953 S.C. (H.L.) 1 77
Cull *v.* Oilfield Inspection Services Group plc, 1990 S.L.T. 205 37
Cumming *v.* Anderson, 1988 S.L.T. 485 .... **208**
Cunningham *v.* Camberwell Health Authority [1990] 2 Med. L.R. 49 9
Cunningham *v.* City of Edinburgh District Council, 1994 G.W.D. 21-1299 15
Cunningham *v.* Harrison [1973] Q.B. 942 52
Cunningham *v.* National Coal Board, 1981 S.L.T. (Notes) 74 .... **293**
Curran *v.* H A T Painters (Scotland) Ltd, 1987 S.L.T. 98 13
Curran *v.* Scottish Gas Board, 1970 S.L.T. (Notes) 33 .... **286**
Currie *v.* Kilmarnock and Loudoun District Council, 1996 S.C. 55 35
Curwen *v.* James [1963] 1 W.L.R. 748 4

Daish *v.* Wanton [1972] 2 Q.B. 262 44
Dalgleish *v.* Glasgow Corporation, 1976 S.C. 32 .... 4, 32, 33
Davidson *v.* Upper Clyde Shipbuilders Ltd, 1990 S.L.T. 329 .... 72, 76, 79, **300**
Davie *v.* Edinburgh Corporation, 1978 S.L.T. (Notes) 37 .... **293**
Davies *v.* Powell Duffryn Associated Collieries Ltd [1942] A.C. 601 .... 75, 76
Davies *v.* Taylor [1974] A.C. 207 .... 5, 6
Denheen *v.* British Railways Board, 1986 S.L.T. 249 and 1988 S.L.T. 320 59
Devlin *v.* J. Howden & Co. Ltd, 1991 S.L.T. 354 .... **222**
Dews *v.* National Coal Board [1988] A.C. 1 .... 40, 48
Dhaliwal *v.* Hunt [1995] P.I.Q.R. Q56 44
Dickson *v.* Edinburgh Corporation, 1970 S.L.T. (Notes) 56 .... 44, **174**
Dickson *v.* Lothian Health Board, 1994 S.L.T. 525 .... **255**
Dingwall *v.* Walter Alexander & Sons (Midland) Ltd,
1982 S.C. (H.L.) 179 .... 71, 72, 75, 76, 78, **294**
Docherty *v.* City of Glasgow District Council, 1996 Rep. L.R. (Quantum) 5 .... 41, **272**
Docherty's Curator Bonis *v.* U.I.E. Shipbuilding (Scotland) Ltd,
1989 S.L.T. 197 .... 50, 59, **210**
Donaldson *v.* Lothian Health Board, 1998 S.L.T. 416 .... **283**
Donnelly *v.* John Russell (Grangemouth) Ltd, 1985 S.L.T. 82 .... **194**
Douglas *v.* National Coal Board, 1977 S.L.T. (Notes) 14 .... **177**
Doyle *v.* Strathclyde Regional Council, 1994 S.L.T. 524 .... **254**
Drummond *v.* Foulis, 1972 S.L.T. (Notes) 11 44
Duffy *v.* Lanarkshire Health Board, 1995 S.L.T. 1312 .... 6, 7, **265**
Duffy *v.* Lanarkshire Health Board, Lord Johnston, July 31, 1998, unreported... 23, 58, 59
Duffy *v.* Mairs, 1997 S.C.L.R. 590 .... **281**
Duffy *v.* Shaw, 1995 S.L.T. 602 .... 50, **261**
Duller *v.* South East Lincs Engineers [1981] C.L.Y. 585 37
Duncan *v.* Glacier Metal Co Ltd, 1988 S.L.T. 479 42
Duncan *v.* Ross Harper & Murphy, 1993 S.L.T. 105 .... **240**
Duncan *v.* Scottish Marine Biological Association, 1992 S.L.T. 554 .... **232**
Dunn *v.* Johnston Castings Engineering Ltd, 1993 S.L.T. 576 .... **240**

Eastman *v.* South West Thames Health Authority [1992] P.I.Q.R. P42 54
Edgar *v.* Strathclyde Buses Ltd, 1994 S.L.T. 563 .... **254**

Fairhurst *v.* St Helens and Knowsley Health Authority [1995] P.I.Q.R. Q1 60
Faith *v.* CBI Constructors Ltd, 1987 S.L.T. 248 .... **203**
Fallan *v.* Lanarkshire Health Board, 1997 S.L.T. 902 .... **277**
Fallow *v.* Greater Glasgow Health Board, 1985 S.L.T. 98 .... 44, **194**

Farrell *v.* British United Trawlers (Granton) Ltd, 1978 S.L.T. (Notes) 16 .... 79, **292**
Farrelly *v.* Yarrow Shipbuilders Ltd, 1994 S.L.T. 1349 .... 43, 59, 64, **252**
Ferguson *v.* McGrandles, 1993 S.L.T. 822 13
Ferguson *v.* Strathclyde Regional Council, 1981 S.L.T. (Notes) 103 .... **185**
Fish *v.* Wilcox [1994] 5 Med. L.R. 230 5
Fletcher *v.* Autocar and Transporters Ltd [1968] 2 Q.B. 322 33
Forbes *v.* British Railways Board, 1971 S.L.T. (Notes) 21 43
Forsyth's Curator Bonis *v.* Govan Shipbuilders Ltd,
1988 S.C. 421 .... 26, 43, 50, 58, 59, 60, **204**
Foster *v.* Tyne & Wear County Council [1986] 1 All E.R. 567 .... 39, 44
Fournier *v.* Canadian National Railway Company [1927] A.C. 167 3
Fowler *v.* Greater Glasgow Health Board, 1990 S.L.T. 303 .... 72, **220**
Fox *v.* N C R (Nederlande) B V, 1987 S.L.T. 401 85
Fraser *v.* Greater Glasgow Health Board, 1997 S.L.T. 554 .... **273**
Frost *v.* Palmer [1993] P.I.Q.R. Q14 39
Fullemann *v.* McInnes's Executors, 1993 S.L.T. 259 .... 3, 37, 40, **244**
Fulton *v.* CPC (United Kingdom) Ltd, 1996 Rep. L.R. (Quantum) 7 .... **272**

G's Curator Bonis *v.* Grampian Health Board, 1995 S.L.T. 652 .... 50, **261**
Galbraith *v.* Marley Buildings Ltd, 1984 S.L.T. 155 .... **192**
Galbraith's Curator ad Litem *v.* Stewart, 1997 S.L.T. 418 59
Gallacher *v.* Deborah Scaffolding (Aberdeen) Ltd, 1988 S.L.T. 345 .... **207**
Gallacher *v.* McDermotts (Scotland) Ltd, 1987 S.L.T. 56 .... **203**
Gallacher *v.* Strathclyde Regional Council, 1986 S.L.T. 53 .... **198**
Gardner *v.* Howard Doris Ltd, 1983 S.L.T. 672 .... 50, **189**
Garland *v.* Fairnington's Executor, 1994 S.L.T. 855 .... 59, 61, **254**
Geddes *v.* British Railways Board, 1990 S.L.T. 696 .... **219**
Geddes *v.* Lothian Health Board, 1992 S.L.T. 986 .... 44, 50, 51, 53, 54, **231**
Gerrard *v.* Swanson's Executor, 1980 S.L.T. (Notes) 43 .... **182**
Gibney *v.* Eric Johnson Stubbs (Scotland) Ltd, 1987 S.L.T. 132 .... 40, 45, 46, **202**
Gibson *v.* Droopy & Browns Ltd, 1989 S.L.T. 172 .... **214**
Gibson *v.* Glasgow Corporation, 1963 S.L.T. (Notes) 16 37
Gillan *v.* McGawn's Motors Limited, 1970 S.L.T. 250 .... **287**
Girvan *v.* Inverness Farmers Dairy, 1998 S.C. (H.L.) 1 .... 33, 34, 72
Glasgow *v.* City of Glasgow District Council, 1983 S.L.T. 65 .... **189**
Goldfinch *v.* Scannell [1993] P.I.Q.R. Q143 53
Goldie *v.* National Coal Board, 1987 S.L.T. 304 .... **202**
Gordon *v.* Muir, 1980 S.L.T. (Notes) 51 .... **182**
Gordon *v.* Wilson, 1992 S.L.T. 849 .... 50, 53, 60, **231**
Gorman *v.* McLaren Building Services Ltd, 1990 S.L.T. 365 .... **219**
Graham *v.* Associated Electrical Industries, 1966 S.L.T. (Notes) 27 75
Graham *v.* Dodds [1983] 1 W.L.R. 808 .... 78, 79
Grainger *v.* Fife Regional Council, 1991 S.L.T. 632 .... 47, 48, **228**
Grant *v.* Highland Health Board, Lord Sutherland, December 20, 1985, unreported 72
Grant *v.* Lothian Regional Council, 1988 S.L.T. 533 .... **207**
Grant *v.* National Coal Board, 1974 S.L.T. (Notes) 71 43
Gray *v.* Allied Ironfounders Limited, 1969 S.L.T. (Notes) 95 .... **285**
Gray *v.* Lanarkshire Health Board, 1996 S.L.T. 390 6
Greenwood *v.* Muir, 1977 S.L.T. (Notes) 71 (Lord Wylie) **292**
Gripper *v.* British Railways Board, 1991 S.L.T. 659 .... **230**

H West & Son Ltd *v.* Shephard [1964] A.C. 326 .... 32, 33, 34
Hale *v.* London Underground [1993] P.I.Q.R. Q30 33
Hamilton *v.* Clark, 1975 S.L.T. (Notes) 44 .... **175**
Hamilton *v.* Fife Health Board, 1993 S.C. 369 .... 67, 73, 80

Handren *v.* Scottish Construction Co Ltd, 1967 S.L.T. (Notes) 21 26
Hanlon *v.* Cuthbertson, 1981 S.L.T. (Notes) 57 .... **185**
Harper *v.* Smillie, 1974 S.L.T. (Notes) 40 .... **290**
Harris *v.* Bright's Asphalt Contractors Ltd [1953] 1 Q.B. 617 52
Harrison *v.* McLean, 1978 S.L.T.(Notes) 68 .... **178**
Harrison *v.* R.B. Tennent Ltd, 1992 S.L.T. 1060 .... 64, **234**
Hartley *v.* Sandholme Iron Co [1975] Q.B. 600 41
Hatherley *v.* Smith, 1989 S.L.T. 316 75
Hearnshaw *v.* English Steel Corpn Ltd (1971) 11 K.I.R. 306 33
Hempsey *v.* Inverclyde District Council, 1985 S.L.T. 348 .... **193**
Henderson *v.* Occidental Petroleum (Caledonia) Ltd, 1990 S.L.T. 314 .... 69, 70
Henderson *v.* South Wales Switchgear Limited, 1969 S.L.T. (Notes) 52 .... **285**
Hewson *v.* Secretary of State for Scotland, 1987 S.L.T 719 .... **202**
Higgins *v.* Tayside Health Board, 1996 S.L.T. 288 .... **267**
Hill *v.* Lovett, 1992 S.L.T. 994 .... **236**
Hill *v.* Wilson, 1997 S.C. 81 .... 27, 39, 44
Hodge *v.* British Coal Corporation (No. 2), 1992 S.L.T. 913 .... 43, **234**
Hodgson *v.* Trapp [1989] 1 A.C. 807 .... 8, 11, 18, 45, 48, 92, 103
Hoey *v.* British Steel Corporation, 1991 S.L.T. 196 .... **229**
Housecroft *v.* Burnett [1986] 1 All E.R. 332 .... 52, 60
Howard *v.* Comex Houlder Diving Ltd, 1987 S.L.T. 344 .... **201**
Howie *v.* Upper Clyde Shipbuilders Ltd, 1991 S.L.T. 2 .... 59, 64, 76, 85, **223, 302**
Howie *v.* Western Scottish Motor Traction Co. Ltd, 1986 S.L.T 81 .... **197**
Hughes *v.* British Railways Board, 1992 S.L.T. 97 .... **232**
Hunt *v.* Severs [1994] 2 A.C. 350 58
Hunter *v.* Clyde Shaw plc, 1995 S.L.T. 474 .... **263**
Hunter *v.* National Coal Board, 1988 S.L.T. 241 .... **207**
Hussain *v.* New Taplow Paper Mills [1988] A.C. 514 42
Hutchison *v.* National Coal Board, 1988 S.L.T 655 .... **207**

Ichard *v.* Frangoulis [1977] 1 W.L.R. 556 33
Ingham *v.* John G Russell (Transport) Ltd, 1991 S.C. 201 .... 63, 64, 85, 86
Irving *v.* Hiddleston, 1998 S.L.T. 912; 1998 S.C.L.R. 350 4

Jack *v.* Alexander McDougall & Co (Engineers), 1973 S.C. 13 36
Jack *v.* City of Glasgow District Council, 1984 S.L.T. 168 .... **192**
Jag Singh *v.* Toong Fong Omnibus Co Ltd [1964] 1 W.L.R. 1382 34
Janardan *v.* East Berks Health Authority [1990] 2 Med. L.R. 1 44
Jobling *v.* Associated Dairies Ltd [1982] A.C. 794 .... 4, 5, 6, 43
Johns *v.* Greater Glasgow Health Board, 1990 S.L.T. 459 .... **219**
Johnstone *v.* Hardie, 1990 S.L.T. 744 .... **218**
Joliffe *v.* Hay, 1991 S.L.T. 151 .... **223**
Jones *v.* Lawrence [1969] 3 All E.R. 267 44
Joyce *v.* Yeomans [1981] 2 All E.R. 21 44

Kane *v.* Norwest Holst Pipework Ltd, 1988 S.L.T. 28 28
Kay *v.* G P Inveresk Corporation, 1988 S.L.T. 711 .... 13, 14
Keicher *v.* National Coal Board, 1988 S.L.T. 318 27
Keith *v.* Fraser and Ors, First Division, October 23, 1973, unreported 32
Kelly *v.* City of Edinburgh District Council, 1983 S.L.T. 71 .... **190**
Kelly *v.* Glasgow Corporation, 1949 S.C. 496; 1951 S.C. (H.L.) 15 72
Kelly *v.* Keith Cardle & Co, 1954 S.L.T. (Notes) 80 44
Kelly *v.* Smillie, 1974 S.L.T. (Notes) 41 .... **291**
Kennedy *v.* Bryan [1984] C.L.Y. 1028 37
Kennedy *v.* Lees of Scotland Ltd, 1997 S.L.T. 510 .... 58, 59, 60, 63, 64, **276**

Kenny *v.* Lightways (Contractors) Ltd, 1994 S.L.T. 306 .... **252**
Kent *v.* British Railways Board [1995] P.I.Q.R. Q42 37
Kent *v.* Gourlay, 1990 S.L.T. 516 .... **218**
Kerr *v.* Newalls Insulation Co Ltd, 1996 S.C.L.R. 1114; 1997 S.L.T. 723 .... **272**
Kirkpatrick *v.* Scott Lithgow Ltd, 1987 S.L.T. 654 .... 45, **201**
Kirkwood *v.* Christie & Vesey Ltd, 1976 S.L.T. (Notes) 56 .... 33, **176**
Kozikowsla *v.* Kozikowski, 1996 S.L.T. 386 58
Kyle *v.* Salvesen, 1980 S.L.T. (Notes) 18 .... **181**

Laidler *v.* Yarrow Shipbuilders Ltd, 1990 S.L.T. 261 .... **218**
Laing *v.* Northern Grouting Engineers Ltd, 1985 S.L.T. 179 .... **194**
Laing *v.* Tayside Health Board, 1996 G.W.D. 10-587 61
Lamb *v.* Glasgow District Council, 1978 S.L.T. (Notes) 64 .... **179**
Lamb's Tutor *v.* Cawthorn-Sinclair Ltd, 1978 S.L.T. (Notes) 31 .... 44, **179**
Lamont *v.* Cameron's Executrix, 1997 S.L.T. 1147 .... 37, **278**
Lang *v.* Fife Health Board, 1990 S.L.T. 626 .... 44, **217**
Lanigan *v.* Derek Crouch Construction Ltd, 1985 S.L.T. 346 .... **193**
Lappin *v.* Britannia Airways Ltd, 1989 S.L.T. 181 24
Laurie *v.* Douglas Reyburn & Co. Ltd, 1990 S.L.T. 513 .... **217**
Laurie *v.* John Laing Construction Ltd, 1984 S.L.T. 312 .... **192**
Lawrie *v.* Lanarkshire Health Board, 1994 S.L.T. 633 .... **251**
Lees *v.* Grahamston Iron Co. Ltd, 1984 S.L.T. 184 .... **192**
Lenaghan *v.* Ayrshire and Arran Health Board, 1994 S.C. 365 .... 33, **246**
Leneghan *v.* Parker, 1979 S.L.T. (Notes) 83 .... **181**
Lennon *v.* Lanarkshire Health Board, 1991 S.L.T 782 .... **223**
Lewicki *v.* Brown & Root Wimpey Highland Fabricators Ltd, 1996 S.C. 200 42
Liffen *v.* Watson [1940] 1 K.B. 556 37
Lim *v.* Camden Health Authority [1980] A.C. 174 .... 5, 33, 40, 52, 103
Little *v.* Miller, 1984 S.L.T. 99 .... **296**
Littlejohn *v.* Clancy, 1974 S.L.T. (Notes) 68 13
Livingstone *v.* The Rawyards Coal Company Limited (1880) 7 R. (H.L.) 1 5
Logan *v.* Monklands District Council, 1987 S.L.T. 557 .... **200**
Longden *v.* British Coal Corporation [1998] 1 All E.R. 289 47
Love *v.* British Railways Board, 1984 S.L.T. 2 .... 44, **193**
Low *v.* Ralston, 1997 S.L.T. 626 .... 58, 59, 60, 63, **276**
Lynedale Fashion Manufacturers *v.* Rich [1973] 1 All E.R. 33 40

McAleenan (and others) *v.* National Coal Board, 1987 S.L.T. 106 .... **199**
McArthur *v.* Raynesway Plant Limited, 1980 S.L.T. (Notes) 79 .... **293**
McBeth *v.* Secretary of State for Scotland, 1976 S.L.T. (Notes) 63 .... **292**
McCabe *v.* British Domestic Appliances Ltd, 1978 S.L.T. (Notes) 31 .... 28, **179**
McCall *v.* Foulis, 1966 S.L.T. 47 44
McCallum *v.* Paterson, 1968 S.C. 280 35
McCallum *v.* Paterson, 1969 S.C. 85 34
McCance *v.* Newalls Insulation Ltd, 1996 S.L.T. 80 .... **270**
McCann *v.* Miller Insulation and Engineering Ltd, 1986 S.L.T. 147 14
McCarvel *v.* Strathclyde Fire Board, 1997 S.L.T. 1015 .... **277**
McCluskey *v.* Lord Advocate, 1994 S.L.T. **250**
McClymont *v.* Glasgow Corporation, 1971 S.L.T. (Notes) 45 .... **174**
McColl *v.* Barnes, 1992 S.L.T. 1188 .... 23, 24
McCrae *v.* Durastic Ltd, 1989 S.C.L.R. 797 .... **213**
McCrum *v.* Ballantyne, 1993 S.L.T. 788 .... 34, 38, 39, 46, **237**
McCuaig *v.* Redpath Dorman Long Limited, 1972 S.L.T. (Notes) 42 .... **289**
McCusker *v.* Davidson and Pickering Limited, 1968 S.L.T. (Notes) 41 .... **285**
McCutcheon *v.* Lothian Regional Council, 1995 S.L.T. 917 .... **265**

McDaid *v.* Clyde Navigation Trustees, 1946 S.C. 462 40
McDermid *v.* Crown House Engineering Ltd, 1993 S.L.T. 543 .... **234**
McDiarmid *v.* Borders Regional Health Board, 1985 S.L.T. 79 .... **196**
McDonald *v.* Whiteford & Robertson Ltd, 1980 S.L.T. (Notes) 2 .... **183**
McFarlane *v.* Greater Glasgow Health Board, 1989 S.C.L.R. 799 .... **214**
McGahan *v.* Greater Glasgow Health Board, 1988 S.L.T 270 .... 43, **206**
McGarrigle *v.* Babcock Energy Ltd, 1996 S.L.T. 471 .... **267**
McGeechan *v.* George Russell (Steel) Ltd, 1970 S.L.T. (Notes) 76 .... **173**
McGilvray *v.* British Insulated Callender's Cables Ltd, 1965 S.L.T. (Notes) 61 .... **172**
McGowan *v.* Air Products (UK) Ltd, 1991 S.L.T 591 .... **230**
McGregor *v.* Webster's Executors, 1976 S.L.T. 29 .... 46, 55
McGunnigal *v.* D.B. Marshall (Newbridge) Ltd, 1993 S.L.T. 769 .... **245**
McHugh *v.* Leslie, 1961 S.L.T. (Notes) 65 .... **172**
McIlroy *v.* Esso Petroleum Co. Ltd, 1986 S.L.T. 552 .... **197**
MacIntosh *v.* National Coal Board, 1987 S.L.T. 116 and 1988 S.L.T. 348 .... 27, 50, 55, **205**
McIntyre *v.* Strathclyde Regional Council, 1994 S.L.T. 933 .... **248**
McKay *v.* Strathclyde Communications Ltd, 1988 S.L.T. 732 .... 45, 46, **206**
McKendrick *v.* Mitchell Swire Ltd, 1976 S.L.T. (Notes) 65 .... **176**
McKenna *v.* Sharp, 1998 S.C. 297 38
McKenzie *v.* Cape Building Products Ltd, 1995 S.L.T 701 .... **259**
Mackenzie *v.* George McLeod Limited, 1973 S.L.T. (Notes) 64 .... **290**
MacKenzie *v.* Mackay, 1989 S.L.T. 810 .... **214**
Mackenzie *v.* Midland Scottish Omnibuses Ltd, 1992 S.L.T. 752 .... **233**
McKeown *v.* Sir William Arrol & Co, 1974 S.C. 97 .... 71, 75
McKew *v.* Holland & Hannen & Cubitts (Scotland) Ltd, 1970 S.C. (H.L.) 20 33
McKinnell *v.* White, 1971 S.L.T. (Notes) 61 .... 44, **174**
McKinnon *v.* British Railways Board, 1972 S.L.T. (Notes) 2 .... 78, **288**
McKinnon *v.* British Telecommunications plc, 1996 S.L.T 798 .... **266**
McKinnon *v.* Reid, 1975 S.C. 233 .... 72, 77
McKirdy *v.* Lothian Regional Council, 1980 S.L.T. (Notes) 74 .... **182**
McLachlan *v.* D.B. Marshall (Newbridge) Ltd, 1992 S.L.T. 131 .... **236**
McLaughlin *v.* British Steel Corporation, 1978 S.L.T. (Notes) 28 .... **179**
McLaughlin *v.* Strathclyde Regional Council, 1984 S.L.T. 99 .... 76, **297**
McLean *v.* Remploy Ltd, 1994 S.L.T. 687 .... 46, **249**
McLeod *v.* Cartwright, 1981 S.L.T. (Notes) 54 .... **186**
MacLeod *v.* Taylor's Executor, 1994 S.L.T. 322 .... 44, **251**
McLoone *v.* British Railways Board, 1981 S.L.T. (Notes) 65 .... **186**
McMahon *v.* British Railways Board, 1995 S.L.T 591 .... **262**
McManus *v.* British Railways Board, 1993 S.C. 557 .... 28, 32, **237**
MacMaster *v.* Caledonian Railway Co (1885) 13 R. 252 .... 4, 43, 53
McMenemy *v.* Argyll Stores Ltd, 1992 S.L.T. 971 .... **233**
McMillan *v.* D.B. Marshall (Newbridge) Ltd, 1991 S.L.T 229 .... **228**
McMillan *v.* McDowall, 1993 S.L.T. 311 .... 37, 50, 51, 52, 53, 54, 60, **238**
McNee *v.* G.R. Stein & Co. Ltd, 1981 S.L.T. (Notes) 31 .... **187**
McNeil *v.* National Coal Board, 1966 S.L.T. (Notes) 4 .... **284**
MacNeil *v.* U.I.E. Shipbuilding (Scotland) Ltd, 1989 S.L.T. 289 .... 45, **213**
McNeill *v.* Roche Products Ltd, 1988 S.C. 77 13
McNeill *v.* Roche Products Ltd, 1989 S.L.T. 498 28
McNicol *v.* Buko, 1986 S.L.T. 12 13
McPhail *v.* British Railways Board, 1981 S.L.T.(Notes) 124 .... **184**
Macrae *v.* Reed and Mallik Ltd, 1961 S.C. 68 27
MacRae *v.* William K. McIntyre & Sons, 1983 S.L.T. 643 .... **190**
MacShannon *v.* Ailsa Perth Shipbuilders Ltd, 1994 S.L.T. 500 .... **245**
McVey *v.* Central Regional Council, 1994 S.L.T. 190 .... **259**
McWhinnie *v.* British Coal Corporation, 1993 S.L.T. 467 .... 46, **241**

McWilliam *v.* British Coal Corporation, 1990 S.L.T. 679 .... **217**
Malcolm *v.* W.H. Rankin Ltd, 1977 S.L.T. (Notes) 45 .... **177**
Maley *v.* Daylay Foods Limited, 1998 S.C. 324 44
Mallett *v.* McMonagle [1970] A.C. 166 .... 5, 6
Malley *v.* National Coal Board, 1981 S.L.T. (Notes) 81 .... **185**
Malyon *v.* Plummer [1964] 1 Q.B. 330 75
Marshall *v.* Bertrams Ltd, 1985 S.L.T. 80 .... 33, **196**
Martin *v.* Grootcon (UK) Ltd, 1990 S.L.T 566 .... **221**
Martin *v.* James and Andrew Chapman (Haulage Contractors) Ltd, 1995 G.W.D. 2-77 .... 35, 45, 50, 51, 54
Martin *v.* McKinsley, 1980 S.L.T. (Notes) 15 13
Maslowski *v.* Bell, 1981 S.L.T. (Notes) 61 .... **186**
Mazs *v.* Dairy Supply Co Ltd, 1979 S.L.T. (Notes) 44 .... **181**
Mearns *v.* Lothian Regional Council, 1991 S.L.T. 338 .... 6, 7, **228**
Meek *v.* Burton's Gold Medal Biscuits Ltd, 1989 S.L.T. 338 .... 24, **210**
Miles *v.* Glasgow District Council, 1981 S.L.T. (Notes) 44 .... **187**
Millar *v.* Fife Regional Council, 1990 S.L.T. 651 .... **217**
Millar *v.* Jamieson McGregor Ltd, 1988 S.L.T. 83 .... 33, **206**
Miller v U.I.E. (Scotland) Ltd, 1988 S.L.T. 536 .... **205**
Miller *v.* British Road Services Ltd [1967] 1 W.L.R. 443 79
Mitchell *v.* Glenrothes Development Corporation, 1991 S.L.T. 284 .... 47, 48, **227**
Mitchell *v.* H A T Contracting Services Ltd (No 3), 1993 S.L.T. 1199 15
Mitchell *v.* Inverclyde District Council, 1997 Rep. L.R. (Quantum) 29 .... 48, 60, **281**
Mitchell *v.* Laing, 1998 S.C. 342 .... 38, 51, 52
Mitchell *v.* Swanson's Executor, 1980 S.L.T. (Notes) 41 .... **182**
Moeliker *v.* A. Reyrole & Co Ltd [1976] I.C.R. 253 .... 39, 44
Molinari *v.* Ministry of Defence [1994] P.I.Q.R. Q33 24
Monteith *v.* Cape Insulation Ltd, 1998 G.W.D. 29–1496 67
Moodie *v.* Maclean, 1981 S.L.T. (Notes) 53 13
Moriarty *v.* McCarthy [1978] 1 W.L.R. 155 .... 33, 51
Morley *v.* Campbell, 1998 S.L.T. 325 .... **282**
Morris *v.* Drysdale, 1992 S.L.T. 186 77
Morris *v.* Pirie, 1983 S.L.T. 659 .... **295**
Morrison *v.* Barton, 1994 S.L.T. 657 .... 46, **246**
Morrison *v.* Forsyth, 1995 S.L.T. 539 71
Morrison *v.* Laidlaw, 1994 S.L.T. 359 .... **249**
Morrison *v.* McDermott Scotland, 1991 S.L.T. 854 .... 45, **226**
Morton *v.* British Aluminium Co Ltd, 1982 S.L.T. 292 41
Mowbray *v.* Steetley Refractories Ltd, 1987 S.L.T. 250 .... **199**
Muckarsie *v.* Dickson (1848) 11 D. 4 5
Muir's Trustee *v.* Braidwood, 1958 S.C. 169 .... 32, 37, 46, 50, 57, 62
Muirhead *v.* Sealink (Scotland) Ltd, 1986 S.L.T. 21 .... **197**
Murdoch *v.* McDermott (Scotland), Second Division, January 17, 1992, unreported 41
Murphy *v.* Lord Advocate, 1981 S.L.T. (Notes) 77 .... **187**
Murray *v.* British Railways Board, 1990 S.L.T 853 .... **216**
Murray *v.* Gent, 1993 S.L.T. 482 .... **242**
Myles *v.* City of Glasgow District Council, 1994 S.C.L.R. 1112 .... 58, 59, **249**

Napier *v.* Burton's Gold Medal Biscuits Ltd, 1992 S.L.T. 1019 .... **233**
Nash *v.* Southmead Health Authority [1993] P.I.Q.R. Q156 60
Neal *v.* Bingle [1998] 2 All E.R. 58 38
Neill *v.* Scottish Omnibuses Ltd, 1961 S.L.T. (Notes) 42 44
Nelson *v.* National Coal Board, 1986 S.L.T. 2 .... **197**
Nisbet *v.* Marley Roof Tile Co Ltd, 1988 S.C. 29 14

O'Brien's Curator Bonis *v.* British Steel plc, 1989 G.W.D. 13-565 13
O'Brien's Curator Bonis *v.* British Steel plc, 1991 S.C. 315 .... 5, 9, 43, 45, 46, 50, 52, 53, 54, 55, 60, 61, 64, 86, **221**
O'Connor *v.* Holst and Company Limited, 1969 S.L.T. (Notes) 66 .... **286**
O'Connor *v.* Matthews, 1996 S.L.T. 408 .... 50, 51, 55, 60, **268**
O'Donnell *v.* D. & R. Ferrying Co. Ltd, 1966 S.L.T. (Notes) 71 .... **283**
O'Neil *v.* British Coal Corporation, 1991 S.L.T. 367 .... 48, **226**
Odgers *v.* British Railways Board, 1967 S.L.T. (Notes) 97 .... **173**
Orr *v.* Metcalfe, 1973 S.C. 57 26
Owen *v.* Martin [1992] P.I.Q.R. Q151 79
Owenson *v.* Rennie's Lion and Comfort Coaches Ltd, 1976 S.L.T. (Notes) 58 .... **176**

Page *v.* Smith [1996] 1 A.C. 155 33
Palmer *v.* Sealink (Scotland) Ltd, 1987 S.L.T. 797 .... **198**
Paris *v.* Scottish Special Housing Association, 1978 S.L.T. (Notes) 50 .... **179**
Parke *v.* Glasgow District Council, 1979 S.L.T. 45 32
Parker *v.* Wigtown District Council, 1981 S.L.T. (Notes) 95 .... **294**
Parry *v.* Cleaver [1970] A.C. 1 .... 5, 40, 42, 47, 52, 76
Paterson *v.* Costain Mining Ltd, 1988 S.L.T. 413 24
Paterson *v.* Hampton, 1994 S.L.T. 1231 .... 58, **250**
Paterson *v.* Kelvin Central Buses Ltd, 1997 S.L.T. 685 .... **273**
Patterson *v.* Ministry of Defence [1987] C.L.Y. 1194 24
Penman *v.* RGC plc, 1994 S.L.T. 805 .... **258**
Phelan *v.* East Cumbrian Health Authority [1991] 2 Med. L.R. 419 33
Phillips *v.* Grampian Health Board (No.2), 1992 S.L.T. 659 .... 72, 76, **303**
Poole *v.* John Laing plc, 1987 S.L.T. 325 .... 43, **199**
Porter *v.* Dickie, 1983 S.L.T. 234 .... 76, 81, 82, **295**
Port-Glasgow and Newark Sailcloth Co *v.* Caledonian Railway Co (1892) 19 R. 608 .... 31, 36, 46, 49, 56, 61
Prentice *v.* Chalmers, 1984 S.L.T. 63 76
Prentice *v.* Chalmers, 1985 S.L.T. 168 .... 27, 71, 75, 76, 78, 82, **297**
Prentice *v.* William Thyne Ltd, 1989 S.L.T. 336 .... 23, 24, **212**
Preston *v.* Grampian Health Board, 1988 S.L.T. 435 .... 27, 28
Purryag *v.* Greater Glasgow Health Board, 1996 S.L.T. 794 27

Rae *v.* Stewart, 1968 S.L.T. (Notes) 62 .... **285**
Rafferty *v.* J. & C. M. Smith (Whiteinch) Ltd, 1987 S.L.T. 538 .... **298**
Reavis *v.* Clan Line Steamers, 1925 S.C. 725 36
Redman *v.* McRae, 1991 S.L.T 785 .... **225**
Reid *v.* Edinburgh Acoustics Ltd, 1995 S.L.T. 659 .... 6, 7, **263**
Reid *v.* J Smart & Co Ltd, 1981 S.L.T. (Notes) 20 14
Reilly *v.* Robert Kellie & Sons Ltd, 1990 S.L.T 78 .... **216**
Reith *v.* Aberdeen Mineral Water Co Ltd, 1987 S.C.L.R. 689 13
Rennicks *v.* Bison Concrete Ltd, 1988 S.L.T. 343 .... **205**
Rennie *v.* Dorans, 1991 S.L.T 443 .... **224**
Rialas *v.* Mitchell, The Times, 17 Jul 1984 (C. A.); (1984) 128 S.J. 704 .... 52, 54
Riddell *v.* James Longmuir & Sons Ltd, 1971 S.L.T. (Notes) 33 .... **288**
Rieley *v.* Kingslaw Riding School, 1975 S.C. 28 .... 4, 35, 43, 53
Roberts *v.* British Railways Board, 1982 S.L.T. 126 .... **188**
Roberts *v.* Johnstone [1989] Q.B. 878 .... 51, 53
Robertson *v.* Aberdeen University, 1984 S.L.T. 341 .... **193**
Robertson *v.* British Bakeries Ltd, 1991 S.L.T. 434 .... 23, 24, **225**
Robertson *v.* Lestrange [1985] 1 All E.R. 950 .... 48, 79
Robertson *v.* Scottish Special Housing Association, 1989 S.L.T. 686 .... 46, **212**
Robertson *v.* Turnbull, 1982 S.C. (H.L.) 1 .... 31, 49

Robertson's Curator Bonis *v.* Anderson, 1996 S.C. 217 .... 4, 39, 43, 44, 47, **265**
Robson *v.* Liverpool City Council [1993] P.I.Q.R. Q78 .... 39, 44
Ross *v.* National Coal Board, 1980 S.L.T. (Notes) 89 33
Routledge *v.* McKenzie [1994] P.I.Q.R. Q49 45
Rubens *v.* Walker, 1946 S.C. 215 52
Ryan *v.* International Distillers and Vintners Export Ltd, 1978 S.L.T. (Notes) 16 .... **180**

Sands *v.* Devan, 1945 S.C. 380 72
Sands *v.* George Waterston & Sons Ltd, 1989 S.L.T. 174 .... **212**
Scott *v.* Kelvin Concrete Ltd, 1993 S.L.T. 935 .... **243**
Sellar's Curator Bonis *v.* Glasgow Victoria and Leverndale Hospitals, 1973 S.L.T. (Notes) 3 .... 39, **175**
Selvanayagam *v.* University of the West Indies [1983] 1 W.L.R. 585 33
Shanks *v.* Gray, 1977 S.L.T. (Notes) 26 52
Shearman *v.* Folland [1950] 1 All E. R. 976 .... 52, 53
Shevchuk *v.* National Coal Board, 1980 S.L.T. (Notes) 65 .... **183**
Simpson *v.* Imperial Chemical Industries Ltd, 1983 S.L.T. 601. 33
Skakle *v.* Downie, 1975 S.L.T. (Notes) 23 .... **175**
Sloan *v.* Triplett, 1985 S.L.T. 294 .... **196**
Smith *v.* Blackwood, 1991 S.L.T. 562 .... **224**
Smith *v.* Chief Constable, Central Scotland Police, 1991 S.L.T. 634 .... **225**
Smith *v.* Colvilles Limited, 1964 S.L.T. (Notes) 91 .... **172**
Smith *v.* Heeps, 1990 S.L.T. 871 .... **216**
Smith *v.* Manchester Corporation [1974] 17 K.I.R. 1 .... 39, 44
Smith *v.* Middleton, 1971 S.L.T. (Notes) 65 .... **288**
Smith *v.* Middleton, 1972 S.C. 30 .... 26, 27, 38
Smith's Curator Bonis *v.* Scottish Gas Board, 1966 S.L.T. (Notes) 71 .... **173**
Smoker *v.* London Fire Authority [1991] 2 A.C. 502 47
Sommerville *v.* Lothian Health Board, 1994 S.L.T. 1207 .... 44, **258**
Spence *v.* City of Glasgow District Council, 1989 S.L.T. 119 .... 44, **212**
Spittle *v.* Bunney [1988] 1 W.L.R. 847 .... 64, 86
Stafford *v.* Renfrew District Council, 1993 S.L.T. 1197 .... **242**
Stark *v.* Nairn Floors Ltd, 1993 S.L.T. 717 .... **242**
Starkey *v.* National Coal Board, 1987 S.L.T. 103 27
Steele *v.* Robert George & Co (1937) Ltd, [1942] A.C. 497 33
Steen *v.* Macnicol, 1968 S.L.T. (Notes) 77 .... 44, **173**
Steven *v.* Broady Norman & Co, 1928 S.C. 351 4
Stevenson *v.* British Coal Corporation, 1989 S.L.T. 136 .... 44, **211**
Stevenson *v.* Pontifex & Wood (1887) 15 R. 125 4
Stevenson *v.* Sweeney, 1995 S.L.T. 29 .... 50, 54, 55, **260**
Steward *v.* Greater Glasgow Health Board, 1976 S.L.T. (Notes) 66 .... **176**
Stewart *v.* Hughes, 1974 S.L.T. (Notes) 19 .... **291**
Stirling *v.* Norwest Holst Ltd, 1997 S.C.L.R. 1196 .... 60, 63, **279**
Stoddard *v.* Topek Roofing Ltd, 1985 S.L.T. 192 .... **195**
Stone *v.* Mountford, 1995 S.L.T. 1279 14
Stuppart *v.* Bonar Textiles Ltd, 1997 S.L.T. 551 .... **274**
Sutherland *v.* North British Steel Group Ltd, 1986 S.L.T.(Sh. Ct.) 29 6
Swan *v.* Hope-Dunbar, 1997 S.L.T. 760 .... **278**

Taggart *v.* Shell (UK) Ltd, 1996 S.L.T. 795 .... 34, **266**
Tait *v.* Pearson [1996] P.I.Q.R. Q92 .... 39, 44
Tannock *v.* British Leyland Motor Company, 1981 S.L.T. (Notes) 49 .... 45, **187**
Taylor *v.* Bristol Omnibus Ltd [1975] 1 W.L.R. 1054; [1975] 2 All E.R. 1107 .... 5, 44
Taylor *v.* Marshalls Food Group, 1997 S.C.L.R. 815 .... 58, **279**
Taylor *v.* O'Connor [1971] A.C. 115 .... 75, 78, 79

Tennant *v.* John Walker & Sons Ltd, 1989 S.L.T. 143 .... 38, **211**
Thom *v.* Bridges (1857) 19 D. 721 32
Thompson's Curator Bonis *v.* Burnett, 1989 S.L.T. 264 13
Timoney *v.* Dunnery, 1984 S.L.T 151 43
Todd *v.* Montgomerie Sealants Ltd, 1983 S.L.T. 354 .... 45, **190**
Traill & Sons *v.* Actieselskabat Dalbeattie Ltd (1904) 6 F. 798 32
Travers *v.* Muirhead, 1991 S.C. 236 .... **222**
Tuttle *v.* Edinburgh University, 1984 S.L.T. 172 .... 50, **190**
Tweedy *v.* Newboult, 1996 S.L.T. 2 .... 44, **269**

Vaughan *v.* Greater Glasgow Passenger Transport Executive, 1984 S.C. 32 37

Walker *v.* Infabco Diving Services Ltd, 1983 S.L.T. 633 15
Wall *v.* Bryant, 1994 S.L.T. 1260 .... 39, 50, 51, **247**
Walledge *v.* Brown, 1996 S.L.T. 95 .... **270**
Ward *v.* City of Glasgow District Council, 1989 S.L.T. 349 .... **211**
Ward *v.* James [1966] 1 Q.B. 273 33
Ward *v.* Newalls Insulation Co Ltd [1998] 2 All E.R. 690 37
Watson *v.* British Railways Board, 1991 S.L.T 657 .... **224**
Watson *v.* City Meat Wholesalers Ltd, 1981 S.L.T. (Notes) 121 .... **188**
Watson *v.* Thompson, 1991 S.C. 447 32
Watt *v.* Clyde Alloy Steel Company Limited, 1966 S.L.T. (Notes) 64 .... **172**
Watts *v.* Russell, 1993 S.L.T. 1227 .... **244**
Waugh *v.* James K Allan Ltd, 1963 S.C. 175 37
Webb *v.* MacAuley, 1988 S.C. 10 37
Webster *v.* Simpson's Motors, 1967 S.L.T. (Notes) 36 .... **284**
Wells *v.* Wells [1997] 1 W.L.R. 652 .... 92, 103
Wells *v.* Wells [1998] 3 W.L.R. 329 .... 9, 18, 45, 53, 54, 55, 92, 106, 308, 350
White *v.* Inveresk Paper Co Ltd, 1987 S.C. 143 .... 23, 24
Whitfield *v.* Ranco Motors Ltd, 1979 S.L.T. (Notes) 15 .... **181**
Whyte *v.* Nestle (U.K.) Ltd, 1997 S.C.L.R. 598 .... **282**
Whyte *v.* University of Dundee, 1990 S.L.T. 545 .... **215**
Will *v.* Charles Will Ltd, 1980 S.L.T. (Notes) 37 .... 45, 54, 61, 64, **183**
Willett *v.* North Bedfordshire Health Authority [1993] P.I.Q.R. Q166 9
Williamson *v.* GB Papers plc, 1994 S.L.T. 173 .... **258**
Willson *v.* Ministry of Defence [1991] 1 All E. R. 638 .... 23, 24
Wilson *v.* Chief Constable, Lothian and Borders Constabulary, 1989 S.L.T. 97 .... 27, 72, 76, 78, 79, **300**
Wilson *v.* Norman J. Stewart & Co (1970) Ltd, 1986 S.L.T. 469 .... **196**
Wilson *v.* Price, 1989 S.L.T. 484 .... 44, **210**
Wise *v.* Kaye [1962] 1 Q.B. 638 33
Wisely *v.* John Fulton (Plumbers) Ltd, 1998 S.L.T. 1026 27
Woodrup *v.* Nicol [1993] P.I.Q.R. Q104 54
Worf *v.* Western S.M.T. Co Ltd, 1987 S.L.T. 317 .... 76, 78, 86, **299**
Wotherspoon *v.* Strathclyde Regional Council, 1992 S.L.T. 1090 .... 71, 76, 86, **303**
Wright *v.* British Railways Board [1983] 2 A.C. 773 .... 3, 4, 27, 33, 34

Young *v.* Greater Glasgow Health Board, 1993 S.L.T. 721 .... 44, **242**
Young *v.* Roche Services Group plc, 1988 G.W.D. 32-1371 37
Young *v.* Roche Services Group plc, 1989 S.L.T 212 .... **215**

TABLE OF STATUTES

A page number in **bold type** indicates that the full text of the provision is reproduced on that page.

Administration of Justice Act 1982 (c. 53)
Part II 71
s. 7 .... 56, 61
s. 8 49
s. 8(1) 56, 53, 59
s. 8(2) 58
s. 8(3) 58, 60
s. 8(4) 56
s. 9(1) 61, 64
s. 9(2) 83
s. 9(3) 63, 85
s. 9(4) 61, 84
s. 10 42
s. 10(a) 47
s. 10(e)(i) 40
s. 10(iv) 41
s. 11 .... 41, 53
s. 12 .... 3, 22, 23
s. 12(2)(a) 325
s. 12(2)(b) 25
s. 12(3) 25
s. 12(4)(b) 25
s. 13(1) 22, 42, 57, 62
s. 13(2) 41
s. 14(2) 49
s. 14(2)(a) 31, 36, 56, 61, 68, 74, 81, 84

Bankruptcy (Scotland) Act 1985 (c. 66)
s. 31(1)(5) 37, 46, 57, 62
s. 32(6) 37, 46, 57, 62

Children (Scotland) Act 1995 (c. 36)
s. 11(1)(d) 3
s. 13 3
s. 13(1) 14

Court of Session Act 1988 (c. 36)
s. 32(1) 4
s. 32(3) 4
s. 37 4

Damages (Scotland) Act 1976 (c. 13) 16, 49, 56, 61
s. 1 .... 26, 67, 71, 73, 74, 80, 81, 84, 340
s. 1(2) 68, 74, 81, 84
s. 1(3) 73, 80, 83
s. 1(4) 71
s. 1(5) 77
s. 1(5A) 68, 74, 76, 81, 84
s. 1(6) 75
s. 1(7) 71
s. 1A 68, 74, 81, 84
s. 2(1) 31, 36, 46, 49, 56, 61
s. 2(2) 49, 56, 61
s. 2(3) 31
s. 2A 49
s. 2A(1)(2). 31, 36, 56, 62, 68, 74, 81
s. 4 .... 31, 36, 49, 56, 61, 68, 74, 81, 84
s. 6 49
s. 6(1)(2) . 31, 37, 62, 68, 74, 81, 84
s. 6(3)(a) 31, 37, 62
s. 6(3)(b) 68, 74, 81, 84
s. 7(2) 16
s. 9(1)(2) 45
s. 9A(1)(2)(3) 32
s. 10(1) 16, 73, 80, 83
s. 10(2) 67
Sched. 1, paras 1, 2 ... 67, 73, 80, 83

Damages (Scotland) Act 1993 (c. 5)
s. 1(1) 71
s. 2 .... 68, 74, 81, 84
s. 2(1)(2) 14
s. 3 .... 31, 36, 49, 56, 61
s. 4 .... 31, 36, 56, 62, 74
s. 5 32
Sched., para. 1 .... 31, 36, 49, 56, 61, 68, 74, 81, 84

Damages Act 1996 (c. 48) 106
s. 1 .... 8, 11, 92
s. 1(1)(2)(3) 19

s. 2 ... 3
s. 2(1)(2)(3) ... 16
s. 4 ... 16
s. 5 ... 16, 17
s. 6 ... 18

Employment Protection (Consolidation) Act 1978 (c. 44)
s. 81 ... 42

Finance Act 1996 (c. 8)
s. 150(1)(2) ... 16, 18
Sched. 26 ... 16, 18

Income and Corporation Taxes Act 1988 (c. 1)
s. 329AA ... 16, 18
s. 329AA(1)(5)(7) ... 16

Interest on Damages (Scotland) Act 1958 (6 & 7 Eliz. 2, c. 61)
s. 1 ... 26, 28
s. 1(1)(1A) ... 26
s. 1(1B) ... 28

Interest on Damages (Scotland) Act 1971 (c. 31)
s. 1 ... 26, 28

International Transport Conventions Act 1983 (c. 14)
s. 1 ... 71

Jobseekers Act 1995 (c. 18) ... 40

Law Reform (Miscellaneous Provisions) Act 1971 (c. 43)
s. 4 ... 72, 77

Law Reform (Parent and Child) (Scotland) Act 1986 (c. 9)
s. 1(1) ... 42, 57, 67, 73, 80, 83

Law Reform (Personal Injuries) Act 1948 (11 & 12 Geo. 6, c. 41)
s. 2(1) ... 42
s. 2(4) ... 52

Road Traffic Act 1988 (c. 52)
s. 157 ... 53
s. 158 ... 53

Sheriff Courts (Scotland) Act 1907 (7 Edw. 7, c. 51)
s. 27 ... 4

Social Security Act 1975 (c. 14) ... 77

Social Security Administration Act 1992 (c. 5)
s. 23 ... 326
s. 50 ... 326
s. 71 ... 329
s. 82(1)(b) ... 347
s. 98 ... 347
s. 189 ... 335
s. 189(4)(5)(6) ... 339
s. 191 ... 326

Social Security Contributions and Benefits Act 1992 (c. 4) ... 334
Pt XI ... 331
s. 103 ... 338
s. 104 ... 51, 338
s. 105 ... 51, 338

Social Security (Recovery of Benefits) Act 1997 (c. 27) ... 27, **317** ***et seq.***
s. 1 ... **319**, 332, 337
s. 1(1)(a) ... 323
s. 2 ... **319**, 336, 347
s. 3 ... **319**
s. 4 ... **320**, 330, 343
s. 4(9) ... 339
s. 5 ... **321**
s. 6 ... **321**, 322, 326, 329, 330, 332, 333, 335, 337, 343, 344, 347
s. 7 ... **322**
s. 7(4)(5) ... 334
s. 8 ... **322**, 323, 324, 327, 328, 329, 330, 338, 337, 343, 344, 346, 347
s. 9 ... **323**
s. 9(1) 7 ... 343
s. 10 ... **324**, 325, 326
s. 11 ... **324**, 325, 326
s. 12 ... **325**, 326
s. 13 ... **326**
s. 14 ... **326**, 329, 335, 346
s. 14(2)(3)(4) ... 339
s. 15 ... 38, 51, 58, **327**
s. 16 ... **327**
s. 16(1)(2) ... 339
s. 17 ... 38, 40, 51, **327**
s. 18 ... **328**, 339
s. 19 ... **329**, 339
s. 20 ... **329**, 335
s. 21 ... **330**
s. 21(3) ... 339
s. 21(3)(a) ... 342
s. 22 ... **330**
s. 23 ... **331**

s. 23(1)(2)(5)(7) 339
s. 24 .... **332**, 335
s. 25 .... **332**
s. 26 .... **332**, 334
s. 27 .... 333, **334**
s. 28 .... **334**
s. 29 .... **334**, 339
s. 30 .... **335**
s. 31 .... **335**
s. 32 .... **336**, 339
s. 33 .... **336**
s. 34 .... **336**
Sched. 1 .... **337**
Sched. 1, para. 4 339
Sched. 1, para. 8 .... 339, 340
Sched. 1, para. 9 335
Sched. 1, Pt. II 319, 328
Sched. 2 .... 322, 332, **338**
Sched. 2, col. 1 38, 51, 327, 328, 344
Sched. 2, col. 2 .... 51, 328, 335, 344

TABLE OF RULES OF THE COURT OF SESSION

R.C.S.
24.1 4
24.2 4
38.21 4
43.1(1)(a) 32, 37, 50, 57, 62
43.1(1)(b) 69
43.1(2) 69
43.2 69
43.3 69
43.4(1) 69
43.4(2)(3) 70
43.5 70
43.6(1)(2)(3)(4) 70
43.7 70
43.8(1)(2) 12
43.9(1)(2) 12
43.9(3)(4)(5) 13
43.9(6) 15
43.9(7) 14
43.9(8) 12
43.10 15
43.12(a) 22
43.12(b)(c) 22
43.13(1) 25
43.13(2)(3)(4) 25
49.88 3

TABLE OF ORDINARY CAUSE RULES

O.C.R.
18.2 4
18.3 4
33.95 3
36.1(1)(a) 32, 37, 50, 57, 62
36.1(1)(b) 69
36.1(2) 69
36.2 69
36.3 69
36.4(1) 69
36.4(2)(3) 70
36.5 70
36.6(1)(2)(3)(4) 70
36.7 70
36.8(1)(2) 12
36.9(1)(2) 12
36.9(3)(4)(5) 13
36.9(6) 15
36.9(7) 14
36.9(8) 12
36.10 15
36.12(a) 22
36.12(b)(c) 22
36.13(1)(2)(3)(4) 25

I. REMEDIES

Chapter 1

LUMP SUM AWARDS

Damages for personal injuries and for the death of a relative from personal injuries may be given by the court by way of lump sum awards, whether as final decrees for damages or as orders for interim payment of damages.

FINAL DECREES FOR DAMAGES

Subject to certain statutory exceptions,[1] any decree for damages for personal injuries or for the death of a relative requires to take the form of an unconditional lump sum award in favour of the claimant.[2] Where the damages are payable to, or for the benefit of, a child under the age of 16 years, the court may make such order relating to the payment and management of the sum for the benefit of the child as it thinks fit.[3] Decree requires to be granted in pounds sterling, except that decree for any pecuniary loss awarded may be expressed in foreign currency with the alternative in sterling at the date of payment or at the date of extract, whichever is the earlier.[4]

Save in the case of awards of provisional damages, awards of damages for personal injuries are governed by the principle that there

---

[1] Damages Act 1996, s. 2 (consent orders for periodical payments), considered in Chap. 2; and Administration of Justice Act 1982, s. 12 (awards of provisional damages), considered in Chap. 3.

[2] *Banbury v. Bank of Montreal* [1918] A.C. 626 at p. 700; *Fournier v. Canadian National Railway Company* [1927] A.C. 167 at p. 168; *Wright v. British Railways Board* [1983] 2 A.C. 773 at p. 777.

[3] Children (Scotland) Act 1995, s. 13(1). Without prejudice to the generality of that provision, the court may (a) appoint a judicial factor to invest, apply or otherwise deal with the money for the benefit of the child concerned; (b) order the money to be paid — (i) to the sheriff clerk or the accountant of court; or (ii) to a parent or guardian of that child, to be invested, applied or otherwise dealt with, under directions of the court, for the benefit of the child; or (c) order the money to be paid directly to that child — s. 13(2). Where payment is made to a person in accordance with an order under s. 13, a receipt given by him shall be a sufficient discharge of the obligation to make the payment — s. 13(3). Where the court has made an order under s. 13, an application by a person for an order by virtue of s. 11(1)(d) of the 1995 Act (administration of child's property) may be made by minute in the process of the cause in which the order under s. 13 was made — R.C.S. 49.88 (Court of Session) and O.C.R. 33.95 (Sheriff Court).

[4] *Fullemann v. McInnes's Executors*, 1993 S.L.T. 259.

should be finality in litigation.[5] Thus damages have to be assessed once and for all, whether they relate to reparation for loss already incurred and capable of accurate computation or to prospective loss where assessment may necessarily include an element of speculation.[6] The injured person is therefore bound to recover all the damages to which he can lay claim in the one action.[7] Accordingly, once he has been awarded damages in an action against one wrongdoer, it is incompetent for him to sue another.[8]

In making the assessment of damages the court must take into consideration all that has happened since the date of the event giving rise to the claim.[9] The court does not speculate when it knows.[10] This enables the principle of finality in litigation to be disapplied, exceptionally, where the award of damages is under appeal.[11] The appellate court has a discretionary power, to be exercised in very exceptional circumstances, to allow amendment of the pleadings in relation to events which have occurred since the date of the trial and to allow additional proof as to these matters.[12]

---

[5] *Rieley v. Kingslaw Riding School,* 1975 S.C. 28 at p. 41. As to provisional damages, see Chap. 3.

[6] *Rieley v. Kingslaw Riding School,* 1975 S.C. 28 at p. 41; *Wright v. British Railways Board* [1983] 2 A.C. 773 at p. 777.

[7] *Stevenson v. Pontifex & Wood* (1887) 15 R. 125 at p. 130; *Balfour v. Baird & Sons,* 1959 S.C. 64 at p. 72.

[8] Erskine, Inst., III, I, 15; *Balfour v. Baird & Sons,* 1959 S.C. 64. The position would be otherwise if the injured person had been unable to get satisfaction under the decree already obtained and was willing to assign that decree to the second wrongdoer — *Steven v. Broady Norman & Co,* 1928 S.C. 351. Note that *Steven* is not authority that a succession of actions against one defender for different items of loss caused by one wrongful act is possible — *Irving v. Hiddleston,* 1998 S.L.T. 912.

[9] *MacMaster v. Caledonian Railway Co* (1885) 13 R. 252 at p. 255, approved by the Full Bench in *Rieley v. Kingslaw Riding School,* 1975 S.C. 28 at p. 40.

[10] *Jobling v. Associated Dairies Ltd* [1982] A.C. 794 at p. 819; *Curwen v. James* [1963] 1 W.L.R. 748 at p. 753.

[11] *Rieley v. Kingslaw Riding School,* 1975 S.C. 28 at pp. 40–41. As to the conditions requiring to be met before an appeal court will interfere with an award of damages, see *Robertson's Curator Bonis v. Anderson*, 1996 S.C. 217 at pp. 219–220 and cases there cited.

[12] *Rieley v. Kingslaw Riding School,* 1975 S.C. 28 at p. 40 (amendment and additional proof as to amputation of leg after trial allowed); *Dalgleish v. Glasgow Corporation,* 1976 S.C. 32 at p. 50 (amendment as to death of injured person after trial allowed but new material left out of account); R.C.S. 24.1, 24.2 and 38.21 (amendment in Court of Session action under appeal to Inner House); Court of Session Act 1988, s. 32(1) (amendment in Sheriff Court action under appeal to Inner House); O.C.R. 18.2 and 18.3 (amendment in Sheriff Court action under appeal to Sheriff Principal); Court of Session Act 1988, s. 37 (additional proof in Court of Session action under appeal to Inner House); Court of Session Act 1988, ss. 32(3) and 37 (additional proof in Sheriff Court action under appeal to Inner House); Sheriff Courts (Scotland) Act 1907, s. 27 (additional proof in Sheriff Court action under appeal to Sheriff Principal).

The separate items which together constitute a total award of damages are interrelated; they are the parts of a whole, which must be fair and reasonable.[13] The court should look at the total figure in the round, so as to be able to cure any overlapping or other source of error.[14] The risk of overlapping lies, however, as between separate heads of pecuniary loss rather than as between pecuniary loss and non-pecuniary loss, which are assessed on different principles and serve different purposes.[15]

Damages which have to be paid for personal injuries are not punitive, still less are they a reward — they are simply compensation and this is as true with regard to solatium as it is with pecuniary loss.[16] The object is to place the injured person in as good a position as he would have been in but for the accident.[17] He is not to be placed in a better position.[18] This process involves a comparison between his circumstances as they would have been if the accident had not occurred and his actual circumstances following the accident.[19] In relation to determining what did or did not occur in the past, the court decides on the balance of probability and anything that is more probable than not is treated as certain.[20] However, it is impossible to prove as a fact what would have happened; all one can do is estimate or evaluate the chance of a particular outcome and the balance of probability test has no application in this regard.[21] A chance may be a probability of over

---

13 *Lim v. Camden Health Authority* [1980] A.C. 174 at p. 191.

14 *Taylor v. Bristol Omnibus Ltd* [1975] 1 W.L.R. 1054 at p. 1057. The totality of the elements should not, however, be open to increase or modification merely on account of a feeling that the total seems unduly large or small — *Wells v. Wells* [1998] 3 W.L.R. 329 at p. 361.

15 Royal Commission on Civil Liability and Compensation for Personal Injury (Cmnd 7054–I), para. 759; *Lim v. Camden Health Authority* [1980] A.C. 174 at p. 192. See *e.g. Fish v. Wilcox* [1994] 5 Med. L.R. 230 (claim in respect of loss of earnings and for services rendered amounted to double recovery) and *Arafa v. Potter* [1994] P.I.Q.R. Q73 at p. Q78 (no need for injured person to give credit for shorter hours and longer holidays in alternative job obtained by him in mitigation of loss of earnings).

16 *Muckarsie v. Dickson* (1848) 11 D. 4; *Black v. The North British Railway Company,* 1908 S.C. 444; *British Transport Commission v. Gourley* [1956] A.C. 185 at p. 208.

17 *Livingstone v. The Rawyards Coal Company Limited* (1880) 7 R. (H.L.) 1 at p. 7; *O'Brien's Curator Bonis v. British Steel plc,* 1991 S.C. 315 at p. 319; *Jobling v. Associated Dairies Ltd* [1982] A.C. 794 at p. 814.

18 *Parry v. Cleaver* [1970] A.C. 1 at p. 13; *Jobling v. Associated Dairies Ltd* [1982] A.C. 794 at p. 814.

19 *Jobling v. Associated Dairies Ltd* [1982] A.C. 794 at p. 814.

20 *Mallett v. McMonagle* [1970] A.C. 166 at p. 176; *Davies v. Taylor* [1974] A.C. 207 at pp. 212–213.

21 *Davies v. Taylor* [1974] A.C. 207 at pp. 212–213 (no significant chance that widow would have returned to estranged husband); *Anderson v. Davis* [1993] P.I.Q.R. Q87 at p. Q98 (injured person's prospects of achieving promotion by a date several years before the trial estimated at 66.7%; and two-thirds of the net additional loss of earnings referable to the lost promotion awarded as damages).

99%, but it is still only a chance.[22] When it is said that there was a chance that a particular event would have occurred, the sole issue is whether that chance was substantial.[23] If it was, it must be evaluated; if it was not (but was merely speculative), it must be ignored.[24]

In the case of loss preceding trial, the comparison between the actual circumstances (proven on the balance of probability) and a hypothetical state of facts (evaluated with the benefit of hindsight, or assumed) may readily result in the claimed loss being treated as certain.[25] In the case of loss after trial, it is not possible to prove as a fact that a future event will happen or that a future event would have happened but for an occurrence in the past and therefore all one can do is to estimate the chances of particular outcomes:

> "But in assessing damages which depend upon its view as to what will happen in the future or would have happened in the future if something had not happened in the past, the court must make an estimate as to what are the chances that a particular thing will or would have happened and reflect those chances, whether they are more or less than even, in the amount of damages which it awards."[26]

The estimation of chances in any given case, therefore, involves assessing prospects whether future or hypothetical. The latter type of contingency is of particular note in the case of an injured person who had a pre-existing weakness or vulnerability which rendered him, but not others, susceptible to sustaining the injury in question or who had a pre-existing disability or condition which was exacerbated by the particular injury.[27] In either case, damages will be awarded for the

---

[22] *Davies v. Taylor* [1974] A.C. 207 at p. 213.

[23] *Ibid.* at p. 212.

[24] *Ibid.* at p. 212.

[25] *British Transport Commission v. Gourley* [1956] A.C. 185 at p. 212. Such applies also *mutatis mutandis* to a finding of no loss, as in the case of a supervening illness incapacitating the claimant irrespective of the personal injury (as in *e.g. Jobling v. Associated Dairies Ltd* [1982] A.C. 794) and to a finding of partial loss, as in the case of a second, unconnected accident increasing the loss of capacity arising out of the personal injury (as in *e.g. Baker v. Willoughby* [1970] A.C. 467).

[26] *Per* Lord Diplock in *Mallett v. McMonagle* [1970] A.C. 166 at p. 176. The more remote in the future the contingency the less confidence there can be in the chances of its occurring and the smaller the allowance to be made for it in the assessment; and as a matter of arithmetic of the calculation of present value, the later the change takes place the less will be its effect upon the total award of damages (*Mallett*, at p. 177).

[27] See *e.g. Bush v. Greater Glasgow Health Board,* 1995 G.W.D. 25–1333 (predisposition to depressive illness); *Duffy v. Lanarkshire Health Board,* 1995 S.L.T. 1312 (predisposition to anxiety and depression); *Mearns v. Lothian Regional Council,* 1991 S.L.T. 338 (pre-existing disability due to previous injury to knee); and *Reid v. Edinburgh Acoustics Ltd,* 1995 S.L.T. 659 (pre-existing degenerative changes in cervical spine). See also *Sutherland v. North British Steel Group Ltd,* 1986 S.L.T. (Sh.Ct.) 29 and *Gray v. Lanarkshire Health Board,* 1996 S.L.T. 390 (injury accelerating process of herniation).

injury and its effects but discounted or scaled down so as to reflect the chances that similar effects would have arisen within the relevant period irrespective of the injury in question.[28]

The principles above described converge in what may be called the annuity approach relative to the assessment of future pecuniary loss in personal injury cases:

> "The underlying principle is, of course, that damages are compensatory. They are not designed to put the [injured person], or his estate in the event of his death, in a better financial position than that in which he would otherwise have been if the accident had not occurred. At the same time, the principle of making a once-for-all award necessarily involves an assessment both of the probable duration and extent of the financial disadvantages resulting from the accident which the [injured person] will suffer in the future and of the present advantage which will accrue to him from payment in the present of a capital sum which he would not otherwise have and which represents his future income loss. In the making of that assessment, account has also to be taken of a number of unpredictable contingencies and in particular that the life expectancy from which the calculation starts may be falsified in the event by supervening illness or accident entirely unconnected with the event for which compensation is being awarded. Such an assessment cannot, therefore, by its nature be a precise science. The presence of so many imponderable factors necessarily renders the process a complex and imprecise one and one which is incapable of producing anything better than an approximate result. Essentially what the court has to do is to calculate as best it can the sum of money which will on the one hand be adequate, by its capital and income, to provide annually for the injured person a sum equal to his estimated annual loss over the whole of the period during which that loss is likely to continue, but which, on the other hand, will not, at the end of that period, leave him in a better

---

[28] See *e.g. Bush v. Greater Glasgow Health Board*, 1995 G.W.D. 25–1333 (20% deduction from total award to reflect realistic possibility of illness being triggered by equivalent event); *Duffy v. Lanarkshire Health Board*, 1995 S.L.T. 1312 (33% deduction from awards of solatium and loss of earnings for the past and 100% deduction from awards of solatium for the future and loss of future earnings to reflect likelihood that symptoms would have arisen before trial anyway irrespective of the injury in question); *Mearns v. Lothian Regional Council*, 1991 S.L.T. 338 (awards for solatium and loss of future earnings reduced to reflect fact that this was a case of acceleration of a disability rather than the creation of a new disability); and *Reid v. Edinburgh Acoustics Ltd*, 1995 S.L.T. 659 (awards for solatium and loss of earnings reduced to reflect fact that a minor incident in the ordinary course of life could have caused similar aggravation).

financial position than he would have been apart from the accident. Hence the conventional approach is to assess the amount notionally required to be laid out in the purchase of an annuity which will provide the annual amount needed for the whole period of loss."[29]

Underlying the annuity approach is the requirement that all future losses be discounted so as to give a present value, since the capital sum awarded is able to be invested and earn compound interest ahead of the dates of those losses.[30] Such a capital sum may be expressed as the product of multiplying an annual sum which represents the annual loss by a number of years' purchase.[31] This latter figure is less than the number of years representing the estimated period of loss since the capital sum will not be exhausted until the end of that period and in the meantime so much as is not exhausted in each year will earn interest from which the loss in that year could in part be met.[32] The number of years' purchase to be used in order to calculate the capital value of an annuity for a given period of years thus depends upon the rate of interest which it is assumed that money would earn during the period.[33] The higher the rate of return, the lower the number of years' purchase.[34] In determining the rate to be expected from the investment of a sum awarded as damages for future pecuniary loss in an action for personal injury, the court must take into account, subject to and in accordance with the relative rules of court, such rate of return (if any) as may from time to time be prescribed by an order made by the Secretary of State.[35] Pending the making of any such order, the appropriate rate of return (based on the assumption

---

[29] *Per* Lord Oliver of Aylmerton in *Hodgson v. Trapp* [1989] A.C. 807 at p. 826. The annuity approach falls to be applied also in the assessment of loss of support in death cases (see *Cookson v. Knowles* [1979] A.C. 556 at p. 576).

[30] Discounting is achieved by the compound interest or present value formula, which is as follows: $P_n = P_o \left(1 + \frac{x}{100}\right)^n$

where P_o is the initial capital invested at x% and P_n is the capital at compound interest at the end of n years.

[31] *Cookson v. Knowles* [1979] A.C. 556 at p. 568.

[32] *Ibid.*

[33] *Ibid.*

[34] *Ibid.*

[35] Damages Act 1996, s. 1(1) and (5). Such does not prevent the court taking a different rate of return into account if any party to the proceedings shows that it is more appropriate in the case in question — s. 1(2). An order made under subs. (1) may prescribe different rates of return for different classes of case — s. 1(3). Before making an order, the Secretary of State requires to consult the Government Actuary and the Treasury; and any order must be made by statutory instrument subject to annulment in pursuance of a resolution of either House of Parliament — s. 1(4).

that the injured person will invest his damages in index-linked government stock, which is tied to the retail price index and hence protected against inflation, and subject to any significant change in the average yield on ILGS over a period) is 3% net.[36]

The annuity approach in practice involves applying a "multiplier" representing an appropriate number of years' purchase to a "multiplicand" representing the amount of the annual loss or expense. It may be that contingencies or imponderables fall to be reflected in the selection of the latter figure, or by taking different multiplicands for different periods covered by the award;[37] or it may be that such adjusting factors are suitably reflected in the multiplier:

> "The function of the multiplier of an annual sum is first to convert one or more annual sums...into a single capital sum. It is, secondly, to allow for the advancement of the payment or payments that are being made. It is, thirdly, to allow for contingencies and other adjusting factors that have to be taken into account. The first and second aspects are essentially mathematically exercises that should be approached in a mathematical fashion. The third is a matter of assessment and has to take into account all the circumstances of the case, including how the multiplicand has been arrived at. Contingencies may already have been allowed for in a multiplicand or the multiplicand may incorporate assumptions which are favourable to [the injured person] and which then need to be discounted in selecting the multiplier in order to arrive at a reasonable and realistic result."[38]

In making the selection of the multiplier, the court should use actuarial tables.[39] In the case of assessing the lump sum appropriate as compensation for a continuing future pecuniary loss or consequential expense, tables prepared by the Government Actuary's Department (the "Ogden Tables") are available.[40] These tables comprise (i) multipliers for persons over a range of ages calculated *with allowance*

---

[36] *Wells v. Wells* [1998] 3 W.L.R. 329.

[37] *Ibid.*

[38] *Per* Hobhouse J in *Willett v. North Bedfordshire Health Authority* [1993] P.I.Q.R. Q166 at pp. Q167–Q168; *Wells v. Wells, cit. supra.*

[39] *O'Brien's Curator Bonis v. British Steel plc,* 1991 S.C. 315; *Wells v. Wells, cit. supra.*

[40] The tables are reproduced in App. IA. It is not fatal to their use that the tables were not referred to in evidence or lodged as productions—*O'Brien's Curator Bonis v. British Steel plc, cit. supra,* at p. 326. Note that Tables 1 to 10 are constructed from historic mortality experience in England and Wales and Tables 11 to 20 from projected mortality there. *Quaere* how the tables should be used in the case of an injured person living in Scotland where mortality experience has been different (*cf.* App. II).

for historic population mortality and rates of interest ranging from 1.5% to 5%, treating males and females separately by reason of their different life expectancy (Tables 1–10); (ii) multipliers for persons over a range of ages calculated *with allowance for projected population mortality* and rates of interest ranging from 1.5% to 5%, treating males and females separately by reason of their different life expectancy (Tables 11–20); (iii) discounting factors for a term certain (*i.e.* factors to discount the value of a multiplier for a period of deferment) with rates of interest ranging from 1.5% to 5% (Table 21); and (iv) multipliers for pecuniary loss for a term certain (*i.e.* multipliers for regular frequent payments for a fixed period) with rates of interest ranging from 1.5% to 5% (Table 22).

The multipliers in Tables 1 to 20 enable the user to assess the present capital value of future annual loss (net of tax) or annual expense calculated on the basis of various assumptions, namely:

(a) that the loss or expense is assumed to begin immediately and to continue for the whole of the rest of the injured person's life allowing for the possibility of early death or prolonged life (Tables 1 and 2 or 11 and 12);
(b) that the loss or expense is assumed to begin immediately but to continue only until the injured person's retirement or earlier death (Tables 3 and 4 or 13 and 14 for retirement age of 65; Tables 5 and 6 or 15 and 16 for retirement age of 60); and
(c) that the loss or expense is assumed not to begin until the injured person reaches retirement but will then continue for the whole of the rest of his or her life allowing for the chance that he may never live to reach the age of retirement (Tables 7 and 8 or 17 and 18 for retirement age of 65;Tables 9 and 10 or 19 and 20 for retirement age of 60).[41]

---

[41] Tables' Explanatory Notes, Section A, paras 2–4. Note that if for some reason the facts in a particular case do not correspond with the assumptions on which one of the tables is based then the tables can only be used by making an appropriate allowance for this difference and the assistance of an actuary should be sought — para. 10. Where the loss or expense is liable to vary, the tables may nonetheless be used by altering the annual figure for loss or expense or by selecting a different rate of interest, and hence a different multiplier, than would otherwise have been chosen — paras 24 and 25. A difference in retiring age may be catered for in accordance with the advice in paras 16 to 18 of the Explanatory Notes. In the case of multipliers for loss of earnings, younger ages (*i.e.* below 16 years) may be catered for in accordance with the advice in para. 20 of the Explanatory Notes. Where there is medical evidence that an injured person's health impairments are equivalent to adding a certain number of years to the current age, or to treating the individual as having a specific age different from the actual age, the advice given in para. 22 of the Explanatory Notes may be followed. For a view that Projected Mortality Tables should not be used, see Explanatory Notes, App. C, paras 7–11.

The court may also use the multipliers in these tables to assess the lump sum appropriate as compensation for continuing loss of support in death cases, making the selection in respect of deceased persons taking their ages at date of death (rather than at date of trial).[42]

Tables 1 to 20 do not allow for contingencies other than mortality but the Government Actuary's Department has provided other information which, if used in conjunction with the appropriate table above, allows for other chances to be taken into account, namely the principal contingencies of unemployment and illness, on a ready reckoner basis.[43] This other information comprises (1) tables which may be used to reduce the multiplier selected, in order to give a basic deduction for contingencies other than mortality, by multiplying it by a fraction chosen from the appropriate column (usually the one headed "Medium") in the appropriate table (Table A for loss of earnings to pension age of 65 (males); Table B for loss of earnings to pension age of 60 (males); Table C for loss of earnings to pension age of 60 (females)); (2) further figures by which the fraction in question may be varied so as to allow for the riskiness of the injured person's occupation as it affects those principal contingencies; and (3) yet other figures by which the fraction in question may be varied or further varied so as to allow for the geographical region in which the injured person resides as it affects those principal contingencies.[44]

In summary, Tables 1 to 20 may be used by taking the following steps:

"(1) Choose the tables relating to the appropriate period of loss or expense.
(2) Choose the table, relating to that period, appropriate to the sex of the [injured person].
(3) Choose the appropriate rate of return, before allowing for the effect of tax on the income to be obtained from the lump sum.[45]
(4) If appropriate, allow for a reduction in the rate of return to reflect the effect of tax on the income from the lump sum.[46]

---

[42] Tables' Explanatory Notes, Section A, paras 1 and 3; Section C, para. 41(5).

[43] Tables' Explanatory Notes, Section A, para. 21 and Section B. For a view that such information should not be used, see Tables' Explanatory Notes, App. C, paras 12–15.

[44] Tables' Explanatory Notes, Section B, paras 26–40.

[45] See following footnote.

[46] For the purposes of stages 3 and 4, taken together, the appropriate rate of interest generally is 3% net, pending the making of any order by the Secretary of State under s. 1 of the Damages Act 1996 (and subject to any significant change in the yield on index-linked government stock in the future)—see n. 36 *supra* and accompanying text. Only in very exceptional circumstances would there fall to be taken into account the effect which higher rates of tax would have on the income from the damages (*Hodgson v. Trapp* [1989] 1 A.C. 807).

(5) Find the figure under the column in the table chosen given against the age at trial (or, in a fatal accident case, at the death) of the [injured person].
(6) Adjust the figure to take account of contingencies other than mortality…
(7) Multiply the annual loss (net of tax) or expense by that figure."[47]

Tables 21 and 22 do not allow for any contingencies at all *including* mortality and are therefore suitable for the assessment of the present value of a loss taking place at a fixed time in the future, whether in respect of a single sum (Table 21) or a series of annual sums (Table 22).[48]

ORDERS FOR INTERIM PAYMENT OF DAMAGES

In an action of damages for personal injuries or the death of a person from personal injuries, a pursuer may, at any time after defences have been lodged, apply by motion for an order for interim payment of damages to him by the defender or, where there are two or more of them, by any one or more of them.[49] The pursuer requires to intimate the motion to every party not less than 14 days before enrolment.[50] A defender, for these purposes, includes a third party against whom the pursuer has a conclusion or crave for damages.[51] No order can be made against a defender unless it appears to the court that the defender is (a) a person who is insured in respect of the claim; (b) a public authority;

---

47 Tables' Explanatory Notes, Section C, para. 41. An example is given in para. 43. Any adjustment for an expected increase in the annual loss or expenses (*not* due to inflation) can be made at stages 3 or 4 (by choosing a lower rate of interest) or at stage 6 (by increasing the figure for annual loss or expense) — para. 42. Where the expected retirement age differs from that assumed in the tables, the procedure set forth in paras 16–18 of the Explanatory Notes should be followed.

48 See also PNBA Tables B1 and B2, with explanatory notes, in App. I. Table B3 in App. I gives multipliers for payment at intervals of years.

49 R.C.S. 43.8(1) and 43.9(1) (Court of Session) and O.C.R. 36.8(1) and 36.9(1) (Sheriff Court). The rule applies with the necessary modifications to a counterclaim for damages for personal injuries made by a defender as it applies to an action in which the pursuer may apply for an order for interim payment of damages — R.C.S. 43.9(8) and O.C.R. 36.9(8). "Personal injuries" for the purposes of the rule includes any disease or impairment of a physical or mental condition — R.C.S. 43.8(2) and O.C.R. 36.8(2).

50 R.C.S. 43.9(2) and O.C.R. 36.9(2).

51 R.C.S. 43.8(2) and O.C.R. 36.8(2).

or (c) a person whose means and resources are such as to enable him to make the interim payment.[52]

On such a motion, the court may, if satisfied that one or other of certain conditions precedent exist in relation to any defender, ordain that defender to make an interim payment to the pursuer of such amount as it thinks fit, not exceeding a reasonable proportion of the damages which, in the opinion of the court, are likely to be recovered by the pursuer.[53] This leaves quantification open to the court short of the ceiling figure but the limit is set at a proportion and so a conservative and moderate approach is necessary, albeit that the size of the proportion must vary from case to case.[54] Damages must be estimated as at the date or likely date of the forthcoming trial and not as at the date of the motion.[55] The estimation falls to be made on the basis of the information available at the time of the application as disclosed by the parties' pleadings and *ex parte* statements.[56] Factors relevant to the exercise of the court's discretion as to whether or not to make an award include proximity to the trial, any effect upon the pursuer of delay in payment of his damages and the occurrence or otherwise to date of the pursuer's losses but not the intended use of the payment.[57]

The conditions precedent to the making of an order for interim payment of damages are that:

> "(a) the defender has admitted liability to the pursuer in the action; or
>
> (b) if the action proceeded to proof, the pursuer would succeed in the action on the question of liability without any substantial finding of contributory negligence on his part,

---

[52] R.C.S. 43.9(5) and O.C.R. 36.9(5). Paragraphs (a) and (c) refer, respectively, to a person who has the benefit of a contract of insurance in his favour or in favour of some other party in terms which cover the risks of the defender and a person who can meet the obligation to pay out of funds which are his or are his to dispose of at will — *Ferguson v. McGrandles*, 1993 S.L.T. 822. The Motor Insurers' Bureau's obligation to satisfy any judgment obtained against a particular defender does not fall within that defender's "means and resources" for the purposes of the rule — *Martin v. McKinsley*, 1980 S.L.T. (Notes) 15.

[53] R.C.S. 43.9(3) and O.C.R. 36.9(3).

[54] *Nisbet v. Marley Roof Tile Co Ltd*, 1988 S.C. 29 at p. 31.

[55] *Nisbet v. Marley Roof Tile Co Ltd*, 1988 S.C. 29; *O'Brien's Curator Bonis v. British Steel plc*, 1989 G.W.D. 13–565.

[56] *Littlejohn v. Clancy*, 1974 S.L.T. (Notes) 68; *Boyle v. Rennies of Dunfermline Ltd*, 1975 S.L.T. (Notes) 13; *Moodie v. Maclean*, 1981 S.L.T. (Notes) 53; *Nisbet v. Marley Roof Tile Co Ltd*, 1988 S.C. 29.

[57] *McNicol v. Buko*, 1986 S.L.T. 12; *Reith v. Aberdeen Mineral Water Co Ltd*, 1987 S.C.L.R. 689; *Curran v. H A T Painters (Scotland) Ltd*, 1987 S.L.T. 98; *Nisbet v. Marley Roof Tile Co Ltd*, 1988 S.C. 29; *McNeill v. Roche Products Ltd*, 1988 S.C. 77; *Kay v. G P Inveresk Corporation*, 1988 S.L.T. 711; *Thompson's Curator Bonis v. Burnett*, 1989 S.L.T. 264.

> or on the part of any person in respect of whose injury or death the claim of the pursuer arises, and would obtain decree for damages against [the] defender."[58]

The court must be satisfied as to either (a) or (b) but either suffices. If condition precedent (a) is met, it is unnecessary to consider any part of condition precedent (b), such as the issue of contributory negligence.[59] In relation to condition precedent (b), the first question which has to be considered by the court is whether it is satisfied that, if the action were to proceed to proof, the pursuer would succeed on the question of liability to any extent.[60] Such requires the court to be satisfied, on the basis of the information contained in the averments, that the pursuer would almost certainly succeed on that question, at least to some extent.[61] If so, and if contributory negligence is pled, the next question for the court is whether it is satisfied, to the required standard, that the finding of contributory negligence will not be so large as to have a material effect on its assessment of the amount which the pursuer is likely to recover as damages.[62] Where material averments are in dispute, the court cannot be satisfied to the requisite standard.[63]

Any interim payment of damages may be ordered to be made in one lump sum or otherwise as the court thinks fit.[64] The court has power also, with the parties' consent, to make an order under which the damages to be paid to the pursuer are wholly or partly to take the form of periodical payments.[65] Unless the court otherwise directs, any interim payment must be made to the pursuer.[66] Where the sum is payable to, or for the benefit of, a child under the age of 16 years, the court may make such order relating to the payment and management of the sum for the benefit of the child as it thinks fit.[67] Notwithstanding the grant or refusal of a motion for an interim

---

[58] R.C.S. 43.9(3) and O.C.R. 36.9(3).

[59] *Kay v. G P Inveresk Corporation,* 1988 S.L.T. 711 at p. 712.

[60] *Cowie v. Atlantic Drilling Co Ltd,* 1995 S.C. 288 at p. 292.

[61] *Ibid.* at p. 292. *Quaere* whether the court is entitled to consider material other than the averments, such as productions lodged in process (*cp. McCann v. Miller Insulation and Engineering Ltd,* 1986 S.L.T. 147; *Stone v. Mountford*, 1995 S.L.T. 1279; *Cleland v. Campbell*, 1998 S.L.T. 642).

[62] *Cowie v. Atlantic Drilling Co Ltd,* 1995 S.C. 288 at p. 294.

[63] *Reid v. J Smart & Co Ltd,* 1981 S.L.T. (Notes) 20; *McCann v. Miller Insulation and Engineering Ltd,* 1986 S.L.T. 147.

[64] R.C.S. 43.9(4) and O.C.R. 36.9(4).

[65] Damages (Scotland) Act 1993, s. 2(1) and (2).

[66] R.C.S. 43.9(7) and O.C.R. 36.9(7).

[67] Children (Scotland) Act 1995, s. 13(1). See n. 3 *supra*.

payment, a subsequent motion may be made where there has been a change of circumstances.[68]

Where a defender has made an interim payment ordered by the court, the court may make such order, when final decree is pronounced, with respect to the interim payment as it thinks fit to give effect to the final liability of that defender to the pursuer.[69] In particular the court may order (a) repayment by the pursuer of any sum by which the interim payment exceeds the amount which that defender is liable to pay the pursuer; or (b) payment by any other defender or a third party of any part of the interim payment which the defender who made it is entitled to recover from him by way of contribution or indemnity or in respect of any remedy or relief relating to, or connected with, the claim of the pursuer.[70] Where an interim payment ordered by the court has been made by a number of defenders, abandonment of the action against one defender results in a final decree, at least against him, and enables the court to order the remaining defenders to pay the amount of his share of the interim payment to him.[71]

---

[68] R.C.S. 43.9(6) and O.C.R. 36.9(6). A "change of circumstances" within the meaning of the rule can only relate to a difference between the factual situation *quoad* the pursuer at the time of the previous award and his present circumstances, rather than to a failure to put full information before the court at that time — *Cunningham v. City of Edinburgh District Council,* 1994 G.W.D. 21–1299.

[69] R.C.S. 43.10 and O.C.R. 36.10.

[70] *Ibid.* The rule applies whether or not the pursuer is successful in his action — *Walker v. Infabco Diving Services Ltd,* 1983 S.L.T. 633 at p. 643. *Quaere* whether the rule allows the court to order payment of interest on the sum ordered to be repaid *(cf. Walker*, at pp. 638 and 640–641).

[71] *Mitchell v. H A T Contracting Services Ltd (No 3),* 1993 S.L.T. 1199.

CHAPTER 2

CONSENT ORDERS FOR PERIODICAL PAYMENTS

THE court awarding damages in an action for personal injury may, with the consent of the parties, make an order under which the damages are wholly or partly to take the form of periodical payments.[1]

Such an order may incorporate the terms of an agreement settling a claim or action for damages for personal injury whereby the damages are to consist wholly or partly of periodical payments.[2] Such an agreement may be a "structured settlement" or a public sector settlement.

Where the person to whom the payments are to be made is to receive them as the annuitant under one or more annuities purchased for him by the person against whom the claim or action is brought or, if he is insured against the claim, by his insurer, the agreement is a "structured settlement".[3] Structured settlements provide an alternative form of damages to lump sum awards:

---

[1] Damages Act 1996, s. 2(1). The provision is without prejudice to any powers exercisable apart from the section — s. 2(3). "Personal injury" has the meaning given by s. 10(1) of the Damages (Scotland) Act 1976 (*viz.* as including any disease or any impairment of a person's physical or mental condition) — s. 7(2). "(Claim or) action for personal injury" is defined for the purposes of s. 329AA of the Income and Corporation Taxes Act 1988 (exemption from income tax for personal injury damages in the form of periodical payments under an agreement or a court order) as including such (claim or) action brought by virtue of the Damages (Scotland) Act 1976 — s. 329AA(6)(c). The provision applies to orders for interim payment of damages — Damages Act 1996, s. 2(2)(*cf.* 1988 Act, s. 329AA(7)).

[2] Income and Corporation Taxes Act 1988, s. 329AA(1), as inserted by the Finance Act 1996, s. 150(1) and (2) and Sched. 26. As to the meaning of "claim or action for personal injury", see preceding footnote. "Personal injury" is defined by s. 329AA(5) as including any disease and any impairment of a person's physical or mental condition.

[3] Damages Act 1996, s. 5(1). The definition of structured settlements is given for the purposes of s. 4 of that Act (enhanced protection for structured settlement annuitants in the event of insurer's liquidation). Note that where (a) an agreement is made settling a claim or action for damages for personal injury on terms whereby the damages are to consist wholly or partly of periodical payments; (b) the person against whom the claim or action is brought (or, if he is insured against the claim, his insurer) purchases one or more annuities; and (c) a subsequent agreement is made under which the annuity is, or the annuities are, assigned in favour of the person entitled to the payments (so as to secure that from a future date he receives the payments as the annuitant under the annuity or annuities), then, for the purposes of s. 4, the agreement settling the claim or action shall be treated as a structured settlement and any such annuity assigned in favour of that

"They usually consist of an initial lump sum part payment followed by a series of further instalments of the damages for which the defendant is liable. The initial lump sum tends to represent compensation for past pain and suffering and costs and expenses already incurred. The defendant or the defendant's insurer uses the balance of the sum due under the settlement to purchase an annuity or a series of annuities from a life insurance company. The payments made under the annuities are used to fund the periodic payments, which usually last for the life of the plaintiff or a specified term, whichever is the longer."[4]

The annuity or annuities in question must be such as to provide the annuitant with sums which as to amount and time of payment correspond to the periodical payments described in the agreement.[5] The periodical payments may be for the life of the claimant, for a specified period or of a specified number or minimum number, or include payments of more than one of those descriptions.[6] The amounts of the periodical payments (which need not be at a uniform rate or payable at uniform intervals) may be — (a) specified in the agreement, with or without provision for increases of specified amounts or percentages; or (b) subject to adjustment in a specified manner so as to preserve their real value; or (c) partly so specified and partly so subject to adjustment.[7] Payments in respect of the annuity or annuities may be received on behalf of the annuitant by another person or received and held on trust for his benefit under a trust of which he is, during his lifetime, the sole beneficiary.[8]

Where a claim or action for damages for personal injury is settled on terms corresponding to those of a structured settlement except that the person to whom the payments are to be made is not to receive them as the annuitant under one or more annuities purchased for him by the person against whom the claim or action is brought or, if he is

---

person shall be treated as an annuity purchased for him pursuant to that settlement — s. 5(8) and (9). Note further that the Secretary of State may by an order made by statutory instrument provide that there shall for the purposes of s. 5 be treated as an insurer any body specified in the order, being a body which, though not an insurer, appears to him to fulfill corresponding functions in relation to damages for personal injury claimed or awarded against persons of any class or description, and the reference in s. 5(1) to a person being insured against the claim and his insurer shall be construed accordingly — s. 5(6) and (7).

[4] The Law Commission, Report on Structured Settlements and Interim and Provisional Damages (Law Com. No. 223), para. 3.1.

[5] Damages Act 1996, s. 5(4).

[6] *Ibid.*, s. 5(2).

[7] *Ibid.*, s. 5(3).

[8] *Ibid.*, s. 5(5).

insured against the claim, by his insurer, the agreement may be a public sector settlement; and if payments are to be made under such agreement or under an order incorporating the terms of such agreement by a designated body, a Minister of the Crown may guarantee those payments.[9]

Whether made under an agreement or a court order, periodical payments are not for the purposes of income tax regarded as the income of any of the following persons (and accordingly require to be paid without any deduction of income tax):

(a) the person ("A") entitled to the damages under the agreement or order;
(b) any person who, whether in pursuance of the agreement or order or otherwise receives the payments or any of them on behalf of A; and
(c) any trustee who, whether in pursuance of the agreement or order or otherwise, receives the payments or any of them on trust for the benefit of A under a trust under which A is during his lifetime the sole beneficiary;[10] and sums paid to, or for the benefit of, A by a trustee or trustees are not regarded as his income for the purposes of income tax if made out of payments which by virtue of the foregoing are not to be regarded for those purposes as income of the trustee or trustees.[11]

By way of contrast, income arising from the investment of a lump sum award is subject to income tax and no specific account may be taken of the incidence of such tax, at least at higher rates, in the assessment of future pecuniary loss.[12] The consequent tax saving to an injured person of an agreement or order whereby the damages are to consist wholly or partly of periodical payments may be quantified by comparing the periodical payments under the agreement or order with an annuity purchased by an injured person out of a lump sum; in the latter only the element representing a return of purchase price would not be chargeable to tax.[13]

---

[9] *Ibid.*, s. 6(1), (2) and (3). As to the details regarding the giving of such guarantees, see s. 6(4), (5), (6), (7), (8) and (9).

[10] Income and Corporation Taxes Act 1988, s. 329AA(1) and (2), as inserted by the Finance Act 1996, s. 150(1) and (2) and Sched. 26. Note that the periodical payments, or any of them, may, if the agreement or court order or a subsequent agreement so provides, consist of payments under one or more annuities purchased or provided for, or for the benefit of, A by the person by whom the payments would otherwise fall to be made — s. 329AA(3), as so inserted. Thus annuities purchased by a third party such as the Motor Insurers' Bureau are included.

[11] Income and Corporation Taxes Act 1988, s. 329AA(4), as inserted by the Finance Act 1996, s. 150(1) and (2) and Sched. 26.

[12] *Hodgson v. Trapp* [1989] 1 A.C. 807; *Wells v. Wells* [1998] 3 W.L.R. 329.

[13] The Law Commission, Report on Structured Settlements and Interim and Provisional Damages (Law Com. No. 224), para. 3.13, n. 10.

The relative rate of return from structuring and lump sums at any particular time may be a significant factor in assessing the desirability or otherwise of a structured settlement. An index-linked annuity will be based on the returns on index-linked gilt edged securities, which may differ from the rate of return on which any multiplier in relation to future loss suffered by the injured person may be based.[14]

The Law Commission has set forth possible advantages and disadvantages of structured settlements as follows:

> "One of the advantages of structuring is said to be that it benefits both parties, thereby encouraging early settlement with attendant savings in cost and time. Parties that are far apart on a lump sum figure, perhaps because of differences over life expectancy, may be able to take a different approach which will eventually lead to an acceptable compromise.
>
> "However, the main advantage cited for plaintiffs is certainty. This consists of a number of elements. The plaintiff is relieved of the burden of managing a large sum of money and is protected from possible dissipation of the funds. There is the assurance of regular payments for life and of payments to dependants if the payments are guaranteed for a period longer than the plaintiff's life, together with the assurance that the payments will not decline in value if they are index-linked. These features make structured settlements particularly appropriate in cases where there are serious injuries and the conventional award would be large, and particularly where the plaintiff is a child and a long period of future care is envisaged. It is regarded as unlikely the state will ever have to step in to provide for the plaintiff where a settlement is structured.
>
> "Flexibility is seen as a further attractive feature of structuring for the plaintiff. The projected settlement can be tailored individually to the plaintiff's needs. Damages are linked to life expectancy without an absolute date having to be specified to provide a cut-off point. Cash flow is also based on projected future cash requirements. Provided these are considered carefully, the annuity package can be set up to provide at the appropriate time for education, changing nursing needs, asset accumulation, housing, marriage and children, and limited work or business prospects, if any. The damages will not be spent before these needs arise. The way to achieve these aims is to include the payment of periodic lump sums at key stages in the

---

[14] Damages Act 1996, s. 1(1), (2) and (3).

plaintiff's life. By this means structuring focuses on the plaintiff's needs, unlike the conventionally assessed lump sum, thereby in principle reducing the adversarial nature of the proceedings.

"Finally, the tax advantages of structured settlements, which have already been outlined, have been the real catalyst for the development of this form of award for both plaintiff and defendant. Tax savings to the plaintiff could in the extreme case and at current levels of tax approach 40% of the periodic payments. It is argued strongly by advocates of structuring that the annuity purchased is able to provide greater benefits in the longer term than a traditional lump sum invested by the plaintiff. The plaintiff is also immunized against future increases in personal tax rates. The tax saving is also a negotiating tool, since it can fund any discount requested by the defendant....

"Structured settlements do, however, have a number of disadvantages. They do not avoid the need for forecasting. In fact they may place an undesirable emphasis on forward planning which is avoided where lump sums are used. Whereas with the latter the plaintiff has to deal with anticipated future needs by managing the lump sum and making payments to meet the needs as required, a structured settlement requires experts and advisers to prepare a complex advance budget for life. Once determined, structured settlements cannot be changed — they only possess initial flexibility. The pressure to 'get it right' at that initial stage is therefore extreme. Payments from annuities may come on stream at the wrong time or not be needed at all. Prognoses may yet prove to be incorrect, affecting decisions previously made about lifestyle. The problem is ameliorated to a degree by building a contingency fund into the structure, but the size of this fund varies a great deal.

"Moreover, structured settlements do not completely remove the risk that the monies provided under them will not in fact be adequate to meet the plaintiff's needs. The plaintiff [may] still be able to squander any monies received even if they are intended for specific purposes. Another aspect of the risk is that although structures are linked to the RPI via the index-linked annuity, this cannot guarantee that costs of future care will always be met. Historically, the cost of care has risen faster than the RPI. To this extent, the shortfall has to be made up from the contingency fund. Structures are by no means perfect.

"Finally, a structured settlement, although apparently benefiting a plaintiff in every way, may simply be undesired by the individual plaintiff. For example, a severely injured plaintiff may wish to take a large lump sum in order to move to another country for family reasons or to take advantage of educational or business opportunities there."[15]

The Association of British Insurers and the Inland Revenue have agreed a standard form agreement (the "Model Agreement") which if used without amendment renders it unnecessary to obtain Inland Revenue approval ensuring tax-free status for the settlement.[16]

---

[15] Report on Structured Settlements and Interim and Provisional Damages (Law Com. No. 224), paras 3.10–3.13 and 3.20–3.22.

[16] The Model Agreement, including its four alternative Schedules, is reproduced in App. III.

CHAPTER 3

PROVISIONAL DAMAGES FOR PERSONAL INJURIES

IN certain actions of damages for personal injuries the court may order that provisional damages be awarded to the injured person and that the injured person may apply for a further award of damages.[1]

AWARDS OF PROVISIONAL DAMAGES

A claim for provisional damages is made by including a conclusion or crave therefor in the summons or initial writ.[2] There requires also to be included, in addition to an appropriate plea-in-law, averments in the condescendence supporting the conclusion, including averments:

> "(a) that there is a risk that, at some definite or indefinite time in the future, the pursuer will, as a result of the act or omission which gave rise to the cause of action, develop some serious disease or suffer some serious deterioration of his physical or mental condition; and
>
> (b) that the defender was, at the time of the act or omission which gave rise to the cause of action, a public authority, public corporation or insured or otherwise indemnified in respect of the claim."[3]

The matters described in paragraphs (a) and (b) constitute the conditions precedent to the making of an award of provisional

---

[1] Administration of Justice Act 1982, s. 12. "Personal injuries" includes any disease or any impairment of a person's physical or mental condition — s. 13(1).

[2] R.C.S. 43.12(a) (Court of Session) and O.C.R. 36.12(a) (Sheriff Court). The conclusion in a Court of Session action requires to be in Form 43.12, which is as follows: "For payment to the pursuer by the defender of the sum of (*amount in words and figures*) as provisional damages."

[3] R.C.S. 43.12(b) and (c) (Court of Session) and O.C.R. 36.12(b) and (c) (Sheriff Court).

damages.[4] In the event that they are satisfied, the court may, on the application of the injured person, order:

(i) that damages assessed on the assumption that the injured person will not develop the disease or suffer the deterioration in question be awarded to the injured person; and
(ii) that the injured person may apply for an award of further damages if he develops the disease or suffers the deterioration; and, if it considers it appropriate, that any such application may be made only within a specified period.[5]

In relation to the condition precedent set forth in (a) above, the court should not impose upon a defender or his insurers a contingent liability for final damages unless the nature and the extent of that liability are clear.[6] Accordingly, if provisional damages are to be awarded, it is essential that the court's determination should make clear to the parties the nature of the disease or deterioration on the occurrence of which the pursuer's right to final damages will arise; and such a determination will also make clear what is being left out in the assessment of provisional damages.[7] This suggests that the stage at which the right to final damages will arise would require to be a clear-cut event or threshold.[8] Provisional damages are thus not warranted in the case of disabilities which follow a developing pattern in which the precise results cannot be foreseen or may take several

---

[4] Administration of Justice Act 1982, s. 12(1)(a) and (b). The Secretary of State may, by order, provide that categories of defenders shall, for the purposes of condition precedent (b), become or cease to be responsible persons, and may make such modifications of that paragraph as appear to him to be necessary for the purpose, and such an order shall be made by statutory instrument subject to annulment in pursuance of a resolution of either House of Parliament — s. 12(6).

[5] 1982 Act, s. 12(2) and (4). Note that nothing in s. 12 shall be construed as affecting the exercise of any power relating to expenses including a power to make rules of court relating to expenses; or as prejudicing any duty of the court under any enactment or rule of law to reduce or limit the total damages which would have been recoverable apart from any such duty — s.12(5).

[6] *Bonar v. Trafalgar House Offshore Fabrication Ltd,* 1996 S.L.T. 548 at p. 550.

[7] *Prentice v. William Thyne Ltd,* 1989 S.L.T. 336 at p. 337; *Bonar v. Trafalgar House Offshore Fabrication Ltd,* 1996 S.L.T. 548 at p. 550.

[8] *White v. Inveresk Paper Co Ltd,* 1987 S.C. 143 at p. 150; *Prentice v. William Thyne Ltd,* 1989 S.L.T. 336 at p. 337; *Bonar v. Trafalgar House Offshore Fabrication Ltd,* 1996 S.L.T. 548 at p. 551; *Willson v. Ministry of Defence* [1991] 1 All E. R. 638 at p. 644. For cases in which such thresholds were identified, see *Robertson v. British Bakeries Ltd,* 1991 S.L.T. 434 (post-traumatic osteo-arthritis), *McColl v. Barnes,* 1992 S.L.T. 1188 (post-traumatic epilepsy) and *Duffy v. Lanarkshire Health Board,* Lord Johnston, July 31, 1998, unreported (post-transplant cancer).

forms, of varying severity, or are disabilities which progress gradually.[9] Further, the risk of serious disease or serious deterioration must be material and not theoretical or remote.[10] The seriousness of the disease or deterioration requires to be assessed by reference to the injured person's circumstances.[11] The development of the disease or the suffering of the deterioration may be shown to result from the act or omission which gave rise to the cause of the action notwithstanding that the development or deterioration is brought about by an interaction between the condition produced by the original act and some future triggering event or other change in the pursuer's circumstances or environment.[12]

Once satisfied as to the conditions precedent, the court may make the award if satisfied that reserving the injured person's right to return would do better justice than a once and for all assessment.[13] Factors relevant to the exercise of the court's discretion in this regard include the practicability of taking the risk of a serious disease or deterioration into account in a once and for all assessment and the degree and consequences of the risk itself.[14] In the event of making the award, the court should in the absence of exceptional circumstances fix a period for any application for further damages.[15]

---

[9] *Willson v. Ministry of Defence* [1991] 1 All E. R. 638 at p. 644; *Meek v. Burton's Gold Medal Biscuits Ltd,* 1989 S.L.T. 338 at p. 340; *Prentice v. William Thyne Ltd,* 1989 S.L.T. 336 at p. 337; *Bonar v. Trafalgar House Offshore Fabrication Ltd,* 1996 S.L.T. 548 at p. 551.

[10] *White v. Inveresk Paper Co Ltd,* 1987 S.C. 143 at pp. 147–149 (1% a material risk but "less than 1%" not a positive quantitative assessment of risk); *Patterson v. Ministry of Defence* [1987] C.L.Y. 1194 (2% to 3% a material risk but 1% not a material risk).

[11] *Robertson v. British Bakeries Ltd,* 1991 S.L.T. 434 at p. 439; *Willson v. Ministry of Defence* [1991] 1 All E. R. 638 at p. 642.

[12] *Meek v. Burton's Gold Medal Biscuits Ltd,* 1989 S.L.T. 338 at p. 340. But see *Paterson v. Costain Mining Ltd,* 1988 S.L.T. 413 and *Bonar v. Trafalgar House Offshore Fabrication Ltd,* 1996 S.L.T. 548 at p. 551.

[13] *Meek v. Burton's Gold Metal Biscuits Ltd,* 1989 S.L.T. 338 at p. 340; *Willson v. Ministry of Defence* [1991] 1 All E. R. 638 at p. 645; *Molinari v. Ministry of Defence* [1994] P.I.Q.R. Q33.

[14] *Robertson v. British Bakeries Ltd,* 1991 S.L.T. 434 at p. 440; *McColl v. Barnes,* 1992 S.L.T. 1188 at p. 1190; *Bonar v. Trafalgar House Offshore Fabrication Ltd,* 1996 S.L.T. 548 at p. 551; *Willson v. Ministry of Defence* [1991] 1 All E. R. 638 at p.644.

[15] *Bonar v. Trafalgar House Offshore Fabrication Ltd,* 1996 S.L.T. 548 at p. 551. For examples of specified periods for the making of an application for further damages, see *White v. Inveresk Paper Co Ltd,* 1987 S.C. 143 at p. 150 (20 years from date of accident); *Lappin v. Britannia Airways Ltd,* 1989 S.L.T. 181 at p. 182 (five years from date of decree); *Robertson v. British Bakeries Ltd,* 1991 S.L.T. 434 at pp. 440–441 (10 years from date of accident); *McColl v. Barnes,* 1992 S.L.T. 1188 at p. 1190 (seven years from date of accident).

FURTHER AWARDS OF DAMAGES

An application for further damages by a pursuer in respect of whom an order under (ii) above has been made requires to be made by minute and must include (a) a conclusion or crave for further damages; (b) averments in the statement of facts supporting that conclusion or crave; and (c) appropriate pleas-in-law.[16]

On lodging such a minute in process, the pursuer must apply by motion for warrant to serve the minute on (a) every other party; and (b) where such other party is insured or otherwise indemnified, his insurer or indemnifier, if known to the pursuer.[17] Any such party, insurer or indemnifier may lodge answers to such a minute in process within 28 days after the date of service on him.[18]

Upon such an application the court may award the pursuer further damages if he has developed the disease or suffered the deterioration in respect of which his right to return was reserved by the court upon granting decree.[19]

---

[16] R.C.S. 43.13(1) (Court of Session) and O.C.R. 36.13(1) (Sheriff Court). The conclusion in a Court of Session action requires to be in Form 43.13A, which is as follows: "For payment to the pursuer by the defender of the sum (*amount in words and figures*) as further damages."

[17] R.C.S. 43.13(2) and O.C.R. 36.13(2). R.C.S. 43.13(3) requires that a notice of intimation in Form 43.13B must be attached to the copy of the minute served on a warrant granted on such a motion in the Court of Session.

[18] R.C.S. 43.13(4) and O.C.R. 36.13(3). O.C.R. 36.13(4) provides that where answers have been lodged, the sheriff may, on the motion of any party, make such further order as to procedure as he thinks fit.

[19] Administration of Justice Act 1982, s. 12(2)(b), (3) and (4)(b).

CHAPTER 4

INTEREST ON DAMAGES

THE court has a statutory power to grant interest on damages for personal injuries or for the death of a relative by including such interest in the decree for damages.[1]

A claim for interest is made by including the amount sought by way of interest in the sum concluded for or craved as damages.[2] Application for interest after decree for damages has been granted is incompetent.[3] Exceptionally, however, the appellate court entertaining an appeal against an award of damages may entertain a motion for interest where no such motion was made to the court of first instance.[4]

Section 1(1A) of the Interest on Damages (Scotland) Act 1958 requires the court in actions of damages for personal injuries to exercise the general power conferred by section 1(1) of the Act (*viz.* to award interest, at such rate or rates as may be specified, on the whole or any part of any damages awarded for the whole or any part of any period between the date when the right of action arose and the date of decree) so as to include in the sum awarded interest on the individual elements of the award or on such part of each as the court thinks appropriate, unless the court is satisfied that there are reasons special to the case why no interest should be given in respect thereof. This is a matter of discretion for the judge of first instance in which he can normally rely upon the good sense of the parties' representatives to assist him by reaching agreement; and when this

---

[1] Interest on Damages (Scotland) Act 1958, s. 1(1) and (1A), as substituted by the Interest on Damages (Scotland) Act 1971, s. 1. The section applies the power to awards of "damages or solatium for personal injuries sustained by the pursuer or any other person". Such has been held to include the common law awards of loss of support and solatium to widows and children of a deceased (*Smith v. Middleton,* 1972 S.C. 30 at p. 35). The replacement of such remedies by statutory awards for relatives under s. 1 of the Damages (Scotland) Act 1976 has not been regarded as altering the position. Note further that nothing in s. 1 authorises the granting of interest on interest, or prejudices any other power of the court as to the granting of interest, or affects the running of any interest which apart from the section would run by virtue of any enactment or rule of law — s. 1(2).

[2] *Orr v. Metcalfe,* 1973 S.C. 57 at p. 60.

[3] *Handren v. Scottish Construction Co Ltd,* 1967 S.L.T. (Notes) 21.

[4] *Forsyth's Curator Bonis v. Govan Shipbuilders Ltd,* 1988 S.C. 421.

does not happen the exercise of his discretion is not open to review save in exceptional circumstances.[5]

The purpose of these provisions is to give the court power to give fuller effect to the cardinal rule in awards of damages, namely to put the injured person, so far as money can do, into the same position as he would have been if he had not been injured.[6] Hence interest should be awarded, in the exercise of that power, upon those parts of the whole sum of damages payment of which has been withheld through the litigation's normal delays, which can never include loss which the pursuer has not yet sustained at the date of trial.[7] Such entails the allocation by the court, whether judge or jury, of certain heads of damage between past and future.[8] In the case of inordinate delay on the part of the pursuer in prosecuting his claim, the pursuer is not in the absence of special circumstances to be deprived of interest on past pecuniary loss, but the rate and period of interest on past non-pecuniary loss in such circumstances may be restricted.[9] The court should disregard benefits deductible from any compensation payment in terms of the Social Security (Recovery of Benefits) Act 1997 when assessing interest on past pecuniary loss.[10]

Interest should not be awarded without regard to the legal rate of interest from time to time prevailing in the period preceding trial.[11] Account may be taken of changes in the legal rate by applying different rates of interest to different parts of the relevant period or by applying an average or adjusted average rate to the whole of the relevant period.[12]

The exercise of the general power requires the adoption of a selective and discriminating approach, which may result in the following:[13]

(i) where a loss is not a cumulative one, as with funeral expenses, interest may be awarded to the date of trial at the legal rate or rates from the date when the loss was incurred;[14]

---

[5] *MacIntosh v. National Coal Board,* 1988 S.L.T. 348 at p. 361.

[6] *Macrae v. Reed and Mallik Ltd,* 1961 S.C. 68 at p. 76; *Smith v. Middleton,* 1972 S.C. 30 at pp. 38–39.

[7] *Macrae v. Reed and Mallik Ltd,* 1961 S.C. 68 at p. 77; *Smith v. Middleton,* 1972 S.C. 30 at pp. 38–39.

[8] *Hill v. Wilson,* 1997 S.C. 81 at p. 82.

[9] *Boots the Chemist Ltd v. G A Estates Ltd,* 1993 S.L.T. 136; *Bhatia v. Tribax Ltd,* 1994 S.L.T. 1201; *Birkett v. Hayes* [1982] 1 W.L.R. 816; *Wright v. British Railways Board* [1983] 2 A.C. 773. *Cf. Purryag v. Greater Glasgow Health Board,* 1996 S.L.T. 794.

[10] *Wisely v. John Fulton (Plumbers) Ltd,* 1998 S.L.T. 1026.

[11] *Starkey v. National Coal Board,* 1987 S.L.T. 103.

[12] *Keicher v. National Coal Board,* 1988 S.L.T. 318 at p. 319; *Preston v. Grampian Health Board,* 1988 S.L.T. 435 at p. 437; *Starkey v. National Coal Board,* 1987 S.L.T. 103; *Wilson v. Chief Constable, Lothian and Borders Constabulary,* 1989 S.L.T. 97 at p. 106.

[13] *Macrae v. Reed and Mallik Ltd,* 1961 S.C. 68; *Smith v. Middleton,* 1972 S.C. 30 at pp. 38–39.

[14] *Prentice v. Chalmers,* 1985 S.L.T. 168 at p. 176.

(ii) where a loss is a cumulative one and is continuing at the date of trial, as with solatium or loss of earnings in some cases, interest may be awarded to the date of trial at about half the legal rate or rates from the date of commencement of the loss;[15]

(iii) where a loss is a cumulative one but has ceased prior to trial, as with solatium or loss of earnings in other cases, interest may be awarded to the date of trial (a) at the legal rate or rates from the date when the loss ceased; or (b) at less than the legal rate or rates from the date of commencement of the loss; or (c) at less than the legal rate or rates from the date of commencement of the loss until the date when the loss ceased and at the legal rate thereafter.[16]

The application of interim payments for the purposes of an award of interest on damages is a matter for the discretion of the court but in the absence of circumstances which indicate that a different approach is appropriate, an interim payment should be applied *primo loco* to loss already occurred as at the date of receipt.[17] The amount treated as the interim payment for these purposes is the interim payment grossed up to include interest at the legal rate from time to time prevailing from the date of the interim payment order.[18]

Where a tender is made in the course of an action, it requires unless otherwise stated therein to be in full satisfaction of any claim to interest thereunder by any person in whose favour the tender is made; and in considering in any such action whether an award is equal to or greater than an amount tendered in the action, the court must take account of the amount of any interest awarded under the 1958 Act, or such part of that interest as the court considers appropriate.[19]

---

[15] *Clark v. Sutherland*, 1993 S.C. 320 at p. 324; *McManus v. British Railways Board*, 1993 S.C. 557 at p. 563.

[16] (a) *e.g. McCabe v. British Domestic Appliances Ltd*, 1978 S.L.T. (Notes) 31 at p. 32; (b) *e.g. Kane v. Norwest Holst Pipework Ltd*, 1988 S.L.T. 28 at p. 28; (c) *e.g. Preston v. Grampian Health Board*, 1988 S.L.T. 435 at p. 437.

[17] *Bhatia v. Tribax Ltd*, 1994 S.L.T. 1201 at p. 1205.

[18] *McNeill v. Roche Products Ltd*, 1989 S.L.T. 498 at p. 507; *Bhatia v. Tribax Ltd*, 1994 S.L.T. 1201 at p. 1205.

[19] Interest on Damages (Scotland) Act 1958, s. 1(1B), as substituted by the Interest on Damages (Scotland) Act 1971, s. 1.

II. HEADS OF CLAIM FOR PERSONAL INJURIES

CHAPTER 5

SOLATIUM

NON-PECUNIARY loss arising from personal injury whether in its positive form, namely pain and suffering, or in its negative form, namely loss of faculties and amenities, may be compensated by an award of solatium.

A claim for solatium may be made in an action of damages for personal injuries by the injured person.[1] His title to sue is unaffected by any insurance arrangements.[2] His right to solatium transmits upon his death to his executor, but in determining the amount of damages payable to the executor, the court shall have regard only to the period ending immediately before the deceased's death.[3] The executor's claim is not excluded by the making of a claim under the Damages (Scotland) Act 1976 by a relative of the deceased or by a deceased relative's executor.[4] For the purpose of enforcing any such right the injured person's executor is entitled — (a) to bring an action; or (b) if an action for that purpose had been brought by the deceased but had not been concluded before his death, to be sisted as pursuer in that action.[5]

---

[1] Claims by third parties for solatium arising out of the personal injuries sustained by the injured person are irrelevant since the losses are too remote — *Robertson v. Turnbull,* 1982 S.C. (H.L.) 1 (claim for solatium by family members for injuries to wife and mother dismissed as irrelevant).

[2] *Port-Glasgow and Newark Sailcloth Co v. Caledonian Railway Co* (1892) 19 R. 608.

[3] Damages (Scotland) Act 1976, s. 2(1) and (3), as substituted by the Damages (Scotland) Act 1993, s. 3. See *e.g. Beggs v. Motherwell Bridge Fabricators Ltd,* 1997 S.C.L.R. 1019 at p. 1033.

[4] 1976 Act, s. 4, as amended by the Administration of Justice Act 1982, s. 14(2)(a) and the Damages (Scotland) Act 1993, Sched., para. 1.

[5] 1976 Act, s. 2A(1), as inserted by the Damages (Scotland) Act 1993, s. 4. For the purposes of s. 2A(1) an action shall not be taken to be concluded while any appeal is competent or before any appeal taken has been disposed of — s. 2A(2). Note that where in an action in which, following the death of the deceased from personal injuries, damages are claimed by the executor of the deceased, in respect of the injuries from which the deceased died, it is shown that by antecedent agreement, compromise or otherwise, the liability arising in relation to a particular defender from the personal injuries in question had, before the deceased's death, been limited to damages of a specified or ascertainable amount, or where that liability is so limited by virtue of any enactment, nothing in the 1976 Act shall make that defender liable to pay damages exceeding that amount; and accordingly where in such an action there are two or more pursuers any damages to which they would respectively be entitled under the Act apart from the said limitation shall, if necessary, be reduced *pro rata* — s. 6(1) and (3)(a). Where two or more such actions are conjoined, the conjoined actions shall be treated for the purposes of the foregoing as if they were a single action — s. 6(2).

In either event the rules of court concerning intimation of the action to connected persons are applicable.[6] In the case of the injured person's bankruptcy, his trustee in sequestration cannot raise an action for solatium arising out of the personal injury without at least having first obtained an assignation of the right from the bankrupt.[7] The trustee is, however, entitled to be sisted as pursuer in the bankrupt's place in any depending action for solatium.[8]

The aspects of non-pecuniary injury for which solatium may be awarded are the following:

(a) pain and suffering (including suffering which an injured person has or is likely to have in consequence of being or becoming aware of the reduction by his injuries of his expectation of life);
(b) loss of faculties and amenities.[9]

The court in making an award of damages by way of solatium is not required to ascribe specifically any part of the award to loss of expectation of life.[10] The general rule is that solatium should be considered and assessed as a single entity, subject only to the requirement to divide the award, where appropriate, into pre-decree and post-decree periods for the purposes of calculation of interest, which is exigible in respect of the former.[11]

In determining compensation for non-pecuniary injury the court should take all factors into account, including the nature and consequences of the injuries, the age of the injured person and the period of life during which he has been deprived of activities and amenities as the case may be.[12]

There is an infinite variety of injuries, as well as diseases, and sequelae which may be compensated, except that the ordinary emotions

---

[6] R.C.S. 43.1(1)(a)(Court of Session) and O.C.R. 36.1(1)(a)(Sheriff Court). The relevant rules are noted in Chap. 9, text accompanying nn. 12–19.

[7] *Muir's Trustee v. Braidwood,* 1958 S.C. 169; *Traill & Sons v. Actieselskabat Dalbeattie Ltd* (1904) 6 F. 798.

[8] *Thom v. Bridges* (1857) 19 D. 721; *Watson v. Thompson,* 1991 S.C. 447; *Bern's Executor v. Montrose Asylum* (1893) 20 R. 859 at p. 863.

[9] *Dalgleish v. Glasgow Corporation,* 1976 S.C. 32 at p. 53 and Damages (Scotland) Act 1976, s. 9A(1), as inserted by the Damages (Scotland) Act 1993, s. 5. Note that no damages by way of solatium are recoverable in respect of loss of expectation of life as such — 1976 Act, s. 9A(2), as so inserted. See also the Scottish Law Commission Report on The Effect of Death on Damages (Scot. Law Com. No. 134), paras 2.3 and 4.13–4.21.

[10] 1976 Act, s. 9A(3), as inserted by the Damages (Scotland) Act 1993, s. 5.

[11] *Keith v. Fraser and Ors,* First Division, October 23, 1973, unreported (quoted in *Parke v. Glasgow District Council,* 1979 S.L.T. 45 at p. 47); *McManus v. British Railways Board,* 1993 S.C. 557. As to interest on damages, see Chap. 4.

[12] *Dalgleish v. Glasgow Corporation,* 1976 S.C. 32 at p. 54; *H West & Son Ltd v. Shephard* [1964] A.C. 326 at p. 346.

of anxiety, fear, grief or transient shock are not conditions for which the law gives compensation as personal injuries.[13] Non-pecuniary injury in its positive form, namely pain and suffering, may exist on its own, as in the case of a person undergoing surgery without anaesthetic.[14] Conversely, as in the case of a person suffering catastrophic brain damage, there may be only negative loss to be compensated, namely for the mutilation of the body and deprivation of the ordinary experiences and amenities of life.[15] The injury or disease itself has always justified and required in law an award of damages according to its extent, gravity and duration.[16] The amenities or pleasures of life lost as a result of personal injuries sound in damages according to their nature and the effect of their loss upon the injured person.[17] It is not relevant in assessing solatium to consider an injured person's economic and social position as such.[18]

An award of solatium is a payment in money for something which cannot be precisely quantified.[19] Awards, at least by judges, are therefore conventional or standard figures derived from experience and from awards in comparable cases.[20] Nevertheless, it is the facts of

---

[13] *Page v. Smith* [1996] 1 A.C. 155 at p. 171; *Simpson v. Imperial Chemical Industries Ltd,* 1983 S.L.T. 601. As to damages for emotions such as grief arising out of the death of a relative, see Chap. 9, text accompanying n. 24 *et seq.*

[14] *Phelan v. East Cumbrian Health Authority* [1991] 2 Med. L.R. 419.

[15] *Dalgleish v. Glasgow Corporation,* 1976 S.C. 32; *Wise v. Kaye* [1962] 1 Q.B. 638; *H West & Son Ltd v. Shephard* [1964] A.C. 326; *Lim v. Camden Health Authority* [1980] A.C. 174.

[16] *Wise v. Kaye* [1962] 1 Q.B. 638 at p. 651. An injured person cannot, however, recover damages for a prolongation or exacerbation of his injury which is attributable to his own wilful act or default (*McKew v. Holland & Hannen & Cubitts (Scotland) Ltd,* 1970 S.C. (H.L.) 20). Such would include an unreasonable refusal to undergo medical treatment (*Steele v. Robert George & Co (1937) Ltd* [1942] A.C. 497; *Selvanayagam v. University of the West Indies* [1983] 1 W.L.R. 585). As to *novus actus interveniens* generally, see textbooks on delictual liability.

[17] Relevant loss of amenities or pleasures include loss of sporting activity or hobby (*Kirkwood v. Christie & Vesey Ltd,* 1976 S.L.T. (Notes) 56; *Ross v. National Coal Board,* 1980 S.L.T. (Notes) 89; *Girvan v. Inverness Farmers Dairy,* 1998 S.C.(H.L.) 1; loss of musical activity or hobby (*Marshall v. Bertrams Ltd,* 1985 S.L.T. 80; *Millar v. Jamieson McGregor Ltd,* 1988 S.L.T. 83); loss of holiday *(Ichard v. Frangoulis* [1977] 1 W.L.R. 556; *Bush v. Phillips* (1989) C.L.Y. 1065); loss of leisure time through having to work longer for same pay (*Hearnshaw v. English Steel Corpn Ltd* (1971) 11 K.I.R. 306); loss of congenial employment or career *(Lenaghan v. Ayrshire and Arran Health Board,* 1994 S.C. 365; *Hale v. London Underground* [1993] P.I.Q.R. Q30); loss of sexual potency (*Cook v. J L Kier & Co Ltd* [1970] 2 All E. R. 513); and loss of marriage prospects (*Moriarty v. McCarthy* [1978] 1 W.L.R. 155).

[18] *Fletcher v. Autocar and Transporters Ltd* [1968] 2 Q.B. 322 at pp. 340–341 and 364.

[19] *Girvan v. Inverness Farmers Dairy,* 1998 S.C.(H.L.) 1 at p. 17.

[20] *Ibid.* at p. 24; *Ward v. James* [1966] 1 Q.B. 273 at p. 303; *Wright v. British Railways Board* [1983] 2 A.C. 773 at p. 777. As to awards by juries, see *Girvan, supra.*

the particular case which have principally and primarily to be taken into account by the court in assessing the claim of an injured person.[21] The current of decisions in similar cases no doubt provides a useful guide to deciding what on the facts of the particular case will be an appropriate award.[22] There must, however, be a discernible trend or clear pattern of awards for use as a good point of reference.[23] Individual awards of solatium in other cases are unreliable guides as comparisons except when the injuries in the one case are virtually identical with the injuries in the other, as in the case of the loss of an eye or a limb.[24] Even there, the common factor (for example, the amputation of a leg) may be attended by totally different factors and considerations.[25] Cases of multiple injuries of varying types or degrees of severity have to be looked at on their own, with regard being had to the cumulative effect of the particular injuries as well as to the general run of awards and judicial experience.[26] In all cases account should be taken of awards in any neighbouring locality where similar social, economic and industrial conditions exist; hence awards of general damages for pain, suffering and loss of amenities in English cases which are comparable on their facts should be taken into account.[27] In considering any previous similar award the court should have regard to any change in the value of money between the date of that award and the date of the

---

[21] *Butler v. Adam Lynn Ltd,* 1965 S.C. 137 at p. 143; *McCallum v. Paterson,* 1969 S.C. 85 at p. 90; *Rieley v. Kingslaw Riding School,* 1975 S.C. 28 at p. 55; *Bowers v. Strathclyde Regional Council,* 1981 S.L.T. 122 at p. 125.

[22] *Butler v. Adam Lynn Ltd,* 1965 S.C. 137 at p. 143; *McCallum v. Paterson,* 1968 S.C. 280 at p. 286; *Bowers v. Strathclyde Regional Council,* 1981 S.L.T. 122 at p. 125; *H West & Son Ltd v. Shephard* [1964] A.C. 326 at p. 346; *Wright v. British Railways Board* [1983] 2 A.C. 773.

[23] *McCrum v. Ballantyne,* 1993 S.L.T. 788 at p. 790; *Jag Singh v. Toong Fong Omnibus Co Ltd* [1964] 1 W.L.R. 1382 at p. 1387.

[24] *Barker v. Murdoch,* 1979 S.L.T. 145 at p. 147; *McCrum v. Ballantyne,* 1993 S.L.T. 788 at p. 790.

[25] *Rieley v. Kingslaw Riding School,* 1975 S.C. 28 at p. 60.

[26] *Barker v. Murdoch,* 1979 S.L.T. 145 at p. 147; *McCrum v. Ballantyne,* 1993 S.L.T. 788 at p. 790.

[27] *Jag Singh v. Toong Fong Omnibus Co Ltd* [1964] 1 W.L.R. 1382 at p. 1385; *Allan v. Scott,* 1972 S.C. 59; *Chan Wai Tong v. Li Ping Sum* [1985] 1 A.C. 446. Reference may be made to the "Guidelines for the Assessment of General Damages in Personal Injury Cases" compiled for the Judicial Studies Board in England (the fourth edition of which is reproduced in App. VII), as was done in *e.g. Taggart v. Shell (UK) Ltd,* 1996 S.L.T. 795 at p. 797 and *Girvan v. Inverness Farmers Dairy,* 1998 S.C.(H.L.) 1 at p. 19. Note, however, that the guidelines are not in themselves law and do not exclude the need to look at the sources rather than merely the summary which the guidelines offer — *Arafa v. Potter* [1994] P.I.Q.R. Q73 at p. Q79. *Cf. Chan Wai Tong v. Li Ping Sum,* cit. supra.

trial in the instant case.[28] Allowance may be made for inflation by means of the use of an inflation table calculated from the Official Retail Prices Index.[29] A significant erosion in the value of money over a period, however, can render illustrative cases obsolete and inapplicable nevertheless.[30]

---

[28] *Rieley v. Kingslaw Riding School,* 1975 S.C. 28 at p. 60.

[29] *Currie v. Kilmarnock and Loudoun District Council,* 1996 S.C. 55 at p. 67.

[30] *McCallum v. Paterson,* 1968 S.C. 280 at p. 286; *Martin v. James and Andrew Chapman (Haulage Contractors) Ltd,* 1995 G.W.D. 2–77.

Chapter 6

LOSS OF EARNINGS AND PENSION RIGHTS

Pecuniary loss arising from personal injury in its negative form, namely deprivation of financial benefit arising from impairment — total or partial, permanent or temporary — of actual or potential capacity to earn, may be compensated by awards for loss of earnings and loss of pension rights.

LOSS OF EARNINGS

A claim for loss of earnings may be made in an action of damages for personal injuries by the injured person.[1] His title to sue is unaffected by any insurance arrangements.[2] His right to damages for loss of earnings transmits upon his death to his executor, but only in respect of loss attributable to the period before death.[3] The executor's claim is not excluded by the making of a claim under the Damages (Scotland) Act 1976 by a relative of the deceased or by a deceased relative's executor.[4] For the purpose of enforcing any such right the injured person's executor is entitled — (a) to bring an action; or (b) if an action for that purpose had been brought by the deceased but had not been concluded before his death, to be sisted as pursuer in that action.[5]

---

[1] Claims by third parties for loss of earnings arising out of the personal injuries sustained by the injured person are irrelevant since the losses are too remote — *Allan v. Barclay* (1864) 2 M. 873 and *Reavis v. Clan Line Steamers,* 1925 S.C. 725 (claim for loss of earnings by employer for injury to employee dismissed in each case as irrelevant) and *Jack v. Alexander McDougall & Co (Engineers),* 1973 S.C. 13 (claim for loss of earnings by wife giving up work to look after injured husband dismissed as irrelevant).

[2] *Port-Glasgow and Newark Sailcloth Co v. Caledonian Railway Co* (1892) 19 R. 608.

[3] Damages (Scotland) Act 1976, s. 2(1) and (2), as substituted by the Damages (Scotland) Act 1993, s. 3.

[4] 1976 Act, s. 4, as amended by the Administration of Justice Act 1982, s. 14(2)(a) and the Damages (Scotland) Act 1993, Sched., para. 1.

[5] 1976 Act, s. 2A(1), as inserted by the Damages (Scotland) Act 1993, s. 4. For the purpose of s. 2A(1) an action shall not be taken to be concluded while any appeal is competent or before any appeal taken has been disposed of — s. 2A(2). Note that where in an action in which, following the death of the deceased from personal injuries, damages are claimed

In either event the rules of court concerning intimation of the action to connected persons are applicable.[6] In the case of the injured person's bankruptcy, his trustee in sequestration has the right to sue for any pecuniary losses arising out of the personal injury.[7]

Damages for loss of earnings may be claimed in respect of earnings derived by the injured person in the form of a wage or salary from an employer, dividends from a limited company, profits from sole trading or an agreed share of partnership profits.[8] Where the losses suffered as a result of the personal injuries have been sustained by a separate legal persona such as a limited company they are not recoverable.[9] A loss of earnings claim does not lie in respect of illegal earnings.[10] An award for loss of earnings may include damages for loss of perquisites and benefits in kind to which the injured person was entitled, provided that a monetary value is placed on them.[11] Overtime payments are

---

by the executor of the deceased, in respect of the injuries from which the deceased died, it is shown that by antecedent agreement, compromise or otherwise, the liability arising in relation to a particular defender from the personal injuries in question had, before the deceased's death, been limited to damages of a specified or ascertainable amount, or where that liability is so limited by virtue of any enactment, nothing in the 1976 Act shall make that defender liable to pay damages exceeding that amount; and accordingly where in such an action there are two or more pursuers any damages to which they would respectively be entitled under the Act apart from the said limitation shall, if necessary, be reduced *pro rata* — s. 6(1) and (3)(a). Where two or more such actions are conjoined, the conjoined actions shall be treated for the purposes of the foregoing as if they were a single action — s. 6(2).

6 R.C.S. 43.1(1)(a)(Court of Session) and O.C.R. 36.1(1)(a)(Sheriff Court). The relevant rules are noted in Chap. 9, text accompanying nn. 12–19.

7 *Muir's Trustee v. Broadwood,* 1958 S.C. 169 at p. 173; Bankruptcy (Scotland) Act 1985, s. 31(1) and (5) or s. 32(6).

8 *Vaughan v. Greater Glasgow Passenger Transport Executive,* 1984 S.C. 32; *Anthony v. Brabbs,* 1998 G.W.D. 28–1437. See also *Kent v. British Railways Board* [1995] P.I.Q.R. Q42 and *Ward v. Newalls Insulation Co Ltd* [1998] 2 All E.R. 690.

9 *Fullemann v. McInnes's Executors,* 1993 S.L.T. 259. See also *Gibson v. Glasgow Corporation,* 1963 S.L.T. (Notes) 16 (claim by partnership dismissed as irrelevant) and cases cited in n. 1 *supra.*

10 *Waugh v. James K Allan Ltd,* 1963 S.C. 175 at p. 183; *Burns v. Edman* [1970] 1 All E. R. 886. It has been held that it would not be proper to take into account payments by an employer which were not declared for tax purposes — *Young v. Roche Services Group plc,* 1988 G.W.D. 32–1371. But see *Duller v. South East Lincs Engineers* [1981] C.L.Y. 585 (failure to declare lawful earnings to the Inland Revenue does not render them illegal and thus irrecoverable).

11 *McMillan v. McDowall,* 1993 S.L.T. 311 and *Liffen v. Watson* [1940] 1 K.B. 556 (free accommodation); *Kennedy v. Bryan* [1984] C.L.Y. 1028 (free company car); *Lamont v. Cameron's Executrix,* 1997 S.L.T. 1147 (free accommodation and car). *Cf. Cull v. Oilfield Inspection Services Group plc,* 1990 S.L.T. 205 (free company car and other fringe benefits). In *Webb v. MacAuley,* 1988 S.C. 10 the injured person was held entitled to recover family income supplement (now family credit), a state benefit paid to low earners to augment family resources, as a loss no different in kind from her loss of wages on which it was entirely consequential. In *Arnott v. Bristol-Myers Co Ltd,* 1998 S.L.T. 110 a

relevantly claimed.[12] An award may be made in respect of a redundancy payment which the injured person would have received but for his injury.[13]

Where an award of damages for personal injuries includes compensation for earnings lost during the relevant period, the court requires to specify in its order the amount of the compensation payment which is attributable to such loss for the purposes of recovery of the relative listed benefits in column 2 of Schedule 2 to the Social Security (Recovery of Benefits) Act 1997, namely disability working allowance, disablement pension payable under section 103 of the Social Security Contributions and Benefits Act 1992, incapacity benefit, income support, invalidity pension and allowance, jobseeker's allowance, reduced earnings allowance, severe disablement allowance, sickness benefit, statutory sick pay (as defined in Note 2 of Schedule 2), unemployability supplement and unemployment benefit.[14] The "relevant period" for which the court requires to specify the amount of compensation is, if it is a case of accident or injury, the period of five years immediately following the day on which the accident or injury in question occurred or, if it is a case of disease, the period of five years beginning with the date on which the claimant first claimed a listed benefit in consequence of the disease.[15] An award of damages for loss of earnings requires to be divided, where appropriate, into pre-decree and post-decree periods for the purposes of calculation of interest, which is exigible in respect of the former.[16]

---

claim for loss of the income support which but for the accident the injured person would have received on a "non-recoupable" basis was held to be relevant. In *McKenna v. Sharp*, 1998 S.C. 297 a claim for loss of the income support which but for the accident the injured person would have continued to receive was held to be relevant. See also *Neal v. Bingle* [1998] 2 All E.R. 58.

[12] *McCrum v. Ballantyne*, 1993 S.L.T. 788 at p. 790.

[13] *Tennant v. John Walker & Sons Ltd*, 1989 S.L.T. 143; *Campbell v. F. & F. Moffat (Transport) Ltd*, 1992 S.L.T. 962.

[14] Social Security (Recovery of Benefits) Act 1997, s. 15 and Sched 2. The Act and relative Regulations are reproduced in App. VI. Court of Session Practice Note No. 3 of 1997 requires that in all cases to which the Act applies, parties seeking decree (except where that decree is sought of consent) must lodge in process a schedule of damages stating the amount of any compensation which is claimed in respect of the relevant period under any of the headings in col. 1 of Sched. 2 to the Act. Such applies to final decrees after proof or jury trial, decrees in absence, decrees by default, summary decrees, interim decrees and decrees for provisional damages. Practice Notes in similar terms have been issued in the Sheriffdoms. For a specimen schedule, see App. IV. As to "the relevant period", see text accompanying following footnote. Note that in assessing damages in respect of any accident, injury or disease, the amount of any listed benefits paid or likely to be paid is to be disregarded — 1997 Act, s. 17.

[15] *Mitchell v. Laing*, 1998 S.C. 342.

[16] *Smith v. Middleton*, 1972 S.C. 30 at pp. 38–39.

The measure of damages for loss of earnings in an action of damages for personal injuries is the sum lost in consequence of the injuries:

> "The basic principle so far as loss of earnings [is] concerned is that the injured person should be placed in the same financial position, so far as can be done by an award of money, as he would have been had the accident not happened."[17]

The basic principle may be applied whether or not the injured person was in employment at the time of the accident. If he was in employment at that time, the injured person may recover damages on the footing that as a result of the accident his earnings have diminished or ceased altogether or will probably diminish or cease altogether.[18] He may recover on the basis that as a result of the accident he has suffered or will probably in the future suffer loss or diminution of opportunity to obtain alternative employment.[19] He may recover on the basis that as a result of the accident he has suffered or will probably in the future suffer loss or diminution of opportunity to obtain better employment.[20] If he was not in employment at the time of the accident, the injured person may recover damages for loss of earnings, whether in respect of the period before or after trial, on the footing that but for the accident he would probably have obtained employment.[21] Alternatively, he may recover such damages, whether in respect of the period before or after trial, on the basis that but for the accident he would probably have had an opportunity or better opportunity or opportunities to obtain employment.[22]

---

[17] *Per* Lord Goddard in *British Transport Commission v. Gourley* [1956] A.C. 185 at p. 206.

[18] As in *e.g. McCrum v. Ballantyne*, 1993 S.L.T. 788.

[19] *Robertson's Curator Bonis v. Anderson,* 1996 S.C. 217 at pp. 224–225; *Hill v. Wilson,* 1997 S.C. 81 at p. 85. *Cf. Smith v. Manchester Corporation* [1974] 17 K.I.R. 1; *Moeliker v. A. Reyrole & Co Ltd* [1976] I.C.R. 253; *Chan Wai Tong v. Li Ping Sum* [1985] 1 A.C. 446 at p. 460; *Foster v. Tyne & Wear County Council* [1986] 1 All E.R. 567; *Robson v. Liverpool City Council* [1993] P.I.Q.R. Q78; *Tait v. Pearson* [1996] P.I.Q.R. Q92. Note that such a case of loss of opportunity (whether described as such, or as a case of "market disadvantage", or as a case of loss of employability), arising as it would out of impairment to an injured person's earning capacity, is not concerned with a single "chance" which must be either in the past or in the future, even theoretically — *Hill v. Wilson, loc. cit.* Note further that it is not wrong in principle to award damages for loss of opportunity, howsoever described, to an injured person who is awarded damages for loss of future earnings — *Hill v. Wilson, loc. cit.*; *Frost v. Palmer* [1993] P.I.Q.R. Q14 at p. Q22.

[20] As in *e.g. Sellar's Curator Bonis v. Glasgow Victoria and Leverndale Hospitals,* 1973 S.L.T. (Notes) 3; *Wall v. Bryant*, 1994 S.L.T. 1260; *Anderson v. Davis* [1993] P.I.Q.R. Q87 at p. Q98.

[21] *Robertson's Curator Bonis v. Anderson,* 1996 S.C. 217.

[22] *Hill v. Wilson,* 1997 S.C. 81.

As a corollary of the basic principle, it is a universal rule that the injured person cannot recover more than he has lost.[23] Accordingly, outgoings which would have been incurred in achieving hypothetical profits fall to be taken into consideration.[24] Allowance must likewise be made for income tax which would have been payable on prospective earnings.[25] Sums which would have been paid in National Insurance contributions require also to be deducted in computing loss of earnings.[26] Similarly, hypothetical contributions to a pension scheme will be taken into account for purposes of a loss of earnings claim, at least where the injured person is also awarded damages for loss of pension rights.[27]

On the same principle, any remuneration or earnings from employment after the date of the accident must be taken into account so as to reduce the amount of damages payable to the injured person.[28]

---

[23] *Parry v. Cleaver* [1970] A.C. 1 at p. 13.

[24] *British Transport Commission v. Gourley* [1956] A.C. 185 at pp. 212–213; *Lynedale Fashion Manufacturers v. Rich* [1973] 1 All E.R. 33 at p. 36; *Lim v. Camden Health Authority* [1980] A.C. 174 at p. 191. *Cf. Dews v. National Coal Board* [1988] A.C. 1 at p. 13 (travelling expenses as a deduction generally to be discouraged).

[25] *McDaid v. Clyde Navigation Trustees,* 1946 S.C. 462; *British Transport Commission v. Gourley* [1956] A.C. 185. In the case of partial loss, the earnings lost are always treated as the top part of the income for the purposes of taking tax into account (*Lynedale Fashion Manufacturers v. Rich* [1973] 1 All E.R. 33). In *Fullemann v. McInnes's Executors,* 1993 S.L.T. 259 an award was made on the basis of the injured person's gross income in respect that under the law of Switzerland awards of damages for loss of earnings and other taxable receipts are subject to income tax. In *Clark v. Sutherland,* 1993 S.C. 320 the court made a deduction of one-third from the injured person's gross salary for tax and national insurance in the absence of evidence as to net earnings.

[26] *Gibney v. Eric Johnson Stubbs (Scotland) Ltd,* 1987 S.L.T. 132; *Cooper v. Firth Brown* [1963] 1 W.L.R. 418.

[27] *Dews v. National Coal Board* [1988] A.C. 1 at p. 18. But see *Anderson v. Gerrard,* 1994 S.L.T. 1326 (deductions for superannuation taken into account so as to reduce damages for loss of earnings even though no claim for loss of pension rights).

[28] Administration of Justice Act 1982, s. 10(i). This does not apply where the recipient of the payments, whether the injured person or any relative of his, is under an obligation to reimburse the employer in the event of damages being recovered in respect of those injuries — 1982 Act, s.10(e). As to the distinction between s. 10(i) and s. 10(a) ("contractual pension or benefit") see n. 33 *infra*. Note also that in terms of s. 10(ii) and (iii) of the Act there requires also to be taken into account in assessing the amount of damages payable to the injured person, so as to reduce that amount, any contribution-based jobseekers allowance (payable under the Jobseekers Act 1995) and any benefit payable from public funds designed to secure to the injured person or any relative of his a minimum level of subsistence (*e.g.* income support) in respect of the period prior to the date of the award of damages (*i.e.* relative to the assessment of past loss). These provisions appear to conflict with the Social Security (Recovery of Benefits) Act 1997, s. 17, which provides that in assessing damages in respect of any accident, injury or disease, the amount of any listed benefits (which include jobseekers allowance and income support) paid or likely to be paid is to be disregarded. See also *Arnott v. Bristol-Myers Co Ltd,* 1998 S.L.T. 110 at p. 112.

If the injured person ought reasonably to have resumed a particular type of employment by a particular time after his accident, account will be taken of the remuneration or earnings which he would have earned thereby had he done so.[29] Any payment of a benevolent character made to the injured person or to any relative of his by the wrongdoer following on the injuries in question, where such a payment is made directly and not through a trust or other fund from which the injured person or his relatives have benefited or may benefit, must also be taken into account so as to reduce the amount of damages payable.[30] Any tax rebate or tax saving resulting from the loss of earnings requires to be set against that loss.[31] Any saving to the injured person which is attributable to his maintenance wholly or partly at public expense in a hospital, nursing home or other institution must be set off against any income lost by him as a result of his injuries.[32]

On the other hand, subject to any agreement to the contrary, there must not be taken into account so as to reduce the amount of damages any of the following:

> "(a) any contractual pension or benefit (including any payment by a friendly society or trade union);[33]

---

[29] *Bowers v. Strathclyde Regional Council,* 1981 S.L.T. 122 at pp. 124–125. An injured plasterer was held to have acted unreasonably in refusing an offer of alternative employment as a security officer in *Docherty v. City of Glasgow District Council,* 1996 Rep. L.R. (Quantum) 5. An injured skimmings collector was held to have acted reasonably in refusing an offer of alternative employment as a lavatory attendant in *Morton v. British Aluminium Co Ltd,* 1982 S.L.T. 292. Note that an injured person who is fit for work may recover damages for loss of earnings in respect of a period during which he is unemployed, provided he reasonably requires the time to find work or has made reasonable efforts during the period to find employment or by reason of his age or other cause is not capable of obtaining work during the period even if technically employable — *Buckley v. Melville Dundas and Whitson Ltd,* 1979 S.L.T. (Notes) 102; *Blair v. F.J.C. Lilley (Marine) Ltd,* 1981 S.L.T. 90 at pp. 91–92; *Murdoch v. McDermott (Scotland),* Second Division, January 17, 1992, unreported.

[30] Administration of Justice Act 1982, s. 10(iv). "Payment" falls to be construed as a reference to payment whether in cash or in kind — s. 13(2). As to "relative", see n. 36 *infra.* Note that what was envisaged by the enactment of s. 10(iv) was that such payments would be deductible from *any* head of damages and not just from loss of earnings — *Hansard,* H.C. (October 19, 1982), Vol. 29, cols 288–291.

[31] *Hartley v. Sandholme Iron Co* [1975] Q.B. 600 (rebate) and *Brayson v. Wilmot-Breedon* [1976] C.L.Y. 682 (saving).

[32] Administration of Justice Act 1982, s. 11.

[33] "Benefit" and "pension" fall to be construed, respectively, as a reference to benefit or pension whether in cash or in kind — Administration of Justice Act 1982, s. 13(2). Note that s. 10(a) ("contractual pension or benefit") and s. 10(i) ("remuneration or earnings from employment") of the 1982 Act are mutually exclusive; so that particular payments made to an injured person cannot properly be regarded as falling at the same time under both heads, the distinction which has to be made depending not on the source but on the intrinsic nature of the payments as disclosed by the contractual documents which created

(b) any pension or retirement benefit payable from public funds other than any pension or benefit to which section 2(1) of the Law Reform (Personal Injuries) Act 1948 applies;
(c) any benefit payable from public funds, in respect of any period after the date of the award of damages, designed to secure to the injured person or any relative of his a minimum level of subsistence;[34]
(d) any redundancy payment under the Employment Protection (Consolidation) Act 1978, or any payment made in circumstances corresponding to those in which a right to a redundancy payment would have accrued if section 81 of that Act had applied;[35]
(e) any payment made to the injured person or to any relative[36] of his by the injured person's employer following upon the injuries in question where the recipient is under an obligation to reimburse the employer in the event of damages being recovered in respect of those injuries;
(f) subject to paragraph (iv) below,[37] any payment[38] of a benevolent character made to the injured person or to any relative of his by any person following upon the injuries in question."[39]

---

the injured person's right to receive them — *Lewicki v. Brown & Root Wimpey Highland Fabricators Ltd,* 1996 S.C. 200 (payments under disability scheme a contractual benefit rather than remuneration). Accident insurance falls within the definition of "contractual benefit" and is therefore not taken into account *(cf. Parry v. Cleaver* [1970] A.C. 1). Wage payments made during illness sourced by an insurance policy taken out for that purpose by the employer amount to remuneration, and not contractual benefit, and therefore fall to be deducted *(Hussain v. New Taplow Paper Mills* [1988] A.C. 514).

[34] Such a benefit is income support; it is to be left out of account in the assessment of future loss. As to such benefit payable in respect of the period prior to the date of the award (*i.e.* relative to the assessment of past loss), see n. 28 *supra.*

[35] A severance payment does not fall within the terms of s. 10(d) of the Administration of Justice Act 1982 and is therefore deductible — *Duncan v. Glacier Metal Co Ltd,* 1988 S.L.T. 479.

[36] "Relative" in relation to the injured person is defined by s. 13(1) of the Administration of Justice Act 1982 as (a) the spouse or divorced spouse; (b) any person, not being the spouse of the injured person who was, at the time of the act or omission giving rise to liability in the responsible person, living with the injured person as husband or wife; (c) any ascendant or descendant; (d) any brother, sister, uncle or aunt; or any issue of any such person; (e) any person accepted by the injured person as a child of his family. In deducing any relationship for the purposes of the foregoing definition — (a) any relationship by affinity is treated as a relationship by consanguinity; any relationship of the half blood is treated as a relationship of the whole blood; and the stepchild of any person is treated as his child; and (b) s. 1(1) of the Law Reform (Parent and Child)(Scotland) Act 1986 (legal equality of children) applies — 1982 Act, s. 13(1).

[37] As to the terms of para. (iv) of s. 10, see text accompanying n. 30 *supra.*

[38] "Payment" falls to be construed as a reference to payment whether in cash or in kind — 1982 Act, s. 13(2).

[39] Administration of Justice Act 1982, s. 10.

In making the assessment with respect to damages for loss of earnings, the court must take into consideration all that has happened since the date of the event giving rise to the claim, whether tending to increase or decrease damages.[40] Thus account falls to be taken, for example, of any changes in the rate of pay relative to the injured person's employment.[41] Similarly, any situation of redundancy relative to the injured person's job must be taken into consideration.[42] Any supervening condition such as illness or disease unrelated to the accident suffered by the injured person must likewise be taken into account.[43] The court accordingly calculates loss of earnings to the date of trial with the full benefit of hindsight.

The method to be adopted in the assessment of loss of future earnings depends on the circumstances of the case, but the means must always be subservient to the end.[44] Given that the purpose is to give effect to the basic principle, what is required is such a sum as may reasonably be expected to achieve this.[45] In making such a calculation the court may adopt the method of a lump sum, or a multiplier, or a combination of both.[46] Where earnings will be lost over a future period of years it will normally be appropriate to resort to the use of a multiplier.[47] However, consideration of the extent of the imponderable elements in a claim may determine which method to choose.[48]

A lump sum award is based on the experience of the judge and may be incapable of precise analysis.[49] It is the appropriate method of assessment wherever the period of loss is so short or the circumstances are so uncertain that it is better to make a broad estimate in the form of a lump sum than to attempt a more sophisticated calculation.[50] A

---

[40] *MacMaster v. Caledonian Railway Co* (1885) 13 R. 252 at p. 255, approved by the Full Bench in *Rieley v. Kingslaw Riding School,* 1975 S.C. 28 at p. 40.

[41] *Forsyth's Curator Bonis v. Govan Shipbuilders Ltd,* 1988 S.C. 421 (but evidence must be led as to wage increases applicable to the injured person's employment, not just as to increases in wages generally).

[42] As in *e.g. Poole v. John Laing plc,* 1987 S.L.T. 325; *Hodge v. British Coal Corporation (No. 2),* 1992 S.L.T. 913; *Farrelly v. Yarrow Shipbuilders Ltd,* 1994 S.L.T. 1349.

[43] *Forbes v. British Railways Board,* 1971 S.L.T. (Notes) 21; *Grant v. National Coal Board,* 1974 S.L.T. (Notes) 71; *Jobling v. Associated Dairies Ltd* [1982] A.C. 794.

[44] *O'Brien's Curator Bonis v. British Steel plc,* 1991 S.C. 315 at p. 319; *Robertson's Curator Bonis v. Anderson,* 1996 S.C. 217 at p. 224.

[45] *O'Brien's Curator Bonis v. British Steel plc,* 1991 S.C. 315 at p. 319.

[46] *Robertson's Curator Bonis v. Anderson,* 1996 S.C. 217 at p. 224.

[47] *O'Brien's Curator Bonis v. British Steel plc,* 1991 S.C. 315 at p. 324.

[48] *Robertson's Curator Bonis v. Anderson,* 1996 S.C. 217 at p. 224; *Blamire v. South Cumbria Health Authority* [1993] P.I.Q.R. Q1 at p. Q6.

[49] *Robertson's Curator Bonis v. Anderson,* 1996 S.C. 217 at p. 224.

[50] *O'Brien's Curator Bonis v. British Steel plc,* 1991 S.C. 315 at p. 319; *Timoney v. Dunnery,* 1984 S.L.T 151 at p. 152; *Blamire v. South Cumbria Health Authority* [1993] P.I.Q.R. Q1. Broad estimates in the form of a lump sum were made in *McGahan v. Greater Glasgow*

broad approach may also be indicated in the case of more remote losses such as loss or diminution of some future opportunity or opportunities for work in the market.[51]

An award made on the basis of a multiplier involves the application of judicial experience within a more scientific framework:

> "Essentially what the court has to do is to calculate as best it can the sum of money which will on the one hand be adequate, by its capital and income, to provide annually for the injured person a sum equal to his estimated annual loss over the whole of the period during which that loss is likely to continue, but which, on the other hand, will not, at the end of that period, leave him in a better financial position than he would have been apart from

---

Health Board, 1988 S.L.T 270; *Stevenson v. British Coal Corporation,* 1989 S.L.T. 136; *Lang v. Fife Health Board,* 1990 S.L.T. 626; *Young v. Greater Glasgow Health Board,* 1993 S.L.T. 721; *MacLeod v. Taylor's Executor,* 1994 S.L.T. 322; *Sommerville v. Lothian Health Board,* 1994 S.L.T. 1207; *Tweedy v. Newboult,* 1996 S.L.T. 2; and *Maley v. Daylay Foods Limited,* 1998 S.C. 324. Claims on behalf of injured children for loss of future earnings have been dealt with on a lump sum basis (*Steen v. Macnicol,* 1968 S.L.T. (Notes) 77; *Lamb's Tutor v. Cawthorn-Sinclair Ltd,* 1978 S.L.T. (Notes) 31; *Brogan's Tutors v. Glasgow District Council,* 1978 S.L.T (Notes) 47; *Anderson's Tutor v. J.Wallace and Sons,* 1989 S.L.T. 150; *Spence v. City of Glasgow District Council,* 1989 S.L.T. 119) or on a multiplier/multiplicand basis (*Dickson v. Edinburgh Corporation,* 1970 S.L.T. (Notes) 56; *McKinnell v. White,* 1971 S.L.T. (Notes) 61; *Chapman v. South of Scotland Electricity Board,* 1983 S.L.T. 456; *Love v. British Railways Board,* 1984 S.L.T. 2; *Fallow v. Greater Glasgow Health Board,* 1985 S.L.T. 98; *Wilson v. Price,* 1989 S.L.T. 484; *Geddes v. Lothian Health Board,* 1992 S.L.T. 986). *Cf. Jones v. Lawrence* [1969] 3 All E.R. 267; *Daish v. Wanton* [1972] 2 Q.B. 262; *Taylor v. Bristol Omnibus Co Ltd* [1975] 2 All E.R. 1107; *Joyce v. Yeomans* [1981] 2 All E.R. 21; *Connolly v. Camden and Islington Area Health Authority* [1981] 3 All E.R. 250; *Croke v. Wiseman* [1981] 3 All E.R. 852; *Janardan v. East Berks Health Authority* [1990] 2 Med. L.R. 1; *Cassel v. Riverside Health Authority* [1992] P.I.Q.R. Q168; *Dhaliwal v. Hunt* [1995] P.I.Q.R. Q56.

51 *Robertson's Curator Bonis v. Anderson,* 1996 S.C. 217 at pp. 224–225; *Hill v. Wilson,* 1997 S.C. 81. *Cf. Smith v. Manchester Corporation* [1974] 17 K.I.R. 1; *Moeliker v. A. Reyrole & Co Ltd* [1976] I.C.R. 253; *Chan Wai Tong v. Li Ping Sum* [1985] 1 A.C. 446 at p. 460; *Foster v. Tyne & Wear County Council* [1986] 1 All E.R. 567; *Robson v. Liverpool City Council* [1993] P.I.Q.R. Q78; *Tait v. Pearson* [1996] P.I.Q.R. Q92. An issue may arise as to whether a claimed loss of financial opportunity is too speculative or remote (*cf. Kelly v. Keith Cardle & Co,* 1954 S.L.T. (Notes) 80 (amateur boxer's loss of prospect of professional earnings not too remote); *Neill v. Scottish Omnibuses Ltd,* 1961 S.L.T. (Notes) 42 (averments indicative of professional boxer's status relevant to issue of his potential purses but speculative enquiry into whether pursuer would have won a U.K. title fight unsuitable for investigation and evaluation by the court and loss of opportunity to fight for world title too remote and speculative); *McCall v. Foulis,* 1966 S.L.T. 47 (insurance clerk's averments relating to enforced delay in sitting professional examination and consequent loss of opportunity to increase earnings relevant but loss of opportunity to play professional football too remote); and *Drummond v. Foulis,* 1972 S.L.T. (Notes) 11 (averment of loss of opportunity to resume as professional dancer or instructor relevant)).

the accident. Hence the conventional approach is to assess the amount notionally required to be laid out in the purchase of an annuity [an investment of money entitling the investor to a series of equal annual sums] which will provide the annual sum needed for the whole period of the loss."[52]

The mechanism by which the capital sum is arrived at is the selection of a multiplicand, as representing the estimated annual loss of earnings as at the date of trial, and a multiplier which, when applied to the multiplicand, will provide the amount which can be expected to achieve the desired result.[53]

The multiplier that is selected represents a number of years' purchase and is applied to the multiplicand from the date of trial.[54] The multiplier may be divided and the portions applied to different annual sums or multiplicands representing different amounts of loss over the period of the multiplier.[55] The multiplicand may be varied to take account of special factors.[56] Where the injured person's expected date of death is earlier than it would have been if he had not sustained the injuries, it must be assumed that he will live until the date when he would have been expected to die if he had not sustained the injuries.[57] To select a multiplier appropriate in general terms to an injured person's age and then to discount it to allow for special factors is a legitimate method

---

52 *Per* Lord Oliver of Aylmerton in *Hodgson v. Trapp* [1989] A.C. 807 at p. 826.

53 *O'Brien's Curator Bonis v. British Steel plc,* 1991 S.C. 315 at p. 319.

54 *Will v. Charles Will Ltd,* 1980 S.L.T. (Notes) 37.

55 *Tannock v. British Leyland Motor Company,* 1981 S.L.T. (Notes) 49; *Routledge v. McKenzie* [1994] P.I.Q.R. Q49. Loss of future earnings was divided into separate periods in *e.g. Kirkpatrick v. Scott Lithgow Ltd,* 1987 S.L.T. 654; *MacNeil v. U.I.E. Shipbuilding (Scotland) Ltd,* 1989 S.L.T. 289 and *Campbell v. City of Glasgow District Council,* 1991 S.L.T. 616.

56 *Wells v. Wells* [1998] 3 W.L.R. 329 at p. 362. See *e.g. Anderson v. Brown,* 1983 S.L.T. 655; *Todd v. Montgomerie Sealants Ltd,* 1983 S.L.T. 354; *Barrett v. Strathclyde Fire Brigade,* 1984 S.L.T. 325; *Gibney v. Eric Johnson Stubbs (Scotland) Ltd,* 1987 S.L.T. 132; *Bird* v. *British Beef Co Ltd,* 1988 S.L.T. 801; *McKay v. Strathclyde Communications Ltd,* 1988 S.L.T. 732 and *Morrison v. McDermott Scotland,* 1991 S.L.T. 854.

57 Damages (Scotland) Act 1976, s. 9(1) and (2)(a). In such a case, the court may have regard to any amount, whether or not it is an amount related to earnings by the pursuer's own labour or other gainful activity, which in its opinion the pursuer, if he had not sustained the injuries in question, would have received in the period up to his notional date of death by way of benefits in money or money's worth, being benefits derived from sources other than the pursuer's own estate; and must have regard to any diminution of any such amount as aforesaid by virtue of expenses which in the opinion of the court the pursuer, if he had not sustained the injuries in question, would reasonably have incurred in the said period by way of living expenses — 1976 Act, s. 9(2)(b) and (c). For an illustration of the application of the provision, see *Martin v. James and Andrew Chapman (Haulage Contractors) Ltd,* 1995 G.W.D. 2–77.

of estimating loss of future earnings.[58] The initial choice of multiplier should also reflect the probable duration of the injured person's working life but for the accident by taking account of the normal retirement age applicable to the injured person's employment.[59] Special factors to be taken into consideration may constitute potential outcomes in a hypothetical state of facts or future prospects or chances.[60] There are many possible variables, such as the risks of accident, illness or redundancy and the prospect of promotion as well as variations in the amount of earnings.[61] Other factors include the chance of future alternative employment such as light work.[62] Where the damages are in respect of a loss of earnings commencing at some distant time in the future, some significant allowance should be made for the fact that the injured person would be receiving his damages for future loss now, and much earlier than the loss would be suffered.[63]

LOSS OF PENSION RIGHTS

A claim for loss of pension rights may be made in an action of damages for personal injuries by the injured person.[64] His title to sue is unaffected by any insurance arrangements.[65] His right to damages for loss of pension rights transmits upon his death to his executor, but only in respect of loss attributable to the period before death.[66] In the case of the injured person's bankruptcy, his trustee in sequestration has the right to sue for any pecuniary losses arising out of the personal injury.[67]

Lost pension rights resulting from personal injury are not strictly speaking lost earnings because a pension is intrinsically of a different

---

[58] *McCrum v. Ballantyne,* 1993 S.L.T. 788 at p. 791.

[59] As in *e.g. McWhinnie v. British Coal Corporation*, 1993 S.L.T. 467; *McLean v. Remploy Ltd,* 1994 S.L.T. 687.

[60] *Cp. Blair v. F.J.C. Lilley (Marine) Ltd,* 1981 S.L.T. 90 (potential outcomes but for accident) and *Morrison v. Barton,* 1994 S.L.T. 657 (future possibilities).

[61] *O'Brien's Curator Bonis v. British Steel plc,* 1991 S.C. 315 at p. 321.

[62] See *e.g. Gibney v. Eric Johnson Stubbs (Scotland) Ltd,* 1987 S.L.T. 132; *McKay v. Strathclyde Communications Ltd,* 1988 S.L.T. 732; and *Robertson v. Scottish Special Housing Association,* 1989 S.L.T. 686.

[63] *McGregor v. Webster's Executors,* 1976 S.L.T. 29 at p. 32.

[64] Claims by third parties for loss of pension rights arising out of the personal injuries sustained by the injured person are irrelevant since the losses are too remote — see n. 1 *supra*.

[65] *Port-Glasgow and Newark Sailcloth Co v. Caledonian Railway Co* (1892) 19 R. 608.

[66] Damages (Scotland) Act 1976, s. 2(1) and (2). And see text accompanying nn. 4–6 *supra*.

[67] *Muir's Trustee v. Broadwood,* 1958 S.C. 169 at p. 173; Bankruptcy (Scotland) Act 1985, s. 31(1) and (5) or s. 32(6).

kind from wages, the latter being a reward for contemporaneous work and the former being the fruit, through insurance, of all the money which was set aside in the past in respect of the injured person's past work.[68] Pensions are nonetheless regarded as earned income since the products of the sums paid into a pension fund are in fact delayed remuneration for current work and losses relative to a pension, whether total or partial, resulting from inability to work due to personal injury are recoverable.[69]

The measure of damages for loss of pension rights in an action of damages for personal injuries is the sum lost in consequence of the injuries. The basic principle so far as such claims are concerned is:

> "What has to be found is such sum of money as will put the pursuer in the same position as he would have been in had he not sustained the injury in question."[70]

As a corollary of the basic principle, it is a universal rule that the injured person cannot recover more than he has lost.[71] Accordingly, any other pension received as a result of the personal injury during the retirement period requires to be set off against the claimed loss.[72] Allowance must be made for income tax which would have been payable on the prospective pension.[73] Any repayment of pension contributions to the injured person must likewise be taken into account.[74]

The method to be adopted in the assessment of loss of pension rights depends on the circumstances of the case, but the means must always be subservient to the end.[75] Given that the purpose is to give

---

[68] *Parry v. Cleaver* [1970] A.C. 1 at p. 16; *Smoker v. London Fire Authority* [1991] 2 A.C. 502.

[69] *Ibid.*; *Auty v. National Coal Board* [1985] W.L.R. 784; *Mitchell v. Glenrothes Development Corporation,* 1991 S.L.T. 284.

[70] *Mitchell v. Glenrothes Development Corporation* 1991 S.L.T. 284 at p. 289.

[71] *Parry v. Cleaver* [1970] A.C. 1 at p. 13.

[72] *Mitchell v. Glenrothes Development Corporation,* 1991 S.L.T. 284 at p. 291; *Cantwell, Petitioner,* Lord Milligan, July 28, 1998, unreported. *Cf. Parry v. Cleaver* [1970] A.C. 1 at pp. 20–21; *Longden v. British Coal Corporation* [1998] 1 All E.R. 289 at p. 301. In *Cantwell* the Lord Ordinary rejected the argument that the common law had been altered by the Administration of Justice Act 1982, s. 10(a) (envisaged as applicable to claims for loss of *earnings* — Scottish Law Commission, Damages for Personal Injuries: Report on (1) Admissibility of Claims for Services; (2) Admissible Deductions (Scot. Law Com. No. 51), Part III, esp. paras 46–47; *Hansard,* H.C. (October 19, 1982), Vol. 29, cols 288–291). Note that on this basis it is right to set against the claim that part of any lump sum pension payment which represented the commutation of a part of the annual payments which the injured person would otherwise have received as income during the retirement period — *Longden v. British Coal Corporation, cit. supra,* at pp. 302–304.

[73] *Grainger v. Fife Regional Council,* 1991 S.L.T. 632.

[74] *Mitchell v. Glenrothes Development Corporation,* 1991 S.L.T. 284 at p. 291.

[75] *Cf. Robertson's Curator Bonis v. Anderson,* 1996 S.C. 217 at p. 224.

effect to the basic principle, what is required is such a sum as may reasonably be expected to achieve this.[76] In some pension schemes, if the period of disability is relatively short, it may be that the injured person can be compensated for the loss by paying him a sum equivalent to the contributions that have not been paid (whether by him or his employer or both) during his disability, so that he can top up the contributions.[77] However, if the injured person has been off work for a substantial period of time or is permanently disabled, a more sophisticated calculation will be required to ascertain the loss.[78] In that regard, the conventional approach is similar to that relating to loss of future earnings, namely to assess the amount notionally required to be laid out in the purchase of an annuity (an investment of money entitling the investor to a series of equal annual sums) which will provide the annual sum needed for the whole period of the loss.[79] The mechanism by which the capital sum is arrived at is the selection of a multiplicand, as representing the estimated annual loss of pension as at the date of trial, and a multiplier which, when applied to the multiplicand, will provide the amount which can be expected to achieve the desired result.[80]

The multiplier that is selected represents a number of years' purchase and is applied to the multiplicand from the date of trial.[81] In estimating the period of loss, the injured person's age and expectation of life at the commencement of the period of loss fall to be taken into account.[82] The multiplier may be modified so as to recognise the imponderables, such as the risk that the injured person would have suffered illness, dismissal or redundancy or the possibility that another pension may be forthcoming.[83] Consideration should be given to the value of any lump sum benefit, on the one hand, and to the deferment in payment of the pension until the age of retirement, on the other.[84]

---

[76] *Dews v. National Coal Board* [1988] A.C. 1 at p. 18.

[77] *Ibid.* at p. 14.

[78] *Ibid.* at p. 15.

[79] *Cf. Hodgson v. Trapp* [1989] A.C. 807 at p. 826.

[80] *Mitchell v. Glenrothes Development Corporation,* 1991 S.L.T. 284 at p. 291; *Grainger v. Fife Regional Council,* 1991 S.L.T. 632.

[81] *Mitchell v. Glenrothes Development Corporation,* 1991 S.L.T. 284 at p. 291.

[82] *Mitchell v. Glenrothes Development Corporation,* 1991 S.L.T. 284; *Auty v. National Coal Board* [1985] 1 W.L.R. 784.

[83] *O'Neil v. British Coal Corporation,* 1991 S.L.T. 367 at p. 370; *Mitchell v. Glenrothes Development Corporation,* 1991 S.L.T. 284 at p. 291; *Grainger v. Fife Regional Council,* 1991 S.L.T. 632 at p. 633; *Mitchell v. Inverclyde District Council,* 1997 Rep. L.R. (Quantum) 29 at p. 31; *Auty v. National Coal Board* [1985] 1 W.L.R. 784 at p. 798.

[84] *Mitchell v. Glenrothes Development Corporation,* 1991 S.L.T. 284 at p. 291; *Robertson v. Lestrange* [1985] 1 All E.R. 950 at p. 958.

Chapter 7

OUTLAYS AND EXPENSES

Pecuniary loss arising from personal injury in its positive form, namely expenditure rendered necessary by the injury or its effects, may be compensated by an award of damages for outlays and expenses.

A claim for outlays and expenses may be made in an action of damages for personal injuries by the injured person.[1] His title to sue is unaffected by any insurance arrangements.[2] His right to damages for outlays and expenses transmits upon his death to his executor, but only in respect of loss attributable to the period before death.[3] The executor's claim is not excluded by the making of a claim under the Damages (Scotland) Act 1976 by a relative of the deceased or by a deceased relative's executor.[4] For the purpose of enforcing any such right the injured person's executor is entitled — (a) to bring an action; or (b) if an action for that purpose had been brought by the deceased but had not been concluded before his death, to be sisted as pursuer in that action.[5] In either event the rules of court concerning intimation of

---

[1] Claims by third parties for outlays and expenses arising out of the personal injuries sustained by the injured person, save in the case of claims under the Administration of Justice Act 1982, s. 8, are irrelevant since the losses are too remote — *Robertson v. Turnbull,* 1982 S.C. (H.L.) 1 (claim for expenses incurred by family members for injuries to wife and mother dismissed as irrelevant).

[2] *Port-Glasgow and Newark Sailcloth Co v. Caledonian Railway Co* (1892) 19 R. 608.

[3] Damages (Scotland) Act 1976, s. 2(1) and (2), as substituted by the Damages (Scotland) Act 1993, s. 3.

[4] 1976 Act, s. 4, as amended by the Administration of Justice Act 1982, s. 14(2)(a) and the Damages (Scotland) Act 1993, Sched., para. 1.

[5] 1976 Act, s. 2A(1), as inserted by the Damages (Scotland) Act 1993, s. 4. For the purpose of s. 2A(1) an action shall not be taken to be concluded while any appeal is competent or before any appeal taken has been disposed of — s. 2A(2). Note that where in an action in which, following the death of the deceased from personal injuries, damages are claimed by the executor of the deceased, in respect of the injuries from which the deceased died, it is shown that by antecedent agreement, compromise or otherwise, the liability arising in relation to a particular defender from the personal injuries in question had, before the deceased's death, been limited to damages of a specified or ascertainable amount, or where that liability is so limited by virtue of any enactment, nothing in the 1976 Act shall make that defender liable to pay damages exceeding that amount; and accordingly where in such an action there are two or more pursuers any damages to which they would respectively be entitled under the Act apart from the said limitation shall, if necessary, be reduced *pro rata* — s. 6(1) and (3)(a). Where two or more such actions are conjoined, the conjoined actions shall be treated for the purposes of the foregoing as if they were a single action — s. 6(2).

the action to connected persons are applicable.[6] In the case of the injured person's bankruptcy, his trustee in sequestration has the right to sue for any pecuniary losses arising out of the personal injury.[7]

Outlays and expenses may be claimed where they are in the form of expenditure on goods or services.[8] Such purchases are recoverable whether they are extraordinary in nature or merely additional expenditure on ordinary items.[9] Capital outlays as well as recurring expenditure may be recovered.[10] Costs incurred in relation to heritable property may also be the subject of a claim.[11]

---

6 R.C.S. 43.1(1)(a) (Court of Session) and O.C.R. 36.1(1)(a) (Sheriff Court). The relevant rules are noted in Chap. 9, text accompanying nn. 12–19.

7 *Muir's Trustee v. Broadwood,* 1958 S.C. 169 at p. 173; Bankruptcy (Scotland) Act 1985, s. 31(1) and (5) or s. 32(6).

8 See *e.g. Gardner v. Howard Doris Ltd,* 1983 S.L.T. 672 (medical supplies; aids, appliances and equipment; nursing and domestic assistance; motor vehicle; clothing); *Tuttle v. Edinburgh University,* 1984 S.L.T. 172 (medical supplies; aids, appliances and equipment; additional motoring expenses; special clothing and dressing; additional running costs of home; recreation and holidays); *MacIntosh v. National Coal Board,* 1987 S.L.T. 116 and 1988 S.L.T. 348 (medical supplies; appliances, aids and equipment; care and attendance; additional motoring expenses; additional running costs of home; holidays and recreation; clothing and dressing); *Forsyth's Curator Bonis v. Govan Shipbuilders Ltd,* 1988 S.C. 421 (expenses of curatory); *Docherty's Curator Bonis v. U I E Shipbuilding (Scotland) Ltd,* 1989 S.L.T. 197 (residential care; expenses of curatory); *O'Brien's Curator Bonis v. British Steel plc,* 1991 S.C. 315 (residential care); *Geddes v. Lothian Health Board,* 1992 S.L.T. 986 (travelling expenses; extra clothing, laundry, telephone, holiday and motoring costs; aids, appliances and equipment; non-residential care and attendance; residential care); *Gordon v. Wilson,* 1992 S.L.T. 849 (extra transport, heating, telephone and holiday costs; special equipment); *McMillan v. McDowall,* 1993 S.L.T. 311 (special equipment; special clothing and dressing; care and attendance; holidays); *Cherry v. Strathclyde Regional Council,* 1994 S.L.T. 494 (extra transport costs); *Wall v. Bryant,* 1994 S.L.T. 1260 (furnishings; appliances; additional motoring expenses); *Stevenson v. Sweeney,* 1995 S.L.T. 29 (aids and equipment; holidays; additional transport costs; care and attendance); *Duffy v. Shaw,* 1995 S.C.L.R. 406 (domestic assistance; extra food and transport costs); *G's Curator Bonis v. Grampian Health Board,* 1995 S.L.T. 652 (expenses of curatory); *Martin v. James and Andrew Chapman (Haulage Contractors) Ltd,* 1995 G.W.D. 2–77 (aids and equipment; holidays; care and attendance); *O'Connor v. Matthews,* 1996 S.L.T. 408 (special aids, equipment and outlays; care and attendance).

9 Contrast *e.g.* curatory expenses (*Forsyth's Curator Bonis v. Govan Shipbuilders Ltd,* 1988 S.C. 421; *Docherty's Curator Bonis v. U I E Shipbuilding (Scotland) Ltd,* 1989 S.L.T. 197; *G's Curator Bonis v. Grampian Health Board,* 1995 S.L.T. 652) with *e.g.* transport costs (*Tuttle v. Edinburgh University,* 1984 S.L.T. 172; *MacIntosh v. National Coal Board,* 1987 S.L.T. 116; *Geddes v. Lothian Health Board,* 1992 S.L.T. 986; *Gordon v. Wilson,* 1992 S.L.T. 849; *Cherry v. Strathclyde Regional Council,* 1994 S.L.T. 494; *Wall v. Bryant,* 1994 S.L.T. 1260; *Stevenson v. Sweeney,* 1995 S.L.T. 29; *Duffy v. Shaw,* 1995 S.L.T. 602).

10 See *e.g. Gardner v. Howard Doris Ltd,* 1983 S.L.T. 672; *Tuttle v. Edinburgh University,* 1984 S.L.T. 172; *MacIntosh v. National Coal Board,* 1987 S.L.T. 116; *Geddes v. Lothian Health Board,* 1992 S.L.T. 986; *Gordon v. Wilson,* 1992 S.L.T. 849; *McMillan v. McDowall* 1993 S.L.T. 311; *Wall v. Bryant,* 1994 S.L.T. 1260; *Stevenson v. Sweeney,* 1995 S.L.T. 29; *O'Connor v. Matthews,* 1996 S.L.T. 408.

11 *Gardner v. Howard Doris Ltd,* 1983 S.L.T. 672 (central heating for existing house); *Tuttle v. Edinburgh University,* 1984 S.L.T. 172 (special adaptations to existing house); *Geddes v.*

Where an award of damages for personal injuries includes compensation for the cost of care incurred during the relevant period, the court requires to specify in its order the amount of the compensation payment which is attributable to such cost for the purposes of recovery of the relative listed benefits in column 2 of Schedule 2 to the Social Security (Recovery of Benefits) Act 1997, namely attendance allowance, the care component of disability living allowance and the disablement pension increase payable under section 104 or section 105 of the Social Security Contributions and Benefits Act 1992.[12] Where such an award includes compensation for loss of mobility during the relevant period, the court requires to specify in its order the amount of the compensation payment which is attributable to such loss for the purposes of recovery of the relative listed benefits in column 2 of Schedule 2 to the 1997 Act, namely mobility allowance and the mobility component of disability living allowance.[13] Whether the compensation is in respect of the cost of care or for loss of mobility, the "relevant period" for which the court requires to specify the amount of compensation is, if it is a case of accident or injury, the period of five years immediately following the day on which the accident or

---

Lothian Health Board, 1992 S.L.T. 986 (acquisition of new house); *McMillan v. McDowall,* 1993 S.L.T. 311 (alterations to existing house); *Wall v. Bryant,* 1994 S.L.T. 1260 (central heating for existing house); *Martin v. James and Andrew Chapman (Haulage Contractors) Ltd,* 1995 G.W.D. 2–77 (acquisition of land for and construction of new house); *Moriarty v. McCarthy* [1978] 1 W.L.R. 155 (alterations to future house); *Roberts v. Johnstone* [1989] Q.B. 878 (acquisition of and alterations to new house); *Almond v. Leeds Western Health Authority* (1990) 1 Med. L.R. 370 (acquisition of and alterations to new house). *Cf. O'Connor v. Matthews,* 1996 S.L.T. 408 at p. 410 (purchase costs for first time house disallowed on footing that no evidence that adequate council house could not be allocated and because loss of earnings claim presupposed that but for accident injured person would have been earning wages which would have been subject to similar housing costs).

12 Social Security (Recovery of Benefits) Act 1997, s. 15. The Act and relative Regulations are reproduced in App. VI. Court of Session Practice Note No. 3 of 1997 requires that in all cases to which the Act applies, parties seeking decree (except where that decree is sought of consent) must lodge in process a schedule of damages stating the amount of any compensation which is claimed in respect of the relevant period under any of the headings in col. 1 of Sched. 2 to the Act. Such applies to final decrees after proof or jury trial, decrees in absence, decrees by default, summary decrees, interim decrees and decrees for provisional damages. Practice Notes in similar terms have been issued in the Sheriffdoms. For a specimen schedule, see App. IV. As to "the relevant period", see text accompanying n.14. Note that in assessing damages in respect of any accident, injury or disease, the amount of any listed benefits paid or likely to be paid is to be disregarded — 1997 Act, s. 17.

13 Social Security (Recovery of Benefits) Act 1997, s. 15. An example of damages for loss of mobility would be the cost of fares for journeys by bus or taxi which the injured person would not have required to take but for the loss of mobility — *Mitchell v. Laing,* 1998 S.C. 342 at p. 352. Note that in the context of the 1997 Act, and especially in the light of Parliament's intention to protect victims' solatium from reduction by any amount of benefits, it would be wrong to construe any of the heads in col. 1 of Sched. 2 to the 1997 Act as including any element of solatium (*cf. Mitchell, loc. cit.*).

injury occurred or, if it is a case of a disease, the period of five years beginning with the date on which the claimant first claimed a listed benefit in consequence of the disease.[14] An award of damages for outlays and expenses requires to be divided, where appropriate, into pre-decree and post-decree periods for the purposes of calculation of interest, which is exigible in respect of the former.[15]

The measure of damages for outlays and expenses in an action of damages for personal injuries is the sum expended in consequence of the injuries:

> "The basic principle so far as...out of pocket expenses are concerned is that the injured person should be placed in the same financial position, so far as can be done by an award of money, as he would have been had the accident not happened."[16]

In applying the basic principle, outlays and expenses are recoverable only if they are reasonably incurred.[17] There requires to be disregarded, in determining the reasonableness of any expenses, the possibility of avoiding those expenses or part of them by taking advantage of National Health Service facilities.[18] Medical expenses cannot be recovered for any period in which the injured person has in fact received or is likely to receive the treatment free of charge.[19] It is a question of circumstances as to whether or not it is reasonable for an injured person to insist on being cared for at home.[20]

As a corollary of the basic principle, it is a universal rule that the injured person cannot recover more than he has lost.[21] Accordingly, any domestic element in the cost of care must be deducted to the extent that it is a cost which would have been incurred by the injured person anyway if there had been no accident.[22] In the case of a householder or lodger who is injured, many of his expenses are fixed charges which continue while he is in hospital and are not deducted.[23] If the injured

---

[14] *Mitchell v. Laing,* 1998 S.C. 342.

[15] *Cf. McMillan v. McDowall,* 1993 S.L.T. 311.

[16] *Per* Lord Goddard in *British Transport Commission v. Gourley* [1956] A.C. 185 at p. 206. Legal expenses incurred prior to litiscontestation cannot however be claimed as damages — *Shanks v. Gray,* 1977 S.L.T. (Notes) 26.

[17] *Anderson v. Forth Valley Health Board,* 1998 S.L.T. 588. Expenses of medical treatment may be reasonably incurred notwithstanding that the treatment turns out to be unnecessary and useless — see *Rubens v. Walker,* 1946 S.C. 215.

[18] Law Reform (Personal Injuries) Act 1948, s. 2(4).

[19] *Harris v. Bright's Asphalt Contractors Ltd* [1953] 1 Q.B. 617; *Cunningham v. Harrison* [1973] Q.B. 942; *Housecroft v. Burnett* [1986] 1 All E.R. 332; *Lim v. Camden Health Authority* [1980] A.C. 174.

[20] *Rialas v. Mitchell, The Times,* 17 Jul 1984 (C. A.); (1984) 128 S.J. 704.

[21] *Parry v. Cleaver* [1970] A.C. 1 at p. 13.

[22] *O'Brien's Curator Bonis v. British Steel plc,* 1991 S.C. 315 at pp. 317–319; *Lim v. Camden Health Authority* [1980] A.C. 174 at pp. 190–192.

[23] *Shearman v. Folland* [1950] 1 All E. R. 976 at p. 979.

person is a dependant, he does not save any living expenses because he incurs none.[24] In the event that the saving to the injured person is attributable to his maintenance wholly or partly at public expense in a hospital, nursing home or other institution, such saving must then be set off against any income lost by him as a result of his injuries.[25] On the same principle, where a new item of property has to be purchased in substitution for an existing one, only the additional cost may be recovered.[26]

In making the assessment of damages the court must take into consideration all that has happened since the date of the event giving rise to the claim.[27] Thus reasonable outlays and expenses arising out of the personal injury which have already been incurred by the time of the trial will be awarded.[28]

With regard to future loss, the method of assessment depends on the circumstances of the case, but the means must always be subservient to the end.[29] Given that the purpose is to give effect to the basic principle, what is required is such a sum of money as may reasonably be expected to achieve this.[30] In making such a calculation, therefore, the court may adopt a method of assessment appropriate to the nature of the outlay.

In relation to the purchase of special accommodation, for example, damages fall to be assessed on the basis of the additional annual cost over the injured person's lifetime of providing that accommodation, such cost to be taken as 3% of the net capital cost (which, if necessarily expended, is not to be reduced by reason of any betterment not required to meet the injured person's needs); and a further sum falls to be awarded for the full capital cost of any conversion works necessary to adapt the property for the injured person's needs, save insofar as they enhance the value of the property.[31]

---

[24] *Ibid.*

[25] Administration of Justice Act 1982, s. 11.

[26] *Geddes v. Lothian Health Board,* 1992 S.L.T. 986 at p. 987 (motor car). *Cf. Goldfinch v. Scannell* [1993] P.I.Q.R. Q143 (damages awarded reflecting difference in capital depreciation between appropriate new car and likely second-hand car but for accident).

[27] *MacMaster v. Caledonian Railway Co* (1885) 13 R. 252 at p. 255, approved by the Full Bench in *Rieley v. Kingslaw Riding School,* 1975 S.C. 28 at p. 40.

[28] It is necessary to show that liability has in fact been incurred but not necessarily that the bill or account has actually been settled (*cf. Gordon v. Wilson,* 1992 S.L.T. 849 at pp. 855–856; *Allen v. Waters & Co* [1935] 1 K.B. 200). Note that, in the case of a motor accident, ss. 157 and 158 of the Road Traffic Act 1988, as amended by the Road Traffic Accidents (Payments for Treatment) Order 1995 (S.I. 1995/889), make provision for payments up to a maximum amount for hospital treatment of traffic casualties (to be made by an owner or insurer of a vehicle the use of which gave rise to the injuries) and for emergency treatment and a medical practitioner's travelling expenses (to be made by the person using such a vehicle).

[29] *O'Brien's Curator Bonis v. British Steel plc,* 1991 S.C. 315 at p. 319.

[30] *Ibid.*

[31] *Geddes v. Lothian Health Board,* 1992 S.L.T. 986 at p. 988; *McMillan v. McDowall,* 1993 S.L.T. 311 at p. 317; *Roberts v. Johnstone* [1989] Q.B. 878; *Almond v. Leeds Western Health Authority* (1990) 1 Med. L.R. 370; *Wells v. Wells* [1998] 3 W.L.R. 329 at p. 348.

In relation to the purchase of goods which require to be replaced during the period of loss, damages require to be assessed at such figure as will, if reduced by the purchase price of the asset, leave a surplus which if invested would enable the injured person to replace the item as many times as necessary within the period of loss, taking into consideration where appropriate its likely trade-in value.[32]

In relation to the purchase of services such as care provision, the court may adopt the method of a lump sum or a multiplier:

> "Since the whole damage must be recovered in one action, the award which the court must make once and for all for the future has to take the form of a capital sum. So that sum should be assessed at such figure as will, if reduced by the annual amount required for the expenditure in question but increased by the interest which it can be expected to earn if invested, provide what is necessary over the entire period [for which the expenditure is needed]. The mechanism by which the capital sum is arrived at is the selection of a multiplicand, as representing the estimated annual cost of the care as at the date of the proof, and a multiplier which, when applied to the multiplicand, will provide the amount which can be expected to achieve the desired result. There may be cases [however] where, because the period is so short or the circumstances are so uncertain, this method is inappropriate and it is better to make a broad estimate of the damages in the form of a lump sum."[33]

The multiplier that is selected represents a number of years' purchase and is applied to the multiplicand from the date of trial.[34] Where the cost of future care will fluctuate, the court may split the multiplier so as to apply different parts thereof to different amounts.[35] In the assessment of the multiplicand, which will necessarily depend significantly on the facts of the particular case, there may be a number of contingencies which ought to be reflected in the figure or figures selected.[36] In estimating the period of loss, the injured person's age

---

[32] *Woodrup v. Nicol* [1993] P.I.Q.R. Q104 at pp. Q108–Q109 (motor car); *Martin v. James and Andrew Chapman (Haulage Contractors) Ltd,* 1995 G.W.D. 2–77 (wheelchair; computer equipment; motor car).

[33] *O'Brien's Curator Bonis v. British Steel plc,* 1991 S.C. 315 at p. 319.

[34] *Will v. Charles Will Ltd,* 1980 S.L.T. (Notes) 37.

[35] *Geddes v. Lothian Health Board,* 1992 S.L.T. 986 at p. 989; *McMillan v. McDowall,* 1993 S.L.T. 311 at pp. 316–317; *Stevenson v. Sweeney,* 1995 S.L.T. 29; *Rialas v. Mitchell, The Times*, 17 Jul 1984 (C. A.); (1984) 128 S.J. 704; *Eastman v. South West Thames Health Authority* [1992] P.I.Q.R. P42; *Bristow v. Judd* [1993] P.I.Q.R. Q117; *Wells v. Wells* [1998] 3 W.L.R. 329 at p. 333.

[36] *Wells v. Wells* [1998] 3 W.L.R. 329 at p. 362.

and expectation of life fall to taken into account.[37] With regard to the latter, the contingency can work in either direction and so no discount falls to be made for premature death in the event that the injured person's expectation of life, taking his individual characteristics into account, is agreed.[38] There are likely to be fewer variables where the cost of care is in issue than in the case of a claim for loss of future earnings.[39] Contingencies such as uncertainties in respect of the injured person's condition in the future may be reflected in the selection of the multiplier.[40]

---

[37] *O'Brien's Curator Bonis v. British Steel plc,* 1991 S.C. 315 at p. 321. In the case of a reduced life expectancy to a particular age, a multiplier for loss for a term certain may be used — *Wells v. Wells, cit. supra,* at p. 347 (whole life multiplier for six-year-old child with a life expectancy to age 60, *i.e.* 54 years' expectation of life, assessed at 26.58). *Cf.* App. I B2, row 54, col. 3% discount rate.

[38] *Wells v. Wells* [1998] 3 W.L.R. 329 at p. 346.

[39] *O'Brien's Curator Bonis v. British Steel plc, cit. supra,* at p. 321.

[40] *MacIntosh v. National Coal Board,* 1988 S.L.T. 348 at p. 360. No discount for contingencies was made in *Stevenson v. Sweeney,* 1995 S.L.T. 29 or in *O'Connor v. Matthews,* 1996 S.L.T. 408.

CHAPTER 8

INJURED PERSON'S SERVICES

WHERE a person has sustained personal injuries as a result of an act or omission giving rise to liability to pay damages, the wrongdoer is also liable to pay damages in respect of (a) any necessary services rendered or likely to be rendered to the injured person by a relative; and (b) any personal services unable to be rendered by the injured person to a relative.[1]

NECESSARY SERVICES

A claim in respect of necessary services may be made in an action of damages for personal injuries by the injured person.[2] His title to sue is unaffected by any insurance arrangements.[3] His right to damages for necessary services transmits upon his death to his executor, but only insofar as attributable to the period before death.[4] The executor's claim is not excluded by the making of a claim under the Damages (Scotland) Act 1976 by a relative of the deceased or by a deceased relative's executor.[5] For the purposes of enforcing any such right the injured person's executor is entitled — (a) to bring an action; or (b) if an action for that purpose had been brought by the deceased but had not been concluded before his death, to be sisted as pursuer in that action.[6]

---

[1] Administration of Justice Act 1982, s. 7.

[2] Administration of Justice Act 1982, ss. 7 and 8(1). A relative has no direct right of action in delict against the wrongdoer in respect of any necessary services or any expenses incurred in connection therewith — s. 8(4).

[3] *Port-Glasgow and Newark Sailcloth Co v. Caledonian Railway Co* (1892) 19 R. 608.

[4] Damages (Scotland) Act 1976, s. 2(1) and (2), as substituted by the Damages (Scotland) Act 1993, s. 3.

[5] 1976 Act, s. 4, as amended by the Administration of Justice Act 1982, s. 14(2)(a) and the Damages (Scotland) Act 1993, Sched., para. 1.

[6] 1976 Act, s. 2A(1), as inserted by the Damages (Scotland) Act 1993, s. 4. For the purposes of s. 2A(1) an action shall not be taken to be concluded while any appeal is competent or before any appeal taken has been disposed of — s. 2A(2). Note that where in an action in which, following the death of the deceased from personal injuries, damages are claimed by the executor of the deceased, in respect of the injuries from which the deceased died, it is shown that by antecedent agreement, compromise or otherwise, the liability arising in relation to a particular defender from the personal injuries in question had, before the

In either event the rules of court concerning intimation of the action to connected persons are applicable.[7] In the case of the injured person's bankruptcy, his trustee in sequestration has the right to sue for any pecuniary losses arising out of the personal injury.[8]

The relatives in relation to whom a claim in respect of necessary services may be made are any of the following (only):

> "(a) the spouse or divorced spouse;
> (b) any person, not being the spouse of the injured person, who was, at the time of the act or omission giving rise to liability in the responsible person, living with the injured person as husband or wife;
> (c) any ascendant or descendant;
> (d) any brother, sister, uncle or aunt; or any issue of any such person;
> (e) any person accepted by the injured person as a child of his family;"[9]

and in deducing any relationship for the purposes of the foregoing definition — (a) any relationship by affinity is treated as a relationship by consanguinity; any relationship of the half blood is treated as a relationship of the whole blood; and the stepchild of any person is treated as his child; and (b) section 1(1) of the Law Reform (Parent and Child)(Scotland) Act 1986 (legal equality of children) applies.[10]

The necessary services for which damages may be claimed by the injured person are —

> (i) necessary services which have been rendered to the injured person by a relative in consequence of the injuries in question, except where the relative has expressly agreed in the knowledge that an action for damages has been raised or is in

---

deceased's death, been limited to damages of a specified or ascertainable amount, or where that liability is so limited by virtue of any enactment, nothing in the 1976 Act shall make that defender liable to pay damages exceeding that amount; and accordingly where in such an action there are two or more pursuers any damages to which they would respectively be entitled under the Act apart from the said limitation shall, if necessary, be reduced *pro rata* — s. 6(1) and (3)(a). Where two or more such actions are conjoined, the conjoined actions shall be treated for the purposes of the foregoing as if they were a single action — s. 6(2).

[7] R.C.S. 43.1(1)(a)(Court of Session) and O.C.R. 36.1(1)(a)(Sheriff Court). The relevant rules are noted in Chap. 9, text accompanying nn.12–19.

[8] *Muir's Trustee v. Broadwood,* 1958 S.C. 169 at p. 173; Bankruptcy (Scotland) Act 1985, s. 31(1) and (5) or s. 32(6).

[9] Administration of Justice Act 1982, s. 13(1).

[10] *Ibid.*

contemplation that no payment should be made in respect of those services;

(ii) necessary services which, at the date of an award of damages in favour of the injured person, it is likely will, after that date, be rendered to him by a relative in consequence of the injuries in question, except where the relative has expressly agreed that no payment shall be made for those services.[11]

The injured person is obliged to account to any relative by whom necessary services have been rendered for any damages recovered in that respect from the wrongdoer.[12] Separate awards for necessary services and personal services are therefore called for.[13] By the same token, any award for necessary services rendered by more than one person falls to be allocated among the relatives concerned.[14] An award for necessary services requires to be divided, where appropriate, into pre-decree and post-decree periods for the purposes of calculation of interest, which is exigible in respect of the former.[15]

A claim under this head can only be made in respect of services which would not have been performed but for the accident and its consequences, that is services which have been rendered necessary by the accident and its consequences.[16] The claim must be refused when the relative testifies that he will not accept any money from the injured person for the services rendered to him even if the injured person recovered the money from a third party.[17] What was envisaged by the enactment of a statutory right to such damages was chiefly services for nursing and attendance.[18] The claim is, however, relevant

---

[11] *Ibid.*, s. 8(1) and (3).

[12] *Ibid.*, s. 8(2). It follows that a claim in respect of services to date of trial is incompetent where the relative in question happens to be the wrongdoer — *Kozikowsla v. Kozikowski,* 1996 S.L.T. 386; *Hunt v. Severs* [1994] 2 A.C. 350. Note that an award in respect of necessary services is not the equivalent of compensation for the cost of care to which s. 15 of the Social Security (Recovery of Benefits) Act 1997 applies — *Duffy v. Lanarkshire Health Board,* Lord Johnston, July 31, 1998, unreported.

[13] *Low v. Ralston,* 1997 S.L.T. 626; *Taylor v. Marshalls Food Group,* 1997 S.C.L.R. 815 at p. 819. As to a method of allocation of damages between the claims, see n. 21 *infra.*

[14] *Kennedy v. Lees of Scotland Ltd,* 1997 S.L.T. 510 at p. 514.

[15] *Forsyth's Curator Bonis v. Govan Shipbuilders Ltd,* 1988 S.C. 421 at p. 438.

[16] *Ibid.* at pp. 427 and 437–438.

[17] *Campbell v. City of Glasgow District Council,* 1991 S.L.T. 616 at p. 624. *Cf. Myles v. City of Glasgow District Council,* 1994 S.C.L.R. 1112.

[18] Scottish Law Commission, Damages for Personal Injuries: Report on (1) Admissibility of Claims for Services; (2) Admissible Deductions (Scot. Law Com. No. 51, 1978), p. 49. See *e.g. Forsyth's Curator Bonis v. Govan Shipbuilders Ltd,* 1988 S.C. 421 at p. 427 (assistance with adjusting the injured person's clothing, with washing, bathing and shaving, with the cutting up of his food, in enabling him to rise after a fall and in accompanying him out of doors); *Paterson v. Hampton,* 1994 S.L.T. 1231 at p. 1234 (helping the injured

where the services are essentially those involved in supporting the injured person emotionally and psychologically, rather than physically.[19] The claim is also relevantly stated where the services comprise or include the performance of household chores on behalf of the injured person insofar as rendered necessary by his injuries.[20]

Where the services consist of normal domestic tasks from which the injured person and the relative benefit, such as where a relative prepares a family meal or does the family laundry, claims for necessary services and in respect of personal services may become almost inextricable and may require to be dealt with by allocating damages between the claims on a broad basis.[21]

Where damages are payable in respect of necessary services which have been rendered, the wrongdoer is liable to pay to the injured person by way of damages such sum as represents reasonable remuneration for those services and repayment of reasonable expenses incurred in connection therewith.[22] In assessing what would be "reasonable remuneration" for the necessary services in question, the court will have regard to the nature, quality and extent of the services and assess a figure which represents their value or at least a reasonable consideration for them.[23] The relative's prior earnings, if he has given up employment to render the services, as well as the kinds of charges

---

person in and out of the bath and up and down stairs and driving him to and from hospital); *Garland v. Fairnington's Executor,* 1994 S.L.T. 855 at p. 857 (feeding the injured person, helping him to get out of bed, bathing him, seeing that he did not fall and driving him).

[19] *Howie v. Upper Clyde Shipbuilders Ltd,* 1991 S.L.T. 2 at p. 4; *Farrelly v. Yarrow Shipbuilders Ltd,* 1994 S.L.T. 1349 at p. 1351.

[20] *Denheen v. British Railways Board,* 1986 S.L.T. 249 and 1988 S.L.T. 320. See *e.g. Myles v. City of Glasgow District Council,* 1994 S.C.L.R. 1112 at p. 1114 (cleaning, washing, ironing, changing bed linen, driving, window-cleaning and grass-cutting); *Cherry v. Strathclyde Regional Council,* 1994 S.L.T. 494 at pp. 494–495 (washing, cleaning, cooking, driving). The provision of transplant organs or transplant material by a relative does not constitute the rendering of necessary services within the meaning of s. 8 — *Duffy v. Lanarkshire Health Board,* Lord Johnston, July 31, 1998, unreported.

[21] *Kennedy v. Lees of Scotland Ltd,* 1997 S.L.T. 510 at p. 513. In *Low v. Ralston,* 1997 S.L.T. 626 the claims were treated separately on an agreed approach, namely that regard should be had to the number of individuals in the household; so that where the household contained four persons, one-quarter of that which was done might be seen as relating to services rendered to the injured person and three-quarters relating to things which, but for his injuries, the injured person might have been expected to do for others.

[22] Administration of Justice Act 1982, s. 8(1). The cost of necessary transport by taxi to visit the incapax was held to be a reasonable expense in *Docherty's Curator Bonis v. U I E Shipbuilding (Scotland) Ltd,* 1989 S.L.T. 197 at p. 198.

[23] *Forsyth's Curator Bonis v. Govan Shipbuilders Ltd,* 1988 S.C. 421 at p. 429; *Galbraith's Curator ad Litem v. Stewart,* 1997 S.L.T. 418 at p. 424 (fatal lack of specification in averments which did not make clear what particular assistance was now required, or its duration per day or over any particular period, nor whether the requirements were continuing or were likely to continue in the future and, if so, for what period of time).

made for the kinds of services in question will be taken into account.[24] The relevant circumstances, however, include the fact that the relative does not have the qualifications of those who provide the services on a commercial basis.[25] It is to be borne in mind in the assessment of services provided by relatives that there are natural ties which should not convert the assessment of any award into a purely commercial transaction and it is therefore inappropriate to adopt commercial rates without question.[26] In the case of family members giving services in their own time for a few minutes or an hour or two here or there, a nominal rate may be applied.[27] In the absence of evidence as to relevant matters, the court will award an amount, if any, which represents the minimum that can reasonably be inferred as appropriate on the basis of such evidence as there is.[28]

Where damages are payable in respect of services which it is likely will be rendered, the wrongdoer is liable to pay to the injured person by way of damages such sum as represents reasonable remuneration for those services and reasonable expenses which are likely to be incurred in connection therewith.[29] Remuneration for future necessary services may be assessed by means of the application of a multiplier referable to the period over which the services are likely to be rendered to a multiplicand representing the annual value of those services.[30] The multiplier that is selected represents a number of years' purchase

---

[24] *Forsyth's Curator Bonis v. Govan Shipbuilders Ltd,* 1988 S.C. 421 at p. 430; *Clark v. Sutherland,* 1993 S.C. 320 at p.323; *McMillan v. McDowall,* 1993 S.L.T. 311 at p.315. *Cf. Housecroft v. Burnett* [1986] 1 All E. R. 332 at p. 343.

[25] *Gordon v. Wilson,* 1992 S.L.T. 849 at p. 855 (rate of pay for home help, as nearest equivalent to relative on the evidence, adopted under deduction of commission, tax and national insurance). See also *McMillan v. McDowall,* 1993 S.L.T. 311 at pp. 315–316 (undiscounted non-commercial rate of pay for unskilled care worker and undiscounted home help rate, making allowance for incidence of taxation and counter allowance for irregular hours of work and responsibility, variously adopted); *Cherry v. Strathclyde Regional Council,*1994 S.L.T. 494 at p. 495 (local authority charges for home help adopted); and *O'Connor v. Matthews,* 1996 S.L.T. 408 at p. 411 (non-commercial rate of pay for unskilled care worker adopted, discounting for tax and for the fact that some services would have been provided irrespective of the injury). *Cf. Nash v. Southmead Health Authority* [1993] P.I.Q.R. Q156 (two-thirds of average non-commercial rate of pay for unskilled care worker adopted) and *Fairhurst v. St Helens and Knowsley Health Authority* [1995] P.I.Q.R. Q1 (three-quarters of non-commercial rate of pay for home helps as accepted by local authorities from time to time adopted).

[26] *Mitchell v. Inverclyde District Council,* 1997 Rep. L.R. (Quantum) 29 at p. 31.

[27] *Kennedy v. Lees of Scotland Ltd,* 1997 S.L.T. 510 at p. 513; *Stirling v. Norwest Holst Ltd,* 1997 S.C.L.R. 1196 at p. 1208.

[28] *Clark v. Sutherland,* 1993 S.C. 320 at pp. 323–324.

[29] Administration of Justice Act 1982, s. 8(3).

[30] *O'Brien's Curator Bonis v. British Steel plc,* 1991 S.C. 315 at p. 332; *Cherry v. Strathclyde Regional Council,* 1994 S.L.T. 494; *Low v. Ralston,* 1997 S.L.T. 626.

and is applied to the multiplicand from the date of trial.[31] In estimating the period of loss, the age and the expectation of life of the injured person and the relative, respectively, fall to be taken into consideration so that the likelihood of the provider of the services continuing to exist and the likelihood of the injured person being alive to benefit from those services may be established.[32] The prospect that the providing capacity of the provider or the needs of the injured person would have been affected or altered by the changes or chances of life either in a positive or in a negative manner must also be taken into account in the selection of the multiplier.[33] The potential for divorce falls to be taken into account in appropriate cases.[34] As an alternative to the multiplier/multiplicand mechanism, the court may make a broad estimate of the damages in the form of a lump sum.[35]

PERSONAL SERVICES

A claim in respect of personal services may be made in an action of damages for personal injuries by the injured person.[36] His title to sue is unaffected by any insurance arrangements.[37] His right to damages in relation to personal services transmits upon his death to his executor, but only insofar as attributable to the period before death.[38] The executor's claim is not excluded by the making of a claim under the Damages (Scotland) Act 1976 by a relative of the deceased or by a deceased relative's executor.[39] For the purposes of enforcing any such right the injured person's executor is entitled — (a) to bring an action; or

---

[31] *Will v. Charles Will Ltd*, 1980 S.L.T. (Notes) 37.

[32] *O'Brien's Curator Bonis v. British Steel plc*, 1991 S.C. 315 at p. 332; *Corbett v. Barking Health Authority* [1991] 2 Q.B. 408 at p. 422. Thus in *e.g. Laing v. Tayside Health Board*, 1996 G.W.D. 10–587, the award of damages for necessary services was calculated having regard to the life expectancy of the relative since it was likely that the injured person would outlive him (whereas in *O'Brien's Curator Bonis* no reduction fell to be made from the multiplier, which was based on the life expectancy of the injured person, since it was likely that the relative would live longer).

[33] *O'Brien's Curator Bonis v. British Steel plc*, 1991 S.C. 315 at p. 332; *Corbett v. Barking Health Authority* [1991] 2 Q.B. 408 at p. 422; *Laing v. Tayside Health Board*, 1996 G.W.D. 10–587.

[34] *O'Brien's Curator Bonis v. British Steel plc*, 1991 S.C. 315 at p. 332.

[35] *Garland v. Fairnington's Executor*, 1994 S.L.T. 855 at p. 857.

[36] Administration of Justice Act 1982, ss. 7 and 9(1). A relative has no direct right of action in delict against the wrongdoer in respect of any personal services — s. 9(4).

[37] *Port-Glasgow and Newark Sailcloth Co v. Caledonian Railway Co* (1892) 19 R. 608.

[38] Damages (Scotland) Act 1976, s. 2(1) and (2), as substituted by the Damages (Scotland) Act 1993, s. 3.

[39] 1976 Act, s. 4. as amended by the Administration of Justice Act 1982, s. 14(2)(a) and the Damages (Scotland) Act 1993, Sched., para. 1.

(b) if an action for that purpose had been brought by the deceased but had not been concluded before his death, to be sisted as pursuer in that action.[40] In either event the rules of court concerning intimation to connected persons are applicable.[41] In the case of the injured person's bankruptcy, his trustee in sequestration has the right to sue for any pecuniary losses arising out of the personal injury.[42]

The relatives in relation to whom a claim in respect of personal services may be made are any of the following (only):

> "(a) the spouse or divorced spouse;
> (b) any person, not being the spouse of the injured person, who was, at the time of the act or omission giving rise to liability in the reponsible person, living with the injured person as husband or wife;
> (c) any ascendant or descendant;
> (d) any brother, sister, uncle or aunt; or any issue of any such person;
> (e) any person accepted by the injured person as a child of his family;"[43]

and in deducing any relationship for the purposes of the foregoing definition — (a) any relationship by affinity is treated as a relationship by consanguinity; any relationship of the half blood is treated as a relationship of the whole blood; and the stepchild of any person is treated as his child; and (b) section 1(1) of the Law Reform (Parent and Child) (Scotland) Act 1986 (legal equality of children) applies.[44]

---

[40] 1976 Act, s. 2A(1), as inserted by the Damages (Scotland) Act 1993, s. 4. For the purposes of s. 2A(1) an action shall not be taken to be concluded while any appeal is competent or before any appeal taken has been disposed of — s. 2A(2). Note that where in an action in which, following the death of the deceased from personal injuries, damages are claimed by the executor of the deceased, in respect of the injuries from which the deceased died, it is shown that by antecedent agreement, compromise or otherwise, the liability arising in relation to a particular defender from the personal injuries in question had, before the deceased's death, been limited to damages of a specified or ascertainable amount, or where that liability is so limited by virtue of any enactment, nothing in the 1976 Act shall make that defender liable to pay damages exceeding that amount; and accordingly where in such an action there are two or more pursuers any damages to which they would respectively be entitled under the Act apart from the said limitation shall, if necessary, be reduced *pro rata* — s. 6(1) and (3)(a). Where two or more such actions are conjoined, the conjoined actions shall be treated for the purposes of the foregoing as if they were a single action — s. 6(2).

[41] R.C.S. 43.1(1)(a) (Court of Session) and O.C.R. 36.1(1)(a) (Sheriff Court). The relevant rules are noted in Chap. 9, text accompanying nn. 12–19.

[42] *Muir's Trustee v. Broadwood,* 1958 S.C. 169 at p. 173; Bankruptcy (Scotland) Act 1985, s. 31(1) and (5) or s. 32(6).

[43] Administration of Justice Act 1982, s. 13(1).

[44] *Ibid.*

The personal services for which damages may be claimed by the injured person arising out of his inability to render them are personal services:

"(a) which were or might have been expected to have been rendered by the injured person before the occurrence of the act or omission giving rise to liability,
(b) of a kind which, when rendered by a person other than a relative, would ordinarily be obtainable on payment, and
(c) which the injured person but for the injuries in question might have been expected to render gratuitously to a relative."[45]

An award in respect of personal services requires to be divided, where appropriate, into pre-decree and post-decree periods for the purposes of calculation of interest, which is exigible in respect of the former.[46]

In any claim in respect of the inability of the injured person to render personal services, it must be shown that the services were or might have been expected to have been rendered (i) for the benefit of the person claiming and (ii) in person by the injured person and not by a third party acting on his behalf.[47] No hard and fast rules as to what categories of work might or might not be personal services can be laid down since circumstances will vary considerably.[48] A whole range of housekeeping and maintenance services may be covered by the expression.[49] Childcare services provided by a parent fall within the definition.[50] Where the services consist of normal domestic tasks from which the injured person and the relative benefit, such as where a relative prepares a family meal or does the family laundry, claims for necessary services and in respect of personal services may become almost inextricable.[51] It is, however, essential that the court makes a separate award in respect of each type of claim in light of the injured person's obligation to account for damages recovered for necessary services which have been rendered by a relative.[52]

---

[45] *Ibid.* s. 9(3).

[46] *Low v. Ralston,* 1997 S.L.T. 626 at p. 629.

[47] *Ingham v. John G Russell (Transport) Ltd*, 1991 S.C. 201 at p. 204.

[48] *Ibid.* at pp. 204–205.

[49] *Ibid.* at p. 204.

[50] *Brown v. Ferguson,* 1990 S.L.T. 274 at p. 276. Such can include taking one's child to the swimming pool or playing football with him — *Stirling v. Norwest Holst Ltd,* 1997 S.C.L.R. 1196 at p. 1211.

[51] *Kennedy v. Lees of Scotland Ltd,* 1997 S.L.T. 510 at p. 513.

[52] *Ibid.* at p. 514. As to a method of allocation of damages between the claims, see n. 21 *supra.*

The wrongdoer is liable to pay to the injured person a reasonable sum by way of damages in respect of the inability to render the personal services in question.[53] In assessing "a reasonable sum", the court requires to make a broad assessment and may do so by reference to an estimate of the average weekly time expended on the services and a suitable hourly rate, which may or may not correlate with any rate of pay commanded by the injured person in employment.[54] Where the relative could reasonably be expected to employ or has in fact reasonably employed someone, such as a housekeeper, to perform the personal services which the injured person is unable to perform, the cost of that employment could be used as a measure of the loss of services provided that the wage payable is not unreasonable.[55] A detailed enquiry involving evidence as to the rates of pay applicable to different household tasks and the number of hours worked in relation to each is never warranted.[56]

The court may make the assessment as regards the future by means of the application of a multiplier referable to the period of the inability to render services to a multiplicand representing the annual value of those services.[57] The multiplier that is selected represents a number of years' purchase and is applied to the multiplicand from the date of trial.[58] In estimating the period of loss, the prospective length of the joint lives of the injured person and the relative fall to be taken into consideration.[59] The prospect that the providing capacity of the injured person or the needs of the relative would have been affected or altered by the changes or chances of life either in a positive or in a negative manner must also be taken into account in the selection of the multiplier.[60] The potential for divorce falls to be taken into account in appropriate cases.[61] Account must be taken of any change in the nature of the personal services over time, as in the case of childcare.[62] As an alternative to the multiplier/multiplicand mechanism, the court may make a broad estimate of the damages in the form of a lump sum.[63]

---

[53] Administration of Justice Act 1982, s. 9(1).

[54] *Ingham v. John G. Russell (Transport) Ltd,* 1991 S.C. 201 at p. 205; *Campbell v. Gillespie,* 1996 S.L.T. 503 at p. 512. *Cf. Howie v. Upper Clyde Shipbuilders Ltd,* 1991 S.L.T. 2 at p. 4.

[55] *Brown v. Ferguson,* 1990 S.L.T. 274 at p. 276 (living out housekeeper); *Spittle v. Bunney* [1988] 1 W.L.R. 847 (nanny for young child).

[56] *Ingham v. John G Russell (Transport) Ltd,* 1991 S.C. 201 at p. 211; *Kennedy v. Lees of Scotland Ltd,* 1997 S.L.T. 510 at p. 513.

[57] *Farrelly v. Yarrow Shipbuilders Ltd,* 1994 S.L.T. 1349 at p. 1352.

[58] *Will v. Charles Will Ltd,* 1980 S.L.T. (Notes) 37.

[59] *Farrelly v. Yarrow Shipbuilders Ltd,* 1994 S.L.T. 1349 at p. 1352; *Corbett v. Barking Health Authority* [1991] 2 Q.B. 408 at p. 422; and see n. 32 *supra.*

[60] *Corbett v. Barking Health Authority* [1991] 2 Q.B. 408 at p. 422.

[61] *Cf. O'Brien's Curator Bonis v. British Steel plc,* 1991 S.C. 315 at p. 332.

[62] *Spittle v. Bunney* [1988] 1 W.L.R. 847 at p. 858.

[63] See *e.g. Harrison v. R.B. Tennent Ltd,* 1992 S.L.T. 1060.

III. HEADS OF CLAIM FOR DEATH OF RELATIVE

CHAPTER 9

LOSS OF SOCIETY

THE damages which a wrongdoer requires to pay to a member of the deceased's[1] immediate family under section 1 of the Damages (Scotland) Act 1976 include, without prejudice to any claim for loss of support or funeral expenses, such sum of damages, if any, as the court thinks just by way of compensation for all or any of certain aspects of non-pecuniary injury as listed hereunder.[2]

A "member of the deceased's immediate family" for this purpose is any of the following (only):

> "(a) any person who immediately before the deceased's death was the spouse of the deceased;
> (aa) any person, not being the spouse of the deceased, who was, immediately before the deceased's death, living with the deceased as husband or wife;
> (b) any person who was a parent or child of the deceased;
> (c) any person not falling within paragraph (b) above who was accepted by the deceased as a child of his family;"[3]

and in deducing any relationship for the purposes of the foregoing definition — (a) any relationship by affinity is treated as a relationship by consanguinity; any relationship of the half blood is treated as a relationship of the whole blood; and the stepchild of any person is treated as his child; and (b) section 1(1) of the Law Reform (Parent and Child) (Scotland) Act 1986 (legal equality of children) applies.[4]

---

[1] A child dying after birth from injuries sustained in the womb is a deceased person for these purposes — *Hamilton v. Fife Health Board,* 1993 S.C. 369.

[2] Damages (Scotland) Act 1976, s. 1(4). These aspects of non-pecuniary injury are listed in the text accompanying n. 24 *infra*. As to circumstances in which liability to pay damages under s. 1 of the 1976 Act may be excluded or limited, see n. 11 and accompanying text *infra.*

[3] 1976 Act, s.10(2) and Sched. 1, para. 1. A posthumous child is a "child" for these purposes — *Cohen v. Shaw,* 1992 S.L.T. 1022.

[4] 1976 Act, Sched. 1, para. 2. This paragraph must be given effect in the construction of the expression "member of the deceased's immediate family"; and, accordingly, any in-laws of the deceased (*i.e.* father-in-law; mother-in-law; son-in-law; daughter-in-law) have title to sue under s. 1(4) of the Act (*Monteith v. Cape Insulation Ltd,* 1998 G.W.D. 29–1496).

The claim by a member of the deceased's immediate family may be brought by way of summons or initial writ or by way of minute in a depending action at the instance of another relative of the deceased or the deceased's executor.[5] Where the claim is brought by way of summons or initial writ, the rules of court concerning intimation of the action to connected persons are applicable.[6] The relative's claim is not excluded by the making of a claim by the deceased's executor for damages in respect of the deceased's personal injuries.[7] The relative's right to damages for non-pecuniary injury transmits upon his death to his executor, but, in determining the amount of damages payable to an executor, the court must have regard only to the period ending immediately before the relative's death.[8] The making of a claim by the deceased's executor for damages in respect of the deceased's personal injuries does not exclude the relative's executor's claim either.[9] For the purposes of enforcing such right the relative's executor is entitled — (a) to bring an action; or (b) if an action for that purpose had been brought by the deceased relative but had not been concluded before his death, to be sisted as pursuer in that action.[10] No liability arises to pay damages to either the relative or the relative's executor if the liability to the deceased or his executor in respect of the act or omission has been excluded or discharged (whether by antecedent agreement or otherwise) by the deceased before his death, or is excluded by virtue of any enactment.[11]

---

[5] See text accompanying nn. 20–23 *infra* regarding claims made by way of minute.

[6] See text accompanying nn. 12–19 *infra*.

[7] Damages (Scotland) Act 1976, s. 4, as amended by the Administration of Justice Act 1982, s. 14(2)(a) and the Damages (Scotland) Act 1993, Sched., para. 1.

[8] 1976 Act, s. 1A, as inserted by the Damages (Scotland) Act 1993, s. 2.

[9] 1976 Act, s. 4, as amended by the Administration of Justice Act 1982, s. 14(2)(a) and the Damages (Scotland) Act 1993, Sched., para. 1.

[10] 1976 Act, s. 2A(1), as inserted by the Damages (Scotland) Act 1993, s. 4. For the purpose of s. 2A(1) an action shall not be taken to be concluded while any appeal is competent or before any appeal taken has been disposed of — s. 2A(2).

[11] 1976 Act, s. 1(2). But where a deceased has been awarded provisional damages, the making of that award does not prevent liability arising under s. 1 of the 1976 Act—s. 1(5A). Note that where, in an action in which, following the death of any person from personal injuries, damages are claimed in respect of the death of the deceased by any relative of his, or, if the relative has died, by the relative's executor, it is shown that by antecedent agreement, compromise or otherwise, the liability arising in relation to a particular defender from the personal injuries in question had, before the deceased's death, been limited to damages of a specified or ascertainable amount, or where that liability is so limited by virtue of any enactment, nothing in the 1976 Act shall make the defender liable to pay damages exceeding that amount; and accordingly where in such an action there are two or more pursuers any damages to which they would respectively be entitled under the Act apart from the said limitation shall, if necessary, be reduced *pro rata*—s. 6(1) and (3)(b). Where two or more such actions are conjoined, the conjoined actions shall be treated for the purposes of the foregoing as if they were a single action—s. 6(2).

In any action of damages in which, following the death of any person from personal injuries, damages are claimed by any relative of the deceased (including members of his immediate family) in respect of the death of the deceased, intimation to connected persons may fall to be made.[12] In such an action the pursuer must aver in the condescendence, as the case may be —

"(a) that there are no connected persons [*viz.* persons, not being parties to the action, who have title to sue the defender in respect of the personal injuries from which the deceased died or in respect of his death[13]];

(b) that there are connected persons, being the persons specified in the warrant (or crave, as the case may be) for intimation;

(c) that there are connected persons in respect of whom intimation should be dispensed with on the ground that —

(i) the names or whereabouts of such persons are not known to, and cannot reasonably be ascertained by, the pursuer; or

(ii) such persons are unlikely to be awarded more than the sum of £200 each."[14]

Where the pursuer makes averments under head (b) above, he requires to insert a warrant for intimation in the summons (or a crave for intimation in the initial writ, as the case may be) and attach a notice of intimation thereto.[15] Where the pursuer makes averments under head (c) above, he requires to apply by motion (or in the case of a sheriff court action, by crave) for an order to dispense with intimation.[16] In determining such a motion (or application by crave), the court must have regard to — (a) the desirability of avoiding multiplicity of actions; and (b) the expense, inconvenience or difficulty likely to be involved

---

[12] R.C.S. 43.1(1)(b)(Court of Session) and O.C.R. 36.1(1)(b)(Sheriff Court).

[13] R.C.S. 43.1(2) and O.C.R. 36.1(2).

[14] R.C.S. 43.2 and O.C.R. 36.2. It is sufficient compliance with the rule, in relation to relatives beyond the immediate family, for the pursuer to aver without giving names that there are connected persons, that no such person was receiving, or is likely to receive, support from the deceased, and that in these circumstances it is believed and averred that none of these persons is likely to be awarded more than the sum of £200 — *Henderson v. Occidental Petroleum (Caledonia) Ltd,* 1990 S.L.T. 314 at p. 316.

[15] R.C.S. 43.3 and O.C.R. 36.3. The terms of the warrant specified in R.C.S. 43.3 are: "Warrant to intimate to (*name and address*) as a person who is believed to have title to sue the defender in an action in respect of the personal injuries from which the late (*name and last place of residence*) died [*or* the death of the late (*name and last place of residence*)]." The notice of intimation requires to be in Form 43.3 (Court of Session) or Form D1 (Sheriff Court).

[16] R.C.S. 43.4(1) and O.C.R. 36.4(1).

in taking steps to ascertain the name or whereabouts of the connected person.[17] Where the court is not satisfied that intimation to a connected person should be dispensed with, it may — (a) order intimation to a connected person whose name and whereabouts are known; (b) order the pursuer to take such further steps as it may specify in the interlocutor to ascertain the name or whereabouts of any connected person; and (c) order that such advertisement be made in such manner, in such place and at such times as it may specify in the interlocutor.[18] Where the name or whereabouts of a person, in respect of whom the court has dispensed with intimation on a ground specified in head (c) above (dispensing with intimation to connected persons), subsequently becomes known to the pursuer while the action is depending before the court, the pursuer must apply by motion for a warrant for intimation to such a person; and the notice of intimation above referred to falls to be attached as aforesaid.[19]

A connected person may apply to the court by minute in the process of the action craving leave to be sisted as an additional pursuer to the action.[20] Such a minute requires also to (a) crave leave of the court to adopt the existing grounds of action and to amend the conclusions (or craves, as the case may be), condescendence and pleas-in-law; or (b) (in the Court of Session only) set out separate conclusions, a statement of facts and appropriate pleas-in-law.[21] Answers to such a minute fall to be lodged within 14 days.[22] Where a connected person to whom intimation is made in accordance with the foregoing — (a) does not apply to be sisted as an additional pursuer to the action, (b) subsequently brings a separate action against the same defender in respect of the same personal injuries or death, and (c) would otherwise be awarded the expenses or part of the expenses of that action, he will not be awarded those expenses except on cause shown.[23]

---

[17] R.C.S. 43.4(2) and O.C.R. 36.4(2). In the ordinary situation of remoter relatives with no nexus of support, intimation would not prevent multiplicity of actions, since actions by such persons would be highly improbable; and ascertainment of the name or whereabouts of any such person, if not already known, would be quite pointless, and even minor expense, inconvenience, or difficulty would accordingly be unjustified; and so all the criteria set out in para. (2) would point to dispensing with intimation to such relatives — *Henderson v. Occidental Petroleum (Caledonia) Ltd,* 1990 S.L.T. 314 at p. 316.

[18] R.C.S. 43.4(3) and O.C.R. 36.4(3).

[19] R.C.S. 43.5 and O.C.R. 36.5.

[20] R.C.S. 43.6(1) and O.C.R. 36.6(1).

[21] R.C.S. 43.6(2) and O.C.R. 36.6(2).

[22] R.C.S. 43.6(4)(specifying that the period runs from the date on which the minute was lodged, that date requiring to be intimated along with the minute in terms of R.C.S. 43.6(3) to every party) and O.C.R. 36.6(3)(specifying that the period runs from the date of intimation of the minute). In terms of O.C.R. 36.6(4), rule 14.13 (procedure following grant of minute) does not apply to such a minute.

[23] R.C.S. 43.7 and O.C.R. 36.7.

The aspects of non-pecuniary injury for which such sum of damages, if any, as the court thinks just may be awarded to a member of the deceased's immediate family by way of compensation are the following:

"(a) distress and anxiety endured by the relative in contemplation of the suffering of the deceased before his death;
(b) grief and sorrow of the relative caused by the deceased's death;
(c) the loss of such non-patrimonial benefit as the relative might have been expected to derive from the deceased's society and guidance if the deceased had not died."[24]

The court in making an award for non-pecuniary injury is not required to ascribe specifically any part of the award to any of paragraphs (a), (b) and (c) above.[25] An award should, however, be divided, where appropriate, into pre-decree and post-decree periods for the purposes of calculation of interest, which is exigible in respect of the former.[26]

In determining compensation for non-pecuniary injury, the court must look at the relationship which existed between the parties involved, their respective ages, the circumstances in which they lived with respect to each other, and any other relevant factor, and from the weighing of these factors determine what in the exercise of its judgment an appropriate award of compensation should be for the loss and what that involves to the individual pursuer, keeping in mind the imponderables.[27]

In applying the foregoing, the extent of contact between the relative and the deceased prior to his death may fall to be examined.[28] Their conduct towards one another so far as disclosing the state of their relationship may be material, but conduct towards others is not

---

[24] 1976 Act, s. 1(4), as amended by the Damages (Scotland) Act 1993, s. 1(1). Note that the intention of the amendment was not to change the basis of the pre-existing loss of society award, as it had come to be interpreted by the courts, but merely to clarify it and secure it legislatively — Scottish Law Commission, Report on The Effect of Death on Damages (Scot. Law Com. No. 134), para. 4.45. Awards made under the unamended legislation are accordingly still relevant for purposes of comparison. Note further that except as provided for in s. 1 of the 1976 Act or in Part II of the Administration of Justice Act 1982 or under s. 1 of the International Transport Conventions Act 1983, no person is entitled by reason of relationship to damages (including damages by way of solatium) in respect of the death of another person — 1976 Act, s. 1(7).

[25] 1976 Act, s. 1(4), as amended by the Damages (Scotland) Act 1993.

[26] *McKeown v. Sir William Arrol & Co,* 1974 S.C. 97; *Prentice v. Chalmers,* 1985 S.L.T. 168. As to interest on damages, see Chap. 4.

[27] *Dingwall v. Walter Alexander & Sons (Midland) Ltd,* 1982 S.C. (H.L.) 179 at p. 209.

[28] *Wotherspoon v. Strathclyde Regional Council,* 1992 S.L.T. 1090 at p.1091(adopted sons not really bothered with deceased awarded small sums); *Morrison v. Forsyth,* 1995 S.L.T. 539 (widow separated but still associating with and affectionate towards deceased awarded discounted sum).

relevant.[29] The number of years of loss of prospective society is an important consideration.[30] In the case of children, this factor is generally reflected by an inverse relationship between age and size of award.[31] For children within one family there is thus a sliding scale of damages, with normally the highest award being for the youngest child and the lowest for the eldest.[32] Age relativity applies also with respect to surviving spouses, benefiting the younger claimant, but against this to some extent is the fact that the length of completed married life will tend to exacerbate grief as well as loss of society, favouring the older claimant, and the bulk of awards will tend to be attributable to the years immediately following death, namely years relevant in the case of surviving spouses of all ages.[33] Where the period of the deceased's life expectancy had always been very short, as in the case of a child born handicapped, the award falls to be restricted.[34] Knowledge of a deceased's reduced life expectation at the time of marriage is not an absolute bar to recovery of damages by the surviving spouse.[35] The court cannot take account of the remarriage of the widow or her prospects of remarriage in assessing her damages.[36] Where a widow has remarried, therefore, the court in assessing damages has to fix a figure based on all relevant considerations but treating the situation as if the widow had not remarried.[37] In the case of children's claims, the court may take account of the subsequent death of the deceased's surviving spouse as a reason for enhancing the awards.[38]

An award for non-pecuniary injury in favour of a relative is a payment in money for something which cannot be precisely quantified.[39] Awards, at least by judges, are therefore conventional or standard figures derived from experience and from awards in comparable cases, taking into account any changes in the value of money.[40] Nevertheless, every case must be considered in relation to its own particular circumstances.[41]

---

[29] *Wilson v. Chief Constable, Lothian and Borders Constabulary,* 1989 S.L.T. 97 at p. 106 (recurring minor episodes and single major incident of drinking and violence by deceased towards widow taken into consideration); *Grant v. Highland Health Board,* Lord Sutherland, December 20, 1985, unreported (anti-social behaviour of deceased towards others to be left out of account).

[30] See *Davidson v. Upper Clyde Shipbuilders Ltd,* 1990 S.L.T. 329 at p. 331.

[31] See *e.g. Kelly v. Glasgow Corporation,* 1949 S.C. 496 at p. 500, approved by the House of Lords (1951 S.C. (H.L.) 15).

[32] *Dingwall v. Walter Alexander & Sons (Midland) Ltd,* 1982 S.C. (H.L.) 179 at p. 208.

[33] *Davidson v. Upper Clyde Shipbuilders Ltd,* 1990 S.L.T. 329 at pp. 331–332.

[34] *Fowler v. Greater Glasgow Health Board,* 1990 S.L.T. 303 at p. 304.

[35] *Phillips v. Grampian Health Board,* 1992 S.L.T. 659 at p. 660.

[36] Law Reform (Miscellaneous Provisions) Act 1971, s. 4.

[37] *McKinnon v. Reid,* 1975 S.C. 233.

[38] *Kelly v. Glasgow Corporation,* 1951 S.C. (H.L.) 15.

[39] *Girvan v. Inverness Farmers Dairy,* 1998 S.C.(H.L.) 1 at p. 9.

[40] *Ibid.*; *Sands v. Devan,* 1945 S.C. 380; *Kelly v. Glasgow Corporation,* 1951 S.C. (H.L.) 15.

[41] *Kelly v. Glasgow Corporation,* 1949 S.C. 496 at p. 502; *Dingwall v. Walter Alexander & Sons (Midland) Ltd,* 1982 S.C. (H.L.) 179 at p. 209.

Chapter 10

LOSS OF SUPPORT

The damages which a wrongdoer requires to pay to a relative of a deceased[1] under section 1 of the Damages (Scotland) Act 1976 shall (subject to the provisions of the Act) be such as will compensate the relative for any loss of support suffered by him since the date of the deceased's death or likely to be suffered by him as a result of the act or omission in question.[2]

A "relative" for this purpose is any of the following (only):

> "(a) any person who immediately before the deceased's death was the spouse of the deceased;
> (aa) any person, not being the spouse of the deceased, who was, immediately before the deceased's death, living with the deceased as husband or wife;
> (b) any person who was a parent or child of the deceased;
> (c) any person not falling within paragraph (b) above who was accepted by the deceased as a child of his family;
> (d) any person who was an ascendant or descendant (other than a parent or child) of the deceased;
> (e) any person who was, or was the issue of, a brother, sister, uncle or aunt of the deceased; and
> (f) any person who, having been a spouse of the deceased, had ceased to be so by virtue of a divorce;"[3]

and in deducing any relationship for the purposes of the foregoing definition — (a) any relationship by affinity is treated as a relationship by consanguinity; any relationship of the half blood is treated as a relationship of the whole blood; and the stepchild of any person is treated as his child; and (b) section 1(1) of the Law Reform (Parent and Child) (Scotland) Act 1986 (legal equality of children) applies.[4]

---

[1] A child dying after birth from injuries sustained in the womb is a deceased person for these purposes — *Hamilton v. Fife Health Board,* 1993 S.C. 369.

[2] Damages (Scotland) Act 1976, s. 1(3). As to circumstances in which liability to pay damages under s. 1 of the 1976 Act may be excluded or limited, see n. 11 and accompanying text *infra.*

[3] 1976 Act, s. 10(1) and Sched. 1, para. 1. A posthumous child is a "child" for these purposes — *Cohen v. Shaw,* 1992 S.L.T. 1022.

[4] 1976 Act, Sched. 1, para. 2.

The relative's claim may be brought by way of summons or initial writ or by way of minute in a depending action at the instance of another relative of the deceased or the deceased's executor.[5] Where the claim is brought by summons or initial writ, the rules of court concerning intimation of the action to connected persons are applicable.[6] The relative's claim is not excluded by the making of a claim by the deceased's executor for damages in respect of the deceased's personal injuries.[7] The relative's right to damages for loss of support transmits upon his death to his executor, but, in determining the amount of damages payable to an executor, the court must have regard only to the period ending immediately before the relative's death.[8] The making of a claim by the deceased's executor for damages in respect of the deceased's personal injuries does not exclude the relative's executor's claim either.[9] For the purposes of enforcing such right the relative's executor is entitled — (a) to bring an action; or (b) if an action for that purpose had been brought by the deceased relative but had not been concluded before his death, to be sisted as pursuer in that action.[10] No liability arises to pay damages to either the relative or the relative's executor if the liability to the deceased or his executor in respect of the act or omission has been excluded or discharged (whether by antecedent agreement or otherwise) by the deceased before his death, or is excluded by virtue of any enactment.[11]

---

[5] See Chap. 9, text accompanying nn. 20–23 regarding claims made by way of minute.

[6] See Chap. 9, text accompanying nn. 12–19.

[7] Damages (Scotland) Act 1976, s. 4, as amended by the Administration of Justice Act 1982, s. 14(2)(a) and the Damages (Scotland) Act 1993, Sched., para. 1.

[8] 1976 Act, s. 1A, as inserted by the Damages (Scotland) Act 1993, s. 2.

[9] 1976 Act, s. 4, as amended by the Administration of Justice Act 1982, s. 14(2)(a) and the Damages (Scotland) Act 1993, Sched., para. 1.

[10] 1976 Act, s. 2A(1), as inserted by the Damages (Scotland) Act 1993, s. 4. For the purposes of s. 2A(1) an action shall not be taken to be concluded while any appeal is competent or before any appeal taken has been disposed of — s. 2A(2).

[11] 1976 Act, s. 1(2). But where a deceased has been awarded provisional damages, the making of that award does not prevent liability arising under s. 1 of the 1976 Act— s. 1(5A). Note that where, in an action in which, following the death of any person from personal injuries, damages are claimed in respect of the death of the deceased by any relative of his, or, if the relative has died, by the relative's executor, it is shown that by antecedent agreement, compromise or otherwise, the liability arising in relation to a particular defender from the personal injuries in question had, before the deceased's death, been limited to damages of a specified or ascertainable amount, or where that liability is so limited by virtue of any enactment, nothing in the 1976 Act shall make the defender liable to pay damages exceeding that amount; and accordingly where in such an action there are two or more pursuers any damages to which they would respectively be entitled under the Act apart from the said limitation shall, if necessary, be reduced *pro rata*—s. 6(1) and (3)(b). Where two or more such actions are conjoined, the conjoined actions shall be treated for the purposes of the foregoing as if they were a single action— s. 6(2).

Loss of support may be claimed in respect of support in the form of money or some other emolument received by the deceased, such as a tied cottage.[12] Support may have been provided by the deceased by applying earned income to or for the benefit of the relative or by nominal employment of him whereby the relative derived unearned income.[13]

An award of damages for loss of support requires to be divided, where appropriate, into pre-decree and post-decree periods for the purposes of calculation of interest, which is exigible in respect of the former.[14]

The measure of damages for loss of support in an action of damages for the death of a relative is the value of the support which has been lost in consequence of the death.[15] The basic principle so far as such claims are concerned is:

> "[The dependants] are entitled to such sum as will make good to them the financial loss which they have suffered and will suffer as a result of the death."[16]

In applying the basic principle, it is generally necessary first to calculate the deceased's net earnings as at the date of his death.[17] Any fluctuations in those earnings may be evened out using a lengthy period in order to obtain an average for the purposes of calculation.[18] Any increases in the rate of pay relative to the deceased's employment between the date of death and the date of trial fall to be taken into consideration.[19] More generally, account may be taken of inflation between the date of death and the date of trial, at least where the deceased was willing and able to maintain in real terms his family's

---

[12] *Hatherley v. Smith,* 1989 S.L.T. 316.

[13] *Bhatia v. Tribax Ltd,* 1993 G.W.D. 35–2257 (whole of child's wage deducted; wife's wage from husband's company undervaluing her services left out of account). *Cf. Malyon v. Plummer* [1964] 1 Q.B. 330 (wife's wage from deceased husband's company part of her dependency to the extent that it exceeded the market value of her services).

[14] *McKeown v. Sir William Arrol & Co,* 1974 S.C. 97; *Prentice v. Chalmers,* 1985 S.L.T. 168. As to interest on damages, see Chap. 4.

[15] *Graham v. Associated Electrical Industries,* 1966 S.L.T. (Notes) 27. Note that in order to establish loss of support it is not essential for a claimant to show that the deceased was, or might have become, subject to a duty in law to provide or contribute to the support of the claimant; but if any such fact is established it may be taken into account in determining whether, and if so to what extent, the deceased, if he had not died, would have been likely to provide or contribute to such support — Damages (Scotland) Act 1976, s. 1(6).

[16] *Per* Lord Reid in *Taylor v. O'Connor* [1971] A.C. 115 at p. 127.

[17] *Dingwall v. Walter Alexander & Sons (Midland) Ltd,* 1982 S.C. (H.L.) 179 at p. 190; *Prentice v. Chalmers,* 1985 S.L.T. 168 at p. 172; *Davies v. Powell Duffryn Associated Collieries Ltd* [1942] A.C. 601 at p. 617.

[18] *Prentice v. Chalmers,* 1985 S.L.T. 168 at p. 172.

[19] *Dingwall v. Walter Alexander & Sons (Midland) Ltd,* 1982 S.C. (H.L.) 179 at p. 190.

standard of living.[20] Where a deceased had been awarded provisional damages, such part of the award relating to future pecuniary loss as was intended to compensate him for a period beyond the date on which he died requires to be taken into account in assessing the amount of the loss of support suffered by a relative.[21]

As a corollary of the basic principle, it is a universal rule that the relative cannot recover more than he has lost.[22] Accordingly, sums required or expended from the deceased's earnings for the deceased's own personal and living expenses must be excluded from the calculation.[23] Such can be achieved by taking a figure representing the deceased's net earnings at the date of death, making an estimate of how much of that sum was for his own expenses either in a particular amount or at a particular percentage of the net earnings and deducting the one from the other; and the dependency is accordingly the resultant figure after deduction of the estimated amount or percentage from the deceased's net earnings.[24] Where both spouses were working and pooling their resources, the estimated amount or percentage is deducted from the spouses' joint net earnings; and the dependency is accordingly the resultant figure after deduction of the estimated amount or percentage from the spouses' joint earnings, less the surviving spouse's net earnings.[25] On the same principle, account falls to be taken of any

---

[20] *Prentice v. Chalmers*, 1985 S.L.T. 168 at p. 173.

[21] Damages (Scotland) Act 1976, s. 1(5A).

[22] *Cf. Parry v. Cleaver* [1970] A.C. 1 at p. 13.

[23] *Davies v. Powell Duffryn Associated Collieries Ltd* [1942] A.C. 601 at p. 617.

[24] See *e.g. Dingwall v. Walter Alexander & Sons (Midland) Ltd,* 1982 S.C. (H.L.) 179 at p. 190 (widow and five children; 30% deduction for deceased's personal expenditure); *Clark v. J.M.J. Contractors Ltd,* 1982 S.L.T. 299 at p. 300 (widow and one child; £7,000 deducted from £22,000 for deceased's personal expenditure); *McLaughlin v. Strathclyde Regional Council,* 1984 S.L.T. 99 (widow and eight children; 20% deduction for deceased's personal expenditure); *Prentice v. Chalmers,* 1984 S.L.T. 63 at p. 64 (widow and three children; 33% deduction for deceased's personal expenditure); *Worf v. Western S.M.T. Co Ltd,* 1987 S.L.T. 317 at p. 319 (widow and three children; 25% deduction for deceased's personal expenditure); *Wilson v. Chief Constable, Lothian and Borders Constabulary,* 1989 S.L.T. 97 at p. 106 (widow and three children; £1,200 deducted from £3,700 for deceased's personal expenditure); *Davidson v. Upper Clyde Shipbuilders Ltd,* 1990 S.L.T. 329 at pp. 332–333 (widow; 45% deduction for deceased's personal expenditure); *Howie v. Upper Clyde Shipbuilders Ltd,* 1991 S.L.T. 2 at p. 5 (widow; 50% deduction for deceased's personal expenditure); *Bhatia v. Tribax Ltd,* 1993 G.W.D.35–2257 (widow and two children; DM65,000 deducted from DM165,000 for deceased's personal expenditure); *Campbell v. Gillespie,* 1996 S.L.T. 503 at pp. 511 and 515–516 (widow and two children; 30% deduction for deceased's personal expenditure, increased to 50% for period of deceased's retirement).

[25] *Porter v. Dickie,* 1983 S.L.T. 234 at p. 235 (widow; 50% of joint net earnings deducted for deceased's personal expenditure); *Brown v. Ferguson,* 1990 S.L.T. 274 at p. 275 (widow and one child; 25% of joint net earnings deducted for deceased's personal expenditure); *Phillips v. Grampian Health Board (No.2),* 1992 S.L.T. 659 at p. 660 (widow; 50% of joint net earnings deducted for deceased's personal expenditure); *Wotherspoon v.*

support provided to the relative after the death of the deceased, such as by another man with whom the surviving spouse and child are now living, so as to reduce the damages.[26]

On the other hand, the court cannot take account of the remarriage of the widow or her prospects of remarriage in assessing her damages.[27] Where a widow has remarried, therefore, the court has to fix a figure based on all relevant considerations but treating the situation as if the widow had not remarried and no account is accordingly taken of any support provided by her new husband.[28] No account is to be taken of a surviving spouse's private means in assessing loss of support.[29] There must also be left out of account in assessing the amount of any loss of support suffered by a relative —

> "(a) any patrimonial gain or advantage which has accrued or will or may accrue to the relative from the deceased or from any other person by way of succession or settlement;
> (b) any insurance money, benefit, pension or gratuity which has been, or will be or may be, paid as a result of the deceased's death."[30]

With regard to the method of assessment, the conventional approach is similar to that relating to loss of future earnings, namely to assess the amount required to be laid out in the purchase of an annuity (an investment of money entitling the investor to a series of equal annual

---

Strathclyde Regional Council, 1992 S.L.T. 1090 (widow and three dependent children; 25% of joint net earnings deducted for deceased's personal expenditure, increased to 30% for the period after trial); *Beggs v. Motherwell Bridge Fabricators Ltd,* 1997 S.C.L.R. 1019 (widow and two children; 25% of joint net earnings deducted for deceased's personal expenditure, increased for the period after trial and further increased to 50% for the period of deceased's retirement).

[26] *Cowan v. Greig,* 1969 S.L.T. (Notes) 34 at p. 35; *Morris v. Drysdale,* 1992 S.L.T. 186 at pp. 187–188.

[27] Law Reform (Miscellaneous Provisions) Act 1971, s. 4.

[28] *McKinnon v. Reid,* 1975 S.C. 233.

[29] *Cruikshank v. Shiels,* 1953 S.C. (H.L.) 1.

[30] Damages (Scotland) Act 1976, s. 1(5). For the purposes of the subsection, "benefit" means benefit under the Social Security Act 1975 or the Social Security (Northern Ireland) Act 1975 and any payment by a friendly society or trade union for the relief or maintenance of a member's dependants; "insurance money" includes a return of premiums; and "pension" includes a return of contributions and any payment of a lump sum in respect of a person's employment — *ibid.* An *ex gratia* payment made by the wrongdoer to the relative was held not to be deductible in *Bews v. Scottish Hydro Electric plc,* 1992 S.L.T. 749. Note that any pension received by the surviving spouse as a result of the death of the deceased falls to be left out of account in relation to loss of support *after* retirement (but prior to the notional date of death) as well as in relation to loss of support *before* retirement — *Davidson v. Upper Clyde Shipbuilders Ltd,* 1990 S.L.T. 329; *Campbell v. Gillespie,* 1996 S.L.T. 503.

sums) which will provide the annual sum needed for the whole period of the loss.[31] The mechanism by which the capital sum is arrived at where damages for loss of support are claimed is to determine a multiplier of a certain number of years and apply that to an annual sum or multiplicand representing the loss of support suffered by the deceased's family, before dividing it up between the respective members of the family.[32]

The multiplier that is selected represents a number of years' purchase and is applied to the multiplicand from the date of death.[33] The multiplier falls to be divided into the period before and after trial for the purely mathematical purpose of calculating interest.[34] The multiplier may be further divided and the portions applied to different annual sums or multiplicands representing different levels of support over the period of the multiplier.[35] In estimating the period of loss, the age and expectation of life of the deceased and the relatives, respectively, fall to be taken into consideration so that the likelihood of the provider of the support continuing to exist and the likelihood of the dependant being alive to benefit from that support may be established.[36] The prospect of the providing capacity of the provider

---

[31] *Cookson v. Knowles* [1979] A.C. 556 at p. 576.

[32] *Dingwall v. Walter Alexander & Sons (Midland) Ltd,* 1982 S.C. (H.L.) 179 at p. 229. As to apportionment between members of the family, see *e.g. McKinnon v. British Railways Board*, 1972 S.L.T. (Notes) 2 (loss of support allocated 80% to widow and 20% to children, subdivided on basis of 42.5% to older child and 57.5% to younger child); *Prentice v. Chalmers*, 1985 S.L.T. 168 at pp. 174, 176 and 178 (loss of support allocated 75% to widow and 25% to children, subdivided on basis of years of dependency up to 21 years); *Worf v. Western S.M.T. Co Ltd*, 1987 S.L.T. 317 (loss of support allocated 70% to widow and 30% to children); *Wilson v. Chief Constable, Lothian and Borders Constabulary*, 1989 S.L.T. 97 (loss of support allocated 50% to widow and 50% to children, subdivided on basis of 4/15 to eldest child, 5/15 to the second child and 6/15 to youngest child); *Bhatia v. Tribax Ltd*, 1993 G.W.D. 35–2257 (loss of support allocated 70% to widow and 30% to children, subdivided equally); *Campbell v. Gillespie*, 1996 S.L.T. 503 (loss of support allocated in respect of the period to date of retirement of deceased 2/3 to widow and 1/3 to children, subdivided equally); and *Beggs v. Motherwell Bridge Fabricators Ltd*, 1997 S.C.L.R. 1019 (loss of support allocated in respect of the period to date of trial 70% to widow and 30% to children, subdivided equally; in respect of the period thereafter to date of retirement of deceased 80% to widow and 20% to children, subdivided equally; and in respect of the period after the retirement of the deceased 100% to widow).

[33] *Dingwall v. Walter Alexander & Sons (Midland) Ltd,* 1982 S.C. (H.L.) 179 at pp. 206, 219 and 229; *Graham v. Dodds* [1983] 1 W.L.R. 808.

[34] *Dingwall v. Walter Alexander & Sons (Midland) Ltd,* 1982 S.C. (H.L.) 179 at p. 229; *Prentice v. Chalmers,* 1985 S.L.T. 168 at pp. 173, 176 and 178.

[35] *Brown v. Ferguson,* 1990 S.L.T. 274.

[36] *Dingwall v. Walter Alexander & Sons (Midland) Ltd,* 1982 S.C. (H.L.) 179 at pp. 205–206; *Taylor v. O'Connor* [1971] A.C. 115 at p. 127; *Cookson v. Knowles* [1979] A.C. 556 at p. 568; *Corbett v. Barking Health Authority* [1991] 2 Q.B. 408 at p. 422. Note that a deceased's expectation of life (rather than his expectation of *working* life) is relevant in

or the needs of the dependant being affected or altered by the changes and chances of life either in a positive or negative manner must also be taken into account in the selection of the multiplier.[37] The potential for divorce falls to be taken into account in appropriate cases.[38] Allowance may be made for the risk that the deceased might have suffered illness or injury, early retirement or unemployment.[39] Conversely, prospective increases in the deceased's earnings arising from promotion or a move to better paid work may be taken into consideration.[40]

---

the assessment of the duration of dependency wherever it may be taken that he would have made ample provision during his working life to enable him to provide support during his retirement (*Taylor v. O'Connor* [1971] A.C. 115 at pp. 127–128). In the event that pension arrangements are made, support may be calculated by reference to (i) the period before retirement and (ii) the period after retirement, applying a multiplier to a multiplicand in respect of each period (*Davidson v. Upper Clyde Shipbuilders Ltd,* 1990 S.L.T. 329 at p. 333; *Campbell v. Gillespie,* 1996 S.L.T. 503 at p. 516).

37 *Cookson v. Knowles* [1979] A.C. 556 at pp. 568–569; *Corbett v. Barking Health Authority* [1991] 2 Q.B. 408 at p. 422.

38 *Farrell v. British United Trawlers (Granton) Ltd,* 1978 S.L.T. (Notes) 16 at p. 17; *Owen v. Martin* [1992] P.I.Q.R. Q151.

39 *Wilson v. Chief Constable, Lothian & Borders Constabulary,* 1989 S.L.T. 97 at p. 106; *Cookson v. Knowles* [1979] A.C. 556 at p. 568; *Graham v. Dodds* [1983] 1W.L.R. 808; *Robertson v. Lestrange* [1985] 1 All E.R. 950 at pp. 954–955.

40 *Cookson v. Knowles* [1979] A.C. 556 at p. 568; *Miller v. British Road Services Ltd* [1967] 1 W.L.R. 443.

Chapter 11

FUNERAL EXPENSES

The damages which a wrongdoer requires to pay to a relative of a deceased[1] under section 1 of the Damages (Scotland) Act 1976 include any reasonable expense incurred by the relative in connection with the deceased's funeral.[2]

A "relative" for this purpose is any of the following (only):

"(a) any person who immediately before the deceased's death was the spouse of the deceased;

(aa) any person, not being the spouse of the deceased, who was, immediately before the deceased's death, living with the deceased as husband or wife;

(b) any person who was a parent or child of the deceased;

(c) any person not falling within paragraph (b) above who was accepted by the deceased as a child of his family;

(d) any person who was an ascendant or descendant (other than a parent or child) of the deceased;

(e) any person who was, or was the issue of, a brother, sister, uncle or aunt of the deceased; and

(f) any person who, having been a spouse of the deceased, had ceased to be so by virtue of a divorce;"[3]

and in deducing any relationship for the purposes of the foregoing definition — (a) any relationship by affinity is treated as a relationship by consanguinity; any relationship of the half blood is treated as a relationship of the whole blood; and the stepchild of any person is treated as his child; and (b) section 1(1) of the Law Reform (Parent and Child)(Scotland) Act 1986 (legal equality of children) applies.[4]

The relative's claim may be brought by way of summons or initial writ or by way of minute in a depending action at the instance of

---

[1] A child dying after birth from injuries sustained in the womb is a deceased person for these purposes — *Hamilton v. Fife Health Board,* 1993 S.C. 369.

[2] Damages (Scotland) Act 1976, s. 1(3). As to circumstances in which liability to pay damages under s. 1 of the 1976 Act may be excluded or limited, see n. 11 and accompanying text *infra.*

[3] 1976 Act, s.10(1) and Sched. 1, para. 1. A posthumous child is a "child" for these purposes — *Cohen v. Shaw,* 1992 S.L.T. 1022.

[4] 1976 Act, Sched. 1, para. 2.

another relative or the deceased's executor.[5] Where the claim is brought by summons or initial writ, the rules of court concerning intimation of the action to connected persons are applicable.[6] The claim is not excluded by the making of a claim by the deceased's executor for damages in respect of the deceased's personal injuries.[7] The relative's right to damages for funeral expenses transmits upon his death to his own executor.[8] The making of a claim by the deceased's executor for damages in respect of the deceased's personal injuries does not exclude the relative's executor's claim either.[9] For the purposes of enforcing such right the relative's executor is entitled — (a) to bring an action; or (b) if an action for that purpose had been brought by the deceased relative but had not been concluded before his death, to be sisted as pursuer in that action.[10] No liability arises to pay damages to either the relative or the relative's executor if the liability to the deceased or his executor in respect of the act or omission has been excluded or discharged (whether by antecedent agreement or otherwise) by the deceased before his death, or is excluded by virtue of any enactment.[11]

The expression "funeral" covers the ceremonies connected with the burial or cremation of the deceased.[12] Expense incurred in connection with the funeral may properly include the undertaker's account, gratuities to the gravediggers and the cost of flowers as well

---

[5] See Chap. 9, text accompanying nn. 20–23 regarding claims made by way of minute.

[6] See Chap. 9, text accompanying nn. 12–19.

[7] Damages (Scotland) Act 1976, s. 4, as amended by the Administration of Justice Act 1982, s. 14(2)(a) and the Damages (Scotland) Act 1993, Sched., para. 1.

[8] 1976 Act, s. 1A, as inserted by the Damages (Scotland) Act 1993, s. 2.

[9] 1976 Act, s. 4, as amended by the Administration of Justice Act 1982, s. 14(2)(a) and the Damages (Scotland) Act 1993, Sched., para. 1.

[10] 1976 Act, s. 2A(1), as inserted by the Damages (Scotland) Act 1993, s. 4. For the purpose of s. 2A(1) an action shall not be taken to be concluded while any appeal is competent or before any appeal taken has been disposed of — s. 2A(2).

[11] 1976 Act, s. 1(2). But where a deceased has been awarded provisional damages, the making of that award does not prevent liability arising under s. 1 of the 1976 Act—s. 1(5A). Note that where, in an action in which, following the death of any person from personal injuries, damages are claimed in respect of the death of the deceased by any relative of his, or, if the relative has died, by the relative's executor, it is shown that by antecedent agreement, compromise or otherwise, the liability arising in relation to a particular defender from the personal injuries in question had, before the deceased's death, been limited to damages of a specified or ascertainable amount, or where that liability is so limited by virtue of any enactment, nothing in the 1976 Act shall make the defender liable to pay damages exceeding that amount; and accordingly where in such an action there are two or more pursuers any damages to which they would respectively be entitled under the Act apart from the said limitation shall, if necessary, be reduced *pro rata*—s. 6(1) and (3)(b). Where two or more such actions are conjoined, the conjoined actions shall be treated for the purposes of the foregoing as if they were a single action—s. 6(2).

[12] *Porter v. Dickie*, 1983 S.L.T. 234 at p. 235.

as the outlay for a headstone irrespective of when it is erected.[13] Whether or not a particular headstone is a reasonable expense is a question of fact.[14]

The relative's claim can only cover expense incurred by the relative himself.[15]

---

[13] *Prentice v. Chalmers,* 1985 S.L.T. 168. Note that in *Bhatia v. Tribax Ltd,* 1993 G.W.D. 35–2257 funeral expenses inclusive of incidental travelling expenses, mourning clothes and transporting of the ashes were agreed.

[14] *Porter v. Dickie,* 1983 S.L.T. 234. The reasonableness or otherwise of the expense might be related to the station in life of the deceased and his family — see *Porter* at p. 235 and *Prentice* at p. 171.

[15] *Bhatia v. Tribax Ltd,* 1993 G.W.D. 35–2257 (state refund of burial costs deducted from award of funeral expenses). Thus funeral expenses met from the deceased's estate require to be claimed by the deceased's executor.

CHAPTER 12

DECEASED PERSON'S SERVICES

WHERE an injured person has died, any relative of his entitled to damages in respect of loss of support under section 1(3) of the Damages (Scotland) Act 1976 is entitled to include as a head of damage under that section a reasonable sum in respect of the loss to him of certain personal services.[1]

A "relative" for this purpose is any of the following (only):

"(a) any person who immediately before the deceased's death was the spouse of the deceased;

(aa) any person, not being the spouse of the deceased, who was immediately before the deceased's death, living with the deceased as husband or wife;

(b) any person who was a parent or child of the deceased;

(c) any person not falling within paragraph (b) above who was accepted by the deceased as a child of his family;

(d) any person who was an ascendant or descendant (other than a parent or child) of the deceased;

(e) any person who was, or was the issue of, a brother, sister, uncle or aunt of the deceased;

(f) any person who, having been a spouse of the deceased, had ceased to be so by virtue of a divorce;"[2]

and in deducing any relationship for the purposes of the foregoing definition — (a) any relationship by affinity is treated as a relationship by consanguinity; any relationship of the half blood is treated as a relationship of the whole blood; and the stepchild of any person is treated as his child; and (b) section 1(1) of the Law Reform (Parent and Child) (Scotland) Act 1986 (legal equality of children) applies.[3]

The relative's claim for loss of personal services falls to be made in the writ by which he claims damages for loss of support.[4] He has

---

[1] Administration of Justice Act 1982, s. 9(2). As to circumstances in which liability to pay damages under s. 1 of the 1976 Act may be excluded or limited, see n. 10 and accompanying text *infra*.

[2] Damages (Scotland) Act 1976, s. 10(1) and Sched. 1, para. 1. A posthumous child is a "child" for these purposes — *Cohen v. Shaw*, 1992 S.L.T. 1022.

[3] 1976 Act, Sched. 1, para. 2.

[4] As to which, see Chap. 10, text accompanying n. 6.

otherwise no direct right of action in delict against the wrongdoer in respect of the loss of personal services.[5] The claim is not excluded by the making of a claim by the deceased's executor for damages in respect of the deceased's personal injuries.[6] The relative's right to damages for loss of personal services transmits upon his death to his executor, but, in determining the amount of damages payable to an executor, the court must have regard only to the period ending immediately before the relative's death.[7] The making of a claim by the deceased's executor for damages in respect of the deceased's personal injuries does not exclude the relative's executor's claim either.[8] The relative's executor's claim falls to be made in the writ by which he claims damages for loss of support.[9] No liability arises to pay damages to either the relative or the relative's executor if the liability to the deceased or his executor in respect of the act or omission has been excluded or discharged (whether by antecedent agreement or otherwise) by the deceased before his death, or is excluded by virtue of any enactment.[10]

The personal services which may be included as a head of damage by a relative entitled to damages for loss of support are personal services:

> "(a) which were or might have been expected to have been rendered by the injured person before the occurrence of the act or omission giving rise to liability,

---

[5] Administration of Justice Act 1982, s. 9(4).

[6] Damages (Scotland) Act 1976, s. 4, as amended by the Administration of Justice Act 1982, s. 14(2)(a) and the Damages (Scotland) Act 1993, Sched., para. 1.

[7] 1976 Act, s. 1A, as inserted by the Damages (Scotland) Act 1993, s. 2.

[8] 1976 Act, s. 4, as amended by the Administration of Justice Act 1982, s. 14(2)(a) and the Damages(Scotland) Act 1993, Sched., para. 1.

[9] As to which, see Chap. 10, text accompanying n. 11.

[10] 1976 Act, s. 1(2). But where a deceased has been awarded provisional damages, the making of that award does not prevent liability arising under s. 1 of the 1976 Act—s. 1(5A). Note that where, in an action in which, following the death of any person from personal injuries, damages are claimed in respect of the death of the deceased by any relative of his, or, if the relative has died, by the relative's executor, it is shown that by antecedent agreement, compromise or otherwise, the liability arising in relation to a particular defender from the personal injuries in question had, before the deceased's death, been limited to damages of a specified or ascertainable amount, or where that liability is so limited by virtue of any enactment, nothing in the 1976 Act shall make the defender liable to pay damages exceeding that amount; and accordingly where in such an action there are two or more pursuers any damages to which they would respectively be entitled under the Act apart from the said limitation shall, if necessary, be reduced *pro rata*—s. 6(1) and (3)(b). Where two or more such actions are conjoined, the conjoined actions shall be treated for the purposes of the foregoing as if they were a single action—s. 6(2).

(b) of a kind which, when rendered by a person other than a relative, would ordinarily be obtainable on payment, and
(c) which the injured person but for the injuries in question might have been expected to render gratuitously to a relative."[11]

An award in respect of personal services requires to be divided, where appropriate, into pre-decree and post-decree periods for the purposes of calculation of interest, which is exigible in respect of the former.[12]

Where a claim is made in respect of loss of personal services, it must be shown that the personal services were or might have been expected to have been rendered (i) for the benefit of the person claiming and (ii) in person by the now deceased and not by a third party acting on his behalf.[13] No hard and fast rules as to what categories of work might or might not be personal services can be laid down since circumstances will vary considerably.[14] A whole range of housekeeping and maintenance services may be covered by the expression.[15] Childcare services provided by a parent fall within the definition.[16] Whether particular benefits lost are to be regarded as lost support or lost services may be a matter of circumstances.[17]

As to what amounts to "a reasonable sum" for the loss of the personal services in question, the court requires to make a broad assessment and may do so by reference to an estimate of the average weekly time expended on the services and a suitable hourly rate, which may or may not correlate with any rate of pay commanded by the deceased in employment.[18] Where a claimant could reasonably be expected to employ or has in fact reasonably employed someone, such as a housekeeper, to perform the lost services the cost of that employment could be used as a measure of the loss of services provided that the wage payable is not unreasonable.[19] A detailed enquiry involving evidence as to the rates of pay applicable to

---

[11] Administration of Justice Act 1982, s. 9(3).

[12] *Bhatia v. Tribax Ltd,* 1994 S.L.T. 1201 at p. 1205.

[13] *Ingham v. John G Russell (Transport) Ltd,* 1991 S.C. 201 at p. 204.

[14] *Ibid.* at pp. 204–205.

[15] *Ibid.* at p. 204.

[16] *Brown v. Ferguson,* 1990 S.L.T. 274 at p. 276.

[17] *Fox v. N C R (Nederlande) B V,* 1987 S.L.T. 401 at p. 404.

[18] *Ingham v. John G Russell (Transport) Ltd,* 1991 S.C. 201 at p. 205; *Campbell v. Gillespie,* 1996 S.L.T. 503 at p. 512. *Cf. Howie v. Upper Clyde Shipbuilders Ltd,* 1991 S.L.T. 2 at p. 4.

[19] *Brown v. Ferguson,* 1990 S.L.T. 274 at p. 276 (living out housekeeper); *Spittle v. Bunney* [1988] 1 W.L.R. 847 (nanny for young child).

different household tasks and the number of hours worked in relation to each is never warranted.[20]

The court may make the assessment by means of the application of a multiplier referable to the period of loss to a multiplicand representing the annual value of the loss.[21] The multiplier that is selected represents a number of years' purchase and is applied to the multiplicand from the date of death.[22] In estimating the period of loss, the prospective length of the joint lives of the deceased and the relative fall to be taken into consideration.[23] The prospect that the providing capacity of the deceased or the needs of the relative would have been affected or altered by the changes or chances of life either in a positive or in a negative manner must also be taken into account in the selection of the multiplier.[24] The potential for divorce falls to be taken into account in appropriate cases.[25] Account must be taken of any change in the nature of the personal services over time, as in the case of childcare.[26] As an alternative to the multiplier/multiplicand mechanism, the court may make a broad estimate of the damages in the form of a lump sum.[27]

---

[20] *Ingham v. John G Russell (Transport) Ltd,* 1991 S.C. 201 at p. 211.

[21] *Worf v.Western S M T Co Ltd,* 1987 S.L.T. 317; *Bhatia v. Tribax Ltd,* 1993 G.W.D. 35–2257; *Campbell v. Gillespie,* 1996 S.L.T. 503 at p. 512; *Beggs v. Motherwell Bridge Fabricators Ltd,* 1997 S.C.L.R. 1019 at p. 1032; *Spittle v. Bunney* [1988] 1 W.L.R. 847.

[22] *Bhatia v. Tribax Ltd,* 1993 G.W.D. 35–2257.

[23] *Spittle v. Bunney* [1988] 1 W.L.R. 847 at p. 855; *Corbett v. Barking Health Authority* [1991] 2 Q.B. 408 at p. 422. And see Chap. 8, n. 32.

[24] *Corbett v. Barking Health Authority* [1991] 2 Q.B. 408 at p. 422.

[25] *Cf. O'Brien's Curator Bonis v. British Steel plc,* 1991 S.C. 315 at p. 332.

[26] *Spittle v. Bunney* [1988] 1 W.L.R. 847 at p. 858.

[27] *Wotherspoon v. Strathclyde Regional Council,* 1992 S.L.T. 1090 at p. 1092.

APPENDICES

Appendix I

TABLES OF MULTIPLIERS

A. OGDEN TABLES

Actuarial tables prepared by the Government Actuary's Department with explanatory notes for use in personal injury and fatal accident cases prepared by an inter-disciplinary working party of actuaries, lawyers, accountants and other interested parties

Third edition

EXPLANATORY NOTES

SECTION A: GENERAL

Purpose of tables

1. The tables have been prepared by the Government Actuary's Department. They provide an aid for those assessing the lump sum appropriate as compensation for a continuing future pecuniary loss or consequential expense in personal injury and fatal accident cases.

Application of tables

2. The tables set out multipliers. These multipliers enable the user to assess the present capital value of future annual loss (net of tax) or annual expense calculated on the basis of various assumptions which are explained below. Accordingly, to find the present capital value of a given annual loss or expense, it is necessary to select the appropriate table, find the appropriate multiplier and then multiply the amount of the annual loss or expense by that figure.

3. Tables 1 to 20 deal with annual loss or annual expense extending over three different periods of time. In each case there are separate tables for men and women.

— In Tables 1, 2, 11 and 12 the loss or expense is assumed to begin immediately and to continue for the whole of the rest of the plaintiff's life, allowing for the possibility of early death or prolonged life. ("The plaintiff" here includes the deceased in fatal accident cases.)

— In Tables 3 to 6 and 13 to 16 the loss or expense is assumed to begin immediately but to continue only until the plaintiff's retirement or earlier death. The age of retirement is assumed to be 65 in Tables 3 and 4 (and 13 and 14) and 60 in Tables 5 and 6 (and 15 and 16).

— In Tables 7 to 10 and 17 to 20 it is assumed that the annual loss or annual expense will not begin until the plaintiff reaches retirement but will then continue for the whole of the rest of his or her life.

4. In Tables 7 and 17 (males) and Tables 8 and 18 (females) the age of retirement is assumed to be 65. In Tables 9 and 19 (males) and Tables 10 and 20 (females) the age of retirement is assumed to be 60. The tables make due allowance for the chance that the plaintiff may not live to reach the age of retirement.

Mortality assumptions for Tables 1 to 10

5. As in previous editions of these tables, Tables 1 to 10 are based on the mortality rates experienced in England and Wales in a three-year period, in this case the years 1990 to 1992, and published by the Government Actuary's Department as English Life Tables No. 15 (ELT 15). Given this assumption about mortality, the accuracy of these tables, which were prepared by the Government Actuary's Department, has been accepted by all the actuaries on the working party, which included actuaries nominated by the Institute and the Faculty of Actuaries, the Association of British Insurers ("ABI") and the Family Law Bar Association. Consequently, the courts can have confidence in the mathematical accuracy of these tables. Members of the working party nominated by the ABI have reservations about the application of the tables and other matters and these are set out in Appendix C.

6. On the basis of some reported cases, it appears that tables for pecuniary loss for life, *e.g.* cost of care, may have been misunderstood. As stated hereafter in paragraph 21, the tables take account of the possibilities that the plaintiff will live for different periods, *e.g.* die soon or live to be very old. The mortality assumptions relate to the general population of England and Wales. Unless there is clear evidence in an individual case to support the view that the individual is atypical and will enjoy longer or shorter than average life, no further increase or reduction is required for mortality alone.

Tables adjusted to take account of projected mortality (Tables 11 to 20)

7. The actuaries on the working party consider that failure to have regard to reasonable projected improvements in mortality rates will

result in plaintiffs receiving awards of damages which are lower than they should be. At Appendix A is an extract from ELT 15 which shows graphs indicating rates of mortality expressed in percentages of 1911 rates on a logarithmic scale. They demonstrate in a stark fashion the improvement in longevity which has taken place since 1911. The sole exception is a small increase recently in the mortality of males in their late twenties and early thirties due to AIDS and increasing numbers of suicides, the same effect being present, but to a lesser degree, for females. Even if this slight worsening of mortality at these ages were to continue, the effect on the tables of multipliers would not be significant. (For comments by the ABI see Appendix C.)

8. The graphs, and the figures on which they are based, point to the conclusion that, on the balance of probabilities, the mortality rates which will actually be experienced in future by those who are alive today will be lower than in ELT15, and increasingly so the further into the future one goes. This, of course, would imply the need for higher multipliers. For the purposes of preparing the official national population projections, the Government Actuary makes a considered estimate of the extent of future improvements in mortality. Tables 11 to 20 show the multipliers which result from the application of these projected mortality rates. The actuaries on the working party (save for the dissenting views expressed at Appendix C) consider that these alternative tables may provide a more appropriate estimate of the value of future income streams than Tables 1 to 10, which are based on historic mortality and almost certainly underestimate future longevity of the population as a whole. The working party therefore recommends the courts to use Tables 11 to 20 rather than Tables 1 to 10.

Use of tables

9. To find the appropriate figure for the present value of a particular loss or expense the user must first choose that table which relates to the period of loss or expense for which the individual plaintiff is to be compensated and to the sex of the plaintiff.

10. If for some reason the facts in a particular case do not correspond with the assumptions on which one of the tables is based (if, for instance, it is known that the plaintiff will have a different retiring age from that assumed in the tables), then the tables can only be used by making an appropriate allowance for this difference; for this purpose the assistance of an actuary should be sought.

Rate of return

11. The basis of the multipliers set out in the tables is that the lump sum will be invested and yield income (but that over the period in

question the plaintiff will gradually reduce the capital sum so that at the end of the period it is exhausted). Accordingly, an essential factor in arriving at the right figure is to choose the appropriate rate of return. The tables set out multipliers based on rates of return ranging from $1^1/_2$% to 5%, as in previous editions.

12. Currently, the rate of return to be applied is 4.5% (*Wells v. Wells* [1997] 1 W.L.R. 652). (N.B. this differs from the figures stated in *Hodgson v. Trapp* [1989] A.C. 807, namely 4% to 5%, which allowed a degree of flexibility according to the prevailing economic circumstances.)[1] After a Commencement Order has been made in respect of the Damages Act 1996, section 1, the rate or rates of return are likely to be specified by the Lord Chancellor after receiving advice from the Government Actuary and the Treasury. Should it become necessary, further tables will be issued.

13. Previous editions of these tables explained how the current yields on index-linked government bonds could be used as an indicator of the appropriate real rate of return for valuing future income streams. Since such considerations could apply again following the commencement of section 1 of the Damages Act 1996, it has been thought desirable to retain tables for a range of possible rates of return, notwithstanding the Appeal Court judgment in *Wells v. Wells*. A description of how to use market rates of return on index-linked gilts to determine the appropriate rate of return is given in Appendix B. In cases outwith the scope of these tables, the advice of an actuary should be sought.

Tax

14. In order to arrive at a true present capital value of the plaintiff's future loss or expense it is necessary to consider whether he or she will have to pay a significant amount of tax on the investment return arising from his compensation. If he or she will pay little or no tax, no adjustment of the rate of return will be required. If he or she will have to pay a significant percentage of that income in tax, then the rate of return chosen to determine the present capital value of the loss or expense should be reduced accordingly. Attention is drawn to the decision of the House of Lords in *Hodgson v. Trapp* [1989] A.C. 807 concerning the treatment of the incidence of higher rate tax on the income arising from a compensatory fund.

15. In cases where the impact of personal income tax and capital gains tax is likely to be significant, more accurate calculation of the value

---

[1] See now *Wells v. Wells* [1998] 3 W.L.R. 329.

net of tax of payments to the individual may be desirable. Such calculations can be carried out by using software of the type referred to in paragraph 45 of the advice of an actuary should be sought.

Different retirement ages

16. In paragraph 10 above, reference was made to the problem that will arise when the plaintiff's retiring age is different from that assumed in the tables. Such a problem may arise in valuing a loss or expense beginning immediately but ending at retirement; or in valuing a loss or expense which will not begin until the plaintiff reaches retirement but will then continue until death. In the former case, that is where the loss or expense to be valued covers the period up to retirement, the following procedure will be found to be satisfactory in most cases. Where the plaintiff's actual retiring age would have been earlier than that assumed in the tables, he or she is treated as correspondingly older than his or her true age. Thus a woman of 42 who would have retired at 55 is treated as though she were 47 and retiring at 60. The appropriate multiplier is then obtained from the table (Table 6 or 16). A further correction should then be made, because the plaintiff's chances of survival are greater at 42 than if she were in fact 47. There should therefore be added to the multiplier one-quarter of one per cent for each year (here 5 years) by which the plaintiff's personal retiring age is earlier than 60. In the case of a man the correction required is a half per cent for each such year. This difference is because, on average, women live longer than men.

17. When the plaintiff would have expected to retire later than the age assumed in the table, the procedure is reversed. Thus a man of 42 who would have retired at 70 is treated as though he were 37 and retiring at 65. The appropriate multiplier is then obtained from the table (in this case Table 3 or 13) and the further correction required is made by reducing the multiplier by one-half of one per cent for each year by which the retiring age of the plaintiff exceeds the retiring age assumed in the table. In the case of a woman the reduction would, of course, be by one-quarter per cent for each year.

18. When the loss or expense to be valued is that from the date of retirement to death, and the plaintiff's date of retirement differs from that assumed in the tables, a different approach is necessary. The first step is to assume that there is a present loss which will continue for the rest of the plaintiff's life and from Table 1 or 2 (or 11 or 12) establish the value of that loss or expense over the whole period from the date of assessment until the plaintiff's death. The second step is to establish the value of such loss or expense over the period from the date of assessment until the plaintiff's expected date of retirement following

the procedure explained in paragraphs 16 and 17 above. The third step is to subtract the second figure from the first. The balance remaining represents the present value of the plaintiff's loss or expense between retirement and death.

Younger ages

19. Tables 1, 2, 11 and 12, which concern pecuniary loss for life, and Tables 7 to 10 and 17 to 20, which concern loss of pension from retirement age, have been extended down to age 0. In some circumstances the multiplier at age 0 is slightly lower than that at age 1; this arises because of the relatively high incidence of deaths immediately after birth.

20. Tables for multipliers for loss of earnings (Table 3 to 6 and 13 to 16) have not been extended below age 16. In order to determine the multiplier for loss of earnings for someone who has not yet started work, it is first necessary to determine an assumed age at which the plaintiff would have commenced work and to find the appropriate multiplier for that age from Tables 3 to 6 or 13 to 16, according to the assumed retirement age. This multiplier should then be multiplied by the deferment factor from Table 21 which corresponds to the appropriate rate of return and the period from the date of the trial to the date on which it is assumed that the plaintiff would have started work. A similar approach can be used for determining a multiplier for pecuniary loss for life where the loss is assumed to commence a fixed period of years from the date of the trial. For simplicity the factors in Table 21 relate purely to the impact of the rate of return and ignore mortality. At ages below 30 this is a reasonable approximation (for example allowance for ELT15 male mortality from age 5 to 25 would only reduce the multiplier by a further 1%) but at higher ages it would normally be appropriate to allow explicitly for mortality and the advice of an actuary should be sought.

Contingencies

21. Tables 1 to 10 have been calculated to take into account the chances that the plaintiff will live for different periods, including the possibility that he or she will die young or live to be very old, based on current levels of population mortality. Tables 11 to 20 make reasonable provision for the levels of mortality which members of the population of England and Wales may expect to experience in future. The tables do not take account of the other risks and vicissitudes of life, such as the possibility that the plaintiff would for periods have ceased to earn due to ill-health or loss of employment. Nor do they take account of

the fact that many people cease work for substantial periods to care for children or other dependants. Section B suggests ways in which allowance may be made to the multipliers for loss of earnings to allow for certain risks other than mortality.

Impaired lives

22. In some cases medical evidence may be available which asserts that a plaintiff's health impairments are equivalent to adding a certain number of years to the current age, or to treating the individual as having a specific age different from the actual age. In such cases, Tables 1, 2, 11 and 12 can be used with respect to the deemed higher age. For the other tables the adjustment is not so straightforward, as adjusting the age will also affect the period up to retirement age, but the procedures described in paragraphs 16 to 18 may be followed, or the advice of an actuary should be sought.

Fixed periods

23. In cases where pecuniary loss is to be valued for a fixed period, the multipliers in Table 22 may be used. These make no allowance for mortality or any other contingency but assume that regular frequent payments will continue throughout the period. These figures should in principle be adjusted to allow for less frequent periodicity of payment, especially if the payments in question are annually in advance or in arrears. An appropriate adjustment is to multiply by one plus half the rate of return for annual payments in advance (*i.e.* by 1.02 for a rate of return of 4%) and to divide the term certain multiplier one plus half the rate of return for annual payments in arrears.

Variable loss or expense

24. The tables do not provide an immediate answer when the loss or expense to be valued is not assumed to be stable; where, for instance, the plaintiff's lost earnings were on a sliding scale or he was expected to achieve promotion. It may be possible to use the tables to deal with such situations by increasing the basic figure of annual loss or expense; or by choosing a lower rate of interest and so a higher multiplier than would otherwise have been chosen. More complicated cases may be suited to the use of the software referred to in paragraph 45.

25. If doubt exists that the tables are appropriate to a particular case which appears to present significant difficulties of substance it would be prudent to take actuarial advice.

SECTION B: CONTINGENCIES OTHER THAN MORTALITY

26. As stated in paragraph 21, the tables for loss of earnings (Tables 3 to 6 and 13 to 16) take no account of risks other than mortality. This section shows how the multipliers in these tables may be reduced to take account of risks other than mortality. This is based on work commissioned by the Institute of Actuaries and carried out by Professor S. Haberman and Mrs D. S. F. Bloomfield. (*Work time lost to sickness, unemployment and stoppages: measurement and application* (1990), Journal of the Institute of Actuaries 117, 533–595.) Although there was some debate within the actuarial profession about the details of this work, and in particular about the scope for developing it further, the findings were broadly accepted and were adopted by the Government Actuary and the other actuaries who were members of the working party when the second edition of the tables was published.

27. Reported cases suggest that the courts have hesitated to accept these findings, which were based on scientific research, and continue to make reductions of as much as 20%, which appears to have been a figure adopted before any work on the subject had been carried out. Since the risk of mortality has already been taken into account in the tables, the principal contingencies in respect of which a further reduction is to be made are illness and unemployment. Even with the effective disappearance of the "job for life" there appears to be no scientific justification in the generality of cases for assuming significantly larger deductions than those given in this section. It should be noted that the authors of the 1990 paper (Professor Haberman and Mrs Bloomfield) wrote "All the results discussed in this paper should be further qualified by the caveat that the underlying models … assume that economic activity rates and labour force separation and accession rates do not vary in the future from the bases chosen. As mentioned already in the text, it is unlikely to be true that the future would be free from marked secular trends." The paper relied on Labour Force Surveys for 1973, 1977, 1981 and 1985 and English Life Tables No. 14 (1980–82). However, although it is now somewhat out of date, it is the best study presently available. It is hoped to commission some further research into the impact of contingencies other than mortality.

28. Specific factors in individual cases may necessitate larger reductions. By contrast, there will also be cases where the standard multipliers should be increased, to take into account positive factors of lifestyle, employment prospects and life expectancy.

29. The extent to which the multiplier needs to be reduced will reflect individual circumstances such as occupation and geographical region. In the short term, levels of economic activity and unemployment, including time lost through industrial action, are relevant. Reductions may be expected to be smaller for clerical workers than for manual workers, for those living in the south rather than the north, and for those in "secure" jobs and in occupations less affected by redundancy or industrial action.

30. The suggestions which follow are intended only to provide a "ready reckoner" as opposed to precise figures.

The basis deduction for contingencies other than mortality

31. Subject to the adjustments which may be made as described below, the multiplier which has been selected from the tables, *i.e.* in respect of risks of mortality only, should be reduced by *multiplying* it by a figure selected from the table below, under the heading "Medium".

Table A
Loss of earnings to pension age 65 (males)

Age at date of trial	High	Medium	Low
20	0.99	0.98	0.97
25	0.99	0.98	0.96
30	0.99	0.97	0.95
35	0.98	0.96	0.93
40	0.98	0.96	0.92
45	0.97	0.95	0.90
50	0.96	0.93	0.87
55	0.95	0.90	0.82
60	0.95	0.90	0.81

Levels of economic activity and employment

32. The medium set of reductions is appropriate if it is anticipated that economic activity is likely to correspond to that in the 1970s and 1980s (ignoring periods of high and low unemployment). The high set is appropriate if higher economic activity and lower unemployment rates are anticipated. The low set is appropriate if lower economic activity and higher unemployment rates are anticipated.

33. Whereas it is possible to reach conclusions about these factors in the short term the courts are not prepared to speculate about such matters beyond the short term (*Auty v. National Coal Board* [1985] 1 W.L.R. 784). Consequently the headings "High" and "Low" may only be of limited value.

Lower pension ages (males)

34. The figures will be higher for a lower pension age. For example, if pension age is 60, the figures should be as shown in Table B.

Table B
Loss of earnings to pension age 60 (males)

Age at date of trial	High	Medium	Low
20	0.99	0.99	0.98
25	0.99	0.99	0.97
30	0.99	0.98	0.97
35	0.99	0.98	0.96
40	0.98	0.97	0.94
45	0.98	0.96	0.93
50	0.97	0.94	0.92
55	0.96	0.93	0.88

Female lives

35. As a rough guide, for female lives between ages 35 and 55 with a pension age of 60, the figures should be as shown in Table C.

Table C
Loss of earnings to pension age 60 (females)

Age at date of trial	High	Medium	Low
35	0.95	0.95	0.94
40	0.93	0.93	0.92
45	0.90	0.90	0.88
50	0.91	0.90	0.88
55	0.95	0.94	0.93

Variations by occupation

36. The risks of illness, injury and disability are less for persons in clerical or similar jobs, *e.g.* civil servants, the professions and financial services industries, and greater for those in manual jobs, *e.g.* construction, mining, quarrying and ship-building. However, what matters is the precise nature of the work undertaken by the person in question; for example, a secretary in the headquarters office of a large construction company may be at no greater risk than a secretary in a solicitor's office.

37. In less risky occupations the figures in Tables A to C should be *increased* by a maximum of the order of 0.01 at age 25, 0.01 at age 40 and 0.03 at age 55.

38. In more risky occupations the figures in Tables A to C should be *reduced* by a maximum of the order of 0.01 at age 25, 0.02 at age 40 and 0.05 at age 55.

Variations by geographical region

39. For persons resident in the south east, East Anglia, south west and East Midlands, the figures in Tables A to C should be *increased* by a maximum of the order of 0.01 at age 25, 0.01 at age 40 and 0.03 at age 55.

40. For persons resident in the north, north west, Wales and Scotland, the figures in Tables A to C should be *reduced* by a maximum of the order of 0.01 at age 25, 0.02 at age 40 and 0.05 at age 55.

SECTION C: SUMMARY

41. To use the tables take the following steps:

(1) Choose the tables relating to the appropriate period of loss or expense.
(2) Choose the table, relating to that period, appropriate to the sex of the plaintiff.
(3) Choose the appropriate rate of return, before allowing for the effect of tax on the income to be obtained from the lump sum.
(4) If appropriate, allow for a reduction in the rate of return to reflect the effect on the income from the lump sum.
(5) Find the figure under the column in the table chosen given against the age at trial (or, in a fatal accident case, at the death) of the plaintiff.

(6) Adjust the figure to take account of contingencies other than mortality, as specified in Section B above.
(7) Multiply the annual loss (net of tax) or expense by that figure.

42. In principle an allowance for an expected increase in the annual loss or expense (not due to inflation) can be made by choosing a lower rate of return or by increasing the figure of annual loss or expense. In cases where the plaintiff's expected age of retirement differs from that assumed in the tables the more complicated procedure explained in paragraphs 16 to 18 should be followed.

43. An example is given below:

EXAMPLE

The plaintiff is female, aged 35. She lives in London and is an established civil servant who was working in an office at a salary of £25,000 net of tax. As a result of her injuries, she has lost her job. The task of estimating her loss of earnings to retirement age of 60 is to be undertaken as follows:

(1) Tables 6 and 16 assume a retirement age of 60 for females. If the projected mortality tables are accepted, then Table 16 is relevant.
(2) The appropriate rate of return is decided to be 4.5% (based on *Wells v. Wells* [1997] 1 W.L.R. 652).[2]
(3) Table 16 shows that, on the basis of a 4.5% rate of return, the multiplier for a female aged 35 is 14.94.
(4) It is now necessary to take account of risks other than mortality. Let us assume that economic activity for the next few years, for the purpose of this exercise, is regarded as being "high". Table C would require 14.94 to be multiplied by 0.95.
(5) Further adjustment is necessary because the plaintiff (a) is in a secure non-manual job, and (b) lives in the south east.

The adjustments should be made as follows:

Basic adjustment to allow for short-term high economic activity (Table C)	0.95
Adjustment to allow for occupation, say	+0.01
	0.96
Adjustment for geographical region, say	+0.01
	0.97

---

[2] See now *Wells v. Wells* [1998] 3 W.L.R. 329.

The original multiplier taken from Table 16, namely 14.94, must therefore be multiplied by 0.97, resulting in a revised multiplier for use of 14.49.

This example takes no account of the incidence of tax on investment return (see paragraph 14) above. It is assumed that this was taken into account when determining the 4.5% rate of return.

Final remarks

44. These tables are designed to assist the courts to arrive at suitable multipliers in a range of possible situations. However, they do not cover all possibilities and in more complex situations advice should be sought from a fellow of the Institute of Actuaries or a fellow of the Faculty of Actuaries.

45. In the Family Division a software program (the Duxbury Method) is used for making similar calculations in complex cases. A similar facility would be useful for more complex personal injury and fatal accident cases and it is intended that such a program will be made available shortly.

Chirstopher Daykin CB, MA, FIA
Government Actuary

London
May, 1998

Appendix A

Rates of mortality expressed as percentages of 1911 rates (logarithmic scale)

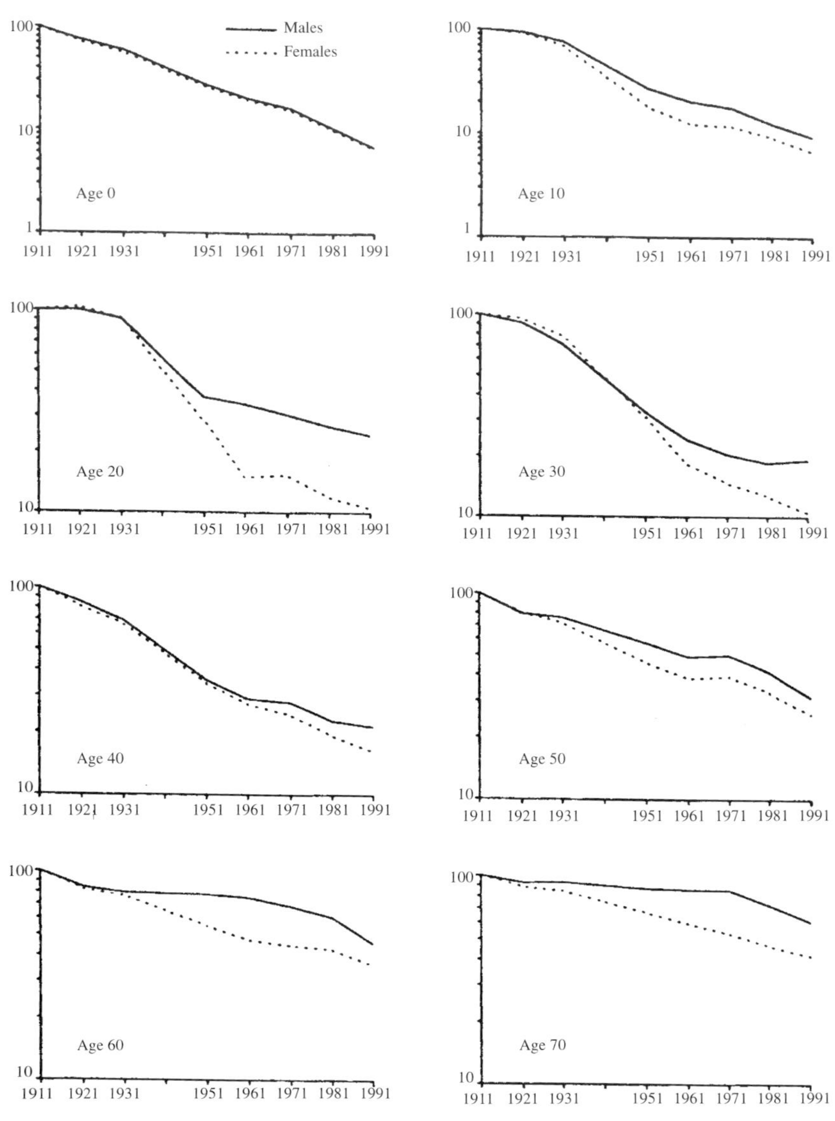

Appendix B

Selecting an appropriate real rate of return based on market considerations

1. The purpose of setting out figures based upon a range of rates of return is to enable the user to choose a rate which reflects the "real rate of return" that can be obtained upon the capital sum. In times of inflation high rates of return can be obtained; these rates compensate the investor in part for the fall in the value of his capital and of the dividends he receives due to inflation. The real rate of return may be defined as part of the actual rate which excludes this element. It has been held that in times of stable currency, when there is little or no inflation, a return on capital of 4% or 5% has been usual (see *Lim v. Camden Health Authority* [1980] A.C. 174, cases cited there and *Hodgson v. Trapp* [1989] A.C. 807). Reference has been made in paragraph 12 of the main text to the judgment of the Court of Appeal in *Wells v. Wells* [1997] 1 W.L.R. 652, which currently requires the use of $4^1/_2$%.

2. However, index-linked government stocks have been available since 1981 and it is accordingly no longer necessary to speculate about either future rates of inflation or the real rate of return obtainable on an investment. The redemption value and dividends of these stocks are adjusted from time to time so as to maintain the real value of the stock in the face of inflation. The current real rates of return on such stocks are published daily in the *Financial Times* and hitherto have fallen into the range of about $2^1/_2$% to $4^1/_2$% (gross, *i.e.* before the impact of taxation). It may be thought that the return on such index-linked government stocks is the most accurate reflection of the real rate of return available to plaintiffs seeking the prudent investment of awards of damages. In any event, when using the tables it will be necessary to use the real rate of return which is deemed the most appropriate for the particular purpose.

3. To identify the real return on such stocks on a particular date, reference should be made to the section of the *Financial Times* for that day entitled "FTSE Actuaries Govt. Securities UK Indices" (abbreviated to "Fixed interest indices" in the Contents list).

4. The most appropriate figures will be found

(a) in the section "Index-linked"
(b) within the sub-section on yields under the column for the day in question within the group of columns headed "Inflation 5%"
(c) in the line "Over 5 Years"

5. This figure is also published at quarterly intervals within the "Data Page" in the Law Society's Gazette; real returns on index-linked securities are generally stable and major fluctuations between the intervals of publication in the Gazette are unusual.

6. The rate thus obtained by reference to the *Financial Times* or Law Society's Gazette makes no allowance for the incidence of tax on the income from a compensation award. Accordingly, the rate should be adjusted if necessary, as described in paragraphs 14 and 15 of Section A, in order to identify the correct column of the table to be used.

Appendix C

Comments by the Association of British Insurers (ABI)

Introduction

1. The Association of British Insurers (ABI) represents companies transacting some 95% of insurance company business in the United Kingdom. The Forum of Insurance Lawyers (FOIL) fully supports the comments made in this appendix. Both ABI and FOIL are pleased to have participated for the first time in the working party which was responsible for the third edition of these tables and explanatory notes.

2. We believe that the central issue in the debate on the calculation of damages for future losses and expenses is ensuring that the plaintiff, the recipient of the compensation, is able to meet his or her future needs and requirements for as long as they arise. There may be a number of ways of calculating what the plaintiff needs for the future. Using multipliers is one. Purchasing an annuity may be another. There is perhaps a danger that the use of any scientific approach in this area may bring a spurious accuracy to a calculation which, almost by definition, will prove wrong in the future.

3. Our contention is that none of the methods above addresses this key question. All that any of the currently used methods do is to calculate a sum of money which is given to the plaintiff to do with as he or she wishes or sees fit. We nonetheless accept that a wider review of the means of addressing future financial provision for the victims of personal injury is outside the scope of this working party.

The tables in the third edition

4. What the tables do is to give a multiplier for a particular individual in his or her particular circumstances which is based on the general

mortality of the population at large. Insurers have no objection to the actuarial principles underlying the tables, because the figures which they include are derived from objective actuarial science applied to real mortality data from current English Life Tables.

5. The figures in the tables have been produced by the Government Actuary. We have no reason to dispute the mathematical accuracy or the rigour of the calculations used to derive any of the figures in any of the tables. What may be open to discussion is the suitability of using data drawn from a population of millions as a tool to predict what may be appropriate for an individual plaintiff in his or her own particular environment.

6. The figures in Tables 1 to 10 could provide a useful starting point for assessment of an individual case, and will need adjustment to reflect accurately the individual circumstances of the persons concerned. As the chairman of this working party noted in the discussions prior to publication of this edition: "People show a marked disinclination to die in strict accordance with their life expectancy."

Projected mortality tables

7. Paragraphs 7 and 8 of the explanatory notes state that Tables 11 to 20 are concerned with projected improvements in mortality rates. It is noted that the Government Actuary makes a considered estimate of the future improvements in mortality for national population projections. We accept that the evidence of the 20th century demonstrates that the mortality of the population as a whole has been improving. We understand that these improvements could provide a basis for projections for the national population as a whole. Nevertheless, we are aware of a number of factors which tend to question the continuation of such improvements.

8. We note that there is no objective evidence to which we have access of how the mortality patterns of a particular injury group are developing. We would strongly suggest that movements in the mortality of the group of victims of personal injury (of which an individual plaintiff in his or her particular circumstances is a member) may not be properly represented by the projected improvement in mortality of the whole of the population of the United Kingdom.

9. For example, whilst the development of improved methods of resuscitation and treatment may result in fewer fatalities, those who survive as a consequence of these procedures may bring with them a heavier pattern of mortality which is at variance with national experience.

10. In our view the use of Tables 11 to 20 is not supportable for two reasons. First, because of uncertainty about the future movements in national mortality and second because of uncertainty about the movement of the mortality of victims of personal injury relative to it.

11. Our conclusion on mortality is that whilst we accept with some reservations the updating of the tables of multipliers represented by Tables 1 to 10, we see no valid argument for further modifying the mortality basis to include speculative assessments of future changes. For these reasons, insurers are unable to recommend the use of Tables 11 to 20 to the courts.

Explanatory notes — Section B: Contingencies other than mortality

12. Paragraphs 26 to 40 attempt to deal with the deductions to be made for contingencies other than mortality, especially the risk of unemployment. A "ready reckoner" to assess the deduction to be made from the multiplier is proposed at paragraphs 31 to 40.

13. A different approach is generally adopted in the courts when assessing the deduction to be made for these contingencies. The practice is to consider all the evidence relating to how the individual is affected in his or her own particular circumstances, and then to decide on an appropriate adjustment which reflects these circumstances.

14. The paper from which Section B is derived is now over eight years old and was based on data which is at least 13 years old. Some of the data analysed in the paper is now 25 years old. It is our considered view that the use of such limited and out of date information which does not accurately reflect economic conditions at the time of trial or settlement is wholly anomalous.

15. Paragraph 27 mentions that further research is being considered. ABI is keen to facilitate and contribute to such research and, at the time of writing, is in discussion with the Government Actuary's Department on this subject.

Rates of return

16. It is not for this working party to advocate the use of any particular rate of return. Under the Damages Act 1996, this is a matter for the Lord Chancellor (if he is so minded) who is likely to make his decision after the House of Lords has given its judgment in *Wells v. Wells*. Until *Wells* is decided and until the Lord Chancellor has considered exercising his power under the Damages Act, we would therefore caution against adoption of the argument in support of index-linked

government stock, proposed in the "Introduction to the First Edition" which is found in this (third) edition at pages 12 to 14 and further discussed in paragraphs 2 to 5 of Appendix B at page 31.

17. FOIL suggests that in changing economic conditions there may be a case for including rates of return beyond the 1 to 5% range, which earlier editions of these tables adopted and which is used in the current edition.

Association of British Insurers
April 6, 1998

Table 1 Multipliers for pecuniary loss for life (males)

Age at date of trial	Multiplier calculated with allowance for population mortality and rate of return of 1.5%	2.0%	2.5%	3.0%	3.5%	4.0%	4.5%	5.0%	Age at date of trial
0	43.97	38.02	32.25	29.38	26.22	23.60	21.41	19.57	0
1	43.98	38.08	33.34	29.49	26.34	23.72	21.53	19.68	1
2	43.66	37.86	33.18	29.38	26.26	23.67	21.49	19.66	2
3	43.32	37.62	33.01	29.26	26.17	23.60	21.45	19.62	3
4	42.98	37.37	32.84	29.13	26.08	23.53	21.40	19.58	4
5	42.63	37.12	32.65	29.00	25.98	23.46	21.34	19.54	5
6	42.27	36.86	32.47	28.86	25.88	23.39	21.28	19.50	6
7	41.90	36.59	32.27	28.72	25.77	23.31	21.22	19.45	7
8	41.53	36.32	32.07	28.57	25.66	23.22	21.16	19.41	8
9	41.16	36.05	31.87	28.42	25.55	23.14	21.10	19.35	9
10	40.77	35.76	31.66	28.26	25.43	23.05	21.03	19.30	10
11	40.38	35.48	31.44	28.10	25.31	22.95	20.95	19.24	11
12	39.99	35.18	31.22	27.93	25.18	22.85	20.88	19.19	12
13	39.59	34.88	30.99	27.76	25.05	22.75	20.80	19.12	13
14	39.19	34.58	30.76	27.58	24.91	22.65	20.72	19.06	14
15	38.78	34.27	30.53	27.41	24.77	22.54	20.63	18.99	15
16	38.37	33.96	30.29	27.22	24.63	22.43	20.55	18.93	16
17	37.96	33.65	30.05	27.04	24.49	22.32	20.46	18.86	17
18	37.55	33.33	29.82	26.86	24.35	22.21	20.38	18.79	18
19	37.13	33.02	29.57	26.67	24.21	22.10	20.29	18.72	19
20	36.71	32.70	29.33	26.48	24.06	21.98	20.20	18.65	20
21	36.29	32.37	29.07	26.28	23.90	21.86	20.10	18.57	21
22	35.86	32.03	28.81	26.08	23.74	21.74	20.00	18.49	22
23	35.42	31.69	28.55	25.87	23.58	21.60	19.90	18.41	23
24	34.97	31.35	28.27	25.65	23.41	21.47	19.79	18.32	24
25	34.52	30.99	27.99	25.43	23.23	21.33	19.67	18.23	25
26	34.06	30.63	27.70	25.20	23.04	21.18	19.55	18.13	26
27	33.59	30.26	27.41	24.96	22.85	21.02	19.43	18.03	27
28	33.12	29.88	27.10	24.72	22.66	20.86	19.30	17.92	28
29	32.64	29.49	26.79	24.47	22.45	20.70	19.16	17.81	29
30	32.15	29.10	26.47	24.21	22.24	20.52	19.02	17.69	30
31	31.65	28.70	26.15	23.94	22.02	20.34	18.87	17.57	31
32	31.15	28.29	25.81	23.67	21.80	20.16	18.71	17.44	32
33	30.64	27.87	25.47	23.38	21.56	19.96	18.55	17.30	33
34	30.12	27.44	25.12	23.09	21.32	19.76	18.38	17.16	34
35	29.60	27.01	24.76	22.80	21.07	19.55	18.21	17.01	35
36	29.07	26.57	24.40	22.49	20.82	19.34	18.03	16.86	36
37	28.54	26.13	24.03	22.18	20.56	19.12	17.84	16.70	37
38	28.00	25.68	23.65	21.86	20.29	18.89	17.64	16.53	38
39	27.45	25.22	23.26	21.54	20.01	18.65	17.44	16.36	39
40	26.90	24.76	22.87	21.20	19.73	18.41	17.23	16.18	40
41	26.34	24.28	22.47	20.86	19.43	18.16	17.02	15.99	41
42	25.78	23.80	22.06	20.51	19.13	17.90	16.79	15.80	42
43	25.21	23.32	21.64	20.15	18.82	17.63	16.56	15.60	43
44	24.63	22.83	21.22	19.79	18.51	17.36	16.32	15.39	44
45	24.05	22.33	20.79	19.41	18.18	17.07	16.07	15.17	45
46	23.47	21.82	20.35	19.03	17.85	16.78	15.82	14.94	46
47	22.89	21.31	19.91	18.65	17.51	16.48	15.55	14.71	47
48	22.30	20.80	19.46	18.25	17.16	16.18	15.28	14.47	48
49	21.71	20.28	19.01	17.85	16.81	15.87	15.01	14.22	49
50	21.11	19.76	18.55	17.45	16.45	15.55	14.72	13.97	50
51	20.52	19.24	18.09	17.04	16.09	15.22	14.43	13.71	51
52	19.93	18.72	17.62	16.62	15.72	14.89	14.14	13.44	52
53	19.33	18.19	17.15	16.20	15.34	14.55	13.83	13.17	53
54	18.74	17.66	16.68	15.78	14.96	14.21	13.52	12.89	54
55	18.15	17.13	16.20	15.35	14.57	13.86	13.21	12.60	55

(*continued*)

Table 1 Multipliers for pecuniary loss for life (males) (*continued*)

Age at date of trial	1.5%	2.0%	2.5%	3.0%	3.5%	4.0%	4.5%	5.0%	Age at date of trial
			Multiplier calculated with allowance for population mortality and rate of return of						
56	17.55	16.60	15.72	14.92	14.18	13.51	12.88	12.31	56
57	16.97	16.07	15.24	14.49	13.79	13.15	12.56	12.01	57
58	16.38	15.54	14.76	14.05	13.39	12.79	12.23	11.71	58
59	15.80	15.01	14.28	13.61	13.00	12.42	11.89	11.40	59
60	15.22	14.49	13.81	13.18	12.60	12.06	11.56	11.09	60
61	14.66	13.97	13.33	12.74	12.20	11.69	11.22	10.78	61
62	14.10	13.45	12.86	12.31	11.80	11.32	10.88	10.46	62
63	13.55	12.95	12.40	11.88	11.40	10.95	10.54	10.15	63
64	13.01	12.45	11.94	11.46	11.01	10.59	10.20	9.83	64
65	12.48	11.97	11.49	11.04	10.62	10.23	9.86	9.52	65
66	11.96	11.49	11.04	10.63	10.24	9.87	9.53	9.21	66
67	11.46	11.02	10.61	10.22	9.86	9.52	9.20	8.90	67
68	10.97	10.56	10.18	9.82	9.49	9.17	8.87	8.59	68
69	10.49	10.11	9.76	9.43	9.12	8.82	8.55	8.28	69
70	10.02	9.67	9.35	9.04	8.75	8.48	8.22	7.98	70
71	9.55	9.24	8.94	8.66	8.39	8.14	7.90	7.68	71
72	9.10	8.81	8.54	8.28	8.04	7.80	7.58	7.37	72
73	8.67	8.40	8.15	7.91	7.69	7.47	7.27	7.08	73
74	8.25	8.00	7.77	7.56	7.35	7.15	6.97	6.79	74
75	7.84	7.62	7.41	7.21	7.02	6.84	6.67	6.50	75
76	7.44	7.24	7.05	6.87	6.69	6.53	6.37	6.22	76
77	7.05	6.87	6.70	6.53	6.37	6.22	6.08	5.94	77
78	6.69	6.52	6.36	6.21	6.07	5.93	5.80	5.67	78
79	6.33	6.18	6.04	5.90	5.77	5.65	5.53	5.41	79
80	5.99	5.86	5.73	5.61	5.49	5.37	5.26	5.16	80
81	5.67	5.55	5.43	5.32	5.21	5.11	5.01	4.91	81
82	5.36	5.25	5.14	5.04	4.94	4.85	4.76	4.67	82
83	5.06	4.96	4.86	4.77	4.68	4.60	4.52	4.44	83
84	4.77	4.68	4.60	4.52	4.44	4.36	4.28	4.21	84
85	4.50	4.42	4.35	4.27	4.20	4.13	4.06	4.00	85
86	4.25	4.17	4.10	4.04	3.97	3.91	3.85	3.79	86
87	4.01	3.94	3.88	3.82	3.76	3.70	3.65	3.59	87
88	3.78	3.72	3.67	3.61	3.56	3.51	3.46	3.41	88
89	3.57	3.52	3.47	3.42	3.37	3.32	3.28	3.24	89
90	3.36	3.31	3.27	3.23	3.18	3.14	3.10	3.06	90
91	3.15	3.11	3.07	3.03	3.00	2.96	2.92	2.89	91
92	2.95	2.92	2.88	2.85	2.81	2.78	2.75	2.72	92
93	2.77	2.74	2.70	2.67	2.64	2.61	2.59	2.56	93
94	2.60	2.57	2.54	2.52	2.49	2.46	2.44	2.41	94
95	2.45	2.42	2.40	2.37	2.35	2.33	2.30	2.28	95
96	2.31	2.29	2.26	2.24	2.22	2.20	2.18	2.16	96
97	2.18	2.16	2.14	2.12	2.10	2.08	2.06	2.04	97
98	2.06	2.04	2.02	2.00	1.98	1.97	1.95	1.93	98
99	1.94	1.92	1.91	1.89	1.87	1.86	1.84	1.83	99
100	1.83	1.81	1.80	1.78	1.77	1.76	1.74	1.73	100

Table 2 Multipliers for pecuniary loss for life (females)

Age at date of trial	1.5%	2.0%	2.5%	3.0%	3.5%	4.0%	4.5%	5.0%	Age at date of trial
	Multiplier calculated with allowance for population mortality and rate of return of								
0	45.85	39.35	34.21	30.08	26.73	23.99	21.70	19.79	0
1	45.82	39.38	34.27	30.16	26.83	24.08	21.80	19.88	1
2	45.53	39.18	34.14	30.07	26.76	24.04	21.77	19.86	2
3	45.21	38.97	33.99	29.97	26.69	23.99	21.73	19.84	3
4	44.90	38.75	33.83	29.86	26.61	23.93	21.69	19.81	4
5	44.57	38.52	33.67	29.75	26.53	23.87	21.65	19.78	5
6	44.24	38.28	33.51	29.63	26.45	23.81	21.61	19.75	6
7	43.90	38.05	33.34	29.51	26.36	23.75	21.56	19.71	7
8	43.56	37.80	33.16	29.38	26.27	23.68	21.51	19.68	8
9	43.21	37.55	32.98	29.25	26.17	23.61	21.46	19.64	9
10	42.86	37.30	32.80	29.12	26.08	23.54	21.41	19.60	10
11	42.50	37.04	32.61	28.98	25.97	23.47	21.35	19.56	11
12	42.13	36.78	32.42	28.84	25.87	23.39	21.29	19.51	12
13	41.76	36.51	32.22	28.69	25.76	23.31	21.23	19.46	13
14	41.39	36.23	32.02	28.54	25.65	23.22	21.17	19.42	14
15	41.01	35.95	31.81	28.39	25.54	23.14	21.10	19.37	15
16	40.63	35.67	31.60	28.23	25.42	23.05	21.03	19.31	16
17	40.24	35.38	31.39	28.07	25.30	22.95	20.96	19.26	17
18	39.85	35.09	31.17	27.91	25.17	22.86	20.89	19.20	18
19	39.45	34.80	30.95	27.74	25.04	22.76	20.82	19.15	19
20	39.05	34.49	30.72	27.57	24.91	22.66	20.74	19.08	20
21	38.64	34.18	30.48	27.39	24.77	22.55	20.65	19.02	21
22	38.22	33.87	30.24	27.20	24.63	22.44	20.57	18.95	22
23	37.80	33.55	30.00	27.01	24.48	22.33	20.48	18.88	23
24	37.37	33.22	29.74	26.82	24.33	22.21	20.38	18.81	24
25	36.94	32.88	29.49	26.61	24.17	22.09	20.29	18.73	25
26	36.50	32.54	29.22	26.41	24.01	21.96	20.18	18.65	26
27	36.05	32.20	28.95	26.19	23.84	21.82	20.08	18.56	27
28	35.59	31.84	28.67	25.97	23.67	21.68	19.97	18.47	28
29	35.13	31.48	28.39	25.75	23.49	21.54	19.85	18.38	29
30	34.67	31.11	28.09	25.52	23.30	21.39	19.73	18.28	30
31	34.20	30.74	27.80	25.28	23.11	21.23	19.60	18.18	31
32	33.72	30.36	27.49	25.03	22.91	21.07	19.47	18.07	32
33	33.23	29.97	27.18	24.78	22.71	20.91	19.34	17.96	33
34	32.74	29.58	26.86	24.53	22.50	20.74	19.20	17.84	34
35	32.25	29.18	26.54	24.26	22.28	20.56	19.05	17.72	35
36	31.75	28.77	26.21	23.99	22.06	20.38	18.90	17.59	36
37	31.24	28.36	25.87	23.71	21.83	20.19	18.74	17.46	37
38	30.73	27.94	25.53	23.43	21.60	19.99	18.58	17.32	38
39	30.21	27.51	25.18	23.14	21.36	19.79	18.41	17.18	39
40	29.68	27.08	24.82	22.84	21.11	19.58	18.23	17.03	40
41	29.15	26.64	24.45	22.54	20.85	19.37	18.05	16.88	41
42	28.61	26.19	24.08	22.22	20.59	19.14	17.86	16.72	42
43	28.07	25.74	23.70	21.91	20.32	18.92	17.67	16.55	43
44	27.53	25.28	23.31	21.58	20.04	18.68	17.46	16.38	44
45	26.98	24.82	22.92	21.25	19.76	18.44	17.25	16.20	45
46	26.42	24.35	22.52	20.91	19.47	18.19	17.04	16.01	46
47	25.86	23.88	22.12	20.56	19.17	17.93	16.82	15.82	47
48	25.30	23.40	21.71	20.21	18.87	17.67	16.59	15.62	48
49	24.73	22.91	21.29	19.85	18.56	17.40	16.36	15.41	49
50	24.16	22.42	20.87	19.48	18.24	17.12	16.11	15.20	50
51	23.59	21.92	20.44	19.11	17.91	16.84	15.86	14.98	51
52	23.01	21.42	20.00	18.73	17.58	16.55	15.61	14.76	52
53	22.43	20.92	19.56	18.34	17.24	16.25	15.35	14.52	53
54	21.84	20.41	19.12	17.95	16.90	15.94	15.07	14.28	54
55	21.26	19.89	18.66	17.55	16.54	15.63	14.80	14.03	55

(*continued*)

Table 2 Multipliers for pecuniary loss for life (females) (*continued*)

Age at date of trial	Multiplier calculated with allowance for population mortality and rate of return of 1.5%	2.0%	2.5%	3.0%	3.5%	4.0%	4.5%	5.0%	Age at date of trial
56	20.67	19.38	18.21	17.15	16.19	15.31	14.51	13.78	56
57	20.08	18.86	17.75	16.74	15.82	14.98	14.22	13.52	57
58	19.49	18.33	17.28	16.33	15.45	14.65	13.92	13.25	58
59	18.91	17.81	16.82	15.91	15.08	14.32	13.62	12.98	59
60	18.32	17.29	16.35	15.49	14.70	13.98	13.31	12.70	60
61	17.74	16.77	15.88	15.07	14.32	13.63	13.00	12.42	61
62	17.16	16.25	15.41	14.64	13.94	13.29	12.69	12.13	62
63	16.58	15.73	14.94	14.22	13.55	12.93	12.36	11.84	63
64	16.01	15.21	14.47	13.79	13.16	12.58	12.04	11.54	64
65	15.45	14.70	14.00	13.37	12.77	12.22	11.71	11.24	65
66	14.89	14.19	13.54	12.94	12.38	11.87	11.38	10.94	66
67	14.33	13.68	13.07	12.51	11.99	11.50	11.05	10.63	67
68	13.77	13.17	12.61	12.08	11.59	11.14	10.71	10.32	68
69	13.23	12.66	12.14	11.65	11.20	10.77	10.37	10.00	69
70	12.68	12.16	11.68	11.23	10.80	10.40	10.03	9.68	70
71	12.14	11.66	11.21	10.79	10.40	10.03	9.68	9.36	71
72	11.61	11.17	10.75	10.36	10.00	9.65	9.33	9.03	72
73	11.09	10.68	10.30	9.94	9.60	9.28	8.98	8.70	73
74	10.58	10.21	9.86	9.53	9.21	8.92	8.64	8.38	74
75	10.08	9.74	9.42	9.11	8.83	8.56	8.30	8.06	75
76	9.58	9.27	8.98	8.70	8.44	8.19	7.95	7.73	76
77	9.09	8.81	8.54	8.29	8.05	7.82	7.60	7.40	77
78	8.62	8.36	8.12	7.89	7.67	7.46	7.26	7.07	78
79	8.16	7.93	7.71	7.50	7.30	7.11	6.93	6.75	79
80	7.72	7.51	7.31	7.12	6.94	6.76	6.60	6.44	80
81	7.29	7.10	6.92	6.75	6.58	6.43	6.28	6.13	81
82	6.88	6.70	6.54	6.39	6.24	6.10	5.96	5.83	82
83	6.47	6.32	6.18	6.04	5.90	5.77	5.65	5.53	83
84	6.09	5.95	5.82	5.69	5.57	5.46	5.35	5.24	84
85	5.71	5.59	5.48	5.36	5.26	5.15	5.05	4.96	85
86	5.36	5.25	5.15	5.05	4.95	4.86	4.77	4.68	86
87	5.04	4.94	4.85	4.76	4.67	4.59	4.51	4.43	87
88	4.72	4.64	4.56	4.48	4.40	4.32	4.25	4.18	88
89	4.42	4.34	4.27	4.20	4.13	4.06	4.00	3.94	89
90	4.14	4.07	4.00	3.94	3.88	3.82	3.76	3.71	90
91	3.87	3.81	3.75	3.70	3.64	3.59	3.54	3.49	91
92	3.63	3.57	3.52	3.47	3.42	3.37	3.33	3.28	92
93	3.40	3.35	3.31	3.26	3.22	3.18	3.13	3.09	93
94	3.19	3.15	3.11	3.07	3.03	2.99	2.95	2.92	94
95	2.99	2.95	2.92	2.88	2.85	2.81	2.78	2.75	95
96	2.82	2.78	2.75	2.72	2.69	2.66	2.63	2.60	96
97	2.66	2.63	2.60	2.57	2.54	2.52	2.49	2.47	97
98	2.50	2.48	2.45	2.43	2.40	2.38	2.35	2.33	98
99	2.35	2.32	2.30	2.28	2.26	2.23	2.21	2.19	99
100	2.20	2.18	2.16	2.14	2.12	2.10	2.08	2.06	100

Table 3 Multipliers for loss of earnings to pension age 65 (males)

Age at date of trial	Multiplier calculated with allowance for population mortality and rate of return of 1.5%	2.0%	2.5%	3.0%	3.5%	4.0%	4.5%	5.0%	Age at date of trial
16	33.54	30.32	27.54	25.14	23.05	21.23	19.63	18.23	16
17	33.05	29.93	27.23	24.89	22.86	21.07	19.51	18.12	17
18	32.56	29.54	26.92	24.65	22.66	20.91	19.38	18.02	18
19	32.07	29.15	26.61	24.39	22.45	20.75	19.24	17.91	19
20	31.57	28.75	26.28	24.13	22.24	20.57	19.10	17.80	20
21	31.07	28.34	25.95	23.86	22.02	20.39	18.96	17.68	21
22	30.55	27.92	25.61	23.58	21.79	20.21	18.80	17.55	22
23	30.03	27.49	25.26	23.29	21.56	20.01	18.64	17.42	23
24	29.50	27.05	24.90	23.00	21.31	19.81	18.48	17.28	24
25	28.96	26.61	24.53	22.69	21.06	19.60	18.30	17.14	25
26	28.41	26.15	24.15	22.38	20.80	19.39	18.12	16.98	26
27	27.85	25.69	23.77	22.05	20.53	19.16	17.93	16.82	27
28	27.29	25.22	23.37	21.72	20.24	18.92	17.73	16.65	28
29	26.71	24.73	22.96	21.38	19.95	18.67	17.52	16.48	29
30	26.13	24.24	22.54	21.02	19.65	18.42	17.30	16.29	30
31	25.54	23.73	22.11	20.66	19.34	18.15	17.07	16.10	31
32	24.94	23.22	21.68	20.28	19.02	17.87	16.84	15.89	32
33	24.33	22.70	21.23	19.89	18.69	17.59	16.59	15.68	33
34	23.71	22.17	20.77	19.50	18.34	17.29	16.33	15.45	34
35	23.08	21.62	20.29	19.09	17.98	16.98	16.06	15.22	35
36	22.45	21.07	19.81	18.67	17.62	16.66	15.78	14.97	36
37	21.81	20.51	19.32	18.24	17.24	16.33	15.49	14.71	37
38	21.16	19.94	18.82	17.79	16.85	15.98	15.18	14.44	38
39	20.50	19.35	18.30	17.34	16.45	15.63	14.87	14.16	39
40	19.83	18.76	17.78	16.87	16.03	15.26	14.54	13.87	40
41	19.15	18.16	17.24	16.39	15.60	14.87	14.19	13.56	41
42	18.47	17.55	16.69	15.90	15.16	14.48	13.84	13.24	42
43	17.78	16.92	16.13	15.39	14.71	14.06	13.47	12.91	43
44	17.07	16.29	15.56	14.87	14.24	13.64	13.08	12.56	44
45	16.36	15.64	14.97	14.34	13.75	13.20	12.68	12.19	45
46	15.64	14.99	14.37	13.79	13.25	12.74	12.26	11.81	46
47	14.92	14.32	13.76	13.23	12.74	12.27	11.83	11.41	47
48	14.18	13.64	13.14	12.66	12.21	11.78	11.37	10.99	48
49	13.44	12.96	12.50	12.07	11.66	11.27	10.91	10.56	49
50	12.69	12.26	11.85	11.47	11.10	10.75	10.42	10.10	50
51	11.93	11.55	11.19	10.85	10.52	10.21	9.92	9.63	51
52	11.16	10.83	10.52	10.22	9.93	9.65	9.39	9.14	52
53	10.38	10.10	9.83	9.56	9.31	9.07	8.84	8.62	53
54	9.60	9.35	9.12	8.90	8.68	8.48	8.28	8.08	54
55	8.80	8.60	8.40	8.21	8.03	7.85	7.68	7.52	55
56	7.99	7.82	7.66	7.51	7.36	7.21	7.07	6.93	56
57	7.17	7.04	6.91	6.78	6.66	6.54	6.43	6.31	57
58	6.34	6.23	6.13	6.04	5.94	5.85	5.76	5.67	58
59	5.49	5.42	5.34	5.27	5.19	5.12	5.05	4.99	59
60	4.63	4.58	4.52	4.47	4.42	4.37	4.32	4.27	60
61	3.75	3.72	3.68	3.65	3.61	3.58	3.55	3.51	61
62	2.85	2.83	2.81	2.79	2.77	2.75	2.73	2.72	62
63	1.93	1.92	1.91	1.90	1.89	1.89	1.88	1.87	63
64	0.98	0.98	0.98	0.97	0.97	0.97	0.97	0.97	64

Table 4 Multipliers for loss of earnings to pension age 65 (females)

Age at date of trial	Multiplier calculated with allowance for population mortality and rate of return of								Age at date of trial
	1.5%	2.0%	2.5%	3.0%	3.5%	4.0%	4.5%	5.0%	
16	34.08	30.78	27.93	25.47	23.34	21.47	19.84	18.41	16
17	33.59	30.39	27.62	25.23	23.14	21.32	19.72	18.31	17
18	33.10	30.00	27.31	24.98	22.94	21.16	19.59	18.21	18
19	32.60	29.60	26.99	24.72	22.73	20.99	19.46	18.10	19
20	32.09	29.19	26.66	24.45	22.52	20.82	19.31	17.98	20
21	31.57	28.77	26.32	24.18	22.30	20.64	19.17	17.86	21
22	31.05	28.34	25.98	23.90	22.07	20.45	19.01	17.74	22
23	30.52	27.91	25.62	23.61	21.83	20.25	18.85	17.61	23
24	29.98	27.47	25.26	23.31	21.58	20.05	18.69	17.47	24
25	29.43	27.02	24.89	23.00	21.33	19.84	18.51	17.32	25
26	28.87	26.56	24.51	22.69	21.07	19.62	18.33	17.17	26
27	28.31	26.09	24.11	22.36	20.79	19.39	18.14	17.01	27
28	27.74	25.61	23.71	22.02	20.51	19.16	17.94	16.84	28
29	27.16	25.12	23.30	21.68	20.22	18.91	17.73	16.66	29
30	26.57	24.62	22.88	21.32	19.92	18.65	17.51	16.48	30
31	25.97	24.12	22.45	20.96	19.61	18.39	17.29	16.29	31
32	25.36	23.60	22.01	20.58	19.28	18.11	17.05	16.08	32
33	24.75	23.07	21.56	20.19	18.95	17.83	16.80	15.87	33
34	24.13	22.54	21.10	19.79	18.61	17.53	16.55	15.65	34
35	23.50	21.99	20.63	19.39	18.26	17.22	16.28	15.42	35
36	22.86	21.44	20.14	18.97	17.89	16.90	16.00	15.17	36
37	22.21	20.87	19.65	18.53	17.51	16.57	15.71	14.92	37
38	21.55	20.30	19.15	18.09	17.12	16.23	15.41	14.65	38
39	20.89	19.71	18.63	17.63	16.72	15.87	15.09	14.37	39
40	20.22	19.11	18.10	17.17	16.30	15.50	14.77	14.08	40
41	19.53	18.51	17.56	16.68	15.87	15.12	14.42	13.78	41
42	18.84	17.89	17.01	16.19	15.43	14.72	14.07	13.46	42
43	18.14	17.26	16.44	15.68	14.97	14.31	13.70	13.12	43
44	17.43	16.62	15.86	15.16	14.50	13.89	13.31	12.77	44
45	16.71	15.97	15.27	14.62	14.01	13.44	12.91	12.41	45
46	15.98	15.31	14.67	14.07	13.51	12.99	12.49	12.02	46
47	15.25	14.63	14.05	13.51	12.99	12.51	12.05	11.62	47
48	14.50	13.95	13.42	12.93	12.46	12.02	11.60	11.21	48
49	13.75	13.25	12.78	12.33	11.91	11.51	11.13	10.77	49
50	12.98	12.54	12.12	11.72	11.34	10.98	10.64	10.31	50
51	12.20	11.81	11.44	11.09	10.75	10.43	10.12	9.83	51
52	11.42	11.08	10.75	10.44	10.15	9.86	9.59	9.33	52
53	10.62	10.33	10.05	9.78	9.52	9.27	9.03	8.81	53
54	9.81	9.56	9.32	9.09	8.87	8.66	8.45	8.25	54
55	8.99	8.79	8.58	8.39	8.20	8.02	7.85	7.68	55
56	8.16	7.99	7.83	7.66	7.51	7.36	7.21	7.07	56
57	7.32	7.18	7.05	6.92	6.79	6.67	6.55	6.44	57
58	6.46	6.36	6.25	6.15	6.05	5.96	5.86	5.77	58
59	5.59	5.51	5.44	5.36	5.29	5.21	5.14	5.07	59
60	4.71	4.65	4.60	5.54	4.49	4.44	4.39	4.34	60
61	3.81	3.77	3.73	3.70	3.66	3.63	3.60	3.56	61
62	2.89	2.87	2.85	2.83	2.81	2.79	2.77	2.75	62
63	1.95	1.94	1.93	1.92	1.91	1.90	1.89	1.88	63
64	0.99	0.98	0.98	0.98	0.98	0.97	0.97	0.97	64

Table 5 Multipliers for loss of earnings to pension age 60 (males)

Age at date of trial	Multiplier calculated with allowance for population mortality and rate of return of								Age at date of trial
	1.5%	2.0%	2.5%	3.0%	3.5%	4.0%	4.5%	5.0%	
16	31.43	28.64	26.20	24.07	22.20	20.55	19.09	17.79	16
17	30.91	28.22	25.86	23.79	21.97	20.36	18.93	17.66	17
18	30.39	27.79	25.51	23.51	21.74	20.17	18.78	17.54	18
19	29.86	27.36	25.16	23.22	21.50	19.98	18.62	17.40	19
20	29.33	26.92	24.80	22.92	21.26	19.77	18.45	17.26	20
21	28.78	26.47	24.43	22.61	21.00	19.56	18.27	17.12	21
22	28.23	26.01	24.05	22.30	20.74	19.34	18.09	16.96	22
23	27.67	25.55	23.66	21.97	20.46	19.11	17.90	16.80	23
24	27.11	25.07	23.26	21.64	20.18	18.87	17.69	16.63	24
25	26.53	24.59	22.85	21.29	19.89	18.62	17.48	16.45	25
26	25.94	24.09	22.43	20.93	19.58	18.37	17.26	16.26	26
27	25.34	23.58	21.99	20.56	19.27	18.10	17.03	16.07	27
28	24.74	23.06	21.55	20.18	18.94	17.82	16.79	15.86	28
29	24.12	22.53	21.09	19.79	18.60	17.52	16.54	15.64	29
30	23.50	21.99	20.63	19.39	18.25	17.22	16.28	15.41	30
31	22.87	21.44	20.15	18.97	17.89	16.91	16.00	15.17	31
32	22.22	20.88	19.66	18.54	17.52	16.58	15.72	14.92	32
33	21.57	20.31	19.16	18.10	17.13	16.24	15.42	14.66	33
34	20.91	19.73	18.64	17.65	16.73	15.88	15.10	14.38	34
35	20.24	19.13	18.12	17.18	16.32	15.52	14.78	14.09	35
36	19.55	18.53	17.58	16.70	15.89	15.14	14.44	13.79	36
37	18.87	17.91	17.03	16.21	15.45	14.74	14.08	13.47	37
38	18.17	17.28	16.47	15.70	14.99	14.33	13.71	13.14	38
39	17.46	16.65	15.89	15.18	14.52	13.91	13.33	12.79	39
40	16.74	16.00	15.30	14.65	14.04	13.46	12.93	12.42	40
41	16.01	15.33	14.70	14.10	13.53	13.01	12.51	12.04	41
42	15.27	14.66	14.08	13.53	13.02	12.53	12.07	11.64	42
43	14.53	13.97	13.44	12.95	12.48	12.04	11.62	11.22	43
44	13.77	13.27	12.80	12.35	11.93	11.53	11.15	10.78	44
45	13.00	12.56	12.14	11.74	11.36	10.99	10.65	10.32	45
46	12.22	11.83	11.46	11.10	10.77	10.44	10.14	9.84	46
47	11.43	11.09	10.77	10.45	10.16	9.87	9.60	9.34	47
48	10.63	10.34	10.06	9.79	9.53	9.28	9.04	8.81	48
49	9.82	9.57	9.33	9.10	8.88	8.67	8.46	8.26	49
50	9.00	8.79	8.59	8.40	8.21	8.03	7.85	7.68	50
51	8.17	8.00	7.83	7.67	7.52	7.37	7.22	7.08	51
52	7.33	7.19	7.05	6.93	6.80	6.68	6.56	6.44	52
53	6.47	6.36	6.26	6.16	6.06	5.96	5.87	5.78	53
54	5.60	5.52	5.44	5.36	5.29	5.22	5.15	5.08	54
55	4.71	4.65	4.60	4.55	4.49	4.44	4.39	4.34	55
56	3.81	3.77	3.74	3.70	3.67	3.63	3.60	3.57	56
57	2.89	2.87	2.85	2.83	2.81	2.79	2.77	2.75	57
58	1.95	1.94	1.93	1.92	1.91	1.90	1.89	1.88	58
59	0.99	0.98	0.98	0.98	0.98	0.97	0.97	0.97	59

Table 6 Multipliers for loss of earnings to pension age 60 (females)

Age at date of trial	Multiplier calculated with allowance for population mortality and rate of return of								Age at date of trial
	1.5%	2.0%	2.5%	3.0%	3.5%	4.0%	4.5%	5.0%	
16	31.81	28.97	26.50	24.33	22.42	20.74	19.26	17.94	16
17	31.29	28.55	26.15	24.05	22.19	20.56	19.11	17.82	17
18	30.76	28.12	25.80	23.76	21.96	20.37	18.95	17.69	18
19	30.23	27.68	25.44	23.47	21.72	20.17	18.79	17.55	19
20	29.68	27.23	25.07	23.16	21.47	19.96	18.62	17.41	20
21	29.13	26.78	24.70	22.85	21.21	19.75	18.44	17.26	21
22	28.57	26.31	24.31	22.53	20.94	19.52	18.25	17.11	22
23	28.00	25.84	23.91	22.20	20.66	19.29	18.06	16.94	23
24	27.42	23.35	23.51	21.86	20.38	19.05	17.85	16.77	24
25	26.83	24.86	23.09	21.50	20.08	18.80	17.64	16.59	25
26	26.24	24.35	22.66	21.14	19.77	18.53	17.42	16.40	26
27	25.63	23.84	22.22	20.77	19.45	18.26	17.18	16.20	27
28	25.02	23.31	21.77	20.38	19.12	17.98	16.94	15.99	28
29	24.40	22.78	21.31	19.99	18.78	17.69	16.69	15.77	29
30	23.77	22.23	20.84	19.58	18.43	17.38	16.42	15.55	30
31	23.12	21.68	20.36	19.16	18.07	17.06	16.15	15.30	31
32	22.47	21.11	19.87	18.73	17.69	16.73	15.86	15.05	32
33	21.82	20.53	19.36	18.29	17.30	16.39	15.56	14.79	33
34	21.15	19.95	18.84	17.83	16.90	16.04	15.24	14.51	34
35	20.47	19.35	18.32	17.36	16.48	15.67	14.92	14.22	35
36	19.78	18.74	17.77	16.88	16.05	15.29	14.58	13.92	36
37	19.09	18.12	17.22	16.38	15.61	14.89	14.22	13.60	37
38	18.38	17.48	16.65	15.87	15.15	14.48	13.85	13.27	38
39	17.67	16.84	16.07	15.35	14.68	14.05	13.47	12.92	39
40	16.94	16.18	15.47	14.81	14.19	13.61	13.06	12.55	40
41	16.21	15.51	14.86	14.26	13.68	13.15	12.64	12.17	41
42	15.46	14.83	14.24	13.69	13.16	12.67	12.20	11.76	42
43	14.70	14.14	13.60	13.10	12.62	12.17	11.75	11.34	43
44	13.94	13.43	12.95	12.49	12.06	11.66	11.27	10.90	44
45	13.16	12.71	12.28	11.87	11.49	11.12	10.77	10.44	45
46	12.37	11.98	11.60	11.24	10.89	10.56	10.25	9.95	46
47	11.58	11.23	10.90	10.58	10.28	9.99	9.71	9.45	47
48	10.77	10.47	10.18	9.91	9.64	9.39	9.15	8.91	48
49	9.95	9.69	9.45	9.21	8.99	8.77	8.56	8.36	49
50	9.11	8.90	8.69	8.50	8.31	8.12	7.94	7.77	50
51	8.27	8.09	7.92	7.76	7.60	7.45	7.30	7.16	51
52	7.41	7.27	7.14	7.00	6.88	6.75	6.63	6.51	52
53	6.54	6.43	6.33	6.22	6.12	6.03	5.93	5.84	53
54	5.65	5.57	5.49	5.42	5.34	5.27	5.20	5.13	54
55	4.75	4.70	4.64	4.59	4.53	4.48	4.43	4.38	55
56	3.84	3.80	3.77	3.73	3.69	3.66	3.63	3.59	56
57	2.91	2.89	2.86	2.84	2.82	2.80	2.78	2.77	57
58	1.96	1.95	1.94	1.93	1.92	1.91	1.90	1.89	58
59	0.99	0.99	0.98	0.98	0.98	0.98	0.97	0.97	59

Table 7 Multipliers for loss of pension commencing age 65 (males)

Age at date of trial	Multiplier calculated with allowance for population mortality and rate of return of								Age at date of trial
	1.5%	2.0%	2.5%	3.0%	3.5%	4.0%	4.5%	5.0%	
0	3.76	2.62	1.83	1.28	0.90	0.63	0.45	0.32	0
1	3.85	2.69	1.89	1.33	0.94	0.66	0.47	0.34	1
2	3.91	2.75	1.94	1.37	0.97	0.69	0.49	0.35	2
3	3.97	2.81	1.99	1.41	1.01	0.72	0.52	0.37	3
4	4.03	2.86	2.04	1.46	1.04	0.75	0.54	0.39	4
5	4.09	2.92	2.09	1.50	1.08	0.78	0.56	0.41	5
6	4.15	2.98	2.14	1.55	1.12	0.81	0.59	0.43	6
7	4.22	3.04	2.20	1.59	1.16	0.84	0.62	0.45	7
8	4.28	3.10	2.25	1.64	1.20	0.88	0.64	0.47	8
9	4.34	3.16	2.31	1.69	1.24	0.91	0.67	0.50	9
10	4.41	3.23	2.37	1.74	1.28	0.95	0.70	0.52	10
11	4.48	3.29	2.43	1.79	1.33	0.99	0.73	0.55	11
12	4.55	3.36	2.49	1.85	1.38	1.03	0.77	0.57	12
13	4.61	3.43	2.55	1.90	1.42	1.07	0.80	0.60	13
14	4.68	3.50	2.62	1.96	1.47	1.11	0.84	0.63	14
15	4.76	3.57	2.68	2.02	1.53	1.15	0.88	0.67	15
16	4.83	3.64	2.75	2.08	1.58	1.20	0.92	0.70	16
17	4.90	3.71	2.82	2.15	1.64	1.25	0.96	0.73	17
18	4.98	3.79	2.89	2.21	1.69	1.30	1.00	0.77	18
19	5.06	3.87	2.97	2.28	1.76	1.35	1.05	0.81	19
20	5.14	3.95	3.04	2.35	1.82	1.41	1.10	0.85	20
21	5.22	4.03	3.12	2.42	1.88	1.47	1.15	0.90	21
22	5.31	4.12	3.20	2.50	1.95	1.53	1.20	0.94	22
23	5.39	4.20	3.29	2.57	2.02	1.59	1.25	0.99	23
24	5.48	4.29	3.37	2.65	2.09	1.66	1.31	1.04	24
25	5.56	4.38	3.46	2.74	2.17	1.72	1.37	1.09	25
26	5.65	4.47	3.55	2.82	2.25	1.79	1.43	1.15	26
27	5.74	4.57	3.64	2.91	2.33	1.87	1.50	1.21	27
28	5.83	4.66	3.73	3.00	2.41	1.94	1.57	1.27	28
29	5.92	4.76	3.83	3.09	2.50	2.02	1.64	1.33	29
30	6.02	4.86	3.93	3.19	2.59	2.11	1.72	1.40	30
31	6.11	4.96	4.03	3.28	2.68	2.19	1.79	1.47	31
32	6.21	5.06	4.14	3.39	2.78	2.28	1.88	1.55	32
33	6.31	5.17	4.24	3.49	2.88	2.37	1.96	1.63	33
34	6.41	5.28	4.35	3.60	2.98	2.47	2.05	1.71	34
35	6.52	5.39	4.47	3.71	3.09	2.57	2.15	1.80	35
36	6.62	5.50	4.59	3.83	3.20	2.68	2.25	1.89	36
37	6.73	5.62	4.71	3.95	3.32	2.79	2.35	1.99	37
38	6.84	5.74	4.83	4.07	3.44	2.91	2.46	2.09	38
39	6.95	5.87	4.96	4.20	3.56	3.03	2.58	2.20	39
40	7.07	5.99	5.09	4.33	3.69	3.15	2.70	2.31	40
41	7.19	6.12	5.23	4.47	3.83	3.28	2.82	2.43	41
42	7.31	6.26	5.37	4.61	3.97	3.42	2.96	2.56	42
43	7.43	6.40	5.51	4.76	4.12	3.57	3.09	2.69	43
44	7.56	6.54	5.66	4.91	4.27	3.72	3.24	2.83	44
45	7.69	6.68	5.82	5.07	4.43	3.88	3.39	2.98	45
46	7.83	6.84	5.98	5.24	4.60	4.04	3.56	3.14	46
47	7.97	6.99	6.15	5.41	4.77	4.22	3.73	3.30	47
48	8.12	7.16	6.32	5.59	4.96	4.40	3.91	3.48	48
49	8.27	7.33	6.50	5.78	5.15	4.59	4.10	3.67	49
50	8.43	7.51	6.70	5.98	5.35	4.80	4.30	3.87	50
51	8.59	7.69	6.89	6.19	5.57	5.01	4.52	4.08	51
52	8.77	7.89	7.10	6.41	5.79	5.24	4.74	4.30	52
53	8.95	8.09	7.32	6.64	6.03	5.48	4.99	4.55	53
54	9.14	8.31	7.56	6.88	6.28	5.74	5.25	4.80	54
55	9.35	8.53	7.80	7.14	6.55	6.01	5.52	5.08	55

(continued)

Table 7 Multipliers for loss of pension commencing age 65 (males) (*continued*)

Age at date of trial	Multiplier calculated with allowance for population mortality and rate of return of 1.5%	2.0%	2.5%	3.0%	3.5%	4.0%	4.5%	5.0%	Age at date of trial
56	9.56	8.77	8.06	7.41	6.83	6.30	5.82	5.38	56
57	9.79	9.03	8.33	7.70	7.13	6.61	6.13	5.70	57
58	10.04	9.30	8.63	8.02	7.45	6.94	6.47	6.04	58
59	10.31	9.59	8.94	8.35	7.80	7.30	6.84	6.41	59
60	10.59	9.91	9.28	8.71	8.18	7.69	7.24	6.82	60
61	10.90	10.25	9.65	9.10	8.58	8.11	7.67	7.26	61
62	11.24	10.62	10.05	9.52	9.02	8.57	8.14	7.75	62
63	11.61	11.03	10.48	9.98	9.51	9.07	8.66	8.28	63
64	12.02	11.47	10.96	10.48	10.04	9.62	9.23	8.87	64
65	12.48	11.97	11.49	11.04	10.62	10.23	9.86	9.52	65

Table 8 Multipliers for loss of pension commencing age 65 (females)

Age at date of trial	Multiplier calculated with allowance for population mortality and rate of return of 1.5%	2.0%	2.5%	3.0%	3.5%	4.0%	4.5%	5.0%	Age at date of trial
0	5.11	3.53	2.45	1.70	1.19	0.83	0.58	0.41	0
1	5.22	3.63	2.53	1.77	1.24	0.87	0.61	0.43	1
2	5.30	3.70	2.59	1.82	1.28	0.91	0.64	0.46	2
3	5.38	3.78	2.66	1.88	1.33	0.94	0.67	0.48	3
4	5.47	3.85	2.72	1.93	1.37	0.98	0.70	0.50	4
5	5.55	3.93	2.79	1.99	1.42	1.02	0.73	0.53	5
6	5.63	4.01	2.86	2.05	1.47	1.06	0.77	0.55	6
7	5.72	4.09	2.94	2.11	1.52	1.10	0.80	0.58	7
8	5.80	4.17	3.01	2.18	1.58	1.15	0.84	0.61	8
9	5.89	4.26	3.09	2.24	1.63	1.19	0.87	0.64	9
10	5.98	4.34	3.16	2.31	1.69	1.24	0.91	0.67	10
11	6.07	4.43	3.24	2.38	1.75	1.29	0.96	0.71	11
12	6.16	4.52	3.32	2.45	1.81	1.34	1.00	0.74	12
13	6.26	4.61	3.41	2.52	1.88	1.40	1.04	0.78	13
14	6.35	4.70	3.49	2.60	1.94	1.45	1.09	0.82	14
15	6.45	4.80	3.58	2.68	2.01	1.51	1.14	0.86	15
16	6.55	4.90	3.67	2.76	2.08	1.57	1.19	0.90	16
17	6.65	5.00	3.76	2.84	2.15	1.64	1.25	0.95	17
18	6.75	5.10	3.86	2.93	2.23	1.70	1.30	1.00	18
19	6.85	5.20	3.96	3.02	2.31	1.77	1.36	1.05	19
20	6.96	5.31	4.06	3.11	2.39	1.84	1.42	1.10	20
21	7.06	5.41	4.16	3.20	2.48	1.92	1.49	1.16	21
22	7.17	5.52	4.27	3.30	2.56	1.99	1.55	1.21	22
23	7.28	5.64	4.37	3.40	2.65	2.07	1.62	1.28	23
24	7.39	5.75	4.48	3.51	2.75	2.16	1.70	1.34	24
25	7.51	5.87	4.60	3.61	2.84	2.24	1.78	1.41	25
26	7.62	5.99	4.71	3.72	2.94	2.34	1.86	1.48	26
27	7.74	6.11	4.83	3.83	3.05	2.43	1.94	1.55	27
28	7.86	6.23	4.96	3.95	3.16	2.53	2.03	1.63	28
29	7.98	6.36	5.08	4.07	3.27	2.63	2.12	1.71	29
30	8.10	6.49	5.21	4.19	3.38	2.74	2.22	1.80	30
31	8.23	6.62	5.34	4.32	3.50	2.85	2.32	1.89	31
32	8.35	6.76	5.48	4.45	3.63	2.96	2.42	1.99	32
33	8.48	6.90	5.62	4.59	3.76	3.08	2.53	2.09	33
34	8.62	7.04	5.76	4.73	3.89	3.21	2.65	2.19	34
35	8.75	7.18	5.91	4.88	4.03	3.34	2.77	2.30	35
36	8.89	7.33	6.06	5.03	4.17	3.47	2.90	2.42	36
37	9.03	7.49	6.22	5.18	4.32	3.61	3.03	2.54	37
38	9.17	7.64	6.38	5.34	4.48	3.76	3.17	2.67	38
39	9.32	7.80	6.55	5.51	4.64	3.92	3.31	2.81	39
40	9.47	7.97	6.72	5.68	4.81	4.08	3.47	2.95	40
41	9.62	8.13	6.89	5.85	4.98	4.24	3.63	3.10	41
42	9.77	8.31	7.07	6.03	5.16	4.42	3.79	3.26	42
43	9.93	8.48	7.26	6.22	5.35	4.60	3.97	3.43	43
44	10.10	8.66	7.45	6.42	5.54	4.79	4.15	3.60	44
45	10.26	8.85	7.65	6.62	5.75	4.99	4.35	3.79	45
46	10.44	9.04	7.85	6.83	5.96	5.20	4.55	3.99	46
47	10.61	9.24	8.07	7.05	6.18	5.42	4.76	4.20	47
48	10.80	9.45	8.29	7.28	6.41	5.65	4.99	4.41	48
49	10.99	9.66	8.51	7.52	6.65	5.89	5.23	4.65	49
50	11.18	9.88	8.75	7.76	6.90	6.14	5.48	4.89	50
51	11.38	10.11	9.00	8.02	7.16	6.41	5.74	5.15	51
52	11.59	10.34	9.25	8.29	7.44	6.68	6.02	5.43	52
53	11.81	10.59	9.52	8.57	7.72	6.98	6.31	5.72	53
54	12.03	10.84	9.79	8.86	8.03	7.28	6.62	6.03	54
55	12.26	11.11	10.08	9.16	8.34	7.61	6.95	6.36	55

(continued)

Table 8 Multipliers for loss of pension commencing age 65 (females) (*continued*)

Age at date of trial	Multiplier calculated with allowance for population mortality and rate of return of								Age at date of trial
	1.5%	2.0%	2.5%	3.0%	3.5%	4.0%	4.5%	5.0%	
56	12.51	11.38	10.38	9.48	8.68	7.95	7.30	6.71	56
57	12.76	11.67	10.70	9.82	9.03	8.31	7.67	7.08	57
58	13.03	11.98	11.03	10.17	9.40	8.70	8.06	7.48	58
59	13.31	12.30	11.38	10.55	9.79	9.10	8.48	7.90	59
60	13.61	12.64	11.75	10.95	10.21	9.54	8.92	8.36	60
61	13.93	13.00	12.15	11.37	10.66	10.00	9.40	8.85	61
62	14.27	13.38	12.57	11.82	11.13	10.50	9.92	9.38	62
63	14.64	13.79	13.01	12.30	11.64	11.03	10.47	9.95	63
64	15.03	14.23	13.49	12.81	12.18	11.60	11.07	10.57	64
65	15.45	14.70	14.00	13.37	12.77	12.22	11.71	11.24	65

Table 9 Multipliers for loss of pension commencing age 60 (males)

Age at date of trial	1.5%	2.0%	2.5%	3.0%	3.5%	4.0%	4.5%	5.0%	Age at date of trial
	Multiplier calculated with allowance for population mortality and rate of return of								
0	5.40	3.83	2.72	1.94	1.39	0.99	0.71	0.51	0
1	5.53	3.94	2.81	2.01	1.45	1.04	0.75	0.55	1
2	5.62	4.02	2.88	2.08	1.50	1.08	0.79	0.57	2
3	5.70	4.10	2.96	2.14	1.55	1.13	0.82	0.60	3
4	5.79	4.18	3.03	2.20	1.61	1.17	0.86	0.63	4
5	5.88	4.27	3.11	2.27	1.66	1.22	0.90	0.66	5
6	5.97	4.35	3.19	2.34	1.72	1.27	0.94	0.70	6
7	6.06	4.44	3.27	2.41	1.78	1.32	0.98	0.73	7
8	6.15	4.53	3.35	2.48	1.84	1.37	1.03	0.77	8
9	6.24	4.62	3.43	2.56	1.91	1.43	1.07	0.81	9
10	6.34	4.72	3.52	2.63	1.98	1.49	1.12	0.85	10
11	6.43	4.81	3.61	2.71	2.05	1.55	1.17	0.89	11
12	6.53	4.91	3.70	2.80	2.12	1.61	1.22	0.93	12
13	6.63	5.01	3.79	2.88	2.19	1.67	1.28	0.98	13
14	6.73	5.11	3.89	2.97	2.27	1.74	1.34	1.03	14
15	6.84	5.21	3.99	3.06	2.35	1.81	1.40	1.08	15
16	6.94	5.32	4.09	3.15	2.43	1.88	1.46	1.14	16
17	7.05	5.43	4.19	3.25	2.52	1.96	1.53	1.20	17
18	7.16	5.54	4.30	3.35	2.61	2.04	1.60	1.26	18
19	7.27	5.66	4.41	3.45	2.70	2.12	1.67	1.32	19
20	7.39	5.78	4.53	3.56	2.80	2.21	1.75	1.39	20
21	7.51	5.90	4.64	3.67	2.90	2.30	1.83	1.46	21
22	7.63	6.02	4.76	3.78	3.01	2.40	1.91	1.53	22
23	7.75	6.15	4.89	3.90	3.11	2.49	2.00	1.61	23
24	7.87	6.27	5.01	4.02	3.23	2.60	2.09	1.69	24
25	7.99	6.41	5.14	4.14	3.34	2.70	2.19	1.78	25
26	8.12	6.54	5.28	4.27	3.46	2.81	2.29	1.87	26
27	8.25	6.68	5.41	4.40	3.59	2.93	2.39	1.96	27
28	8.38	6.81	5.55	4.54	3.71	3.05	2.50	2.06	28
29	8.51	6.96	5.70	4.68	3.85	3.17	2.62	2.17	29
30	8.65	7.10	5.85	4.82	3.99	3.30	2.74	2.28	30
31	8.79	7.25	6.00	4.97	4.13	3.44	2.87	2.39	31
32	8.93	7.40	6.15	5.12	4.28	3.58	3.00	2.52	32
33	9.07	7.56	6.31	5.28	4.43	3.72	3.14	2.65	33
34	9.22	7.72	6.48	5.45	4.59	3.88	3.28	2.78	34
35	9.36	7.88	6.65	5.62	4.76	4.04	3.43	2.92	35
36	9.52	8.05	6.82	5.79	4.93	4.20	3.59	3.07	36
37	9.67	8.22	7.00	5.97	5.11	4.38	3.76	3.23	37
38	9.83	8.39	7.18	6.16	5.29	4.56	3.93	3.40	38
39	9.99	8.57	7.37	6.36	5.49	4.75	4.11	3.57	39
40	10.16	8.76	7.57	6.56	5.69	4.94	4.31	3.76	40
41	10.33	8.95	7.77	6.76	5.90	5.15	4.51	3.95	41
42	10.50	9.15	7.98	6.98	6.12	5.37	4.72	4.16	42
43	10.68	9.35	8.20	7.20	6.34	5.59	4.94	4.37	43
44	10.87	9.56	8.42	7.44	6.58	5.83	5.17	4.60	44
45	11.05	9.77	8.65	7.68	6.83	6.08	5.42	4.84	45
46	11.25	9.99	8.89	7.93	7.08	6.34	5.68	5.10	46
47	11.45	10.22	9.14	8.19	7.35	6.61	5.95	5.37	47
48	11.66	10.46	9.40	8.47	7.64	6.90	6.24	5.66	48
49	11.88	10.71	9.67	8.75	7.93	7.20	6.55	5.96	49
50	12.11	10.97	9.96	9.05	8.24	7.52	6.87	6.29	50
51	12.35	11.24	10.25	9.37	8.57	7.86	7.21	6.63	51
52	12.60	11.53	10.56	9.70	8.92	8.21	7.58	7.00	52
53	12.86	11.83	10.89	10.05	9.28	8.59	7.96	7.39	53
54	13.14	12.14	11.24	10.42	9.67	8.99	8.38	7.81	54
55	13.43	12.47	11.60	10.81	10.08	9.42	8.82	8.26	55

(*continued*)

Table 9 Multipliers for loss of pension commencing age 60 (males) (*continued*)

Age at date of trial	Multiplier calculated with allowance for population mortality and rate of return of								Age at date of trial
	1.5%	2.0%	2.5%	3.0%	3.5%	4.0%	4.5%	5.0%	
56	13.75	12.82	11.99	11.22	10.52	9.88	9.29	8.74	56
57	14.08	13.20	12.40	11.66	10.98	10.36	9.79	9.26	57
58	14.43	13.60	12.83	12.13	11.48	10.89	10.33	9.82	58
59	14.81	14.03	13.30	12.63	12.02	11.45	10.92	10.43	59
60	15.22	14.49	13.81	13.18	12.60	12.06	11.56	11.09	60

Table 10 Multipliers for loss of pension commencing age 60 (females)

Age at date of trial	Multiplier calculated with allowance for population mortality and rate of return of								Age at date of trial
	1.5%	2.0%	2.5%	3.0%	3.5%	4.0%	4.5%	5.0%	
0	6.88	4.83	3.41	2.41	1.71	1.22	0.87	0.62	0
1	7.03	4.96	3.52	2.50	1.78	1.28	0.92	0.66	1
2	7.14	5.06	3.61	2.58	1.85	1.33	0.96	0.69	2
3	7.25	5.17	3.70	2.65	1.91	1.38	1.00	0.73	3
4	7.36	5.27	3.79	2.73	1.98	1.44	1.05	0.76	4
5	7.47	5.38	3.89	2.82	2.05	1.49	1.09	0.80	5
6	7.58	5.49	3.98	2.90	2.12	1.55	1.14	0.84	6
7	7.70	5.60	4.08	2.99	2.20	1.62	1.19	0.88	7
8	7.81	5.71	4.19	3.08	2.27	1.68	1.25	0.93	8
9	7.93	5.82	4.29	3.17	2.35	1.75	1.30	0.98	9
10	8.05	5.94	4.40	3.27	2.43	1.82	1.36	1.02	10
11	8.17	6.06	4.51	3.37	2.52	1.89	1.42	1.08	11
12	8.30	6.18	4.62	3.47	2.61	1.97	1.49	1.13	12
13	8.42	6.31	4.74	3.57	2.70	2.05	1.56	1.19	13
14	8.55	6.44	4.86	3.68	2.80	2.13	1.63	1.25	14
15	8.68	6.57	4.98	3.79	2.89	2.22	1.70	1.31	15
16	8.81	6.70	5.11	3.91	3.00	2.30	1.78	1.37	16
17	8.95	6.83	5.24	4.02	3.10	2.40	1.86	1.44	17
18	9.08	6.97	5.37	4.15	3.21	2.49	1.94	1.52	18
19	9.22	7.11	5.50	4.27	3.32	2.59	2.03	1.59	19
20	9.36	7.26	5.64	4.40	3.44	2.70	2.12	1.67	20
21	9.51	7.41	5.79	4.53	3.56	2.81	2.22	1.76	21
22	9.65	7.56	5.93	4.67	3.69	2.92	2.32	1.84	22
23	9.80	7.71	6.08	4.81	3.82	3.04	2.42	1.94	23
24	9.95	7.87	6.24	4.96	3.95	3.16	2.53	2.04	24
25	10.10	8.03	6.40	5.11	4.09	3.29	2.65	2.14	25
26	10.26	8.19	6.56	5.27	4.24	3.42	2.77	2.25	26
27	10.41	8.36	6.72	5.43	4.39	3.56	2.89	2.36	27
28	10.57	8.53	6.90	5.59	4.54	3.70	3.03	2.48	28
29	10.74	8.70	7.07	5.76	4.71	3.85	3.16	2.60	29
30	10.90	8.88	7.25	5.94	4.87	4.01	3.31	2.73	30
31	11.07	9.06	7.43	6.12	5.04	4.17	3.46	2.87	31
32	11.24	9.25	7.62	6.30	5.22	4.34	3.61	3.02	32
33	11.42	9.44	7.82	6.50	5.41	4.52	3.78	3.17	33
34	11.60	9.63	8.02	6.69	5.60	4.70	3.95	3.33	34
35	11.78	9.83	8.22	6.90	5.80	4.89	4.13	3.50	35
36	11.96	10.03	8.44	7.11	6.01	5.09	4.32	3.67	36
37	12.15	10.24	8.65	7.33	6.22	5.30	4.52	3.86	37
38	12.34	10.45	8.88	7.56	6.45	5.51	4.72	4.06	38
39	12.54	10.67	9.11	7.79	6.68	5.74	4.95	4.26	39
40	12.74	10.90	9.34	8.03	6.92	5.97	5.17	4.48	40
41	12.94	11.13	9.59	8.28	7.17	6.22	5.41	4.71	41
42	13.15	11.36	9.84	8.54	7.43	6.48	5.66	4.95	42
43	13.37	11.60	10.10	8.81	7.70	6.74	5.92	5.21	43
44	13.59	11.85	10.36	9.08	7.98	7.02	6.19	5.48	44
45	13.81	12.11	10.64	9.37	8.27	7.32	6.48	5.76	45
46	14.05	12.37	10.93	9.67	8.58	7.62	6.79	6.06	46
47	14.28	12.65	11.22	9.98	8.89	7.94	7.11	6.37	47
48	14.53	12.93	11.53	10.30	9.23	8.28	7.44	6.71	48
49	14.78	13.22	11.84	10.64	9.57	8.63	7.80	7.06	49
50	15.05	13.52	12.17	10.98	9.93	9.00	8.17	7.43	50
51	15.32	13.83	12.51	11.35	10.31	9.39	8.56	7.82	51
52	15.60	14.15	12.87	11.73	10.71	9.79	8.98	8.24	52
53	15.89	14.49	13.24	12.12	11.12	10.22	9.41	8.69	53
54	16.19	14.83	13.62	12.53	11.56	10.67	9.88	9.16	54
55	16.50	15.20	14.02	12.97	12.01	11.15	10.37	9.66	55

(*continued*)

Table 10 Multipliers for loss of pension commencing age 60 (females) (*continued*)

Age at date of trial	Multiplier calculated with allowance for population mortality and rate of return of								Age at date of trial
	1.5%	2.0%	2.5%	3.0%	3.5%	4.0%	4.5%	5.0%	
56	16.83	15.57	14.44	13.42	12.49	11.65	10.88	10.19	56
57	17.17	15.97	14.88	13.89	13.00	12.18	11.43	10.75	57
58	17.54	16.39	15.34	14.40	13.53	12.74	12.02	11.36	58
59	17.92	16.83	15.83	14.93	14.10	13.34	12.64	12.00	59
60	18.32	17.29	16.35	15.49	14.70	13.98	13.31	12.70	60

Table 11 Multipliers for pecuniary loss for life (males)

Age at date of trial	Multiplier calculated with allowance for projected mortality from the 1996-based population projections and rate of return of								Age at date of trial
	1.5%	2.0%	2.5%	3.0%	3.5%	4.0%	4.5%	5.0%	
0	45.80	39.31	34.17	30.05	26.70	23.96	21.68	19.77	0
1	45.73	39.31	34.20	30.10	26.77	24.04	21.76	19.85	1
2	45.43	39.09	34.06	30.00	26.70	23.99	21.73	19.83	2
3	45.11	38.87	33.90	29.89	26.62	23.93	21.69	19.80	3
4	44.78	38.64	33.74	29.78	26.54	23.87	21.64	19.76	4
5	44.45	38.41	35.57	29.66	26.46	23.81	21.60	19.73	5
6	44.11	38.17	33.40	29.54	26.37	23.74	21.55	19.69	6
7	43.76	37.92	33.22	29.41	26.27	23.67	21.50	19.65	7
8	43.41	37.67	33.04	29.28	26.18	23.60	21.44	19.61	8
9	43.05	37.41	32.86	29.14	26.08	23.53	21.38	19.57	9
10	42.69	37.15	32.67	29.00	25.97	23.45	21.33	19.53	10
11	42.32	36.88	32.47	28.85	25.86	23.37	21.26	19.48	11
12	41.94	36.61	32.27	28.70	25.75	23.28	21.20	19.43	12
13	41.57	36.33	32.06	28.55	25.64	23.20	21.13	19.38	13
14	41.18	36.05	31.85	28.40	25.52	23.11	21.06	19.32	14
15	40.79	35.76	31.64	28.24	25.40	23.01	20.99	19.27	15
16	40.40	35.47	31.42	28.07	25.27	22.92	20.92	19.21	16
17	40.01	35.18	31.20	27.91	25.15	22.82	20.84	19.15	17
18	39.62	34.89	30.98	27.74	25.02	22.72	20.77	19.09	18
19	39.22	34.59	30.76	27.57	24.90	22.63	20.70	19.04	19
20	38.83	34.30	30.54	27.40	24.77	22.53	20.62	18.98	20
21	38.42	33.99	30.31	27.23	24.63	22.43	20.54	18.91	21
22	38.02	33.68	30.08	27.05	24.49	22.32	20.46	18.85	22
23	37.60	33.37	29.83	26.87	24.35	22.21	20.37	18.78	23
24	37.18	33.04	29.59	26.67	24.20	22.09	20.28	18.71	24
25	36.75	32.71	29.33	26.48	24.05	21.97	20.18	18.63	25
26	36.31	32.38	29.07	26.27	23.89	21.85	20.08	18.55	26
27	35.87	32.04	28.80	26.06	23.72	21.72	19.98	18.47	27
28	35.42	31.69	28.53	25.85	23.55	21.58	19.87	18.38	28
29	34.97	31.33	28.25	25.63	23.38	21.44	19.76	18.29	29
30	34.50	30.96	27.96	25.40	23.19	21.29	19.64	18.20	30
31	34.02	30.59	27.66	25.16	23.00	21.14	19.51	18.10	31
32	33.54	30.20	27.36	24.91	22.81	20.98	19.38	17.99	32
33	33.05	29.81	27.04	24.66	22.60	20.81	19.25	17.88	33
34	32.56	29.42	26.72	24.40	22.39	20.64	19.11	17.76	34
35	32.05	29.01	26.39	24.13	22.17	20.46	18.96	17.64	35
36	31.54	28.59	26.05	23.85	21.94	20.27	18.80	17.51	36
37	31.01	28.16	25.70	23.57	21.70	20.07	18.64	17.37	37
38	30.48	27.73	25.34	23.27	21.46	19.87	18.47	17.23	38
39	29.94	27.29	24.98	22.97	21.21	19.66	18.29	17.08	39
40	29.40	26.84	24.61	22.66	20.95	19.44	18.11	16.92	40
41	28.85	26.38	24.23	22.34	20.68	19.22	17.92	16.76	41
42	28.29	25.92	23.84	22.02	20.41	18.98	17.72	16.59	42
43	27.73	25.44	23.44	21.68	20.13	18.74	17.52	16.42	43
44	27.15	24.96	23.04	21.34	19.83	18.49	17.30	16.23	44
45	26.57	24.47	22.62	20.98	19.53	18.23	17.08	16.04	45
46	25.98	23.96	22.19	20.61	19.21	17.96	16.84	15.84	46
47	25.37	23.45	21.75	20.23	18.89	17.68	16.60	15.62	47
48	24.76	22.93	21.30	19.85	18.55	17.39	16.34	15.40	48
49	24.14	22.39	20.84	19.45	18.20	17.08	16.08	15.16	49
50	23.52	21.86	20.37	19.04	17.85	16.78	15.80	14.93	50
51	22.90	21.32	19.90	18.63	17.49	16.46	15.53	14.68	51
52	22.28	20.78	19.43	18.22	17.12	16.14	15.24	14.43	52
53	21.65	20.23	18.95	17.79	16.75	15.80	14.95	14.16	53
54	21.02	19.67	18.46	17.36	16.37	15.46	14.64	13.89	54
55	20.38	19.11	17.96	16.92	15.98	15.12	14.33	13.62	55

(*continued*)

Table 11 Multipliers for pecuniary loss for life (males) (*continued*)

Age at date of trial	Multiplier calculated with allowance for projected mortality from the 1996-based population projections and rate of return of 1.5%	2.0%	2.5%	3.0%	3.5%	4.0%	4.5%	5.0%	Age at date of trial
56	19.75	18.55	17.47	16.48	15.58	14.77	14.02	13.33	56
57	19.12	17.99	16.97	16.04	15.19	14.41	13.70	13.04	57
58	18.50	17.44	16.47	15.59	14.78	14.05	13.37	12.74	58
59	17.87	16.87	15.97	15.14	14.38	13.68	13.03	12.44	59
60	17.24	16.31	15.46	14.68	13.96	13.30	12.69	12.13	60
61	16.61	15.74	14.94	14.21	13.54	12.92	12.34	11.81	61
62	15.98	15.17	14.43	13.74	13.11	12.52	11.98	11.48	62
63	15.35	14.60	13.90	13.26	12.67	12.12	11.62	11.14	63
64	14.72	14.02	13.38	12.78	12.23	11.72	11.24	10.80	64
65	14.09	13.45	12.85	12.30	11.78	11.31	10.86	10.45	65
66	13.46	12.87	12.32	11.81	11.33	10.89	10.48	10.09	66
67	12.85	12.30	11.80	11.32	10.88	10.47	10.09	9.73	67
68	12.24	11.74	11.28	10.84	10.44	10.06	9.70	9.36	68
69	11.64	11.19	10.76	10.36	9.99	9.64	9.31	9.00	69
70	11.06	10.65	10.26	9.89	9.55	9.23	8.92	8.64	70
71	10.51	10.13	9.77	9.44	9.12	8.83	8.55	8.29	71
72	9.97	9.63	9.30	9.00	8.71	8.44	8.18	7.94	72
73	9.45	9.14	8.84	8.56	8.30	8.05	7.82	7.59	73
74	8.95	8.67	8.40	8.15	7.91	7.68	7.46	7.26	74
75	8.46	8.21	7.97	7.74	7.52	7.31	7.11	6.93	75
76	8.00	7.77	7.55	7.34	7.14	6.95	6.77	6.60	76
77	7.56	7.35	7.15	6.96	6.78	6.61	6.45	6.29	77
78	7.14	6.95	6.77	6.60	6.43	6.28	6.13	5.99	78
79	6.73	6.56	6.40	6.25	6.10	5.96	5.82	5.70	79
80	6.35	6.20	6.06	5.92	5.78	5.65	5.53	5.41	80
81	6.00	5.86	5.73	5.60	5.48	5.36	5.25	5.14	81
82	5.66	5.54	5.42	5.30	5.19	5.09	4.99	4.89	82
83	5.35	5.24	5.13	5.03	4.93	4.83	4.74	4.65	83
84	5.07	4.97	4.87	4.78	4.69	4.60	4.52	4.53	84
85	4.81	4.72	4.63	4.54	4.46	4.38	4.30	4.23	85
86	4.56	4.48	4.40	4.32	4.24	4.17	4.10	4.04	86
87	4.32	4.24	4.17	4.10	4.03	3.96	3.90	3.84	87
88	4.07	4.01	3.94	3.88	3.82	3.76	3.70	3.64	88
89	3.84	3.78	3.72	3.66	3.61	3.56	3.50	3.45	89
90	3.62	3.56	3.51	3.46	3.41	3.36	3.32	3.27	90
91	3.40	3.35	3.31	3.26	3.22	3.17	3.13	3.09	91
92	3.19	3.14	3.10	3.06	3.02	2.99	2.95	2.91	92
93	2.99	2.96	2.92	2.88	2.85	2.81	2.78	2.75	93
94	2.82	2.78	2.75	2.72	2.69	2.66	2.63	2.60	94
95	2.65	2.62	2.59	2.56	2.53	2.50	2.48	2.45	95
96	2.48	2.45	2.43	2.40	2.38	2.35	2.33	2.31	96
97	2.32	2.29	2.27	2.25	2.23	2.21	2.19	2.16	97
98	2.15	2.13	2.11	2.10	2.08	2.06	2.04	2.02	98
99	1.99	1.98	1.96	1.94	1.93	1.91	1.90	1.88	99
100	1.83	1.82	1.81	1.79	1.78	1.76	1.75	1.74	100

Table 12 Multipliers for pecuniary loss for life (females)

Age at date of trial	Multiplier calculated with allowance for projected mortality from the 1996-based population mortality and rate of return of								Age at date of trial
	1.5%	2.0%	2.5%	3.0%	3.5%	4.0%	4.5%	5.0%	
0	47.34	40.38	34.93	30.59	27.10	24.25	21.90	19.94	0
1	47.25	40.36	34.95	30.64	27.16	24.31	21.97	20.01	1
2	46.97	40.18	34.82	30.55	27.10	24.28	21.94	19.99	2
3	46.67	39.97	34.69	30.46	27.04	24.23	21.91	19.97	3
4	46.37	39.77	34.54	30.36	26.97	24.18	21.88	19.94	4
5	46.06	39.55	34.40	30.26	26.89	24.13	21.84	19.92	5
6	45.74	39.34	34.24	30.15	26.82	24.08	21.80	19.89	6
7	45.42	39.11	34.09	30.04	26.74	24.02	21.76	19.86	7
8	45.09	38.88	33.93	29.93	26.66	23.97	21.72	19.83	8
9	44.76	38.65	33.76	29.81	26.58	23.91	21.68	19.80	9
10	44.42	38.41	33.59	29.69	26.49	23.84	21.63	19.76	10
11	44.08	38.17	33.42	29.56	26.40	23.78	21.58	19.72	11
12	43.73	37.92	33.24	29.44	26.31	23.71	21.53	19.69	12
13	43.38	37.67	33.06	29.30	26.21	23.64	21.48	19.65	13
14	43.02	37.41	32.87	29.17	26.11	23.56	21.42	19.60	14
15	42.65	37.15	32.68	29.03	26.01	23.48	21.36	19.56	15
16	42.29	36.88	32.49	28.89	25.90	23.41	21.30	19.52	16
17	41.91	36.61	32.29	28.74	25.79	23.32	21.24	19.47	17
18	41.54	36.34	32.09	28.59	25.68	23.24	21.18	19.42	18
19	41.15	36.05	31.88	28.43	25.56	23.15	21.11	19.37	19
20	40.77	35.77	31.67	28.28	25.44	23.06	21.04	19.32	20
21	40.37	35.48	31.45	28.11	25.32	22.97	20.97	19.26	21
22	39.97	35.18	31.23	27.94	25.19	22.87	20.90	19.20	22
23	39.57	34.88	31.00	27.77	25.06	22.77	20.82	19.14	23
24	39.16	34.57	30.77	27.59	24.93	22.67	20.74	19.08	24
25	38.74	34.25	30.53	27.41	24.79	22.56	20.65	19.01	25
26	38.32	33.93	30.28	27.22	24.64	22.44	20.56	18.94	26
27	37.89	33.61	30.03	27.03	24.49	22.33	20.47	18.87	27
28	37.46	33.27	29.78	26.83	24.34	22.21	20.38	18.79	28
29	37.01	32.93	29.51	26.63	24.18	22.08	20.28	18.71	29
30	36.57	32.59	29.24	26.42	24.01	21.95	20.17	18.63	30
31	36.11	32.23	28.97	26.20	23.84	21.81	20.06	18.54	31
32	35.65	31.87	28.68	25.98	23.66	21.67	19.95	18.45	32
33	35.18	31.50	28.39	25.75	23.48	21.52	19.83	18.35	33
34	34.70	31.13	28.10	25.51	23.29	21.37	19.71	18.25	34
35	34.22	30.74	27.79	25.26	23.09	21.21	19.58	18.15	35
36	33.73	30.35	27.48	25.01	22.89	21.05	19.44	18.04	36
37	33.23	29.96	27.16	24.75	22.68	20.88	19.30	17.92	37
38	32.72	29.55	26.83	24.49	22.46	20.70	19.16	17.80	38
39	32.21	29.14	26.50	24.22	22.24	20.51	19.00	17.67	39
40	31.69	28.72	26.16	23.94	22.01	20.33	18.85	17.54	40
41	31.17	28.29	25.81	23.65	21.77	20.13	18.68	17.41	41
42	30.64	27.86	25.45	23.36	21.53	19.93	18.51	17.26	42
43	30.10	27.42	25.09	23.06	21.28	19.72	18.34	17.12	43
44	29.56	26.97	24.71	22.75	21.02	19.50	18.16	16.96	44
45	29.00	26.51	24.33	22.43	20.75	19.28	17.97	16.80	45
46	28.44	26.04	23.94	22.10	20.48	19.04	17.77	16.63	46
47	27.88	25.57	23.55	21.77	20.20	18.80	17.56	16.46	47
48	27.30	25.09	23.14	21.42	19.90	18.55	17.35	16.27	48
49	26.72	24.60	22.73	21.07	19.60	18.30	17.13	16.08	49
50	26.14	24.10	22.30	20.71	19.30	18.03	16.90	15.88	50
51	25.54	23.60	21.87	20.34	18.98	17.76	16.66	15.68	51
52	24.95	23.09	21.44	19.97	18.65	17.48	16.42	15.47	52
53	24.36	22.58	21.00	19.59	18.33	17.20	16.17	15.25	53
54	23.78	22.09	20.58	19.22	18.01	16.92	15.93	15.04	54
55	23.21	21.59	20.15	18.85	17.69	16.64	15.68	14.82	55

(*continued*)

Table 12 Multipliers for pecuniary loss for life (females) (*continued*)

Age at date of trial	Multiplier calculated with allowance for projected mortality from the 1996-based population mortality and rate of return of								Age at date of trial
	1.5%	2.0%	2.5%	3.0%	3.5%	4.0%	4.5%	5.0%	
56	22.63	21.10	19.72	18.47	17.36	16.35	15.43	14.60	56
57	22.05	20.59	19.27	18.09	17.02	16.05	15.16	14.36	57
58	21.46	20.07	18.82	17.69	16.66	15.74	14.89	14.12	58
59	20.85	19.54	18.35	17.27	16.30	15.41	14.60	13.86	59
60	20.22	18.98	17.86	16.84	15.91	15.07	14.29	13.58	60
61	19.57	18.40	17.35	16.38	15.50	14.70	13.97	13.29	61
62	18.90	17.81	16.81	15.91	15.08	14.32	13.62	12.98	62
63	18.21	17.19	16.26	15.41	14.63	13.92	13.26	12.65	63
64	17.52	16.57	15.70	14.90	14.17	13.50	12.88	12.31	64
65	16.81	15.94	15.13	14.39	13.70	13.07	12.49	11.95	65
66	16.11	15.30	14.55	13.86	13.23	12.64	12.09	11.59	66
67	15.42	14.67	13.98	13.34	12.75	12.20	11.69	11.22	67
68	14.75	14.05	13.42	12.82	12.27	11.76	11.29	10.85	68
69	14.08	13.45	12.86	12.31	11.80	11.33	10.89	10.47	69
70	13.44	12.85	12.31	11.81	11.34	10.90	10.49	10.11	70
71	12.8	12.28	11.79	11.32	10.89	10.48	10.10	9.74	71
72	12.2	11.74	11.28	10.85	10.45	10.08	9.72	9.39	72
73	11.7	11.21	11.79	10.40	10.03	9.68	9.35	9.05	73
74	11.1	10.69	10.31	9.94	9.60	9.28	8.98	8.70	74
75	10.6	10.18	9.83	9.50	9.19	8.89	8.61	8.35	75
76	10.0	9.68	9.36	9.06	8.77	8.50	8.25	8.00	76
77	9.5	9.19	8.90	8.62	8.36	8.11	7.88	7.66	77
78	9.0	8.70	8.44	8.19	7.95	7.73	7.51	7.31	78
79	8.5	8.22	7.99	7.76	7.55	7.34	7.15	6.96	79
80	8.0	7.76	7.55	7.34	7.15	6.96	6.79	6.62	80
81	7.5	7.32	7.12	6.94	6.76	6.60	6.44	6.28	81
82	7.1	6.89	6.72	6.55	6.39	6.24	6.10	5.96	82
83	6.7	6.49	6.33	6.19	6.04	5.91	5.78	5.65	83
84	6.3	6.12	5.98	5.85	5.72	5.59	5.47	5.36	84
85	5.9	5.78	5.65	5.53	5.42	5.30	5.20	5.09	85
86	5.6	5.46	5.35	5.24	5.13	5.03	4.93	4.84	86
87	5.3	5.16	5.06	4.96	4.86	4.77	4.68	4.60	87
88	5.0	4.88	4.79	4.70	4.61	4.53	4.45	4.37	88
89	4.7	4.62	4.53	4.45	4.37	4.30	4.22	4.15	89
90	4.5	4.37	4.30	4.22	4.15	4.08	4.02	3.95	90
91	4.2	4.13	4.07	4.00	3.93	3.87	3.81	3.75	91
92	4.0	3.90	3.84	3.78	3.72	3.67	3.61	3.56	92
93	3.7	3.68	3.62	3.57	3.52	3.47	3.42	3.37	93
94	3.5	3.46	3.41	3.36	3.32	3.27	3.23	3.18	94
95	3.3	3.25	3.21	3.16	3.12	3.08	3.04	3.00	95
96	3.1	3.05	3.01	2.97	2.93	2.90	2.86	2.83	96
97	2.9	2.87	2.83	2.80	2.77	2.73	2.70	2.67	97
98	2.7	2.70	2.67	2.64	2.61	2.58	2.55	2.53	98
99	2.6	2.53	2.51	2.48	2.45	2.43	2.40	2.38	99
100	2.4	2.37	2.34	2.32	2.29	2.27	2.25	2.23	100

Table 13 Multipliers for loss of earnings to pension age 65 (males)

Age at date of trial	Multiplier calculated with allowance for projected mortality from the 1996-based population mortality and rate of return of								Age at date of trial
	1.5%	2.0%	2.5%	3.0%	3.5%	4.0%	4.5%	5.0%	
16	33.83	30.56	27.74	25.30	23.19	21.34	19.72	18.30	16
17	33.34	30.17	27.43	25.05	22.99	21.18	19.59	18.20	17
18	32.85	29.78	27.12	24.80	22.79	21.02	19.47	18.09	18
19	32.36	29.38	26.80	24.55	22.58	20.85	19.33	17.99	19
20	31.86	28.98	26.48	24.29	22.37	20.68	19.19	17.87	20
21	31.35	28.57	26.15	24.02	22.15	20.51	19.05	17.76	21
22	30.84	28.16	25.81	23.75	21.93	20.32	18.90	17.63	22
23	30.32	27.73	25.46	23.46	21.70	20.13	18.74	17.50	23
24	29.78	27.29	25.10	23.17	21.46	19.93	18.58	17.37	24
25	29.25	26.85	24.74	22.87	21.21	19.73	18.41	17.23	25
26	28.70	26.40	24.36	22.56	20.95	19.51	18.23	17.08	26
27	28.15	25.94	23.98	22.24	20.68	19.29	18.04	16.92	27
28	27.58	25.47	23.59	21.91	20.41	19.06	17.85	16.76	28
29	27.01	24.99	23.18	21.57	20.12	18.82	17.64	16.59	29
30	26.43	24.50	22.77	21.22	19.82	18.57	17.43	16.40	30
31	25.84	24.00	22.34	20.86	19.52	18.30	17.21	16.21	31
32	25.24	23.49	21.91	20.49	19.20	18.03	16.98	16.01	32
33	24.63	22.97	21.46	20.10	18.87	17.75	16.73	15.80	33
34	24.02	22.44	21.01	19.71	18.53	17.46	16.48	15.59	34
35	23.39	21.90	20.54	19.30	18.18	17.15	16.21	15.36	35
36	22.76	21.34	20.06	18.89	17.81	16.83	15.94	15.11	36
37	22.11	20.78	19.56	18.45	17.44	16.50	15.65	14.86	37
38	21.45	20.20	19.06	18.01	17.05	16.16	15.34	14.59	38
39	20.79	19.62	18.54	17.55	16.64	15.80	15.03	14.31	39
40	20.12	19.02	18.02	17.09	16.23	15.44	14.70	14.02	40
41	19.44	18.42	17.48	16.61	15.80	15.05	14.36	13.72	41
42	18.75	17.80	16.93	16.12	15.36	14.66	14.01	13.40	42
43	18.05	17.18	16.37	15.61	14.91	14.25	13.64	13.07	43
44	17.34	16.54	15.79	15.09	14.44	13.82	13.25	12.72	44
45	16.63	15.89	15.20	14.55	13.95	13.38	12.85	12.35	45
46	15.90	15.22	14.59	14.00	13.44	12.92	12.43	11.97	46
47	15.15	14.54	13.97	13.43	12.92	12.44	11.99	11.56	47
48	14.40	13.85	13.33	12.84	12.38	11.94	11.53	11.14	48
49	13.64	13.15	12.69	12.24	11.83	11.43	11.05	10.70	49
50	12.88	12.44	12.02	11.63	11.25	10.90	10.56	10.24	50
51	12.10	11.72	11.35	11.00	10.67	10.35	10.04	9.76	51
52	11.32	10.98	10.66	10.35	10.06	9.78	9.51	9.25	52
53	10.52	10.23	9.96	9.69	9.44	9.19	8.96	8.73	53
54	9.72	9.48	9.24	9.01	8.79	8.58	8.38	8.18	54
55	8.91	8.70	8.50	8.31	8.13	7.95	7.78	7.61	55
56	8.09	7.92	7.75	7.59	7.44	7.29	7.15	7.01	56
57	7.25	7.12	6.99	6.86	6.73	6.61	6.50	6.38	57
58	6.41	6.30	6.20	6.10	6.00	5.91	5.81	5.72	58
59	5.55	5.47	5.39	5.32	5.24	5.17	5.10	5.03	59
60	4.67	4.62	4.56	4.51	4.46	4.41	4.36	4.31	60
61	3.78	3.75	3.71	3.67	3.64	3.61	3.57	3.54	61
62	2.87	2.85	2.83	2.81	2.79	2.77	2.75	2.73	62
63	1.94	1.93	1.92	1.91	1.90	1.89	1.89	1.88	63
64	0.98	0.98	0.98	0.98	0.97	0.97	0.97	0.97	64

Table 14 Multipliers for loss of earnings to pension age 65 (females)

Age at date of trial	Multiplier calculated with allowance for projected mortality from the 1996-based population projections and rate of return of								Age at date of trial
	1.5%	2.0%	2.5%	3.0%	3.5%	4.0%	4.5%	5.0%	
16	34.22	30.89	28.03	25.55	23.40	21.53	19.89	18.45	16
17	33.73	30.50	27.72	25.31	23.21	21.37	19.76	18.35	17
18	33.23	30.11	27.40	25.05	23.01	21.21	19.63	18.24	18
19	32.73	29.70	27.08	24.79	22.80	21.04	19.50	18.13	19
20	32.22	29.29	26.75	24.53	22.58	20.87	19.36	18.02	20
21	31.70	28.87	26.41	24.25	22.36	20.69	19.21	17.90	21
22	31.17	28.45	26.06	23.97	22.13	20.50	19.06	17.77	22
23	30.64	28.01	25.71	23.68	21.89	20.30	18.90	17.64	23
24	30.10	27.57	25.34	23.38	21.64	20.10	18.73	17.50	24
25	29.55	27.12	24.97	23.07	21.39	19.89	18.55	17.36	25
26	28.99	26.66	24.59	22.76	21.13	19.67	18.37	17.21	26
27	28.43	26.19	24.20	22.43	20.86	19.45	18.18	17.05	27
28	27.86	25.71	23.80	22.10	20.58	19.21	17.99	16.88	28
29	27.28	25.22	23.39	21.75	20.29	18.97	17.78	16.71	29
30	26.69	24.73	22.97	21.40	19.99	18.71	17.56	16.52	30
31	26.09	24.22	22.54	21.03	19.68	18.45	17.34	16.33	31
32	25.48	23.70	22.10	20.66	19.35	18.17	17.10	16.13	32
33	24.87	23.18	21.65	20.27	19.02	17.89	16.86	15.92	33
34	24.24	22.64	21.19	19.87	18.68	17.59	16.60	15.70	34
35	23.61	22.09	20.72	19.47	18.33	17.29	16.33	15.47	35
36	22.97	21.54	20.23	19.04	17.96	16.97	16.06	15.22	36
37	22.32	20.97	19.74	18.61	17.58	16.64	15.77	14.97	37
38	21.66	20.39	19.23	18.17	17.19	16.29	15.46	14.70	38
39	20.99	19.81	18.71	17.71	16.79	15.94	15.15	14.42	39
40	20.32	19.21	18.19	17.24	16.37	15.57	14.82	14.13	40
41	19.63	18.60	17.64	16.76	15.94	15.18	14.48	13.83	41
42	18.94	17.98	17.09	16.27	15.50	14.79	14.13	13.51	42
43	18.24	17.35	16.53	15.76	15.04	14.38	13.76	13.18	43
44	17.53	16.71	15.95	15.24	14.57	13.95	13.37	12.83	44
45	16.81	16.06	15.35	14.70	14.08	13.51	12.97	12.46	45
46	16.08	15.39	14.75	14.15	13.58	13.05	12.55	12.08	46
47	15.33	14.71	14.13	13.58	13.06	12.57	12.11	11.68	47
48	14.58	14.02	13.49	13.00	12.52	12.08	11.66	11.26	48
49	13.82	13.32	12.85	12.40	11.97	11.57	11.18	10.82	49
50	13.05	12.61	12.18	11.78	11.40	11.03	10.69	10.36	50
51	12.27	11.88	11.50	11.15	10.81	10.48	10.17	9.88	51
52	11.48	11.14	10.81	10.49	10.20	9.91	9.64	9.37	52
53	10.68	10.38	10.10	9.83	9.57	9.32	9.08	8.85	53
54	9.87	9.62	9.38	9.14	8.92	8.70	8.50	8.30	54
55	9.05	8.84	8.63	8.44	8.25	8.07	7.89	7.72	55
56	8.21	8.04	7.87	7.71	7.55	7.40	7.26	7.11	56
57	7.37	7.23	7.09	6.96	6.84	6.71	6.59	6.48	57
58	6.50	6.40	6.29	6.19	6.09	5.99	5.90	5.81	58
59	5.63	5.55	5.47	5.39	5.32	5.24	5.17	5.10	59
60	4.73	4.68	4.62	4.57	4.51	4.46	4.41	4.36	60
61	3.82	3.79	3.75	3.72	3.68	3.65	3.61	3.58	61
62	2.90	2.88	2.86	2.84	2.82	2.80	2.78	2.76	62
63	1.95	1.94	1.93	1.92	1.92	1.91	1.90	1.89	63
64	0.99	0.99	0.98	0.98	0.98	0.98	0.97	0.97	64

Table 15 Multipliers for loss of earnings to pension age 60 (males)

Age at date of trial	Multiplier calculated with allowance for projected mortality from the 1996-based population projections and rate of return of 1.5%	2.0%	2.5%	3.0%	3.5%	4.0%	4.5%	5.0%	Age at date of trial
16	31.58	28.77	26.31	24.16	22.28	20.61	19.14	17.84	16
17	31.06	28.34	25.97	23.88	22.05	20.42	18.99	17.71	17
18	30.53	27.91	25.62	23.60	21.81	20.23	18.83	17.58	18
19	30.00	27.48	25.26	23.30	21.57	20.04	18.67	17.45	19
20	29.47	27.04	24.90	23.01	21.33	19.83	18.50	17.31	20
21	28.92	26.59	24.53	22.70	21.07	19.62	18.32	17.16	21
22	28.37	26.13	24.15	22.38	20.81	19.40	18.14	17.01	22
23	27.81	25.67	23.76	22.06	20.54	19.17	17.95	16.85	23
24	27.24	25.19	23.36	21.72	20.25	18.94	17.75	16.68	24
25	26.66	24.70	22.95	21.38	19.96	18.69	17.54	16.50	25
26	26.08	24.21	22.53	21.02	19.66	18.43	17.32	16.31	26
27	25.48	23.70	22.10	20.65	19.35	18.17	17.09	16.12	27
28	24.88	23.19	21.66	20.28	19.02	17.89	16.86	15.92	28
29	24.27	22.66	21.21	19.89	18.69	17.60	16.61	15.70	29
30	23.64	22.12	20.74	19.49	18.34	17.30	16.35	15.48	30
31	23.01	21.57	20.26	19.07	17.98	16.99	16.08	15.24	31
32	22.37	21.01	19.78	18.65	17.61	16.66	15.79	14.99	32
33	21.72	20.44	19.28	18.21	17.23	16.32	15.49	14.73	33
34	21.06	19.86	18.77	17.76	16.83	15.97	15.18	14.46	34
35	20.38	19.27	18.24	17.29	16.42	15.61	14.86	14.17	35
36	19.70	18.66	17.70	16.81	15.99	15.23	14.52	13.86	36
37	19.01	18,04	17.15	16.32	15.55	14.83	14.17	13.55	37
38	18.30	17.41	16.58	15.81	15.09	14.42	13.80	13.21	38
39	17.59	16.77	16.00	15.29	14.62	14.00	13.41	12.87	39
40	16.87	16.12	15.41	14.75	14.13	13.55	13.01	12.50	40
41	16.14	15.45	14.81	14.20	13.63	13.10	12.59	12.12	41
42	15.40	14.77	14.19	13.63	13.11	12.62	12.16	11.72	42
43	14.65	14.08	13.55	13.05	12.58	12.13	11.70	11.30	43
44	13.89	13.38	12.90	12.45	12.02	11.62	11.23	10.86	44
45	13.11	12.66	12.24	11.83	11.45	11.08	10.73	10.40	45
46	12.33	11.93	11.55	11.19	10.85	10.53	10.22	9.92	46
47	11.53	11.18	10.85	10.54	10.24	9.95	9.67	9.41	47
48	10.72	10.42	10.13	9.86	9.60	9.35	9.11	8.88	48
49	9.90	9.64	9.40	9.17	8.94	8.73	8.52	8.32	49
50	9.07	8.85	8.65	8.45	8.26	8.08	7.90	7.73	50
51	8.22	8.05	7.88	7.72	7.56	7.41	7.26	7.12	51
52	7.37	7.23	7.10	6.97	6.84	6.72	6.60	6.48	52
53	6.50	6.40	6.29	6.19	6.09	5.99	5.90	5.81	53
54	5.62	5.54	5.47	5.39	5.32	5.24	5.17	5.10	54
55	4.73	4.67	4.62	4.57	4.51	4.46	4.41	4.36	55
56	3.82	3.79	3.75	3.71	3.68	3.65	3.61	3.58	56
57	2.90	2.88	2.85	2.83	2.81	2.79	2.78	2.76	57
58	1.95	1.94	1.93	1.92	1.92	1.91	1.90	1.89	58
59	0.99	0.99	0.98	0.98	0.98	0.98	0.97	0.97	59

Table 16 Multipliers for loss of earnings to pension age 60 (females)

Age at date of trial	Multiplier calculated with allowance for projected mortality from the 1996-based population projections and rate of return of								Age at date of trial
	1.5%	2.0%	2.5%	3.0%	3.5%	4.0%	4.5%	5.0%	
16	31.88	29.03	26.55	24.37	22.46	20.77	19.28	17.96	16
17	31.36	28.61	26.20	24.09	22.23	20.59	19.13	17.84	17
18	30.83	28.17	25.85	23.80	21.99	20.40	18.98	17.71	18
19	30.29	27.73	25.49	23.50	21.75	20.19	18.81	17.57	19
20	29.74	27.28	25.11	23.20	21.50	19.99	18.64	17.43	20
21	29.18	26.82	24.73	22.88	21.24	19.77	18.46	17.28	21
22	28.62	26.35	24.35	22.56	20.97	19.55	18.27	17.12	22
23	28.05	25.88	23.95	22.23	20.69	19.31	18.07	16.96	23
24	27.47	25.39	23.54	21.88	20.40	19.07	17.87	16.79	24
25	26.88	24.90	23.12	21.53	20.10	18.82	17.66	16.61	25
26	26.28	24.39	22.69	21.17	19.80	18.56	17.43	16.42	26
27	25.68	23.88	22.26	20.80	19.48	18.28	17.20	16.22	27
28	25.06	23.35	21.81	20.41	19.15	18.00	16.96	16.01	28
29	24.44	22.82	21.35	20.02	18.81	17.71	16.71	15.79	29
30	23.81	22.27	20.88	19.61	18.46	17.41	16.44	15.56	30
31	23.17	21.72	20.40	19.19	18.09	17.09	16.17	15.32	31
32	22.52	21.15	19.90	18.76	17.72	16.76	15.88	15.07	32
33	21.86	20.57	19.40	18.32	17.33	16.42	15.58	14.81	33
34	21.19	19.98	18.88	17.86	16.93	16.06	15.27	14.53	34
35	20.51	19.38	18.35	17.39	16.51	15.69	14.94	14.24	35
36	19.82	18.77	17.80	16.91	16.08	15.31	14.60	13.94	36
37	19.12	18.15	17.25	16.41	15.64	14.91	14.24	13.62	37
38	18.42	17.52	16.68	15.90	15.18	14.50	13.87	13.28	38
39	17.70	16.87	16.10	15.38	14.70	14.07	13.48	12.93	39
40	16.97	16.21	15.50	14.84	14.21	13.63	13.08	12.57	40
41	16.24	15.54	14.89	14.28	13.71	13.17	12.66	12.18	41
42	15.49	14.86	14.27	13.71	13.18	12.69	12.22	11.78	42
43	14.73	14.17	13.63	13.12	12.64	12.19	11.77	11.36	43
44	13.97	13.46	12.98	12.52	12.09	11.68	11.29	10.92	44
45	13.19	12.74	12.31	11.90	11.51	11.14	10.79	10.46	45
46	12.40	12.00	11.62	11.26	10.91	10.59	10.27	9.97	46
47	11.60	11.25	10.92	10.60	10.30	10.01	9.73	9.46	47
48	10.79	10.49	10.20	9.93	9.66	9.41	9.16	8.93	48
49	9.97	9.71	9.46	9.23	9.00	8.78	8.57	8.37	49
50	9.13	8.92	8.71	8.51	8.32	8.14	7.96	7.79	50
51	8.28	8.11	7.94	7.77	7.62	7.46	7.31	7.17	51
52	7.42	7.28	7.15	7.01	6.89	6.76	6.64	6.52	52
53	6.55	6.44	6.34	6.23	6.13	6.03	5.94	5.85	53
54	5.66	5.58	5.50	5.43	5.35	5.28	5.21	5.13	54
55	4.76	4.71	4.65	4.59	4.54	4.49	4.44	4.39	55
56	3.84	3.81	3.77	3.74	3.70	3.67	3.63	3.60	56
57	2.91	2.89	2.87	2.85	2.83	2.81	2.79	2.77	57
58	1.96	1.95	1.94	1.93	1.92	1.91	1.90	1.90	58
59	0.99	0.99	0.98	0.98	0.98	0.98	0.98	0.97	59

Table 17 Multipliers for loss of pension commencing age 65 (males)

Age at date of trial	Multiplier calculated with allowance for projected mortality from the 1996-based population projections and rate of return of								Age at date of trial
	1.5%	2.0%	2.5%	3.0%	3.5%	4.0%	4.5%	5.0%	
0	5.17	3.58	2.48	1.72	1.20	0.84	0.59	0.42	0
1	5.28	3.67	2.55	1.79	1.25	0.88	0.62	0.44	1
2	5.36	3.74	2.62	1.84	1.30	0.91	0.65	0.46	2
3	5.44	3.81	2.68	1.89	1.34	0.95	0.68	0.48	3
4	5.52	3.89	2.75	1.95	1.39	0.99	0.71	0.51	4
5	5.60	3.97	2.82	2.01	1.44	1.03	0.74	0.53	5
6	5.68	4.05	2.89	2.07	1.48	1.07	0.77	0.56	6
7	5.77	4.13	2.96	2.13	1.54	1.11	0.81	0.59	7
8	5.85	4.21	3.03	2.19	1.59	1.16	0.84	0.62	8
9	5.94	4.29	3.11	2.26	1.64	1.20	0.88	0.65	9
10	6.02	4.37	3.18	2.32	1.70	1.25	0.92	0.68	10
11	6.11	4.46	3.26	2.39	1.76	1.30	0.96	0.71	11
12	6.20	4.55	3.34	2.46	1.82	1.35	1.00	0.75	12
13	6.29	4.63	3.42	2.54	1.88	1.40	1.05	0.78	13
14	6.38	4.73	3.51	2.61	1.95	1.46	1.09	0.82	14
15	6.48	4.82	3.59	2.69	2.02	1.52	1.14	0.86	15
16	6.57	4.91	3.68	2.77	2.09	1.58	1.19	0.91	16
17	6.67	5.01	3.77	2.85	2.16	1.64	1.25	0.95	17
18	6.77	5.11	3.87	2.94	2.23	1.70	1.30	1.00	18
19	6.87	5.21	2.96	3.02	2.31	1.77	1.36	1.05	19
20	6.97	5.31	4.06	3.11	2.39	1.84	1.42	1.10	20
21	7.07	5.42	4.17	3.21	2.48	1.92	1.49	1.16	21
22	7.18	5.53	4.27	3.30	2.56	1.99	1.56	1.22	22
23	7.29	5.64	4.38	3.40	2.65	2.07	1.63	1.28	23
24	7.39	5.75	4.48	3.50	2.75	2.16	1.70	1.34	24
25	7.50	5.86	4.60	3.61	2.84	2.24	1.77	1.41	25
26	7.61	5.98	4.71	3.72	2.94	2.33	1.85	1.48	26
27	7.73	6.10	4.83	3.83	3.04	2.43	1.94	1.55	27
28	7.84	6.22	4.94	3.94	3.15	2.52	2.02	1.63	28
29	7.95	6.34	5.07	4.06	3.26	2.62	2.11	1.71	29
30	8.07	6.46	5.19	4.18	3.37	2.73	2.21	1.79	30
31	8.18	6.59	5.32	4.30	3.49	2.83	2.31	1.88	31
32	8.30	6.72	5.45	4.43	3.61	2.94	2.41	1.97	32
33	8.42	6.85	5.58	4.56	3.73	3.06	2.52	2.07	33
34	8.54	6.98	5.72	4.69	3.86	3.18	2.63	2.17	34
35	8.66	7.11	5.85	4.83	3.99	3.31	2.74	2.28	35
36	8.78	7.25	5.99	4.97	4.13	3.44	2.87	2.39	36
37	8.90	7.39	6.14	5.11	4.27	3.57	2.99	2.51	37
38	9.03	7.53	6.29	5.26	4.41	3.71	3.12	2.64	38
39	9.15	7.67	6.44	5.41	4.56	3.85	3.26	2.77	39
40	9.28	7.81	6.59	5.57	4.72	4.01	3.41	2.90	40
41	9.41	7.96	6.75	5.73	4.88	4.16	3.56	3.04	41
42	9.54	8.11	6.91	5.90	5.05	4.33	3.71	3.19	42
43	9.67	8.27	7.08	6.07	5.22	4.49	3.88	3.35	43
44	9.81	8.42	7.25	6.25	5.40	4.67	4.05	3.52	44
45	9.94	8.58	7.42	6.43	5.58	4.85	4.23	3.69	45
46	10.08	8.74	7.60	6.61	5.77	5.04	4.41	3.87	46
47	10.22	8.91	7.78	6.80	5.96	5.24	4.61	4.06	47
48	10.36	9.07	7.96	7.00	6.17	5.44	4.81	4.26	48
49	10.50	9.24	8.15	7.20	6.38	5.65	5.02	4.47	49
50	10.65	9.42	8.35	7.42	6.60	5.88	5.25	4.69	50
51	10.80	9.60	8.56	7.64	6.83	6.11	5.48	4.92	51
52	10.96	9.79	8.77	7.86	7.07	6.36	5.73	5.17	52
53	11.12	9.99	8.99	8.10	7.31	6.61	5.99	5.43	53
54	11.29	10.20	9.22	8.35	7.58	6.88	6.27	5.71	54
55	11.47	10.41	9.46	8.61	7.85	7.17	6.56	6.01	55

(continued)

Table 17 Multipliers for loss of pension commencing age 65 (males) (*continued*)

Age at date of trial	Multiplier calculated with allowance for projected mortality from the 1996-based population projections and rate of return of								Age at date of trial
	1.5%	2.0%	2.5%	3.0%	3.5%	4.0%	4.5%	5.0%	
56	11.67	10.64	9.71	8.89	8.14	7.47	6.87	6.32	56
57	11.87	10.88	9.98	9.18	8.45	7.80	7.20	6.66	57
58	12.09	11.13	10.27	9.49	8.78	8.14	7.55	7.02	58
59	12.32	11.41	10.57	9.82	9.13	8.50	7.93	7.41	59
60	12.57	11.69	10.90	10.17	9.50	8.89	8.34	7.82	60
61	12.83	12.00	11.23	10.54	9.90	9.31	8.77	8.27	61
62	13.11	12.32	11.60	10.93	10.32	9.75	9.23	8.75	62
63	13.41	12.67	11.98	11.35	10.77	10.23	9.73	9.27	63
64	13.73	13.04	12.40	11.81	11.26	10.75	10.27	9.83	64
65	14.09	13.45	12.85	12.30	11.78	11.31	10.86	10.45	65

Table 18 Multipliers for loss of pension commencing age 65 (females)

Age at date of trial	Multiplier calculated with allowance for projected mortality from the 1996-based population projections and rate of return of								Age at date of trial
	1.5%	2.0%	2.5%	3.0%	3.5%	4.0%	4.5%	5.0%	
0	6.35	4.36	3.00	2.08	1.44	1.00	0.70	0.49	0
1	6.47	4.47	3.09	2.15	1.50	1.05	0.73	0.52	1
2	6.57	4.56	3.17	2.21	1.55	1.09	0.77	0.54	2
3	6.67	4.65	3.25	2.28	1.60	1.13	0.80	0.57	3
4	6.77	4.74	3.33	2.35	1.66	1.18	0.84	0.60	4
5	6.87	4.83	3.41	2.42	1.72	1.22	0.87	0.63	5
6	6.97	4.93	3.50	2.49	1.78	1.27	0.91	0.66	6
7	7.07	5.03	3.58	2.56	1.84	1.32	0.95	0.69	7
8	7.18	5.13	3.67	2.64	1.90	1.38	1.00	0.73	8
9	7.28	5.23	3.76	2.72	1.97	1.43	1.04	0.76	9
10	7.39	5.33	3.86	2.80	2.04	1.49	1.09	0.80	10
11	7.50	5.43	3.95	2.88	2.11	1.55	1.14	0.84	11
12	7.61	5.54	4.05	2.97	2.18	1.61	1.19	0.88	12
13	7.72	5.65	4.15	3.05	2.26	1.67	1.24	0.92	13
14	7.83	5.76	4.25	3.14	2.33	1.74	1.30	0.97	14
15	7.95	5.87	4.35	3.24	2.41	1.81	1.35	1.02	15
16	8.07	5.99	4.46	3.33	2.50	1.88	1.41	1.07	16
17	8.18	6.11	4.57	3.43	2.58	1.95	1.48	1.12	17
18	8.30	6.23	4.69	3.53	2.67	2.03	1.54	1.18	18
19	8.43	6.35	4.80	3.64	2.77	2.11	1.61	1.24	19
20	8.55	6.48	4.92	3.75	2.86	2.19	1.69	1.30	20
21	8.67	6.60	5.04	3.86	2.96	2.28	1.76	1.36	21
22	8.80	6.73	5.16	3.97	3.07	2.37	1.84	1.43	22
23	8.93	6.86	5.29	4.09	3.17	2.47	1.92	1.50	23
24	9.06	7.00	5.42	4.21	3.28	2.56	2.01	1.58	24
25	9.19	7.14	5.56	4.34	3.40	2.66	2.10	1.65	25
26	9.33	7.28	5.69	4.47	3.51	2.77	2.19	1.74	26
27	9.46	7.42	5.83	4.60	3.63	2.88	2.29	1.82	27
28	9.60	7.56	5.98	4.73	3.76	2.99	2.39	1.91	28
29	9.74	7.71	6.12	4.87	3.89	3.11	2.50	2.01	29
30	9.88	7.86	6.27	5.02	4.02	3.24	2.61	2.11	30
31	10.02	8.01	6.43	5.17	4.16	3.36	2.72	2.21	31
32	10.17	8.17	6.58	5.32	4.31	3.50	2.85	2.32	32
33	10.31	8.33	6.74	5.47	4.45	3.63	2.97	2.44	33
34	10.46	8.49	6.91	5.63	4.61	3.78	3.10	2.56	34
35	10.61	8.65	7.07	5.80	4.77	3.93	3.24	2.68	35
36	10.76	8.82	7.25	5.97	4.93	4.08	3.38	2.81	36
37	10.91	8.99	7.42	6.14	5.10	4.24	3.53	2.95	37
38	11.06	9.16	7.60	6.32	5.27	4.41	3.69	3.10	38
39	11.22	9.33	7.78	6.51	5.45	4.58	3.85	3.25	39
40	11.38	9.51	7.97	6.70	5.64	4.76	4.02	3.41	40
41	11.54	9.69	8.16	6.89	5.83	4.95	4.20	3.58	41
42	11.70	9.88	8.36	7.09	6.03	5.14	4.39	3.76	42
43	11.86	10.06	8.56	7.30	6.24	5.34	4.58	3.94	43
44	12.03	10.26	8.77	7.51	6.45	5.55	4.79	4.14	44
45	12.20	10.45	8.98	7.73	6.67	5.77	5.00	4.34	45
46	12.37	10.65	9.20	7.96	6.90	5.99	5.22	4.55	46
47	12.54	10.86	9.42	8.19	7.14	6.23	5.45	4.78	47
48	12.72	11.06	9.65	8.43	7.38	6.48	5.69	5.02	48
49	12.90	11.28	9.88	8.68	7.63	6.73	5.95	5.26	49
50	13.08	11.50	10.12	8.93	7.90	7.00	6.21	5.53	50
51	13.27	11.72	10.37	9.20	8.17	7.28	6.49	5.80	51
52	13.47	11.95	10.63	9.47	8.46	7.57	6.78	6.09	52
53	13.68	12.20	10.90	9.77	8.76	7.88	7.10	6.40	53
54	13.92	12.47	11.20	10.08	9.09	8.21	7.44	6.74	54
55	14.16	12.76	11.52	10.42	9.44	8.57	7.79	7.10	55

(continued)

Table 18 Multipliers for loss of pension commencing age 65 (females) (*continued*)

Age at date of trial	Multiplier calculated with allowance for projected mortality from the 1996-based population projections and rate of return of 1.5%	2.0%	2.5%	3.0%	3.5%	4.0%	4.5%	5.0%	Age at date of trial
56	14.42	13.05	11.84	10.76	9.80	8.94	8.17	7.48	56
57	14.68	13.36	12.18	11.13	10.18	9.33	8.57	7.89	57
58	14.95	13.67	12.53	11.50	10.57	9.74	8.99	8.31	58
59	15.22	13.99	12.88	11.88	10.98	10.17	9.43	8.76	59
60	15.49	14.30	13.24	12.27	11.40	10.60	9.88	9.22	60
61	15.75	14.62	13.59	12.67	11.82	11.05	10.35	9.71	61
62	16.00	14.93	13.96	13.07	12.26	11.52	10.84	10.22	62
63	16.26	15.25	14.33	13.49	12.72	12.01	11.36	10.76	63
64	16.53	15.58	14.72	13.92	13.20	12.52	11.91	11.33	64
65	16.81	15.94	15.13	14.39	13.70	13.07	12.49	11.95	65

Table 19 Multipliers for loss of pension commencing age 60 (males)

Age at date of trial	Multiplier calculated with allowance for projected mortality from the 1996-based population projections and rate of return of								Age at date of trial
	1.5%	2.0%	2.5%	3.0%	3.5%	4.0%	4.5%	5.0%	
0	6.94	4.88	3.44	2.43	1.73	1.23	0.88	0.63	0
1	7.08	5.00	3.54	2.52	1.80	1.28	0.92	0.66	1
2	7.19	5.10	3.63	2.59	1.86	1.34	0.96	0.70	2
3	7.30	5.20	3.72	2.67	1.92	1.39	1.01	0.73	3
4	7.41	5.31	3.81	2.75	1.99	1.44	1.05	0.77	4
5	7.52	5.41	3.91	2.83	2.06	1.50	1.10	0.81	5
6	7.63	5.52	4.01	2.92	2.13	1.56	1.15	0.85	6
7	7.74	5.63	4.10	3.00	2.20	1.62	1.20	0.89	7
8	7.85	5.74	4.21	3.09	2.28	1.69	1.25	0.93	8
9	7.97	5.85	4.31	3.18	2.36	1.75	1.31	0.98	9
10	8.08	5.97	4.42	3.28	2.44	1.82	1.37	1.03	10
11	8.20	6.08	4.52	3.38	2.53	1.90	1.43	1.08	11
12	8.32	6.20	4.64	3.48	2.61	1.97	1.49	1.13	12
13	8.44	6.32	4.75	3.58	2.71	2.05	1.56	1.19	13
14	8.57	6.45	4.87	3.69	2.80	2.13	1.63	1.25	14
15	8.69	6.57	4.99	3.80	2.90	2.22	1.70	1.31	15
16	8.82	6.70	5.11	3.91	3.00	2.30	1.78	1.37	16
17	8.95	6.84	5.24	4.02	3.10	2.40	1.86	1.44	17
18	9.08	6.97	5.37	4.14	3.21	2.49	1.94	1.51	18
19	9.22	7.11	5.50	4.27	3.32	2.59	2.03	1.59	19
20	9.36	7.26	5.64	4.40	3.44	2.70	2.12	1.67	20
21	9.50	7.40	5.78	4.53	3.56	2.80	2.21	1.75	21
22	9.65	7.55	5.93	4.67	3.68	2.92	2.31	1.84	22
23	9.79	7.70	6.08	4.81	3.81	3.03	2.42	1.93	23
24	9.94	7.86	6.23	4.95	3.95	3.16	2.53	2.03	24
25	10.08	8.01	6.38	5.10	4.09	3.28	2.64	2.13	25
26	10.24	8.17	6.54	5.25	4.23	3.41	2.76	2.24	26
27	10.39	8.33	6.71	5.41	4.38	3.55	2.89	2.35	27
28	10.54	8.50	6.87	5.57	4.53	3.69	3.02	2.47	28
29	10.70	8.67	7.04	5.74	4.69	3.84	3.15	2.59	29
30	10.86	8.84	7.22	5.91	4.85	3.99	3.29	2.72	30
31	11.01	9.01	7.40	6.09	5.02	4.15	3.44	2.86	31
32	11.18	9.19	7.58	6.27	5.19	4.32	3.59	3.00	32
33	11.34	9.37	7.77	6.45	5.37	4.49	3.75	3.15	33
34	11.50	9.55	7.96	6.64	5.56	4.67	3.92	3.31	34
35	11.67	9.74	8.15	6.84	5.75	4.85	4.10	3.47	35
36	11.84	9.93	8.35	7.04	5.95	5.04	4.28	3.64	36
37	12.01	10.12	8.56	7.25	6.16	5.24	4.47	3.82	37
38	12.18	10.32	8.76	7.46	6.37	5.45	4.67	4.01	38
39	12.35	10.52	8.98	7.68	6.59	5.66	4.88	4.21	39
40	12.53	10.72	9.20	7.91	6.82	5.89	5.10	4.42	40
41	12.71	10.93	9.42	8.14	7.05	6.12	5.32	4.64	41
42	12.89	11.14	9.65	8.38	7.30	6.36	5.56	4.87	42
43	13.08	11.36	9.89	8.63	7.55	6.62	5.81	5.11	43
44	13.27	11.58	10.13	8.89	7.81	6.88	6.07	5.37	44
45	13.46	11.81	10.38	9.15	8.08	7.15	6.34	5.64	45
46	13.65	12.03	10.64	9.42	8.36	7.44	6.63	5.92	46
47	13.84	12.27	10.89	9.70	8.65	7.73	6.92	6.21	47
48	14.04	12.51	11.16	9.98	8.95	8.04	7.23	6.52	48
49	14.25	12.75	11.44	10.28	9.26	8.36	7.56	6.85	49
50	14.46	13.01	11.72	10.59	9.59	8.70	7.90	7.19	50
51	14.68	13.27	12.02	10.91	9.93	9.05	8.26	7.56	51
52	14.91	13.54	12.33	11.25	10.29	9.42	8.64	7.95	52
53	15.14	13.83	12.65	11.60	10.66	9.81	9.05	8.36	53
54	15.39	14.13	12.99	11.97	11.05	10.22	9.47	8.79	54
55	15.65	14.44	13.34	12.36	11.47	10.66	9.92	9.26	55

(continued)

Table 19 Multipliers for loss of pension commencing age 60 (males) (*continued*)

Age at date of trial	Multiplier calculated with allowance for projected mortality from the 1996-based population projections and rate of return of								Age at date of trial
	1.5%	2.0%	2.5%	3.0%	3.5%	4.0%	4.5%	5.0%	
56	15.93	14.77	13.72	12.77	11.91	11.12	10.41	9.75	56
57	16.23	15.12	14.12	13.20	12.37	11.61	10.92	10.28	57
58	16.54	15.49	14.54	13.67	12.87	12.14	11.47	10.86	58
59	16.88	15.89	14.98	14.16	13.40	12.70	12.06	11.47	59
60	17.24	16.31	15.46	14.68	13.96	13.30	12.69	12.13	60

Table 20 Multipliers for loss of pension age 60 (females)

Age at date of trial	Multiplier calculated with allowance for projected mortality from the 1996-based population projections and rate of return of								Age at date of trial
	1.5%	2.0%	2.5%	3.0%	3.5%	4.0%	4.5%	5.0%	
0	8.19	5.71	4.00	2.81	1.98	1.40	1.00	0.71	0
1	8.34	5.85	4.12	2.91	2.06	1.47	1.05	0.75	1
2	8.47	5.97	4.22	2.99	2.13	1.52	1.09	0.79	2
3	8.60	6.09	4.32	3.08	2.21	1.59	1.14	0.83	3
4	8.73	6.21	4.43	3.18	2.28	1.65	1.19	0.87	4
5	8.85	6.33	4.54	3.27	2.36	1.71	1.25	0.91	5
6	8.99	6.46	4.65	3.37	2.45	1.78	1.30	0.96	6
7	9.12	6.58	4.77	3.47	2.53	1.85	1.36	1.00	7
8	9.25	6.71	4.89	3.57	2.62	1.93	1.42	1.05	8
9	9.39	6.85	5.01	3.68	2.71	2.00	1.49	1.11	9
10	9.53	6.98	5.13	3.79	2.80	2.08	1.55	1.16	10
11	9.67	7.12	5.26	3.90	2.90	2.17	1.62	1.22	11
12	9.81	7.26	5.39	4.02	3.00	2.25	1.69	1.28	12
13	9.96	7.40	5.52	4.14	3.11	2.34	1.77	1.34	13
14	10.10	7.55	5.66	4.26	3.21	2.43	1.85	1.41	14
15	10.25	7.70	5.80	4.39	3.33	2.53	1.93	1.48	15
16	10.40	7.85	5.94	4.52	3.44	2.63	2.02	1.55	16
17	10.55	8.00	6.09	4.65	3.56	2.74	2.11	1.63	17
18	10.71	8.16	6.24	4.79	3.69	2.85	2.20	1.71	18
19	10.87	8.32	6.40	4.93	3.81	2.96	2.30	1.80	19
20	11.03	8.49	6.55	5.08	3.95	3.08	2.41	1.89	20
21	11.19	8.65	6.72	5.23	4.08	3.20	2.51	1.98	21
22	11.35	8.83	6.88	5.38	4.23	3.33	2.63	2.08	22
23	11.52	9.00	7.05	5.54	4.37	3.46	2.74	2.18	23
24	11.69	9.18	7.23	5.71	4.52	3.60	2.87	2.29	24
25	11.86	9.36	7.41	5.88	4.68	3.74	2.99	2.40	25
26	12.04	9.54	7.59	6.05	4.84	3.89	3.13	2.52	26
27	12.21	9.73	7.78	6.23	5.01	4.04	3.27	2.65	27
28	12.39	9.92	7.97	6.42	5.19	4.20	3.41	2.78	28
29	12.57	10.12	8.16	6.61	5.37	4.37	3.57	2.92	29
30	12.76	10.31	8.37	6.81	5.55	4.54	3.73	3.07	30
31	12.94	10.52	8.57	7.01	5.74	4.72	3.89	3.22	31
32	13.13	10.72	8.78	7.21	5.94	4.91	4.07	3.38	32
33	13.32	10.93	9.00	7.43	6.15	5.10	4.25	3.55	33
34	13.51	11.14	9.22	7.65	6.36	5.31	4.44	3.72	34
35	13.71	11.36	9.44	7.87	6.58	5.52	4.64	3.91	35
36	13.91	11.58	9.67	8.10	6.81	5.73	4.84	4.10	36
37	14.11	11.81	9.91	8.34	7.04	5.96	5.06	4.30	37
38	14.31	12.03	10.15	8.59	7.29	6.20	5.28	4.52	38
39	14.51	12.27	10.40	8.84	7.54	6.44	5.52	4.74	39
40	14.72	12.51	10.66	9.10	7.80	6.70	5.77	4.98	40
41	14.93	12.75	10.92	9.37	8.07	6.96	6.02	5.22	41
42	15.15	13.00	11.18	9.65	8.35	7.24	6.29	5.48	42
43	15.37	13.25	11.46	9.93	8.64	7.52	6.57	5.76	43
44	15.59	13.51	11.74	10.23	8.93	7.82	6.87	6.04	44
45	15.81	13.77	12.03	10.53	9.24	8.13	7.18	6.34	45
46	16.04	14.04	12.32	10.84	9.57	8.46	7.50	6.66	46
47	16.28	14.32	12.63	11.17	9.90	8.80	7.83	6.99	47
48	16.51	14.60	12.94	11.50	10.24	9.15	8.19	7.34	48
49	16.76	14.89	13.26	11.84	10.60	9.51	8.56	7.71	49
50	17.01	15.18	13.59	12.20	10.98	9.90	8.94	8.10	50
51	17.26	15.49	13.94	12.57	11.36	10.30	9.35	8.51	51
52	17.52	15.80	14.29	12.95	11.77	10.72	9.78	8.94	52
53	17.81	16.14	14.67	13.36	12.20	11.16	10.24	9.40	53
54	18.12	16.51	15.07	13.80	12.66	11.64	10.73	9.90	54
55	18.45	16.89	15.50	14.26	13.15	12.15	11.25	10.43	55

(*continued*)

Table 20 Multipliers for loss of pension age 60 (females) (*continued*)

Age at date of trial	1.5%	2.0%	2.5%	3.0%	3.5%	4.0%	4.5%	5.0%	Age at date of trial
	Multiplier calculated with allowance for projected mortality from the 1996-based population projections and rate of return of								
56	18.79	17.29	15.94	14.74	13.66	12.68	11.80	11.00	56
57	19.14	17.70	16.40	15.24	14.19	13.24	12.38	11.59	57
58	19.50	18.12	16.88	15.76	14.74	13.82	12.99	12.22	58
59	19.86	18.55	17.36	16.29	15.32	14.43	13.62	12.89	59
60	20.22	18.98	17.86	16.84	15.91	15.07	14.29	13.58	60

Table 21 Discounting factors for term certain

Term	1.5%	2.0%	2.5%	3.0%	3.5%	4.0%	4.5%	5.0%	Term
	Factor to discount value of multiplier for a period of deferment								
1	0.9852	0.9804	0.9756	0.9709	0.9662	0.9615	0.9569	0.9524	1
2	0.9707	0.9612	0.9518	0.9426	0.9335	0.9246	0.9157	0.9070	2
3	0.9563	0.9423	0.9286	0.9151	0.9019	0.8890	0.8763	0.8638	3
4	0.9422	0.9238	0.9060	0.8885	0.8714	0.8548	0.8386	0.8227	4
5	0.9283	0.9057	0.8839	0.8626	0.8420	0.8219	0.8025	0.7835	5
6	0.9145	0.8880	0.8623	0.8375	0.8135	0.7903	0.7679	0.7462	6
7	0.9010	0.8706	0.8413	0.8131	0.7860	0.7599	0.7348	0.7107	7
8	0.8877	0.8535	0.8207	0.7894	0.7594	0.7307	0.7032	0.6768	8
9	0.8746	0.8368	0.8007	0.7664	0.7337	0.7026	0.6729	0.6446	9
10	0.8617	0.8203	0.7812	0.7441	0.7089	0.6756	0.6439	0.6139	10
11	0.8489	0.8043	0.7621	0.7224	0.6849	0.6496	0.6162	0.5847	11
12	0.8364	0.7885	0.7436	0.7014	0.6618	0.6246	0.5897	0.5568	12
13	0.8240	0.7730	0.7254	0.6810	0.6394	0.6006	0.5643	0.5303	13
14	0.8118	0.7579	0.7077	0.6611	0.6178	0.5775	0.5400	0.5051	14
15	0.7999	0.7430	0.6905	0.6419	0.5969	0.5553	0.5167	0.4810	15
16	0.7880	0.7284	0.6736	0.6232	0.5767	0.5339	0.4945	0.4581	16
17	0.7764	0.7142	0.6572	0.6050	0.5572	0.5134	0.4732	0.4363	17
18	0.7649	0.7002	0.6412	0.5874	0.5384	0.4936	0.4528	0.4155	18
19	0.7536	0.6864	0.6255	0.5703	0.5202	0.4746	0.4333	0.3957	19
20	0.7425	0.6730	0.6103	0.5537	0.5026	0.4564	0.4146	0.3769	20
21	0.7315	0.6598	0.5954	0.5375	0.4856	0.4388	0.3968	0.3589	21
22	0.7207	0.6468	0.5809	0.5219	0.4692	0.4220	0.3797	0.3418	22
23	0.7100	0.6342	0.5667	0.5067	0.4533	0.4057	0.3634	0.3256	23
24	0.6995	0.6217	0.5529	0.4919	0.4380	0.3901	0.3477	0.3101	24
25	0.6892	0.6095	0.5394	0.4776	0.4231	0.3751	0.3327	0.2953	25
26	0.6790	0.5976	0.5262	0.4637	0.4088	0.3607	0.3184	0.2812	26
27	0.6690	0.5859	0.5134	0.4502	0.3950	0.3468	0.3047	0.2678	27
28	0.6591	0.5744	0.5009	0.4371	0.3817	0.3335	0.2916	0.2551	28
29	0.6494	0.5631	0.4887	0.4243	0.3687	0.3207	0.2790	0.2429	29
30	0.6398	0.5521	0.4767	0.4120	0.3563	0.3083	0.2670	0.2314	30

Table 22 Multipliers for pecuniary loss for term certain

Term	Multiplier for regular frequent payments for a term certain at rate of return of 1.5%	2.0%	2.5%	3.0%	3.5%	4.0%	4.5%	5.0%	Term
1	0.99	0.99	0.99	0.99	0.98	0.98	0.98	0.98	1
2	1.97	1.96	1.95	1.94	1.93	1.92	1.91	1.91	2
3	2.93	2.91	2.89	2.87	2.85	2.83	2.81	2.79	3
4	3.88	3.85	3.81	3.77	3.74	3.70	3.67	3.63	4
5	4.82	4.76	4.70	4.65	4.59	4.54	4.49	4.44	5
6	5.74	5.66	5.58	5.50	5.42	5.35	5.27	5.20	6
7	6.65	6.54	6.43	6.32	6.22	6.12	6.02	5.93	7
8	7.54	7.40	7.26	7.12	6.99	6.87	6.74	6.62	8
9	8.42	8.24	8.07	7.90	7.74	7.58	7.43	7.28	9
10	9.29	9.07	8.86	8.66	8.46	8.27	8.09	7.91	10
11	10.15	9.88	9.63	9.39	9.16	8.93	8.72	8.51	11
12	10.99	10.68	10.39	10.10	9.83	9.57	9.32	9.08	12
13	11.82	11.46	11.12	10.79	10.48	10.18	9.90	9.63	13
14	12.64	12.23	11.84	11.46	11.11	10.77	10.45	10.14	14
15	13.44	12.98	12.54	12.12	11.72	11.34	10.98	10.64	15
16	14.24	13.71	13.22	12.75	12.30	11.88	11.48	11.11	16
17	15.02	14.43	13.88	13.36	12.87	12.41	11.97	11.55	17
18	15.79	15.14	14.53	13.96	13.42	12.91	12.43	11.98	18
19	16.55	15.83	15.17	14.54	13.95	13.39	12.87	12.38	19
20	17.30	16.51	15.78	15.10	14.46	13.86	13.30	12.77	20
21	18.03	17.18	16.39	15.65	14.95	14.31	13.70	13.14	21
22	18.76	17.83	16.97	16.17	15.43	14.74	14.09	13.49	22
23	19.48	18.47	17.55	16.69	15.89	15.15	14.46	13.82	23
24	20.18	19.10	18.11	17.19	16.34	15.55	14.82	14.14	24
25	20.87	19.72	18.65	17.67	16.77	15.93	15.16	14.44	25
26	21.56	20.32	19.19	18.14	17.18	16.30	15.48	14.73	26
27	22.23	20.91	19.71	18.60	17.59	16.65	15.80	15.01	27
28	22.90	21.49	20.21	19.04	17.97	16.99	16.09	15.27	28
29	23.55	22.06	20.71	19.47	18.35	17.32	16.38	15.52	29
30	24.20	22.62	21.19	19.89	18.71	17.64	16.65	15.75	30
31	24.83	23.17	21.66	20.30	19.06	17.94	16.91	15.98	31
32	25.46	23.70	22.12	20.69	19.40	18.23	17.16	16.19	32
33	26.07	24.23	22.57	21.08	19.73	18.51	17.40	16.40	33
34	26.68	24.74	23.01	21.45	20.04	18.78	17.63	16.59	34
35	27.28	25.25	23.43	21.81	20.35	19.04	17.85	16.78	35
36	27.87	25.74	23.85	22.16	20.64	19.28	18.06	16.96	36
37	28.45	26.23	24.26	22.50	20.93	19.52	18.26	17.13	37
38	29.02	26.70	24.65	22.83	21.20	19.75	18.45	17.29	38
39	29.58	27.17	25.04	23.15	21.47	19.97	18.64	17.44	39
40	30.14	27.63	25.42	23.46	21.73	20.19	18.81	17.58	40

ACTUARIAL FORMULAE AND BASIS

The functions tabled are:

Tables 1, 2, 11 and 12	$\bar{a}_x$
Tables 3, 4, 13 and 14	$\bar{a}_{x:\overline{65-x}\rceil}$
Tables 5, 6, 15 and 16	$\bar{a}_{x:\overline{60-x}\rceil}$
Tables 7, 8, 17 and 18	$_{(65-x)\vert}\bar{a}_{65}$
Tables 9, 10, 19 and 20	$_{(60-x)\vert}\bar{a}_{60}$
Table 21:	$1/(1+i)^n$
Table 22:	$\bar{a}_{\overline{n}\rceil}$

Mortality: English Life Tables No. 15 (Tables 1 to 10)
Mortality assumptions for 1996-based official population projections for England and Wales (Tables 11 to 20)

Loadings: None

Rate of return: As stated in the Tables

B. PNBA TABLES

Prepared by Peter Jennings, Barrister

EXPLANATORY NOTES

The purpose of these notes is to show, for each of a number of rates of discount, the present capital value of a loss taking place at a fixed time in the future.

The first table (B1) gives the multiplier for a single payment in *n* years' time at various rates of discount.[1] (Thus the appropriate multiplier at the 2% discount for a single payment in 10 years' time is 0.82.)

The second table (B2) similarly gives the multiplier of a series of annual payments for *n* years.[2] (Thus the appropriate multiplier at the 2% discount for a series of annual payments for 10 years is 8.98.)

Each of the remaining tables (B3) is for a single rate of discount and contains a number of columns: the number of years; the multiplier for a single payment (as per B1); the multiplier for annual payments (as per B2); and [periodic multipliers] for payments at intervals of 2, 3, 4 and so on years. (Thus the appropriate multiplier at the 2% discount for payments over a period of 10 years at intervals of 2 years is 4.45.)

The multiplier is that appropriate to expenditure at the end of the relevant year or years.

Thus at 2% discount:
£100 paid after 10 years has a present value of £82;
£100 at the end of each of the next 10 years has a present value of £898;
£100 at the end of 2, 4, 6, 8 and 10 years has a present value of £445 (row 10, 2-yearly column); and
£100 at the end of 3, 6 and 9 years has a present value of £267 (row 9, 3-yearly column).

If an immediate payment is needed in addition to the recurring payments, add 1 to the multiplier....

The tables make no discount for contingencies.

---

[1] This is the same table as Table 21 in App. IA (to one less decimal place).

[2] This is the same table as Table 22 in App. IA (subject to the adjustment referred to latterly in para. 23 in Section A of the Tables' Explanatory Notes, namely dividing the multiplier by one plus half the rate of return for annual payments in arrears).

Modifications

Intermediate rates of discount can be derived by interpolation, thus: For annual payments for 10 years multipliers at 2% and 2.5% discount are 8.98 and 8.75. That at 2.25% discount is $^1/_2$ (8.98 + 8.75) = 8.87.

Payments more frequent than yearly, for example weekly. The true multiplier will be higher as on average payments are advanced by about half a year. A sufficient approximation to the multiplier for weekly payments for n years can be obtained, if desired, by multiplying by (1 + $^1/_2$ the discount rate). Thus at 2% discount the multiplier for annual payments for 10 years is 8.98. That for weekly payments for 10 years is approximately 8.98 x (1.01) = 9.07.

Periods other than entire years can then be obtained by interpolation. For annual payments for 10 and 11 years the multipliers at 2% discount are 8.98 and 9.79. That for weekly payments for 10$^1/_2$ years is approximately $^1/_2$ (8.98 + 9.79) x (1.01) = 9.48.

Periods greater than 70 years. Multipliers can be derived as follows. At 2%:
For single payments by simple multiplication:
Multiplier for one payment after 40 years is 0.453;
That for one payment after 80 years is 0.453 x 0.453 = 0.205.
For recurring payments by adding a discount factor from the single payment column:
Multiplier for annual payments for 40 years is 27.36;
Multiplier for five-yearly payments for 40 years is 5.22;
That for annual payments for 80 years is 27.36 x 1.453 = 39.75;
and for five-yearly payments for 80 years is 5.22 x 1.453 + 7.58.

Payments beginning after a deferred period can be derived by subtraction or by multiplying by a factor from the single payment column. At 2%:
Multipliers for five-yearly payments for 15 and 20 years are 2.43 and 6.00;
That for five-yearly payments from years 20 to 50 inclusive is 6.00–2.43 = 3.57;
Multiplier for one payment after 18 years is 0.700;
That for five-yearly payments from years 23 to 68 inclusive is 6.00 x 0.700 + 4.20.

Irregular payments: Multipliers can be found by adding individual multipliers from the single payment column.

B1: Multipliers for future single payments

Tables showing the present value of £1 in *n* years' time at a discount of *p*% per year

p_n	2.0%	2.5%	3.0%	3.5%	4.0%	4.5%	5.0%
1	0.980	0.976	0.971	0.966	0.962	0.957	0.952
2	0.961	0.952	0.943	0.934	0.925	0.916	0.907
3	0.942	0.929	0.915	0.902	0.889	0.876	0.864
4	0.924	0.906	0.888	0.871	0.855	0.839	0.823
5	0.906	0.884	0.863	0.842	0.822	0.808	0.784
6	0.888	0.862	0.837	0.814	0.790	0.768	0.746
7	0.871	0.841	0.813	0.786	0.760	0.735	0.711
8	0.853	0.821	0.789	0.759	0.731	0.703	0.677
9	0.837	0.801	0.766	0.734	0.703	0.673	0.645
10	0.820	0.781	0.744	0.709	0.676	0.644	0.614
11	0.804	0.762	0.722	0.685	0.650	0.616	0.585
12	0.788	0.744	0.701	0.662	0.625	0.590	0.557
13	0.773	0.725	0.681	0.639	0.601	0.564	0.530
14	0.759	0.708	0.661	0.618	0.577	0.540	0.505
15	0.743	0.690	0.642	0.597	0.555	0.517	0.481
16	0.728	0.674	0.623	0.577	0.534	0.494	0.458
17	0.714	0.657	0.605	0.557	0.513	0.473	0.436
18	0.700	0.641	0.587	0.538	0.494	0.453	0.416
19	0.686	0.626	0.570	0.520	0.475	0.433	0.396
20	0.673	0.610	0.554	0.503	0.456	0.415	0.377
21	0.660	0.595	0.538	0.486	0.439	0.397	0.359
22	0.647	0.581	0.522	0.469	0.422	0.380	0.342
23	0.634	0.567	0.507	0.453	0.406	0.363	0.326
24	0.622	0.553	0.492	0.438	0.390	0.348	0.310
25	0.610	0.539	0.478	0.423	0.375	0.333	0.295
26	0.598	0.526	0.464	0.409	0.361	0.318	0.281
27	0.589	0.513	0.450	0.395	0.347	0.305	0.268
28	0.574	0.501	0.437	0.382	0.333	0.292	0.255
29	0.563	0.489	0.424	0.369	0.321	0.279	0.243
30	0.552	0.477	0.412	0.356	0.308	0.267	0.231
31	0.541	0.465	0.400	0.344	0.296	0.256	0.220
32	0.531	0.454	0.388	0.333	0.285	0.244	0.210
33	0.520	0.443	0.377	0.321	0.274	0.234	0.200
34	0.510	0.432	0.366	0.310	0.264	0.224	0.190
35	0.500	0.421	0.355	0.300	0.253	0.214	0.181
36	0.490	0.411	0.345	0.290	0.244	0.205	0.173
37	0.481	0.401	0.335	0.280	0.234	0.196	0.164
38	0.471	0.391	0.325	0.271	0.225	0.188	0.157
39	0.462	0.382	0.316	0.261	0.217	0.180	0.149
40	0.453	0.372	0.307	0.253	0.208	0.172	0.142
41	0.444	0.363	0.298	0.244	0.200	0.165	0.135
42	0.435	0.354	0.289	0.236	0.193	0.157	0.129
43	0.427	0.346	0.281	0.228	0.185	0.151	0.123
44	0.418	0.337	0.272	0.220	0.178	0.144	0.117
45	0.410	0.329	0.264	0.213	0.171	0.138	0.111
46	0.402	0.321	0.257	0.205	0.165	0.132	0.106
47	0.394	0.313	0.249	0.199	0.158	0.126	0.101
48	0.387	0.306	0.242	0.192	0.152	0.121	0.096
49	0.379	0.298	0.235	0.185	0.146	0.116	0.092
50	0.372	0.291	0.228	0.179	0.141	0.111	0.087
51	0.364	0.284	0.221	0.173	0.135	0.106	0.083
52	0.357	0.277	0.215	0.167	0.130	0.101	0.079
53	0.350	0.270	0.209	0.161	0.125	0.097	0.075
54	0.343	0.264	0.203	0.156	0.120	0.093	0.072
55	0.337	0.257	0.197	0.151	0.116	0.089	0.068

(*continued*)

B1: Multipliers for future single payments (*continued*)

Tables showing the present value of £1 in *n* years' time at a discount of *p*% per year

p_n	2.0%	2.5%	3.0%	3.5%	4.0%	4.5%	5.0%
56	0.330	0.251	0.191	0.146	0.111	0.085	0.065
57	0.323	0.245	0.185	0.141	0.107	0.081	0.062
58	0.317	0.239	0.180	0.136	0.103	0.078	0.059
59	0.311	0.233	0.175	0.131	0.099	0.074	0.056
60	0.305	0.227	0.170	0.127	0.095	0.071	0.054
61	0.299	0.222	0.165	0.123	0.091	0.068	0.051
62	0.293	0.216	0.160	0.118	0.088	0.065	0.049
63	0.287	0.211	0.155	0.114	0.085	0.062	0.046
64	0.282	0.206	0.151	0.111	0.081	0.060	0.044
65	0.276	0.201	0.146	0.107	0.078	0.057	0.042
66	0.271	0.196	0.142	0.103	0.075	0.055	0.040
67	0.265	0.191	0.138	0.100	0.072	0.052	0.038
68	0.260	0.187	0.134	0.096	0.069	0.050	0.036
69	0.255	0.182	0.130	0.093	0.067	0.048	0.035
70	0.250	0.178	0.126	0.090	0.064	0.046	0.033

Larger figures can be obtained by simple multiplication of factors:

Present value of £1 in 90 years at 2% discount: £1 x 0.250 x 0.673 = 0.168

Intermediate rates can be found by interpolation:
£1 in 10 years at 2.25%: £1 x (0.820 + 0.781) x 0.5 = 0.800

B2: Multipliers for annual payments for fixed periods

Tables showing the present value of £1 per year for n years at a discount of p% per year

p_n	2.0%	2.5%	3.0%	3.5%	4.0%	4.5%	5.0%
1	0.98	0.98	0.97	0.97	0.96	0.96	0.95
2	1.94	1.93	1.91	1.90	1.89	1.87	1.86
3	2.88	2.86	2.83	2.80	2.78	2.75	2.72
4	3.81	3.76	3.72	3.67	3.63	3.59	3.55
5	4.71	4.65	4.58	4.52	4.45	4.39	4.33
6	5.60	5.51	5.42	5.33	5.24	5.16	5.08
7	6.47	6.35	6.23	6.11	6.00	5.89	5.79
8	7.33	7.17	7.02	6.87	6.73	6.60	6.46
9	8.16	7.97	7.79	7.61	7.44	7.27	7.11
10	8.98	8.75	8.53	8.32	8.11	7.91	7.72
11	9.79	9.51	9.25	9.00	8.76	8.53	8.31
12	10.58	10.26	9.95	9.66	9.39	9.12	8.86
13	11.35	10.98	10.63	10.30	9.99	9.68	9.39
14	12.11	11.69	11.30	10.92	10.56	10.22	9.90
15	12.85	12.38	11.94	11.52	11.12	10.74	10.38
16	13.56	13.06	12.56	12.09	11.65	11.23	10.84
17	14.29	13.71	13.17	12.65	12.17	11.71	11.27
18	14.99	14.35	13.75	13.19	12.66	12.16	11.69
19	15.68	14.98	14.32	13.71	13.13	12.59	12.09
20	16.35	15.59	14.88	14.21	13.59	13.01	12.46
21	17.01	16.18	15.42	14.70	14.03	13.40	12.82
22	17.66	16.77	15.94	15.17	14.45	13.78	13.16
23	18.29	17.33	16.44	15.62	14.86	14.15	13.49
24	18.91	17.88	16.94	16.06	15.25	14.50	13.80
25	19.52	18.42	17.41	16.48	15.62	14.83	14.09
26	20.12	18.95	17.88	16.89	15.98	15.15	14.38
27	20.71	19.46	18.33	17.29	16.33	15.45	14.64
28	21.28	19.96	18.76	17.67	16.66	15.74	14.90
29	21.84	20.45	19.19	18.04	16.98	16.02	15.14
30	22.40	20.93	19.60	18.39	17.29	16.29	15.37
31	22.94	21.40	20.00	18.74	17.59	16.54	15.59
32	23.47	21.85	20.39	19.07	17.87	16.79	15.80
33	23.99	22.29	20.77	19.39	18.15	17.02	16.00
34	24.50	22.72	21.13	19.70	18.41	17.25	16.19
35	25.00	23.15	21.49	20.00	18.66	17.46	16.37
36	25.49	23.56	21.83	20.29	18.91	17.67	16.55
37	25.97	23.96	22.17	20.57	19.14	17.86	16.71
38	26.44	24.35	22.49	20.84	19.37	18.05	16.87
39	26.90	24.73	22.81	21.10	19.58	18.23	17.02
40	27.36	25.10	23.11	21.36	19.79	18.40	17.16
41	27.80	25.47	23.41	21.60	19.99	18.57	17.29
42	28.23	25.82	23.70	21.83	20.19	18.72	17.42
43	28.66	26.17	23.98	22.06	20.37	18.87	17.55
44	29.08	26.50	24.25	22.28	20.55	19.02	17.66
45	29.49	26.83	24.52	22.50	20.72	19.16	17.77
46	29.89	27.15	24.78	22.70	20.88	19.29	17.88
47	30.29	27.47	25.02	22.90	21.04	19.41	17.98
48	30.67	27.77	25.27	23.09	21.20	19.54	18.08
49	31.05	28.07	25.50	23.28	21.34	19.65	18.17
50	31.42	28.36	25.73	23.46	21.48	19.76	18.26
51	31.79	28.65	25.95	23.63	21.62	19.87	18.34
52	32.14	28.92	26.17	23.80	21.75	19.97	18.42
53	32.49	29.19	26.37	23.96	21.87	20.07	18.49
54	32.84	29.46	26.58	24.11	21.99	20.16	18.57
55	33.17	29.71	26.77	24.26	22.11	20.25	18.63

(continued)

B2: Multipliers for annual payments for fixed periods (*continued*)

Tables showing the present value of £1 per year for *n* years at a discount of *p*% per year

p_n	2.0%	2.5%	3.0%	3.5%	4.0%	4.5%	5.0%
56	33.50	29.96	26.97	24.41	22.22	20.33	18.70
57	33.83	30.21	27.15	24.55	22.33	20.41	18.76
58	34.15	30.45	27.33	24.69	22.43	20.49	18.82
59	33.46	30.68	27.51	24.82	22.53	20.57	18.88
60	34.76	30.91	27.68	24.94	22.62	20.64	18.93
61	35.06	31.13	27.84	25.07	22.71	20.71	18.98
62	33.35	31.35	28.00	25.19	22.80	20.77	19.03
63	35.64	31.56	28.16	25.30	22.89	20.83	19.08
64	35.92	31.76	28.31	25.41	22.97	20.89	19.12
65	36.20	31.96	28.45	25.52	23.05	20.95	19.16
66	36.47	32.16	28.60	25.62	23.12	21.01	19.20
67	36.73	32.35	28.73	25.72	23.19	21.06	19.24
68	36.99	32.54	28.87	25.82	23.26	21.11	19.28
69	37.25	32.72	29.00	25.91	23.33	21.16	19.31
70	37.50	32.90	29.12	26.00	23.39	21.20	19.34

Larger figures can be obtained by multiplication and addition of factors

Present value of £1 for 90 years at 2% discount:
£1 x (Multiplier for 45 years) x (1 + discount for 45 years) = £1 x 29.49 x (1 + 0.410) = 41.58

Intermediate rates can be found by interpolation:
£1 for 10 years at 2.25%: £1 x (8.98 + 8.75) x 0.5 = 8.87

B3: Periodic multipliers

Periodic multipliers at 2% discount

	Factor	Frequency of payments in years											
n		1	2	3	4	5	6	7	8	10	12	15	20
1	0.980	0.98											
2	0.961	1.94	0.96										
3	0.942	2.88		0.94									
4	0.924	3.81	1.88		0.92								
5	0.906	4.71				0.91							
6	0.888	5.60	2.77	1.83			0.89						
7	0.871	6.47						0.87					
8	0.853	7.33	3.63		1.78				0.85				
9	0.837	8.16		2.67									
10	0.820	8.98	4.45			1.69				0.82			
11	0.804	9.79											
12	0.788	10.58	5.23	3.46	2.57		1.68				0.79		
13	0.773	11.35											
14	0.759	12.11	5.99					1.63					
15	0.743	12.85		4.20		2.43						0.74	
16	0.728	13.56	6.72		3.29				1.58				
17	0.714	14.29											
18	0.700	14.99	7.42	4.90			2.38						
19	0.686	15.68											
20	0.673	16.35	8.09		3.97	3.10				1.49			0.67
21	0.660	17.01		5.56				2.29					
22	0.647	17.66	8.74										
23	0.634	18.29											
24	0.622	18.91	9.36	6.18	4.59		3.00		2.20		1.41		
25	0.610	19.52				3.71							
26	0.598	20.12	9.96										
27	0.589	20.71		6.77									
28	0.574	21.28	10.54		5.16			2.86					
29	0.563	21.84											
30	0.552	22.40	11.09	7.32		4.27	3.55			2.25		1.30	
31	0.541	22.94											
32	0.531	23.47	11.62		5.69				2.73				
33	0.520	23.99		7.84									
34	0.510	24.50	12.13										
35	0.500	25.00				4.77		3.36					
36	0.490	25.49	12.62	8.33	6.18		4.04				1.90		
37	0.481	25.97											
38	0.471	26.44	13.09										
39	0.462	26.90		8.79									
40	0.453	27.36	13.54		6.64	5.22			3.19	2.50			1.13
41	0.444	27.80											
42	0.435	28.23	13.98	9.23			4.48	3.80					
43	0.427	28.66											
44	0.418	29.08	14.40		7.05								
45	0.410	29.49		9.64		5.63						1.71	
46	0.402	29.89	14.80										
47	0.394	30.29											
48	0.387	30.67	15.18	10.03	7.44		4.86		3.57		2.29		
49	0.379	31.05						4.18					
50	0.372	31.42	15.56			6.00				3.24			

(*continued*)

B3: Periodic multipliers (*continued*)

Periodic multipliers at 2% discount (continued)

	Factor	Frequency of payments in years											
n		1	2	3	4	5	6	7	8	10	12	15	20
51	0.364	31.79		10.39									
52	0.357	32.14	15.91		7.80								
53	0.350	32.49											
54	0.343	32.84	16.26	10.73			5.21						
55	0.337	33.17				6.34							
56	0.330	33.50	16.59		8.13			4.51	3.90				
57	0.323	33.83		11.06									
58	0.317	34.15	16.90										
59	0.311	34.46											
60	0.305	34.76	17.21	11.36	8.43	6.64	5.51			3.55	2.59	2.01	1.43
61	0.299	35.06											
62	0.293	35.35	17.50										
63	0.287	35.64		11.65				4.80					
64	0.282	35.92	17.78		8.72				4.19				
65	0.276	36.20				6.92							
66	0.271	36.47	18.05	11.92			5.78						
67	0.265	36.73											
68	0.260	36.99	18.31		8.98								
69	0.255	37.25		12.17									
70	0.250	37.50	18.56			7.17		5.05		3.80			

B3: Periodic multipliers (*continued*)

Periodic multipliers at 2.5% discount

	Factor	Frequency of payments in years											
n		1	2	3	4	5	6	7	8	10	12	15	20
1	0.976	0.98											
2	0.952	1.93	0.95										
3	0.929	2.86		0.93									
4	0.906	3.76	1.86		0.91								
5	0.884	4.65				0.88							
6	0.862	5.51	2.72	1.79			0.86						
7	0.841	6.35						0.84					
8	0.821	7.17	3.54		1.73				0.82				
9	0.801	7.97		2.59									
10	0.781	8.75	4.32			1.67				0.78			
11	0.762	9.51											
12	0.744	10.26	5.07	3.34	2.47		1.61				0.74		
13	0.725	10.98											
14	0.708	11.69	5.77					1.55					
15	0.690	12.38		4.03		2.36						0.69	
16	0.674	13.06	6.45		3.15				1.50				
17	0.657	13.71											
18	0.641	14.35	7.09	4.67			2.25						
19	0.626	14.98											
20	0.610	15.59	7.70		3.76	2.97				1.39			0.61
21	0.595	16.18		5.26				2.14					
22	0.581	16.77	8.28										
23	0.567	17.33											
24	0.553	17.88	8.83	5.82	4.31		2.80		2.05		1.30		
25	0.539	18.42				3.50							
26	0.526	18.95	9.36										
27	0.513	19.46		6.33									
28	0.501	19.96	9.86		4.81			2.65					
29	0.489	20.45											
30	0.477	20.93	10.34	6.81		3.98	3.28			1.87		1.17	
31	0.465	21.40											
32	0.454	21.85	10.79		5.26				2.50				
33	0.443	22.29		7.25									
34	0.432	22.72	11.22										
35	0.421	23.15				4.40		3.07					
36	0.411	23.56	11.63	7.66	5.67		3.69				1.71		
37	0.401	23.96											
38	0.391	24.35	12.03										
39	0.382	24.73		8.04									
40	0.372	25.10	12.40		6.05	4.77			2.87	2.24			2.71
41	0.363	25.47											
42	0.354	25.82	12.75	8.40			4.04	3.42					
43	0.346	26.17											
44	0.337	26.50	13.09		6.38								
45	0.329	29.83		8.72		5.10						1.50	
46	0.321	27.15	13.41										
47	0.313	27.47											
48	0.306	27.77	13.72	9.03	6.69		4.35		3.18		2.01		
49	0.298	28.07						3.72					
50	0.291	28.36	14.01			5.39				2.53			

(*continued*)

B3: Periodic multipliers (*continued*)

Periodic multipliers at 2.5% discount (continued)

	Factor	Frequency of payments in years											
n		1	2	3	4	5	6	7	8	10	12	15	20
51	0.284	28.65		9.31									
52	0.277	28.92	14.28		6.97								
53	0.270	29.19											
54	0.264	29.46	14.55	9.58			4.61						
55	0.257	29.71				5.65							
56	0.251	29.96	14.80		7.22			3.97	3.43				
57	0.245	30.21		9.82									
58	0.239	30.45	15.04										
59	0.233	30.68											
60	0.227	30.91	15.26	10.05	7.44	5.88	4.84			2.76	2.24	1.72	2.93
61	0.222	31.13											
62	0.216	31.35	15.48										
63	0.211	31.56		10.26				4.18					
64	0.206	31.76	15.69		7.64				3.64				
65	0.201	31.96				6.08							
66	0.196	32.16	15.88	10.46			5.04						
67	0.191	32.35											
68	0.187	32.54	16.07		7.84								
69	0.182	32.72		10.64									
70	0.178	32.90	16.25			6.26		4.36		2.94			

B3: Periodic multipliers (*continued*)

Periodic multipliers at 3% discount

n	Factor	Frequency of payments in years: 1	2	3	4	5	6	7	8	10	12	15	20
1	0.971	0.97											
2	0.943	1.91	0.94										
3	0.915	2.83		0.92									
4	0.888	3.72	1.83		0.89								
5	0.863	4.58				0.86							
6	0.837	5.42	2.67	1.75			0.84						
7	0.813	6.23						0.81					
8	0.789	7.02	3.46		1.68				0.79				
9	0.766	7.79		2.52									
10	0.744	8.53	4.20			1.61				0.74			
11	0.722	9.25											
12	0.701	9.95	4.90	3.22	2.38		1.54				0.70		
13	0.681	10.63											
14	0.661	11.30	5.56					1.47					
15	0.642	11.94		3.86		2.25						0.64	
16	0.623	12.56	6.19		3.00				1.41				
17	0.605	13.17											
18	0.587	13.75	6.77	4.45			2.13						
19	0.570	14.32											
20	0.554	14.88	7.33		3.56	2.80				1.30			0.55
21	0.538	15.42		4.99				2.01					
22	0.522	15.94	7.85										
23	0.507	16.44											
24	0.492	16.94	8.34	5.48	4.05		2.62		1.90		1.19		
25	0.478	17.41				3.28							
26	0.464	17.88	8.81										
27	0.450	18.33		5.93									
28	0.437	18.76	9.24		4.48			2.45					
29	0.424	19.19											
30	0.412	19.60	9.65	6.24		3.69	3.03			1.71		1.05	
31	0.400	20.00											
32	0.388	20.39	10.04		4.87				2.29				
33	0.377	20.77		6.72									
34	0.366	21.13	10.41										
35	0.355	21.49				4.05		2.80					
36	0.345	21.83	10.75	7.06	5.22		3.37				1.54		
37	0.335	22.17											
38	0.325	22.49	11.08										
39	0.316	22.81		7.38									
40	0.307	23.11	11.39		5.52	4.36			2.60	2.02			0.86
41	0.298	23.41											
42	0.289	23.70	11.67	7.67			3.66	3.09					
43	0.281	23.98											
44	0.272	24.25	11.95		5.80								
45	0.264	24.52		7.93		4.62						1.32	
46	0.257	24.78	12.20										
47	0.249	25.02											
48	0.242	25.27	12.45	8.17	6.04		3.91		2.84		1.78		
49	0.235	25.50						3.33					
50	0.228	25.73	12.67			4.85				2.25			

(*continued*)

B3: Periodic multipliers (*continued*)

Periodic multipliers at 3% discount (continued)

n	Factor	1	2	3	4	5	6	7	8	10	12	15	20
		Frequency of payments in years											
51	0.221	25.95		8.39									
52	0.215	26.17	12.89		6.25								
53	0.209	26.37											
54	0.203	26.58	13.09	8.60			4.11						
55	0.197	26.77				5.04							
56	0.191	29.97	13.28		6.44			3.52	3.03				
57	0.185	27.15		8.78									
58	0.180	27.33	13.46										
59	0.175	27.51											
60	0.170	27.68	13.63	8.95	6.61	5.21	4.28			2.41	1.95	1.49	1.03
61	0.165	27.84											
62	0.160	28.00	13.79										
63	0.155	28.16		9.11				3.67					
64	0.151	28.31	13.94		6.77				3.19				
65	0.146	28.45				5.36							
66	0.142	28.60	14.09	9.25			4.42						
67	0.138	28.73											
68	0.134	28.87	14.22		6.90								
69	0.130	29.00		9.38									
70	0.126	29.12	14.35			5.49		3.80		2.54			

B3: Periodic multipliers (*continued*)

Periodic multipliers at 3.5% discount

	Factor	Frequency of payments in years											
n		1	2	3	4	5	6	7	8	10	12	15	20
1	0.966	0.97											
2	0.934	1.90	0.93										
3	0.902	2.80		0.90									
4	0.871	3.67	1.81		0.87								
5	0.842	4.52				0.84							
6	0.814	5.33	2.62	1.72			0.81						
7	0.786	6.11						0.79					
8	0.759	6.87	3.38		1.63				0.76				
9	0.734	7.61		2.45									
10	0.709	8.32	4.09			1.55				0.71			
11	0.685	9.00											
12	0.662	9.66	4.75	3.11	2.29		1.48				0.66		
13	0.639	10.30											
14	0.618	10.92	5.37					1.40					
15	0.597	11.52		3.71		2.15						0.60	
16	0.577	12.09	5.94		2.87				1.34				
17	0.557	12.65											
18	0.538	13.19	6.48	4.25			2.01						
19	0.520	13.71											
20	0.503	14.21	6.99		3.37	2.65				1.21			0.50
21	0.486	14.70		4.73				1.89					
22	0.469	15.17	7.45										
23	0.453	15.62											
24	0.438	16.06	7.89	5.17	3.81		2.45		1.77		1.10		
25	0.423	16.48				3.07							
26	0.409	16.89	8.30										
27	0.395	17.29		5.57									
28	0.382	17.67	8.68		4.19			2.27					
29	0.369	18.04											
30	0.356	18.39	9.04	5.92		3.43	2.81			1.57		0.95	
31	0.344	18.74											
32	0.333	19.07	9.37		4.53				2.11				
33	0.321	19.39		6.24									
34	0.310	19.70	9.68										
35	0.300	20.00				3.73		2.57					
36	0.290	20.29	9.97	6.53	4.82		3.10				1.39		
37	0.280	20.57											
38	0.271	20.84	10.24										
39	0.261	21.10		6.79									
40	0.253	21.36	10.50		5.07	3.98			2.36	1.82			0.76
41	0.244	21.60											
42	0.236	21.83	10.73	7.03			3.33	2.81					
43	0.228	22.06											
44	0.220	22.28	10.95		5.29								
45	0.213	22.50		7.24		4.20						1.17	
46	0.205	22.70	11.16										
47	0.199	22.90											
48	0.192	23.09	11.35	7.44	5.48		3.53		2.55		1.58		
49	0.185	23.28						2.99					
50	0.179	23.46	11.53			4.38				2.00			

(*continued*)

B3: Periodic multipliers (*continued*)

Periodic multipliers at 3.5% discount (continued)

n	Factor	1	2	3	4	5	6	7	8	10	12	15	20
						Frequency of payments in years							
51	0.173	23.63		7.61									
52	0.167	23.80	11.70		5.65								
53	0.161	23.96											
54	0.156	24.11	11.85	7.76			3.68						
55	0.151	24.26				4.53							
56	0.146	24.41	12.00		5.79			3.14	2.70				
57	0.141	24.55		7.91									
58	0.136	24.69	12.13										
59	0.131	24.82											
60	0.127	24.94	12.26	8.03	5.92	4.65	3.81			2.13	1.75	1.29	0.88
61	0.123	25.07											
62	0.118	25.19	12.38										
63	0.114	25.30		8.15				3.25					
64	0.111	25.41	12.49		6.03				2.81				
65	0.107	25.52				4.76							
66	0.103	25.62	12.59	8.25			3.91						
67	0.100	25.72											
68	0.096	25.82	12.69		6.13								
69	0.093	25.91		8.34									
70	0.090	26.00	12.78			4.85		3.34		2.22			

B3: Periodic multipliers (*continued*)

Periodic multipliers at 4% discount

	Factor	Frequency of payments in years											
n		1	2	3	4	5	6	7	8	10	12	15	20
1	0.962	0.96											
2	0.925	1.89	0.93										
3	0.889	2.78		0.89									
4	0.855	3.63	1.78		0.86								
5	0.822	4.45				0.82							
6	0.790	5.24	2.57	1.68			0.79						
7	0.760	6.00						0.76					
8	0.731	6.73	3.30		1.59				0.73				
9	0.703	7.44		2.38									
10	0.676	8.11	3.98			1.50				0.68			
11	0.650	8.76											
12	0.625	9.39	4.60	3.01	2.21		1.42				0.63		
13	0.601	9.99											
14	0.577	10.56	5.18					1.34					
15	0.555	11.12		3.56		2.05						0.56	
16	0.534	11.65	5.71		2.75				1.27				
17	0.513	12.17											
18	0.494	12.66	6.21	4.06			1.91						
19	0.475	13.13											
20	0.456	13.59	6.66		3.20	2.51				1.13			0.46
21	0.439	14.03		4.50				1.78					
22	0.422	14.45	7.09										
23	0.406	14.86											
24	0.390	15.25	7.48	4.89	3.59		2.30		1.66		1.02		
25	0.375	15.62				2.88							
26	0.361	15.98	7.84										
27	0.347	16.33		5.23									
28	0.333	16.66	8.17		3.92			2.11					
29	0.321	16.98											
30	0.308	17.29	8.48	5.54		3.19	2.61			1.44		0.86	
31	0.296	17.59											
32	0.285	17.87	8.76		4.21				1.94				
33	0.274	18.15		5.81									
34	0.264	18.41	9.03										
35	0.253	18.66				3.45		2.36					
36	0.244	18.91	9.27	6.06	4.45		2.85				1.26		
37	0.234	19.14											
38	0.225	19.37	9.50										
39	0.217	19.58		6.28									
40	0.208	19.79	9.70		4.66	3.65			2.15	1.65			0.67
41	0.200	19.99											
42	0.193	20.19	9.90	6.47			3.04	2.56					
43	0.185	20.37											
44	0.178	20.55	10.07		4.84								
45	0.171	20.72		6.64		3.82						1.03	
46	0.165	20.88	10.24										
47	0.158	21.04											
48	0.152	21.20	10.39	6.79	4.99		3.20		2.30		1.41		
49	0.146	21.34						2.70					
50	0.141	21.48	10.53			3.97				1.79			

(continued)

B3: Periodic multipliers (*continued*)

Periodic multipliers at 4% discount (continued)

	Factor	Frequency of payments in years											
n		1	2	3	4	5	6	7	8	10	12	15	20
51	0.135	21.62		6.93									
52	0.130	21.75	10.66		5.12								
53	0.125	21.87											
54	0.120	21.99	10.78	7.05			3.32						
55	0.116	22.11				4.08							
56	0.111	22.22	10.89		5.23			2.81	2.41				
57	0.107	22.33		7.15									
58	0.103	22.43	11.00										
59	0.099	22.53											
60	0.095	22.62	11.09	7.25	5.33	4.18	3.41			1.88	1.51	1.13	0.76
61	0.091	22.71											
62	0.088	22.80	11.17										
63	0.085	22.89		7.33				2.90					
64	0.081	22.97	11.25		5.41				2.49				
65	0.078	23.05				4.25							
66	0.075	23.12	11.33	7.41			3.49						
67	0.072	23.19											
68	0.069	23.26	11.40		5.48								
69	0.067	23.33		7.48									
70	0.064	23.39	11.46			4.32		2.96		1.95			

B3: Periodic multipliers (*continued*)

Periodic multipliers at 4.5% discount

n	Factor	Frequency of payments in years: 1	2	3	4	5	6	7	8	10	12	15	20
1	0.957	0.96											
2	0.916	1.87	0.92										
3	0.876	2.75		0.88									
4	0.839	3.59	1.76		0.84								
5	0.808	4.39				0.81							
6	0.768	5.16	2.52	1.64			0.77						
7	0.735	5.89						0.74					
8	0.703	6.60	3.23		1.54				0.70				
9	0.673	7.27		2.32									
10	0.644	7.91	3.87			1.45				0.64			
11	0.616	8.53											
12	0.590	9.12	4.46	2.91	2.13		1.36				0.59		
13	0.564	9.68											
14	0.540	10.22	5.00					1.28					
15	0.517	10.74		3.42		1.97						0.52	
16	0.494	11.23	5.49		2.63				1.20				
17	0.473	11.71											
18	0.453	12.16	5.95	3.88			1.81						
19	0.433	12.59											
20	0.415	13.01	6.36		3.04	2.38				1.06			0.42
21	0.397	13.40		4.27				1.67					
22	0.380	13.78	6.74										
23	0.363	14.15											
24	0.348	14.50	7.09	4.62	3.39		2.16		1.55		0.94		
25	0.333	14.83				2.72							
26	0.318	15.15	7.41										
27	0.305	15.45		4.93									
28	0.292	15.74	7.70		3.68			1.96					
29	0.279	16.02											
30	0.267	16.29	7.97	5.20		2.98	2.43			1.33		0.78	
31	0.256	16.54											
32	0.244	16.79	8.21		3.93				1.79				
33	0.234	17.02		5.43									
34	0.224	17.25	8.44										
35	0.214	17.46				3.20		2.18					
36	0.205	17.67	8.64	5.63	4.13		2.63				1.14		
37	0.196	17.86											
38	0.188	18.05	8.83										
39	0.180	18.23		5.81									
40	0.172	18.40	9.00		4.30	3.37			1.96	1.50			0.59
41	0.165	18.57											
42	0.157	18.72	9.16	5.97			2.79	2.34					
43	0.151	18.87											
44	0.144	19.02	9.30		4.45								
45	0.138	19.16		6.11		3.51						0.92	
46	0.132	19.29	9.43										
47	0.126	19.41											
48	0.121	19.54	9.55	6.23	4.57		2.91		2.08		1.26		
49	0.116	19.65						2.45					
50	0.111	19.76	9.67			3.62				1.61			

(*continued*)

B3: Periodic multipliers (*continued*)

Periodic multipliers at 4.5% discount (continued)

	Factor	Frequency of payments in years											
n		1	2	3	4	5	6	7	8	10	12	15	20
51	0.106	19.87		6.34									
52	0.101	19.97	9.77		4.67								
53	0.097	20.07											
54	0.093	20.16	9.86	6.43			3.00						
55	0.089	20.25				3.71							
56	0.085	20.33	9.94		4.75			2.54	2.17				
57	0.081	20.41		6.51									
58	0.078	20.49	10.02										
59	0.074	20.57											
60	0.071	20.64	10.09	6.58	4.82	3.78	3.07			1.68	1.34	0.99	0.66
61	0.068	20.71											
62	0.065	20.77	10.16										
63	0.062	20.83		6.64				2.60					
64	0.060	20.79	10.22		4.88				2.23				
65	0.057	20.95				3.84							
66	0.055	21.01	10.27	6.70			3.13						
67	0.052	21.06											
68	0.050	21.11	10.32		4.93								
69	0.048	21.16		6.75									
70	0.046	21.20	10.37			3.88		2.64		1.73			

B3: Periodic multipliers (*continued*)

Periodic multipliers at 5% discount

	Factor	Frequency of payments in years											
n		1	2	3	4	5	6	7	8	10	12	15	20
1	0.952	0.95											
2	0.907	1.86	0.91										
3	0.864	2.72		0.86									
4	0.823	3.55	1.73		0.82								
5	0.784	4.33				0.78							
6	0.746	5.08	2.48	1.61			0.75						
7	0.711	5.79						0.71					
8	0.677	6.46	3.15		1.50				0.68				
9	0.645	7.11		2.26									
10	0.614	7.72	3.77			1.40				0.61			
11	0.585	8.31											
12	0.557	8.86	4,32	2.81	2.06		1.30				0.58		
13	0.530	9.39											
14	0.505	9.90	4.83					1.22					
15	0.481	10.38		3.29		1.88						0.48	
16	0.458	10.84	5.29		2.52				1.14				
17	0.436	11.27											
18	0.416	11.69	5.70	3.71			1.72						
19	0.396	12.09											
20	0.377	12.46	6.08		2.89	2.26				0.99			0.38
21	0.359	12.82		4.07				1.58					
22	0.342	13.16	6.42										
23	0.326	13.49											
24	0.310	13.80	6.73	4.38	3.20		2.03		1.45		0.87		
25	0.295	14.09				2.65							
26	0.281	14.38	7.01										
27	0.268	14.64		4.65									
28	0.255	14.90	7.27		3.46			1.83					
29	0.243	15.14											
30	0.231	15.37	7.50	4.88		2.88	2.26			1.22		0.71	
31	0.220	15.59											
32	0.210	15.80	7.71		3.67				1.66				
33	0.200	16.00		508									
34	0.190	16.19	7.90										
35	0.181	16.37				3.06		2.01					
36	0.173	16.55	8.07	5.25	3.84		2.43				1.04		
37	0.164	16.71											
38	0.157	16.87	8.23										
39	0.149	17.02		5.40									
40	0.142	17.16	8.37		3.98	3.21			1.80	1.36			0.52
41	0.135	17.29											
42	0.129	17.42	8.50	5.53			2.56	2.14					
43	0.123	17.55											
44	0.117	17.66	8.62		4.10								
45	0.111	17.77		5.64		3.32						0.82	
46	0.106	17.88	8.72										
47	0.101	17.98											
48	0.096	18.08	8.82	5.74	4.20				1.89		1.14		
49	0.092	18.17					2.66	2.23					
50	0.087	18.26	8.91			3.40				1.45			

(*continued*)

B3: Periodic multipliers (*continued*)

Periodic multipliers at 5% discount (continued)

	Factor	Frequency of payments in years											
n		1	2	3	4	5	6	7	8	10	12	15	20
51	0.083	18.34		5.82									
52	0.079	18.42	8.99		4.27								
53	0.075	18.49											
54	0.072	18.57	9.06	5.89			2.73						
55	0.068	18.63				3.47							
56	0.065	18.70	9.12		4.34			2.30	1.96				
57	0.062	18.76		5.95									
58	0.059	18.82	9.18										
59	0.056	18.88											
60	0.054	18.93	9.24	6.01	4.39	3.53	2.78			1.51	1.19	0.88	0.57
61	0.051	18.98											
62	0.049	19.03	9.28										
63	0.046	19.08		6.05				2.34					
64	0.044	19.12	9.33		4.44				2.00				
65	0.042	19.16				3.57							
66	0.040	19.20	9.37	6.09			2.82						
67	0.038	19.24											
68	0.036	19.28	9.40		4.47								
69	0.035	19.31		6.13									
70	0.033	19.34	9.44			3.60		2.37		1.54			

APPENDIX II

LIFE TABLES

Prepared by the Government Actuary's Department

Explanatory note: Column lx shows the number who would survive to exact age (x), out of 10,000 or 100,000 born, who were subject throughout their lives to the death rates experienced in the three-year period indicated. Column ex is "the expectation of life", that is, the average future lifetime which would be lived by a person aged exactly x if likewise subject to the death rates experienced in the three-year period indicated.

Tables based on 1993–95 experience

	United Kingdom				England and Wales			
	Males		Females		Males		Females	
	lx	ex	lx	ex	lx	ex	lx	ex
Age (x)								
0 years	100,000	73.9	100,000	79.2	100,000	74.2	100,000	79.4
5 years	99,185	69.5	99,352	74.7	99,188	69.8	99,357	74.9
10 years	99,105	64.6	99,293	69.8	99,109	64.8	99,300	70.0
15 years	99,003	59.6	99,222	64.8	99,011	59.9	99,230	65.0
20 years	98,714	54.8	99,095	59.9	98,740	55.0	99,105	60.1
25 years	98,296	50.0	98,943	55.0	98,339	50.3	98,957	55.2
30 years	97,864	45.2	98,760	50.1	97,927	45.5	98,778	50.3
35 years	97,360	40.5	98.498	45.2	97,438	40.7	98,524	45.4
40 years	96,710	35.7	98,103	40.4	96,797	35.9	98,139	40.6
45 years	95,725	31.1	97,438	35.6	95,837	31.3	97,491	35.8
50 years	94,223	26.5	96,396	31.0	94,383	26.7	96,470	31.2
55 years	91,607	22.2	94,675	26.5	91,845	22.4	94,979	26.7
60 years	87,315	18.2	92,010	22.2	87,683	18.3	92,207	22.4
65 years	80,293	14.5	87,617	18.2	80,831	14.6	87,937	18.3
70 years	69,449	11.4	80,627	14.5	70,148	11.4	81,083	14.6
75 years	54,848	8.7	70,313	11.3	55,610	8.8	70,911	11.4
80 years	37,573	6.5	56,187	8.4	38,273	6.6	56,907	8.5
85 years	20,691	4.8	38,354	6.2	21,189	4.9	39,027	6.2

	Scotland				Northern Ireland			
	Males		Females		Males		Females	
	lx	ex	lx	ex	lx	ex	lx	ex
Age (x)								
0 years	10,000	71.9	10,000	77.4	10,000	72.9	10,000	78.4
5 years	9,919	67.5	9,932	72.9	9,911	68.6	9,927	74.0
10 years	9,909	62.5	9,926	67.9	9,902	63.6	9,919	69.0
15 years	9,898	57.6	9,919	63.0	9,886	58.7	9,911	64.1
20 years	9,858	52.8	9,904	58.1	9,842	54.0	9,897	59.2
25 years	9,804	48.1	9,886	53.2	9,784	49.3	9,881	54.3
30 years	9,745	43.4	9,863	48.3	9,732	44.5	9,863	49.4
35 years	9,680	38.7	9,828	43.5	9,675	39.8	9,838	44.5
40 years	9,607	33.9	9,781	38.7	9,610	35.0	9,797	39.7
45 years	9,482	29.3	9,699	34.0	9,514	30.3	9,723	34.9
50 years	9,283	24.9	9,575	29.4	9,630	25.8	9,614	30.3
55 years	8,944	20.8	9,361	25.0	9,093	21.5	9,424	25.9
60 years	8,404	16.9	9,034	20.8	8,614	17.5	9,129	21.6
65 years	7,560	13.5	8,494	16.9	7,843	14.0	8,653	17.7
70 years	6,333	10.6	7,670	13.5	6,738	10.9	7,954	14.0
75 years	4,818	8.1	6,513	10.4	5,239	8.2	6.876	10.8
80 years	3,157	6.1	4.994	7.8	3,489	6.1	5,435	7.9
85 years	1,651	4.5	3,263	5.6	1,844	4.3	3.615	5.6

Interim life tables, 1994–96

	United Kingdom				England and Wales			
	Males		Females		Males		Females	
	lx	ex	lx	ex	lx	ex	lx	ex
Age (x)								
0 years	100,000	74.1	100,000	79.4	100,000	74.4	100,000	79.6
5 years	99,192	69.7	99,360	74.9	99,191	70.0	99,363	75.1
10 years	99,117	64.8	99,304	69.9	99,117	65.0	99,307	70.1
15 years	99,017	59.8	99,238	65.0	99,020	60.1	99,234	65.2
20 years	98,713	55.0	99,106	60.1	96,734	55.2	99,111	60.3
25 years	98,283	50.3	98,952	55.1	98,321	50.5	98,961	55.3
30 years	97,835	45.5	98,764	50.2	97,891	45.7	98,776	50.4
35 years	97,315	40.7	98,501	45.4	97,387	40.9	98,518	45.6
40 years	96,660	36.0	98.098	40.5	96,746	36.2	98,124	40.7
45 years	95,668	31.3	97,440	35.8	95,774	31.5	97,480	36.0
50 years	94,173	25.8	96,410	31.2	94,325	26.9	96,475	31.3
55 years	91,639	22.4	94,715	26.7	91,859	22.6	94,829	26.8
60 years	87,448	18.4	92,096	22.4	87,798	18.5	92,280	22.5
65 years	80,633	14.7	87,852	18.3	81,158	14.8	88,164	18.4
70 years	70,126	11.5	81,017	14.6	70,806	11.6	81,461	14.7
75 years	55,697	8.8	70,809	11.3	55,439	8.9	71,378	11.4
80 years	38,531	6.6	56,783	8.5	39,212	6.6	57,442	8.6
85 years	21,458	4.9	38,937	6.2	21,945	4.9	39,552	6.3

Interim life tables, 1994–96

	Scotland				Northern Ireland			
	Males		Females		Males		Females	
	lx	ex	lx	ex	lx	ex	lx	ex
Age (x)								
0 years	10,000	72.1	10,000	77.6	10,000	73.3	10,000	78.7
5 years	9,921	67.7	9,935	73.2	9,918	68.9	9,933	74.2
10 years	9,913	62.7	9,929	68.2	9,909	63.9	9,925	69.3
15 years	9,901	57.8	9,922	63.2	9,896	59.0	9,919	64.3
20 years	9,857	53.1	9,907	58.3	9,855	54.3	9,905	59.4
25 years	9,803	48.3	9,888	53.4	9,800	49.6	9,892	54.5
30 years	9,740	43.6	9,865	48.6	9,754	44.8	9,875	49.6
35 years	9,673	38.9	9,834	43.7	9,695	40.0	9,847	44.7
40 years	9,595	34.2	9,786	38.9	9,625	35.3	9,805	39.9
45 years	8,476	29.6	9,706	34.2	9,528	30.6	9,739	35.1
50 years	9,279	25.2	9,579	29.6	9,377	26.1	9,630	30.5
55 years	8,956	21.0	9,386	25.2	9,122	21.7	9,443	26.0
60 years	8,421	17.2	9,041	21.0	8,667	17.7	9,175	21.7
65 years	7,594	13.7	8,516	17.2	7,927	14.2	8,705	17.8
70 years	6,405	10.8	7,714	13.7	6,845	11.0	8,014	14.0
75 years	4,909	8.3	6,582	10.6	5,373	8.3	6,957	10.8
80 years	3,258	6.2	5,103	7.9	3,625	6.0	5,518	7.9
85 years	1,734	4.6	3,369	5.7	1,924	4.2	3,681	5.6

Appendix III

MODEL STRUCTURED SETTLEMENT

Explanatory note: The model agreement, including its four alternative Schedules, is available as a form in duplicate with notes for guidance prepared by the Association of British Insurers, reference C/156/001.

MODEL AGREEMENT

PARTIES: (1) ("the Claimant")
(2) ("the Insurer")

WHEREAS:

(1) The Claimant has made a claim against .... ("the Insured") arising out of .... ("the Claim").

(2) It is agreed that the Claim shall be settled for £......................

AGREED:

1 The Insurer shall be substituted for the Insured to the intent that any liability of the Insured to the Claimant in respect of the Claim shall attach to and be the sole responsibility of the Insurer and that the Insured shall be discharged from any such liability.

2 By way of settlement of the Claim the Insurer shall pay or procure to be paid to the Claimant the sum of £........ and the Claimant shall accept such sum in full and final settlement of the Claim, which is discharged.

3 Subject to the Claimant complying with clause 4 to the satisfaction of the Insurer, the debt of £......... arising under clause 2 shall be discharged by payments by the Insurer to the claimant in accordance with the Schedule.

4.1 The Claimant shall forthwith take all necessary steps to discontinue any proceedings which have been begun or threatened against the Insurer or the Insured in connection with the Claim.

4.2 The Claimant shall not institute any proceedings against the Insurer or the Insured in connection with the Claim.

DATED ....

SIGNED: (1) .... (the Claimant)

(2) .... (for the Insurer)

Form (a)

BASIC TERMS

THE SCHEDULE

Amount	Date for payment

Form (b)

INDEXED TERMS

THE SCHEDULE

Amount	Date for payment

Amounts payable under this Schedule shall be increased annually on or after the date of each anniversary of this agreement in proportion to the increase if any in the figure for the General Index of Retail Prices (all items) for the relevant month over the figures for the same month of the preceding year. For the first anniversary the relevant month shall be that for which the monthly Index was last published by the Department of Employment before that anniversary; for the second and subsequent anniversaries the relevant month in the year of the anniversary in question shall be the same as that used in calculating the increase due on the first anniversary. These increases shall take effect each year on the anniversary of this agreement, or on the date of publication of the Index figure for the relevant month, whichever is later.

In the event that in any year the figure for the General Index of Retail prices (all items) for the relevant month is lower than the figure for the same month of the preceding year (the "Base Figure"), then:

(1) In that year, the amounts payable under this Schedule shall be the same amount ("the fixed amounts") as were paid in the previous year.

(2) In subsequent years, the amounts payable under this Schedule shall remain at the fixed amounts until in any subsequent year (a "year of RPI increase") the figure for the General Index of Retail Prices (all items) for the relevant month is higher than the Base Figure.

(3) In such a year of RPI increase, the amounts payable under the Schedule shall be increased on or after the date of the anniversary of this agreement in proportion to the increase in the figure for the General Index of Retail Prices (all items) for the relevant month over the Base Figure. Such an increase shall take effect in accordance with the terms of this Schedule.

Form (c)

TERMS FOR LIFE

THE SCHEDULE

Amount	Date for payment

A minimum of £......... payments shall be made under this Schedule, regardless of the date of the Claimant, but subject to this no amounts shall be payable after the date of death of the Claimant.

Form (d)

INDEXED TERMS FOR LIFE

THE SCHEDULE

Amount	Date for payment

Amounts payable under this Schedule shall be increased annually on or after the date of each anniversary of this agreement in proportion to the increase if any in the figure for the General Index of Retail Prices (all terms) for the relevant month over the figure for the same month of the preceding year. For the first anniversary the relevant month shall be that for which the monthly Index was last published by the Department of Employment before that anniversary; for the second and subsequent anniversaries the relevant month in the year of the anniversary in question shall be the same as that used in calculating the increase due on the first anniversary. These increases shall take effect each year on the anniversary of this agreement, or on the date of publication of the Index figures for the relevant month, whichever is later.

In the event that in any year the figure for the General Index of Retail Prices (all items) for the relevant month is lower than the figure for the same month of the preceding year (the "Base Figure") then:

(1) In that year, the amounts payable under this Schedule shall be the same amount ("the fixed amounts") as were paid in the previous year.

(2) In subsequent years, the amounts payable under this Schedule shall remain at the fixed amounts until in any subsequent year (a "year of RPI increase") the figure for the General Index of Retail Prices (all times) for the relevant month is higher than the Base Figure.

(3) In such a year of RPI increase, the amounts under the Schedule shall be increased on or after the date of the anniversary of this agreement in proportion to the increase in the figure for the General Index of Retail Prices (all times) for the relevant month over the Base Figure. Such an increase shall take effect in accordance with the terms of this Schedule.

A minimum of .... payments shall be made under this Schedule, regardless of the date of death of the Claimant, but subject to this no amounts shall be payable after the date of death of the Claimant.

Appendix IV

SPECIMEN SCHEDULE OF DAMAGES (RECOVERY OF BENEFITS)

IN THE COURT OF SESSION

SCHEDULE OF DAMAGES
for purposes of the Social Security
(Recovery of Benefits) Act 1997

in the cause

JOHN BROWN, residing at 3
Black Street, Aytown
PURSUER

against

PETER SMITH, residing at 4
Green Road, Beetown
DEFENDER

The amount of compensation claimed in respect of the relevant period, namely between 15 July 1993 and 15 July 1998, is as follows:

1. Compensation for earnings lost during the relevant period: £26,843.

2. Compensation for cost of care incurred during the relevant period: nil.

3. Compensation for loss of mobility during the relevant period: nil.

Appendix V

REPORTED CASES INVOLVING PECUNIARY CLAIMS

A. PERSONAL INJURY CASES

(1) **McHugh v. Leslie,** 1961 S.L.T. (Notes) 65 (Lord Wheatley)

Pursuer aged 42 at date of trial — Injury causing loss of eye — Evidence showed period of adjustment to monocular vision nearly over and pursuer prepared to get back to pre-accident work — Damages of £250 *awarded* for **possible loss of wage-earning potential in the future**.

(2) **Smith v. Colvilles Limited,** 1964 S.L.T. (Notes) 91 (Lord Milligan)

Pursuer aged 28 at date of trial — Serious injury rendering the pursuer paraplegic — Evidence that the pursuer was an electrician to trade; that his pre-accident net weekly wage was £15 13s 6d; and that his expectation of life was 30 to 40 years — Damages of £10,000 *awarded* for **loss of future earnings**, having regard to the ordinary vicissitudes of life and also to the fact that a pursuer had not only the income from the sum awarded but also the capital.

(3) **McGilvray v. British Insulated Callender's Cables Ltd,** 1965 S.L.T. (Notes) 61 (Lord Johnston)

Pursuer aged 40 at date of trial — Injury rendering the pursuer blind — Evidence that the pursuer's average weekly net pre-accident wage was £11 15s — **Loss of earnings to date of trial and beyond,** for a period of about six months, agreed and damages *awarded* accordingly — Damages of £5,000 *awarded* for **loss of future earnings** thereafter, on the basis of a multiplicand of £500 and a multiplier of 10, having regard to the prospect that had the accident not occurred the pursuer might reasonably have looked forward to 20 or 25 years of employment and, set against that, the possibility of illness and accident.

(4) **Watt v. Clyde Alloy Steel Company Limited,** 1966 S.L.T. (Notes) 64 (Lord Thomson)

Pursuer aged 52 at date of trial — Respiratory disease involving breathlessness and tiredness — Evidence that the pursuer would be likely to earn reduced wages so long as he was able to work in the future; and that he would probably have to give up working at an earlier age than he would otherwise have had to do — **Loss of earnings to date of trial** calculated and damages *awarded* accordingly — Damages of 650, being five years at £130, and £750, being approximately one year's present earnings, *awarded* for **loss of future earnings**.

(5) **Smith's Curator Bonis v. Scottish Gas Board,** 1966 S.L.T. (Notes) 71 (Lord Fraser)

Ward aged c.39 at date of trial — Very severe brain damage resulting in total incapacity for work — Estimated annual earnings c.£850 — **Loss of earnings to date of trial** calculated and damages *assessed* accordingly — Damages of £8,500 *assessed* for **loss of future earning capacity**, taking account of the probability that pursuer would be maintained without charge in hospital for the rest of his life.

(6) **Odgers v. British Railways Board,** 1967 S.L.T. (Notes) 97 (Second Division)

Pursuer suffering skin disease — Evidence that the pursuer's dermatitis had diminished the resistance of his skin to the ordinary wear of life; and that he was a poor risk for working under conditions of bad ventilation, sweating and dust — Damages of £300 *awarded* for **diminution in the pursuer's value in the labour market**.

(7) **Steen v. Macnicol,** 1968 S.L.T. (Notes) 77 (Lord Stott)

Child aged nine at time of accident — Severe head and brain damage rendering it not at all likely that he would ever be able to work — Damages of £12,000 *awarded* for **loss of future earnings**, taking full account of the imponderables.

(8) **McGeechan v. George Russell (Steel) Ltd,** 1970 S.L.T. (Notes) 76 (Lord Leechman)

Pursuer aged 43 at date of trial — Severe injuries resulting in continuing disability and rendering the pursuer unfit for his pre-accident employment as a lorry driver — Evidence that osteo-arthritis had established itself in the pursuer's hip joint and the prognosis was that it might likewise affect his knee joint and possibly his ankle; that the condition would deteriorate and the pursuer's restricted working capacity would be further impaired; that any alternative work which he might obtain would in all probability not exceed his unemployment by more than 30s a week; that the pursuer would have been discharged from his employment in any event; and that following that he would have in all probability been employed again but for his physical incapacity resulting from his injuries — **Loss of earnings to date of**

trial calculated for the whole period and damages *awarded* accordingly — Damages of £2,860 *awarded* for **loss of future earnings** on the basis of a multiplicand of £260 and a multiplier of 11.

(9) **Dickson v. Edinburgh Corporation,** 1970 S.L.T. (Notes) 56 (Lord Leechman)

Child aged 14 at time of accident — Serious brain damage rendering him unable to concentrate or shoulder any degree of responsibility and unable to continue with his studies, with consequent severely limited prospects of employment — Evidence that from comparatively early age would probably have earned £30– £40 per week and that in his post-accident state his earnings would be at most £10– £15 per week — Damages of £13,125 *awarded* for **loss of future earnings** on the basis of a multiplicand of £875 per annum and a multiplier of 15.

(10) **McClymont v. Glasgow Corporation,** 1971 S.L.T. (Notes) 45 (Lord Robertson)

Pursuer aged 63 at date of trial — Injury causing psychological and neurotic illness and traumatic cervical spondylosis and rendering him permanently unfit for work — Evidence that general deterioration in health might have prevented him from working until retiring age in any event — Damages *awarded* for **loss of future earnings** for period ending shortly prior to prospective date of retirement.

(11) **McKinnell v. White,** 1971 S.L.T. (Notes) 61 (Lord Fraser)

Child aged seven at date of trial — Serious brain damage rendering him unable to live an independent life and requiring almost certainly to have to spend his whole life in an institution — No evidence as to what his likely earning capacity might have been when he grew up apart from his pre-accident intelligence and fact that his father in business as a building contractor — Damages of £15,000 *awarded* for **loss of earning capacity** on the basis of a multiplicand of £1,000 and a multiplier of 15.

(12) **Brown v. Glasgow Corporation,** 1973 S.L.T. (Notes) 45 (Lord Maxwell)

Pursuer aged 57 at date of trial — Injuries to neck, shoulder and arm resulting in continuing disability — Evidence that the pursuer was still in work; that he no longer worked overtime, which was in the order of £8 per week; that the accident had precipitated symptoms from an underlying condition; and that he had unrelated leg trouble as at the date of trial — Damages of £300 for **loss of future earnings**, having regard to (i) the real risk of some further interruption of work attributable to the accident; (ii) the possibility, albeit speculative, that the pursuer might have to give up work somewhat earlier than he otherwise would have done; and (iii) the prospect that the symptoms, if they had not been initiated by the accident, might well have been initiated in some other way; and £250 for **loss of overtime payment in the future**, having regard to the uncertainty as to whether the loss was due to the attributable injuries as opposed to advancing years and other disabilities such as the recent trouble with his leg, *awarded*.

(13) **Sellar's Curator Bonis v. Glasgow Victoria and Leverndale Hospitals,** 1973 S.L.T. (Notes) 3 (Lord Leechman)

Ward a newly qualified nurse — Serious brain damage leaving her in a physical state of spastic quadriplegia — Evidence of normal progression of nursing careers indicating likely attainment of status of ward sister by date of trial **— Loss of earnings to date of trial** calculated on that basis and damages *awarded* accordingly — Damages of £17,000 *awarded* for **loss of future earnings** on the basis of a multiplicand of £1,700 and a multiplier of 10 — Damages of £12,000 *awarded* for **future care costs** on the basis of three and a half years at home and thereafter for visits home from institution where she would probably have to go ultimately.

(14) **Hamilton v. Clark,** 1975 S.L.T. (Notes) 44 (Lord Dunpark)

Pursuer aged c.49 at date of trial — Injury to head resulting in loss of sight in one eye and damage to the other — Evidence that the pursuer was a principal in the civil service; that he would probably be able to continue to work as a civil servant until retirement at the age of 62; that but for his accident he would probably have been promoted to assistant secretary by about between one and five years after the date of trial; that he would require a serious and delicate operation to his right eye by about three years after the date of trial **— Loss of earnings to date of trial** agreed and damages *awarded* accordingly — Damages of £1,150 *awarded* for **loss of future earnings** on the basis that the pursuer would have been promoted one year after the date of trial and that his promotion would be deferred by two years until after the operation, meaning that he would lose two years' differential between the salaries at £575 a year.

(15) **Skakle v. Downie,** 1975 S.L.T. (Notes) 23 (Lord Maxwell)

Pursuer aged c.25 at date of trial — Serious head injury causing severe and permanent change of personality and leaving him childish, unstable, irresponsible and lacking in interest and enthusiasm — Evidence that now unable to practise former craft of carpentry, albeit holding down lower paid unskilled employment, but uncertainties as to wage differential — Damages of £1,000 for **loss of future earnings** and £3,000 for **employment insecurity** *awarded*.

(16) **Bennett v. Dexion Ltd,** 1976 S.L.T. (Notes) 69 (Lord Brand)

Pursuer a young man — Severe fractures to leg sustained at work — Evidence that pursuer had very poor pre-accident work record and was unemployed at date of trial although had been fit for light work for two years **— Loss of earnings to date of trial** calculated and damages *assessed* accordingly — Damages of £1,000 *assessed* for **prospective future loss of earning capacity**.

(17) **Kirkwood v. Christie & Vesey Ltd,** 1976 S.L.T. (Notes) 56 (Lord Grieve)

Pursuer a woodcutting machinist — Serious and permanent injuries to left hand, including traumatic amputations resulting in residual disability — Evidence that pursuer continuing to work as machinist but with restrictions — Damages of £1,500 *awarded* for **loss of earning capacity**.

(18) **McKendrick v. Mitchell Swire Ltd,** 1976 S.L.T. (Notes) 65 (Lord Brand)

Pursuer aged 40 at date of trial — Severe crushing injuries leaving pursuer fit only for light work — Evidence that pursuer's job was temporary and other employees who lost their jobs unable to find alternative work **— Loss of earnings to date of trial** calculated and damages *assessed* accordingly subject to deduction of 30% — Damages of £5,000 *assessed* for **future loss of earnings** on the basis of a multiplicand of £500 and a multiplier of 10, taking account of the prospect that the diminished earning capacity would cease to be operative by the time the pursuer was 50.

(19) **Owenson v. Rennie's Lion and Comfort Coaches Ltd,** 1976 S.L.T. (Notes) 58 (Lord Brand)

Pursuer aged 48 at date of trial — Serious injuries to pelvis resulting in limited mobility, frequent headaches and psychological upset — Evidence that pursuer an active hard-working woman who owned and managed a grocer's shop which she required to sell after her accident — **Loss of profits to date of trial** agreed as to amount and damages *awarded* accordingly — Damages of £10,000 *awarded* for **future loss of profits** on the basis of a multiplicand of £2,000, being the difference between her likely net profit and the investment income from the sale proceeds of the business, and a multiplier of five, taking account of (i) the chances of life; (ii) the fact that the pursuer would be receiving the money now; and (iii) the estimation that she would have handed over the business to her grand-daughter after about eight years from the date of trial.

(20) **Steward v. Greater Glasgow Health Board,** 1976 S.L.T. (Notes) 66 (Lord Keith)

Child aged three at date of trial — Serious brain damage leaving her suffering from spastic tetraplegia and gross mental retardation — Damages of £18,000 *assessed* for **future care costs** on the basis of an agreed multiplicand of £1,500 and a multiplier of 12, taking account of real possibility that in the end of the day child would have to be handed over to institutional care — Damages for **future loss of earnings** would have been *refused* as too speculative.

(21) **Cartledge v. Clydeside Steel Fabrications Ltd,** 1977 S.L.T. (Notes) 69 (Lord Allanbridge)

Pursuer aged 42 at date of trial — Injury to back causing quite severe pain and limitation of movement — Evidence that pursuer told to get sedentary job but had made no attempt to do so **— Loss of earnings to date of trial** calculated, on a broad basis, on the assumption that the pursuer should have taken at least some steps to try to obtain sedentary work and damages *assessed* accordingly — Damages of £2,000 *assessed* for **future loss of earnings** on the basis of the pursuer's age and permanent unfitness for heavy work.

(22) **Clues v. Western S.M.T. Co. Ltd,** 1977 S.L.T. (Notes) 51 (Lord Maxwell)

Pursuer aged c.62 at date of trial — Injury to leg resulting in minor residual disability but preventing her from doing a job involving much standing or climbing of stairs — Evidence that prior to the accident she worked in a hotel — Damages for **loss of earnings to date of trial** and for one year's **future loss of earnings** *awarded*, taking into account the pursuer's age.

(23) **Douglas v. National Coal Board,** 1977 S.L.T. (Notes) 14 (Lord Keith)

Pursuer aged 35 at date of trial — Injury to back involving the protrusion of an intervertebral disc in the lumbar region — Evidence that pursuer's doctor was continuing to certify him as unfit for any work and that the pursuer was permanently unfit for heavy work, with his prospects of obtaining suitable light work uncertain; and that the pursuer had had a certain history of back trouble prior to the accident, with the prospect that renewed back trouble in some shape or form might in any event have reduced his capacity to work **— Loss of earnings to date of trial** agreed as to amount and damages therefor *assessed* on the basis that the pursuer had not acted unreasonably in not seeking light work to date — Damages of £3,000 *assessed* for **loss of future earnings**.

(24) **Malcolm v. W.H. Rankin Ltd,** 1977 S.L.T. (Notes) 45 (Lord Robertson)

Pursuer aged c.20 at date of trial — Severe brain damage resulting in partial paralysis and complete change of personality — Evidence that had it not been for the accident the pursuer would probably, on completion of his apprenticeship with his father's firm, have earned as a qualified joiner £50 per week, plus overtime, and eventually one-half of the net profits at the end of the financial year but now had no hope of becoming a successful tradesman and business man, having only the possibility of doing general clerical work if he could obtain a course in this line — **Loss of earnings to date of trial** agreed and damages *awarded* accordingly — Damages of £26,250 *awarded* for **loss of future earnings** on the basis of a multiplicand of £1,750, taking account of the possibility that the pursuer might be able to earn something in the future, and a multiplier of 15, having regard to his age.

(25) **Brogan's Tutors v. Glasgow District Council,** 1978 S.L.T. (Notes) 47 (Lord Wylie)

Child aged seven at date of trial — Severe burning injury to right hand resulting in permanent disability and leaving him very severely restricted in the range of employment open to him in adult life, being unfit for jobs involving heavy work or intricate movements of the hand and fingers — Damages of £3,000 *awarded* for **loss of earning capacity**.

(26) **Cook v. National Coal Board,** 1978 S.L.T. (Notes) 19 (Lord Stott)

Pursuer aged c.53 at date of trial — Severe injury to leg resulting in eventual amputation and leaving the pursuer, a maintenance engineer, fit for bench work only — Evidence that pursuer considered himself fit for bench work for two years preceding the trial but his doctor had given certificates of total incapacity throughout, albeit telling him that as from three months before the date of trial he would no longer be entitled to sit back and expect his wage loss to be made good by the defenders **— Loss of earnings to date of trial** calculated and damages therefor *awarded* subject to a deduction for the differential between a maintenance engineer's earnings and that of a bench worker over the three months' period — Damages of £3,000 *awarded* for **loss of future earnings**, applying the same differential and taking into account deductible benefits of £600.

(27) **Harrison v. McLean,** 1978 S.L.T.(Notes) 68 (Lord Grieve)

Pursuer aged 52 at date of trial — Minor injury allegedly causing continuing pain and disability — Evidence, however, not supportive of causal link between accident and continuing symptoms — On hypothesis that such link established, no **loss of earnings to date of trial** proved in any event but, as to **loss of future earnings**, damages of £7,000 would have been *awarded* on the basis of a multiplicand of £1,768 and a multiplier of four, taking into account her present age and a retirement age of 60 as well as the fact that the prospect of her finding any form of employment in the future was extremely remote.

(28) **Lamb v. Glasgow District Council,** 1978 S.L.T. (Notes) 64 (Lord Grieve)

Pursuer aged 35 at date of trial — Severe burning injuries leaving her with loss of grip in left hand — Evidence that she had worked for two months each year before the accident, earning about £130 per annum but was now unfit for work of any sort — Damages of £850 *awarded* for **loss of earning capacity**, taking account of possibility that she might have worked for another 10 years at least but might not have worked for two months each year.

(29) **Lamb's Tutor v. Cawthorn-Sinclair Ltd,** 1978 S.L.T. (Notes) 31 (Lord Stewart)

Child aged c.10 at date of trial — Serious injuries resulting in total paralysis from waist down — Damages of £5,000 *assessed* for **loss of future earnings**, taking into account all the vicissitudes of life to which the boy would in any event have been subject.

(30) **McCabe v. British Domestic Appliances Ltd,** 1978 S.L.T. (Notes) 31 (Lord Grieve)

Pursuer aged c.47 at date of trial — Injury involving disc in spine — Evidence that the pursuer's employers went out of business and pursuer made redundant; and that the pursuer acted unreasonably in refusing surgical operation which had reasonably good prospects of complete success — **Loss of earnings to date of trial** calculated on the basis of the period until the date upon which, after the proposed surgical operation, the pursuer would have been fit for employment and damages therefor *awarded*, account not being taken of the closure of the defenders' business.

(31) **McLaughlin v. British Steel Corporation,** 1978 S.L.T. (Notes) 28 (Lord Ross)

Pursuer aged 45 at date of trial — Back injury resulting in very serious consequences and leaving the pursuer unfit for work and unlikely ever to be fit for work again — **Loss of earnings to date of trial** agreed and damages *awarded* accordingly — Damages of £29,120 *awarded* for **loss of future earnings** on the basis of a multiplicand of £2,912 and a multiplier of 10, having regard to the pursuer's age and the fairly pessimistic medical evidence.

(32) **Paris v. Scottish Special Housing Association,** 1978 S.L.T. (Notes) 50 (Lord Stott)

Pursuer aged 59 at date of trial — Injury to wrist resulting in continuing disability and leaving her unfit for her pre-accident employment as an auxiliary nurse — Evidence that the pursuer had been fit for light work after a period and that she had made no attempt to find such work, but the prospects for her having been able to find such work could not have been very great at her age and with her disability; and that she had since the accident remarried and moved house and it might be doubtful that she would have chosen to continue in employment in any event — **Loss of earnings to date of trial** calculated and damages therefor *awarded* making some allowance for the possibility of light work having been available — Damages of £500 *awarded* for **loss of future earnings**, looking at the matter broadly.

(33) **Ryan v. International Distillers and Vintners Export Ltd,** 1978 S.L.T. (Notes) 16 (Lord Allanbridge)

Pursuer aged c.48 at date of trial — Injury to back resulting in residual disability and leaving the pursuer permanently unfit for heavy work — Damages of £750 *awarded* for **loss of future earning capacity**, upon a broad assessment.

(34) **Byrnes v. Fife Health Board,** 1979 S.C. 415 (Second Division; Lord Ross)

Pursuer aged 46 at date of trial — Injury comprising negligent high amputation about mid-thigh instead of below-knee amputation — Evidence that difference between the amputations had a minimal effect on the pursuer's wage-earning capacity and that the pursuer had had a variable work record prior to his injury and had lost the habit of regular gainful employment, albeit that he had worked for about 40 months out of the nine and a half years since the accident — **Loss of earnings to date of trial** allowed in respect of two and a half years out of a total of five and three quarters non-earning years, on the basis that he was to be regarded as a man who would have worked only half the year, and damages *awarded* accordingly — Damages of £5,000 *awarded* for **loss of future earning capacity and potential in the wage-earning field**.

(35) **Buckley v. Melville Dundas and Whitson Ltd,** 1979 S.L.T. (Notes) 102 (Lord Ross)

Pursuer aged c.54 at date of trial — Crushing injury to finger resulting in fusion operation — Evidence that the pursuer should have been able to resume his pre-accident work within nine months after the operation for fusion; that he lost his employment about three months after his operation; that he might not have found it easy to obtain alternative employment because of his stiff finger once he had become fit for work; and that he ought to have been able to obtain comparable work at a comparable wage within a further period of six months after becoming fit for work — **Loss of earnings to date of trial** calculated for the period from the date of the accident until a date fifteen months after the operation and damages *awarded* accordingly — Damages for **loss of future earnings** *refused*.

(36) **Leneghan v. Parker,** 1979 S.L.T. (Notes) 83 (Lord Stewart)
Pursuer aged 21 at date of trial — Injuries to arm resulting in loss of lifting power and leaving the pursuer restricted in his capacity for physical effort — Evidence that the pursuer not bright and from a community where there was no regular work and that he had attended a technical school for a time and at the time of the trial was engaged in light work — **Loss of earnings to date of trial** calculated and damages therefor *awarded* on the basis of an estimated loss of about three months' earnings per year for four years.

(37) **Mazs v. Dairy Supply Co Ltd,** 1979 S.L.T. (Notes) 44 (Lord Cowie)
Pursuer aged c.39 at date of trial — Serious injuries resulting in paralysis from the waist down — Evidence that the pursuer would have gone back to site work but for the accident where earnings would have been greater but less regular — **Loss of earnings to date of trial** calculated and damages therefor *assessed* on the basis of an overall average weekly figure, allowing for all the normal contingencies of life, less the sums which he had in fact earned since his accident — Damages of £30,000 *assessed* for **loss of future earnings** on the basis of a multiplicand of £2,500, representing the differential between the average wage which he would have been able to earn but for the accident and his actual wage, and a multiplier of 12.

(38) **Whitfield v. Ranco Motors Ltd,** 1979 S.L.T. (Notes) 15 (Lord Grieve)
Pursuer aged c.44 at date of trial — Injury to finger resulting in partial amputation and leaving her with a residual disability — **Loss of earnings to date of trial** agreed and damages *awarded* accordingly — Evidence unclear as to whether any ongoing loss of earnings — Damages of £300 *awarded* for **loss of future earning capacity**.

(39) **Kyle v. Salvesen,** 1980 S.L.T. (Notes) 18 (Lord Grieve)
Pursuer aged 31 at date of trial — Serious back injuries resulting in significant disability in locomotion and leaving him unable to resume employment as a merchant seaman and fit only for sedentary work — **Loss of earnings to date of trial** agreed and damages *awarded* accordingly — Damages of £33,174 *awarded* for **loss of future earnings** on the basis of a multiplicand of £3,686 and a multiplier of nine, upon the assumption that he would succeed in getting some form of gainful employment.

(40) **Barclay v. J. & W. Henderson Ltd,** 1980 S.L.T. (Notes) 71 (Lord McDonald)
Pursuer aged c.30 at date of trial — Multiple fractures resulting in failed arthrodesis to wrist and leaving the pursuer unable to resume

work as a scaffolder but able to hold down driving job — **Loss of earnings to date of trial** agreed and damages *awarded* accordingly — Damages of £24,000 *awarded* for **loss of future earnings** on the basis of a multiplicand of £2,000, representing the differential between the pursuer's pre-accident and post-accident employment, and a multiplier of 12, having regard to the pursuer's age.

(41) **Mitchell v. Swanson's Executor,** 1980 S.L.T. (Notes) 41 (Lord Allanbridge)

Pursuer aged 21 at date of trial — Severe brain injury leaving him seriously physically handicapped with a substantial reduction in his ability to concentrate and very limited working capacity for the future — **Loss of earnings to date of trial** agreed and damages *awarded* accordingly — Damages of £39,000, less benefits, *awarded* for **loss of future earnings** on the basis of a multiplicand of £3,000 and a multiplier of 13, after making a deduction for probable future earnings of £3,000.

(42) **Gerrard v. Swanson's Executor,** 1980 S.L.T. (Notes) 43 (Lord Allanbridge)

Pursuer aged 23 at date of trial — Severe brain injury leaving the pursuer physically and mentally handicapped and very limited working capacity for the future as well as little likelihood of marriage — **Loss of earnings to date of trial** agreed and damages *awarded* accordingly — Damages of £26,000, less benefits, *awarded* for **loss of future earnings** on the basis of a multiplicand of £2,000 and a multiplier of 13, after making a deduction for possible but unlikely events of future employment and future marriage of £2,000.

(43) **Gordon v. Muir,** 1980 S.L.T. (Notes) 51 (Lord Kincraig)

Pursuer aged c.65 at date of trial — Severe head injury and other injuries transforming the pursuer into a mental and physical invalid — Evidence that pursuer would probably have to employ someone to look after him, as his wife now did but might not always do, but not sufficient to allow a reasonably accurate assessment to be made — Damages of £500 *awarded* for **future care costs**.

(44) **McKirdy v. Lothian Regional Council,** 1980 S.L.T. (Notes) 74 (Lord Kissen)

Pursuer aged 60 at date of trial — Injury to shoulder and right median nerve — Evidence that the pursuer would have been unfit for his employment as a bus driver irrespective of the accident but no evidence as to the kinds of alternative employment which he might then have had, the earnings in any such kinds of employment or the availability of such employment — **Loss of earnings to date of trial** calculated as a rough estimate and damages *awarded* accordingly — Damages of £1,000 *awarded* for **prejudice of future earning capacity**, allowing for the possibility of the continuation of benefits.

(45) **McDonald v. Whiteford & Robertson Ltd,** 1980 S.L.T. (Notes) 2 (Lord Cowie)

Pursuer aged c.67 at date of trial — Severe exacerbation of pre-existing degenerative back condition leaving the pursuer unfit for work — Evidence that he would not have been fit for anything but light work after his 65th birthday irrespective of his accident and that he had had previous back trouble and had to wear a corset at the time of his accident, but no evidence that he could have got light work at his age — Damages for **loss of earnings** after 65th birthday *refused.*

(46) **Shevchuk v. National Coal Board,** 1980 S.L.T. (Notes) 65 (Lord Stott)

Pursuer aged 51 at date of trial — Injury to neck leaving the pursuer with severe limitation of neck movement and pain from time to time and unfit for his pre-accident work — Evidence that pursuer had pre-existing degenerative changes which might have given rise to symptoms in any event **— Loss of earnings to date of trial** agreed and damages *awarded* accordingly — Damages of £5,690, less benefits, *awarded* for **loss of future earnings**, taking into account the differential between his former and his present earnings of £1,600 as well as the possibility that the symptoms would have emerged in any event, being one of the imponderables which had to be kept in view.

(47) **Will v. Charles Will Ltd,** 1980 S.L.T. (Notes) 37 (Lord Ross)

Pursuer aged 25 at date of trial — Serious injury to leg resulting in below-knee amputation — Evidence that after completing a course the pursuer, before his accident a farm worker and casual stevedore, was hoping to obtain a clerical job and that he should be able to do so within about eight months, averaging about £2,000 per annum — Damages of £30,000, less benefits, *awarded* for **loss of future earnings** on the basis of a multiplicand of £2,000, representing a probable income but for the accident of £4,000 less his likely future earnings of £2,000, and a multiplier of 15, taking into account the pursuer's age, the normal vicissitudes of life and the chances of his capacity deteriorating, his health suffering or his employment ceasing as well as the fact that there would be increased loss for the initial period of eight months.

(48) **Blair v. F.J.C. Lilley (Marine) Ltd,** 1981 S.L.T. 90 (Second Division; Lord Cowie)

Pursuer aged 52 at date of trial — Injury involving traumatic amputation of arm above elbow and leaving the pursuer unfit for his previous work as a labourer — Evidence that the pursuer had been in almost constant employment during the whole of his working life but had virtually always obtained employment which enabled him to stay at home; that when he changed jobs it was to improve his earnings but in that respect had been dependent on others for transport where the work was not local; and that there was now a lack of suitable work locally for him in his post-accident state — **Loss of earnings to date of trial** calculated on appeal on the basis of both (i) the pursuer's wage-earning capacity in the construction industry generally, with its built-in overtime advantages; and (ii) the more limited wage-earning potential in his locality, as reflecting situations which were liable to have occurred during the remainder of his working life, there being possibilities that the pursuer might have obtained employment elsewhere with transport provided, given his record in seeking better paid work, or might have obtained employment locally, or might not have been able to obtain or undertake such employment and damages *awarded* accordingly — Damages of £19,500, less benefits, *awarded* on appeal for **loss of future earnings** on the basis of a multiplicand of £3,900, reflecting the competing situations by taking an adjusted average of the differing net weekly earnings on a broad axe basis, and a multiplier of five.

(49) **Bowers v. Strathclyde Regional Council,** 1981 S.L.T. 122 (First Division; Lord Ross)

Pursuer aged 34 at date of trial — Minor physical injuries resulting in anxiety state with phobic content — Evidence that the pursuer should have been able to resume employment of a suitable kind by the third anniversary of his accident, albeit that he might not have found it easy to obtain employment, and no suggestion in the evidence that he would have been liable to periods of unemployment once he had resumed work — **Loss of earnings to date of trial** calculated on the footing that the period of loss ended three years after the accident and damages *awarded* accordingly — Damages for **loss of future earnings** *refused.*

(50) **McPhail v. British Railways Board,** 1981 S.L.T.(Notes) 124 (Lord Wylie)

Pursuer aged 63 at date of trial — Injury to leg involving fracture of thigh bone resulting in probable acceleration of the onset of arthritis — Evidence that the retirement age for the pursuer's employment was 65 years — **Loss of earnings** calculated on the basis that but for the accident the pursuer would have been able to continue in his employment until aged 63 and damages *assessed* accordingly.

(51) **Bruce v. British Transport Hotels Ltd,** 1981 S.L.T. (Notes) 77 (Lord Brand)

Pursuer aged 59 at date of trial — Comparatively trivial injury to ankle resulting in disability which was largely due to the effects of a pre-existing injury and obesity — **Loss of earnings to date of trial** agreed and damages *assessed* accordingly — Damages for **loss of future earnings** would have been *refused*.

(52) **Comerford v. P.S.C. Equipment Ltd,** 1981 S.L.T. (Notes) 52 (Lord Cowie)

Pursuer sustaining minor physical injuries resulting in a post-traumatic neurosis and leaving him unable to work at heights for some time to come — Evidence that pursuer had been unfit for work for three and a half years after his accident, when he obtained light work, and that his pre-accident employment would have come to an end in any event within two years of his accident although there was no evidence to prove that he would then have obtained a similar job elsewhere — **Loss of earnings to date of trial** calculated on the basis of the pursuer's pre-accident earnings up to the date that he obtained light work (there being no doubt that the pursuer would have found some form of employment when made redundant) but not for the period thereafter and damages *assessed* accordingly — Damages of £2,500 *assessed* for **loss of wage-earning capacity**.

(53) **Ferguson v. Strathclyde Regional Council,** 1981 S.L.T. (Notes) 103 (Lord Allanbridge)

Pursuer aged c.53 at date of trial — Severe head injury resulting in post-traumatic epilepsy and significant change of personality and leaving it extremely difficult if not impossible for her to get a job — Evidence that the pursuer had had various jobs at one time or another albeit that at the time of her accident she was not employed — Damages of £1,000 *awarded* for **loss of earning capacity**.

(54) **Hanlon v. Cuthbertson,** 1981 S.L.T. (Notes) 57 (Lord Allanbridge)

Pursuer aged c.43 at date of trial — Injuries to arm and shoulder with both mental and physical effects, including substantial restriction of use of the left arm and fingers — Evidence that the pursuer retained as employee in husband's business at pre-accident level of earnings — No loss of earnings to date of trial — Damages of £2,000 *awarded* for **reduction in future earning capacity**.

(55) **Malley v. National Coal Board,** 1981 S.L.T. (Notes) 81 (Lord Wylie)

Pursuer aged 42 at date of trial — Injury to leg resulting in amputation — Evidence suggestive of uncertainty that the pursuer's earnings at the time of the accident would have held up; and evidence that the pursuer had resumed employment after his accident at a lower rate of pay — **Loss of earnings to date of trial** agreed and damages *awarded* accordingly — Damages of £5,200, less benefits, *awarded* for **loss of future earnings** on the basis of a multiplicand of £520 per annum, representing the differential between the pre-accident and post-accident earnings, and a multiplier of 10, taking account of the pursuer's age and the uncertainty as to his pre-accident earnings.

(56) **Maslowski v. Bell,** 1981 S.L.T. (Notes) 61 (Lord Murray)

Pursuer aged c.33 at date of trial — Severe internal injuries and multiple fractures resulting in restrictions in mobility and loss of concentration and ability to remember leaving him with a permanent continuing loss of working capacity — Evidence that but for the accident the pursuer would have become a partner in his father's firm by which he was employed at the time, that the pursuer would probably now become a partner within a few months after trial and that his incapacity would be of progressively decreasing importance in the long-term arrangements of the firm **— Loss of earnings to date of trial and beyond** for the period thereafter until the pursuer's probable assumption as a partner calculated and damages *awarded* accordingly — Damages of £11,200 *awarded* for **loss of future earnings** after the pursuer's assumption on the basis of a multiplicand of £1,400, representing the net loss to the pursuer of his one-third share of the firm's profits calculated on the footing of the cost of employing substitutes for him, and a multiplier of eight, having regard to the nature of the pursuer's permanent incapacity and its probable diminishing importance in the long term in the setting of the partnership.

(57) **McLeod v. Cartwright,** 1981 S.L.T. (Notes) 54 (Lord Stewart)

Pursuer aged c.58 at date of trial — Very severe injuries to leg resulting in amputation at mid-thigh and leaving him unfit for any kind of work **— Loss of earnings to date of trial** agreed and damages *awarded* accordingly — Damages of £11,024, less benefits, *awarded* for **loss of future earnings** on the basis of a multiplicand of £2,756 and a multiplier of four.

(58) **McLoone v. British Railways Board,** 1981 S.L.T. (Notes) 65 (Lord Ross)

Pursuer aged 23 at date of trial — Severe injuries to legs resulting in a double above-knee amputation — Evidence that the pursuer might have been promoted but for his accident and that in his post-accident state he was fit for sedentary employment **— Loss of earnings to date of trial** calculated and damages *awarded* accordingly — Damages of £37,180, less benefits, *awarded* for **loss of future earnings** on the basis of a multiplicand of £2,860, representing a wage loss at a rate about half-way between the pursuer's pre-accident job and the promoted position, and a multiplier of 13, taking account of the fact that the pursuer was apparently fit for some forms of employment.

(59) **McNee v. G.R. Stein & Co. Ltd,** 1981 S.L.T. (Notes) 31 (Lord Murray)

Pursuer aged 49 at date of trial — Disease affecting skin on hand — Damages of £500 *assessed* for **restriction on future employment prospects**, the effects on such prospects in this case being minimal.

(60) **Miles v. Glasgow District Council,** 1981 S.L.T. (Notes) 44 (Lord Ross)

Pursuer aged 33 at date of trial — Serious injuries to foot and leg resulting in loss of mobility, including the ability to walk on rough ground — Damages of £1,000 *assessed* for **future disadvantage on the labour market**.

(61) **Murphy v. Lord Advocate,** 1981 S.L.T. (Notes) 77 (Lord Cowie)

Pursuer a forestry worker sustaining vibration-induced white finger — Evidence that pursuer receiving a lower rate of pay in post-accident employment as a result of his injuries **— Loss of earnings to date of trial** calculated and damages *assessed* accordingly — Damages of £2,500 *assessed* for **loss of future earnings** on the basis of a continuing loss of £13 per week.

(62) **Tannock v. British Leyland Motor Company,** 1981 S.L.T. (Notes) 49 (Lord Jauncey)

Pursuer aged c.32 at date of trial — Injury to neck and back resulting in some disability and leaving the pursuer fit for moderately heavy industrial employment but not for his pre-accident employment as a machine operator nor for any other job which involved heavy lifting — Evidence that the pursuer in post-accident clerical employment earning less than he had as a machine operator, that he was not happy in that job and wanted to do a driving job, which was difficult to obtain in the defenders' factory, and that there was a possibility that some further improvement might occur in his condition **— Loss of earnings to date of trial** agreed and damages *awarded* accordingly — Damages of £6,250 *awarded* for **loss of future earnings** on the basis of (i) a multiplicand of £1,150, representing the differential between his post-accident and pre-accident earnings, and a multiplier of four; and (ii) a multiplicand of £550, representing the differential between a future, better paid job and his pre-accident employment (having regard to the medical evidence as to the pursuer's fitness for moderately heavy work and the possibility of some further improvement in his condition), and a multiplier of three.

(63) **Watson v. City Meat Wholesalers Ltd,** 1981 S.L.T. (Notes) 121 (Lord Cowie)

Pursuer aged 41 at date of trial — Disease sustained by pursuer leaving him unfit for his pre-accident employment as a slaughterman — Evidence that the pursuer now in employment at a lower rate of pay but subject to some talk of redundancy shortly before trial, the risk thereof having passed for the time being **— Loss of earnings to date of trial** agreed and damages *awarded* accordingly — Damages of £31,200 *awarded* for **loss of future earnings** on the basis of a multiplicand of £2,600, representing the differential between his pre-accident and post-accident earnings, and a multiplier of 12, taking account of the pursuer's age and the normal vicissitudes of life as well as the possibility of redundancy from his present job.

(64) **Roberts v. British Railways Board,** 1982 S.L.T. 126 (Lord Cowie)

Pursuer aged c.29 at date of trial — Injury to knee resulting in the pursuer being unfit for his pre-accident employment as an engine driver for the foreseeable future but fit for some form of work **— Loss of earnings to date of trial** agreed and damages *assessed* accordingly — Damages of £40,880.32, less benefits, *assessed* for **loss of future earnings** on the basis of a multiplicand of £5,110.04, being what the pursuer's earnings would have been as at the date of trial, and a multiplier of eight, taking account of the possibility of the pursuer obtaining some form of employment in the future.

(65) **Anderson v. Brown,** 1983 S.L.T. 655 (Lord Stewart)

Pursuer aged c.30 at date of trial — Injury comprising severe neurological disability arising from negligent misdiagnosis of subarachnoid haemorrhage resulting in serious physical deterioration, mental handicap and personality change — Evidence that the pursuer might have gained promotion from her pre-accident employment as a staff nurse and that although she might have left work in order to have a family, it was likely that, if she could, she would have returned to nursing, which she loved — Evidence that the pursuer was not a person who could cope adequately with life on her own but because of her husband, himself ill, she was not in present need of nursing care but there was a possibility that she might in the future find herself on her own **— Loss of earnings to date of trial** agreed and damages *awarded* accordingly — Damages of £36,000 *awarded* for **loss of future earnings** on the basis of a multiplicand of £4,000, representing what the pursuer's earnings as a staff nurse would have been as at the date of trial less an allowance for the possibility that the pursuer even in her disabled state might be able to earn something, perhaps by some form of part time work, and a multiplier of nine —

Damages of £3,000 *awarded* for the **cost of future assistance of a general domestic kind**.

(66) **Gardner v. Howard Doris Ltd,** 1983 S.L.T. 672 (Lord Grieve)
Pursuer aged 42 at date of trial — Injury to spine resulting in paraplegia — Evidence that the pursuer would have been made redundant from his pre-accident job as a craft operative irrespective of his accident but that he had seldom been out of work before his accident and had skills which would have made regular employment a probability for him — Evidence that the pursuer required more heat in his home by reason of his paraplegia and needed to expend funds on his central heating system for that purpose; that he required to incur as a necessity costs in connection with the purchase, replacement and running of a car; that he required care and attendance for both nursing and domestic and the provision of medical supplies and equipment; and that he required certain alterations to his house as a result of his condition **— Loss of earnings to date of trial** calculated and damages *awarded* accordingly — Damages of £62,000 *awarded* for **loss of future earnings** on the basis of a multiplicand of £6,200, representing what the pursuer's earnings would have been as at the date of trial, and a multiplier of 10, having regard to the pursuer's age, work record and skills — Damages of £3,000 for **central heating costs**; £6,000 for **motor vehicle provision, replacement and running costs**, on a lump sum basis; £10,000 for **nursing and domestic assistance and special equipment costs**, on a lump sum basis; and £3,500 for **house alteration costs** *awarded.*

(67) **Chapman v. South of Scotland Electricity Board,** 1983 S.L.T. 456 (Lord McDonald)
Pursuer aged c.16 at date of trial — Severe electrical burning injuries over various parts of his body resulting in an above-knee amputation of his left leg — Damages of £22,500 *awarded* for **loss of future earnings** on the basis of a multiplicand of £1,500, representing the extent to which the pursuer's future annual earning capacity had been diminished by reason of his injuries, and a multiplier of 15, having regard to the various imponderable factors implicit in an exercise of such nature.

(68) **Glasgow v. City of Glasgow District Council,** 1983 S.L.T. 65 (Lord Allanbridge)
Pursuer aged 26 at date of trial — Severe injuries to spine and ribs resulting in permanent disabilities and leaving him unfit to return to heavy work but capable of work of a light or sedentary nature, albeit that he might not find such work easy to get **— Loss of earnings to date of trial** agreed and damages *awarded* accordingly — Damages

of £30,000 *awarded* for **loss of future earnings** as being the approximate mid-point between the sums of £33,328 (an amount calculated on the basis of a multiplicand of £3,328, representing what the pursuer's earnings would have been as at the date of trial, and a multiplier of 10, being two-thirds of the multiplier which would have been appropriate if the pursuer had had no prospects of further employment rather than, as was the case, reasonable prospects of some future employment at a lower wage) and £28,000 (an amount calculated on the basis of a three-year period of no employment in the future and a continuing wage loss for the remaining 12 years at the rate of £1,500 per annum).

(69) **Kelly v. City of Edinburgh District Council,** 1983 S.L.T. 71 (Lord Murray)

Pursuer aged 21 at date of trial — Serious skeletal injuries resulting in fitness for light work only in the future — **Loss of earnings to date of trial** agreed and damages *assessed* accordingly — Damages of £42,000 *awarded* for **loss of future earnings** on the basis of a multiplicand of £3,000, representing what the pursuer's earnings would have been as at the date of trial less 40% to take account of his fitness for light work, and a multiplier of 14.

(70) **MacRae v. William K. McIntyre & Sons,** 1983 S.L.T. 643 (Lord Brand)

Pursuer aged 21 at date of trial — Very serious injury to hand and fingers resulting in amputation of index finger in dominant hand and limiting the range of employment open to the pursuer in the future — Damages of £3,000 *awarded* for **loss of earning capacity**.

(71) **Todd v. Montgomerie Sealants Ltd,** 1983 S.L.T. 354 (Lord Murray)

Pursuer aged 34 at date of trial — Injury to wrist resulting in need for arthrodesis and reducing manipulative ability and grip of the hand — **Loss of earnings to date of trial** calculated, taking account of second unconnected accident, and damages *awarded* accordingly — Damages of £24,336 *awarded* for **loss of future earnings** on the basis of a multiplicand of £3,042, representing what the pursuer's earnings would have been as at the date of trial less a discount of 35% to take account of the prospect of his obtaining light work in the future, and a multiplier of eight, taking account of his age and limited disability.

(72) **Tuttle v. Edinburgh University,** 1984 S.L.T. 172 (Lord McDonald)

Pursuer aged 24 at date of trial — Severe injuries resulting in paraplegia — Evidence that the pursuer had lost a period of potential employment of up to a year prior to trial and that while he was not working full time at present, he was in continuing receipt of a full time salary and should be able to work full time in due course — Evidence that the pursuer required certain aids, appliances and equipment, some of which might require replacement from time to time; that he required regular assistance in keeping his house and maintaining the small garden, a need which would increase as he grew older; that he would require over time to replace his car, which had been provided and adapted through the generosity of his friends, and would incur additional running costs by reason of requiring to use the car more often than would a person who was not disabled; that he required certain adaptations to his home and would incur additional running costs in relation to his home beyond what was normally to be expected with regard to heating costs and fuel bills; and that he required special clothing and dressing — **Loss of earnings to date of trial** calculated and damages *awarded* accordingly — Damages of £30,000 *awarded* for **potential loss of opportunity in well-remunerated active employment**, particularly overseas — Damages of £3,000 for **aids, appliances and equipment costs**; £30,000 for **future care and attendance costs** on the basis of a multiplicand of £2,000 and a multiplier of 10, supplemented by a further sum of £10,000 in recognition of the fact that this was a need which would increase as the pursuer grew older; £6,000 for **car replacement costs**; £10,000 for **additional motoring costs** on the basis of a multiplicand of £1,000 and a multiplier of 10; £13,000 for **home adaptation costs**, allowing for receipt of local authority grants; £4,000 for the **additional home running costs** on the basis of a multiplicand of £260 and a multiplier of 15, rounded up; and £1,500 for **special clothing and dressing costs** *awarded.*

(73) **Barrett v. Strathclyde Fire Brigade,** 1984 S.L.T. 325 (Lord Brand)
Pursuer aged 31 at date of trial — Severe head injury resulting in epilepsy and leaving the pursuer unfit for his pre-accident employment as a fireman — Evidence that the pursuer would have been promoted by the date of trial and might have been promoted further in the future; that he would have had to retire from the fire service at age 48 in any event; and that it was probable that after a period of retraining he would be fit for some kind of work, possibly in protected employment — **Loss of earnings to date of trial** agreed and damages *awarded* accordingly — Damages of £37,000, less benefits, *awarded* for **loss of future earnings** on the basis of (i) a multiplicand of £6,000, representing what the pursuer's current earnings would have been as at the date of trial, and a multiplier of two; and (ii) a multiplicand of £3,000, representing those earnings less a discount of 50% to take account of the probability that after retraining he would be fit for some

kind of work, and a multiplier of eight; and (iii) a lump sum of £1,000 to allow for what would have been the pursuer's prospects of promotion.

(74) **Galbraith v. Marley Buildings Ltd,** 1984 S.L.T. 155 (Lord Allanbridge)

Pursuer aged 49 at date of trial — Injury to back aggravating a pre-existing disc disease — Evidence that there was a very substantial risk that even without his accident the pursuer's back condition might well have prevented him from doing heavy work up to the date of his retirement at the age of 65 years and that the pursuer now doing light work during the summer months — **Loss of earnings to date of trial** agreed and damages *awarded* accordingly — Damages of £18,382 *awarded* for **loss of future earnings** on the basis of a multiplicand of £5,252 and a multiplier of three and a half, taking into account the very substantial risk arising from the pursuer's pre-existing back condition and his post-accident earnings.

(75) **Jack v. City of Glasgow District Council,** 1984 S.L.T. 168 (Lord Allanbridge)

Pursuer aged 35 at date of trial — Very serious injury to ulnar nerve resulting in disability with uncertain prognosis and rendering the pursuer unfit for any kind of work, including his pre-accident employment as a joiner, albeit with the possibility of becoming fit for light work in the future — Evidence that the level of the pursuer's pre-accident earnings inflated by temporary factors — **Loss of earnings to date of trial** agreed and damages *awarded* accordingly — Damages of £62,608 *awarded* for **loss of future earnings** on the basis of a multiplicand of £8,944, representing what the pursuer's earnings would have been as at the date of trial, and a multiplier of seven, taking account of the fact that the level of the pursuer's pre-accident earnings was temporarily inflated and that the pursuer might become fit for light work in the future.

(76) **Lees v. Grahamston Iron Co. Ltd,** 1984 S.L.T. 184 (Lord Stewart)

Pursuer aged c.21 at date of trial — Injury to eye resulting in loss of sight in that eye — Damages of £4,500, less benefits, *awarded* for **diminished prospects of employment in the future**.

(77) **Laurie v. John Laing Construction Ltd,** 1984 S.L.T. 312 (Lord McDonald)

Pursuer a young man — Injury to arm resulting in minor permanent disability — Evidence that the pursuer had been made redundant after a period but neither that nor his subsequent inability to get work related to his disability — **Loss of earnings to date of trial** agreed and damages *assessed* accordingly — Damages of £2,000 *assessed* for **disadvantage on the labour market**.

(78) **Love v. British Railways Board,** 1984 S.L.T. 2 (Lord Ross)

Pursuer aged c.14 at date of trial — Very severe injuries involving burns to 53% of the body surface and resulting in amputations of the right hand and leg — Damages of £22,500 *assessed* for **future loss of wage-earning capacity** on the basis of a multiplicand of £1,500, representing a regular weekly wage of £30 to take account of (i) the fact that there were a variety of forms of employment for which the pursuer would be suited, such as working as a storeman or a clerk doing simple clerking or a lift attendant or the like; (ii) the fact that it was far from clear that even if the pursuer had not had his accident he would have obtained permanent employment; and (iii) the fact that the pursuer was subject to all the normal contingencies of life, and a multiplier of 15.

(79) **Robertson v. Aberdeen University,** 1984 S.L.T. 341 (Lord Kincraig)

Pursuer in his early 50s at date of trial — Injury to back exacerbating pre-existing degenerative arthritic changes in the lumbar spine and leaving the pursuer unfit for his pre-accident employment but fit for light work — Evidence that the pre-existing condition was progressive and would have gradually got worse to the extent that he would have become incapable of carrying out his work at some stage irrespective of his accident **— Loss of earnings to date of trial** agreed and damages *assessed* accordingly — Damages of £16,620 *assessed* for **loss of future earnings** on the basis of a multiplicand of £5,540 and a multiplier of three, taking account of (i) the probability that the pursuer would have had to give up his usual work before normal retirement age anyway; and (ii) the probability that he would now find light work at some time before the age of 65.

(80) **Lanigan v. Derek Crouch Construction Ltd,** 1985 S.L.T. 346 (Lord Mackay of Clashfern)

Pursuer aged 51 at date of trial — Injury to foot and ankle resulting in permanent disability — Evidence that the pursuer prepared to suffer the pain from his disability rather than not work — Damages of £1,000 *assessed* for **loss of future earning capacity**.

(81) **Hempsey v. Inverclyde District Council,** 1985 S.L.T. 348 (Lord Cowie)

Pursuer aged c.24 at date of trial — Injury to eye rendering it almost useless — Evidence that a fellow-plumber also one-eyed **— Loss of earnings to date of trial** agreed and damages *assessed* accordingly — Damages for **loss of earning capacity** *refused* on the footing that there was nothing in his present condition to suggest that he would be unable to carry on his trade successfully and compete with other plumbers in the labour market.

(82) **Donnelly v. John Russell (Grangemouth) Ltd,** 1985 S.L.T. 82 (Lord Mayfield)

Pursuer aged 38 at date of trial — Injuries to arm and hand resulting in restricted movement of the arm and loss of grip in the hand and leaving him unfit for his pre-accident employment as a heavy goods driver but fit to drive a van or car — **Loss of earnings to date of trial** calculated by reference to an adjusted average weekly figure to take account of the probability that the pursuer would have been made redundant and later re-engaged irrespective of the accident and damages *awarded* accordingly — Damages of £35,000 *awarded* for **loss of future earnings** on the basis of a multiplicand of £5,000, based on the pursuer's pre-accident wage, and a multiplier of seven, taking into account the fact that the pursuer might obtain a form of light work although his prospects were limited.

(83) **Fallow v. Greater Glasgow Health Board,** 1985 S.L.T. 98 (Lord Grieve)

Pursuer aged c.20 at date of trial — Injury arising from the negligent application of a plaster to a fractured wrist resulting in limitation of the ability to clench his fist fully or to grip objects firmly and leaving the pursuer restricted in his ability to get work — Evidence that the pursuer had wanted to be a glazier but had never worked, sustaining his injury while still at school, and that the average weekly wage for a third-year apprentice, which the pursuer could be regarded as at the date of trial, was about £80 — **Loss of earnings to date of trial** agreed and damages *assessed* accordingly — Damages of £30,000 *assessed* for **loss of future earnings** on the basis of a multiplicand of £2,000, representing an average weekly wage of £40, rounded down, and a multiplier of 15.

(84) **Laing v. Northern Grouting Engineers Ltd,** 1985 S.L.T. 179 (Lord Allanbridge)

Pursuer aged 35 at date of trial — Injury to wrist causing degenerative arthritis and resulting in disability including loss of grip in the hand and restriction of movement in the wrist, leaving the pursuer unable to carry on as a joiner and fit for light work only — **Loss of earnings to date of trial** calculated, having regard to earnings derived by the pursuer since his accident, and damages *awarded* accordingly — Damages of £7,500 *awarded* for **loss of future earnings** on a lump sum basis, taking account of (i) the fact that the pursuer had a substantial handicap on the labour market in the future, albeit not in respect of his dominant hand; and (ii) the fact that there had been a lack of continuity in his pre-accident employment, albeit that being a good worker he might well be able in the future, as he had done in the past, to get casual work; the assessment being the equivalent of a net loss of £15 per week for 10 years.

(85) **Caven v. McEwan,** 1985 S.L.T. 83 (Lord Davidson)
Pursuer aged 31 at trial — Severe injury to leg resulting in knee-level amputation and leaving the pursuer unfit for his pre-accident work and fit only for light work not involving sitting or standing for long periods, heavy or moderate lifting, much going up or down stairs or kneeling — Evidence that the pursuer had failed to take reasonable steps to improve his job prospects and thereby mitigate his loss but that, even if he had taken those steps, he would probably not have obtained gainful employment prior to the date of trial, although he would have been better equipped to get work **— Loss of earnings to date of trial** agreed as to amount and damages *awarded* accordingly — Damages of £26,250, less benefits, *awarded* for **loss of future earnings** on the basis of a multiplicand of £4,420 and a multiplier of six, having regard to (i) the pursuer's failure to take steps to improve his job prospects; (ii) his personal qualities, which would enable him to adapt well to new working conditions; (iii) the likelihood that in the next five years he would obtain an offer of employment suitable for his condition; (iv) the likelihood that in the course of the next few years his mobility was likely to improve; and (v) the fact that any employment offered to him might be at a lower rate of remuneration than that pertaining to his pre-accident employment.

(86) **Convery v. Kirkwood,** 1985 S.L.T. 483 (Lord McDonald)
Pursuer aged 25 at date of trial — Severe injury to head rendering the pursuer virtually unemployable by reason of mental deterioration and personality change **— Loss of earnings to date of trial** agreed as to amount and damages *assessed* accordingly — Damages of £50,960, less benefits, *assessed* for **loss of future earnings** on the basis of a multiplicand of £3,640 and a multiplier of 14, having regard to the pursuer's complete inability to get on with other people with the result that no one was likely to employ him.

(87) **Stoddard v. Topek Roofing Ltd,** 1985 S.L.T. 192 (Lord Stott)
Pursuer aged 42 at date of trial — Injury to back rendering him unfit for his pre-accident work as a roofer but fit for moderately heavy work but only on the level and for comparatively short periods — Evidence that the pursuer had worked as a roofer for 23 years; was hoping to attend a rehabilitation course in which he would be trained for some form of lighter work; but had little prospect of obtaining

such work in the foreseeable future, it being almost impossible to find in his locality — **Loss of earnings to date of trial** agreed and damages *awarded* accordingly — Damages of £54,208 (sic) *awarded* for **loss of future earnings** on the basis of a multiplicand of £7,748 and a multiplier of seven, taking into consideration the somewhat remote possibility that work would become available to the pursuer.

(88) **Sloan v. Triplett,** 1985 S.L.T. 294 (Lord Allanbridge)

Pursuer aged 26 at date of trial — Injury to eye resulting in double vision — **Loss of earnings to date of trial** agreed and damages *assessed* accordingly — Damages of £3,000 *assessed* for **future disability on the labour market**, having regard to the fact that his double vision could affect his ability to work safely at heights.

(89) **Marshall v. Bertrams Ltd,** 1985 S.L.T. 80 (Lord Allanbridge)

Pursuer aged 39 at date of trial — Injury to hand resulting in disability involving his grip and leaving the pursuer unfit for work involving heavy lifting or tools and limiting his capacity to play the drums, as he had sometimes done professionally before his accident — Evidence that the pursuer was made redundant shortly after returning to work for reasons unconnected with his accident but no satisfactory evidence as to what earnings he would have derived thereafter had he not had his accident — **Loss of earnings to date of trial** agreed on the basis of loss terminating upon redundancy and damages *awarded* accordingly — Damages of £15,000, less benefits, *awarded* on a lump sum basis for **restriction on the pursuer's past and future earning capacity** as a skilled moulder (or even labourer) or drummer, having regard to his age and the nature of his disability; the assessment being the equivalent of a net loss of about £30 per week for 10 years or £20 per week for 15 years.

(90) **McDiarmid v. Borders Regional Health Board,** 1985 S.L.T. 79 (Lord Davidson)

Pursuer aged 59 at date of trial — Injury comprising neurological damage arising from the negligent misdiagnosis of a neck fracture — Evidence that the pursuer's incapacity for work was attributable both to the neurological damage and to an unconnected disabling frozen shoulder condition — Damages for **loss of earnings** *refused* in these circumstances.

(91) **Wilson v. Norman J. Stewart & Co (1970) Ltd,** 1986 S.L.T. 469 (Lord Dunpark)

Pursuer aged 35 at date of trial — Injuries from fall resulting in a post-traumatic anxiety state with depression and a personality change — Evidence that the pursuer unlikely to recover to enable him to perform any remunerative work in the future — **Loss of earnings to date of trial** agreed and damages *awarded* accordingly — Damages of £64,000 *awarded* for **loss of future earnings** on the basis of a multiplicand of £8,000, representing what the pursuer would have been earning as at the date of trial, and a multiplier of eight, having regard to the pursuer's age, the medical evidence and the hazards of the pursuer's former employment as a steel erector.

(92) **Nelson v. National Coal Board,** 1986 S.L.T. 2 (Lord Stewart)
Pursuer aged c.56 at date of trial — Injury to chest resulting in recurrent coronary spasm causing severe chest pain at infrequent but unpredictable times — Evidence that the pursuer would have been unfit for work as a miner for an unrelated reason for a period preceding the date of trial and that a number of miners retired at the age of 55 — **Loss of earnings to date of trial** calculated and damages *awarded* accordingly — Damages for **loss of future earnings** *refused*.

(93) **Muirhead v. Sealink (Scotland) Ltd,** 1986 S.L.T. 21 (Lord Mackay of Clashfern)
Pursuer aged 63 at date of trial — Injury to foot and knee rendering him unfit for his pre-accident employment as a nightwatchman — **Loss of earnings to date of trial** calculated and damages *awarded* accordingly — Damages of £6,000 *awarded* for **loss of future earnings**, representing about one year's net earnings, to take account of (i) the fact that the pursuer still had about one and a half years to go to reach his normal retirement age; (ii) the contingencies of life; (iii) the fact that the pursuer would be receiving damages now in respect of earnings that would accrue over a tract of future time; and (iv) the fairly remote possibility that the pursuer would obtain some form of employment over that period.

(94) **McIlroy v. Esso Petroleum Co. Ltd,** 1986 S.L.T. 552 (Lord Mayfield)
Pursuer aged 45 at date of trial — Disease affecting skin on face and trunk and from time to time other parts of his body and resulting in the loss of his pre-accident employment — **Loss of earnings to date of trial** agreed and damages *assessed* accordingly — Damages of £88,000 *assessed* for **loss of future earnings** on the basis of a multiplicand of £11,000 and a multiplier of eight.

(95) **Howie v. Western Scottish Motor Traction Co. Ltd,** 1986 S.L.T 81 (Lord Davidson)
Pursuer aged 47 at date of trial — Injury to spine resulting in backache and a serious worsening of a pre-existing melancholia, which had not prevented him from working prior to his accident, amounting

to a serious personality change and leaving him at present unfit for employment — Evidence that the pursuer's pre-accident assessment indicated that his potential did not extend beyond labouring work, it being notorious that such work was scarce in his locality, and that the pursuer's employers' business had closed two years after his accident, but no evidence as to how the pursuer's fellow-employees made redundant by the closure had subsequently fared — Damages of £5,000 for **loss of earnings to date of trial** and £10,000 for **loss of future earnings** *awarded*, each on a lump sum basis, taking the many imponderables into consideration and reflecting the fact that as a result of the accident the pursuer's chances of obtaining suitable work were reduced; the assessment being the equivalent of the product of a multiplicand of £3,276 and a multiplier of between 12 and 13, discounted to take account of the pursuer's pre-accident assessment and the notorious scarcity of labouring work in the pursuer's locality.

(96) **Gallacher v. Strathclyde Regional Council,** 1986 S.L.T. 53 (Lord McDonald)

Pursuer aged c.34 at date of trial — Injury to knee a precipitating cause of new symptoms in an already troublesome joint — Evidence that even had there been no accident the condition of the knee was such that it would have obliged him in any event to have given up work as a fireman within a number of years from the date of the accident **— Loss of earnings to date of trial** calculated and *assessed* on that basis — Damages of £3,500, less benefits, *assessed* for **loss of future earnings**, representing half a year's earnings.

(97) **Brodie v. British Railways Board,** 1986 S.L.T 208 (Lord Kincraig)

Pursuer aged 53 at date of trial — Injury resulting in permanent unfitness for pre-accident employment — Evidence that the pursuer would have been likely to have retired at the age of 60 but might have worked on until aged 65 **— Loss of earnings to date of trial** agreed and damages *assessed* accordingly — Damages of £2,500 *assessed* for **loss of future earnings** on the basis of a multiplicand of £500 and a multiplier of five, having regard to the age of the pursuer and the prospects of his going on working until he was possibly 65 but more likely 60.

(98) **Palmer v. Sealink (Scotland) Ltd,** 1987 S.L.T. 797 (Lord Murray)

Pursuer aged 58 at date of trial — Injury rendering the pursuer permanently unfit for employment — Evidence that the pursuer had relatively demanding duties in his pre-accident employment as a nightwatchman but would have continued to work until he was 65 **— Loss of earnings to date of trial** agreed and damages *awarded* accordingly — Damages of £18,390 *awarded* for **loss of future earnings** on the basis of a multiplicand of £6,130 and a multiplier of three.

(99) **Poole v. John Laing plc,** 1987 S.L.T. 325 (Lord Morison)

Pursuer aged c.57 at date of trial — Injury to knee resulting in meniscectomy — Evidence that the degenerative condition of the cartilage was such as predisposed the pursuer to the kind of injury which occurred; that his knee was probably now materially affected by the progression of his pre-existing osteo-arthritic condition; that from a date shortly after the accident the pursuer suffered from a variety of conditions unconnected with it which restricted his earning capacity in any event; and that he would anyway have been made redundant shortly after the date of the accident — **Loss of earnings to date of trial** calculated on the basis that the pursuer had failed to establish that the accident caused him to lose wages for more than a year during the whole of the period during which he was unemployed prior to the date of trial and damages *awarded* accordingly.

(100) **Mowbray v. Steetley Refractories Ltd,** 1987 S.L.T. 250 (Lord Allanbridge)

Pursuer aged 64 at date of trial — Injury to leg resulting in unfitness for work — Evidence that the pursuer would have been made redundant in any event at the age of 60, about 16 months after the accident — **Loss of earnings to date of trial** calculated on a lump sum basis, taking into account the pursuer's age at the date of redundancy and the problems created by unemployment during the intervening years, and damages *assessed* accordingly.

(101) **McAleenan (and others) v. National Coal Board,** 1987 S.L.T. 106 (Lord Jauncey)

McAleenan

Pursuer aged 46 at trial — Burning injuries resulting in certain post-traumatic anxiety symptoms — Evidence that the pursuer worked after his accident, had been made redundant for reasons unrelated to his accident but had made no attempt to obtain other employment since then — Damages for **disadvantage in the labour market** *refused.*

Grant

Pursuer aged 58 at date of trial — Injuries involving burns and the acceleration of an existing progressive deterioration in lung function resulting in a post-traumatic neurosis — Evidence that the pursuer had been made redundant for reasons unrelated to his accident and that but for the accident he would then have been seeking part time work — **Damages for future loss of earning capacity** *refused* in the absence of evidence that such a very restricted labour market, *viz.* for persons near retiring age seeking only part time work, existed at all.

Allardyce
Pursuer aged 31 at date of trial — Burning injuries resulting in panic attacks — Evidence that the pursuer had returned to above-surface work after his accident at a lower rate of pay and had not unreasonably chosen redundancy thereafter — **Loss of earnings to date of trial and beyond,** to the expiry of the quinquennium agreed as to amount and damages therefor *awarded* on the basis that the pursuer had acted reasonably — Damages of £2,000 *awarded* for **loss of future earnings** thereafter on a lump sum basis, there being no evidence that the pursuer would suffer loss in any particular amount in employment outwith the mining industry.

Murphy
Pursuer aged 47 at date of trial — Injuries involving burns and damage to lungs resulting in dyspnoea — Evidence that but for his accident the pursuer would have retired at the age of 55 — **Loss of earnings to date of trial** agreed and damages *awarded* accordingly — Damages of £20,131 *awarded* for **loss of future earnings** on the basis of a multiplicand of c.£4,736 and a multiplier of about four and a quarter.

Cushley
Pursuer aged 57 at date of trial — Injuries involving burns and ensuing internal haemorrhage and resulting in depression — Evidence that the pursuer accepted redundancy after his accident although there was neither mental or physical reason why he could not have undertaken the light work which was then available to him — **Loss of earnings to date of trial** calculated on the basis that no loss after the date of redundancy had been established and damages *awarded* accordingly.

(102) **Logan v. Monklands District Council,** 1987 S.L.T. 557 (Lord Jauncey)

Pursuer aged 42 at date of trial — Injury to arm resulting in permanent unfitness for pre-accident heavy labouring work and leaving the pursuer fit only for light work or work of a supervisory nature which did not involve frequent use of his arm — Evidence that the pursuer had some prior experience of supervisory work and that he had made no attempt since his accident to find other employment or have himself retrained for other employment — **Loss of earnings to date of trial** agreed and damages *awarded* accordingly — Damages *awarded* for **loss of future earnings** on the basis of an agreed multiplicand and a multiplier of eight, having regard to (i) the fact that he had made so small an effort to find suitable employment; and (ii) his prior experience in a supervisory capacity.

(103) **Kirkpatrick v. Scott Lithgow Ltd,** 1987 S.L.T. 654 (Lord McCluskey)

Pursuer aged c.47 at date of trial — Injuries to legs resulting in double amputation below the knee — Evidence that the pursuer had been unfit for work to date of trial; that he would be offered an office job upon recovery from a forthcoming operation which it would be reasonable to expect him to undertake; that on no view was he likely to be able to continue to a normal retiring age having regard to the effort involved in getting about; that the long term future of his employers' business was rather uncertain and thus the pursuer's long term working future was similarly uncertain, and having regard to his disabilities he had poor prospects in the medium and long term of earning his living, accepting that as a skilled tradesman they could not be dismissed as negligible, particularly in view of the fact that he lived in an area of high unemployment; that by the same token the pursuer's high earnings in his pre-accident employment might not have been maintained over the long term irrespective of his accident — **Loss of earnings to date of trial and beyond,** to the date when the pursuer should have returned to work, agreed and damages *awarded* accordingly — Damages of £48,653 *awarded* for **loss of future earnings** after the date of the pursuer's return to work, comprising (i) an award of £6,875 for the period of about 16 months immediately following his likely return to work, being a period during which the pursuer could reasonably confidently be expected to work for his employers, at a rate representing the differential between the pursuer's pre-accident and likely post-accident jobs; and (ii) an award of £41,778 for the period thereafter, being one-half of the product of a multiplicand of £13,926 (what the pursuer's earnings would have been as at the date of the trial) and a multiplier of six, the discount being appropriate in view of the fact that the pursuer could not have been certain of remaining in his pre-accident job until the end of his working days regardless of his accident.

(104) **Howard v. Comex Houlder Diving Ltd,** 1987 S.L.T. 344 (Lord Allanbridge)

Pursuer aged c.30 at date of trial — Injury comprising damage to lungs and rendering the pursuer unfit to return to his pre-accident employment as a saturation diver — Evidence that the pursuer would not have been fully employed as a diver during the period to date of trial because of the undoubted drop in North Sea oil activity and that he would probably not have carried on with saturation diving beyond the age of 40 anyway **— Loss of earnings to date of trial** calculated on the basis of a deduction of about 30% to take account of the fact that the pursuer might have found it difficult to obtain such work during that period and damages *assessed* accordingly — Damages of £41,000 *assessed* for **loss of future earnings** on the basis, rounded up, of a multiplicand of £13,622 and a multiplier of three, having regard to the pursuer's probable retirement date and all the uncertainties at present of work being available in the oil industry.

(105) **Hewson v. Secretary of State for Scotland,** 1987 S.L.T 719 (Lord Cowie)

Pursuer aged 38 at date of trial — Injuries to leg, ankle and foot rendering the pursuer fit only for sedentary work — Evidence that the pursuer was a painter and decorator to trade but had a very bad criminal record at the time of his accident and was likely to have continued in that way of life — Damages of £10,608 *awarded* for **loss of future earnings** on the basis of a multiplicand of £5,304, representing what the pursuer's earnings would have been as a painter and decorator as at the date of trial, and a multiplier of two, having regard to the pursuer's past history and the difficulties he would have had in any event in obtaining employment of any sort.

(106) **Goldie v. National Coal Board,** 1987 S.L.T. 304 (Lord Jauncey)

Pursuer aged c.26 at date of trial — Injury to leg rendering the pursuer unfit for his pre-accident job and for any regular heavy manual work — Damages of £1,200 *awarded* for **disadvantage on the labour market**.

(107) **Gibney v. Eric Johnson Stubbs (Scotland) Ltd,** 1987 S.L.T. 132 (Lord McCluskey)

Pursuer aged 50 at date of trial — Injuries to arm, neck and back rendering the pursuer permanently unfit for his pre-accident work as a rigger/erector but fit for light work as a clerical officer — Evidence that the pursuer had a relatively poor physique for one engaged in such employment and was most unlikely to have continued in regular employment as a rigger/erector until the age of 65, being likely to have retired at the age of 60 or even earlier; that he had a pre-existing tendency to suffer from smoking-related bronchitis and from minor back trouble; and that it was likely that he would have lost a few weeks' work from time to time as he changed jobs **— Loss of earnings to date of trial** calculated on the basis of a 47 week year, having regard to the prospect that he would have lost time off work by reason of his bronchitis, back trouble and job changes, and damages *awarded* accordingly — Damages of £33,105, less benefits, *awarded* for **loss of future earnings** on the basis of a multiplicand of £6,621, representing what the pursuer's earnings would have been as at the date of trial discounted for contingencies related to possible future minor ill health, and a multiplier of five, taking account of (i) the likelihood, arising out of the pursuer's age and health, that he would have retired at the age of 60 or even earlier; and (ii) the possibility, though it was not a strong one, that he might yet return to paid employment (albeit at a reduced wage).

(108) **Gallacher v. McDermotts (Scotland) Ltd,** 1987 S.L.T. 56 (Lord Davidson)

Pursuer aged 45 at date of trial — Crushing injury to leg and chest resulting in permanent disability and personality change — Evidence that the pursuer had returned to his pre-accident employment after a period at a basic weekly wage of £205 and that his future there was not secure by reason of recession in the off-shore oil industry — **Loss of earnings to date of trial** agreed and damages *awarded* accordingly — Damages of £4,000 *awarded* for **loss of future earning capacity**, having regard to the risk of redundancy, the current state of the labour market and the amount of the pursuer's current weekly wage.

(109) **Faith v. CBI Constructors Ltd,** 1987 S.L.T. 248 (Lord Sutherland)

Pursuer aged c.39 at date of trial — Injuries to arm and shoulder rendering him permanently unfit for his pre-accident employment as a caulker/burner — Evidence that the pursuer would have been made redundant but would have obtained alternative work forthwith; that he had eventually obtained light work, just before the date of trial; and that his failure to obtain light work sooner was not his responsibility — **Loss of earnings to date of trial** calculated for the period until the pursuer's commencement of light work, without discount (and for the period thereafter as part of the damages awarded on the basis of a multiplier and multiplicand) and damages *awarded* accordingly — Damages of £13,000 *awarded* for **loss of future earnings** (as well as for the loss of earnings for the short period immediately preceding the date of trial) on the basis of a multiplicand of £2,600, representing the differential between the pursuer's pre-accident and post-accident jobs, and a multiplier of five, having regard to the uncertainties of continuing employment for caulkers/burners.

(110) **Bruce v. Ailsa Vacuum Extraction Ltd,** 1987 S.L.T. 464 (Lord McCluskey)

Pursuer aged 50 at date of trial — Burning injuries to legs resulting in the acceleration by two or three years of arthritic symptoms in the pursuer's knee rendering him restricted in his capacity to carry out his pre-accident work as a fitter/welder — Evidence that the pursuer had an unsatisfactory pre-accident work record, having been variously dismissed and out of work for some period of time; that he would have been made redundant within a few months of the date of his accident in any event; that he was fit to look for work about one year after his accident but had not done so; and that he was apprehensive about the possibility of further injuries to the skin of his legs — **Loss of earnings to date of trial** calculated on the basis of what he would have been earning had he remained in employment, totalling £14,000, less a discount of £3,000 to take account of his failure to seek work and his pre-accident work record, and damages *assessed* accordingly — Damages of £2,000 *assessed* for **prejudice to earning capacity** on the basis that the pursuer would by now have begun to suffer from osteo-arthritis and it was largely that condition (rather than the condition of his skin) which limited the range of work that he might be able to do.

(111) **Anderson v. Thames Case Ltd,** 1987 S.L.T. 564 (Lord Jauncey)
Pursuer aged 54 at date of trial — Injury to thumb involving partial amputation — Damages of £200 *awarded* for **diminished capacity in the labour market**.

(112) **Forsyth's Curator Bonis v. Govan Shipbuilders Ltd,** 1988 S.C. 421 (Second Division; Lord Clyde)
Ward aged c.35 at date of trial — Head injury involving serious brain damage with consequences of very considerable severity, the permanent residual disability being one of the most serious forms of disability possible — Evidence as to the ward's earnings as at the time of the accident and as to increases in wages generally but not as to any increases applicable to the ward's situation — Evidence as to services carried out for the ward by his wife, including giving assistance with adjusting his clothing, with washing, bathing and shaving, with the cutting up of his food, in enabling him to rise after a fall and in accompanying him out of doors, and of her prior earnings but not of the kinds of charges for the kinds of services which were required — Evidence that the pursuer had incurred and would incur expense in administering the curatory estate — **Loss of earnings to date of trial** calculated on the basis of the ward's earnings as at the time of the accident only and damages *awarded* accordingly — Damages of £84,240 *awarded* for **loss of future earnings** on the basis of a multiplicand of £7,020, representing the earnings of the ward as at the time of the accident, and a multiplier of 12, having regard to the probable difficulty in finding employment if he had ceased work with his employers — Remuneration for **necessary services to date of trial** calculated on the basis of the wife's prior earnings of £2,000 per annum and the lapse of four and a quarter years from the date of the

ward's departure from hospital and damages *awarded* accordingly — Damages of £39,150 *awarded* for **curatory expenses**, comprising a sum in respect of past expense, namely £150, and a sum in respect of future costs, namely £39,000, on the basis of a multiplicand of £3,000, representing the annual administration expenses, and a multiplier of 13, having regard to (i) the ward's life expectancy; (ii) the tax relief available in respect of such expenses; and (iii) the larger fees chargeable in the initial stages, but not to the progressive reduction in the curatory estate as capital and income were spent since such did not necessarily entail any diminution in the content of the curator's work.

(113) **MacIntosh v. National Coal Board,** 1988 S.L.T. 348 (Second Division; Lord Stewart)

Pursuer aged 48 at date of trial — Serious back injury rendering the pursuer paraplegic — Evidence that she would require care and attendance provision to a certain extent over the next five years but that after reaching the age of 55 she would probably require to spend much more annually on such provision — Damages of £55,000, subject to 50% deduction for contributory negligence, *awarded* on appeal for **future care and attendance costs**, comprising (i) a sum of £5,000 to cover the next five years at £1,000 per annum; and (ii) a sum of £50,000 for the period thereafter on the basis of a multiplicand of £10,000 and a multiplier of five, having regard to the fact that there were more than the usual number of imponderables in the exercise including the possibility that (a) the pursuer might not survive for five years; (b) her condition might not deteriorate as quickly as estimated; and (c) her need for extra care and maintenance provision might not materialise when anticipated.

(114) **Rennicks v. Bison Concrete Ltd,** 1988 S.L.T. 343 (Lord Davidson)

Pursuer aged 45 at date of trial — Crush injury to fingers resulting in permanent reduction in manual dexterity and leaving the pursuer unfit for heavy work — Evidence that the pursuer in alternative employment at a lower rate of pay but insufficient evidence as to details of current earnings — Damages of £2,000 *awarded* for **loss of future earnings** on a lump sum basis.

(115) **Miller v U.I.E. (Scotland) Ltd,** 1988 S.L.T. 536 (Lord Clyde)

Pursuer aged c.50 at date of trial — Injury to foot rendering the pursuer unfit for his pre-accident employment as a welding inspector — Evidence that since the accident the pursuer had obtained work as a welding instructor at a lower rate of pay but with greater security than his pre-accident job, albeit that the probabilities were that he would have continued work as a welding inspector but for the accident — **Loss of earnings to date of trial** agreed and damages *awarded* accordingly — Damages of £10,400 *awarded* for **loss of future earnings** on the basis of a multiplicand of £2,600, representing the differential between the pre-accident and post-accident jobs, and a multiplier of four, having regard to the pursuer's age, the uncertainties of finding employment and the whole circumstances of the case.

(116) **Millar v. Jameson McGregor Ltd,** 1988 S.L.T. 83 (Lord Jauncey)
Pursuer aged 44 at date of trial — Injuries to leg and back rendering it likely that there would be an occasional day or two in the future when the pursuer's back would trouble him to the extent of preventing his working **— Loss of earnings to date of trial** agreed and damages therefor *awarded* accordingly — Damages of £500 *awarded* for **loss of future earnings**.

(117) **McKay v. Strathclyde Communications Ltd,** 1988 S.L.T. 732 (Lord Prosser)
Pursuer aged c.52 at date of trial — Injuries to head and arm rendering the pursuer physically unfit for heavier work such as he had previously done as a coded welder and in a mental state such as to disable him from work — Evidence that the pursuer had been certified as unfit for work until about a year before the date of trial and had then made some enquiries but no sustained effort to find a new type of work; but since it could not be presumed that work was available for a man of the pursuer's age, with a history of disability and some persisting limitation of capacity, it was unlikely that he could have found light work by the date of trial anyway, even if he had felt able mentally to put all possible effort into the search for work since being signed off by his doctor **— Loss of earnings to date of trial** calculated on the basis of the net wage the pursuer was earning as at the time of the accident and on the footing that the whole loss to date was attributable to the accident and damages *awarded* accordingly — Damages of £17,680 *awarded* for **loss of future earnings** on the basis of a multiplicand of £4,420, representing a rounding up of the pre-accident net wage figure with account being taken of the major change in his working pattern prior to his accident, and a multiplier of four, having regard to (i) the general problem as to the availability of work; (ii) the prospect that the pursuer would find it difficult to seek out, accept and remain in employment, having regard to the impact which the accident had had on his whole attitude of mind; and (iii) the chances, not very good, that the pursuer would in fact yet find employment.

(118) **McGahan v. Greater Glasgow Health Board,** 1988 S.L.T. 270 (Lord Allanbridge)
Pursuer aged 29 at date of trial — Injury to back rendering the pursuer unfit for her pre-accident employment as a nurse — Evidence

that the pursuer had had some earlier unrelated health problems, albeit that she was well motivated to nurse, and that she was now a clerical officer at a rate of pay which was increasingly less than her pre-accident earnings — Damages of £2,000 *awarded* for **loss of future earnings** on a lump sum basis, having regard to the uncertainties of the case including the pursuer's previous health and the fluctuations in the annual loss.

(119) **Hutchison v. National Coal Board,** 1988 S.L.T 655 (Lord Dervaird)
Pursuer aged 44 at date of trial — Injury to back involving a prolapsed disc rendering the pursuer unfit for his pre-accident employment as a miner and fit only for light work — Evidence that the pursuer had a pre-existing arthritic condition; that by 10–15 years after the date of trial he would have been so disabled by reason of that problem as not to be fit for heavy work; that episodes of back pain would in any event have continued in the interim and been liable to be more frequent and longer in duration; and that the pursuer, having left his job on the ground of his incapacity for heavy work, had made substantial efforts to find light work but without success — **Loss of earnings to date of trial** agreed and damages *awarded* accordingly — Damages of £18,000 *awarded* for the pursuer's **lack of employability**, having regard to the various imponderables; the assessment being the equivalent of four years' future loss, allowing for at least six weeks' absence per annum because of the underlying back condition.

(120) **Hunter v. National Coal Board,** 1988 S.L.T. 241 (Lord Weir)
Pursuer aged c.45 at date of trial — Injury to neck causing emergence of symptoms of cervical spondylosis — Evidence of more serious symptoms at a later date but no causal connection with the effects of the accident established — Damages of £3,000 *assessed* for **loss of value on the labour market**, having regard to the prospect that the pursuer might obtain a clerical post and bearing in mind the uncertainties.

(121) **Grant v. Lothian Regional Council,** 1988 S.L.T. 533 (Lord Prosser)
Pursuer aged c.24 at trial — Injury to elbows rendering the pursuer incapable of caring for herself for about three weeks — Evidence that her mother had cared for her during that period, assisting with dressing and feeding and with her personal toilet and hygiene requirements — Damages of £250 *assessed* for **necessary services**.

(122) **Gallacher v. Deborah Scaffolding (Aberdeen) Ltd,** 1988 S.L.T. 345 (Lord Kirkwood)
Pursuer aged 32 at date of trial — Injuries to spine, pelvis and ankle rendering the pursuer permanently unfit for his pre-accident

employment as an offshore scaffolder and fit only for some forms of light work, such as bench assembly work, or clerical work, or driving — Evidence that even if the pursuer had been working as a scaffolder there would have been periods between contracts when he was not working and there was a likelihood that he would have had to take onshore work at some stage and in that event suffer a significant reduction in his earnings; and that the pursuer had made no attempt to obtain any form of employment since his accident but had enrolled in the Open University, though it was not possible at this stage to say whether he would graduate and, if so, what type of employment, if any, such a degree would be likely to enable him to obtain — **Loss of earnings to date of trial** calculated on the basis of the pursuer's pre-accident income discounted for (i) his failure to make any effort to obtain remunerative employment; and (ii) the periods between contracts when he would not have been working and damages *assessed* accordingly — Damages of £72,000, less benefits, *assessed* for **loss of future earnings** on the basis of a multiplicand of £12,000 and a multiplier of six, taking account of (a) the likelihood that the pursuer would have had to take less remunerative onshore work at some stage; and (b) the pursuer's failure to take reasonable steps to minimise his loss by seeking light work for which he was fit.

(123) **Cumming v. Anderson,** 1988 S.L.T. 485 (Lord Jauncey)

Pursuer aged c.32 at date of trial — Injuries to head, legs and arms rendering the pursuer unfit to return to scaffolding or heavy construction work — Evidence that the pursuer had switched to working as a salesman just prior to his accident in order to be at home with his young son; that he had had periods out of work because he wished to be at home with his family; and that after his accident he had obtained employment selling life insurance, in respect of which there was a very high turnover of persons doing similar work — **Loss of earnings to date of trial** calculated on the basis of an adjusted average net weekly wage, taking into account the various imponderables, and making a deduction of 10% to reflect the possibility of periods of voluntary unemployment at home and damages *assessed* accordingly — Damages of £5,000 *assessed* for **future loss**, having regard to (i) the insecurity of the pursuer's present work; but (ii) his desire to make a success of it, and balancing (a) the possibility that the pursuer might not make a long term success of his present work and then have greater difficulty in finding suitable work with (b) the possibility that he would make a success of it and be able to continue with such work for so long as he wished.

(124) **Clews v. B.A. Chemicals Ltd,** 1988 S.L.T. 29 (Lord McCluskey)

Pursuer aged 41 at date of trial — Injury to fingers resulting in partial amputations — Evidence that the pursuer as a fitter was earning about £150 for a flat week and about £230 for an overtime week with the result that his loss would build up quite quickly if he were to lose his present job and have difficulty in securing another one; that for disablement benefit purposes he was judged to be 20% disabled; and that he was plainly an able man with good work experience and a good work record so that one would not expect his difficulty in obtaining new work to be very much greater as a result of the accident — Damages of £2,500 *awarded* for **prospective difficulty in finding employment** should that prove necessary on some indeterminate date in the future, having regard to the pursuer's age, earnings, working history and disability.

(125) **Bird v. British Beef Co. Ltd,** 1988 S.L.T. 801 (Lord Dervaird)
Pursuer aged 26 at date of trial — Injury to back rendering the pursuer unfit for heavy work — Evidence that the pursuer had a pre-existing spondylosis of the lumbar vertebra which was symptom free and would probably not have prevented him from working until normal retiring age; and that the pursuer was now working as a barman three evenings per week but could do more — **Loss of earnings to date of trial** calculated and damages *awarded* accordingly — Damages of £40,000 *awarded* for **loss of future earnings** on the basis, rounded down, of a multiplicand of £3,400, representing the differential between the pursuer's pre-accident earnings and his earnings as a barman working more hours than he was in fact doing, and a multiplier of 12, taking into account the pursuer's age and medical circumstances.

(126) **Baillie v. Grahamston Iron Co. Ltd,** 1988 S.L.T. 429 (Lord McCluskey)
Pursuer aged 41 at date of trial — Disease affecting skin on hands and body — Evidence that the pursuer was continuing in his pre-accident job because he felt he had no choice, notwithstanding that such was not helping his dermatitis; that his employers might or might not be able to relocate him; that if the pursuer were to lose his present job he would great difficulty in finding another one; that he was likely to have periods off work and if he did for as much as eight weeks in any one year would lose £1,000 — **Loss of earnings to date of trial** agreed and damages *awarded* accordingly — Damages of £5,000 *awarded* for **future loss or prejudice to earning capacity**, having regard to the circumstances and the uncertainties concerning (i) the prospects of the pursuer's obtaining different work with his employers; (ii) the prospects of his obtaining work with another employer; and (iii) the extent to which he would in the future be incapacitated by his dermatitis as he had plainly been during the previous year.

(127) **Docherty's Curator Bonis v. U.I.E. Shipbuilding (Scotland) Ltd,** 1989 S.L.T. 197 (Lord Morison)

Ward aged 64 at date of trial — Head injury involving severe brain damage with serious consequences including a drastic personality change — Evidence that the hospital in which he was now residing was inappropriate and unnecessarily unpleasant for him, that it was quite impracticable for him to be sent home even if nursing support were provided for him there and that residence in a nursing home would provide the nursing care which was required, a secure and stable environment, a degree of privacy, pleasant surroundings and the opportunity for some social communication and outings — Evidence that expenses would be incurred in the administration of the curatory estate — **Loss of earnings** and **transport costs** arising from visits from relatives which had been beneficial for the ward agreed and damages *awarded* accordingly — Damages of £79,560 *awarded* for **future nursing home treatment costs** on the basis of a multiplicand of £13,260, representing the present annual cost of residence in a particular nursing home which was suitable, and a multiplier of six, having regard to the ward's age and the ordinary chances of life as well as the slight possibility that he would react unfavourably to his new environment — Damages of £16,500 *awarded* for **curatory expenses**, having regard to (i) the annual figure of £3,000; (ii) the progressive diminution of the ward's estate; (iii) the age of the ward; and (iv) the interest which would be derived from the investment of a capital sum awarded for future expenditure.

(128) **Meek v. Burton's Gold Medal Biscuits Ltd,** 1989 S.L.T. 338 (Lord Prosser)

Pursuer aged c.46 at date of trial — Injury to back resulting in weakened lumbar disc liable to future prolapse — Evidence that there was a wide variation of future possibilities, ranging from the very disabling to the relatively tolerable, so that no sensible line could be drawn between those future disabilities which were not to be regarded as a serious deterioration and those which were; and that, even if there was a prolapse, it might not be serious — Damages of £4,000 *awarded* for **diminution in future working capacity**, having regard to the variety of possibilities in the future, and order for **provisional damages** *refused*.

(129) **Wilson v. Price,** 1989 S.L.T. 484 (Lord Milligan)

Pursuer aged 20 at date of trial — Severe cranio-facial injuries resulting in impairment of senses, behavioural difficulties and epilepsy — Evidence that pursuer at school at time of accident and had doubtful employment prospects at that time; that he had since undergone youth training when he was judged a good trier but lacking in concentration;

that he wanted to be in catering, albeit that such might not be possible having regard to his handicaps; and that his prospects of long term employment now were very slim — **Loss of earnings to date of trial** agreed and damages *assessed* accordingly — Damages of £18,750 *assessed* for **loss of future earnings** on the basis of a multiplicand of £1,250 and a multiplier of 15.

(130) **Ward v. City of Glasgow District Council,** 1989 S.L.T. 349 (Lord Prosser)

Pursuer aged c.41 at date of trial — Injuries to heelbones with severe consequences leaving the pursuer permanently very disabled — **Loss of earnings to date of trial** agreed and damages *awarded* accordingly — Damages of £44,128, less benefits, *awarded* for **loss of future earnings** on the basis of a multiplicand of £5,516, representing what the pursuer's earnings would have been as at the date of trial, and a multiplier of eight, a small discount being made for the very poor prospect that the pursuer would find sedentary work.

(131) **Tennant v. John Walker & Sons Ltd,** 1989 S.L.T. 143 (Lord Sutherland)

Pursuer aged in his late 30s at date of trial — Injury to elbow resulting in substantial restriction in the nature of employment open to the pursuer — Evidence that the pursuer was fit for some form of light work but such would have been very restricted and it was very doubtful that there was any such work available and the pursuer in any event had ongoing symptoms at the time which required operative treatment; and that the pursuer would have been made redundant from his employment as a cooper upon the closure of the employers' business in any event and it was unlikely that he would have been able to obtain further employment as a cooper — **Loss of earnings to date of trial** agreed for the period until redundancy and for the period thereafter calculated, and **loss of the redundancy payment** which the pursuer would have received but for his accident agreed, and damages *awarded* accordingly — Damages of £3,000 *awarded* for **loss of earning capacity**, having regard to the fact that the pursuer was substantially restricted in the employment open to him.

(132) **Stevenson v. British Coal Corporation,** 1989 S.L.T. 136 (Lord Prosser)

Pursuer aged 50 at date of trial — Injury to back rendering the pursuer unfit for his pre-accident employment and fit only for light work — Evidence that the pursuer had strong personal qualities and was undergoing training for light work but that the prospects of his obtaining long term employment were gloomy, having regard to the state of his back, his age and the likely need for further training once employed — **Loss of earnings to date of trial** agreed and damages *awarded* accordingly — Damages of £30,000 *awarded* for **loss of future earnings** on a lump sum basis; the assessment being the broad equivalent of a multiplicand of £9,256, representing what the pursuer's earnings would have been as at the date of trial, and a multiplier of three, taking account of the pursuer's personal state and circumstances.

(133) **Spence v. City of Glasgow District Council,** 1989 S.L.T. 119 (Lord Sutherland)

Pursuer aged c.18 at date of trial — Head injury involving damage to cranial nerves resulting in facial paralysis, speech difficulty, partial deafness and inability to close his left eye — Damages of £500 *awarded* for **diminished employment prospects**, there being no medical evidence to suggest that the pursuer would be in any way physically impaired from obtaining employment albeit that his appearance and speech difficulty might be slightly off-putting to a prospective employer and that if the pursuer were to obtain work in the open air he might have difficulty with his left eye in cold winds or in dusty conditions in the summer.

(134) **Sands v. George Waterston & Sons Ltd,** 1989 S.L.T. 174 (Lord Weir)

Pursuer aged c.54 at date of trial — Bruising injury to back causing pain and lingering discomfort — Evidence that the pursuer had been off work for six weeks, during which time her husband had provided services by way of housework and other personal assistance — Damages of £100 *awarded* for **necessary services**.

(135) **Robertson v. Scottish Special Housing Association,** 1989 S.L.T 686 (Lord Cameron of Lochbroom)

Pursuer aged 28 at date of trial — Injury to foot resulting in permanent unfitness for pre-accident employment as a slater and roughcaster and fit only for light work not involving standing or walking for any distance — Evidence that the pursuer had been unable to find any suitable form of light work to date despite attempts to do so, albeit that there was some prospect that he would be able to find some suitable employment at some stage — **Loss of earnings to date of trial** agreed and damages *awarded* accordingly — Damages of £67,600 *awarded* for **loss of future earnings** on the basis of a multiplicand of £6,700 and a multiplier of 10, having regard to the prospect of the pursuer obtaining future employment.

(136) **Prentice v. William Thyne Ltd,** 1989 S.L.T. 336 (Lord Dervaird)

Pursuer aged c.32 at date of trial — Injury to leg resulting in restrictions of hip movements — Evidence that it was likely that the pursuer would develop degenerative changes in the hip joint amounting to a worsening of the condition from which he was already suffering, so that it was virtually impossible to say at what point along the line of possible developments the condition already present and causing some problems would be classifiable as a serious deterioration from the existing condition — Evidence that the pursuer's wife performed services for him during a portion of the time when he was required to rest at home — Damages of £5,000 *assessed* for **loss of employability in the future** and an order for **provisional damages** would have been *refused* — Damages of £400 *assessed* on a broad basis for **necessary services**.

(137) **McCrae v. Durastic Ltd,** 1989 S.C.L.R. 797 (Lord Cameron of Lochbroom)

Pursuer aged 48 at date of trial — Shoulder injury resulting in residual disability and a very marked change in personality leaving the pursuer unfit for his pre-accident employment — Evidence that the pursuer had bronchitic condition which could in the fullness of time have affected his earning capacity; that his work experience was limited to a trade to which he could not now return; and that his physical limitations and more generally the limited range of suitable work for which he was capable made his future prospects of returning to gainful employment very uncertain, albeit that it could not be said that he would never resume employment of any kind **— Loss of earnings to date of trial** agreed and damages *awarded* accordingly — Damages of £48,000 *awarded* for **loss of future earnings** on the basis of a multiplicand of £6,000 and a multiplier of eight, having regard to the prospects for future employment.

(138) **MacNeil v. U.I.E. Shipbuilding (Scotland) Ltd,** 1989 S.L.T. 289 (Lord Weir)

Pursuer aged 51 at date of trial — Injuries to face and hearing resulting in a post-traumatic neurosis which caused a personality change and rendered the pursuer permanently unfit to continue his employment as a welder — Evidence that welders tended to move around doing short term contract work with intervening periods of unemployment; that the gaps between jobs might be considerable where the inclination was to work near home, as had been the case with the pursuer; that the pursuer had worked on after his accident until his contract of employment had come to an end but not thereafter because of his mental state; that he was now on the point of starting in part time employment as a sales assistant but it could not be predicted how long the job would last or where it would lead to; and that his general attitude to work and disposition made it likely that he would obtain full time employment at some stage in the future (say after a year), although his wages would never approach that which he would have enjoyed as a welder — **Loss of earnings to date of trial** calculated on the basis that the pursuer would have worked as a welder for 12 out of the past 21 months and damages *awarded* accordingly — Damages of £39,000 *awarded* for **loss of future earnings**, comprising (i) the sum of £7,800, being the differential between the pursuer's pre-accident earnings and his new job's earnings for one year; and (ii) the sum of £31,200, calculated on the basis of a multiplicand of £5,200, representing the differential between the pursuer's pre-accident earnings and his earnings from a future full time position, and a multiplier of six, having regard to the probable periods of unemployment between contracts.

(139) **McFarlane v. Greater Glasgow Health Board,** 1989 S.C.L.R. 799 (Lord Cameron of Lochbroom)

Pursuer a hospital domestic — Shoulder injury resulting in disability likely to remain for a further year after trial — Evidence that as at the date of trial the pursuer would have been earning £75 per week but was unemployed for unrelated reasons — Evidence that services rendered to the pursuer for about eight hours per week in the early stages after her accident but decreasing thereafter — Damages of £1,000 *assessed* for **loss of future earnings** — Damages of £2,500 *assessed* for **necessary services**.

(140) **MacKenzie v. Mackay,** 1989 S.L.T. 810 (Lord Weir)

Pursuer aged 26 at date of trial — Injuries to leg, arms and thumb resulting in continuing disability rendering him unfit for his pre-accident employment as an apprentice fitter — Evidence that the pursuer had obtained work of a clerical nature since his accident but had no qualifications and suitable job opportunities in his area were very limited **— Loss of earnings to date of trial** agreed and damages *awarded* accordingly — Damages of £14,000 *awarded* for **loss of future earnings** on the basis of a multiplicand of £1,000 and a multiplier of 14 — Damages of £2,000 *awarded* for **loss of prospects**, it being agreed that the pursuer was entitled to a further sum in that regard.

(141) **Gibson v. Droopy & Browns Ltd,** 1989 S.L.T. 172 (Lord Clyde)

Pursuer aged 24 at date of trial — Injury to back and leg rendering her unfit to return to her pre-accident employment as an assistant manageress and fit only for a clerical or desk job — Evidence that the pursuer had the personality and the ability to undertake work successfully within the limitations which she had and that she could have obtained such work by the date of trial, albeit after some difficulty **— Loss of earnings to date of trial** agreed as to amount and damages therefor *assessed* for the whole of the period to date of trial — Damages of £3,000 *awarded* for **general prejudice to employment prospects**.

(142) **Anderson's Tutor v. J. Wallace and Sons,** 1989 S.L.T. 150 (Lord Cowie)

Child aged c.13 at date of trial — Injury to eye resulting in loss of sight in that eye — Evidence that the child wanted to be a farm worker and drive tractors but no medical reason why he should not do so — Damages of £4,000 *assessed* for **prospective loss due to a reduction in ability to obtain employment**.

(143) **Young v. Roche Services Group plc,** 1989 S.L.T 212 (Lord Wylie)

Pursuer aged 29 at date of trial — Multiple injuries involving fractures resulting in a below knee amputation and rendering the pursuer unfit for his pre-accident employment and leaving him fit only for sedentary work or at least work which did not require prolonged standing or walking about — Evidence that the pursuer's prospects of employment were extremely limited **— Loss of earnings to date of trial** calculated and damages *awarded* accordingly — Damages of £50,000, less benefits, *awarded* for **loss of future earnings** on the basis of a multiplicand of £5,000 and a multiplier of 10, having regard to the pursuer's age.

(144) **Calder v. Lummus Crest Ltd,** 1989 S.L.T. 689 (Lord Clyde)

Pursuer aged 55 at date of trial — Injuries to arm and shoulder rendering the pursuer unfit for his pre-accident employment, which he would probably remain incapable of doing — Evidence that the pursuer had been fit for light work for about two years but had made no attempt to find any work; and that any such work would probably be less well remunerated than his pre-accident employment **— Loss of earnings to date of trial** calculated and damages *awarded* accordingly — Damages of £10,000 *awarded* for **loss of future earnings** on the basis of between one and two years' earnings relative to his pre-accident work, taking into account the pursuer's age and the question of how long he would have remained in work even if the accident had not occurred.

(145) **Whyte v. University of Dundee,** 1990 S.L.T. 545 (Lord Kirkwood)

Pursuer aged 44 at date of trial — Injury to eye and face resulting in a marked reduction of his vision in that eye — No evidence that the pursuer in any real danger of losing his job but if he were to become unemployed he would be at a considerable disadvantage if he was in the position of having to compete for alternative employment — Evidence that the pursuer had required to cancel a holiday because of his injuries — Evidence that the pursuer's wife looked after him when he came back from hospital and, for example, administered his drugs and eye drops, drove him about for a period of several months, particularly to keep hospital appointments, and carried out a number of household duties which were normally carried out by the pursuer as well as a certain amount of paper work resulting from the accident — Damages of £2,000 *awarded* for **prospective loss of future earning capacity — Holiday cancellation costs** agreed and damages *awarded* accordingly — Damages of £500 *awarded* for **necessary services**.

(146) **Smith v. Heeps,** 1990 S.L.T. 871 (Lord Cameron of Lochbroom)

Pursuer aged 47 at date of trial — Injuries to hip and knee resulting in osteo-arthritic degeneration likely to require surgical intervention about two years after the date of trial — Evidence that the pursuer was continuing in his pre-accident work as a shuttering joiner but would require to switch to less well paid employment as a bench joiner after his return to work some three to six months after such surgery — Evidence that the pursuer's wife had provided services to him over a short period and would provide such in the future **— Loss of earnings to date of trial** agreed and damages *awarded* accordingly — Damages of £42,000 *awarded* for **loss of future earnings** on the basis of a multiplicand of £7,000, representing the differential between what the pursuer would be earning as a shuttering joiner and as a bench joiner, and a multiplier of six, having regard to the pursuer's age, the uncertain prospect of future employment and the factor of the present award for loss accruing in the future — Damages of £100 for **necessary services to date of trial** and £150 for **future necessary services**, discounted for the fact that it was being paid now, *awarded.*

(147) **Reilly v. Robert Kellie & Sons Ltd,** 1990 S.L.T 78 (Lord Milligan)

Pursuer aged 30 at date of trial — Respiratory disease involving asthma — Damages of £2,000 *awarded* of consent for **disadvantage on the labour market**.

(148) **Murray v. British Railways Board,** 1990 S.L.T 853 (Lord Kirkwood)

Pursuer aged 43 at date of trial — Injury to back rendering the pursuer unfit for his pre-accident employment and fit only for light work — Evidence that the pursuer had worked intermittently after the accident but there was uncertainty as to what types of light work he would be able to undertake or what work would be available for him **— Loss of earnings to date of trial** and beyond, for a period of one year, agreed and damages *assessed* accordingly — Damages of £6,000 *assessed* for **loss of earning capacity** for the period thereafter, having regard to the pursuer's uncertain employment prospects.

(149) **Millar v. Fife Regional Council,** 1990 S.L.T. 651 (Lord Morton of Shuna)

Pursuer aged c.42 at date of trial — Injury to ankle — Evidence that the pursuer's wife had rendered services to him consisting of taking his dog for a walk and driving the car to the shops when the pursuer was unable because of his ankle plaster to do either of these actions — Damages of £10 *awarded* for **necessary services**, such being so minimal that anything other than a token award was inappropriate.

(150) **McWilliam v. British Coal Corporation,** 1990 S.L.T. 679 (Lord Cameron of Lochbroom)

Pursuer aged c.36 at date of trial — Minor injury to leg — Evidence that the pursuer's wife had for a short period after the accident assisted him in moving around the house and in bathing and dressing — Damages of £50 *awarded* for **necessary services**.

(151) **Laurie v. Douglas Reyburn & Co. Ltd,** 1990 S.L.T. 513 (Lord Morison)

Pursuer aged 54 at date of trial — Respiratory disease involving asthma associated with chronic bronchitis and emphysema unrelated to the pursuer's work — Evidence that the pursuer was severely disabled by the unrelated conditions **— Loss of earnings to date of trial** restricted to a period of two years from the date of cessation of her employment and damages *assessed* accordingly — Damages for **loss of future earnings** *refused* — If the present and future disablement were to be regarded as caused only by occupational asthma, past and future wages would have been *assessed* on the basis of the parties' agreement with a multiplier of three and a half, having regard to the pursuer's age.

(152) **Lang v. Fife Health Board,** 1990 S.L.T. 626 (Lord Caplan)

Pursuer aged c.44 at date of trial — Injury to neck and shoulder advancing the onset of symptoms of pre-existing asymptomatic degenerative changes and rendering the pursuer unfit for his pre-accident employment, for which he was unlikely ever to be fit again, or any other work involving heavy lifting — Evidence that it was probable that but for the accident the degenerative condition would not have become symptomatic at least until retirement age; that the pursuer had been fit for light work for a period of about eighteen months preceding the date of trial but had been certified by his doctor as unfit for work; and that he had taken virtually no steps to find light work, which would take time to find, and instead had in mind seeking entry to a social work course; but no evidence as to the local work situation, the jobs which might be available to him or the likely wage rate for such employment as he could hope to secure nor as to the grants to which he might be entitled if he did decide to study — **Loss of earnings to date of trial** calculated on the basis that the pursuer entitled to the whole of his net wage loss to date and damages *awarded* accordingly — Damages of £15,000 *awarded* for **loss of future earnings** on a lump sum basis (the future for the pursuer being so full of conjecture and uncertainty that compensation for him had to be determined on a broad basis), with allowance for (i) his dilatoriness in looking for other work; (ii) the fact that even in his pre-accident job his pay was relatively modest; and (iii) the prospect that certain deductions would require to be made in respect of benefits.

(153) **Laidler v. Yarrow Shipbuilders Ltd,** 1990 S.L.T. 261 (Lord Kirkwood)

Pursuer aged 30 at date of trial — Injury to ear resulting in tinnitus which would be a permanent but not significant disability — Evidence that the pursuer had made no effort to return to work or to obtain alternative employment, such being unreasonable in the circumstances — **Loss of earnings to date of trial** calculated on the basis that the pursuer would be entitled to three months' loss of earnings and damages *assessed* accordingly — Damages of £2,000 *assessed* for **potential loss of earning capacity**.

(154) **Kent v. Gourlay,** 1990 S.L.T. 516 (Lord Cameron of Lochbroom)

Pursuer aged 22 at date of trial — Injuries to arm and leg rendering the pursuer unfit for work involving substantial lifting, walking or climbing and thus unable to take on heavy labouring work or work on construction sites and leaving him at best fit for work which was largely sedentary — Evidence that the pursuer was unemployed at the time of the accident and had had no settled employment prior thereto and that since his accident he had sought light work but had had only casual or temporary work — **Loss of earnings to date of trial** *refused* on the basis that such would not exceed the total amount which he would have earned but for the accident and the deductible benefits — Damages of £15,000 *awarded* for **loss of employability for the future**, having regard to (i) the pursuer's age; and (ii) the fact that his incapacity was substantial and permanent and had affected and would affect adversely his employment prospects throughout his working life; the assessment being the equivalent of a net loss of £15 per week for 20 years.

(155) **Johnstone v. Hardie,** 1990 S.L.T. 744 (Lord Morton of Shuna)

Pursuer aged 42 at date of trial — Minor injuries with physical and psychological effects rendering the pursuer unfit for her pre-accident employment as a hospital domestic, it being probable that she would continue to be unfit for heavy work — Evidence that the pursuer had done virtually no housework or shopping since the accident and that this had been done by her unemployed husband for a number of hours per day, the work being in part necessary services rendered to the pursuer and in part personal services which she was unable to render to her family by reason of her injuries — Damages of £14,600, less benefits, *awarded* for **loss of future earnings** on the basis, rounded down, of a multiplicand of £2,920.32 and a multiplier of five — Damages of £3,000 *awarded* for **necessary services** and the pursuer's **inability to render personal services**.

(156) **Johns v. Greater Glasgow Health Board,** 1990 S.L.T. 459 (Lord Cameron of Lochbroom)

Pursuer aged 49 at date of trial — Injury comprising un-united fractures of wrists arising from a negligent failure to diagnose at the time of the pursuer's accident rendering her unable to resume her pre-accident employment as a silver service waitress or any other kind of work — Evidence that operative treatment to fuse one of the wrists had not been successful but that there was still hope that success would be achieved and if both wrists were fused there was a prospect that the pursuer could return to silver service waitressing — **Loss of earnings to date of trial** agreed and damages *awarded* accordingly — Damages of £14,280 *awarded* for **loss of future earnings** on the basis of a multiplicand of £3,570 and a multiplier of four, having regard to (i) the doubt as to the likely success of the operative treatment; and (ii) the possibility that the pursuer would be enabled to return to employment at some future date.

(157) **Gorman v. McLaren Building Services Ltd,** 1990 S.L.T. 365 (Lord Dervaird)

Pursuer aged c.25 at date of trial — Injury to back leaving the pursuer at increased risk of having further episodes of significant back pain in the future — Evidence that the pursuer might not have been in continous employment in any event — **Loss of earnings to date of trial** calculated on the basis of a modest reduction to take account of the risk that the pursuer would have been out of work for a period anyway and damages *assessed* accordingly — Damages of £2,000 *assessed* for **disadvantage on the labour market**.

(158) **Geddes v. British Railways Board,** 1990 S.L.T. 696 (Lord Weir)

Pursuer aged 47 at date of trial — Injury to back resulting in the pursuer's temporary unfitness for his pre-accident employment — Evidence that the pursuer was obese and over the years prior to his accident was off work from time to time but did not have an extensive and recurring health problem; that his employers unjustifiably took the opportunity of his accident to decline to allow him to return to his duties upon recovering from his injuries; that despite his efforts to find work the pursuer remained unemployed as at the date of trial; and that the pursuer was learning to be a driving instructor and hoped to qualify within about four months **— Loss of earnings to date of trial** calculated on the basis that the pursuer was entitled to recover for the whole of the period to that date and damages *awarded* accordingly — Damages of £11,400 *awarded* for **loss of future earnings**, comprising (i) the sum of £1,400 for the period until the pursuer's possible qualification as a driving instructor; and (ii) the sum of £10,000 for the pursuer's loss on the labour market, taking into account all the imponderables, including (a) the fact that the pursuer had been unfit from time to time in the past and might not have been able to work at his former employment beyond the age of 60; (b) the fact that his weight was an adverse factor in obtaining alternative employment; and (c) the prospect that he might suffer little or no loss if he qualified as a driving instructor and managed to obtain employment as such in the future.

(159) **Fowler v. Greater Glasgow Health Board,** 1990 S.L.T. 303 (Lord Morison)

Pursuers suing as executors of child aged about 21 months at date of death — Severe brain damage resulting in coma — Evidence that for last ten months of the child's life his parents had cared for him at home, the care including the sucking out of his tracheostomy tube, the cleaning of the hole, the administration of drugs, feeding him by means of a naso-gastral tube, and physiotherapy, as well as keeping a constant watch on him — Damages of £5,000 *assessed* for **necessary services**, taking into account the amount of care which ordinarily has to be afforded to a baby by his parents.

(160) **Aitken v. Midlothian District Council (No. 2),** 1990 S.L.T 41 (Lord Sutherland)

Pursuer aged c.30 at date of trial — Injury to knee rendering the pursuer unfit for any heavy or labouring work and fit only for light or sedentary employment — Evidence that it was probable that the pursuer would have progressive degenerative changes in the knee which might cause progressive symptoms; that it was unlikely that he would require further medical attention for several years although it was possible that he would develop such severe degenerative changes that he would require further reconstruction of the knee in 20 or 30 years' time; that the pursuer was in employment as a storeman as at the date of trial; and that he was optimistic about continuing in the job and about the possibility of obtaining further work as a storeman should anything go wrong with his present position — **Loss of earnings to date of trial** agreed and damages *awarded* accordingly — Damages of £1,500 *awarded* for **future loss of earning capacity**, having regard to (i) the fact that the pursuer's capacity in the labour market in the future was undoubtedly restricted; (ii) the possibility that his working life would be cut short because of progressive degenerative changes in his knee; (iii) that if he lost his present employment he would make every effort to obtain other work and because of his determination would be likely to be successful; and (iv) the consideration that any award in respect of possible inability to work in the long term future must inevitably be heavily discounted in view of the fact that the damages would be payable so long in advance.

(161) **Clarke v. McFadyen,** 1990 S.L.T. 277 (Lord Kirkwood)
Pursuer aged c.23 at trial — Injuries to head, leg and pelvis resulting in continuing disability which interfere with her work — **Loss of earnings to date of trial** calculated and damages *awarded* accordingly — Damages of £1,500 *awarded* for **loss of earning capacity**.

(162) **Martin v. Grootcon (UK) Ltd,** 1990 S.L.T 566 (Lord Morton of Shuna)
Pursuer aged 59 at date of trial — Minor bruising injury to back and chest resulting in continuing symptoms of pain, anxiety and depression and complaints of inability to sit for any length of time or to walk any material distance — Evidence that the pursuer had a long history of medical problems evidencing a strongly hypochondriacal nature; that he had nevertheless worked for over 15 years after the first neurosis symptom was recorded; but that an event such as the accident could have occurred to trigger such incapacity at any time, the accident being like the straw that broke the camel's back — **Loss of earnings to date of trial** calculated on the basis that (i) the pursuer would have worked a further five years but for his accident and (ii) during that five year period he would have had periods of short term incapacity and unemployment such as had previously occurred or perhaps rather higher, such being taken into consideration by assessing the loss by reference to the earnings of the pursuer's younger and fitter former workmate, discounted by 40%, and damages *awarded* accordingly.

(163) **O'Brien's Curator Bonis v. British Steel plc,** 1991 S.C. 315 (First Division; Lord Weir)
Ward aged 41 at date of trial — Very serious injuries resulting in permanent and severe disablement — Evidence that the ward requiring residential care at an epilepsy centre, returning home to his wife and family for a visit on alternate weekends and an occasional week-long stay, and would need institutional care for the rest of his life; that the ward might need more costly care in the future; that the annual charge

for residence at the centre was £11,200 (whereof the sum of £7,280 was attributable to staff costs and the sum of £3,920 was for personal costs, the latter comprising £1,000 for food and the balance for clothing, heating and lighting); that, subject to the effect of the ward's epilepsy, his expectation of life remained much as it was before the accident and he would require care for a period of about 30 years from the date of trial; and that the epilepsy might lead to a shortening of the ward's life due to accident — Evidence that the ward's wife, who was about the same age as the ward, had provided services to him in the form of care and that the marriage, which had lasted for about 23 years, would survive — Damages of £165,000 *awarded* on appeal for **future care costs** on the basis of a multiplicand of £11,000, representing the annual charge for residence at the centre reduced by the cost of food (only) but increased to take account of the possibility that the ward might need more costly care in the future, and a multiplier of 15, having regard to the ward's life expectancy and the risk of epilepsy leading to a shortening of the ward's life due to accident — Damages of £9,000 *awarded* on appeal for **future necessary services** on the basis of a multiplicand of £600 and a multiplier of 15, having regard to the multiplier selected for the cost of future care.

(164) **Travers v. Muirhead,** 1991 S.C. 236 (First Division; Sheriff Principal at Dundee)

Pursuer aged 33 at date of trial — Serious injury to heel resulting in substantial continuing disability and rendering the pursuer unfit for his pre-accident work or any work involving walking on rough or uneven surfaces or on stairs or slopes or driving some types of vehicle — Evidence that although the pursuer had taken part in training courses he had been unable to find work suitable to his condition following the accident **— Loss of earnings to date of trial** calculated and damages *awarded* accordingly — Damages of £15,000 *awarded* for **loss of future earnings**, which could be analysed as the product of a multiplicand of £2,500, representing what the pursuer would have been earning as at the date of trial, and a multiplier of six.

(165) **Devlin v. J. Howden & Co. Ltd,** 1991 S.L.T. 354 (Lord Weir)

Pursuer aged c.64 at date of trial — Injury to back rendering the pursuer unfit for his pre-accident work — Evidence that the pursuer's retirement age was 65 but that he had had episodes of back trouble prior to his accident **— Loss of earnings to date of trial** calculated on the basis of a cut-off date 18 months before the pursuer's 65th birthday to take account of the possibility that with his history sooner or later the pursuer would have sustained at work a similar sort of injury and damages *assessed* accordingly.

(166) **Howie v. Upper Clyde Shipbuilders Ltd,** 1991 S.L.T 2 (Lord Cameron of Lochbroom)

Pursuer suing as executor of husband aged 61 at date of death — Respiratory disease resulting in increasing disablement, including breathlessness and loss of mobility — Evidence that the pursuer rendered services to the deceased for the last two and a half years of his life, in the course of which period she gave up her employment as a hospital domestic; and that she provided him with comfort and support, took steps to give him physical support in overcoming his breathlessness and lack of strength and in giving him medication and undertook more concentrated nursing in the course of the last six months of his life — Damages of £6,810 *awarded* for **necessary services** (as being services which went beyond what might be given by reason of the bond of affection naturally arising from the marriage relationship), the amount awarded corresponding to the earnings which the pursuer would otherwise have received if she had remained in constant employment during the material period.

(167) **Joliffe v. Hay,** 1991 S.L.T. 151 (Lord Caplan)

Pursuer aged c.55 at date of trial — Injuries to chest, back and neck resulting in disabilities which were likely to be permanent and rendering the pursuer unfit for his pre-accident as a warehouseman and stockkeeper or for any work involving lifting, prolonged sitting, bending or substantial walking — Evidence that the pursuer had been in regular employment and was a satisfactory employee before his accident; that his pre-accident job was secure and was likely to have remained open until he reached the age of 65, albeit that he might have felt unwilling to carry on with a job which involved heavy duties such as heavy lifting until he was 65; that since his accident the pursuer had been considered by his doctor to be unfit for work, albeit that he might now be fit for light work; that his prospect of obtaining something suitable in the future must be very doubtful, any such job being likely to be at a much lower wage than he would otherwise have earned; and that as at the date of trial the pursuer would have been earning £8,320 per annum **— Loss of earnings to date of trial** calculated on the basis that the whole of the loss to date should be attributed to the accident and damages *awarded* accordingly — Damages of £20,000 *awarded* for **loss of future earnings**, having regard to (i) the very doubtful prospect of the pursuer obtaining suitable work in the future; and (ii) the uncertainties which could have surrounded his position even if the accident had not occurred, such as whether he would have wanted to work on until the age of 65.

(168) **Lennon v. Lanarkshire Health Board,** 1991 S.L.T 782 (Lord Prosser)

Pursuer aged c.41 at date of trial — Injury to wrist resulting in minor disability — Evidence that there was a real risk that the pursuer might become unemployed — Damages of £3,000 *assessed* for **loss of employability** on the basis that although the disability was not great the marginal might become crucial in the search for work.

(169) **Rennie v. Dorans,** 1991 S.L.T 443 (Lord Cameron of Lochbroom)
Pursuer aged 48 at date of trial — Injury to foot resulting in continuing disability and substantially restricting the pursuer in his choice of future work — Evidence that the pursuer had not worked for some four years prior to his accident and that any prospects of employment in his locality were slim — Evidence that the pursuer's wife had provided services to him for six weeks after the accident when he was lying at home and required to be assisted in more than the usual way — Damages of £2,000 *awarded* for **loss of employability** — Damages of £100 *awarded* for **necessary services**.

(170) **Smith v. Blackwood,** 1991 S.L.T. 562 (Lord Clyde)
Pursuer aged 26 at date of trial — Injuries to back and knee rendering the pursuer unfit for his pre-accident employment or any other heavy work but fit for lighter work — Evidence that the pursuer was in continous employment with his pre-accident employers and in all probability would have been earning a labourer's wage with them but for the accident, amounting to £5,300 per annum; that work was not easy to find in the pursuer's locality as at the date of trial; that it was not clear whether the earnings from any such employment would be more or less than those which he would have been receiving from his pre-accident employment; and that on the other hand the pursuer was clearly an intelligent, articulate and energetic individual within the range of his capacity and had the motivation and interest to extend that range by further education in appropriate directions **— Loss of earnings to date of trial** calculated and damages *awarded* accordingly — Damages of £15,000 *awarded* for **loss of future earnings** on a lump sum basis, the award not being open to precise calculation because of the imponderables involved; the assessment being the equivalent of a little less than three years of the suggested multiplicand of £5,300.

(171) **Watson v. British Railways Board,** 1991 S.L.T 657 (Lord Marnoch)
Pursuer aged c.43 at date of trial — Injury to ankle resulting in continuing disability attributable to psychiatric condition rendering the pursuer unfit for his pre-accident employment — Evidence that the pursuer's employers had kept him on their books and would review his case in about a year after the date of trial; that his condition was likely to improve over the next year or so; and that he would then be seen to be fit to return to his former or some comparable employment

— **Loss of earnings to date of trial and beyond** to the date of the forthcoming review calculated and damages *awarded* accordingly.

(172) **Redman v. McRae,** 1991 S.L.T 785 (Lord Weir)

Pursuer aged 48 at date of trial — Injuries to ribs, pelvis and hip and haemothorax resulting in severe continuing disability and rendering the pursuer unfit for his pre-accident employment — Evidence that the pursuer was unable to stand for long without having to sit down and unable to sit for long without being compelled to stand; that the range of alternative jobs open to him must be extremely limited; and that the chances of obtaining work again had to be considered as unlikely — **Loss of earnings to date of trial** agreed and damages *awarded* accordingly — Damages of £44,200 *awarded* for **loss of future earnings** on the basis of a multiplicand of £8,840, representing what the pursuer would have been earning as at the date of trial (including the variables of overtime, holiday pay and some travelling expenses), and a multiplier of five, having regard to the pursuer's age and, while not ruling it out, the remoteness of his prospects in obtaining any alternative work.

(173) **Robertson v. British Bakeries Ltd,** 1991 S.L.T. 434 (Lord Osborne)

Pursuer aged 47 at date of trial — Injury to ankle resulting in continuing disability — Evidence that it was likely that within a relatively short period of time after trial the pursuer would begin to suffer from post-traumatic osteo-arthritis and that such was likely to mean that he could not continue with his existing employment which even now he carried on with some difficulty — **Loss of earnings to date of trial** agreed and **provisional damages** therefor *awarded*, with an order that the pursuer might apply for an award of further damages if he developed post-traumatic osteo-arthritis in his right ankle within a period of 10 years from the date of the accident — Damages *assessed* in the alternative, on a conventional basis, for (i) the agreed **loss of earnings to date of trial**; and (ii) the pursuer's **diminished value on the labour market**, in the sum of £16,000, such being roughly twice the pursuer's present rate of net remuneration.

(174) **Smith v. Chief Constable, Central Scotland Police,** 1991 S.L.T. 634 (Lord Marnoch)

Pursuer aged c.36 at date of trial — Injury to neck resulting in continuing disability — Evidence that the pursuer's husband had provided services to her after the accident; that in the early months he was very greatly involved in the running of the home to the extent even of coming home during his dinner hour and even now, three years later, he contributed much in the way of moving furniture, hoovering, lifting the children and the like — Damages of £1,000 *awarded* for **necessary services**.

(175) **O'Neil v. British Coal Corporation,** 1991 S.L.T. 367 (Lord McCluskey)

Pursuer aged 40 at date of trial — Injury to back resulting in the pursuer becoming extremely anxious and obsessed with his condition and rendering him unfit for his pre-accident employment as a miner — Evidence that the pursuer was fit for lighter work; that he had unreasonably declined an offer of employment shortly prior to the date of trial, but no evidence as to the level of earnings which he would have enjoyed in respect of that job; and that the pursuer was unlikely for a long time to come to feel confidence in his ability to do heavy work or to engage in any kind of strenuous physical activity — Evidence that the pursuer had had other, albeit minor, episodes of ill health but that there was no reason to suppose that he would not have continued in his pre-accident employment but for his accident, subject to the notorious fact that the coal industry had been contracting for a number of years and there was great uncertainty about the future of the industry — Evidence that the pursuer's wife had provided services to him by nursing him, taking a week off work, and carrying out duties rendered necessary by the accident, albeit for less than two hours per day **— Loss of earnings to date of trial** calculated on the basis that the pursuer was entitled to recover his loss until the date of refusal by him of the offer of employment and damages *awarded* accordingly — Damages of £10,000 *awarded* for **loss of future earnings** on a lump sum basis, having regard to the absence of evidence as to the likely difference between the pursuer's earnings if he had continued in work and what he might earn in lighter, skilled work — Damages of £5,000 *awarded* for **loss of pension rights** on the basis of a discount for the various circumstances which might well have prevented the pursuer's continuing to work in the coal industry until the age of 60 — Damages of £500 *awarded* for **necessary services** on a lump sum basis.

(176) **Morrison v. McDermott Scotland,** 1991 S.L.T 854 (Lord Milligan)

Pursuer aged 54 at date of trial — Injuries to wrists and knee rendering the pursuer unfit for his pre-accident employment as a supervisor involving extensive climbing around structures — Evidence that if the pursuer had not been laid off from his pre-accident job he would now be earning £350 per week; that he was now employed elsewhere doing light work for £132 per week; that shortly prior to trial the pursuer had been advised by his previous employers that he might be offered work by them at a rate of around £200 per week, including overtime; that but for the accident his prospective retirement age was 65; that while he worked in an industry where job security was not statistically high, he would still probably have been in his pre-accident job as at the date of trial and would by then have been working for his employers constantly for more than 17 years; and that his pre-accident employment did not involve manual work and apparently was a job for which there was a reasonable prospect of employment to that age — **Loss of earnings to date** of trial agreed and damages *awarded* accordingly — Damages of £46,800 *awarded* for **loss of future earnings** on the basis of a multiplicand of £10,400, representing the differential between what the pursuer would have been earning as at the date of trial and what he was in fact earning, less some allowance for the prospect that he might obtain the better paid job referred to by his former employers, and a multiplier of four and a half, having regard to the pursuer's age and the fact that his pre-accident work was a job for which there was a reasonable prospect of employment to the age of 65.

(177) **Mitchell v. Glenrothes Development Corporation,** 1991 S.L.T. 284 (Lord Clyde)

Pursuer aged 48 at date of trial — Injury to shoulder rendering the pursuer unfit for his pre-accident employment or any other work involving heavy lifting — Evidence that the pursuer had been fit for light work for about three years as at the date of trial but despite repeated efforts he had been unable to find any work; that the pursuer had been accepted into the enterprise allowance scheme and intended to start up a business with his wife operating a mobile second hand bookshop throughout the region, hoping to derive a joint profit therefrom of £140 per week; but that the prospects of the new venture were uncertain — Evidence that the pursuer's wife had provided him with services, helping him in and out of the bath, massaging his arm from time to time and helping him to put on his clothes — Evidence that the pursuer's likely retiring age in his pre-accident employment was 65; that he would have received at that time pension benefits under the local authority scheme had he remained in that employment; that the sums that he would then have received, based on the level of wage prevailing as at the date of trial, comprised (i) an annual pension of £3,011; and (ii) a lump sum of £9,034; and that about two years before the date of trial he had been refunded pension contributions in the sum of £2,821 — **Loss of earnings to date of trial** calculated and damages *awarded* accordingly — Damages of £35,568 *awarded* for **loss of future earnings** on the basis of a multiplicand of £7,904 and a multiplier of four and a half, having regard to the uncertainties of the new work and the future benefit which the pursuer might derive therefrom — Damages of £100 *awarded* for **necessary services** — Damages of £15,000 *awarded* for **loss of pension rights** on the basis of a multiplicand of £3,011 and a multiplier of six, less the sum refunded to the pursuer in respect of his pension contributions, together with interest over the period which had elapsed since it was paid, there being a rough balance between the other considerations, *viz.*(i) the imponderables in the case, in particular the possibility of another pension being forthcoming, and the deferment in payment of the pension until age 65; and (ii) the value of the lump sum benefit.

(178) **Grainger v. Fife Regional Council,** 1991 S.L.T. 632 (Lord Cullen)

Pursuer aged c.56 at date of trial — Injury resulting in enforced early retirement — Evidence that as a result the pursuer would suffer a diminution of his pension; that the prospective period during which he would suffer such diminution, assuming his survival, was 20 years between the ages of 55 and 75; and that the amount of diminution after a deduction in respect of income tax was £440 per annum — Damages of £4,840 *awarded* for **loss of pension rights** on the basis of a multiplicand of £440 and a multiplier of 11, making allowance for contingencies.

(179) **Mearns v. Lothian Regional Council,** 1991 S.L.T. 338 (Lord Sutherland)

Pursuer aged c.40 at date of trial — Injury to knee comprising the complete severance of the anterior cruciate ligament and rendering the pursuer unfit for his pre-accident work as a motorman — Evidence that the pursuer, who was not unintelligent, was now fit for light work but had not been able to find anything suitable; and that he had had a meniscectomy some years before the accident and would thereby develop degenerative changes in the knee as a result of which he would probably have only been able to work as a motorman until the age of 50 to 55 in any event **— Loss of earnings to date of trial** agreed and damages *awarded* accordingly — Damages of £36,608 *awarded* for **loss of future earnings** on the basis of a multiplicand of £9,152 and a multiplier of four, having regard to the pursuer's not unreasonable prospects of attaining some suitable employment in the future.

(180) **McMillan v. D.B. Marshall (Newbridge) Ltd,** 1991 S.L.T. 229 (Lord Cameron of Lochbroom)

Pursuer aged 44 at date of trial — Injury to back resulting in continuing disability and rendering the pursuer unfit for her pre-accident employment — Evidence that the pursuer now able to carry out the majority of her household duties but was substantially limited in the kind of employment for which she could now look — Evidence that before the accident the pursuer's husband had been accustomed to making a very substantial contribution to the running of the household; that after the accident he required to spend more time in doing household work which the pursuer had become unable to do, such as cleaning windows, cleaning the house and hanging out the washing as required; and that the most demanding time in that respect was in the period of just over a year after the accident **— Loss of**

earnings to date of trial calculated and damages *awarded* accordingly — Damages of £12,500 *awarded* for **future loss of employment**, having regard to the various factors which might have affected the pursuer's employment even had she not sustained her accident — Damages of £350 *awarded* for the pursuer's **inability to render personal services**.

(181) **Hoey v. British Steel Corporation,** 1991 S.L.T. 196 (Lord MacLean)

Pursuer aged 44 at date of trial — Injury to hearing resulting in partial one-sided deafness — Evidence that only 40% of the hearing loss was sensori-neural in nature — Damages of £6,000 *assessed* for **loss of employability**, discounted to reflect the fact that only 40% of the loss was sensori-neural.

(182) **Campbell v. City of Glasgow District Council,** 1991 S.L.T 616 (Lord Caplan)

Pursuer aged 40 at date of trial — Injuries to wrists and face resulting in continuing disabilities and rendering the pursuer unfit for his pre-accident employment as a scaffolder or any manual employment of a heavy nature — Evidence that the pursuer had been a scaffolder with his employers for 12 years before his accident; that that employment might have its own uncertainties, in that (a) it could lead to accidents in a variety of ways; (b) as the pursuer became older he might have lost his capacity or appetite for such work; and (c) there was also the risk of a downturn in the building industry leading to unemployment; that the pursuer was now fit only for light work; that he had the advantage of a reasonably wide range of job prospects locally; that he had made no attempt to date of trial to find or train for alternative employment; that he was advised by a consultant over a year before the date of trial that he was fit for lighter work but was then still receiving treatment for his injuries and his general practitioner was prepared to continue to certify him as unfit for work; and that even if the pursuer had moved more positively it was doubtful whether he could have equipped himself for alternative work and obtained such work in the time available — Evidence that the pursuer's sister had rendered services to him after the accident in respect that she had him to stay with her for five weeks immediately after his release from hospital when he was totally helpless, then when he returned to his own home she visited him almost every day for a period to help him with his domestic responsibilities and cooking, and finally for about seven months preceding the date of trial she had been calling at his home two or three times a week spending a few hours with him on each occasion and rendering him some help with the domestic tasks which he found difficult; and that she would not accept any payment therefor even if the pursuer recovered the money from a third party — **Loss of earnings to date of trial** calculated on the basis that the earnings lost to date could be regarded as an inevitable consequence of the accident and damages *awarded* accordingly — Damages of £30,912, less benefits, *awarded* for **loss of future earnings**, comprising (i) the sum of £15,912, being two years' net wage loss in respect of total loss of work, on the footing that allowing for the need to find suitable work, possible retraining, and the risk that if he was unemployed in the future then opportunities for alternative work would be reduced, it was reasonable to suppose that his accident had exposed him to a period of two or three years without any work at all from the time when he was ready to look for alternative work and allowing for the fact that he should have begun his efforts to find work rather sooner; and (ii) the sum of £15,000, being net wage loss in respect of what would be likely to be less well paid work, on the basis of a multiplicand of £1,500, representing the pursuer's continuing permanent loss (pitched at that amount in the absence of guidance from the evidence), and a multiplier of 10, having regard to the uncertainties which might in any event have affected the pursuer's working prospects — Damages for **necessary services**, which were reasonably quantified in the sum of £3,500, *refused* in view of the pursuer's sister's insistence that she would not accept any money therefor.

(183) **Gripper v. British Railways Board,** 1991 S.L.T. 659 (Lord Cullen)

Pursuer aged c.55 at date of trial — Injuries to wrist and foot — Evidence that the pursuer's wife had rendered services to him when he was wearing a wrist plaster by assisting him with shaving, dressing and washing and that as a result of his accident the pursuer was unable to carry out gardening which he had previously done two or three times a week — Damages of £200 *awarded* for **necessary** and **personal services**.

(184) **McGowan v. Air Products (UK) Ltd,** 1991 S.L.T 591 (Lord Sutherland)

Pursuer aged c.54 at date of trial — Injury to neck resulting in depression leading to genuine exaggeration of symptoms and rendering the pursuer unfit for employment — Evidence that the pursuer's wife had rendered services to him some of which might be described as being of a nursing nature, and that the pursuer was no longer able to perform services, mainly of a domestic nature, for her — Damages of £750 for **necessary services** and £250 for the pursuer's **inability to perform personal services** *awarded.*

(185) **Campbell v. D.B. Marshall (Newbridge) Ltd,** 1991 S.L.T. 837 (Lord Morton of Shuna)

Pursuer aged c.24 at date of trial — Injury to foot restricting ability to stand for whole shift — Damages of £750 *awarded* for **loss of employability**.

(186) **Geddes v. Lothian Health Board,** 1992 S.L.T. 986 (Lord Milligan)

Child aged seven at date of trial — Injury involving severe neurological damage at about the time of birth — Evidence that the pursuers, suing as the child's tutors and administrators at law, intended to sell the family home (for about £105,000) and build a more expensive property suitable for the child's needs (for about £160,000); that in relation to the use of the family car substantial additional mileage, with substantial additional motoring costs, would result from the child's disability, albeit that such was not clearly quantified and did not adequately distinguish the use which would have been made of the car in any event; that the child undertook trips abroad for treatment at a foreign institution which did not necessarily benefit him; and that the pursuers would require to purchase non-residential care for the child until he was 18 to 20 years of age at which time it was their wish that he be cared for in an institution — Evidence that average non-manual earnings as at date of trial amounted to £11,019.71 — Damages of £27,500 for the **cost of acquisition of a substitute house** (there being no evidence to enable the calculation to be carried out on the correct principle, namely on the basis of annualised cost), £15,000 for the **extra transport costs** on the basis of a multiplicand of £1,000 and a multiplier of 15 (there being insufficient evidence to enable a higher award to be made), £10,000 for the **cost of trips abroad** on the basis that it was not necessarily reasonable to expect abrupt termination of the involvement of the foreign institution and £138,315 for **future care costs**, comprising (i) the sum of £86,215 for the period of non-residential care on the basis of a multiplicand of £7,497 and a multiplier of 11.5; and (ii) the sum of £52,500 for the period of residential care on the basis of a multiplicand of £15,000 and a multiplier of three and a half *assessed* — Damages of £126,727 *assessed* for **loss of earnings** to be incurred from age 18 until retirement on the basis of a multiplicand of £11,019.71 and a multiplier of 11.5, having regard to the element of duplication arising from the assessment with respect to future care costs.

(187) **Gordon v. Wilson,** 1992 S.L.T. 849 (Lord Penrose)

Pursuer aged c.43 at date of trial — Injury involving loss of function of cranial nerves with consequent loss of hearing and facial sensation and unsteadiness in the limbs arising from alleged negligent delay in diagnosis — Evidence that for a period the pursuer's husband had provided services to the pursuer akin to those provided by a home help for about 40 hours per week and as to home help rates net of commission, tax and national insurance; that the pursuer would require care in the future; and that the pursuer had incurred or would incur extra transport, telephone and holiday costs and would require to incur the cost of installation of a shower, but insufficient evidence as to the actual costs incurred or to be incurred — Remuneration for **necessary services to date of trial** calculated on the basis of home help rates net of commission, tax and national insurance and damages *assessed* accordingly — Damages of £27,090 *assessed* for **future care** on the basis of a multiplicand of £1,806 and a multiplier of 15 — Damages for **extra costs**, save insofar as spoken to by the pursuer, would have been *refused.*

(188) **Duncan v. Scottish Marine Biological Association,** 1992 S.L.T. 554 (Lord Cameron of Lochbroom)

Pursuer aged 51 at date of trial — Injury to back involving acute disc prolapse rendering him unfit for his pre-accident work as a deckhand or any other work of a heavy manual kind and fit only for light work — Evidence that the pursuer had previously worked part time as a taxi driver; and that he had been unable to resume such work or find other work for which he was fit despite taking reasonable steps to test the employment market **— Loss of earnings to date of trial** calculated on the basis of the whole period to date but taking no account of the prospect of earnings from taxi-driving as being too speculative — Damages of £45,000 *awarded* for **loss of future earnings** on the basis of a multiplicand of £9,000 and a multiplier of five, having regard to the prospect that the pursuer might obtain limited employment in the future, albeit that those prospects were poor.

(189) **Hughes v. British Railways Board,** 1992 S.L.T. 97 (Lord Coulsfield)

Pursuer aged 38 at date of trial — Injury to neck rendering the pursuer permanently unfit for his pre-accident employment as a wagon repairer — Evidence that the pursuer was now employed as a storeman at a lower wage and that there was a possibility of his becoming redundant, although the risk was not an imminent one **— Loss of earnings to date of trial** agreed and damages *assessed* accordingly — Damages of £4,200 for **loss of future earnings** on the basis of a multiplicand of £350, representing the differential between the pursuer's pre-accident and post-accident jobs, and a multiplier of 12, having regard to his age, and £1,000 for **disadvantage in the labour market** *assessed.*

(190) **Mackenzie** v. **Midland Scottish Omnibuses Ltd**, 1992 S.L.T. 752 (Temporary Judge J.M.S.Horsburgh Q.C.)

Pursuer aged c.33 at date of trial — Injury to neck resulting in considerable disability and rendering her unfit for her pre-accident vocation as a nurse — Evidence that the pursuer had worked since her accident but had been unable to cope; that she had made a number of unsuccessful applications for other work; that in order now to work she would require very sympathetic surroundings and would have to avoid heavy work; and that while she was determined to find employment her prospects of doing so must be slight — **Loss of earnings and other patrimonial loss to date of trial** agreed and damages *awarded* accordingly — Damages of £2,000 *awarded* for **future treatment costs** — Damages of £57,500 *awarded* for **loss of future earnings** on the basis of a multiplicand of £9,583, representing the net midpoint of the nursing and midwifery staff's pay scale upon which the pursuer was paid when she ceased work, and a multiplier of six, having regard to the pursuer's determination and her restricted prospects of work.

(191) **Napier v. Burton's Gold Medal Biscuits Ltd,** 1992 S.L.T. 1019 (Lord Kirkwood)

Pursuer aged c.55 at date of trial — Injury to back resulting in temporary disability — Evidence that the pursuer off work for 10 weeks, during which time her husband had performed the household duties such as ironing, hoovering, making beds, cleaning windows and carrying the shopping normally discharged by the pursuer — Damages of £100 *assessed* for **necessary services**.

(192) **McMenemy v. Argyll Stores Ltd,** 1992 S.L.T. 971 (Lord Coulsfield)

Pursuer aged 33 at date of trial — Injury to elbow resulting in continuing disability — Evidence that there might be some deterioration in the condition of the elbow; that the pursuer had never earned any income at all but had always had an ambition to be a social worker; that as at the date of trial the lowest range of social work salaries was in the region of £11,000 per annum; that the pursuer had intended to obtain employment when her children had reached an age to permit her to do so; and that they were of such an age as at the date of trial — Damages of £8,000 *awarded* for **loss of future earnings**, having regard to (i) the fact that the pursuer had never worked; (ii) the fact that she had not until now taken positive steps towards achieving her career ambitions; (iii) the high degree of uncertainty as to the extent to which, and the time at which, she would have been able to undertake remunerative employment, even if the accident had not happened; (iv) the pursuer's genuine aspirations to work in some social work capacity; and (v) the likelihood that she would have been looking for some form of employment and **provisional damages** *refused.*

(193) **Hodge v. British Coal Corporation (No. 2),** 1992 S.L.T. 913 (Lord Morison)

Pursuer aged c.42 at date of trial — Injury to finger resulting in amputations and rendering the pursuer unfit for his pre-accident employment as a miner or any other work involving heavy lifting or labouring — Evidence that the pursuer would in any event have become redundant upon the closure of his colliery about two years before the date of trial; and that he had developed an unrelated condition of recurrent swelling affecting the same hand and his forearm — Damages of £7,500 *assessed* for **diminution of prospects of obtaining employment** since the date at which the pursuer would have been made redundant, having regard to (i) the fact that the pursuer's disability substantially affected his prospects of obtaining work; (ii) the fact that the pursuer might have had difficulty in obtaining employment even if he had been fully fit; and (iii) the fact that his disability was partly caused by the unrelated recurrent swelling.

(194) **Harrison v. R.B. Tennent Ltd,** 1992 S.L.T. 1060 (Lord Cameron of Lochbroom)

Pursuer aged 45 at date of trial — Injury to back resulting in continuing disability — Evidence that the pursuer was able only to undertake lighter duties; that there was a possibility that because of his inability to carry out all the heavy duties of a burner he might be moved to another job which was less well paid; that there was also a possibility of other changes in the allocation of work which might involve a change in the pursuer's job; and that any change could involve a drop in the pursuer's earnings of £2,500 per annum — Evidence that the pursuer's wife had rendered services to him for a very short period; that a gardener was now employed at £5 per week to do any necessary gardening jobs; and that from time to time in the future decorating jobs in the house would require to be done by others and be paid for instead of being done by the pursuer himself — **Loss of earnings to date of trial** agreed and damages *awarded* accordingly — Damages of £7,500 *awarded* for **loss of future earnings,** there being warrant for holding that if at the very least the pursuer were to be moved or have to move to a lighter job he would suffer some loss of earnings and that there was a reasonable prospect that this might occur at some stage during the pursuer's working life; the assessment being the equivalent of £2,500 for three years — Damages of £50 for **necessary services** and £1,000 for the pursuer's **inability to render personal services** *awarded.*

(195) **Comber v. Greater Glasgow Health Board,** 1992 S.L.T. 22 (Lord Milligan)

Pursuer aged 30 at date of trial — Injury involving misshapen face arising out of allegedly negligent surgical intervention during childhood and resulting in numerous operations disrupting her adolescence — Evidence that the pursuer would have liked to have qualified for a career in nursing but had only been able to obtain two jobs, one an administrative clerical job and the other involving switchboard and typing work **— Loss of earnings to date of trial** agreed and damages *assessed* accordingly — Damages of £24,000 *assessed* for **loss of future earnings** on the basis of a multiplicand of £3,000 and a multiplier of eight, having regard to the reasonable prospect that the pursuer would have been able to undertake a career in, for example, nursing.

(196) **Breslin v. Britoil plc,** 1992 S.L.T. 414 (Lord MacLean)

Pursuer aged 49 at date of trial — Injury to back rendering the pursuer unfit for his pre-accident employment as a rigger and, while objectively he might be fit for light to moderate work of a sedentary nature, he suffered from a behavioural illness resulting from the accident which rendered him a permanent invalid — Evidence that had the accident not happened the pursuer would have gone on working offshore for a number of years, perhaps until his early to mid-50s and thereafter might have continued as a rigger on shore — Evidence that the pursuer's wife had rendered services to the pursuer and that the pursuer had been unable to perform services such as one particular piece of home decorating or generally to help in and around the house **— Loss of earnings to date of trial** agreed and damages *awarded* accordingly — Damages of £108,000 *awarded* for **loss of future earnings** on the basis of a multiplicand of £18,000 and a multiplier of six, having regard to the probable future course of the pursuer's career had he not had his accident — Damages of £800 for **necessary services** and £1,000 for the pursuer's **inability to render personal services** *awarded.*

(197) **Collins v. Gates Rubber Co. Ltd,** 1992 S.L.T. 622 (Lord Milligan)

Pursuer aged c.42 at date of trial — Injury to back rendering the pursuer unfit for his pre-accident employment and fit only for light work, including light intermittent driving — Evidence that but for the accident the pursuer would have been able to work on as an HGV driver for a further 10 years after the date of trial, at least **— Loss of earnings to date of trial** agreed as to amount and damages *awarded* accordingly — Damages of £74,250 *awarded* for **loss of future earnings** on the basis of a multiplicand of £13,500 and a multiplier of five and a half.

(198) **McLachlan v. D.B. Marshall (Newbridge) Ltd,** 1992 S.L.T. 131 (Lord Coulsfield)

Pursuer aged 26 at date of trial — Injury to back resulting in continuing disability and rendering her unfit to carry out work which involved any degree of bending or lifting — Evidence that there was a real and substantial risk that the pursuer would not be able to continue with her present employment indefinitely, she having required to show considerable determination to continue to work as she had done and she might well not be able to do so in the future — Damages of £2,500 *awarded* for **disadvantage in the labour market**.

(199) **Hill v. Lovett,** 1992 S.L.T. 994 (Lord Weir)

Pursuer aged c.36 at date of trial — Injury comprising dog bite to leg resulting in amputation and rendering her fit only for essentially sedentary work — Evidence that the pursuer was originally trained as a dental nurse; that she was planning to resume full time employment as her children had reached an age when she was in a position to start work again; that she had, however, been unable to obtain full time employment and was working part time at the time of her injury; and that at the date of trial she was in the course of completing a degree and hoped to undertake a further course leading to a doctorate **— Loss of earnings to date of trial** calculated on the basis of an assumption that she would at some stage have obtained full time employment and that she might have earned a total figure from part time and full time employment equivalent to the amount of deductible benefits and damages *refused* accordingly — Damages of £12,000 *awarded* for **loss of employability**, having regard to (i) the possibility that the pursuer would eventually obtain well paid employment, albeit that the prospects must be said to be doubtful; and (ii) the possibility that she might obtain full time employment in some sedentary but less well paid work, albeit that in the circumstances, unless good fortune attended her, she would not be able to obtain employment with ease.

(200) **Clark v. Sutherland,** 1993 S.C. 320 (Second Division; Temporary Judge T.G.Coutts Q.C.)

Pursuer aged c.39 at date of trial — Injuries to ankles and leg resulting in the development of osteo-arthritis — Evidence that the pursuer was not employed at the time of the accident; that she had been intending to return to work as a medical secretary when the age of her children permitted; that she would probably have been employed by a date about nine months after the accident; that the effects of the accident disabled her from working full time for a period of two years from that date; that for the remaining two years before the trial she would only have worked part time as a result of her back condition which was not proved to be associated with the accident; that the gross amount which she would have earned by working full time would have been £6,000–£7,000 per annum, according to the pursuer, or £6,800–£9,000 per annum, according to a consultant surgeon, but no evidence as to net earnings — Evidence that the pursuer required considerable assistance in caring for her children and her household from her husband, mother and mother-in-law; that she required to have assistance to change bed linen and to do the washing and only did very limited shopping, her husband doing most of the cooking and home decorating and her mother and mother-in-law doing ironing; and that at least 14 hours a week would have been devoted to the necessary services during the first year after the accident with proportionately less during the next two years and a fraction thereof during the final period before the trial but no evidence as to sums which required to be paid to outsiders for services **— Loss of earnings to date of trial** calculated (in the absence of evidence as to net earnings) on the basis of two-thirds of the minimum amount of gross earnings which the pursuer must have lost, the minimum requiring to be taken as £6,400 per annum, and damages *awarded* on appeal accordingly — Damages of £6,000 *awarded* for **loss of earning capacity** — Remuneration for **necessary services to date of trial** calculated (the evidence being imprecise) on the basis of the minimum reasonable rate of remuneration for the services in question, namely £3 per hour, and after deduction of benefits, damages therefor *refused* on appeal — Damages of £1,000 *awarded* for the pursuer's **inability to render personal services to date of trial** — Damages for the pursuer's **future inability to render personal services**, taking into account deductible benefits, *refused.*

(201) **McManus v. British Railways Board,** 1993 S.C. 557 (Second Division; Lord Penrose)

Pursuer aged c.31 at date of trial — Post-traumatic stress disorder with serious and continuing effects — Evidence that the pursuer was recognised by the adjudicating medical authority as being 25% disabled for life — Damages of £2,500 *awarded* on appeal for **future loss of earning capacity.**

(202) **McCrum v. Ballantyne,** 1993 S.L.T. 788 (First Division; Lord Sutherland)

Pursuer aged 26 at date of trial — Multiple injuries resulting in permanent disability and rendering the pursuer unfit for his pre-accident employment as a welder, except at a bench — Evidence that if the pursuer had still been in his pre-accident employment he would have been working a 59 hour week for which he would earn £203.50 net; that there was a possibility of a reduction in available overtime in that employment; that the pursuer had another job as at the date of trial earning £100 net per week; that he would take a better paid job if he could find it; that there might be light welding jobs around, albeit that none could be identified; that there was no realistic prospect of the pursuer finding such a job in the immediate or indeed foreseeable future; and that the longer he went on without having a welding job the more difficult it would be for him to get back into that kind of work **— Loss of earnings to date of trial** calculated and damages *awarded* accordingly — Damages of £54,648 *awarded* for **loss of future earnings** on the basis of a multiplicand of £4,968, representing the differential on a 48 week year between the pursuer's pre-accident and post-accident earnings, and a multiplier of 11, having regard to (i) the pursuer's age; (ii) the possibility, however remote, that the pursuer might return to welding; (iii) the possible reduction in available overtime in his pre-accident employment; and (iv) the possibility that the pursuer might change his job as he would take a better paid job if he could find it.

(203) **McMillan v. McDowall,** 1993 S.L.T. 311 (Temporary Judge T.G.Coutts Q.C.)

Pursuer aged 24 at date of trial — Injury to spine rendering the pursuer paraplegic — Evidence that but for his accident the pursuer, then a shepherd, would have become entitled to a house with his employment; that after his accident he was provided with accommodation by his parents in their farmhouse; that but for his accident the pursuer might have become a farm manager; and that after his accident he had some prospects of remunerative employment in the future — Evidence that the pursuer's father had incurred costs in relation to alterations to the parents' home, which were necessitated by the pursuer's injuries and did not enhance the value of the property, and a buggy and replacement buggy for the pursuer; that the pursuer required to incur capital costs in relation to certain equipment as well as annual outlays in relation to replacement and maintenance costs and additional washing and clothing requirements and additional holidays; that up until the date of trial and for a short time thereafter, until his own house was built near to his parents' house (at a cost of £143,500), the pursuer had been and would be cared for by his parents and in particular by his mother; that the services, so far as necessary, amounted in all to about one and a half hours a day, being provided at odd times and not necessarily at one extended period, with the level of care being high (virtually 24 hours a day) in the initial stages for such time as the pursuer spent at home and thereafter progressively diminishing to one and a half hours per day; that for the future the pursuer would initially require nothing beyond what he presently needed other than the presence of an emergency backup service when he acquired his own home and independence; that thereafter he would require progressively more care which his mother would be less able to provide, until ultimately he would require a resident housekeeper (in about 20–25 years' time); and that the different levels of care could be provided by an outside agency such as a non-profit-making organisation not setting out to provide skilled nursing care — **Loss of earnings to date of trial** calculated on the basis (a) that the free accommodation to which the pursuer would have become entitled but for his accident formed part of his remuneration; and (b) that the accommodation provided by his parents after his accident was a gratuitous benefit and thus fell to be left out of account, and damages *awarded* accordingly — Damages of £97,760 *awarded* for **loss of future earnings** on the basis of a multiplicand of £7,250 and a multiplier of 13, having regard to (i) the prospect that the pursuer might obtain remunerative work in the future; and (ii) the prospect that but for his accident the pursuer might have advanced to the hoped for position as farm manager — Remuneration for **necessary services to date of trial** calculated on the basis of undiscounted non-profit-making care and home help rates, making allowance for the incidence of taxation and a counter allowance for the irregular hours of work and responsibility, and damages *awarded* accordingly — Damages of £2,241 for the **farmhouse alteration costs**; £2,390 for the **buggy and replacement buggy costs**; £1,850 for **capital outlays**; £13,500 for **replacement and other special costs** on the basis of a multiplicand of £750, representing such annual expense over normal that the pursuer would have, and a multiplier of 18; £23,816 for **future care costs** over the next 20 years on the basis of a multiplicand of £1,642.50, representing one and a half hours per day at £3 hourly, and a multiplier of 14.5; £23,649 for **future care costs** thereafter on the basis of a multiplicand of £7,883, representing the annual cost of a housekeeper at £2,600, a carer with living expenses of £3,261 and a relief help at £2,022, and a multiplier of three; the assessment in respect of future care utilising an overall multiplier of 17.5; £41,700 (sic) for **accommodation costs** on the basis of a multiplicand of £2,870, representing 2% per annum of the cost of the house, and a multiplier of 15, bearing in mind that the outlay had not yet been incurred and might not be for a further year; and £5,200 for the **additional holiday costs** on the basis of a multiplicand of £400 and a multiplier of 13, bearing in mind that the pursuer's ability to go away on holiday would become restricted as he required full time residential care, *awarded.*

(204) **Ballantyne v. Tesco Stores Ltd,** 1993 S.L.T. 678 (Lord Kirkwood)

Pursuer aged c.50 at date of trial — Injury to ankle resulting in temporary disability — Evidence that the pursuer's husband had left his job and returned home to assist her, making the meals and doing all the housework and that it was about two months before the pursuer could resume her normal household duties — Damages of £250 *awarded* for **necessary services**.

(205) **Buchanan v. Lanarkshire Health Board,** 1993 S.L.T. 456 (Lord Kirkwood)

Pursuer aged 53 at date of trial — Injury to back resulting in continuing disability and rendering the pursuer unfit for her pre-accident employment as an auxiliary nurse — Evidence that the pursuer intended to work on until the age of 65 and that there was nothing in her medical records which would be likely to have prevented her from working on until that age **— Loss of earnings to date of trial** agreed and damages awarded accordingly — Damages of £34,122.40 *awarded* for **loss of future earnings** on the basis of a multiplicand of £6,824.48, representing what the pursuer would be earning if she were still in her pre-accident employment, and a multiplier of five, having regard to (i) the nature of the pursuer's disabilities, which made her unlikely to be able to take any other form of gainful employment in the foreseeable future; and (ii) the fact that it must be, to some extent, a matter of conjecture whether she would have been able to work on until the age of 65.

(206) **Duncan v. Ross Harper & Murphy,** 1993 S.L.T. 105 (Lord Kirkwood)

Pursuer aged 25 at date of trial — Serious injury to pelvis with associated internal injuries rendering the pursuer fit only for light work — Evidence that the pursuer had had casual farming work for about six months each year prior to his accident but no evidence as to how much he had been earning in that regard; and that he had not worked since the accident, albeit that he had tried unsuccessfully to obtain light work — Damages of £8,000 *assessed* for **loss of earning capacity**, having regard to the pursuer's age.

(207) **Dunn v. Johnston Castings Engineering Ltd,** 1993 S.L.T. 576 (Lord Weir)

Pursuer aged c.40 at date of trial — Injury to back rendering the pursuer permanently unfit for his pre-accident employment and fit only for light work — Evidence that the pursuer had been earning about £165 per week in his pre-accident job; that his qualifications were related to work which involved a degree of exertion for which he was incapacitated; that on the other hand he was a man of considerable intelligence and his varied work experience suggested a degree of versatility and adaptability towards other forms of employment; and that he should be capable of obtaining work within the next year or so after trial, albeit that it could not be assumed that he would earn as much as previously — **Loss of earnings to date of trial** agreed as to amount and damages *awarded* accordingly — Damages of £12,500 *awarded* on a lump sum basis for the **diminution of employment prospects for the future**, bearing in mind the pursuer's pre-accident wage.

(208) **Campbell v. Campbell & Isherwood Ltd,** 1993 S.L.T. 1095 (Lord Weir)

Pursuer aged 73 at date of trial — Respiratory disease resulting in breathlessness and rendering the pursuer unable to do anything involving any level of exertion — Evidence that the pursuer's disability was contributed to by unrelated medical conditions; that his life expectancy was about five years from the date of trial; that the pursuer's wife had provided services involving extra work of a domestic and a nursing character and would continue to do so; that these services would have had to be performed in a substantial measure even if the disease had not emerged; and that the services were liable to become more onerous as time went by — Damages of £4,000 *awarded* for **necessary services** — Damages for the pursuer's **inability to render personal services** *refused* on the basis that any loss was no more than *de minimis*.

(209) **McWhinnie** v. **British Coal Corporation**, 1993 S.L.T. 467 (Temporary Judge D.B. Robertson Q.C.)

Pursuer aged 44 at date of trial — Injury to back with physical and psychological consequences rendering the pursuer unfit for his pre-accident employment as a miner or any job requiring more than the slightest physical agility — Evidence that the normal retirement age in the pursuer's pre-accident employment was 62; that he could have taken early retirement at the age of 53, but having regard to the pursuer's attitude to his work and the fact that he was a single man with few outside interests it was unlikely that he would have done so; that so far as sedentary work was concerned, the pursuer was unable to sustain the sitting position for any length of time without acute discomfort and in any event lacked any real skills or intellectual capacity for most non-manual occupations; and that the likelihood of the pursuer being able for light work was low and from the medical evidence he must be regarded as being unlikely ever to work again — **Loss of earnings to date of trial** agreed and damages *awarded* accordingly — Damages of £84,393 *awarded* for **loss of future earnings** on the basis of a multiplicand of £9,377 and a multiplier of nine, having regard to the probability that the the pursuer would have retired at the age of 62, which would have given 18 working years till retirement.

(210) **Murray v. Gent,** 1993 S.L.T. 482 (Temporary Judge R.G.McEwan Q.C.)

Pursuer aged c.59 at date of trial — Injury to finger resulting in permanent disability with a very slight risk that if he lost his job the pursuer would be at a disadvantage in the labour market — Damages of £200 *assessed* for **loss of prospects**.

(211) **Stafford v. Renfrew District Council,** 1993 S.L.T. 1197 (Lord Osborne)

Pursuer aged 44 at date of trial — Injury to left wrist and arm rendering the pursuer unfit for his pre-accident employment as a slater — Evidence that the consequences of the wrist injury were permanent and significant; that the pursuer was, however, a right handed individual; and that he could well follow a number of different types of employment at the present time **— Loss of earnings to date of trial** agreed as to amount and damages *awarded* accordingly — Damages of £12,000 *awarded* for the pursuer's **diminished value in the labour market**.

(212) **Stark v. Nairn Floors Ltd,** 1993 S.L.T. 717 (Lord Osborne)

Pursuer aged c.41 at date of trial — Injury to hand and fingers resulting in partial amputation — Evidence that for about four months after the accident the pursuer's wife had had to to do a number of jobs which the pursuer normally did, such as lighting fires and chopping sticks as well as dealing with the consequences of a rewiring operation in the house and perform a number of additional tasks for him, namely a range of personal duties such as dressing and undressing the pursuer, washing and drying him, attending to his shoes and the like — Damages of £500 *assessed* for **necessary services**.

(213) **Young v. Greater Glasgow Health Board**, 1993 S.L.T. 721 (Lord Cameron of Lochbroom)

Pursuer aged c.46 at date of trial — Injury to back in a fall resulting in persistent symptoms — Evidence that at the time of the accident the pursuer, an auxiliary nurse, had pre-existing minor degenerative changes and a history of back injuries which rendered her already vulnerable to further back injury; that she had sustained another back injury in a second fall just under a year later which resulted in an exacerbation of the existing lesion in her back; that while the symptoms of back pain had eased prior to the second fall, they were still of a character such as to suggest that they were persistent and would have taken some time to clear up; that the consequence of the first fall was to make the effects of the second fall more acute than they would otherwise have been; and that even if the pursuer had not suffered the first fall it was probable that the combination of her prior back condition and a further back injury such as she sustained in the second fall would have affected her continuing to work as an auxiliary nurse — **Loss of earnings to date of trial** agreed and damages *assessed* accordingly — Damages of £2,000 *assessed* for **loss of future earnings** on a broad view, it being likely that, having regard to the nature of the pursuer's prior back complaints and the material contribution of the second fall to her present state, even by the date of trial or at least in the reasonably short term future she would have required to give up employment as an auxiliary nurse.

(214) **Scott v. Kelvin Concrete Ltd,** 1993 S.L.T. 935 (Lord Coulsfield)
Pursuer aged 40 at date of trial — Injuries to legs resulting in below-knee amputation and continuing disability in the remaining ankle — Evidence that the pursuer was in employment as at the date of trial and earning £100 per week less than in his pre-accident employment; and that his present employment was with employers who were working under a limited contract — Evidence that the pursuer's wife required to give a considerable amount of assistance to him and also that the pursuer had been considerably restricted in the extent to which he could carry out household tasks and such other tasks as decorating or other D.I.Y. work — **Loss of earnings to date of trial** agreed and damages *awarded* accordingly — Damages of £62,400 for **loss of future earnings** on the basis of a multiplicand of £5,200 and a multiplier of 12, having regard to the pursuer's age; and £10,000 for **disadvantage in the labour market** *awarded* — Damages of £2,000 *awarded* for **necessary services** — Damages of £2,000 *awarded* for the pursuer's **inability to render personal services**.

(215) **McDermid v. Crown House Engineering Ltd,** 1993 S.L.T. 543 (Lord Morton of Shuna)
Pursuer aged c.33 at date of trial — Injury to eye resulting in loss of sight in that eye — Evidence that at the time of the accident the pursuer was employed as an electrician's labourer working from scaffolding; that prior thereto he had worked on building contracts which was an area of work which had recently had particular difficulty; that after his accident he had been offered re-employment on another contract but did not take it up as he felt he was unfit to work from scaffolding; that since then he had not worked although he had made various attempts to obtain work; and that he had not received any medical or other advice as to what type of work he should or should not do — **Loss of earnings to date of trial** agreed as to amount and damages *awarded* accordingly — Damages of £79,000 *awarded* for **loss of future earnings,** as a broad guess, on the basis of a multiplicand of £10,000, representing his net wage loss as at the date of trial, and a multiplier of five, having regard to the absence of evidence from any

witness apart from the pursuer as to what an electrician's labourer with only one eye could reasonably be expected to do, or as to whether a person with one eye would ever be employed as an electrician's labourer, or as to what the pursuer in particular could be retrained to do.

(216) **Fullemann v. McInnes's Executors,** 1993 S.L.T. 259 (Lord Cullen)
Pursuer aged 47 at date of trial — Injuries to brain, face and back resulting in a number of neurological deficits, severe neuro-psychological deficits and a change of personality as well as residual physical disability — Evidence that the pursuer owned 99% of the share capital of a limited company which operated a garage business; that he received remuneration from the company at a level fixed by himself each year under reference to the profits of the company; that in the years immediately preceding his accident the pursuer's average remuneration from the company was SF75,000 and the average value of the benefits he received from the company was SF28,499; that but for his accident the pursuer's remuneration would have progressively increased over the following years until reaching the sum of SF140,000 per annum as at the date of trial; that there was no predetermined limit to the pursuer's working life and it was likely that, given that he was fit to do so, he would have taken whatever opportunity he had to go on working after the age of 65 and as the major shareholder in a garage company was less vulnerable to loss of employment for reasons to do with business conditions; that as a result of his accident the pursuer had had to sell his shares in the company; and that the pursuer was to be regarded as a Swiss resident for Swiss federal tax purposes and under the law of Switzerland awards of damages in respect of loss of earnings and other taxable receipts were subject to income tax — **Loss of earnings to date of trial** calculated on the basis of the gross remuneration as well as the value of the benefits which the pursuer would have received from the company over the whole period, less certain payments and benefits actually received, and damages in Swiss francs *awarded* accordingly — Damages of SF1,853,489 *awarded* for **loss of future earnings** on the basis of a multiplicand of SF168,499, representing the combined total of (a) what the pursuer's gross remuneration from the company would have been as at the date of trial; and (b) the value of his benefits from the company, and a multiplier of 11, having regard to the pursuer's work prospects.

(217) **Watts v. Russell,** 1993 S.L.T. 1227 (Lord MacLean)
Pursuer aged c.53 at date of trial — Injury to toe resulting in residual disability — Evidence that the pursuer was not working at the time of her accident; that her previous employment was seasonal and intermittent but she always had work when she wanted it; that she had been unfit for work until about nine months after her accident when

she resumed employment for a period; and that thereafter she had worked intermittently — Evidence that the pursuer's husband provided services to her within and without the home; that these services comprised doing the cooking, shopping and the housework, helping the pursuer in the shower and driving her to and from the hospital; and that these services were provided for about 12 weeks and were intensive for the first half of that period but became less so as the pursuer recovered mobility — **Loss of earnings to date of trial** calculated broadly on the basis of a lump sum for the period to the date of resumption of employment and damages *awarded* accordingly — Damages of £1,750 *awarded* for **loss of employability** — Damages of £750 *awarded* for **necessary services**.

(218) **McGunnigal v. D.B. Marshall (Newbridge) Ltd,** 1993 S.L.T. 769 (Temporary Judge T.G.Coutts Q.C.)

Pursuer aged 30 at date of trial — Minor physical injury resulting in recognisable psychological disturbance — Evidence that the pursuer returned to work about four months after her accident and worked for about eight months; and that she was fit for work thereafter but did not in fact work — Damages of £4,000 *awarded* for **loss of employability** from the date of cessation of work on the basis that the pursuer had and might well continue to have some difficulty in coping with machinery such as that involved in her accident.

(219) **Baird v. Sellars,** 1993 S.L.T. 856 (Temporary Judge J.M.S.Horsburgh Q.C.)

Pursuer aged c.41 at date of trial — Injury to neck, shoulder, head and chest resulting in continuing disability and rendering the pursuer unfit for her pre-accident employment as a chambermaid and fit only for light work — Evidence that prior to her accident the pursuer had been in part time employment only and was a low wage earner; that she had, however, had plans to attend to her own life in the future, much of her past having been devoted to looking after the older and younger generations of her family; and that her chances of finding suitable light work in an area of the country where few opportunities for this existed, were very slim — **Loss of earnings to date of trial** calculated and damages *awarded* accordingly — Damages of £5,000 *awarded* for **loss of future earnings**.

(220) **MacShannon v. Ailsa Perth Shipbuilders Ltd,** 1994 S.L.T. 500 (Lord MacLean)

Pursuer aged 58 at date of trial — Injury to knee activating symptom-free osteo-arthritis already present and rendering the pursuer unfit for his pre-accident employment as a rigger and leaving him fit only for sedentary jobs — Evidence that the pursuer might find suitable employment but if he did, the difference in earnings between his former job and any light work he might get was likely to result in a shortfall of about £90 net per week; that notwithstanding the pursuer's wish to have gone on working until the age of 65, there was no guarantee that there would continue to be full employment at the yard at which he had worked; and that it was likely that the osteo-arthritis in the pursuer's knee would have become activated before the age of 65, leading to his earlier retirement, irrespective of his accident — Evidence that the pursuer's wife had provided services to him such as helping him out of the bath and would continue to do so especially after his proposed knee replacement operation; and that the pursuer was now unable to perform services such as decoration and painting, in respect of which an outside contractor now had to be employed **— Loss of earnings to date of trial** agreed and damages *awarded* accordingly — Damages of £22,268 *awarded* for **loss of future earnings** on the basis of a multiplicand of £8,907.08, representing the pursuer's probable annual net earnings at the date of trial, and a multiplier of two and a half, having regard to (i) the pursuer's wish to go on working until the age of 65; (ii) the fact that there was no guarantee that there would continue to be full employment at the yard, albeit that there was no evidence of lay-offs; (iii) the likelihood that the osteo-arthritis would have become activated before the age of 65, leading to his earlier retirement; and (iv) the possibility that the pursuer might find suitable employment, albeit at the lower rate of pay — Damages of £1,250 *awarded* for **necessary and personal services** as a whole.

(221) **Morrison v. Barton,** 1994 S.L.T. 657 (First Division; Temporary Judge H.J. Aronson Q.C.)

Pursuer aged 31 at date of trial — Injury to knee resulting in continuing disability due to pain and rendering the pursuer unfit for his pre-accident employment as a teacher for the foreseeable future — Evidence that the pain was genuine, albeit without physical explanation, but no evidence from which it could be inferred that the pain was likely to be permanent — Damages of £86,688 *awarded* for **loss of future earnings** on the basis of a multiplicand of £14,448 and a multiplier of six, having regard to (i) the prospect of continuing disability due to pain for some time in the future; (ii) the difficulties which the pursuer might encounter in obtaining employment when he was fit for that; and (iii) the prospect that any employment offered to him might be at a lower rate of remuneration than that in a senior post as a teacher.

(222) **Lenaghan v. Ayrshire and Arran Health Board,** 1994 S.C. 365 (Extra Division; Lord Weir)

Pursuer aged 45 at date of trial — Injury to back causing functional overlay rendering the pursuer unfit for her pre-accident employment as a hospital catering assistant — Evidence from orthopaedic surgeons that the pursuer would never be fit for work of any sort but no evidence from a specialist in the field of psychological distress or functional overlay — Damages of £38,400 *awarded* on appeal for **loss of future earnings** on the basis of a multiplicand of £6,400 and a multiplier of six.

(223) **Cherry v. Strathclyde Regional Council,** 1994 S.L.T. 494 (Temporary Judge G.H. Gordon Q.C.)

Pursuer aged 62 at date of trial — Injury to hip resulting in continuing disability — Evidence that since the accident the pursuer's husband had provided services to her, comprising the normal household tasks of washing, cooking and cleaning, for five hours a day for the first six weeks and for two hours a day thereafter and would continue to do so, subject to the outcome of a proposed hip replacement operation likely to take place in the next five years and be successful; and that the local authority scale of charges for the provision of home helps gave a rate of £3.33 an hour as at the date of trial — Evidence that the pursuer had required as a result of her disability to incur additional transport costs in respect of a distance of 50 miles a week for the first three weeks and seven miles a week thereafter and would continue to do so; and that the A.A. rate for a car with a capacity of between 1001 and 1400cc with an annual mileage of 5,000 was 56.9 pence — Remuneration for **necessary services to date of trial** calculated on the basis of the hours worked and the local authority scale rate for the provision of home helps and damages *awarded* accordingly — Damages of £14,545.44 *awarded* for **future necessary services** on the basis of a multiplicand of £2,424.24, representing 52 weeks at two hours a day, seven days a week, at the rate of £3.33 an hour, and a multiplier of six, having regard to the likelihood that the hip replacement would take place fairly soon, would be successful and would improve considerably the pursuer's mobility **— Increased transport costs to date of trial** calculated on the basis of the additional miles travelled as a result of the pursuer's disability and the relative A.A. mileage rate and damages *awarded* accordingly — Damages of £1,242.66 *awarded* for **future increased transport costs** on the basis of a multiplicand of £207.11, representing 52 weeks at seven miles a week at the rate of 56.9 pence a mile, and a multiplier of six.

(224) **Wall v. Bryant,** 1994 S.L.T. 1260 (Lord Sutherland)

Pursuer aged 38 at date of trial — Injuries to head, arm and legs resulting in continuing disabilities and rendering him unfit for his pre-accident employment as a dark room technician and fit only for very light work — Evidence that the pursuer would have been promoted to the post of senior technical officer by the date of trial; and that he and his wife might in the future operate a bed and breakfast establishment from which he would derive a living — Evidence that the pursuer required to incur certain costs in relation to the installation of central heating, the acquisition of a three piece suite and the purchase of certain appliances, including an electrical wheelchair which might not be needed for some time; and that he required to incur additional motoring costs in respect that his annual mileage was higher than it otherwise would have been for personal motoring — Evidence that prior to his accident the pursuer helped with household chores which now fell entirely on the shoulders of his wife — **Loss of earnings to date of trial** agreed as to amount and damages *awarded* accordingly — Damages of £79,145 *awarded* for **loss of future earnings** on the basis of a multiplicand of £7,195, representing what the pursuer would have been earning as a senior technical officer as at the date of trial, and a multiplier of 11, having regard to the possibility that the pursuer might be able at some future time to find some very light work which he would be capable of doing, albeit that it was doubtful that any such job would be very remunerative (but taking no account of the possible bed and breakfast venture as being speculative and which, in any event, would require the pursuer to use his capital therefor and any profit he made would be largely in the form of a return on capital not otherwise earning interest) — Damages of £3,500 for the **central heating and three piece suite costs**; £4,000 for the **electric wheelchair cost**, to including running costs; and £7,500 for the **additional motoring costs** on the basis of a multiplicand of £500 and a multiplier of 15 *awarded* — Remuneration for **necessary services** and the pursuer's **inability to render personal services to date of trial** calculated and damages *awarded* accordingly — Damages of £15,000 *awarded* for **future necessary services** and the pursuer's **future inability to render personal services** on the basis of a multiplicand of £1,000 and a multiplier of 15.

(225) **McIntyre v. Strathclyde Regional Council,** 1994 S.L.T. 933 (Lord Penrose)

Pursuer aged c.42 at date of trial — Injury to foot causing nerve damage and rendering the pursuer unfit for work due to pain up to the date of trial — Evidence that the pursuer had continuing pain, albeit exaggerated by virtue of the outstanding litigation; that it was unlikely that he would be able to return to full time employment as a joiner without difficulty in the immediate future; and that his ability to carry out full time work must necessarily be affected by his long period of disability — **Loss of earnings to date of trial** calculated and damages *awarded* accordingly — Damages of £30,000, less benefits, for **loss in respect of continuing wage loss** on the basis of a multiplicand of £6,000 and a multiplier of five, having regard to the pursuer's prospects of returning to remunerative employment in the short term; and £5,000 for **loss in respect of long term employability** *awarded.*

(226) **McLean v. Remploy Ltd,** 1994 S.L.T. 687 (Lord Cameron of Lochbroom)

Pursuer aged 54 at date of trial — Injury to head causing a recurrence of epileptic fits which the pursuer had not suffered since childhood rendering her unfit for her pre-accident work and leaving her fit only for certain types of employment — Evidence that the pursuer would have been bound to cease employment at the age of 60 in any event; that any injury or severe trauma could cause fits; that since losing her job the pursuer had attempted unsuccessfully to obtain suitable alternative employment; and that there was no reasonable prospect of her obtaining employment in the future **— Loss of earnings to date of trial** agreed as to amount and damages *assessed* accordingly — Damages of £18,198 *assessed* for **loss of future earnings** on the basis of a multiplicand of £6,066 and a multiplier of three, having regard to (i) the pursuer's age; (ii) the fact that there was no reasonable prospect of her obtaining employment in the future; (iii) the possibility that the epilepsy could have recurred for other reasons; and (iv) the fact that the pursuer would have been bound to cease employment at the age of 60.

(227) **Morrison v. Laidlaw,** 1994 S.L.T. 359 (Lord Prosser)

Pursuer aged 50 at date of trial — Injury to leg and substantial psychological damage resulting in the loss of the pursuer's pre-accident employment, albeit that he was fit for such work — Evidence that by reason of the pursuer's age the prospects of substantial work, even on a casual basis, were poor **— Loss of earnings to date of trial** agreed and damages *awarded* accordingly — Damages of £58,200 *awarded* for **loss of future earnings** on the basis of a multiplicand of £9,700, representing what the pursuer would have been earning had he continued to work for his previous employers, and a multiplier of six, having regard to the pursuer's poor prospects of finding substantial work.

(228) **Myles v. City of Glasgow District Council,** 1994 S.C.L.R. 1112 (Lord Abernethy)

Pursuer aged 55 at date of trial — Respiratory disease resulting in serious continuing disability involving breathlessness which rendered the pursuer unfit for his pre-accident employment as a slater's labourer — Evidence that the pursuer also suffered from obesity and asthma which contributed to his breathlessness — Evidence that the pursuer's son and daughter-in-law rendered services to him, doing housework two to three times a week, cleaning, washing and ironing, changing the bed linen when necessary, sometimes taking food for him, taking him shopping, cleaning his windows, cutting the grass in his garden and taking him to visit his elderly parents and on other excursions — Evidence that the pursuer had difficulty in getting in and out of the bath and required to install a shower **— Loss of earnings to date of trial** agreed and damages *awarded* accordingly — Damages of £31,149 *awarded* for **loss of future earnings** on the basis of a multiplicand of £6,922 and a multiplier of four and a half — Remuneration for **necessary services to date of trial** calculated on the basis that the level of services provided was reasonable, save for the claim for the whole running costs of the son's car only part of which would be allowed, and damages *awarded* accordingly — Damages of £25,000 *awarded*, on a lump sum basis, for **future necessary services**, having regard to (i) an annual cost for the services of about £2,600 and for transport costs of £200; (ii) the likelihood that the pursuer would get significantly worse; and (iii) the fact that the pursuer would have the money in his hand now; the assessment being the equivalent of the product of a multiplicand of £2,800 and a multiplier of a little under nine — Damages of £2,000 *awarded* for the **shower installation cost**.

(229) **Paterson v. Hampton,** 1994 S.L.T. 1231 (Lord Kirkwood)

Pursuer aged 30 at date of trial — Injuries to leg resulting in below-knee amputation and rendering the pursuer unfit for his pre-accident employment as a night porter or his previous job as a chef — Evidence that the pursuer had a good work record before his accident; that he was now fit for some form of light or sedentary employment; and that, apart from registering at the Job Centre, he had not made any positive attempt to obtain work since his leg was amputated so that there was no way of knowing what type of employment he would eventually obtain or how much he was likely to earn — Evidence that the pursuer's parents had rendered services to him in consequence of his injuries; that after the accident he lived at home for a period, one or other of his parents helping him in and out of the bath two or three times a week, his mother helping him up and down the stairs, and his father driving him to and from the hospital for just over a year — **Loss of earnings to date of trial** agreed and damages *assessed* accordingly — Damages of £24,000 *assessed* for **loss of employability** — Damages of £450 for **necessary services** rendered by the pursuer's father and £250 for **necessary services** rendered by the pursuer's mother *assessed.*

(230) **McCluskey v. Lord Advocate,** 1994 S.L.T. (Lord Kirkwood)

Pursuer aged c.25 at date of trial — Injury to spine resulting in some continuing back pain, particularly after standing for long periods — Evidence that at the time of her accident the pursuer was a part time hairdresser; that but for her accident she would have continued in part time employment before switching to full time work for a short period prior to having a baby; and that the pursuer's disability was likely to have only a relatively minor effect on her ability to work as a hairdresser — Evidence that the pursuer's husband and mother had rendered services to her after the accident, the husband doing all the cooking and the housework for about three months and the mother visiting most evenings and helping with the washing and housework, as well as the shopping and any heavy lifting which was required, for several months — **Loss of earnings to date of trial** calculated and damages *assessed* accordingly — Damages of £750 *assessed* for **future loss of earning capacity** — Damages of £300 for **necessary services** rendered by the pursuer's husband and £300 for **necessary services** rendered by the pursuer's mother *assessed.*

(231) **MacLeod v. Taylor's Executor,** 1994 S.L.T. 322 (Lord Kirkwood)

Pursuer aged 29 at date of trial — Injuries to elbow, ankle and hand resulting in residual disabilities, particularly in the elbow — Evidence that but for his accident the pursuer would have continued with seasonal employment, depending on the availability of work, as well as his small business; that the pursuer was now unemployed but was fit for light work on a full time basis and had worked from time to time since his accident; that, while there was considerable local unemployment, the pursuer had not made adequate efforts to find suitable alternative employment and had sold his business because he felt he would be better off drawing social security benefits; that it was probable that the condition of the pursuer's elbow would deteriorate but a considerable degree of uncertainty existed as to the extent to which the function would deteriorate and as to the timescale of the deterioration — **Loss of earnings to date of trial** calculated and damages *awarded* accordingly — Damages of £18,000 *awarded* for **loss of future earnings** on a lump sum basis.

(232) **Lawrie v. Lanarkshire Health Board,** 1994 S.L.T. 633 (Temporary Judge J.F. Wheatley Q.C.)

Pursuer aged c.45 at date of trial — Injury to back resulting in permanent but limited disability rendering the pursuer unfit for heavy work — Evidence that the pursuer had been rendered services by his sister who assisted with household tasks and even with dressing him and by his nephew who had cut the grass throughout the summer months — Damages of £1,500 *awarded* for **disadvantage in the labour market** — Damages of £200 for **necessary services** rendered by his sister and £100 for **necessary services** rendered by his nephew *awarded.*

(233) **Kenny v. Lightways (Contractors) Ltd,** 1994 S.L.T. 306 (Lord Coulsfield)

Pursuer aged c.37 at date of trial — Injury to ankle with residual disability and leading to the development of osteo-arthritis — Evidence that the pursuer's ankle function would slowly deteriorate; that the rate and severity of the deterioration were unpredictable; that there was a strong possibility that he would require further surgery, probably in the form of an arthrodesis, which would leave him with a stiffened ankle and therefore considerable awkwardness; but that he should be able to continue to manage his work as a painter, including working from ladders **— Loss of earnings to date of trial** agreed and damages *assessed* accordingly — Damages of £7,500 *assessed* in respect of the **risk of future loss** on the basis that the risk of future absence from work and loss of capacity was substantial.

(234) **Farrelly v. Yarrow Shipbuilders Ltd,** 1994 S.L.T. 1349 (Lord Prosser)

Pursuer aged 62 at date of trial — Respiratory disease rendering the pursuer unfit for employment — Evidence that the pursuer had been employed as a foreman electrician in the shipyards since 1947; that there was a real risk that if the pursuer had not retired because of ill health he might in any event have lost his job through compulsory redundancy; that if he had lost his job comparable new jobs were available locally; that, more generally, both within the shipbuilding industry and on major construction sites particular contracts would give rise to a need for skills like the pursuer's; that while the pursuer himself had spent many years with the one employer, electricians had a nomadic tradition and would look for and find work where it arose throughout the country; that the pursuer impressed as a resourceful man, someone who would be very keen to find work and would accept inconveniences such as having to stay away from home, if this proved necessary in obtaining a job; that as an alternative to finding actual employment in industry many electricians would turn to self-employed work, either of a maintenance and fitting type in relation to buildings or in maintaining and repairing domestic appliances and the like; that on the other hand finding work, perhaps particularly in the pursuer's region, would be difficult in the prevailing economic climate; and overall the pursuer's age would be somewhat against him; and that upon the basis that the pursuer would have not have been made redundant he had suffered a loss of pension rights in the sum of £6,000 — Evidence that the pursuer's wife had rendered services to him; that she gave up work when his condition was diagnosed; that she had been earning about £7,500 per annum in her employment; that it would cost £50 a week to obtain relief help at the rate of two hours a day; that the services so far provided were essentially those involved in supporting the pursuer emotionally and psychologically, rather than physically; that it was reasonable to proceed on the basis that the pursuer would survive a further year after trial; that there would be a difficult three month terminal period during which more care would be required than during the first nine months; that it would cost about £5.15 per hour to obtain the services of an appropriate carer for the first nine months; that during that period the need might rise from about two hours per day initially to about six hours per day towards the end of the period; that by taking an average of four hours per day, giving 28 hours a week, one arrived at a weekly rate of about £145; that for the final three month period the need for a carer should be taken as having risen to six hours, or about £30 per day; that in addition nursing care would be required for about four hours per day, costing about £25; and that therefore to obtain both the general care and the necessary nursing would cost £55 per day or £385 per week — Evidence that the pursuer had been a general handyman, who devoted time to maintenance and improvement work in the family home; that over a year he probably did 21 days' work of this kind; that assuming an eight hour day at a rate of £5 per hour the annual rate for these services was £840; that the pursuer spent about one and a half hours per day on domestic work about the house, including help with preparing the evening meal; and that it would cost £ 3.50 per hour to obtain such domestic services for the same length of time each day — Damages of £24,000 *awarded* for **past and future loss of earnings** and **loss of pension rights**, as being one-half of what the combined losses would be on the basis that the pursuer would not have been made redundant (namely £14,000 for past loss of earnings, £28,000 for future loss of earnings on the basis of a multiplicand of £14,000 and a multiplier of two, and £6,000 for loss of pension rights), the award being a fair reflection of the position overall and appearing reasonable against all individual tests, no single test giving a reliable answer — Remuneration for **necessary services to date of trial** calculated on the basis of a lump sum, there being no firm logic in this matter and damages *awarded* accordingly — Damages of £13,275 awarded for **future necessary services**, comprising (i) the sum of £5,655 for the initial nine month (or 39 week) period on the basis of a weekly rate of £145; and (ii) the sum of £4,620 for the final three month (or 12 week) period on the basis of a weekly rate of £385 — Damages of £14,000 *awarded* for the pursuer's **inability to render personal services** on the basis of a multiplicand of £2,000, representing the combined total of (a) the annual rate of £840 for the handyman services; and (b) a figure of £1,160 as a reasonable amount for the domestic work which, done while otherwise at leisure, should be valued at rather below what it would cost to obtain domestic services for the same length of time each day, and a multiplier of seven, having regard to the nature of the services and the pursuer's age and the inference therefrom that he might well have gone on rendering these services for 10 years.

(235) **Garland v. Fairnington's Executor,** 1994 S.L.T. 855 (Lord Milligan)

Pursuer aged c.70 at date of trial — Serious injuries to legs and pelvis resulting in residual disabilities — Evidence that the pursuer's wife had performed very considerable services for him and would continue to do so; that she was by occupation a midwife and her professional general nursing expertise, coupled with her undoubted dedication to do all she could for the pursuer, meant that the services provided for him have been of an exceptional order; that she had incurred certain expenses in relation to visiting him in hospital; that she had provided care to the pursuer both in hospital where he was being treated and at home; that in hospital she had cleaned his mouth and done small things for him when he was in intensive care and thereafter had washed his hair, sponged him down and done other duties which nursing staff would normally do but which the nursing staff were not doing for him; that at home she bathed him for about half an hour and washed his hair, drove him about, such as to church and to monthly meetings, and now did all the cooking, shopping and gardening; that the pursuer's condition was expected to deteriorate and more time caring for him would therefore require to be spent; and that nurses were paid £5 to £6 gross per hour locally, nursing auxiliaries about £4 per hour and auxiliary care nurses £5.54 per hour for a weekday and £6.09 per hour for a weekend day — Remuneration for **necessary services to date of trial** calculated and damages *awarded* accordingly — Damages of £12,000 *awarded* for **future necessary services** on a lump sum basis (the award being particularly difficult to quantify in respect of the imponderables involved), having regard to the whole evidence and in particular that relating to the pursuer's prospective medical condition.

(236) **Edgar v. Strathclyde Buses Ltd,** 1994 S.L.T. 563 (Lord Cameron of Lochbroom)

Pursuer aged 57 at date of trial — Injury to finger of non-dominant hand resulting in amputation resulting in loss of grip strength and obvious cosmetic disability — Evidence that the pursuer a motor mechanic but no indication that he was likely to lose his present employment before retirement age — Damages for **loss of employability** *refused*.

(237) **Doyle v. Strathclyde Regional Council,** 1994 S.L.T. 524 (Lord Sutherland)

Pursuer aged c.36 at date of trial — Injury to brachial plexus of non-dominant arm rendering the pursuer unfit for his pre-accident employment as a fireman — Evidence that the pursuer now a first year student at college taking a two year course in business management with a possible third year at university leading to a degree; that his student grant was £3,500 per annum; that the pursuer was well motivated and would be employable in a new sphere where his disability would be of no importance; but that it was unknown what form of employment he would be able to obtain nor what level of remuneration he would get — **Loss of earnings to date of trial** agreed and damages *assessed* accordingly — Damages of £31,692 *assessed* for **loss of future earnings**, comprising (i) the sum of £42,192, being the product of a multiplicand of £10,548 and a multiplier of four (covering all the eventualities, looking at the matter broadly); less (ii) the sum of £10,500, being the total of three years' grants.

(238) **Coull v. Lothian Regional Council,** 1994 S.L.T. 377 (Lord Clyde)
Pursuer aged c.60 at date of trial — Injury to foot resulting in partial amputation — Evidence that the pursuer had been unemployed at the time of the accident for some one and a half years but was then looking for employment; that she had previously worked as a supervisor, earning about £50 net per week, and would probably have obtained some work for a period had the accident not happened; but that the period for which the pursuer would have obtained it and the extent of the remuneration remained uncertain — Evidence that the pursuer's daughter and son had rendered services to her since the accident and were continuing to do so; that such comprised most of the pursuer's shopping, the heavier housework, the gardening and general help; and that the pursuer received mobility allowance but no evidence as to the amount received nor as to the period over which she had received it — **Loss of earnings to date of trial** calculated on a lump sum basis, bearing in mind the level of her former earnings but also the relative uncertainty after her period of unemployment both of the period for which she would have found employment and the level of wage which she would have earned, and damages *awarded* accordingly — Damages for **necessary services** *refused*, having regard to the concession that allowance had to be made for the pursuer's mobility allowance, which was likely to exceed what might be estimated as a reasonable remuneration for the services which she had received.

(239) **Dickson v. Lothian Health Board,** 1994 S.L.T. 525 (Lord Penrose)
Pursuer aged c.45 at date of trial — Injury to back precipitating the onset of symptoms from pre-existing degenerative changes — Evidence that as regards those degenerative changes the pursuer would have been able to work on for five years but for her accident but would have become incapacitated at about that time, after experiencing progressive pain and discomfort; that the pursuer had suffered further

incidents of injury to her back after the accident, one of which was not a direct and natural consequence of the accident; but that that incident was a neutral event typical of the general category of events to be anticipated once back pain had begun **— Loss of earnings to date of trial** calculated on the basis of five years' net loss of wages and damages *awarded* accordingly.

(240) **Brien v. British Telecommunications plc,** 1994 S.L.T. 629 (Lord Cameron of Lochbroom)

Pursuer aged 47 at date of trial — Injury to back involving disc prolapse rendering the pursuer unfit for his pre-accident employment as a storeman and fit only for work not involving heavy lifting — Evidence that the pursuer would have been entitled to work in his pre-accident job until he was 60; that prior to his accident he had had back trouble; that since being retired compulsorily on health grounds the pursuer had attempted to obtain employment, but without success; and that it was reasonable, however, to anticipate that the pursuer would obtain employment in future of some kind, but no evidence as to the earnings which the pursuer might obtain if he were to find employment **— Loss of earnings to date of trial** agreed as to amount and damages *awarded* accordingly — Damages of £59,000 *awarded* for **loss of future earnings** on the basis, rounded down, of a multiplicand of £17,102, representing what the pursuer would have been earning as at the date of trial but for his accident, and a multiplier of three and a half, having regard to the pursuer's age and future prospects, from which it was reasonable to infer, on a broad view of the matter, that any future employment would be unlikely to bring in much more than half what the pursuer was earning in his pre-accident employment.

(241) **Binnie v. Kwik-Fit (GB) Ltd,** 1994 S.L.T. 742 (Lord Morton of Shuna)

Pursuer aged 43 at date of trial — Injury to knee resulting in continuing disability and rendering the pursuer unfit for his pre-accident work as a self-employed joiner — Evidence that there was a recession in the building trade; that the pursuer had now been assessed as fit for work avoiding walking on rough surfaces, climbing ladders or kneeling and fit only for work with restricted lifting; that any such work would involve some form of retraining but no evidence as to the type of work for which the pursuer might be suitably retrained which would probably require to be sedentary work; and that a further attempt should be made to improve the function of the knee before any retraining was considered — Evidence that the pursuer's cousins had provided services to him in the form of gardening during the summer months for one hour a week and driving the pursuer to and from hospital for several months, respectively, and that the pursuer had had his house completely redecorated outside and inside, a job he was no longer able to do himself — **Loss of earnings to date of trial** calculated on the basis of a discount of just under a third to take account of the recession in the building trade and damages *awarded* accordingly — Damages of £42,000 *awarded* for **loss of future earnings** on the basis of a multiplicand of £7,000, representing the pursuer's net earnings at the time of the accident, and a multiplier of six, having regard to the probability that the pursuer would obtain some form of work after retraining and after he had investigated the possibility of further medical treatment — Damages of £400 for **necessary services** rendered by the pursuer's cousins and £3,000 for **decoration costs**, both past and future *awarded.*

(242) **Armstrong v. Grampian Health Board,** 1994 S.L.T. 380 (Lord Cullen)

Pursuer aged c.50 at date of trial — Injury to leg and ankle resulting in continuing disability — Evidence that the pursuer's wife had cared for him during his recovery, doing all the housekeeping, helping him move around the house and changing his dressing, doing the decorating and the major parts of the gardening for him and that the pursuer had been unable to take any part in looking after the house or carrying out shopping — Damages of £250 *assessed* for **necessary services** and the pursuer's **inability to render personal services**.

(243) **Anderson v. Gerrard,** 1994 S.L.T. 1326 (Lord Cameron of Lochbroom)

Pursuer aged c.46 at date of trial — Injuries to shoulder and knee rendering the pursuer unfit for his pre-accident employment as a police motorcyclist — Evidence that but for the accident the pursuer would have been able to continue in employment as a police officer until the age of 55 at which time he would have retired; that he would have had the prospect of regular increments to his salary; that he would have had deductions for superannuation; that he had now commenced in business as a self-employed traffic consultant; that he considered that his business prospects might well improve in future; and that he was now pursuing an occupation to which his talents were well fitted and so far as possible represented the kind of work which he would have wanted to undertake in any event — **Loss of earnings to date of trial** agreed and damages *awarded* accordingly — Damages of £52,500 *awarded* for **loss of future earnings** on the basis of a multiplicand of £15,000, representing the differential, rounded up, between a net salary as a police officer less deductions for superannuation (£19,754–£2,614=£17,140) and the pursuer's projected earnings (£2,500), and a multiplier of three and a half, to take account upon a broad view of the various imponderables such as (i) the prospect that the pursuer's continuing loss would not be as great as he was suggesting; and (ii) the prospect that if he had remained in employment as a traffic police officer he would have had the security of settled employment and the prospect of regular increments to his salary.

(244) **Williamson v. GB Papers plc,** 1994 S.L.T. 173 (Lord Cullen)
Pursuer aged c.56 at date of trial — Injury to ankle, neck and shoulder resulting in disability arising from previously asymptomatic arthritic changes — Evidence that the pursuer's husband and son had rendered services to her since the accident in dealing with activities such as washing, ironing and shopping — Damages of £400 for **necessary services to date of trial** and £100 for **future necessary services** *awarded.*

(245) **Sommerville v. Lothian Health Board,** 1994 S.L.T. 1207 (Lord Cullen)
Pursuer aged 38 at date of trial — Injury to back rendering the pursuer unfit for her pre-accident employment as a nursing auxiliary — Evidence that the pursuer had obtained part time work in a local authority crèche and was now fit for moderately heavy work, experiencing a substantial remission in the pain which she had from time to time, but no evidence as to her future earning capacity nor as to the time which was likely to elapse before she was able to achieve the most that she could **— Loss of earnings to date of trial** agreed and damages *assessed* accordingly — Damages of £10,000 for **loss of future earnings** *assessed* on a lump sum basis (in respect that her present earnings could not be taken as an accurate representation of the level of earnings which she was likely to be able to receive), no account being taken of any prospective loss of earnings as a nurse as too speculative a matter to be reflected in any assessment.

(246) **Penman v. RGC plc,** 1994 S.L.T. 805 (Lord Morton of Shuna)
Pursuer aged 50 at date of trial — Injury to neck aggravating previously asymptomatic degenerative changes and post-traumatic stress disorder rendering the pursuer permanently unfit for employment — Evidence that subject to the normal exigencies of life and to the risk of deterioration in the degenerative changes in his neck the pursuer would have been able to work as a steel erector until the age of 65 **— Loss of earnings to date of trial** calculated on the basis that the pursuer's earnings would have increased since the date of accident and damages *awarded* accordingly — Damages of £106,800 *awarded* for **loss of future earnings** on the basis of a multiplicand of £17,800, representing what the pursuer would have been earning as at the date of trial but for the accident, and a multiplier of six, having regard to the pursuer's age and taking all the factors into account, including the pre-existing degenerative changes in his neck.

(247) **Clark v. Scottish Power plc,** 1994 S.L.T. 924 (Lord Morton of Shuna)

Pursuer aged c.65 at date of trial — Injury involving psychiatric symptoms in an already very vulnerable personality and considerable distress — Evidence that the pursuer's daughter went to live with her after the injury, was still living with her as at the date of trial and was providing services to her; that the need for many of the daughter's services had no relation to the injury; but that the pursuer required the services of her daughter if for nothing else than the comfort of having somebody else living in the house with her; and that the pursuer unreasonably refused medical treatment and thereby substantially contributed to the continuation of the symptoms from which she suffered — Damages of £1,000 *awarded* for **necessary services to date of trial**, restricted to a period of about three years, such being the cut-off caused by the pursuer's refusal of medical treatment.

(248) **McVey v. Central Regional Council,** 1994 S.L.T. 190 (Temporary Judge R.G. McEwan Q.C.)

Pursuer aged c.38 at date of trial — Injury to foot resulting in continuing disability and rendering the pursuer unfit for work involving prolonged walking or standing — Evidence that the pursuer fit for sedentary work and had made two unsuccessful applications for work; and that he had a justifiably negative attitude to re-employment, having regard to his age and where he lived — Damages of £63,190 *awarded* for **loss of future earnings** on the basis of a multiplicand of £12,638 and a multiplier of five.

(249) **McKenzie v. Cape Building Products Ltd**, 1995 S.L.T 701 (Second Division; Lord Penrose)

Pursuer aged 52 at date of trial — Respiratory disease resulting in minor disability involving breathlessness on taking strenuous exercise — Evidence that the pursuer was also suffering from an unrelated asthmatic condition which contributed equally to his breathlessness; that the pursuer was not thereby disabled from working as a joiner; that a wide range of other factors, both medical and psychological, had contributed to the pursuer's inability to work for a long period of time, notwithstanding that the opportunity to work had presented itself; that his prospects of obtaining employment quite apart from his breathlessness could not have been good, it being at the present stage only, having in effect reformed his way of life, that the pursuer would in any event have become a candidate for work; and that, nevertheless, having altered his way of life, as a qualified joiner he would be able to earn at least the figure of £112.50 per week identified by the Council of Building Trades if he were to overcome his belief that he could not work — Evidence that the pursuer was unable to contribute to the ordinary routine tasks of maintenance of the household; that his contribution, however, had never been great; and that a stage was likely to come when the pursuer would require intensive care and it was possible that at some stage his wife might be faced with a choice between continuing to work at her employment and providing care for husband — **Loss of earnings to date of trial** *refused* on the basis that there was no reliable evidence that the pursuer had lost any wages which could be attributed to his breathlessness — Damages of £15,000 *awarded* for **loss of employability** and **future loss of wages** taken as a whole, reflecting the diminution of the pursuer's prospects of employment against a background in which other contributory factors, both medical and psychological, militated against his employability and his capacity to sustain employment in the future — Damages of £1,500 for **necessary services** and £1,500 for the pursuer's **inability to render personal services** *awarded.*

(250) **Stevenson v. Sweeney,** 1995 S.L.T. 29 (Lord Morton of Shuna)
Pursuer aged 19 at date of trial — Serious injury to spine resulting in permanent severe disablement including gross spasticity of his limbs — Evidence that during the period of about 14 months preceding the date of trial the pursuer's mother had been providing services in the form of care to the pursuer; that the present care was at the level of six hours per day; that a trained care assistant would require to spend a daily average of three and a quarter hours per day to fulfil the various tasks; that the care needed required the carer to be available to help when required; and that the appropriate rate of remuneration was £4 per hour, less deductions in respect of tax and national insurance — Evidence that the pursuer intended to remain at home under his mother's care until he was 25; that he intended to live independently of his parents thereafter; that the annual rate for a carer providing care at the current level, inclusive of four weeks' respite care, was £9,105, before deduction of tax; that the annual rate for the provision of gardening services, household decoration and such maintenance costs was £648; that the annual rate for a live-in carer with provision for relief at overtime weekend rates, respite care and for a nurse or equivalent to deal with bowel function three times a week was £22,766 — Evidence that after training the pursuer could obtain paid work, albeit that he lived in an area of high unemployment which would make his prospects of finding suitable work more difficult, but that only a very low proportion of those who had suffered spinal injuries did get any form of paid work and that these tended to be those who had already completed training before their injury — Remuneration for **necessary services to date of trial** agreed for the initial period and, for the 14 month period immediately preceding the date of trial, calculated on the basis that the case required the equivalent of one full

time job spread over 24 hours each day seven days a week, including the ability of the carer to be out of the house for periods in each day by arrangement, and damages *awarded* accordingly — Damages of £318,327 *awarded* for the **cost of future care** on the basis of a multiplier of 20, having regard to the pursuer's age only (there being no circumstances other than premature death that would diminish the quantity of care that the pursuer would require), the award comprising (i) the sum of £50,077 with respect to the initial period of five and a half years at an annual rate of £9,105, it not being appropriate to base future care assessment in this case on a net of tax basis; and (ii) the sum of £268,250 with respect to the remaining period of the 20 year multiplier at an annual rate of £18,500, inclusive of the sum of £648 for handyman costs, there being no warrant for inclusion of separate provision for bowel management or the provision of relief at overtime weekend rates — Damages of £122,010 *awarded* for **loss of future earnings** on the basis of a multiplicand of £8,715 and a multiplier of 14, having regard to the very slight chance of some future paid work.

(251) **Duffy v. Shaw,** 1995 S.L.T. 602 (Lord Johnston)

Pursuer aged 52 at date of trial — Injury to back resulting in permanent disability — Evidence that there was a real risk that the pursuer would not be able to work out his normal span until 65 — Evidence that the pursuer would incur costs in the future in respect of additional housekeeping and gardening and house maintenance; and that the pursuer's disability restricted his culinary ability which would increase his food costs if he had to buy convenience foods — Damages of £15,000 *awarded* for **loss of future earnings** on the basis that it was unreasonable to award a sum of less than one year's salary, rounded up — Damages of £17,200 *awarded* for **future costs** on the basis of a multiplicand of £1,720 and a multiplier of 10.

(252) **G's Curator Bonis v. Grampian Health Board,** 1995 S.L.T. 652 (Lord Johnston)

Ward aged 44 at date of trial — Catastrophic injury to brain resulting in irreversible and irreparable damage — Evidence that the pursuer's life expectancy was probably not affected; that she was likely to be institutionalised for the rest of her life; that the pursuer's husband and daughter had provided services to her during home visits for parts of weeks between certain dates prior to trial and also two holidays; that the husband had actually paid certain sums in respect of assistance which he required to obtain beyond what he and his daughter were providing to help with the care of the pursuer when she was at home; that the services that were provided were closer to nursing than home help but encompassed all the usual things that a person requires who is being looked after on the domestic front; and as to the rates which the services would have cost if hired — Evidence that the pursuer had a pre-existing depressive illness which would have continued to occur or manifest itself from time to time, probably more frequently as she got older, with the result that there would be times when she would have been disabled from fully acting as a wife and mother; that the pursuer was now unable to perform domestic duties such as home cleaning, cooking and laundry, as well as child care and the normal supply of emotional needs that a mother gives to children; that the average duration of the services was four hours per day to the date of trial and two hours per day for the future in view of the diminishing pressure on a parent, although not on a wife, as the years pass; and as to the rates for such services — Evidence that curatory costs would be 2.5% of the whole fund in the first year and 1.2% of that fund thereafter — Remuneration for **necessary services to date of trial** rendered by the pursuer's husband and daughter calculated on a lump sum basis, taking account of (i) what the award would be if specified rates, albeit on an average and broad axe basis, were set against the periods in question; and (ii) the figure actually paid by the pursuer's husband, and damages *awarded* accordingly — Loss of the pursuer's **personal services to date of trial** calculated on the basis of specified rates applied to a four hour day but discounted by 20% to take account of the pursuer's pre-existing depressive illness and damages *awarded* accordingly — Damages of £31,770 *awarded* for the pursuer's **future inability to render personal services**, made up of (i) the sum of £39,150, being the product of a multiplicand of £2,610 (representing an annual rate for such services on the basis of an hourly rate of £3.59 and a two hour day) and a multiplier of 15, having regard to the pursuer's age; less (ii) the sum of £7,380, being a 20% deduction in respect of the pursuer's pre-existing depressive illness — **Curatory costs** *awarded* on the basis of a multiplier of 15, the first year costs being 2.5% of the fund and the remaining 14 years' costs being 1.2% of the fund.

(253) **McMahon v. British Railways Board,** 1995 S.L.T 591 (Lord Cameron of Lochbroom)

Pursuer aged 55 at date of trial — Minor injury to back as well as post-traumatic stress disorder and depressive illness rendering the pursuer emotionally vulnerable and liable to suffer a major recurrence of symptomatology as a result of even a very minor negative life event — Evidence that the pursuer could have expected in normal circumstances to work on with his present employers until the age of 65; that while it was true to say that by reason of the privatisation of the railways there was no certainty that he would necessarily have remained in his employment until that age, nevertheless in the event that he were to be made redundant, possibly in one year's time, he would be likely to be placed on the labour market with a disability that he would not have had but for the accident; and that, furthermore, the pursuer's condition was such that if he were to be made redundant that disability could well be substantially exacerbated — Damages of £5,000 *awarded* for the pursuer's **disadvantage in the labour market,** having regard to the fact that the pursuer's redundancy could arise in a year's time and looking to the fact that the pursuer might otherwise have continued to work until he was 65.

(254) **Hunter v. Clyde Shaw plc,** 1995 S.L.T. 474 (Temporary Judge T.G.Coutts Q.C.)

Pursuer aged 48 at date of trial — Injury to both elbows resulting in continuing disability rendering the pursuer unfit for work — Evidence that the pursuer did not previously have either a particularly secure or a particularly unsettled form of employment; that he was made redundant after about six months of becoming unfit for work; that he had had two offers of alternative employment thereafter, for which he was not fit; that a full recovery was expected within five years of the date of trial; and that the pursuer was likely to be able to resume full employment within that period, albeit no evidence as to what level or when he would be able to resume some employment — Evidence that the pursuer's wife had attended to certain matters and required to do additional things such as gardening which she did not previously require to do while the pursuer's arms were in slings for a period; and that the pursuer had been unable to assist in caring for his mother-in-law or do things about the house or garden **— Loss of earnings to date of trial** calculated on the basis that the pursuer would have obtained alternative employment after his redundancy and damages *awarded* accordingly — Damages of £30,000 for **loss of future earnings**, having regard to the likelihood that the pursuer would be able to resume full employment within five years, *awarded*; the assessment being the equivalent of a three year multiplier applied to a multiplicand of £10,000, being the pursuer's likely earnings in alternative employment — Damages for **necessary services** *refused* — Damages of £1,000, inclusive of interest to date of trial, *awarded* for the pursuer's **inability to render personal services**.

(255) **Reid v. Edinburgh Acoustics Ltd,** 1995 S.L.T 659 (Lord MacLean)

Pursuer aged 65 at date of trial — Injuries to neck and shoulder exacerbating pre-existing degenerative changes in the cervical spine and rendering the pursuer unfit for her pre-accident employment as an area supervisor — Evidence that the degenerative changes were not dormant at the time of the pursuer's accident; that nevertheless she was scarcely ever out of work and her employment record was very good; that a minor incident in the course of ordinary life could have aggravated the degenerative changes; and that accordingly the pursuer might not have been able to work in any event for the whole of the five year period from the date of her accident until she was 65 — Evidence that the pursuer's husband had to do practically everything in the house for a substantial period after the accident; that he did not require to continue to do all such things; and that some of the pursuer's problems would probably have appeared in any event — **Loss of earnings to date of trial** calculated on the basis that the pursuer was entitled to wage loss for a period of three and a half years from the date of her accident, having regard to the normal vicissitudes of life and the condition from which she was already suffering, and damages *awarded* accordingly — Damages of £1,750 for (i) **necessary services to date of trial**; and (ii) the pursuer's **inability to render personal services to date of trial**; and £500 for (i) **future necessary services**; and (ii) the pursuer's **future inability to render personal services** *awarded*.

(256) **Cole v. Weir Pumps Ltd,** 1995 S.L.T. 12 (Lord Johnston)
Pursuer aged 48 at date of trial — Injury to arm causing brachial neuritis resulting in permanent disability — Evidence that the pursuer's relatives had rendered services to him immediately after his accident — Evidence that the pursuer would be restricted in what other work would be available to him, particularly with regard to driving; and that the pursuer's present employers were anxious to keep him despite the restriction on driving — Damages of £500 *awarded* for **necessary services** — Damages of £2,500 *awarded* for **devaluation in the labour market**.

(257) **Cavanagh v. BP Chemicals Ltd,** 1995 S.L.T. 1287 (Lord Clyde)
Pursuer aged c.53 at date of trial — Injuries to arm and leg resulting in continuing disabilities and rendering the pursuer unfit for employment — Evidence that the pursuer would have continued in his pre-accident work as a self-employed shuttering joiner until his late 50s or 60s; and that he would be unable to be looking for light work for about two years from the date of trial — Evidence that the pursuer's wife had to help him with such tasks as bathing and eating when he was severely disabled, arranging for his meals to be conveniently available for him with the telephone at hand while she was out at work; that more care was required for him during the four periods following on his operations; and that the pursuer's wife gave up certain overtime at her work in order to help him — **Loss of earnings to date of trial** calculated on the basis of the pursuer's pre-accident earnings and damages *awarded* accordingly — Damages of £42,500 *awarded* for **loss of future earnings** on the basis, rounded

down, of a multiplicand of £12,151, representing the pursuer's pre-accident earnings, and a multiplier of three and a half — Damages of £1,000 *awarded* for **necessary services**.

(258) **McCutcheon v. Lothian Regional Council,** 1995 S.L.T. 917 (Temporary Judge T.G.Coutts Q.C.)

Pursuer aged c.31 at date of trial — Injury to forearm resulting in continuing disability in dominant hand — Evidence that the pursuer was a janitor; and that he had permanent weakness in his dominant hand and was therefore less able to lift heavy weights, use the hand dextrously and climb ladders — Evidence that the pursuer's wife had performed some services for him since his accident — Damages of £500 *assessed* for **loss of earning capacity** — Damages of £500, inclusive of interest, *assessed* for **necessary services**.

(259) **Duffy v. Lanarkshire Health Board,** 1995 S.L.T. 1312 (Lord Cullen)

Pursuer aged 49 at date of trial — Injury to back resulting in symptoms of anxiety and depression rendering the pursuer unfit for her pre-accident employment as a nursing auxiliary — Evidence that the pursuer was a person who was predisposed to develop such symptoms; that it was likely that even if the pursuer had not sustained her accident, she would have been likely before the date of trial to develop symptoms of anxiety and depression, especially arising out of her concern for husband's state of health, and to have been disabled from work on that account — Evidence that the pursuer's relatives rendered services to the pursuer over a period of between two and four years for several hours per week; and as to certain hourly rates — **Loss of earnings to date of trial** calculated on the basis that the pursuer would have become disabled from working by then in any event, discounting the agreed figure for the whole period by one-third, and damages *assessed* accordingly — Damages for **loss of future earnings** would have been *refused* — Damages of £2,500 for **necessary services to date of trial** and £250 for the pursuer's **inability to render personal services to date of trial** *assessed*, a discount of one-third having been made in each instance.

(260) **Robertson's Curator Bonis v. Anderson,** 1996 S.C. 217 (Extra Division; Lord MacLean)

Ward aged 31 at date of trial — Serious head injury involving brain damage resulting in permanent deficits and rendering the pursuer unemployable — Evidence that the pursuer was a man of strong personality with initiative, ambition, energy and dedication; that prior to his accident he had had an unsettled work pattern; that he was not employed at the time of his accident but was instead closely involved in voluntary work in the community; that there was opportunity for him to undertake employment as an unqualified day care centre officer at an adult mental health training centre; that just prior to his accident he had made an initial inquiry of a college with a view to qualifying himself for paid employment; that he would probably not have been accepted by that college; that but for his accident he probably would have taken up the unqualifed employment at some point; and that the annual net earnings of an unqualified day care officer were about £6,500 at the time of the pursuer's accident and about £9,400 as at the date of trial seven and a half years later — **Loss of earnings to date of trial** calculated on a broad basis, which could be analysed broadly as two and a half years' loss of net earnings at the rate of £6,500 per annum with interest to the date of trial, and damages *awarded* accordingly — Damages of £80,000 *awarded* for **loss of future earnings**, which could be analysed as about nine years at the rate of £9,400 per annum.

(261) **Taggart v. Shell (UK) Ltd,** 1996 S.L.T. 795 (Lord MacLean)
Pursuer aged 46 at date of trial — Injury to foot resulting in substantial continuing disability — Evidence that the pursuer, a determined individual, was able meantime to work as an offshore operations technician earning about £31,000 net per annum; that the condition of his foot was likely to deteriorate over time; that it was inconceivable that he could continue to work offshore until retiral age of 60; that he was likely to continue in such work until his mid-50s, at most; and that thereafter he would obtain other, less remunerative, employment — Evidence that the pursuer would lose about £750 per annum in pension rights for each year of service lost before retiral age — Loss of earnings to date of trial agreed and damages awarded accordingly — Damages of £15,000 *awarded* for **loss of future earnings** on a lump sum basis, corresponding to a multiplicand of £10,000 as a reasonable estimate of the future salary differential, and a multiplier of one and a half — Damages of £1,100 *awarded* for **loss of pension rights**.

(262) **McKinnon v. British Telecommunications plc,** 1996 S.L.T 798 (Lord Rodger of Earlsferry)
Pursuer aged c.44 at date of trial — Injury to back either of transient effect or the cause of a subsequent prolapsed disc which rendered the pursuer permanently unfit for heavy manual work and fit only for light work which would allow him to stand up and sit down from time to time to ease the pain — Evidence that the pursuer had a vulnerable personality; that he now had no real prospect of obtaining employment in the future; that he had pre-existing degenerative changes in the spine which rendered the disc in question susceptible to prolapse; that

such prolapses could occur even with very slight traumata; and that there must therefore have been a risk that the pursuer would have suffered the same type of prolapsed disc even if the accident had not occurred — **Loss of earnings to date of trial** calculated, in the alternative, on the basis that the pursuer would have worked to date of trial and damages *assessed* accordingly — Damages of £50,000 *assessed* for **loss of future earnings** on the alternative basis, rounded up, of a multiplicand of £12,400 and a multiplier of four.

(263) **McGarrigle v. Babcock Energy Ltd,** 1996 S.L.T. 471 (Lord MacLean)

Pursuer aged 46 at date of trial — Serious crush injuries to pelvis and legs resulting in continuing disabilities rendering the pursuer unfit for work — Evidence that the pursuer was in employment at the time of his accident; that he had had a good work record; and that he might in the future become fit for and obtain some form of light work — Evidence that the pursuer's wife had attended to all his needs for six to seven weeks after the accident, giving up her work as a barmaid to do so; that she continued to look after him to some extent; that the pursuer had prior to his accident done all the repair and maintenance work, including the electrical work, in the family home; that he had also repaired the family car and had done the gardening; and that he was now unable to do any of these tasks **— Loss of earnings to date of trial** agreed and damages *awarded* accordingly — Damages of £93,750 *awarded* for **loss of future earnings** on the basis of a multiplicand of £12,500, representing what the pursuer would have been earning in his pre-accident employment as at the date of trial, and a multiplier of seven and a half, having regard to the possibility that the pursuer might be fit for and obtain some form of light work in the future — Damages of £500 for **necessary services** and £750 for the pursuer's **inability to render personal services** *awarded.*

(264) **Higgins v. Tayside Health Board,** 1996 S.L.T. 288 (Lord Weir)

Pursuer aged 49 at date of trial — Injury to back involving back strain rendering the pursuer unfit for her pre-accident employment as a nurse or for any other work of a strenuous physical character — Evidence that the pursuer was predisposed to back injury; that in all probability she would have suffered an equally disabling incident at some time in any event; and that she would have been able to work but for the accident for a period of about five years after that date before she would have encountered similar disabling symptoms — Evidence that the pursuer's husband had helped her with the shopping, with moving furniture and other lifting tasks after her accident — **Loss of earnings to date of trial** agreed as to amount and damages *awarded* accordingly — Damages of £9,675 *awarded* for **loss of future**

earnings on the basis of an annual figure of £6,450 multiplied by 18 months, being the unexpired portion of the period of five years from the date of the accident — Damages of £500 *awarded* for **necessary services**.

(265) **O'Connor v. Matthews,** 1996 S.L.T. 408 (Lord Marnoch)

Pursuer aged 19 at date of trial — Very severe brain injury resulting in marked physical and intellectual disabilities — Evidence that the pursuer resided with his parents; that he hoped and intended to obtain, in due course, independent accommodation in the form of a ground floor flat — Evidence that the pursuer required to incur additional private transport costs; that by virtue of being indoors to a greater extent than the ordinary citizen he would incur additional heating costs; that inevitable spillages and occasional incontinence would lead to slightly increased laundry costs; that the pursuer, by dragging his feet, might be harder than the average man on footwear; that the pursuer would incur additional costs at a weekly rate of £8.93 in respect of wear and tear; that he would incur costs in respect of D.I.Y.; that he would incur costs in respect of the purchase of a computer; and that he would require miscellaneous aids and appliances — Evidence that the pursuer had been looked after by his parents since his accident at an average of seven and a half hours a day over the whole period of six and a quarter years; that the pursuer would remain at home looked after by his parents over the next five years or so, by which time, hopefully, he would have completed his higher education and obtained whatever qualifications were within his reach; that for care provided for a period of four to six hours a day the annual rate charged by a charity was £10,505; that the pursuer would be capable of living an independent life, which it was in his best interests to do, from about the age of 25 years; and that for care provided for four hours per day and for home help provided for two hours per day the annual rate charged by the British Nursing Association was £13,100 — Evidence that the pursuer's father had been unemployed for a number of years; that there was a fair measure of unemployment in the pursuer's locality; that at the time of his accident the pursuer, then a schoolboy, had hopes of becoming a professional boxer, which failing a manual labourer; that prior to his accident the pursuer was something of a tearaway, but the character of perseverance illustrated by his response to his disabilities and his willingness to learn new tasks must always have been present and would have stood him in good stead in attempts to obtain and find and remain in employment; that since his accident the pursuer had succeeded in obtaining a number of Standard Grade passes and had recently commenced a National Certificate course in computer application at a local college; and that there was, however, no real prospect of the pursuer obtaining profitable employment in the future

— Damages for additional housing costs *refused* on the ground that (i) there was no evidence that a perfectly adequate council house could not be allocated to the pursuer; and (ii) the loss of earnings claim presupposed that, but for the accident, the pursuer would have been earning wages which, had they been earned, would have been subject to the same or similar costs — **Additional transport costs to date of trial** agreed; **additional heating, clothing and laundry costs to date of trial** calculated on a lump sum basis; **wear and tear costs to date of trial** calculated on the basis of a weekly figure; and **care costs to date of trial** calculated on the basis of the charity's care rate discounted for (i) the effects of taxation; (ii) the fact that the calculation proceeded on today's rates rather than on those from time to time prevailing since the time of the accident; and (iii) the fact that even without the accident the pursuer's parents would have been rendering some part of the same services to the pursuer as he grew up in the household; and damages *awarded* accordingly — Damages of £20,800 for **future additional transport costs**, on the basis of a multiplicand of £1,040 and a multiplier of 20; £4,000 for **future additional heating, clothing and laundry costs**, on a lump sum basis; £9,280 for **future wear and tear**, on the basis of a multiplicand of £464 and a multiplier of 20; £3,000 for **D.I.Y.**, on a lump sum basis; £3,000 for the agreed **cost of a computer**; and £1,000 for **other aids and appliances**, on a lump sum basis; *awarded* — Damages of £207,400 *awarded* for **future care costs**, comprising (i) the sum of £24,000 for future care over the next five years on the basis of a multiplicand of £6,000, representing the annual rate of £10,505, discounted for the same factors as pertained to care costs to date of trial and in respect that the assumed extent of care was on the high side, and a multiplier of four; and (ii) the sum of £183,400 for future care thereafter on the basis of a multiplicand of £13,100 and a multiplier of 14, having regard to the fact that the appropriate overall multiplier would be 20; that having already applied four years thereof in the assessment of immediate future care, the balance would be 16; but that that figure fell to be discounted for the fact that the balance of the overall multiplier was being applied to an increased annual sum which would not be incurred for at least a further five years — **Loss of earnings to date of trial** calculated on a lump sum basis and damages *awarded* accordingly — Damages of £116,808 *awarded* for **loss of future earnings** on the basis of a multiplicand of £9,734 and a multiplier of 12.

(266) **Tweedy v. Newboult,** 1996 S.L.T. 2 (Lord Abernethy)

Pursuers aged c.54 and c.48 at date of trial — Injuries to husband's hand, wrist and elbow and to wife's ankle — Evidence that at the time of the accident the pursuers had a business comprising a small village shop run by the husband and an adjoining café run by the wife; that

(271) **Docherty v. City of Glasgow District Council,** 1996 Rep. L.R. (Quantum) 5 (Lord Cameron of Lochbroom)

Pursuer aged 52 at date of trial — Injury to wrist rendering the pursuer unfit for his pre-accident employment as a plasterer — Evidence that the pursuer was medically retired from work about two years after his accident; that just prior thereto he had refused an offer of alternative employment as a security officer; that he had had no good reason to refuse the offer; and that he had not made any serious attempt to find employment or seek advice about doing so since his retirement — Evidence that the pursuer had been unable to render services, principally gardening, since his accident but no evidence as to the sums being paid to the third party carrying out the gardening in his place **— Loss of earnings to date of trial** calculated to the date of the pursuer's retirement on medical grounds and damages *awarded* accordingly — Damages for **loss of future earnings** *refused* — Damages of £400 *awarded* for the pursuer's **inability to render personal services**.

(272) **Fulton v. CPC (United Kingdom) Ltd,** 1996 Rep. L.R. (Quantum) 7 (Lord Osborne)

Pursuer aged 46 at date of trial — Injuries rendering the pursuer unfit for work other than sedentary employment — Evidence that the pursuer had been in steady employment all her adult life notwithstanding that she had borne six children; that had she not sustained her accident she would have been made redundant in any event about one year after the accident; that at that date she was in fact pregnant again; that she had no experience of sedentary work; and that since her accident she had lacked confidence **— Loss of earnings to date of trial** calculated on the basis that the pursuer would have found alternative employment several months after giving birth, with no discount in respect of her failure to obtain sedentary employment, and damages *assessed* accordingly — Damages of £12,000 *assessed* for **loss of future earnings** on a lump sum basis.

(273) **Kerr v. Newalls Insulation Co Ltd**, 1996 S.C.L.R. 1114; 1997 S.L.T. 723 (Lord Hamilton)

Pursuer aged 58 at date of trial — Respiratory disease involving asbestosis — Evidence that the pursuer had unrelated chest, leg and back pain; that the pursuer's wife had provided services to him in physical terms, assisting him when he took a bath, about once a week, or washed in his bedroom, disposing of urine evacuated by him in the bedroom, bringing food to him there, and on occasions assisting him when dressing or when negotiating the stair to the bathroom and lavatory, all such being largely but not wholly by reason of his asbestosis related disability; that she provided emotional support, especially when he became distressed at night; that she had difficulty discussing the pursuer's health and future with him and therefore the psychological support which she was able to provide him was limited but nonetheless important; that her presence in the household was necessary not only for her availability to deal with the pursuer's physical needs but also for his reassurance; and that the current hourly carer's fee rate, exclusive of agency commission, VAT and National Insurance contribution as published by the B.N.A., was £3.74 — Remuneration for **necessary services to date of trial** calculated on the basis of an estimate of the time devoted by the pursuer's wife to his asbestosis related needs (physical, emotional and monitoring) at about one and a half hours per day on average over a two and a quarter year period and damages *awarded* accordingly — Damages of £19,060 *awarded* for **future necessary services** on the basis, rounded up, of a multiplicand of £2,722.72, representing two hours per day at the rate of £3.74 per hour, and a multiplier of seven.

(274) **Paterson v. Kelvin Central Buses Ltd,** 1997 S.L.T. 685 (Lord Dawson)

Pursuer aged 35 at date of trial — Injury to neck resulting in permanent disability and rendering the pursuer unfit for his pre-accident employment as a taxi driver — Evidence that prior to his accident the pursuer had done little else but driving; that he would have continued in that occupation had it not been for the accident; and that he suffered from dyslexia which meant that he could not write **— Loss of earnings to date of trial** calculated on the basis that the pursuer was entitled to recover for the whole period since the date of his accident and damages *awarded* accordingly — Damages of £126,000 *awarded* for **loss of future earnings** on the basis of a multiplicand of £12,600, representing what the pursuer would have earned as a taxi driver as at the date of trial, and a multiplier of 10, having regard to the perhaps remote possibility of some form of work becoming available to the pursuer in the future.

(275) **Fraser v. Greater Glasgow Health Board**, 1997 S.L.T. 554 (Lord MacLean)

Pursuer aged c.43 at date of trial — Injury to back involving muscular strain resulting in minor residual disability — Evidence that the pursuer was no longer able to be involved in lifting and was thus restricted in the range of work she could undertake as a nursing auxiliary — Evidence that while the pursuer was off work after her accident the pursuer's daughter looked after her and did all the housework, including the messages; that after the pursuer went back to work her daughter still did most things in the house, whereas before the accident they had shared the housework, and carried the messages;

services rendered by the pursuer's sister-in-law; £1,000 for **necessary services** rendered by the pursuer's mother-in-law; and £500 for **necessary services** rendered by the pursuer's husband *awarded*.

(279) **Low v. Ralston**, 1997 S.L.T. 626 (Lord Osborne)

Pursuer aged 41 at date of trial — Injury to neck and spine resulting in permanent disability — Evidence that the pursuer lived with her husband and two children; that she had been and remained incapacitated for the performance of ordinary housework, which was instead done by her husband and her mother, now 80 years old; that they had between them rendered such assistance for about two hours per day seven days per week; that the equivalent home help rate was £3.50 per hour net of any income tax or national insurance which might be payable; and that the pursuer had expended the sum of £250 for decoration work in the house which but for her accident she would have done herself and would require to make such payments in the future — **Remuneration for necessary services to date of trial** and damages for the pursuer's **inability to render personal services to date of trial** calculated on the basis of 14 hours per week at the net home help rate for the whole period from the date of the accident, allocated between the two claims on the basis (derived from the number of persons in the household) of one-quarter being in respect of necessary services rendered to the pursuer and three-quarters being in respect of her inability to render personal services, and damages *awarded* accordingly — Damages of £17,472, comprising the sum of £4,368 for **future necessary services** and the sum of £13,104 for the pursuer's **future inability to render personal services**, *awarded* on the basis of a multiplicand of £1,456, representing the annual value of the services at the rate of £3.50 per hour for eight hours per week (leaving the pursuer's mother out of consideration by reason of her age and taking into account the fact that the pursuer's children would assist more as they grew older), and a multiplier of 12, having regard to the pursuer's age, the relatively stable nature of her condition and the fact that medical evidence suggested that improvement was now unlikely, together with the sum of £750 for the pursuer's **past and future inability to render personal services** in respect of decoration.

(280) **Kennedy v. Lees of Scotland Ltd**, 1997 S.L.T. 510 (Lord Gill)

Pursuer aged c.43 at date of trial — Injury to wrist resulting in continuing disability and rendering her unfit for her pre-accident employment as a production line worker — Evidence that the pursuer was now unfit for most of the jobs that would be available to her; that she had been advised to have an operation for fusion of the bones in her wrist; that with waiting time and recovery time it would be about 18 months from the date of trial, at the earliest, before she was fit to look for work; that when women in the pursuer's age group in her locality became unemployed, there was a significant chance that they would remain so in the long term; and that the pursuer's disability and her lack of specialist skill or experience would inhibit her prospects — Evidence that for about six weeks, while her arm was in plaster, the pursuer had had to rely on her husband, daughter and sister for day to day help in dressing and bathing; that it was reasonable to allow 24 hours weekly for all services during that period; that since her plaster was removed, the pursuer's family had assisted her in numerous household tasks and her sister still helped her from day to day, shopping with her, doing some housework and cleaning her windows and would continue to do so until after the pursuer had recovered from her operation; that for this period the need was 10 hours weekly overall; and that the B.N.A. hourly rate for home help services rendered by unqualified persons was £4 — Loss of earnings to date of trial agreed as to amount and damages awarded accordingly — Damages of £9,000, based on a net annual figure representing the current rate of wage loss, for **loss of future earnings** for the period of 18 months from the date of trial, and £8,500, representing net wages at the current rate of wage loss for a period of between one and two years, for **loss of employability** *awarded* — Damages of £1,829 for **necessary services** and £3,658 for the pursuer's **inability to render personal services** *awarded,* the combined sums comprising (i) the sum of £288 for the initial period, applying the rate of £2 per hour to a period of 24 hours per week for six weeks; and (ii) the sum of £5,200 for the period thereafter, ending with the pursuer's recovery from her operation, applying the rate of £2 per hour to a period of 10 hours per week for five years.

(281) **Fallan v. Lanarkshire Health Board,** 1997 S.L.T. 902 (Lord Abernethy)

Pursuer aged 44 at date of trial — Injury to back resulting in permanent disability and rendering the pursuer unfit for her pre-accident employment as a laundry worker — Evidence that the pursuer's symptoms were at least to some degree not now due to the accident but to degenerative changes in the spine; that the pursuer was now fit only for light work; and that the likelihood of the pursuer getting light work in her locality was slim **— Loss of earnings to date of trial** agreed and damages *awarded* accordingly — Damages of £51,300 *awarded* for **loss of future earnings** on the basis of a multiplicand of £5,700 and a multiplier of nine.

(282) **McCarvel v. Strathclyde Fire Board,** 1997 S.L.T. 1015 (Lord Macfadyen)

Pursuer aged 44 at date of trial — Injury to back precipitating symptoms in an abnormal and vulnerable, but hitherto trouble free, back — Evidence that the pursuer would have become disabled by reason of the emergence of symptoms, irrespective of the accident by the date of trial — Evidence that the pursuer's sister had provided services to him for about two hours a day for five months after the accident; and that the appropriate rate of remuneration was £4 per hour — **Loss of earnings to date of trial** calculated to the date of trial and damages *awarded* accordingly — Damages for **loss of future earnings** *refused* — Damages of £1,200 *awarded* for **necessary services**.

(283) **Swan v. Hope-Dunbar,** 1997 S.L.T. 760 (Lord Dawson)

Pursuer aged c.43 at date of trial — Multiple injuries resulting in continuing disability and rendering the pursuer unfit for his pre-accident employment as a part time fireman and restricting his capacity to work as a self-employed monumental sculptor — Evidence that the pursuer would have continued in the fire service, if able, until compulsory retirement at the age of 55 **— Loss of earnings and loss of profits to date of trial** calculated and damages *awarded* accordingly — Damages of £27,750 for **loss of future earnings**, on the basis of a multiplicand of £2,775 and a multiplier of 10, and £60,630 for **loss of future profits**, on the basis of a multiplicand of £4,042 and a multiplier of 15, *awarded.*

(284) **Lamont v. Cameron's Executrix,** 1997 S.L.T. 1147 (Lord Rodger of Earlsferry)

Pursuer aged 29 at date of trial — Severe injuries to face and leg resulting in continuing disability — Evidence that the pursuer was a veterinary surgeon in practice; that at the time of her accident she had been about to take up a new full time appointment; that the remuneration would have included free car and accommodation; that the job offer had been withdrawn as a result of her accident; that she had instead been off work for a period through her injuries and had thereafter worked only part time as a locum, having a baby in the meantime; that but for the accident she would have continued to work after a period of a few months off; and that, apart from a continuing reluctance to drive, the effects of the accident would be exhausted by about a year after the accident **— Loss of earnings to date of trial** calculated and damages *awarded* accordingly — Damages of £9,400, comprising (i) the sum of £2,500 for the loss of salary; (ii) the sum of £3,300 for the loss of the car; and (iii) the sum of £3,600 for the loss of the accommodation, *awarded* for **loss of future earnings** for the period until the expiry of one year from the date of trial — Damages of £5,000 *awarded* for **damage to the pursuer's earning capacity**, having regard to (i) the fact that the progress of her career had been affected and she had not gained the experience and seniority in her profession which she could have expected if the accident had not happened; and (ii) the fact that her difficulties in driving might restrict the kinds of jobs for which she could apply.

(285) **Taylor v. Marshalls Food Group,** 1997 S.C.L.R. 815 (Lord Macfadyen)

Pursuer aged 52 at date of trial — Injury to back precipitating symptoms in a degenerative but symptom-free spine and rendering the pursuer unfit for his pre-accident employment and fit only for light work — Evidence that the pursuer was now fit for light work; that he had not attempted to find such work; that the pursuer's prospects of obtaining suitable employment were very poor; and that, but for the accident, the pursuer would have been likely to have continued to be fit for his former work for up to eight years before being reduced, by emerging symptoms attributable to the degenerative condition, to the degree of disability which he now had — Evidence that the pursuer's son had rendered services to him in connection with (i) a caravan holiday; (ii) the maintenance of his car; and (iii) gardening; and that the accident had prevented the pursuer from doing much that he had previously done about the house to assist his wife because of her disability — **Loss of earnings to date of trial** agreed as to amount and damages *awarded*, in full, accordingly — Damages of £18,200 *awarded* for **loss of future earnings** on the basis of a multiplicand of £7,280 and a multiplier of two and a half, having regard to (i) the prospect that, without his accident, the pursuer's working capacity would have been affected in due course by the emergence of symptoms of the degenerative condition of his back; and (ii) the prospect that the pursuer might obtain light work in the future — Damages of £750 for **necessary services to date of trial** and £500 for **future necessary services** *awarded* — Damages of £2,000 for the pursuer's **inability to render personal services to date of trial** and £2,000 for the pursuer's **future inability to render personal services** *awarded*.

(286) **Stirling v. Norwest Holst Ltd**, 1997 S.C.L.R. 1196 (Lord Eassie)

Pursuer aged 39 at date of trial — Crush injury to ankle and foot resulting in continuing disability and rendering the pursuer unfit for his pre-accident employment as a labourer in the construction industry — Evidence that the pursuer would have been made redundant from his pre-accident employment about three years after the accident in any event; that he would have found further employment as a labourer in the construction industry with relative ease on his being made redundant; that he was now fit for sedentary or semi-sedentary employment only, which was likely to be less well paid than his pre-accident work; that he had not sought employment since his accident; that he had been receiving a succession of medical treatments; that he was certified by his doctor as 65% disabled; and that he had never been advised that he was fit for work or that it was time to seek such employment — Evidence that the pursuer's partner had provided him with services following his accident, visiting him in hospital frequently and after his return home assisting him with his toilet, bathing and cleaning him, dressing him and fetching and carrying meals and other things, all of which went beyond the normal activities which one would expect her to perform as a housewife had the pursuer not been injured; that as the pursuer's condition improved, the need for him to receive such services diminished accordingly; and that as at the date of trial the principal relevant services being provided by the pursuer's partner were assistance with bathing and negotiating the stairs — Evidence that the pursuer was no longer able to render services in respect of window cleaning, gardening, home decoration and general household repairs; and that he was no longer able to take his son to the swimming pool or play football with him — Evidence that the pursuer required to install a shower cabinet to enable him to bathe independently; that his condition was likely to worsen and the stage might soon be reached where the installation of a stair lift was reasonably necessary, which would make him independent of any assistance from his partner; and that he would incur a small amount of additional travel costs by reason of his injuries — **Loss of earnings to date of trial** calculated for the whole period to the date of trial and damages *awarded* accordingly — Damages of £105,000 *awarded* for **loss of future earnings** on the basis of a multiplicand of £15,000 and a multiplier of seven — Damages of £5,675 for **necessary services to date of trial** on a lump sum basis, it not being appropriate in this case, where the service provider was living in household with the injured person, to proceed on the basis of so many hours per week and apply the hourly rate for home helps; and £7,500 for **future necessary services** on a lump sum basis, having regard to (i) the award in respect of equipment, which would reduce the pursuer's dependence upon the services provided by his partner; and (ii) the prospect that there might, in other respects, be an increase in the help which the pursuer required, *awarded* — Damages of £3,200 for the pursuer's **inability to render personal services to date of trial** on the basis of valuing the services, including ordinary domestic or household services, and his services to his son, at £800 per annum for the four year period to date of trial; and £8,000 for the pursuer's **future inability to render personal services**, bearing in mind that the pursuer's son as he grows older might irrespective of the occurrence of the accident reasonably be expected to take over a substantial proportion of the services, *awarded* — Damages of £8,800 for the estimated **cost of installing the shower and the stair lift** and £750 for **future additional travel costs**, on a lump sum basis, *awarded*.

(287) **Mitchell v. Inverclyde District Council**, 1997 Rep. L.R. (Quantum) 29 (Lord Cameron of Lochbroom)

Pursuer aged 46 at date of trial — Injury to shoulder resulting in continuing disability and rendering the pursuer unfit for his pre-accident employment as a gardener — Evidence that prior to his accident the pursuer had had in mind to retire when he reached the age of about 57; that since his retirement on medical grounds he had not attempted to look for light work; but that any work of the kind which he was fit to do was unlikely to have been available to him since he retired — Evidence that the maximum pension loss suffered by the pursuer on the assumption that he would have retired at 60 was £12,000 — Evidence that since his accident the pursuer required assistance in the toilet, getting out of bed and dressing himself, washing his hair, cutting up food and moving furniture, the amount of help varying from time to time — Evidence that the pursuer was now wholly unable to do a lot of the painting and decorating and other household repair and improvement work that he had done in the past as well as gardening; that the pursuer's house had two sitting rooms and two bedrooms; and that the pursuer's wife had expended between £100 and £150 on decorating one room within the house in the past five years and £1,000 on the installation of a new kitchen **— Loss of earnings to date of trial** calculated for the whole period and damages *awarded* accordingly — Damages of £53,000 *awarded* for **loss of future earnings** on the basis, rounded down, of a multiplicand of £8,890 and a multiplier of six, having regard to (i) the likelihood that the pursuer would have retired before he reached the age of 60; (ii) the prospect that other reasons such as ill health or the like might have emerged which would have led to his stopping work before that age; and (iii) the fact that the evidence did not provide much by way of optimism for future employment — Damages of £8,000 *awarded* for **loss of pension**, taking into account that the more likely age on which the pursuer would have sought retirement was at the age of 57 and that other exigencies of life might have forced an earlier retirement — Damages of £1,750 for **necessary services to date of trial**, taking a broad view, and £7,000 for **future necessary services** *awarded* — Damages of £750 for the pursuer's **inability to render personal services to date of trial** and £3,000 for the pursuer's **future inability to render personal services** *awarded*.

(288) **Duffy v. Mairs**, 1997 S.C.L.R. 590; 1998 S.L.T. 433 (Lord Hamilton)

Pursuer aged 20 at date of trial — Disease arising from negligent failure in diagnosis when the pursuer was 15 years old rendering the pursuer unfit for some forms of employment, such as those involving significant manual lifting — Evidence that the pursuer had had in mind leaving school at the age of 17 and obtaining employment in the construction trade; that extremely tentative arrangements had been made in that regard for him to work at a firm at which his brother and sister's boyfriend were employed; that had he obtained employment in that trade he might initially have worked in a training scheme with restricted remuneration and might also have been subject to periods of unemployment; and as to what might have been earned by a person in the construction trade and what range of earnings the pursuer might now and in the future be able to command **— Loss of earnings to date of trial** calculated on the basis of what might have been earned by a person in the construction trade, discounted for initially restricted remuneration and periods of unemployment, and damages *awarded* accordingly — Damages of £22,500 *awarded* for **loss of future earnings** on the basis of a multiplicand of £1,500, representing the annual prospective loss of earnings, and a multiplier of 15.

(289) **Whyte v. Nestle (U.K.) Ltd**, 1997 S.C.L.R. 598 (Temporary Judge J.F.Wheatley Q.C.)

Pursuer a lorry driver — Minor physical injury causing post-traumatic stress disorder resulting in continuing disability — Evidence that the pursuer would recover in about three years after the date of trial; that his pre-accident employment would be available to him at that time; that he would in any event be able to find other employment then if necessary — Evidence that the pursuer's wife required to apply a lotion to the site of the injury on a daily basis and also required to drive him about — Evidence that the pursuer could no longer grow vegetables or raise tomatoes in his greenhouse, decorate or work in the home or get in the coal; and that such took no more than three hours of work each week **— Loss of earnings to date of trial** agreed and damages *awarded* accordingly — Damages of £23,502 *awarded* for **loss of future earnings** on the basis of a multiplicand of £7,834 and a multiplier of three — Damages of £650 *awarded* for **necessary services** — Damages of £514.80 *awarded* for the pursuer's **inability to render personal services to date of trial** on the basis of three hours per week at the rate of £3.30 over three years — Damages of £514.80 *awarded* for the pursuer's **future inability to render personal services** on the basis of a multiplicand of £171.60, representing three hours per week at the rate of £3.30, and a multiplier of three.

(290) **Morley v. Campbell,** 1998 S.L.T. 325 (Temporary Judge T.G.Coutts Q.C.)

Pursuer aged 21 at date of trial — Severe burning injuries resulting in permanent psychological difficulty inhibiting the pursuer in obtaining employment — Evidence that at the time of the accident the pursuer, who was then 14 years old, wanted to be a motor mechanic;

that but for his accident he would have promptly qualified as such; that he would have earned about £300 per week gross in that capacity; that as a result of his injuries the puruser was wholly incapable of any work or even able to proceed to any qualifications for 12 to 18 months; that he had not by the date of trial obtained any employment or even qualified for skilled or semi-skilled work; that he could in fact obtain qualifications and employment; but that he had been held back by the somewhat negative attitude of his parents — Damages of £45,000, comprising (i) the sum of £40,000 for **loss of earnings**, representing four years out of his full earnings as a motor mechanic; and (ii) the sum of £5,000 for **loss of earning capacity** *assessed.*

(291) **Donaldson v. Lothian Health Board,** 1998 S.L.T. 416 (Lord Abernethy)

Pursuer aged c.51 at date of trial — Injuries to arms rendering the pursuer unfit for her pre-accident employment as a laundry assistant — Evidence that the pursuer had obtained alternative employment which was due to come to an end about six months after the date of trial — Evidence that in the initial period of weeks following her accident the pursuer could do very little for herself; that her partner and sister had assisted her in this period with such matters as toilet and feeding; and that thereafter she had required help with shopping and other tasks such as hanging out washing, cleaning windows and hanging curtains and continued to receive such help from her partner **— Loss of earnings to date of trial** agreed and damages *assessed* accordingly — Damages of £3,000 *assessed* for **disadvantage on the labour market** — Damages of £1,300 for **necessary services to date of trial** and £1,000 for **future necessary services** *assessed.*

B. DEATH CASES

(1) **O'Donnell v. D. & R. Ferrying Co. Ltd,** 1966 S.L.T. (Notes) 71 (Lord Hunter)

Deceased aged 37 at date of death, survived by widow aged 33 and nine children aged 12, 11, nine, seven, six, five, four, two and one years — Evidence that the deceased earned a wage ranging from about £17 to £22 per week, out of which he handed about £15 or £16 a week to his wife; that he had enjoyed good health; and that it was probable that he would have spent many more years in employment earning a fairly high wage — Damages for **loss of support**, calculated approximately from £15 per week over a period of 10 years, *awarded* in the total sum of £7,750, comprising: (i) £3,000 for the widow; (ii) £350 for the eldest child; (iii) £400 for the second child; (iv) £450 for the third child; (v) £500 for the fourth child; (vi) £500 for the fifth child; (vii) £550 for the sixth child; (viii) £600 for the seventh child; (ix) £650 for the eighth child; and (x) £750 for the youngest child.

(2) **McNeil v. National Coal Board,** 1966 S.L.T. (Notes) 4 (Lord Guthrie)

Deceased aged 49 at date of death, survived by widow aged 43 and daughter aged 12 — Evidence that the deceased's net weekly wage averaged £16 15s 2d; that his wife had had about £14 10s weekly available for household expenses and the support of the family of three; that of that sum £3 could be attributed to the support of the child and £5 15s to the support of each of the deceased and the widow; that the weekly wage rate for workers in the deceased's grade had increased by approximately £2 in the period between the date of death and the date of trial; that the deceased had had prospects of promotion; and that just prior to the date of trial the daughter had left school and was in employment — Damages for **loss of support** *awarded* as follows: (i) £3,000 for the widow, being £300 per annum for 10 years; and (ii) £400 for the daughter in respect of the period between her father's death and the time when she commenced work on her own account.

(3) **Webster v. Simpson's Motors,** 1967 S.L.T. (Notes) 36 (Lord Robertson)

Deceased aged 46 at date of death, survived by widow aged 44 and three children aged 15, 14 and four — Evidence that the deceased was managing owner and skipper of a trawler; that he had an average net annual income of £1,750; that the earnings of comparable fishing skippers rose considerably over the years subsequent to the deceased's death and were still on a rising trend; and that on the basis of records from a large number of vessels and skippers comparable with the deceased's trawler, the deceased's net earnings for each year to date of trial could have been £2,249, £2,223 and £2,845, respectively — Damages for **loss of support**, calculated on the basis of a multiplier of 10 (having regard to various factors such as the age and health of the parties and the type of the deceased's employment), divided into (a) a period of three years from the date of death until the date of trial; and (b) the period of seven years thereafter, and an annual figure for loss of support of £1,850 (after deducting the sum of £500, as an arbitrary figure representing the deceased's own support, from the sum of £2,350, as an inexact but fair annual net earnings figure on the evidence) *awarded* in the total sum of £18,500, comprising (i) £6,100 for the initial period; and (ii) £12,400 for the second period, and *allocated* in the proportions: (1) to the widow, £14,250; (2) to the eldest child, £750; (3) to the second child (who left school earlier), £500; and (4) to the youngest child, £3,000.

(4) **McCusker v. Davidson and Pickering Limited,** 1968 S.L.T. (Notes) 41 (Lord Kissen)

Deceased aged 37 at date of death, survived by widow aged 31 and two children aged 10 and two years — Evidence that the deceased's earnings for the year prior to his death were £893 out of which the sum of £800 was available for the support of the family; and that £175 from that sum was applied in respect of food for the deceased, when he was at home, for his clothes and for holidays — Damages for **loss of support**, calculated on the basis of an annual sum of £625 and a multiplier of 10, *awarded* in the total sum of £6,250, comprising (i) £4,250 for the widow; (ii) £1,300 for the elder child; and (iii) £700 for the younger child.

(5) **Rae v. Stewart,** 1968 S.L.T. (Notes) 62 (Lord Stott)

Deceased aged 38 at date of death, survived by widow and two children — Evidence that the deceased was earning a net weekly wage of £13, all but 10s of which he handed over to his wife for household expenses, and also did odd jobs in his spare time; and that there was more than a possibility of the widow's remarriage — Damages for **loss of support** *awarded* as follows: (i) £1,250 for the widow; (ii) £900 for the elder child; and (iii) £1,200 for the younger child.

(6) **Gray v. Allied Ironfounders Limited,** 1969 S.L.T. (Notes) 95 (Lord Johnston)

Deceased aged 36 at date of death, survived by widow aged c.35 and two children aged c.13 and c.11 — Evidence that the deceased's wages for the year prior to his death were £1,000 of which he gave between £750 and £800 to his wife for family maintenance; that his health was good; that his prospects of employment were excellent; that about two years after the date of trial, if he had lived, the deceased would have been promoted supervisor at a salary of about £1,400; that he would then have given between £1,100 and £1,150 to his wife; and that after the death of the deceased the widow went out to work for a period — Damages for **loss of support**, calculated on the basis of an overall multiplier of 10 divided into (a) two and a half years at £700 a year; and (b) seven and a half years at £1,050 a year, *awarded* in the total sum of £9,625, comprising (i) £7,125 for the widow; (ii) £1,250 for the elder child; and (iii) £1,250 for the younger child

(7) **Henderson v. South Wales Switchgear Limited,** 1969 S.L.T. (Notes) 52 (Lord Fraser)

Deceased survived by a widow and two children — Evidence that the deceased's average net weekly earnings were about £16 per week; that about £6 per week was required for his support and pocket money; that the net loss to the family was about £10 per week or £500 per annum; that the loss could be apportioned as to £6 per week or £300 per annum to the widow and £2 per week or £100 per annum to each of the children — Damages for **loss of support** *awarded* as follows: (i) £3,000 for the widow on the basis of an estimated annual loss of £300 and a multiplier of 10; (ii) £900 for the elder child on the basis of an estimated annual loss of £100 and a multiplier of nine; and (iii) £1,000 for the younger child on the basis of an estimated annual loss of £100 and a multiplier of 10.

(8) **O'Connor v. Holst and Company Limited,** 1969 S.L.T. (Notes) 66 (Lord Robertson)

Deceased survived by widow aged 23, two children aged three and one and a third, posthumous child — Evidence that the deceased's annual net earnings were £1,430 from which an amount for his own support fell to be deducted; and that the pursuer was likely to remarry — Damages for **loss of support**, calculated on the basis of a multiplicand of £1,100 (annual net earnings of £1,430 less £330 per annum for the deceased's own support) and a multiplier of eight, *awarded* in the total sum of £8,800, comprising (i) £4,400 for the widow; (ii) £1,200 for the eldest child; (iii) £1,400 for the second child; and (iv) £1,800 for the youngest child.

(9) **Cowan v. Grieg,** 1969 S.L.T. (Notes) 34 (Lord Johnston)

Deceased aged 21 at date of death, survived by widow and baby — Evidence that the widow remarried about three and a half years after the death of the deceased; and that the child was being supported by the second husband **— Loss of support** calculated for the period between death and remarriage in the sum of £1,500 and damages *awarded* accordingly — Damages for **loss of support** *awarded* for the child in the sum of £250, having regard to the possibility that, although the probability was that the child would be supported by his stepfather in the future, circumstances might change and the child might require the support which he would otherwise have had from the deceased.

(10) **Curran v. Scottish Gas Board,** 1970 S.L.T. (Notes) 33 (Lord Johnston)

Deceased aged 55 at date of death, survived by widow and eight children — Evidence that the deceased suffering from a heart condition; that it was unlikely that he would have been able to continue in remunerative employment for more than five years after the date of his death; that his weekly wage was £17 11s 6d net; that he gave the whole of his wages to his wife and received back about £2 for pocket money and bus fares; that about £3 a week was required for his keep and about £12 a week (about £3,000 over a five year period) was available for the maintenance of the other members of the household; that the widow was and continued to be employed as a teacher, contributing her salary to the maintenance of her household; and that the eldest two children were independent, the next four partially dependent and the youngest two wholly dependent and would continue to be so for some years — Damages for **loss of support** *awarded* in the total sum of £3,000, comprising (i) £1,500 for the widow; (ii) £100 for the third child; (iii) £100 for the fourth child; (iv) £200 for the fifth child; (v) £200 for the sixth child; (vi) £300 for the seventh child; and (vii) £600 for the eighth child.

(11) **Gillan v. McGawn's Motors Limited,** 1970 S.L.T. 250 (Lord Robertson)

Deceased aged 32 at date of death, survived by widow aged 31 and children aged six and four — Evidence that the deceased was a young farmer of exceptional ability, industry and promise; that he had a very high reputation as a farmer and as a judge of livestock; that he surpassed his neighbours in farming efficiency; that he had already built up a prosperous business by his own efforts, aided by his wife; that they had, however, lived simply and had put back into the business of the farm a substantial amount of the profits, the net profits of the business over the last five years of the deceased's life being £2,158, £2,074, £1,192, £1,638 and (as adjusted) £4,630, while his drawings for personal expenditure averaged only £800, with his wife receiving £220 "wages"; that during the first four of these years bank overdrafts and a loan from the deceased's father had been eliminated and there was also considerable expenditure in non-recurring items of capital outlay on buildings, equipment, etc., the effect of which was to reduce the profits for these years and to enhance the relative profit in the final year; that by the date of his death the deceased had by his efforts built up a business which was approaching the maximum, his initial enterprise having borne fruit and leaving him poised to make larger profits; that he would have increased the size of his farm by purchasing more land and within another 20 years would probably have become one of the leading farmers in his area, with a position like that of his father-in-law, who had a farm of about 436 acres making a gross profit of about £8,500 per year; that at the deceased's age the next 10 years would have been the most vigorous and productive of his life; that over that period, in order to reach the maximum, the deceased would have required to continue to plough back some of his profits into his business, for the purchase of more land and the improvement of his buildings, land and equipment; and that he might soon have reached the level of surtax — Damages for **loss of support**, calculated on the basis of a multiplier of 10 (taking account of the possibility of the widow's remarriage) and an annual figure for loss of support of £2,500 (based on a probable average net income of the deceased over the period of 10 years after his death of £4,000, less (a) a round figure for what would have been expended on the deceased's own support, namely £500; and (b) another round figure for what would have probably been expended by the deceased upon capital improvements such as buying other land and putting in new equipment, namely £1,000), *awarded* in the total sum of £25,000 and *allocated* (subject to another matter) in the proportions: (1) to the widow, £18,000; (2) to the elder child, £3,500; and (3) to the younger child, £3,500.

(12) **Smith v. Middleton,** 1971 S.L.T. (Notes) 65 (Lord Emslie)

Deceased survived by widow and two children — Evidence that the deceased's earnings were on average about £27 a week; that out of his wages the wife was accustomed to get from £17 to £27 a week, depending upon the amount of the deceased's overtime in any given week; and that the amount spent on the deceased's keep was about £6 per week — Damages for **loss of support**, calculated on the basis that £750 per annum was available for the support of the deceased's widow and children, *awarded* in the total sum of £9,000, comprising (i) £6,000 for the widow; (ii) £1,250 for the elder child; and (iii) £1,750 for the younger child.

(13) **Riddell v. James Longmuir & Sons Ltd,** 1971 S.L.T. (Notes) 33 (Lord Hunter)

Deceased aged 41 at date of death, survived by widow aged c.37, four children aged 15, 12, eight and five and a fifth, posthumous child — Evidence that the deceased was a robust man; that he had for a good many years been in regular employment as a lorry driver; that it was probable that apart from accident or illness he had a considerable span of working life before him; that his net average weekly pre-accident wage was £13 2s 0d; that the weekly amount used for the family's support was £11; and that as at the date of trial the elder children were self-supporting — Damages for **loss of support**, calculated on the basis, rounded down, of a figure of £575 per annum and a multiplier of 14, *assessed* in the total sum of £8,000, comprising (i) £5,250 for the widow; (ii) £100 for the eldest child; (iii) £250 for the second child; (iv) £650 for the third child; (v) £750 for the fourth child; (vi) £1,000 for the fifth child.

(14) **McKinnon v. British Railways Board,** 1972 S.L.T. (Notes) 2 (Lord Keith)

Deceased aged 47 at date of death, survived by widow aged 41 and two children aged 14 and 10 — Evidence that as at the date of trial the widow was in part time employment at a wage of £8.50 per week, the elder child was a student in receipt of a grant of £350 per annum and the younger child was still at school; and that the total loss of support suffered by all three was £10,000 — Damages for **loss of support** *assessed* by agreement in the total sum of £10,000 and *allocated* in the proportions: (1) to the widow, £8,000; (2) to the elder child, £850; and (3) to the younger child, £1,150.

(15) **McCuaig v. Redpath Dorman Long Limited**, 1972 S.L.T. (Notes) 42 (Lord Dunpark)

Deceased aged 43 at date of death, survived by widow aged 39 and two children aged 16 and 14 — Evidence that the deceased's average net weekly wage was £30 which he gave to his wife, she returning £5 to him for pocket money; that of the wage retained by the wife a further £5 per week was expended on the deceased's support; that as at the date of death the elder son was working and contributing £2 per week towards his own keep; and that, some months after the death of the deceased, the younger son left school and thereafter also contributed £2 per week to the household expenses — Damages for **loss of support**, calculated on the basis of a multiplier of 10 (having regard to the likelihood of the deceased claiming a larger share of his weekly earnings as his sons became self-supporting) and an annual figure of £1,050 (based on £20 per week), *awarded* in the total sum of £10,500 and *allocated* in the proportions: (1) to the widow, £10,000 (£3,900 to the past); (2) to the elder child, £200 (all to the past); and (3) to the younger child, £300 (all to the past).

(16) **Alexander v. J. Smart & Co. Ltd,** 1973 S.L.T. (Notes) 22 (Lord Robertson)

Deceased aged 60 at date of death, survived by widow aged 55 — Evidence that the deceased, a bricklayer, provided support to his wife at the annual rate of £470; that there had been a rise of 66% in wage rates for bricklayers during the three year period between the date of death and the date of trial; but that taking into account rising prices, expenses, inflation, etc. the amount of the wife's dependency would probably not have risen by the same amount — Damages of £2,500 *awarded* for **loss of support**, on the basis, rounded up, of allowing three years at £470 and a further year and a half at £700.

(17) **Cameron v. Kidd,** 1973 S.L.T. (Notes) 74 (Lord Dunpark)

Deceased aged 57 at date of death, survived by widow aged c.49, adult son and daughter aged 15 — Evidence that the deceased's take home pay was about £21 per week; that out of that sum the deceased gave his wife £12.50 for domestic expenses; that he did not spend the balance on himself, paying for new furniture on hire purchase, redecoration of the house and extras for his daughter such as ski-ing and pony trekking holidays; that since the date of death wages had risen; that from about 20 months after the date of death, when the daughter became self-supporting, the deceased would have been taking home an estimated average of £24 per week; and that the deceased would have retired at the age of 65 — Damages for **loss of support**, calculated on the basis (a) that for the initial period of 20 months after the date of death the whole of the £12.50 per week would have been applied as support for the wife and daughter; (b) that for a period of five years thereafter one-half of the £24 per week would have been applied as support for the wife; and (c) that, had he survived, the deceased would have given his daughter money for special purposes in the future, *awarded* in the total sum of £4,158. comprising (i) £3,588 for the widow (made up of £588 for the initial period, £450 for the period thereafter to date of trial and £2,550 for the balance of the five year period); and (ii) £579 for the daughter (made up of £420 for the initial period and £150 for future gifts).

(18) **Mackenzie v. George McLeod Limited,** 1973 S.L.T. (Notes) 64 (Lord Dunpark)

Deceased aged 15 at date of death, survived by parents — Evidence that the deceased had only worked for four weeks prior to his death, during which he earned less than £6 per week net; that he gave his weekly wage to his mother and received £1 per week as pocket money; and that he was looking for a place to serve an apprenticeship as a toolmaker — Damages for **loss of support** *refused* on the basis that it had to be doubted that the deceased would have earned more than enough to maintain himself for some years and on this evidence the parents had not established their claim for loss of potential future support.

(19) **Harper v. Smillie,** 1974 S.L.T. (Notes) 40 (Lord McDonald)

Deceased aged 28 at date of death, survived by widow aged 29 — Evidence that the deceased was a lorry driver employed at a carpet factory earning a net average weekly wage of £19.37; that he contributed therefrom some £14 towards the maintenance of the household; that, after allowing for the deceased's food and clothing, the net weekly sum available for the wife was £9; that the weekly wages of lorry drivers of the deceased's employers had increased each year since the date of his death, to £25, £30, £37 and £40, respectively; and that had the deceased survived, the wife could have expected net weekly sums to be available to her each year after his death of £11, £14, £17 and £19, respectively — Damages for **loss of support**, calculated on the basis of an overall multiplier of 14 divided into (a) a period of four and a half years from the date of death until the date of trial; and (b) a period of nine and a half years thereafter, *awarded* in the sum of £12,532, comprising (i) £3,146 for the initial period, taking into account the annual increases in support; and (ii) £9,386 for the second period, at the current annual rate of loss of £988.

(20) **Kelly v. Smillie,** 1974 S.L.T. (Notes) 41 (Lord McDonald)

Deceased aged 43 at date of death, survived by widow aged 43, three adult children and three younger children aged 10, seven and six — Evidence that the deceased was a miner; that he was a steady worker who enjoyed good health; that his average net wage was £21.75 per week; that from this sum he gave his wife £17 or £18; that two of the older children contributed £2 or £3 each; that the wife had the family allowance which she used to pay the rent; that she spent £3 or £4 per week on food for the deceased and also bought his clothing; that the extent of the dependency of the wife and family on the contribution of the deceased could reasonably be taken at £14 per week or £730 per annum; that the deceased's wage would have increased from time to time between the date of death and the date of trial; that the dependency would likewise have increased; and that after allowing for tax and other expenses, including the deceased's own maintenance, the wife could have anticipated receiving £29 or £30 per week, or about £1,500 per annum, for maintenance of herself and the family had the deceased been alive as at the date of trial — Damages for **loss of support**, calculated on the basis of an overall multiplier of 12, having regard to the arduous occupation of the deceased, divided into (a) a period of four and a half years from the date of death until the date of trial; and (b) a period of nine and a half years thereafter, *awarded* in the total sum of £15,250, comprising (i) £4,000 for the initial period, taking into account the increases in miners' wages and consequent increases in support; and (ii) £11,250 for the second period, at the current annual rate of loss of £1,500, and *allocated* in the proportions: (1) to the widow, £9,250; (2) to each of the three older children, £750; (3) to the fourth child, £1,500; (4) to the fifth child, £1,750; and (5) to the youngest child, £2,000.

(21) **Stewart v. Hughes,** 1974 S.L.T. (Notes) 19 (Lord Robertson)

Deceased a young man, survived by parents — Evidence that the deceased contributed towards the profits of his parents' business by his services but did not directly support them; that the business was prosperous; that the parents had two other sons and a daughter; and that there was a custom for the family to look after old and indigent members out of the business — Damages of £100 *awarded* to each of the parents for **loss of potential support** upon the hypothesis that, if at any time in the future the parents, or either of them, became impoverished and unable to support themselves, the son could have been called upon to support them, or one of them, and the claim might have been successful if the son was then in a position to contribute support.

(22) **McBeth v. Secretary of State for Scotland**, 1976 S.L.T. (Notes) 63 (Lord Stewart)

Deceased aged 40 at date of death, survived by widow and two sons aged c.14 — Evidence that the support of which the family had been deprived was £370 per annum; that the elder son was a trainee solicitor who might require some degree of support in the future; and that the younger son was in the deceased's business and might well be earning more if his father were still alive — Damages for **loss of support** calculated on the basis, rounded up, of a multiplier of 14 applied to the annual figure of £370, *awarded* in the total sum of £5,200, comprising (i) £3,200 for the widow; (ii) £1,000 for the elder son; and (iii) £1,000 for the younger son, with the awards relating approximately two-thirds to the past.

(23) **Greenwood v. Muir,** 1977 S.L.T. (Notes) 71 (Lord Wylie)

Deceased aged c.56 at date of death, survived by four children aged c.32, c.26, c.20 and c.11 — Evidence that the youngest child was living with her father as at the date of death; that, having regard to the fact that she was equipped to take advantage of further education after school, she was likely to have continued to rely on his support for some time; that the deceased might have retired at about the age of 62; that the deceased's total earnings between date of death and date of trial would have been £9,480; and that his current earning capacity as at the date of trial would have been £2,900 per annum — Damages for **loss of support** *awarded* to the youngest child in the sum of £4,300, comprising (i) £2,370, being one-quarter of the deceased's earnings during the period of three and a half years between date of death and date of trial; and (ii) £1,930, being one-third of the deceased's current earning capacity for two years thereafter.

(24) **Farrell v. British United Trawlers (Granton) Ltd,** 1978 S.L.T. (Notes) 16 (Lord Allanbridge)

Deceased aged 34 at date of death, survived by widow aged c.46 — Evidence that the deceased had been away at sea for most of the marriage; that the marriage had had its ups and downs as there was trouble if the deceased had been drinking; that on occasion the wife had left the matrimonial home because the deceased had been drinking; that the wife nevertheless considered the marriage had been a happy one and she was very upset by the death of the deceased and had a nervous breakdown; that the wife received £15 per week, about half the deceased's net wage, for rent, food and looking after herself when her husband was at sea; that when he was at home from sea she provided his food and clothing out of this £15 per week, but he used to give her money if she needed it — Damages **for loss of support**, calculated on the basis of an overall multiplier of nine, having regard to the fact that the wife was 12 years older than the deceased and to the other circumstances of the marriage, divided into (a) a period of four years from the date of death until about six months after the date of trial; and (b) a period of five years thereafter, *awarded* in the sum of £10,300, comprising (i) £4,300 for the initial period, taking account of agreed increases in support; and (ii) £6,000 for the second period, at the current rate of loss of £1,200.

(25) **Davie v. Edinburgh Corporation,** 1978 S.L.T. (Notes) 37 (Lord Wylie)

Deceased aged 39 at date of death, survived by widow and child aged c.10 — Evidence that the deceased was in a reasonably secure and physically safe occupation as a post office worker; that out of his earnings of £54 a week the amount used for the support of his wife and child was £30; that the deceased would be earning £62 a week as at the date of trial, of which £37 would be allocated to support — Damages for **loss of support**, calculated on the basis of an overall multiplier of 12, having regard to the deceased's age and the nature of his employment, divided into (a) a period of just over four years from the date of death until the date of trial; and (b) a period of just under eight years thereafter, *assessed* in the total sum of £20,900, comprising (i) £7,548 for the initial period, interpolating the figure of £33.50 a week as the loss of support element for that period; and (ii) £13,355 for the second period, and *allocated* in the proportions: (1) to the widow, £15,675 (75%); and (2) to the child, £5,225 (25%).

(26) **McArthur v. Raynesway Plant Limited,** 1980 S.L.T. (Notes) 79 (Lord Jauncey)

Deceased aged 24 at date of death, survived by widow of the same age and child — Evidence that the deceased's net average weekly wage was £37 of which he kept £10 for pocket money, giving the balance of £27 to his wife for the family's maintenance; that, after deducting expenditure for behoof of the deceased and the child, the appropriate proportion attributable to the wife's support was £15 per week or £780 per annum; and that the figure for support fell to be increased by 5% for each year to date to take account of inflation — Damages for **loss of support**, calculated on the basis of an overall multiplier of 15 having regard to the age of the deceased and the widow at date of death, *awarded* to the widow in the sum of £14,260, comprising (i) £5,305 for the period of six years from the date of death until the date of trial; and (ii) £8,955 for the period of nine years thereafter.

(27) **Cunningham v. National Coal Board,** 1981 S.L.T. (Notes) 74 (Lord Brand)

Deceased aged 34 at date of death, survived by widow aged 43, daughter aged 14 and son aged seven — Evidence that the annual sum which but for his death would have been provided by the deceased for his wife and children was £1,820 for the period between the date of his death and the date of trial and £2,080 for the period thereafter; and that the daughter had married at the age of 16 — Damages for **loss of support**, calculated on the basis of an overall multiplier of nine, *assessed* in the total sum of £27,470, comprising (i) £8,750 for the period of five years from the date of death until the date of trial; and (ii) £18,720 for the four year period thereafter, *allocated* in the proportions: (1) to the daughter, £500; and (2) to the widow and son, £18,220 (apportioned 75% to the widow and 25% to the son).

(28) **Parker v. Wigtown District Council,** 1981 S.L.T. (Notes) 95 (Lord McDonald)

Deceased aged 57 at date of death, survived by widow aged c.61 and adult children — Evidence that the deceased contributed some £20 per week to the support of the family; that the wife was dependent on the deceased for support to the extent of about £12 per week; that as the years passed the extent of support would increase; and that the deceased's job had ceased to exist by the date of trial — Damages for **loss of support**, calculated on the basis of a multiplier of six applied to an annual figure of £624, *awarded* to the widow in the sum of £3,744, with one-half attributable to the past.

(29) **Dingwall v. Walter Alexander & Sons (Midland) Ltd,** 1982 S.C. (H.L.) 179 (Second Division; Lord Jauncey)

Deceased aged 42 at date of death, survived by widow aged 38 and five children aged 15, 13, 11, eight and five — Evidence that the deceased was a bus driver earning about £45 in a normal week but every second week during the season he was on tour work which brought him in somewhere between £50 and £60; that he gave the greater part of his wages to his wife, never less than £40 when he was earning £45, and a correspondingly higher figure when his wages were between £50 and £60; that had he continued to work for his employers to the date of trial his net loss of wages would have been £11,340 and his average net wage at that date would have been £80.92 per week, or £4,207.84 per annum; that the deceased had been physically fit; and that there appeared to be no reason why he should not have continued to work for his employers for the foreseeable future — Damages for **loss of support**, calculated on the basis of an overall multiplier of 13, divided into (a) a period of 3.1 years from the date of death until the date of trial; and (b) a period of 9.9 years thereafter, *awarded* in the total sum, rounded up, of £38,500, comprising (i) £7,938 for the initial period, being seven-tenths of the deceased's net earnings for the period; and (ii) £29,155.50 for the second period at the annual rate of loss of support of £2,945 (being seven-tenths of £4,207.84), plus interest on the loss of support to date of trial in the sum of £1,310, and *allocated* (inclusive of interest) in the proportions: (1) to the widow, £28,500; (2) to the eldest child, £700; (3) to the second child, £1,200; (4) to the third child, £1,800; (5) to the fourth child, £2,700; and (6) to the fifth child, £3,600.

(30) **Clark v. J.M.J. Contractors Ltd,** 1982 S.L.T. 299 (Lord Grieve)
Deceased aged 37 at date of death, survived by widow of the same age and child aged c.11 — Evidence that the deceased was an electrical maintenance engineer earning £4,273 a year; that having regard to the increases in the deceased's salary the total sum available for the support of the whole family to the date of trial was £22,000; that of that sum £7,000 fell to be deducted for the deceased's own support; that as at the date of trial the deceased's annual gross wage would have been £9,716; and that of that sum £5,716 fell to be deducted for tax and the deceased's own support — Damages for **loss of support**, calculated on the basis of an overall multiplier of 13, divided into (a) a period of five years from the date of death until the date of trial; and (b) a period of eight years thereafter, *awarded* in the total sum of £47,000, comprising (i) £15,000 for the initial period, deducting the amount for the deceased's own support from the total sum available for the support of the whole family; and (ii) £32,000 for the second period at the annual rate of loss of support of £4,000, and *allocated* in the proportions: (1) to the widow, £42,000; and (2) to the child, £5,000.

(31) **Morris v. Pirie,** 1983 S.L.T. 659 (Lord Stewart)
Deceased aged 50 at date of death, survived by widow aged c.49 and two daughters aged c.13 and nine — Evidence that deceased spent only a small amount upon himself, applying seven-tenths of his net earnings to the support of the family — Damages for **loss of support**, calculated on the basis of a multiplier of nine, *awarded* in the total sum of £43,750 and *allocated* as follows: (1) to the widow, £30,000; (2) to the elder daughter, £5,750; and (3) to the younger daughter, £8,000.

(32) **Porter v. Dickie,** 1983 S.L.T. 234 (Lord Ross)
Deceased aged 49 at date of death, survived by widower aged 50 and daughter aged 16 — Evidence that as at the date of death both the deceased and her husband were in employment, earning a net wage of £46 per week and £58 per week, respectively; that they pooled their resources, each requiring one-half of the joint income for support; that about three and a half years after the death of the deceased the widower was made redundant; that he had tried without success to get work and in view of his age and the current economic climate was not likely to obtain employment again; that he was entitled to

unemployment benefit for one year from the date of redundancy at the rate of £30 per week for the first six months and at the rate of £22.50 thereafter; that during that period the deceased would have been earning about £65 per week; that if he had not become redundant, the widower would have hoped to continue working until the age of 65; that if the deceased had not been killed, she would have hoped to continue working until the age of 60; and that when the widower became redundant the deceased would have continued working and would not have been made redundant — Damages for **loss of support**, calculated on the basis of an overall multiplier of six and a half (the period of the deceased's expectation of working life being a relatively short one), divided into (a) an initial period of three and a half years from the date of death; (b) a second period of one year thereafter, ending at about the date of trial; and (c) a third period of two years after that, *awarded* in the total sum of £4,394, comprising (i) nil for the initial period (in respect that the widower suffered no loss since he still had his own earnings of £58 per week, which was more than half of the joint earnings); (ii) £1,014 for the second period (in respect that if the deceased had not been killed, the joint earnings to be shared equally would have been £95 per week for the first six months and £87 per week for the second six months, whereas the widower had in fact only received the unemployment benefit and accordingly had lost £17.50 per week in the first six months and £21.50 per week in the second six months); and (iii) £3,380 for the third period (in respect that if the deceased had not been killed, she would have been earning £65 per week at this time, of which one-half, namely £32.50 per week, would have been available for the widower's support for the whole of the two year period).

(33) **Little v. Miller,** 1985 S.L.T. 99 (Lord Allanbridge)

Deceased aged 44 at date of death, survived by widow aged 45, son aged 20 and daughter aged c.18 — Evidence that the annual future loss of support suffered by the widow was £2,940; that the son had been paying £15 per week for his board and lodging and suffered no loss of support; and that the daughter had been paying only £40 per month when living with her parents and had married two and a half years after the death of the deceased — Damages for **loss of support** by the widow, calculated on the basis of a multiplier of 10.5, divided into (a) a period of three and a half years from the date of death until the date of trial; and (b) the period of seven years thereafter, *assessed* in the sum of £29,915, comprising (i) £9,335, an agreed sum, for the initial period; and (ii) £20,580, at the annual rate of loss of support of £2,940, for the second period; and for **loss of support** by the daughter *assessed* in the sum of £750.

(34) **McLaughlin v. Strathclyde Regional Council,** 1984 S.L.T. 99 (Lord Mayfield)

Deceased aged 45 at date of death, survived by widow aged 45 and eight children aged 23, 22, 20, 17, 16, 14, 13 and five — Evidence that the deceased was physically fit and had been in regular employment for many years; that there was no reason why he should not have continued to work for the family for many years; that as at date of death he was earning about £74 per week; that he gave £50 per week to his wife and occasionally £20 for bills; that the deceased's wife was herself working and contributed about £38 per week; that the four eldest children contributed £5 per week to the family income; that the three next eldest children each contributed £5 per week when they became 16; that as at the date of trial two of the children had left the family home and two contributed £10 per week; that the deceased retained £24 out of his wage of £74; that he was himself supported out of the family total; that the deceased's wages would have increased; that as at the date of trial he would have handed over £84 per week, being about two-thirds of his weekly wage — Damages for **loss of support**, calculated on the basis of an overall multiplier of 11, divided into (a) an initial period of four and a half years from the date of death until the date of trial; and (b) the period of six and a half years thereafter, *assessed* in the total sum of £37,000, rounded up, comprising (i) £17,046 for the initial period; and (ii) £28,327 for the second period, at an annual figure for loss of support of £4,358 (sic), less one-fifth, and *allocated* in the proportions: (1) to the widow, £30,000; (2) to the sixth child, £750; (3) to the seventh child, £1,250; and (4) to the eighth child, £5,000.

(35) **Prentice v. Chalmers,** 1985 S.L.T 168 (Second Division; Lord Murray)

Deceased aged 42 at date of death, survived by widow aged 41 and three children aged 16, nearly 14 and nearly five — Evidence that the deceased was one of the two experienced and successful partners in a prosperous business from which he drew a salary and cash from time to time; that he was not ungenerous towards his wife and family, readily meeting all their reasonable needs in such things as food and clothing, enabling the family to enjoy a very good standard of living; that he was financially cautious and lived frugally, albeit that he had a weakness for vintage cars; that one-third of his earnings went on his own needs; that as at the date of death the annual drawings of the deceased from his business totalled £15,000; that the deceased's spending on the family had probably increased, even in real terms, during the two or three years before his death; that the retail price index had increased by a total of 57.28% during the period of four years between the date of death and a date three months before the date of trial — Damages for **loss of support**, calculated on the basis of a multiplier of 12, divided into (a) a period of four and a third years from the date of death until the date of trial; and (b) the period of seven and two-thirds years thereafter, *awarded* on appeal in the total sum, rounded down, of £176,030, comprising (i) £55,680 for the initial period on the basis, rounded down, of an annual figure for loss of support during that period of £12,850 (being the product of multiplying the annual loss of support figure as at the date of death (£10,000) by one-half of the percentage increase in prices (57.28%) and adding the resultant sum to that annual amount of £10,000); and (ii) £120,350 for the second period on the basis, rounded down, of an annual figure for loss of support as at the date of trial of £15,700 (being the product of multiplying the annual loss of support figure as at the date of death (£10,000) by the percentage increase in prices (57.28%) and adding the resultant sum to that annual amount of £10,000), and *allocated* in the proportions: (1) to the widow, £132,022, rounded off at £132,020 (75%); (2) to the three children, £44,008, rounded up to £44,110 (25%), subdivided in proportion to the number of years of their dependence from the date of the deceased's death until reaching 21, namely five, seven and 12 (sic) years, respectively, giving a total years of dependency figure of 24 (sic), on the basis of which the eldest child would receive £9,168.75 (5/24ths), rounded off at £9,170; the second child would receive £12,839 (7/24ths), rounded off at £12,840; and the youngest child would receive £22,005 (12/24ths), rounded off at £22,000.

(36) **Rafferty v. J. & C. M. Smith (Whiteinch) Ltd,** 1987 S.L.T. 538 (Lord Weir)

Deceased aged 32 at date of death, survived by two children aged six and two — Evidence that the deceased lived with his children and their mother, to whom he was not married; that the annual median net weekly wage of the deceased was £150; that he required little money for his own support; that the loss of support to the family, including the deceased's cohabitant, was £100 per week; and that the deceased was well regarded as an employee, his health was good and his prospects of continuing in steady employment were excellent — Damages for **loss of support**, calculated on the basis of a multiplier of 13, divided into (a) a period of eight years from the date of death until the date of trial; and (b) the period of five years thereafter, *assessed* in the total sum of £27,040, comprising (i) £16,640 for the initial period at an annual rate of loss of support of £2,080 (being 40% of the annual loss of support to the family of £5,200, the cohabitant receiving 60% of the support); and (ii) £10,400 for the second period at the same annual rate of £2,080, and *allocated* in the proportions: (1) to the elder child, £16,334 (15/34ths); and (2) to the younger child, £20,690 (19/34ths).

(37) **Worf v. Western S.M.T. Co. Ltd,** 1987 S.L.T. 317 (Lord Mayfield)
Deceased aged 32 at date of death, survived by widow aged c.31 and three children aged seven, five and one — Evidence that the deceased carried out substantial improvements and repairs to the matrimonial accommodation in relation to such matters as joinery work, central heating and other domestic appliances; that he constructed and repaired furniture, provided mathematical tuition to the children and prepared his own tax report; that he was also an active gardener; that the widow's brother, a carpenter, had spent about 200 hours a year in various household tasks which the deceased would have done; that the estimated cost of such work was about 6,000 dollars; that most of the tasks which the deceased did now involved the widow in expense; and that she also now had to pay for a security patrol service — Evidence that the deceased was employed as an electronics engineer; that his base salary was 28,200 dollars; that had he survived, there would have been annual progressions of his salary over the period of six and a quarter years between the date of his death and the date of trial; that the net loss of earnings to the date of trial was 242,028 dollars; that he also received fringe benefits, namely medical and dental care both for himself and for his family, pension provisions, life insurance provisions, a stock option and investment plan provision, valued at 15% of salary; that the percentage of the earnings for the deceased's own support was 30%; that the deceased's retirement date was at age 65; that since the commencement of employment the deceased had steadily advanced in relation to promotion of his professional status within the firm and by regular increases in salary; that he was well regarded and would have continued to progress up the salary scale; that annual salary increases would amount to a figure in the region of 4%; that his net salary as at the date of trial would have been 48,548 dollars — Damages for **loss of the deceased's services**, calculated on the basis of a multiplier of 10 and an annual sum of 8,000 dollars, *awarded* in the sum of 80,000 dollars — Damages for **loss of support**, calculated on the basis of an overall multiplier of 15, divided into (a) an initial period of six and a quarter years from the date of death until the date of trial; and (b) the period of eight and three quarter years thereafter, *awarded* in the sum of 648,749 dollars, comprising (i) 208,749 dollars for the initial period, being 75% of 278,332 dollars (the sum of the net loss of earnings for the period (242,028 dollars) plus 15% for fringe benefits for the period (36,304 dollars)); and (ii) 440,000 dollars for the second period, made up of (A) 366,386 dollars at an annual rate of loss of support of 41,872.65 dollars, being 75% of 55,830.20 dollars (the sum of the annual net salary as at the date of trial (48,548 dollars) plus 15% for fringe benefits (7,282.20 dollars)); and (B) 73,614 dollars in respect of the prospect of promotion, and *allocated* in the proportions: (1) to the widow, 70%; and (2) to the children, 30%.

(38) **Wilson v. Chief Constable, Lothian and Borders Constabulary,** 1989 S.L.T. 97 (Lord McCluskey)

Deceased aged c.26 at date of death, survived by widow aged c.26 and three children aged seven years, four years and nine months — Evidence that the deceased earned £3,700 net per annum; that making due allowance for the deceased's upkeep and allowances, the loss of support to the family was £2,500 per year; that the deceased from time to time exhibited violent and drunken behaviour towards his wife; and that there was a real risk that the employment of the deceased could have been interrupted by the general economic problems which affected employment prospects as at the date of trial — Damages for **loss of support**, calculated on the basis of a multiplier of 13 and an annual sum of £2,500, *awarded* in the total sum of £32,500 (with interest on past loss of support of £3,800) and the total (with interest of £36,300) *allocated* in the proportions: (1) to the widow, £18,150 (50%); and (2) to the children, £18,150 (50%), subdivided so as to award: to the eldest child, £4,840 (4/15ths); to the second child, £6,050 (5/15ths); and to the youngest child, £7,260 (6/15ths).

(39) **Davidson v. Upper Clyde Shipbuilders Ltd,** 1990 S.L.T. 329 (Lord Milligan)

Deceased aged 58 at date of death, survived by widow of same age — Evidence that the deceased was a month short of his 59th birthday at the date of his death; that he ordinarily would have retired at 65; that his employment would not have ceased before then; that he earned £6,261 net per annum at the time of his death; that had he survived to his retirement date, the deceased would have received an annual pension thereafter amounting to 13/60ths of his salary at date of retirement; that his annual earnings as at that date would have been about £12,000, which would give an annual pension of about £2,700 at retirement; that thereafter, if the wife survived him, she would have received an annual widow's pension of one-half of the pension which he had been receiving; that the pensions concerned would have been flat rate pensions and not index linked or otherwise increasing annually; that had the deceased survived normal retiring age, he could have expected to live thereafter for a further 13 years according to agreed life expectancy tables; that in the events which happened, the widow received *inter alia* a widow's pension at an annual rate which started at £840 and had been rising and would continue to do so until the date when the deceased would have retired at 65; and that thereafter, the widow would receive half the pension which the deceased would have received had he worked to retirement age, namely half of a prospective £2,700, namely £1,350 annually — Damages for **loss of support**, calculated on the basis of (a) a multiplier of five relative to the period from the date of death until the date of the deceased's expected retirement at age 65 (c.6 years); and (b) a multiplier of six and a half relative to the period of the deceased's expected retirement (13 years) thereafter, *awarded* in the total sum of £26,867, comprising (i) £17,215 for the initial period at an annual figure of loss of support of £3,443, being 55% (reflecting the extent of the wife's dependency) of £6,261 (the deceased's net annual earnings at the date of death); and (ii) £9,652 for the second period at an annual figure of £1,485, being 55% (reflecting the extent of the wife's dependency) of £2,700 (the pension the deceased would have been receiving).

(40) **Brown v. Ferguson,** 1990 S.L.T. 274 (Lord Sutherland)

Deceased aged 33 at date of death, survived by widower and child aged three — Evidence that the deceased had been a teacher and had worked until the birth of her child; that it had been her intention to resume work when the child reached school age about three years after the date of the deceased's death; that the deceased would have been able to obtain employment as a teacher when the child reached school age had she so wished; that if she had been so employed, her net earnings would have been £5,950, £7,350, £8,310, £8,793 and £9,572 in the academic years from that date; that in all probability the deceased would have resumed such employment when her child reached school age and would have continued to be so employed for the foreseeable future since she enjoyed teaching and would have no intention of retiring before she had to; that just prior to her death the deceased had bought a plot of land on which it was intended to build a house to the value of about £40,000 to £50,000, the title to which would be held in joint names; that the idea was that the deceased's first year's earnings would be used as a deposit with the balance of the cost being obtained on mortgage; that the deceased's earnings would then be used to pay off the mortgage as quickly as possible, probably in about seven years; that the husband was a self-employed agricultural contractor earning on average about £9,000–£10,000 gross (about £7,500 net) per annum; and that the family would have been maintained out of his earnings while the house was being paid off — Evidence that the widower now looked after himself with some assistance from the deceased's mother who lived some miles away; that the child now lived with the deceased's mother, visiting the widower at weekends except during the summer when he worked seven days a week; that in order to make this arrangement the deceased's mother required to give up her employment as a school cook; that the widower paid her £100 per month for looking after the child and made other payments to her amounting to about £500 per annum; that in addition he had bought a car for her for which he paid the running costs; that the widower was accordingly paying the deceased's mother something over £2,000 per annum, although that sum included the cost of maintenance of the child; that the cost of employing a housekeeper prepared to look after the child as at the date of trial would be about £60 per week living in or £70 per week living out; and that such cost as at the date of death would have been respectively £45 and £50; that in respect of a living in housekeeper there would also be the cost of keep — Damages for **loss of support**, calculated on the basis of a multiplier of 12, divided into (a) a period of four and five-sixths years from the date of death until the date of trial; (b) the period of three and one-sixth years thereafter; (c) the period of two years after that; and (d) a final period of two years thereafter, *awarded* in the total sum of £14,652, comprising (i) -£3,940 *(i.e.* a negative loss of £3,940) for the initial period, in respect that where for seven years the deceased's earnings would have been spent on the house, to be held in joint names, the appropriate way of dealing with the case was to take half of the deceased's earnings for seven years from the date of probable commencement of employment as a teacher and the whole of her earnings thereafter, add the resultant figure to the widower's earnings to represent the joint income, and deduct 25% from the product for the deceased's own maintenance; and, on that basis, there would be a net saving to the widower of £3,940; and (ii) £18,592 for the second, third and fourth periods, on the basis of taking half of the deceased's earnings for the second and third periods and the whole of her earnings for the fourth period, together with the whole of the widower's earnings for those periods, and deducting 25% for the deceased's own maintenance, and *allocated* in the proportions: (1) to the widower, £12,000; and (2) to the child, £2,652 — Damages for **loss of the deceased's services** *awarded* in the total sum of £40,000, comprising (i) £15,000 for the period of four and five-sixths years from the date of death until the date of trial, taking the living out figure (as this would be much the same as the living in wage plus keep) averaged over the period, namely £60 per week; and (ii) £25,000 for the period of seven years thereafter, taking the figure of £70 per week, and *allocated*, along with interest of £5,438, in the proportions: (1) to the widower, £34,078 (75%); and (2) to the child, £11,360 (25%).

(41) **Howie v. Upper Clyde Shipbuilders Ltd,** 1991 S.L.T. 2 (Lord Cameron of Lochbroom)

Deceased aged 61 at date of death, survived by widow and adult children — Evidence that the deceased's net annual income was £6,250; that apart from his fatal condition he was otherwise in good health; that he intended to work on until he was 65; that while he was in employment the deceased was accustomed to make over his whole pay packet to his wife who became responsible for the payment of all bills and other household expenses; that she provided her husband with petrol money of between £10 and £12 per week and other limited pocket money for newspapers and social expenses; and that when they went to live with their daughter, they agreed to meet one-half of the mortgage payments, initially some £60 per month and latterly £80 per month, and one-half of the general household expenses — Damages for **loss of support**, calculated on the basis of a multiplier of three, divided into (a) a period of just under 18 months from the date of death; and (b) the period of just over 18 months thereafter, *awarded* in the sum of £9,375, comprising (i) £4,167 for the initial period, at an annual rate of loss of support of £3,125 (being 50% of the deceased's annual net earnings); and (ii) £5,208 for the second period, at the same annual rate of loss of support.

(42) **Phillips v. Grampian Health Board (No. 2),** 1992 S.L.T. 659 (Lord Clyde)

Deceased aged 26 at date of death, survived by widow aged c.22 — Evidence that the deceased was in the R.A.F.; that he was regarded by his superiors as keen and competent, happiest when busy, self-confident, determined and reliable; that but for his fatal illness the likelihood was that he would have remained in that career; that the current wage he would now be earning was about £7,100 net per annum; that had he remained in the R.A.F. the deceased would have earned by the date of trial £27,500; that the wife was earning about £40 per week during their married life but since the time of the deceased's death she had been earning some £80 per week; that they had pooled their earnings, defraying their expenses from the pool; and that the wife would have continued to work if the deceased had survived — Damages for **loss of support**, calculated on the basis of a multiplier of 15, divided into (a) a period of four and a quarter years from the date of death until the date of trial; and (b) the period of 10.75 years thereafter, *awarded* in the sum of £20,712, comprising (i) £4,910 for the initial period, on the basis of adding together the deceased's earnings over the period (£27,500) and the widow's earnings over the same period (£17,680), halving the total (50% of £45,180= £22,590) and deducting therefrom the figure of her earnings (£17,680); and (ii) £15,802 for the second period on the basis of taking the multiplicand as a half of the joint earnings less the widow's earnings, namely £1,470, and applying thereto the balance of the multiplier, namely 10.75.

(43) **Wotherspoon v. Strathclyde Regional Council,** 1992 S.L.T. 1090 (Lord Abernethy)

Deceased aged 40 at date of death, survived by widow aged 33, three adult children and three younger children aged 15, eight and five — Evidence that the deceased's average net weekly pay was £153.33; that this would have increased to £165.40 about nine months after the date of his death and to £174.79, the current rate, one year after that; that from the date of death until the date of trial the net loss of income was £21,070; that at the time of the deceased's death his wife was also working, doing secretarial work in a solicitor's office six hours a day, five days a week and earning approximately £350 per month net, a little under £81 per week; that this would have increased to a rate of £90 per week net as at the date of trial; that since the deceased's death the widow had had to cut her hours of work due to the increased demands that the family now made on her, but this would not have happened if the deceased had not died; that assuming some increase in the rate of pay for the widow's job, her net income from the date of death until the date of trial would have totalled £10,970; that the combined total of the family income would therefore have been £32,040 net; and that the 15-year-old did not live with the deceased, who paid £15 per week for her maintenance and also gave her pocket money from time to time when he met her in the street — Evidence that the deceased did general repairs about the house which the widow now had to pay other people to do; that he also did some gardening in respect of which the widow now had to get someone in for two to three hours per week from April to October at a cost of £3 per hour — Damages for **loss of support**, calculated on the basis of a multiplier of 14, divided into (a) a period of two years, five and a half months from the date of death until the date of trial; and (b) the period of 11 years, six and a half months thereafter, *awarded* to the widow and the youngest two children in the total sum of £124,290, comprising (i) £13,060 for the initial period, on the basis of deducting 25% for the deceased's maintenance from the combined total of the family income for the period (25% of £32,040= £8,010) so as to give a figure of £24,030 and deducting the widow's net income of £10,970 from the resultant sum; and (ii) £111,230 for the second period, at an annual rate of £9,089.08, being the combined annual net incomes of the deceased and the widow as at the date of trial, less 30% for the deceased's maintenance in view of the fact that the children would be adult before this period expired, and *allocated,* in respect of past loss of support (along with interest of £2,410), rounded off, in the proportions: (1) to the widow, £10,380 (70%); (2) to the second youngest child, £2,320 (15%); and (3) to the youngest child, £2,320 (15%) and, in respect of future support, rounded off, in the proportions: (1) to the widow, £77,860 (70%); (2) to the second youngest child, £13,905 (12.5%); and (3) to the youngest child, £19,465 (17.5%), and for **loss of support** *awarded* to the third youngest child in the sum of £500, inclusive of interest — Damages for **loss of the deceased's services** *awarded* in the sum of £1,500, inclusive of interest.

(44) **Campbell v. Gillespie,** 1996 S.L.T. 503 (Temporary Judge D.B. Robertson Q.C.)

Deceased aged 37 at date of death, survived by widow aged 27 and two children aged four and two — Evidence that the deceased provided substantial services of a D.I.Y. nature, including decoration and general maintenance, and rendered the usual domestic assistance at home; that at the time of his death the deceased was also renovating a croft-house which he had inherited; that over the course of a year the deceased spent one hour per day in rendering services at both houses — Evidence that the deceased was in employment at the time of his death; that the dependency element of the deceased's earnings was 70%; that the total figure for the dependency for the family from the date of death until the date of trial amounted to £45,270; that the annual rate of future loss of support was £9,236; that the deceased would have retired at age 60; that the retiral pension would have been £6,472 per annum and a lump sum of £25,886; that on the basis of life expectancy tables the deceased would have lived on for a further 18 years; and that since the date of death the widow had been in receipt of a widow's pension — Damages for **loss of the deceased's services**, calculated on the basis of a multiplier of 13, divided into (a) a period of five years from the date of death until the date of trial; and (b) the period of eight years thereafter, *awarded* in the total sum of £21,060, comprising (i) £8,100 for the initial period at an annual rate of £1,620 (being 360 hours at £4.50 per hour); and (ii) £12,960 for the second period at the same annual rate, and *allocated* in the proportions: (1) to the widow, £10,040 (2/3rds); (2) to the elder child, £3,510 (1/6th); and (3) to the younger child, £3,510 (1/6th) — Damages for **loss of support**, calculated on the basis of (a) a total multiplier of 13 relative to the period from the date of death until the deceased's retiral date, divided into (aa) a period of five years from the date of death until the date of trial; and (aaa) the period of eight years thereafter; and (b) a multiplier of five relative to the period after the deceased's retiral date, *awarded* in respect of period (a) in the total sum of £119,158, comprising (i) £45,270 for the period (aa); and (ii) £73,888 for the period (aaa), at an annual rate of loss of support of £9,236, and *awarded* in respect of the period (b) in the sum of £24,809, comprising (i) £16,180 for dependency insofar as the deceased's pension was concerned, on the basis of an annual rate of loss of support of £3,236 (being 50% of the retiral pension payable to the deceased from age 60); and £8,629 for dependency insofar as the deceased's pension lump sum payment was concerned, on the basis of discounting by one-third for accelerated payment the sum of £12,943 (being 50% of the deceased's pension lump sum payment payable at age 60), and *allocated*, in respect of period (aa), in the proportions: (1) to the widow, £30,180 (2/3rds); (2) to the elder child, £7,545 (1/6th); and (3) to the younger child, £7,545 (1/6th); in respect of period (aaa), in the proportions: (1) to the widow, £49,260 (2/3rds); (2) to the elder child, £12,314 (1/6th); and (3) to the younger child, £12,314 (1/6th); and, in respect of the period (b), in the proportions: (1) to the widow, £24,809 (100%); (2) to the elder child, nil; and (3) to the younger child, nil.

(45) **Beggs v. Motherwell Bridge Fabricators Ltd,** 1997 S.C.L.R. 1019 (Lord Eassie)

Deceased aged 38 at date of death, survived by widow of broadly similar age and two children aged 14 and 13 — Evidence that the deceased's annual net wage, averaged over the 26 week period preceding death, was £12,480; that the wife was also in employment; that as at the date of trial the elder child was working in a local factory and the younger child was still at school, having a part time job which gave him some pocket money, and hoping to go to college; that the deceased's retiral date was at age 65; that the annual pension payable to the deceased upon retiral, on the basis of the salary payable at the date of death, was £10,099 gross or about £8,000 net of tax — Evidence that the deceased was a normal married man living in family who did the correspondingly normal, average things which a father and husband did around the house, the garden and the family car, being services to compensate for which the widow would no doubt have to have greater recourse to tradesmen than would be necessary if the deceased were still within the household — Damages for **loss of support**, calculated on the basis of (a) a total multiplier of 14 relative to the period from the date of death until the deceased's retiral date, divided into (aa) a period of about four and a half years from the date of death until the date of trial; and (aaa) the period of nine and a half years thereafter; and (b) a multiplier of 3.8 relative to the period after the deceased's retiral date, *awarded* in respect of period (a) in the total sum of £118,400, comprising (i) £40,500 for the period (aa), on the basis of an annual rate of loss of support of £8,970, say, £9,000 (being the product of adding the deceased's earnings to those of the widow and deducting from that total both an amount equal to 25% thereof and the amount of the widow's earnings); and (ii) £77,900 for the period (aaa), on the basis of an annual rate of loss of support of £8,200 (allowing some increase in the proportion attributable to the deceased's own personal support and expenditure), and *awarded* in respect of the period (b) in the sum of £15,200 on the basis of an annual rate of loss of support of £4,000 (being 50% of the deceased's net annual pension on retiral, and *allocated*, in respect of period (aa), in the proportions: (1) to the widow, £33,460 (70%); (2) to the elder child, £7,170 (15%); and (3) to the younger child, £7,170 (15%); in respect of period (aaa), in the proportions: (1) to the widow, £62,320 (80%); (2) to the elder child, £7,790 (10%); and (3) to the younger child, £7,790 (10%); and, in respect of period of (b), in the proportions: (1) to the widow, £15,200 (100%); (2) to the elder child, nil; and (3) to the younger child, nil — Damages for **loss of the deceased's services** *awarded* in the sum of £9,800, on the basis of a multiplier of 14 and an annual figure of £700.

C. INDEX OF MULTIPLIERS SELECTED

Explanatory note: These multipliers predate the House of Lords decision in *Wells v. Wells* [1998] 3 W.L.R. 329.

1. LOSS OF FUTURE EARNINGS

*denotes partial award

Age at trial	*Case*	*Multiplier*
7	McKinnell (11)	15
7	Geddes (186)	11.5
14	Dickson (9)	15
c.14	Love (78)	15
c.16	Chapman (67)	15
19	Stevenson (250)	14
19	O'Connor (265)	12
c.20	Malcolm (24)	15
c.20	Fallow (83)	15
20	Wilson (129)	15
20	Duffy (288)	15
21	Mitchell (41)	13
21	Kelly (69)	14
23	Gerrard (42)	13
23	McLoone (58)	13
24	McMillan (203)	13
25	Will (47)	15
25	Convery (86)	14
26	Bird (125)	12
26	McKenzie (140)	14*
26	McCrum (202)	11
28	Robertson (135)	10
28	Blackhall (278)	8
c.29	Roberts (64)	8
29	Young (143)	10
29	Lamont (284)	1*
c.30	Anderson (65)	9
c.30	Barclay (40)	12
c.30	Howard (104)	3
30	Comber (195)	8
31	Kyle (39)	9
31	Barrett (73)	2 and 8*
31	Caven (85)	6
31	Morrison (221)	6
31	Robertson's C.B. (260)	c.9
32	Gallacher (122)	6
c.32	Tannock (62)	4 and 3
c.33	Maslowski (56)	8*
33	Travers (164)	6
c.33	McKenzie (190)	6
c.33	McDermid (215)	5
34	Todd (71)	8
c.34	Gallacher (96)	0.5
35	Jack (75)	7
35	Wilson (91)	8
c.35	Forsyth's C.B. (112)	12
35	Paterson (274)	10
c.36	Doyle (237)	4
38	Donnelly (82)	7
38	Hewson (105)	2
38	Hughes (189)	12*
38	Wall (224)	11
c.38	McVey (248)	5
c.39	Mazs (37)	12
c.39	Faith (109)	5
39	Stirling (286)	7
40	McKendrick (18)	10
40	McGilvray (3)	10*
c.40	Mearns (179)	4
40	Campbell (182)	2 and 10
40	Scott (214)	12*
41	Watson (63)	12

Age at trial	*Case*	*Multiplier*	*Age at trial*	*Case*	*Multiplier*
c.41	Ward (130)	8	49	Galbraith (74)	3.5
42	Malley (55)	10	c.49	Hamilton (14)	2
42	Gardner (66)	10	49	Johns (156)	4
42	Stoddard (87)	7	49	Breslin (196)	6
42	Logan (102)	8	49	Higgins (264)	1.5
42	Johnstone (155)	5	50	Gibney (107)	5
c.42	Collins (197)	5.5	c.50	Miller (115)	4
c.42	McIntyre (225)	5*	50	Penman (246)	6
43	McGeechan (8)	11	early 50s	Robertson (79)	3
43	Binnie (241)	6	50	Morrison (227)	6
c.43	Kennedy (280)	1.5*	c.50	Ballantyne (269)	3.5
c.43	Swan (283)	10, 15	50	Burns (277)	7
44	McWhinnie (209)	9	51	MacNeil (138)	1 and 6
c.44	McKinnon (262)	4	51	Duncan (188)	5
44	Fallan (281)	9	52	Harrison (27)	4
45	McLaughlin (31)	10	52	Blair (48)	5
45	McIlroy (94)	8	c.52	McKay (117)	4
45	Lenaghan (222)	6	52	Taylor (285)	2.5
c.46	Anderson (243)	3.5	53	Brodie (97)	5
46	McGarrigle (263)	7.5	53	Buchanan (205)	5
46	Mitchell (287)	6	c.53	Cavanagh (257)	3.5
47	Murphy (101)	c.4.25	54	Morrison (176)	4.5
c.47	Kirkpatrick (103)	1.33 and 6*	54	McLean (226)	3
			55	Calder (144)	1–2
47	Smith (146)	6	55	Myles (228)	4.5
47	Fulleman (216)	11	58	Palmer (98)	3
47	Brien (240)	3.5	c.58	McLeod (57)	4
48	Owenson (19)	5	58	MacShannon (220)	2.5
48	McCrae (137)	8	c.62	Clues (22)	1
48	Redman (172)	5	62	Farrelly (234)	1
48	Mitchell (176)	4.5	63	Muirhead (93)	c.1
48	Stuppart (276)	8*			

2. *LOSS OF PENSION RIGHTS*

Age at trial	*Case*	*Multiplier*	*Age at trial*	*Case*	*Multiplier*
48	Mitchell (177)	6	c.56	Grainger (178)	11
50	Burns (277)	10			

3. FUTURE OUTLAYS AND EXPENSES

Age at trial	*Case*	*Multiplier*	*Age at trial*	*Case*	*Multiplier*
7	Geddes (186)	15, 11.5 and 3.5	c.35	Forsyth's C.B. (112)	13
			36	Bonar (270)	16
19	Stevenson (250)	20	38	Wall (224)	15
19	O'Connor (265)	20, 20, 4 and 14	41	O'Brien's C.B. (163)	15
24	Tuttle (72)	10*, 10, 15	c.43	Gordon (187)	15
			44	G's C.B. (252)	15
24	McMillan (203)	18, 14.5 and 3, 15, 13	48	McIntosh (113)	5 and 5
			62	Cherry (223)	6
			64	Docherty's C.B. (127)	6

4. FUTURE NECESSARY SERVICES

Age at trial	*Case*	*Multiplier*	*Age at trial*	*Case*	*Multiplier*
38	Wall (224)	15	50	Burns (277)	10
41	O'Brien's C.B. (163)	15	58	Kerr (273)	7
41	Low (279)	12	62	Cherry (223)	6

5. FUTURE INABILITY TO RENDER PERSONAL SERVICES

Age at trial	*Case*	*Multiplier*	*Age at trial*	*Case*	*Multiplier*
38	Wall (224)	15	44	G's C.B.(252)	15
41	Low (279)	12			

6. LOSS OF SUPPORT

Age at death	*Case*	*Multiplier*	*Age at death*	*Case*	*Multiplier*
24	McArthur (26)	15	32	Gillan (11)	10
c.26	Wilson (38)	13	32	Rafferty (36)	13
26	Phillips (42)	15	32	Worf (37)	15
28	Harper (19)	14	33	Brown (40)	12

Age at death	Case	Multiplier	Age at death	Case	Multiplier
34	Farrell (24)	9	43	McCuaig (15)	10
34	Cunningham (27)	9	43	Kelly (20)	12
36	Gray (6)	10	44	Little (33)	10.5
37	O'Donnell (1)	10	45	McLaughlin (34)	11
37	McCusker (4)	10	46	Webster (3)	10
37	Clark (30)	13	49	McNeil (2)	10*
37	Campbell (44)	13 and 5	49	Porter (32)	6.5
38	Beggs (45)	14 and 3.8	50	Morris (31)	9
39	Davie (25)	12	c.56	Greenwood (23)	5.5
40	McBeth (22)	14	57	Cameron (17)	6.66
40	Wotherspoon (43)	14*	57	Parker (28)	6
41	Riddell (13)	14	58	Davidson (39)	5 and 6.5
42	Dingwall (29)	13	60	Alexander (16)	4.5
42	Prentice (35)	12	61	Howie (41)	3

7. LOSS OF DECEASED'S SERVICES

Age at death	Case	Multiplier	Age at death	Case	Multiplier
32	Worf (37)	10	37	Campbell (44)	13
33	Brown (40)	11.83	38	Beggs (45)	14

D. INDEX OF LUMP SUM AWARDS FOR LOSS OF FUTURE EARNINGS

* denotes partial award

Age at trial	*Case*	*Amount*
7	Brogan's Tutor (25)	£3,000
9	Steen (7)	£12,000
c.10	Lamb's Tutor (29)	£5,000
c.13	Anderson's Tutor (142)	£4,000
c.18	Spence (133)	£500
21	MacRae (70)	£3,000
c.21	Lees (76)	£4,500
21	Morley (290)	£45,000
22	Kent (154)	£15,000
c.23	Clarke (161)	£1,500
24	Tuttle (72)	£30,000
24	Gibson (141)	£3,000
c.24	Campbell (185)	£750
c.25	Skakle (15)	£1,000 and £3,000
c.25	Gorman (157)	£2,000
25	Duncan (206)	£8,000
25	McCluskey (230)	£750
26	Glasgow (68)	£30,000
26	Sloan (88)	£3,000
c.26	Goldie (106)	£1,200
26	Smith (170)	£15,000
26	McLachlan (198)	£2,500
26	McKenzie (140)	£2,000*
28	Smith (2)	£10,000
29	McGahan (118)	£2,000
29	MacLeod (231)	£18,000
29	Lamont (284)	£5,000*
30	Reilly (147)	£2,000
30	Laidler (153)	£2,000
c.30	Aitken (160)	£1,500
30	McGunnigal (218)	£4,000
30	Paterson (229)	£24,000
31	Allardyce (101)	£2,000*
c.31	McManus (201)	£2,500
c.31	McCutcheon (258)	£500
31	Barrett (73)	£1,000*
c.32	Cumming (123)	£5,000
c.32	Prentice (136)	£5,000
33	Miles (60)	£1,000
33	McMenemy (192)	£8,000
35	Douglas (23)	£3,000
35	Lamb (28)	£850
35	Laing (84)	£7,500
c.36	Hill (199)	£12,000
36	Bonar (270)	£20,000
c.37	Kenny (233)	£7,500
38	Sommerville (245)	£10,000
38	Hughes (189)	£1,000*
c.39	Smith's C.B.(5)	£8,500
39	Marshall (89)	£15,000
c.39	Clark (200)	£6,000
late 30s	Tennant (131)	£3,000
40	O'Neil (175)	£10,000
c.40	Dunn (207)	£12,500
40	Walledge (267)	£4,000
40	Scott (214)	£10,000*
41	Clews (124)	£2,500
41	Baillie (126)	£5,000
c.41	Lennon (168)	£3,000
c.41	Baird (219)	£5,000
42	McHugh (1)	£250
42	Cartledge (21)	£2,000
c.42	Hodge (193)	£7,500
c.42	McIntyre (225)	£5,000*
c.43	Hanlon (54)	£2,000
43	Murray (148)	£6,000*
c.43	Kennedy (280)	£8,500*
c.44	Whitfield (38)	£300
44	Millar (116)	£500
44	Hutchison (119)	£18,000

Age at trial	*Case*	*Amount*	*Age at trial*	*Case*	*Amount*
44	Whyte (145)	£2,000	48	Cole (256)	£2,500
c.44	Lang (152)	£15,000	48	Stuppart (276)	£2,500*
44	McMillan (180)	£12,500	49	McNee (59)	£500
44	Hoey (181)	£6,000	50	Bruce (110)	£2,000
44	Stafford (211)	£12,000	50	Stevenson (132)	£30,000
45	Gallacher (108)	£4,000	51	Shevchuk (46)	£5,690
45	Rennicks (114)	£2,000	51	Lanigan (80)	£1,000
c.45	Hunter (120)	£3,000	c.51	Donaldson (291)	£3,000
45	Harrison (194)	£7,500	52	McKenzie (249)	£15,000
c.45	Lawrie (232)	£1,500	52	Duffy (251)	£15,000
46	Byrnes (34)	£5,000	c.53	Cook (26)	£3,000
c.46	Meek (128)	£4,000	c.53	Ferguson (53)	£1,000
c.46	Young (213)	£2,000	c.53	Watts (217)	£1,750
46	Taggart (261)	£15,000	54	Anderson (111)	£200
46	Fulton (272)	£12,000	c.55	Joliffe (167)	£20,000
47	Howie (95)	£10,000	55	McMahon (253)	£5,000
47	Geddes (158)	£11,400	57	Brown (12)	£300 and £250
47	Robertson (173)	£16,000			
c.48	Ryan (33)	£750	59	Paris (32)	£500
48	Rennie (169)	£2,000	c.59	Murray (210)	£200
48	Hunter (254)	£30,000	60	McKirdy (44)	£1,000

E. INDEX OF AWARDS FOR SERVICES

Description	*Case*	*Amount*
Necessary (past)	Millar (149)	£10
Necessary (past)	McWilliam (150)	£50
Necessary (past)	Harrison (194)	£50
Necessary (past)	Sands (134)	£100
Necessary (past)	Smith (146)	£100
Necessary (past)	Rennie (169)	£100
Necessary (past)	Mitchell (177)	£100
Necessary (past)	Napier (191)	£100
Necessary (past)	Lawrie (232)	£100
Necessary (future)	Williamson (244)	£100
Necessary (future)	Smith (146)	£150
Necessary and Personal (past)	Gripper (183)	£200
Necessary (past)	Lawrie (232)	£200
Necessary (past)	Grant (121)	£250
Personal	McGowan (184)	£250
Necessary (past)	Ballantyne (204)	£250
Necessary (past)	Paterson (229)	£250
Necessary and Personal (past)	Armstrong (242)	£250
Personal (past)	Duffy (259)	£250
Personal (past)	Stuppart (276)	£250
Necessary (past)	McCluskey (230)	£300
Personal (past)	McMillan (180)	£350
Necessary (past)	Prentice (136)	£400
Necessary (past)	Binnie (241)	£400
Necessary (past)	Williamson (244)	£400
Personal (past)	Docherty (271)	£400
Necessary (past)	Paterson (229)	£450
Necessary (past)	Blackhall (278)	£472.50
Necessary (past)	Stark (212)	£500
Necessary (past)	Whyte (145)	£500
Necessary (past)	O'Neil (175)	£500
Necessary and Personal (future)	Reid (255)	£500
Necessary (past)	Cole (256)	£500
Necessary	McGarrigle (263)	£500
Necessary (past)	Higgins (264)	£500
Necessary (past)	Blackhall (278)	£500
Necessary (future)	Taylor (285)	£500

Description	*Case*	*Amount*
Personal (past)	Whyte (289)	£514.80
Personal (future)	Whyte (289)	£514.80
Necessary	Whyte (289)	£650
Necessary (past)	Taylor (285)	£750
Personal	McGarrigle (263)	£750
Necessary (past)	McGowan (184)	£750
Necessary (past)	Watts (217)	£750
Personal (past)	Mitchell (287)	£750
Necessary (past)	Breslin (196)	£800
Necessary (past)	Smith (174)	£1,000
Personal (past and future)	Harrison (194)	£1,000
Personal (past)	Breslin (196)	£1,000
Personal (past)	Clark (200)	£1,000
Necessary (past)	Clark (247)	£1,000
Necessary (past)	Cavanagh (257)	£1,000
Necessary (past)	Blackhall (278)	£1,000
Necessary (future)	Donaldson (291)	£1,000
Necessary (past)	McCarvel (282)	£1,200
Necessary and Personal	MacShannon (220)	£1,250
Personal (future)	Stuppart (276)	£1,250
Necessary (past)	Donaldson (291)	£1,300
Necessary (future)	McKenzie (249)	£1,500
Personal (future)	McKenzie (249)	£1,500
Necessary (past)	Stuppart (276)	£1,500
Necessary and Personal (past)	Reid (255)	£1,750
Necessary (past)	Mitchell (287)	£1,750
Necessary (past)	Kennedy (280)	£1,829
Necessary (past)	Low (279)	£1,965
Necessary	Scott (214)	£2,000
Personal	Scott (214)	£2,000
Necessary (future)	Burns (277)	£2,000
Personal (past)	Taylor (285)	£2,000
Personal (future)	Taylor (285)	£2,000
Necessary (past)	McFarlane (139)	£2,500
Necessary (past)	G's C.B. (252)	£2,500
Necessary (past)	Duffy (259)	£2,500
Necessary (past)	Burns (277)	£2,500
Necessary and Personal	Johnstone (155)	£3,000
Necessary (past)	Farrelly (234)	£3,000

Description	*Case*	*Amount*
Personal (future)	Mitchell (287)	£3,000
Personal (past)	Stirling (286)	£3,200
Necessary (past)	Cherry (223)	£3,202.29
Necessary (future)	Stuppart (276)	£3,500
Personal (past)	Kennedy (280)	£3,658
Necessary (past and future)	Campbell (208)	£4,000
Necessary and Personal (past)	Wall (224)	£4,000
Necessary (future)	McCance (268)	£4,000
Necessary (future)	Low (279)	£4,368
Necessary (past)	Kerr (273)	£4,575
Necessary (past)	Fowler (159)	£5,000
Necessary (past)	G's C.B. (252)	£5,000
Necessary (past)	Stirling (286)	£5,675
Personal (past)	Low (279)	£5,895
Necessary (past)	Howie (166)	£6,810
Necessary (future)	Mitchell (287)	£7,000
Necessary (future)	Stirling (286)	£7,500
Necessary (past)	Myles (228)	£7,800
Necessary (past)	Garland (235)	£8,000
Personal (future)	Stirling (286)	£8,000
Necessary (future)	O'Brien's C.B.(163)	£9,000
Necessary (past)	McMillan (203)	£9,200
Necessary (future)	Garland (235)	£12,000
Personal (future)	Low (279)	£13,104
Necessary (future)	Farrelly (234)	£13,275
Personal	Farrelly (234)	£14,000
Necessary (future)	Cherry (223)	£14,545.44
Necessary and Personal (future)	Wall (224)	£15,000
Necessary (past)	Stevenson (250)	£16,000
Necessary (future)	Kerr (273)	£19,060
Personal (past)	G's C.B. (252)	£20,000
Necessary (future)	McMillan (203)	£23,816
Necessary (future)	O'Connor (265)	£24,000
Necessary (future)	Myles (228)	£25,000
Personal (future)	G's C.B. (252)	£31,770
Necessary (past)	O'Connor (265)	£60,000

APPENDIX VI

RECOVERY OF BENEFITS LEGISLATION

A. THE SOCIAL SECURITY (RECOVERY OF BENEFITS) ACT 1997

ARRANGEMENT OF SECTIONS

Introductory

SECT

1. Cases in which this Act applies.
2. Compensation payments to which this Act applies.
3. "The relevant period".

Certificates of recoverable benefits

4. Applications for certificates of recoverable benefits.
5. Information contained in certificates.

Liability of person paying compensation

6. Liability to pay Secretary of State amount of benefits.
7. Recovery of payments due under section 6.

Reduction of compensation payment

8. Reduction of compensation payment.
9. Section 8: supplementary.

Reviews and appeals

10. Review of certificates of recoverable benefits.
11. Appeals against certificates of recoverable benefits.
12. Reference of questions to medical appeal tribunal.
13. Appeal to Social Security Commissioner.
14. Reviews and appeals: supplementary.

Courts

15. Court orders.
16. Payments into court.
17. Benefits irrelevant to assessment of damages.

Reduction of compensation: complex cases

18. Lump sum and periodical payments.
19. Payments by more than one person.

Miscellaneous

20. Amounts overpaid under section 6.
21. Compensation payments to be disregarded.
22. Liability of insurers.
23. Provision of information.
24. Power to amend Schedule 2.

Provisions relating to Northern Ireland

25. Corresponding provision for Northern Ireland.
26. Residence of the injured person.
27. Jurisdiction of courts.

General

28. The Crown.
29. General interpretation.
30. Regulations and orders.
31. Financial arrangements.
32. Power to make transitional, consequential etc. provisions.
33. Consequential amendments and repeals.
34. Short title, commencement and extent.

SCHEDULES:
Schedule 1— Compensation payments.
Part I— Exempted payments.
Part II— Power to disregard small payments.
Schedule 2— Calculation of compensation payment.
Schedule 3— Consequential amendments.
Schedule 4— Repeals.

An Act to re-state, with amendments, Part IV of the Social Security Administration Act 1992. [19th March 1997]

Cases in which this Act applies

1.—(1) This Act applies in cases where —

(a) a person makes a payment (whether on his own behalf or not) to or in respect of any other person in consequence of any accident, injury or disease suffered by the other, and

(b) any listed benefits have been, or are likely to be, paid to or for the other during the relevant period in respect of the accident, injury or disease.

(2) The reference above to a payment in consequence of any accident, injury or disease is to a payment made—

(a) by or on behalf of a person who is, or is alleged to be, liable to any extent in respect of the accident, injury or disease, or

(b) in pursuance of a compensation scheme for motor accidents;

but does not include a payment mentioned in Part I of Schedule 1.

(3) Subsection (1)(a) applies to a payment made—

(a) voluntarily, or in pursuance of a court order or an agreement, or otherwise, and

(b) in the United Kingdom or elsewhere.

(4) In a case where this Act applies—

(a) the "injured person" is the person who suffered the accident, injury or disease,

(b) the "compensation payment" is the payment within subsection (1)(a), and

(c) "recoverable benefit" is any listed benefit which has been or is likely to be paid as mentioned in subsection (1)(b).

Compensation payments to which this Act applies

2. This Act applies in relation to compensation payments made on or after the day on which this section comes into force, unless they are made in pursuance of a court order or agreement made before that day.

"The relevant period"

3.—(1) In relation to a person ("the claimant") who has suffered any accident, injury or disease, "the relevant period" has the meaning given by the following subsections.

(2) Subject to subsection (4), if it is a case of accident or injury, the relevant period is the period of five years immediately following the day on which the accident or injury in question occurred.

(3) Subject to subsection (4), if it is a case of disease, the relevant period is the period of five years beginning with the date on which the claimant first claims a listed benefit in consequence of the disease.

(4) If at any time before the end of the period referred to in subsection (2) or (3) —

(a) a person makes a compensation payment in final discharge of any claim made by or in respect of the claimant and arising out of the accident, injury or disease, or

(b) an agreement is made under which an earlier compensation payment is treated as having been made in final discharge of any such claim,

the relevant period ends at that time.

Certificates of recoverable benefits

Applications for certificates of recoverable benefits

4.—(1) Before a person ("the compensator") makes a compensation payment he must apply to the Secretary of State for a certificate of recoverable benefits.

(2) Where the compensator applies for a certificate of recoverable benefits, the Secretary of State must —

(a) send to him a written acknowledgement of receipt of his application, and

(b) subject to subsection (7), issue the certificate before the end of the following period.

(3) The period is —

(a) the prescribed period, or

(b) if there is no prescribed period, the period of four weeks;

which begins with the day following the day on which the application is received.

(4) The certificate is to remain in force until the date specified in it for that purpose.

(5) The compensator may apply for fresh certificates from time to time.

(6) Where a certificate of recoverable benefits ceases to be in force, the Secretary of State may issue a fresh certificate without an application for one being made.

(7) Where the compensator applies for a fresh certificate while a certificate ("the existing certificate") remains in force, the Secretary of State must issue the fresh certificate before the end of the following period.

(8) The period is —

(a) the prescribed period, or

(b) if there is no prescribed period, the period of four weeks,

which begins with the day following the day on which the existing certificate ceases to be in force.

(9) For the purposes of this Act, regulations may provide for the day on which an application for a certificate of recoverable benefits is to be treated as received.

Information contained in certificates

5.—(1) A certificate of recoverable benefits must specify, for each recoverable benefit —

(a) the amount which has been or is likely to have been paid on or before a specified date, and

(b) if the benefit is paid or likely to be paid after the specified date, the rate and period for which, and the intervals at which, it is or is likely to be so paid.

(2) In a case where the relevant period has ended before the day on which the Secretary of State receives the application for the certificate, the date specified in the certificate for the purposes of subsection (1) must be the day on which the relevant period ended.

(3) In any other case, the date specified for those purposes must not be earlier than the day on which the Secretary of State received the application.

(4) The Secretary of State may estimate, in such manner as he thinks fit, any of the amounts, rates or periods specified in the certificate.

(5) Where the Secretary of State issues a certificate of recoverable benefits, he must provide the information contained in the certificate to —

(a) the person who appears to him to be the injured person, or

(b) any person who he thinks will receive a compensation payment in respect of the injured person.

(6) A person to whom a certificate of recoverable benefits is issued or who is provided with information under subsection (5) is entitled to particulars of the manner in which any amount, rate or period specified in the certificate has been determined, if he applies to the Secretary of State for those particulars.

Liability of person paying compensation

Liability to pay Secretary of State amount of benefits

6.—(1) A person who makes a compensation payment in any case is liable to pay to the Secretary of State an amount equal to the total amount of the recoverable benefits.

(2) The liability referred to in subsection (1) arises immediately before the compensation payment or, if there is more than one, the first of them is made.

(3) No amount becomes payable under this section before the end of the period of 14 days following the day on which the liability arises.

(4) Subject to subsection (3), an amount becomes payable under this section at the end of the period of 14 days beginning with the day on which a certificate of recoverable benefits is first issued showing that the amount of recoverable benefit to which it relates has been or is likely to have been paid before a specified date.

Recovery of payments due under section 6

7.—(1) This section applies where a person has made a compensation payment but —

(a) has not applied for a certificate of recoverable benefits, or

(b) has not made a payment to the Secretary of State under section 6 before the end of the period allowed under that section.

(2) The Secretary of State may —

(a) issue the person who made the compensation payment with a certificate of recoverable benefits, if none has been issued, or

(b) issue him with a copy of the certificate of recoverable benefits or (if more than one has been issued) the most recent one,

and (in either case) issue him with a demand that payment of any amount due under section 6 be made immediately.

(3) The Secretary of State may, in accordance with subsections (4) and (5), recover the amount for which a demand for payment is made under subsection (2) from the person who made the compensation payment.

(4) If the person who made the compensation payment resides or carries on business in England and Wales and a county court so orders, any amount recoverable under subsection (3) is recoverable by execution issued from the county court or otherwise as if it were payable under an order of that court.

(5) If the person who made the payment resides or carries on business in Scotland, any amount recoverable under subsection (3) may be enforced in like manner as an extract registered decree arbitral bearing a warrant for execution issued by the sheriff court of any sheriffdom in Scotland.

(6) A document bearing a certificate which —

(a) is signed by a person authorised to do so by the Secretary of State, and

(b) states that the document, apart from the certificate, is a record of the amount recoverable under subsection (3),

is conclusive evidence that that amount is so recoverable.

(7) A certificate under subsection (6) purporting to be signed by a person authorised to do so by the Secretary of State is to be treated as so signed unless the contrary is proved.

Reduction of compensation payment

Reduction of compensation payment

8.—(1) This section applies in a case where, in relation to any head of compensation listed in column 1 of Schedule 2—

(a) any of the compensation payment is attributable to that head, and

(b) any recoverable benefit is shown against that head in column 2 of the Schedule.

(2) In such a case, any claim of a person to receive the compensation payment is to be treated for all purposes as discharged if —

(a) he is paid the amount (if any) of the compensation payment calculated in accordance with this section, and

(b) if the amount of the compensation payment so calculated is nil, he is given a statement saying so by the person who (apart from this section) would have paid the gross amount of the compensation payment.

(3) For each head of compensation listed in column 1 of the Schedule for which paragraphs (a) and (b) of subsection (1) are met, so much of the gross amount of the compensation payment as is attributable to that head is to be reduced (to nil, if necessary) by deducting the amount of the recoverable benefit or, as the case may be, the aggregate amount of the recoverable benefits shown against it.

(4) Subsection (3) is to have effect as if a requirement to reduce a payment by deducting an amount which exceeds that payment were a requirement to reduce that payment to nil.

(5) The amount of the compensation payment calculated in accordance with this action is —

(a) the gross amount of the compensation payment,

less

(b) the sum of the reductions made under subsection (3),

(and, accordingly, the amount may be nil).

Section 8: supplementary

9.—(1) A person who makes a compensation payment calculated in accordance with section 8 must inform the person to whom the payment is made —

(a) that the payment has been so calculated, and

(b) of the date for payment by reference to which the calculation has been made.

(2) If the amount of a compensation payment calculated in accordance with section 8 is nil, a person giving a statement saying so is to be treated for the purposes of this Act as making a payment within section 1(1)(a) on the day on which he gives the statement.

(3) Where a person —

(a) makes a compensation payment calculated in accordance with section 8, and

(b) if the amount of the compensation payment so calculated is nil, gives a statement saying so,

he is to be treated, for the purpose of determining any rights and liabilities in respect of contribution or indemnity, as having paid the gross amount of the compensation payment.

(4) For the purposes of this Act —

(a) the gross amount of the compensation payment is the amount of the compensation payment apart from section 8, and

(b) the amount of any recoverable benefit is the amount determined in accordance with the certificate of recoverable benefits.

Reviews and appeals

Review of certificates of recoverable benefits

10.—(1) The Secretary of State may review any certificate of recoverable benefits if he is satisfied —

(a) that it was issued in ignorance of, or was based on a mistake as to, a material fact, or

(b) that a mistake (whether in computation or otherwise) has occurred in its preparation.

(2) On a review under this section the Secretary of State may either —

(a) confirm the certificate, or

(b) (subject to subsection (3)) issue a fresh certificate containing such variations as he considers appropriate.

(3) The Secretary of State may not vary the certificate so as to increase the total amount of the recoverable benefits unless it appears to him that the variation is required as a result of the person who applied for the certificate supplying him with incorrect or insufficient information.

Appeals against certificates of recoverable benefits

11.—(1) An appeal against a certificate of recoverable benefits may be made on the ground—

(a) that any amount, rate or period specified in the certificate is incorrect, or

(b) that listed benefits which have been, or are likely to be, paid otherwise than in respect of the accident, injury or disease in question have been brought into account.

(2) An appeal under this section may be made by —

(a) the person who applied for the certificate of recoverable benefits, or

(b) (in a case where the amount of the compensation payment has been calculated under section 8) the injured person or other person to whom the payment is made.

(3) No appeal may be made under this section until —

(a) the claim giving rise to the compensation payment has been finally disposed of, and

(b) the liability under section 6 has been discharged.

(4) For the purposes of subsection (3)(a), if an award of damages in respect of a claim has been made under or by virtue of —

(a) section 32A(2)(a) of the Supreme Court Act 1981,

(b) section 12(2)(a) of the Administration of Justice Act 1982, or

(c) section 51(2)(a) of the County Courts Act 1984,

(orders for provisional damages in personal injury cases), the claim is to be treated as having been finally disposed of.

(5) Regulations may make provision—

(a) as to the manner in which, and the time within which, appeals under this section may be made,

(b) as to the procedure to be followed where such an appeal is made, and

(c) for the purpose of enabling any such appeal to be treated as an application for review under section 10.

(6) Regulations under subsection (5)(c) may (among other things) provide that the circumstances in which a review may be carried out are not to be restricted to those specified in section 10(1).

Reference of questions to medical appeal tribunal

12.—(1) The Secretary of State must refer to a medical appeal tribunal any question mentioned in subsection (2) arising for determination on an appeal under section 11.

(2) The questions are any concerning—

(a) any amount, rate or period specified in the certificate of recoverable benefits, or

(b) whether listed benefits which have been, or are likely to be, paid otherwise than in respect of the accident, injury or disease in question have been brought into account.

(3) In determining any question referred to it under subsection (1), the tribunal must take into account any decision of a court relating to the same, or any similar, issue arising in connection with the accident, injury or disease in question.

(4) On a reference under subsection (1) a medical appeal tribunal may either—

(a) confirm the amounts, rates and periods specified in the certificate of recoverable benefits, or

(b) specify any variations which are to be made on the issue of a fresh certificate under subsection (5).

(5) When the Secretary of State has received the decisions of the tribunal on the questions referred to it under subsection (1), he must in accordance with those decisions either —

(a) confirm the certificate against which the appeal was brought, or

(b) issue a fresh certificate.

(6) Regulations may make provision —

(a) as to the manner in which, and the time within which, a reference under subsection (1) is to be made, and

(b) as to the procedure to be followed where such a reference is made.

(7) Regulations under subsection (6)(b) may (among other things) provide for the non-disclosure of medical advice or medical evidence given or submitted following a reference under subsection (1).

(8) In this section "medical appeal tribunal" means a medical appeal tribunal constituted under section 50 of the Social Security Administration Act 1992.

Appeal to Social Security Commissioner

13.—(1) An appeal may be made to a Commissioner against any decision of a medical appeal tribunal under section 12 on the ground that the decision was erroneous in point of law.

(2) An appeal under this section may be made by—

(a) the Secretary of State,

(b) the person who applied for the certificate of recoverable benefits, or

(c) (in a case where the amount of the compensation payment has been calculated in accordance with section 8) the injured person or other person to whom the payment is made.

(3) Subsections (7) to (10) of section 23 of the Social Security Administration Act 1992 apply to appeals under this section as they apply to appeals under that section.

(4) In this section "Commissioner" has the same meaning as in the Social Security Administration Act 1992 (see section 191).

Reviews and appeals: supplementary

14.—(1) This section applies in cases where a fresh certificate of recoverable benefits is issued as a result of a review under section 10 or an appeal under section 11.

(2) If—

(a) a person has made one or more payments to the Secretary of State under section 6, and

(b) in consequence of the review or appeal, it appears that the total amount paid is more than the amount that ought to have been paid,

regulations may provide for the Secretary of State to pay the difference to that person, or to the person to whom the compensation payment is made, or partly to one and partly to the other.

(3) If —

(a) a person has made one or more payments to the Secretary of State under section 6, and

(b) in consequence of the review or appeal, it appears that the total amount paid is less than the amount that ought to have been paid,

regulations may provide for that person to pay the difference to the Secretary of State.

(4) Regulations under this section may provide —

(a) for the re-calculation in accordance with section 8 of the amount of any compensation payment,

(b) for giving credit for amounts already paid, and

(c) for the payment by any person of any balance or the recovery from any person of any excess,

and may provide for any matter by modifying this Act.

Courts

Court orders

15.—(1) This section applies where a court makes an order for a compensation payment to be made in any case, unless the order is made with the consent of the injured person and the person by whom the payment is to be made.

(2) The court must, in the case of each head of compensation listed in column 1 of Schedule 2 to which any of the compensation payment is attributable, specify in the order the amount of the compensation payment which is attributable to that head.

Payments into court

16.—(1) Regulations may make provision (including provision modifying this Act) for any case in which a payment into court is made.

(2) The regulations may (among other things) provide —

(a) for the making of a payment into court to be treated in prescribed circumstances as the making of a compensation payment,

(b) for application for, and issue of, certificates of recoverable benefits, and

(c) for the relevant period to be treated as ending on a date determined in accordance with the regulations.

(3) Rules of court may make provision governing practice and procedure in such cases.

(4) This section does not extend to Scotland.

Benefits irrelevant to assessment of damages

17. In assessing damages in respect of any accident, injury or disease, the amount of any listed benefits paid or likely to be paid is to be disregarded.

Reduction of compensation: complex cases

Lump sum and periodical payments

18.—(1) Regulations may make provision (including provision modifying this Act) for any case in which two or more compensation payments in the form of lump sums are made by the same person to or in respect of the injured person in consequence of the same accident, injury or disease.

(2) The regulations may (among other things) provide —

(a) for the re-calculation in accordance with section 8 of the amount of any compensation payment,

(b) for giving credit for amounts already paid, and

(c) for the payment by any person of any balance or the recovery from any person of any excess.

(3) For the purposes of subsection (2), the regulations may provide for the gross amounts of the compensation payments to be aggregated and for —

(a) the aggregate amount to be taken to be the gross amount of the compensation payment for the purposes of section 8,

(b) so much of the aggregate amount as is attributable to a head of compensation listed in column 1 of Schedule 2 to be taken to be the part of the gross amount which is attributable to that head;

and for the amount of any recoverable benefit shown against any head in column 2 of that Schedule to be taken to be the amount determined in accordance with the most recent certificate of recoverable benefits.

(4) Regulations may make provision (including provision modifying this Act) for any case in which, in final settlement of the injured person's claim, an agreement is entered into for the making of —

(a) periodical compensation payments (whether of an income or capital nature), or

(b) periodical compensation payments and lump sum compensation payments.

(5) Regulations made by virtue of subsection (4) may (among other things) provide —

(a) for the relevant period to be treated as ending at a prescribed time,

(b) for the person who is to make the payments under the agreement to be treated for the purposes of this Act as if he had made a single compensation payment on a prescribed date.

(6) A periodical payment may be a compensation payment for the purposes of this section even though it is a small payment (as defined in Part II of Schedule 1).

Payments by more than one person

19.—(1) Regulations may make provision (including provision modifying this Act) for any case in which two or more persons ("the compensators") make compensation payments to or in respect of the same injured person in consequence of the same accident, injury or disease.

(2) In such a case, the sum of the liabilities of the compensators under section 6 is not to exceed the total amount of the recoverable benefits, and the regulations may provide for determining the respective liabilities under that section of each of the compensators.

(3) The regulations may (among other things) provide in the case of each compensator —

- (a) for determining or re-determining the part of the recoverable benefits which may be taken into account in his case,
- (b) for calculating or re-calculating in accordance with section 8 the amount of any compensation payment,
- (c) for giving credit for amounts already paid, and
- (d) for the payment by any person of any balance or the recovery from any person of any excess.

Miscellaneous

Amounts overpaid under section 6

20.—(1) Regulations may make provision (including provision modifying this Act) for cases where a person has paid to the Secretary of State under section 6 any amount ("the amount of the overpayment") which he was not liable to pay.

(2) The regulations may provide —

- (a) for the Secretary of State to pay the amount of the overpayment to that person, or to the person to whom the compensation payment is made, or partly to one and partly to the other, or
- (b) for the receipt by the Secretary of State of the amount of the overpayment to be treated as the recovery of that amount.

(3) Regulations made by virtue of subsection (2)(b) are to have effect in spite of anything in section 71 of the Social Security Administration Act 1992 (overpayments – general).

(4) The regulations may also (among other things) provide —

- (a) for the re-calculation in accordance with section 8 of the amount of any compensation payment,
- (b) for giving credit for amounts already paid, and
- (c) for the payment by any person of any balance or the recovery from any person of any excess.

(5) This section does not apply in a case where section 14 applies.

Compensation payments to be disregarded

21.—(1) If, when a compensation payment is made, the first and second conditions are met, the payment is to be disregarded for the purposes of sections 6 and 8.

(2) The first condition is that the person making the payment —

(a) has made an application for a certificate of recoverable benefits which complies with subsection (3), and

(b) has in his possession a written acknowledgment of the receipt of his application.

(3) An application complies with this subsection if it —

(a) accurately states the prescribed particulars relating to the injured person and the accident, injury or disease in question, and

(b) specifies the name and address of the person to whom the certificate is to be sent.

(4) The second condition is that the Secretary of State has not sent the certificate to the person, at the address, specified in the application, before the end of the period allowed under section 4.

(5) In any case where —

(a) by virtue of subsection (1), a compensation payment is disregarded for the purposes of sections 6 and 8, but

(b) the person who made the compensation payment nevertheless makes a payment to the Secretary of State for which (but for subsection (1)) he would be liable under section 6,

subsection (1) is to cease to apply in relation to the compensation payment.

(6) If, in the opinion of the Secretary of State, circumstances have arisen which adversely affect normal methods of communication —

(a) he may by order provide that subsection (1) is not to apply during a specified period not exceeding three months, and

(b) he may continue any such order in force for further periods not exceeding three months at a time.

Liability of insurers

22.—(1) If a compensation payment is made in a case where —

(a) a person is liable to any extent in respect of the accident, injury or disease, and

(b) the liability is covered to any extent by a policy of insurance,

the policy is also to be treated as covering any liability of that person under section 6.

(2) Liability imposed on the insurers by subsection (1) cannot be excluded or restricted.

(3) For that purpose excluding or restricting liability includes —

(a) making the liability or its enforcement subject to restrictive or onerous conditions,

(b) excluding or restricting any right or remedy in respect of the liability, or subjecting a person to any prejudice in consequence of his pursuing any such right or remedy, or

(c) excluding or restricting rules of evidence or procedure.

(4) Regulations may in prescribed cases limit the amount of the liability imposed on the insurer by subsection (1).

(5) This section applies to policies of insurance issued before (as well as those issued after) its coming into force.

(6) References in this section to policies of insurance and their issue include references to contracts of insurance and their making.

Provision of information

23.—(1) Where compensation is sought in respect of any accident, injury or disease suffered by any person ("the injured person"), the following persons must give the Secretary of State the prescribed information about the injured person —

(a) anyone who is, or is alleged to be, liable in respect of the accident, injury or disease, and

(b) anyone acting on behalf of such a person.

(2) A person who receives or claims a listed benefit which is or is likely to be paid in respect of an accident, injury or disease suffered by him, must give the Secretary of State the prescribed information about the accident, injury or disease.

(3) Where a person who has received a listed benefit dies, the duty in subsection (2) is imposed on his personal representative.

(4) Any person who makes a payment (whether on his own behalf or not) —

(a) in consequence of, or

(b) which is referable to any costs (in Scotland, expenses) incurred by reason of,

any accident, injury or disease, or any damage to property, must, if the Secretary of State requests him in writing to do so, give the Secretary of State such particulars relating to the size and composition of the payment as are specified in the request.

(5) The employer of a person who suffers or has suffered an accident, injury or disease, and anyone who has been the employer of such a person at any time during the relevant period, must give the Secretary of State the prescribed information about the payment of statutory sick pay in respect of that person.

(6) In subsection (5) "employer" has the same meaning as it has in Part XI of the Social Security Contributions and Benefits Act 1992.

(7) A person who is required to give information under this section must do so in the prescribed manner, at the prescribed place and within the prescribed time.

(8) Section 1 does not apply in relation to this section.

Power to amend Schedule 2

24.—(1) The Secretary of State may by regulations amend Schedule 2.

(2) A statutory instrument which contains such regulations shall not be made unless a draft of the instrument has been laid before and approved by resolution of each House of Parliament.

Provisions relating to Northern Ireland

Corresponding provision for Northern Ireland

25. An order in Council made under paragraph 1(1)(b) of Schedule 1 to the Northern Ireland Act 1974 which contains a statement that it is made only for purposes corresponding to those of the provisions of this Act —

- (a) shall not be subject to sub-paragraphs (4) and (5) of paragraph 1 of that Schedule (affirmative resolution of both Houses of Parliament), but
- (b) shall be subject to annulment in pursuance of a resolution of either House of Parliament.

Residence of the injured person

26.—(1) In a case where this Act applies, if the injured person's address is in Northern ireland —

- (a) the person making the compensation payment must apply for a certificate under the Northern Ireland provisions, and may not make any separate application for a certificate of recoverable benefits,
- (b) any certificate issued as a result under the Northern Ireland provisions —
  - (i) is to be treated as including a certificate of recoverable benefits,
  - (ii) must state that it is to be so treated, and
  - (iii) must state that any payment required to be made to the Secretary of State under this Act is to be made to the Northern Ireland Department as his agent, and
- (c) any payment made pursuant to a certificate so issued is to be applied —
  - (i) first towards discharging the liability of the person making the compensation payment under the Northern Ireland provisions, and
  - (ii) then, as respects any remaining balance, towards discharging his liability under section 6.

(2) In a case where the Northern Ireland provisions apply, if the injured person's address is in any part of Great Britain —

(a) the person making the compensation payment must apply for a certificate of recoverable benefits, and may not make any separate application for a certificate under the Northern Ireland provisions,

(b) any certificate of recoverable benefits issued as a result —

  (i) is to be treated as including a certificate under the Northern Ireland provisions,

  (ii) must state that it is to be so treated, and

  (iii) must state that any payment required to be made to the Northern Ireland Department under the Northern Ireland provisions is to be made to the Secretary of State as its agent, and

(c) any payment made pursuant to a certificate of recoverable benefits so issued is to be applied —

  (i) first towards discharging the liability of the person making the compensation payment under section 6, and

  (ii) then, as respects any remaining balance, towards discharging his liability under the Northern Ireland provisions.

(3) In this section —

(a) "the injured person's address" is the address first notified in writing to the person making the payment by or on behalf of the injured person as his residence (or, if he has died, by or on behalf of the person entitled to receive the compensation payment as the injured person's last residence),

(b) "Northern Ireland Department" means the Department of Health and Social Services for Northern Ireland,

(c) "the Northern Ireland provisions" means —

  (i) any legislation corresponding to this Act (other than this section and section 27) and having effect in Northern Ireland, and

  (ii) this section and section 27,

and

(d) any reference in relation to the Northern Ireland provisions to —

  (i) the injured person, means the injured person within the meaning of those provisions,

  (ii) a certificate, means a certificate under those provisions corresponding to the certificate of recoverable benefits, and

  (iii) a compensation payment, means a compensation payment within the meaning of those provisions.

Jurisdiction of courts

27.—(1) In a case where this Act applies, if immediately before making a compensation payment a person —

(a) is not resident and does not have a place of business in Great Britain, but

(b) is resident or has a place of business in Northern Ireland,

subsections (4) and (5) of section 7 apply in relation to him as if at that time he were resident or had a place of business in the relevant part of Great Britain.

(2) In a case where the Northern Ireland provisions apply, if immediately before making a compensation payment a person —

(a) is not resident and does not have a place of business in Northern Ireland, but

(b) is resident or has a place of business in any part of Great Britain,

any provision of the Northern Ireland provisions corresponding to subsection (4) or (5) of section 7 applies in relation to him as if at that time he were resident or had a place of business in Northern Ireland.

(3) In this section —

(a) "the relevant part of Great Britain" means —

(i) the part of Great Britain in which the injured person is or was most recently resident (as determined by any written statement given to the person making the payment by or on behalf of the injured person or, if he has died, by or on behalf of the person entitled to receive the compensation payment), or

(ii) if no such statement has been given, such part of Great Britain as may be prescribed, and

(b) "the Northern Ireland provisions" and references to compensation payments in relation to such provisions have the same meaning as in section 26.

General

The Crown

28. This Act applies to the Crown.

General interpretation

29. In this Act —

"benefit" means any benefit under the Social Security Contributions and Benefits Act 1992, a jobseeker's allowance or mobility allowance, "compensation scheme for motor accidents" means any scheme or arrangement under which funds are available for the payment of compensation in respect of motor accidents caused, or alleged to have been caused, by uninsured or unidentified persons,

"listed benefit" means a benefit listed in column 2 of Schedule 2,

"payment" means payment in money or money's worth, and related expressions are to be interpreted accordingly,

"prescribed" means prescribed by regulations, and

"regulations" means regulations made by the Secretary of State.

Regulations and orders

30.—(1) Any power under this Act to make regulations or an order is exercisable by statutory instrument.

(2) A statutory instrument containing regulations or an order under this Act (other than regulations under section 24 or an order under section 34) shall be subject to annulment in pursuance of a resolution of either House of Parliament.

(3) Regulations under section 20, under section 24 amending the list of benefits in column 2 of Schedule 2 or under paragraph 9 of Schedule 1 may not be made without the consent of the Treasury.

(4) Subsections (4), (5), (6) and (9) of section 189 of the Social Security Administration Act 1992 (regulations and orders – general) apply for the purposes of this Act as they apply for the purposes of that.

Financial arrangements

31.—(1) There are to be paid out of the National Insurance Fund any expenses of the Secretary of State in making payments under section 14 or 20 to the extent that he estimates that those payments relate to sums paid out of that Fund.

(2) There are to be paid out of money provided by Parliament —

(a) any expenses of the Secretary of State in making payments under section 14 or 20 to the extent that he estimates that those payments relate to sums paid out of the Consolidated Fund, and

(b) (subject to subsection (1)) any other expenses of the Secretary of State incurred in consequence of this Act.

(3) Any sums paid to the Secretary of State under section 6 or 14 are to be paid —

(a) into the Consolidated Fund, to the extent that the Secretary of State estimates that the sums relate to payments out of money provided by Parliament, and
(b) into the National Fund, to the extent that he estimates that they relate to payments out of that Fund.

Power to make transitional, consequential etc. provisions

32.—(1) Regulations may make such transitional and consequential provisions, and such savings, as the Secretary of State considers necessary or expedient in preparation for, in connection with, or in consequence of —

(a) the coming into force of any provision of this Act, or
(b) the operation of any enactment repealed or amended by a provision of this Act during any period when the repeal or amendment is not wholly in force.

(2) Regulations under this section may (among other things) provide —

(a) for compensation payments in relation to which, by virtue of section 2, this Act does not apply to be treated as payments in relation to which this act applies,
(b) for compensation payments in relation to which, by virtue of section 2, this Act applies to be treated as payments in relation to which this Act does not apply, and
(c) for the modification of any enactment contained in this Act or referred to in subsection (1)(b) in its application to any compensation payment.

Consequential amendments and repeals

33.—(1) Schedule 3 (which makes consequential amendments) is to have effect.

(2) The enactments shown in Schedule 4 are repealed to the extent specified in the third column.

Short title, commencement and extent

34.—(1) This Act may be cited as the Social Security (Recovery of Benefits) Act 1997.

(2) Sections 1 to 24, 26 to 28 and 33 are to come into force on such day as the Secretary of State may by order appoint, and different days may be appointed for different purposes.

(3) Apart from sections 25 to 27, section 33 so far as it relates to any enactment which extends to Northern Ireland, and this section this Act does not extend to Northern Ireland.

SCHEDULES

Section 1

SCHEDULE 1

Compensation payments

Part I

Exempted payments

1. Any small payment (defined in Part II of this Schedule).

2. Any payment made to or for the injured person under section 35 of the Powers of Criminal Courts Act 1973 or section 249 of the Criminal Procedure (Scotland) Act 1995 (compensation orders against convicted persons).

3. Any payment made in the exercise of a discretion out of property held subject to a trust in a case where no more than 50 per cent by value of the capital contributed to the trust was directly or indirectly provided by persons who are, or are alleged to be, liable in respect of —

(a) the accident, injury or disease suffered by the injured person, or

(b) the same or any connected accident, injury or disease suffered by another.

4. Any payment made out of property held for the purposes of any prescribed trust (whether the payment also falls within paragraph 3 or not).

5. Any payment made to the injured person by an insurance company within the meaning of the Insurance Companies Act 1982 under the terms of any contract of insurance entered into between the injured person and the company before —

(a) the date on which the injured person first claims a listed benefit in consequence of the disease in question, or

(b) the occurrence of the accident or injury in question.

6. Any redundancy payment falling to be taken into account in the assessment of damages in respect of an accident, injury or disease.

7. So much of any payment as is referable to costs.

8. Any prescribed payment.

Part II

Power to disregard small payments

9.—(1) Regulations may make provision for compensation payments to be disregarded for the purposes of sections 6 and 8 in prescribed cases where the amount of the compensation payment, or the aggregate amount of two or more connected compensation payments, does not exceed the prescribed sum.

(2) A compensation payment disregarded by virtue of this paragraph is referred to in paragraph 1 as a "small payment",

(3) For the purposes of this paragraph —

(a) two or more compensation payments are "connected" if each is made to or in respect of the same injured person and in respect of the same accident, injury or disease, and

(b) any reference to a compensation payment is a reference to a payment which would be such a payment apart from paragraph 1.

Section 8

SCHEDULE 2

CALCULATION OF COMPENSATION PAYMENT

(1) *Head of compensation*	(2) *Benefit*
1. Compensation for earnings lost during the relevant period	Disability working allowance Disablement pension payable under section 103 of the 1992 Act Incapacity benefit Income support Invalidity pension and allowance Jobseeker's allowance Reduced earnings allowance Severe disablement allowance Sickness benefit Statutory sick pay Unemployability supplement Unemployment benefit
2. Compensation for cost of care incurred during the relevant period	Attendance allowance Care component of disability living allowance Disablement pension increase payable under section 104 or 105 of the 1992 Act
3. Compensation for loss of mobility during the relevant period	Mobility allowance Mobility component of disability living allowance

NOTES

1.—(1) References to incapacity benefit, invalidity pension and allowance, severe disablement allowance, sickness benefit and unemployment benefit also include any income support paid with each of those benefits on the same instrument of payment or paid concurrently with each of those benefits by means of an instrument for benefit payment.

(2) For the purpose of this Note, income support includes personal expenses addition, special transitional additions and transitional addition as defined in the Income Support (Transitional) Regulations 1987.

2.—Any reference to statutory sick pay —

(a) includes only 80 per cent of payments made between 6th April 1991 and 5th April 1994, and

(b) does not include payments made on or after 6th April 1994.

3.—In this Schedule "the 1992 Act" means the Social Security Contributions and Benefits Act 1992.

[remaining schedules not reproduced]

B. THE SOCIAL SECURITY (RECOVERY OF BENEFITS) REGULATIONS 1997

Made	*10th September 1997*
Laid before Parliament	*15th September 1997*
Coming into force	*6th October 1997*

The Secretary of State for Social Security, in exercise of the powers conferred by section 189(4), (5) and (6) of the Social Security Administration Act 1992 and sections 4(9), 14(2), (3) and (4), 16(1) and (2), 18, 19, 21(3), 23(1), (2), (5) and (7), 29 and 32 of, and paragraphs 4 and 8 of Schedule 1 to, the Social Security (Recovery of Benefits) Act 1997, and of all other powers enabling her in that behalf, hereby makes the following Regulations:

Citation, commencement and interpretation

1.—(1) These Regulations may be cited as the Social Security (Recovery of Benefits) Regulations 1997 and shall come into force on 6th October 1997.

(2) In these Regulations —

"the 1992 Act" means the Social Security Administration Act 1992;

"the 1997 Act" means the Social Security (Recovery of Benefits) Act 1997;

"commencement day" means the day these Regulations come into force;

"compensator" means a person making a compensation payment;

"Compensation Recovery Unit" means the Compensation Recovery Unit of the Department of Social Security at Reyrolle Building, Hebburn, Tyne and Wear NE31 1XB.

(3) A reference in these Regulations to a numbered section or Schedule is a reference, unless the context otherwise requires, to that section of or Schedule to the 1997 Act.

Exempted trusts and payments

2.—(1) The following trusts are prescribed for the purposes of paragraph 4 of Schedule 1:

(a) the Macfarlane Trust established on 10th March 1988 partly out of funds provided by the Secretary of State to the

Haemophilia Society for the relief of poverty or distress among those suffering from haemophilia;

(b) the Macfarlane (Special Payments) Trust established on 29th January 1990 partly out of funds provided by the Secretary of State, for the benefit of certain persons suffering from haemophilia;

(c) the Macfarlane (Special Payments) (No. 2) Trust established on 3rd May 1991 partly out of funds provided by the Secretary of State for the benefit of certain persons suffering from haemophilia and other beneficiaries;

(d) the Eileen Trust established on 29th March 1993 but out of funds provided by the Secretary of State for the benefit of persons eligible for payment in accordance with its provisions.

(2) The following payments are prescribed for the purposes of paragraph 8 of Schedule 1:

(a) any payment to the extent that it is made —
  (i) in consequence of an action under the Fatal Accidents Act 1976; or
  (ii) in circumstances where, had an action been brought, it would have been brought under that Act;

(b) any payment to the extent that it is made in respect of a liability arising by virtue of section 1 of the Damages (Scotland) Act 1976;

(c) any payment made under the Vaccine Damage Payments Act 1979 to or in respect of the injured person;

(d) any award of compensation made to or in respect of the injured person under the Criminal Injuries Compensation Act 1995 or by the Criminal Injuries Compensation Board under the Criminal Injuries Compensation Scheme 1990 or any earlier scheme;

(e) any compensation payment made by British Coal in accordance with the NCB Pneumoconiosis Compensation Scheme set out in the Schedule to an agreement made on the 13th September 1974 between the National Coal Board, the National Union of Mine Workers, the National Association of Colliery Overmen Deputies and Shot-firers and the British Association of Colliery Management;

(f) any payment made to the injured person in respect of sensorineural hearing loss where the loss is less than 50 dB in one or both ears;

(g) any contractual amount paid to an employee by an employer of his in respect of a period of incapacity of work;

(h) any payment made under the National Health Service (Injury Benefits) Regulations 1995 or the National Health Service (Scotland) (Injury Benefits) Regulations 1974;

(i) any payment made by or on behalf of the Secretary of State for the benefit of persons eligible for payment in accordance with the provisions of a scheme established by him on 24th April 1992 or, in Scotland, on 10th April 1992.

Information to be provided by the compensator

3. The following information is prescribed for the purposes of section 23(1):

(a) the full name and address of the injured person;
(b) where known, the date of birth or national insurance number of that person, or both if both are known;
(c) where the liability arises, or is alleged to arise, in respect of an accident or injury, the date of the accident or injury;
(d) the nature of the accident, injury or disease; and
(e) where known, and where the relevant period may include a period prior to 6th April 1994, whether, at the time of the accident or injury or diagnosis of the disease, the person was employed under a contract of service, and, if he was, the name and address of his employer at that time and the person's payroll number.

Information to be provided by the injured person

4. The following information is prescribed for the purposes of section 23(2):

(a) whether the accident, injury or disease resulted from any action taken by another person, or from any failure of another person to act, and, if so, the full name and address of that other person;
(b) whether the injured person has claimed or may claim a compensation payment, and, if so, the full name and address of the person against whom the claim was or may be made;
(c) the amount of any compensation payment and the date on which it was made;
(d) the listed benefits claimed, and for each benefit the date from which it was first claimed and the amount received in the period beginning with that date and ending with the date the information is sent;
(e) in the case of a person who has received statutory sick pay during the relevant period and prior to 6th April 1994, the name and address of any employer who made those payments to him during the relevant period and the dates the employment with that employer began and ended; and
(f) any changes in the medical diagnosis relating to the condition arising from the accident, injury or disease.

Information to be provided by the employer

5. The following information is prescribed for the purposes of section 23(5):

- (a) the amount of any statutory sick pay the employer has paid to the injured person since the first day of the relevant period and before 6th April 1994;
- (b) the date the liability to pay such statutory sick pay first arose and the rate at which it was payable;
- (c) the date on which such liability terminated; and
- (d) the causes of incapacity for work during any period of entitlement to statutory sick pay during the relevant period and prior to 6th April 1994.

Provision of information

6. A person required to give information to the Secretary of State under regulations 3 to 5 shall do so by sending it to the Compensation Recovery Unit not later than 14 days after —

- (a) where he is a person to whom regulation 3 applies, the date on which he receives a claim for compensation from the injured person in respect of the accident, injury or disease;
- (b) where he is a person to whom regulation 4 or 5 applies, the date on which the Secretary of State requests the information from him.

Application for a certificate of recoverable benefits

7.—(1) The following particulars are prescribed for the purposes of section 21(3)(a) (particulars to be included in an application for a certificate of recoverable benefits):

- (a) the full name and address of the injured person;
- (b) the date of birth and, where known, the national insurance number of that person;
- (c) where the liability arises or is alleged to arise in respect of an accident of injury, the date of the accident or injury;
- (d) the nature of the accident, injury or disease;
- (c) where the person liable, or alleged to be liable, in respect of the accident, injury or disease, is the employer of the injured person, or has been such an employer, the information prescribed by regulation 5.

(2) An application for a certificate of recoverable benefits is to be treated for the purposes of the 1997 Act as received by the Secretary of State on the day on which it is received by the Compensation Recovery Unit, or if the application is received after normal business hours, or on a day which is not a normal business day at that office, on the next such day.

Payments into court

8.—(1) Subject to the provisions of this regulation, where a party to an action makes a payment into court which, had it been paid directly to another party to the action ("the relevant party"), would have constituted a compensation payment —

(a) the making of that payment shall be treated for the purposes of the 1997 Act as the making of a compensation payment;
(b) a current certificate of recoverable benefits shall be lodged with the payment; and
(c) where the payment is calculated under section 8, the compensator must give the relevant party the information specified in section 9(1), instead of the person to whom the payment is made.

(2) The liability under section 6(1) to pay an amount equal to the total amount of the recoverable benefits shall not arise until the person making the payment into court has been notified that the whole or any part of the payment into court has been paid out of court to or for the relevant party.

(3) Where a payment into court in satisfaction of his claim is accepted by the relevant party in the initial period, then as respects the compensator in question, the relevant period shall be taken to have ended, if it has not done so already, on the day on which the payment into court (or if there were two or more such payments, the last of them) was made.

(4) Where, after the expiry of the initial period, the payment into court is accepted in satisfaction of the relevant party's claim by consent between the parties, the relevant period shall end, if it has not done so already, on the date on which application to the court for the payment is made.

(5) Where, after the expiry of the initial period, payment out of court is made wholly or partly to or for the relevant party in accordance with an order of the court and in satisfaction of his claim, the relevant period shall end, if it has not done so already, on the date of that order.

(6) In paragraphs (3), (4) and (5), "the initial period" means the period of 21 days after the receipt by the relevant party to the action of notice of the payment into court having been made.

(7) Where a payment into court is paid out wholly to or for the party who made the payment (otherwise than to or for the relevant party to the action) the making of the payment into court shall cease to be regarded as the making of a compensation payment.

(8) A current certificate of recoverable benefits in paragraph (1) means one that is in force as described in section 4(4).

Reduction of compensation: complex cases

9.—(1) This regulation applies where —

(a) a compensation payment in the form of a lump sum (an "earlier payment") has been made to or in respect of the injured person; and

(b) subsequently another such payment (a "later payment") is made to or in respect of the same injured person in consequence of the same accident, injury or disease.

(2) In determining the liability under section 6(1) arising in connection with the making of the later payment, the amount referred to in that subsection shall be reduced by any amount paid in satisfaction of that liability as it arose in connection with the earlier payment.

(3) Where —

(a) a payment made in satisfaction of the liability under section 6(1) arising in connection with an earlier payment is not reflected in the certificate of recoverable benefits in force at the time of a later payment, and

(b) in consequence, the aggregate of payments made in satisfaction of the liability exceeds what it would have been had that payment been so reflected,

the Secretary of State shall pay the compensator who made the later payment an amount equal to the excess.

(4) Where —

(a) a compensator receives a payment under paragraph (3), and

(b) the amount of the compensation payment made by him was calculated under section 8,

then the compensation payment shall be recalculated under section 8, and the compensator shall pay the amount of the increase (if any) to the person to whom the compensation payment was made.

(5) Where both are earlier payment and the later payment are made by the same compensator, he may —

(a) aggregate the gross amounts of the payments made by him;

(b) calculate what would have been the reduction made under section 8(3) if that aggregate amount had been paid at the date of the last payment on the basis that —

  (i) so much of the aggregate amount as is attributable to a head of compensation listed in column (1) of Schedule 2 shall be taken to be the part of the gross amount which is attributable to that head, and

  (ii) the amount of any recoverable benefits shown against any head in column (2) of that Schedule shall be taken to be the amount determined in accordance with the most recent certificate of recoverable benefits;

(c) deduct from that reduction calculated under sub-paragraph (b) the amount of the reduction under section 8(3) from any earlier payment; and

(d) deduct from the latest gross payment the net reduction calculated under sub-paragraph (c) (and accordingly the latest payment may be nil).

(6) Where the Secretary of State is making a refund under paragraph (3), he shall send to the compensator (with the refund) and to the person to whom the compensation payment was made a statement showing —

- (a) the total amount that has already been paid by that compensator to the Secretary of State;
- (b) the amount that ought to have been paid by that compensator; and
- (c) the amount to be repaid to that compensator by the Secretary of State.

(7) Where the reduction of a compensation payment is recalculated by virtue of paragraph (4) or (5) the compensator shall give notice of the calculation to the injured person.

Structured settlements

10.—(1) This regulation applies where —

- (a) in final settlement of an injured person's claim, an agreement is entered into —
  - (i) for the making of periodical payments (whether of an income or capital nature); or
  - (ii) for the making of such payments and lump sum payments; and
- (b) apart from the provisions of this regulation, those payments would fall to be treated for the purposes of the 1997 Act as compensation payments.

(2) Where this regulation applies, the provisions of the 1997 Act and these Regulations shall be modified in the following way —

- (a) the compensator in question shall be taken to have made on that day a single compensation payment;
- (b) the relevant period in the case of the compensator in question shall be taken to end (if it has not done so already) on the day of settlement;
- (c) payments under the agreement referred to in paragraph (1)(a) shall be taken not to be compensation payments;
- (d) paragraphs (5) and (7) of regulation 11 shall not apply.

(3) Where any further payment falls to be made to or in respect of the injured person otherwise than under the agreement in question, paragraph (2) shall be disregarded for the purpose of determining the end of the relevant period in relation to that further payment.

(4) In any case where —

- (a) the person making the periodical payments ("the secondary party") does so in pursuance of arrangements entered into with another ("the primary party") (as in a case where the primary party purchases an annuity for the injured person from the secondary party), and

(b) apart from those arrangements, the primary party would have been regarded as the compensator,

then for the purposes of the 1997 Act, the primary party shall be regarded as the compensator and the secondary party shall not be so regarded.

(5) In this regulation "the day of settlement" means —

(a) if the agreement referred to in paragraph (1)(a) is approved by a court, the day on which that approval is given; and

(b) in any other case, the day on which the agreement is entered into.

Adjustments

11.—(1) Where the conditions specified in subsection (1) and paragraphs (a) and (b) of subsection (2) of section 14 are satisfied, the Secretary of State shall pay the difference between the amount that has been paid and the amount that ought to have been paid to the compensator.

(2) Where the conditions specified in subsection (1) and paragraphs (a) and (b) of subsection (3) of section 14 are satisfied, the compensator shall pay the difference between the total amounts paid and the amount that ought to have been paid to the Secretary of State.

(3) Where the Secretary of State is making a refund under paragraph (1), or demanding payment of a further amount under paragraph (2), he shall send to the compensator (with the refund or demand) and to the person to whom the compensation payment was made a statement showing —

(a) the total amount that has already been paid to the Secretary of State;

(b) the amount that ought to have been paid; and

(c) the difference, and whether a repayment by the Secretary of State or a further payment to him is required.

(4) This paragraph applies where —

(a) the amount of the compensation payment made by the compensator was calculated under section 8; and

(b) the Secretary of State has made a payment under paragraph (1).

(5) Where paragraph (4) applies, the amount of the compensation payment shall be recalculated under section 8 to take account of the fresh certificate of recoverable benefits and the compensator shall pay the amount of the increase (if any) to the person to whom the compensation payment was made.

(6) This paragraph applies where —

(a) the amount of the compensation payment made by the compensator was calculated under section 8;

(b) the compensator has made a payment under paragraph (2); and

(c) the fresh certificate of recoverable benefits issued after the review or appeal was required as a result of the injured person or other person to whom the compensation payment was made supplying to the compensator information knowing it to be incorrect or insufficient with the intent of enhancing the compensation payment calculated under section 8, and the compensator supplying that information to the Secretary of State without knowing it to be incorrect or insufficient.

(7) Where paragraph (6) applies, the compensator may recalculate the compensation payment under section 8 to take account of the fresh certificate of recoverable benefits and may require the repayment to him by the person to whom he made the compensation payment of the difference (if any) between the payment made and the payment as so recalculated.

Transitional provisions

12.—(1) In relation to a compensation payment to which by virtue of section 2 the 1997 Act applies and subject to paragraph (2), a certificate of total benefit issued under Part IV of the 1992 Act shall be treated on or after the commencement date as a certificate of recoverable benefits issued under the 1997 Act and the amount of total benefit treated as that of recoverable benefits.

(2) Paragraph (1) shall not apply to a certificate of total benefit which specifies an amount in respect of disability living allowance without specifying whether that amount was, or is likely to be, paid wholly by way of the care component or the mobility component or (if not wholly one of them) specifying the relevant amount for each component.

(3) Any appeal under section 98 of the 1992 Act made on or after the commencement date shall be referred to and determined by a medical appeal tribunal notwithstanding that it would otherwise have been referred by the Secretary of State to a social security appeal tribunal.

(4) Paragraph (5) applies where —

(a) an amount has been paid to the Secretary of State under section 82(1)(b) of the 1992 Act,

(b) liability arises on or after the commencement day to make a payment under section 6(1), and

(c) the compensation payments which give rise to the liability to make both payments are to or in respect of the same injured person in consequence of the same accident, injury or disease.

(5) Where this paragraph applies, the liability under section 6 shall be reduced by the payment (or aggregate of the payments, if more than one) described in paragraph (4)(a).

(6) Where —

(a) a payment into court has been made on a date prior to the commencement day but the initial period, as defined in section 93(6) of the 1992 Act, in relation to that payment, expires on or after the commencement day; and

(b) the payment into court is accepted by the other party to the action in the initial period,

that payment into court shall be treated as a compensation payment to which the 1992 Act, and not the 1997 Act, applies.

(7) Where a payment into court has been made prior to the commencement day, remains in court on that day and paragraph (6) does not apply, that payment into court shall be treated as a payment to which the 1997 Act applies, but paragraph (1)(b) and (c) of regulation 8 shall not apply.

Appendix VII

JUDICIAL STUDIES BOARD GUIDELINES

Guidelines for the Assessment of General Damages in Personal Injury Cases

Compiled for the Judicial Studies Board by John Cherry, Q.C.; Edwin Glasgow, Q.C.; D. A. K. Hughes, Solicitor; R. J. Sutcliffe, Solicitor; His Honour Judge Roger Cox

Fourth edition

INTRODUCTION

In producing the fourth edition of this book the working party set up by the Judicial Studies Board in 1990 has looked anew at definitions and brackets, though it must be said that in many areas there are no decisions to indicate that the original figures need revision save to the extent that inflation must be considered.

The members of the working party are sincerely grateful for the comments, contributions, and criticisms, which have been received from friends and colleagues at all levels of the profession. They feel the need, however, perhaps more than before, to remind themselves and those who use and comment on these guidelines (for that is all that they are intended to be) of the task that they were originally given by the Civil and Family Committee of the Judicial Studies Board. That was, and remains, to distil guidelines from awards which have in fact been made; it is not and never was to promote any views which they may have as to what the level of those awards *ought* to be. Thus, in working through the material which has been collated (and it is substantial) and in considering the generous help which has been offered by others, the working party has had frequently to resist the temptation to adjust or alter particular figures or brackets simply because its members, and sometimes others who have greater experience, think that they *seem* to be "out of line".

The working party has therefore concentrated on actual awards made by the courts or the Criminal Injuries Compensation Board. It has, of course, looked carefully, as it did for previous editions, at settlements of the details of which its members have been made aware, especially where they have been the subject of court approval. However, in view of the help which has been received from so many quarters the need is felt to say something about the care with which such settlements have been regarded, whether the information has come from the collective experience of the working party or from the contributions of others.

In recent years the process of settling actions for damages for personal injuries in all but the least complex of cases has been complicated by doubts as to the basis on which multipliers for future losses were to be calculated. While these doubts have now been resolved by the decision of the House of Lords in *Wells v. Wells*, they resulted in settlements being agreed for general damages for pain, suffering and loss of amenity which did not necessarily reflect a ruthlessly objective evaluation of those elements in the assessment of the overall value of the case. General damages, particularly in the most serious cases, often represent but a comparatively small part of the global award or settlement. Thus, it is the experience of the working party and that of those from whom soundings have been taken, that parties have been prepared to agree settlements including figures for general damages where the overall compromise figure has been attractive, despite the fact that one or other of the parties did not consider that a court would have been likely to award as general damages on a contested trial of the action the sum which was agreed in respect of that element. Accordingly, the members of the working party have been careful not to allow themselves to be over-influenced by information received as to settlement figures which do not appear to accord with the results of their researches into decided cases. This apparent reluctance to move away from the brackets which reflect actual decisions should not be taken as indicating any ingratitude on the part of the working party for the information which has been provided, for all of it has been carefully considered. It would be most unfortunate if these guidelines were to make agreement on an overall figure, which experienced practitioners honestly and reasonably felt to be right in a particular case, more difficult. Rather, it is hoped that these guidelines will be used, as the Master of the Rolls indicated in his Foreword to the third edition, as "the starting off point rather than the last word … in any particular case".

The working party has not overlooked the danger that "guidelines" may come to be regarded as self-fulfilling prophecies. It should be emphasised that it is for the courts to set the levels of damages and for this book to reflect them. It is not possible in a work such as this minutely to define every injury or state of affairs which will be compensated and it would defeat the purpose of this book were its definitions to be stretched by others to apply to that for which they do not provide. If it is the case that the brackets which have been distilled from the cases are no longer thought to be appropriate, it must be for the courts and not for this working party to signal a change.

The members of the working party would like to express their gratitude to all those who have contributed to their researches, to the Judicial Studies Board for its unstinting support and, in particular, to Andrea Dowsett, its publications co-ordinator, for the immense help which she has given.

The figures in this edition are based on awards up to August 1998.

1. Injuries involving Paralysis

(a) Quadriplegia

£120,000 to £150,000

The level of the award within the bracket will be affected by the following considerations:

(i) The extent of any residential movement

(ii) The presence and extent of pain

(iii) Depression

(iv) Age and life expectancy

The top of the bracket will be appropriate only where there is significant effect on senses.

(b) Paraplegia

£90,000 to £110,000

The level of the award within the bracket will be affected by the following considerations:

(i) The presence and extent of pain

(ii) Depression

(iii) Age and life expectancy

The presence of increasing paralysis or the degree of risk that this will occur, for example from syringomyelia, might take the case above this bracket.

2. Head Injuries

(A) Brain Damage

(a) Very Severe Brain Damage £110,000 to £150,000

In the most severe cases the person injured will have a degree of insight. There may be some ability to follow basic commands, recovery of eye opening and return of sleep and waking patterns and postural reflex movement. There will be little, if any, evidence of meaningful response to environment, little or no language function, double incontinence and the need for full-time nursing care.

The level of the award within the bracket will be affected by:

(i) The degree of insight

(ii) Life expectancy

(iii) The extent of physical limitations

The top of the bracket will be appropriate only where there is significant effect on the senses.

Where there is a persistent vegetative state and/or death occurs very soon after the injuries were suffered and there has been no awareness by the person injured of his condition the award will be solely for loss of amenity and will fall substantially below the above bracket.

(b) Moderately Severe Brain Damage £90,000 to £110,000

The person injured will be very seriously disabled. There will be substantial dependence on others and a need for constant care. Disabilities may be physical, *e.g.*, limb paralysis, or cognitive, with marked impairment of intellect and personality. Cases otherwise within (a) above may fall into this bracket if life expectancy has been greatly reduced.

The level of the award within the bracket will be affected by the following considerations:

(i) The degree of insight

(ii) Life expectancy

(iii) The extent of physical limitations

(iv) The degree of dependence on others

(v) Behavioural abnormality

(c) Moderate Brain Damage

This category is distinguished from (b) by the fact that the degree of dependence is markedly lower.

(i) Cases in which there is moderate to severe intellectual deficit, a personality change, an effect on sight, speech and senses with a significant risk of epilepsy. £65,000 to £90,000

(ii) Cases in which there is a moderate to modest intellectual deficit, the ability to work is greatly reduced if not removed and there is some risk of epilepsy. £40,000 to £65,000

(iii) Cases in which concentration and memory are affected, the ability to work is reduced, where there is a small risk of epilepsy and any dependence on others is very limited £20,000 to £40,000

(d) Minor Brain Damage £7,500 to £20,000

In these cases the person injured will have made a good recovery and will be able to take part in normal social life and to return to work. There may not have been a restoration of all normal functions so there may still be persisting problems such as poor concentration and memory or disinhibition of mood, which may interfere with lifestyle, leisure activities and future work prospects.

The level of the award within the bracket will be affected by:

(i) The extent and severity of the initial injury

(ii) The extent of any continuing and possible permanent disability

(iii) The extent of any personality change

(B) Minor Head Injury £1,000 to £6,000

In these cases brain damage, if any, will have been minimal.

The level of the award will be affected by the following considerations:

(i) The severity of the initial injury

(ii) The period taken to recover from any severe symptoms

(iii) The extent of continuing symptoms

(iv) The presence or absence of headaches

(C) Epilepsy

(a) Established Grand Mal £45,000 to £65,000

(b) Established Petit Mal £25,000 to £55,000

The level of the award within the brackets will be affected by the following factors:

(i) Whether attacks are successfully controlled by medication and the extent to which the need for medication is likely to persist.

(ii) The extent to which the appreciation of life is blunted by such medication.

(iii) The effect on working and/or social life.

(iv) The existence of associated behavioural problems.

(c) Other Epileptic Incidents £5,000 to £12,500

Cases where there are one or two discrete epileptic episodes and there is no risk of recurrence beyond the percentage risk applicable to the population at large. The level of the award within the bracket will be affected by the extent of any consequences of the attacks on, *e.g.*, education, sporting activities, working and social life, and their duration.

3. Psychiatric Damage

In the first part of this chapter some of the brackets contain an element of compensation for post-traumatic stress disorder. This is, of course, not a universal feature of cases of psychiatric injury and hence a number of the awards upon which the brackets are based did not reflect it. Where it does figure any award will tend towards the upper end of the bracket. Cases where post-traumatic stress disorder is the sole psychiatric condition are dealt with in the second part of this chapter.

(A) Psychiatric Damage Generally

The factors to be taken into account in valuing claims of this nature are as follows:

- (i) The injured person's ability to cope with life and work
- (ii) The effect on the injured person's relationships with his family, friends and those with whom he comes into contact
- (iii) The extent to which treatment would be successful
- (iv) Future vulnerability
- (v) Prognosis
- (vi) Whether medical help has been sought

(a) Severe Psychiatric Damage — £25,000 to £50,000

In these cases the person injured will have marked problems with respect to factors (i) to (iv) above and the prognosis will be very poor.

(b) Moderately Severe Psychiatric Damage £9,000 to £25,000

In these cases there will be significant problems associated with factors (i) to (iv) above but the prognosis will generally be much more optimistic. While there are awards which support both extremes of this bracket, the majority were between £15,000 and £17,500

(c) Moderate Psychiatric Damage £3,000 to £9,000

While there may have been the sort of problems associated with factors (i) to (iv) above there will have been marked improvement by trial and the prognosis will be good.

(d) Minor Psychiatric Damage £500 to £2,250

Considerations as to the level of the award will include the length of the period of disability and the extent to which daily activities and sleep were affected.

(B) Post-traumatic Stress Disorder

Cases within this category are exclusively those where there is a specific diagnosis of a reactive psychiatric disorder in which characteristic symptoms are displayed following a psychologically distressing event which was outside the range of normal human experience and which would be markedly distressing to almost anyone. The guidelines below have been compiled by reference to cases which variously reflect the criteria established in the fourth edition of *Diagnostic and Statistical Manual of Mental Disorders* (DSM IV). The symptoms affect basic functions such as breathing, pulse rate and bowel and/or bladder control. They also involve persistent re-experience of the relevant event, difficulty in controlling temper, in concentrating and sleeping, and exaggerated startled response.

(a) Severe £28,500 to £40,000

Such cases will involve permanent effects which prevent the person injured from working at all or at least from functioning at anything approaching the pre-trauma level. All aspects of the life of the person injured will be badly affected.

(b) Moderately Severe £12,500 to £25,000

This category is distinct from (a) above because of the better prognosis which will be for some recovery with professional help. However, the effects are still likely to cause significant disability for the foreseeable future.

(c) Moderate £3,500 to £9,500

In these cases the person injured is largely recovered and any continuing effects are not grossly disabling.

(d) Minor £1,750 to £3,500

In these cases a virtually full recovery is made within one or two years and only minor symptoms persist over any longer period.

4. Injuries Affecting the Senses

(A) Injuries Affecting Sight

(a) Total Blindness and Deafness £150,000

Such cases must be considered as ranking with the most devastating injuries.

(b) Total Blindness £105,000

(c) Loss of Sight in One Eye with Reduced Vision in the Remaining Eye

(i) Where there is serious risk of further deterioration in the remaining eye, going beyond the normal risk of sympathetic ophthalmia. £42,500 to £75,000

(ii) Where there is reduced vision in the remaining eye and/or additional problems such as double vision. £28,500 to £48,500

(d) Total Loss of One Eye £26,000 to £30,000

The level of the award within the bracket will depend on age and cosmetic effect.

(e) Complete Loss of Sight in One Eye £22,500 to £25,000

This award takes account of the risk of sympathetic ophthalmia. The upper end of the bracket is appropriate where there is scarring in the region of the eye which is not sufficiently serious to merit a separate award.

(f) Cases of serious but incomplete loss of vision in one eye without significant risk of loss of or reduction of vision in the remaining eye, or where there is constant double vision. £11,500 to £18,250

(g) Minor but permanent impairment of vision in one eye, including cases where there is some double vision which may not be constant. £6,000 to £10,000

(h) Minor Eye Injuries £1,850 to £4,000

In this bracket fall cases of minor injuries, such as being struck in the eye, exposure to fumes including smoke, or being splashed by liquids, causing initial pain and some interference with vision, but no lasting effects.

(i) Transient Eye Injuries £1,000 to £1,850

In these cases the person injured will have recovered completely within a few weeks.

(B) Deafness

The word "deafness" is used to embrace total and partial hearing loss. In assessing awards for hearing loss regard must be had to the following:

(i) Whether the injury is one that has an immediate effect, allowing no opportunity to adapt, or whether it occurred over a period of time, as in noise exposure cases.

(ii) Whether the injury or disability is one which the person injured suffered at an early age so that it has had or will have an effect on his speech, or if it is one that is suffered in later life.

(iii) Whether the injury or disability affects balance.

(iv) In cases of Noise Induced Hearing Loss (NIHL) age is of particular relevance as noted in paragraph (d) below.

(a) Total Deafness and Loss of Speech £47,500 to £60,000

Such cases arise, for example, where deafness has occurred at an early age (*e.g.*, rubella infection) so as to prevent or seriously affect the development of normal speech.

(b) Total Deafness £40,000 to £47,500

The lower end of the bracket is appropriate for cases where there is no speech deficit or tinnitus. The higher end is appropriate for cases involving both of these.

(c) Total Loss of Hearing in One Ear £15,000 to £21,500

Cases will tend towards the higher end of the bracket where there are associated problems, such as tinnitus, dizziness or headaches.

(d) Partial Hearing Loss/Tinnitus

This category covers the bulk of deafness cases which usually result from exposure to noise over a prolonged period. The disability is not to be judged simply by the degree of hearing loss; there is often a degree of tinnitus present. Age is particularly relevant because impairment of hearing affects most people in the fullness of time and impacts both upon causation and upon valuation.

(i) Severe tinnitus/hearing loss £13,750 to £21,250

(ii) Moderate tinnitus/hearing loss £7,000 to £13,750

(iii) Mild tinnitus with some hearing loss — £6,000 to £7,000

(iv) Slight or occasional tinnitus with slight hearing loss — £3,500 to £6,000

Note: Tariff schemes agreed between unions and insurers have been operating for some years. These tariffs provide scales for compensation measured by precise decibel loss and degree of tinnitus at differing ages. In assessing the above brackets, which reflect decided cases, these schemes have not been adopted because none of them has achieved general judicial approval and they are currently being replaced by simpler schemes based on conventional brackets of compensation for decibel loss, principally affected by age.

(C) Impairment of Taste and Smell

(a) Total Loss of Taste and Smell — £18,250

(b) Total Loss of Smell and Significant Loss of Taste — £15,500 to £18,000

It must be remembered that in nearly all cases of loss of smell there is some impairment of taste. Such cases fall into the next bracket.

(c) Loss of Smell — £12,000 to £15,500

(d) Loss of Taste — £9,000 to £12,000

5. Injuries to Internal Organs

(A) Chest Injuries

This is a specially difficult area because the majority of awards relate to industrial *disease* as distinct from traumatic *injury* and the level of the appropriate award for lung disease necessarily, and often principally, reflects the prognosis for what is frequently a worsening condition and/or the risk of the development of secondary sequelae (such as mesothelioma in asbestos-related cases). Cases of traumatic damage to, or loss of, a lung are comparatively rare: the range is as wide as £1,000 to £65,000.

The levels of awards within the brackets set out below will be affected by:

(i) Age and gender

(ii) Scarring

(iii) The effect on the capacity to work and enjoy life

(iv) The effect on life expectancy

(a) The very worst case will be of total removal of one lung and/or serious heart damage with serious and prolonged pain and suffering and permanent significant scarring. £45,000 to £65,000

(b) Traumatic injury to chest, lung(s) and/or heart causing permanent damage, impairment of function, physical disability and reduction of life expectancy. £30,000 to £45,000

(c) Damage to chest and lung(s) causing some continuing disability. £15,000 to £25,000

(d)	A relatively simple injury (such as a single penetrating wound) causing some permanent damage to tissue but with no significant long-term effect on lung function.	£6,000 to £8,500
(e)	Toxic fume/smoke inhalation, leaving some residual damage, not serious enough permanently to interfere with lung function.	£2,750 to £6,000
(f)	Injuries leading to collapsed lungs from which a full and uncomplicated recovery is made.	£1,000 to £2,500
(g)	Fractures of ribs, causing serious pain and disability over a period of weeks only.	Up to £1,750

(B) Lung Disease

Most of the reported cases are of asbestos-related disease but, save for asthma (which is dealt with separately) the brackets set out below are intended to encompass all lung disease cases irrespective of causation. In many cases falling under this head provisional awards will be appropriate, save at the upper end of the range where serious disabling consequences will already be present and the prognosis is likely to be relatively clear.

(a)	For a young person with serious disability where there is a probability of progressive worsening leading to premature death.	£45,000 to £55,000
(b)	Mesothelioma (typically in an older person), lung cancer or asbestosis causing severe impairment both of function and of quality of life.	£35,000 to £45,000

(c)	Disease causing significant and worsening lung function and impairment of breathing, prolonged and frequent coughing, sleep disturbance and restriction of physical activity and employment — including the more serious cases of pleural thickening.	£25,000 to £35,000
(d)	Breathing difficulties (short of disabling breathlessness) requiring fairly frequent use of an inhaler, where there is inability to tolerate smoky environment, significant pleural thickening and an uncertain prognosis but already significant effect on social and working life.	£15,000 to £25,000
(e)	Bronchitis and wheezing; pleural plaques or thickening not causing serious symptoms; little or no serious or permanent effect on working or social life; varying levels of anxiety about the future.	£10,000 to £15,000
(f)	Some slight breathlessness with no effect on working life and the likelihood of substantial and permanent recovery within a few years of exposure to the cause or aggravation of an existing condition.	£5,000 to £10,000
(g)	Provisional awards for cases otherwise falling within (f), or the least serious cases within (e) where the provisional award excludes any risk of malignancy or of asbestosis.	£2,500 to £5,000
(h)	Temporary aggravation of bronchitis or other chest problems resolving within very few months	£1,000 to £2,500

(C) Asthma

(a)	Severe and permanent disabling asthma, causing prolonged and regular coughing, disturbance of sleep, severe impairment of physical activity and enjoyment of life and where employment prospects, if any, are grossly restricted.	£20,000 to £30,000
(b)	Chronic asthma causing breathing difficulties, the need to use an inhaler from time to time and restriction of employment prospects, with uncertain prognosis.	£12,500 to £20,000
(c)	Bronchitic wheezing, affecting working or social life, with the likelihood of substantial recovery within a few years of the exposure to the cause.	£9,000 to £12,500
(d)	Restrictive Airways Dysfunction Syndrome (RADS). Relatively mild asthma-like symptoms resulting from a single exposure to harmful irritating vapour.	£5,000 to £9,000
(e)	Mild asthma, bronchitis, colds and chest problems (usually resulting from unfit housing or similar exposure, particularly in cases of young children) treated by a general practitioner and resolving within a few months.	Up to £2,250

(D) Digestive System

It is to be noted that the risk of associated damage to the reproductive organs is frequently encountered in cases of this nature and requires separate consideration.

(a)	Severe damage with continuing pain and discomfort.	£20,000 to £28,500

(b) Serious non-penetrating injury causing long-standing or permanent complications, *e.g.*, severe indigestion, aggravated by physical strain. £8,000 to £13,250

(c) Penetrating stab wounds or industrial laceration or serious seat-belt pressure cases. £3,000 to £6,000

(E) Reproductive System

Male

(a) Impotence

(i) Total impotence and loss of sexual function and sterility in the case of a young man

The level of the award will depend on:

(1) age,

(2) psychological reaction and the effect on social and domestic life. In the region of £62,500

(ii) Impotence which is likely to be permanent, in the case of a middle-aged man with children. £20,000 to £35,000

(b) Cases of sterility usually fall into one of two categories: surgical, chemical and disease cases (which involve no traumatic injury or scarring) and traumatic injuries (frequently caused by assaults) which are often aggravated by scarring.

(i) The most serious cases merit awards approaching £58,500

(ii) The bottom of the range is the case of the much older man and merits an award of about £9,000

(c)	An uncomplicated case of infertility without any aggravating features for a young man without children.	£26,500 to £32,500
(d)	A similar case but involving a family man who might have intended to have more children.	£11,500 to £14,500
(e)	Cases where the infertility amounts to little more than an "insult". In the region of	£2,500

Female

The level of awards in this area will typically depend on:

- (i) Whether or not the affected woman already has children and/or whether the intended family was complete
- (ii) Scarring
- (iii) Depression or psychological scarring
- (iv) Whether a foetus was aborted

(a)	Infertility whether by reason of injury or disease, with associated depression and anxiety, pain and scarring	£50,000 to £70,000
(b)	Infertility without any medical complication and where the injured person already has children. The upper end of the bracket is appropriate in cases where there is significant psychological damage.	£8,500 to £17,250
(c)	Infertility where the person injured would not have had children in any event (for example, because of age)	£3,000 to £6,000
(d)	Failed sterilisation leading to unwanted pregnancy where there is no serious psychological impact or depression.	£3,000 to £4,000

(F) Kidney

(a)	Serious and permanent damage to or loss of both kidneys.	£70,000 to £85,000
(b)	Where there is a significant risk of future urinary tract infection or other total loss of natural kidney function the range is up to	£28,500
	Such cases will invariably carry with them substantial future medical expenses, which in this field are particularly high.	
(c)	Loss of one kidney with no damage to the other.	£14,500 to £20,000

(G) Bowels

(a)	Total loss of natural function and dependence on colostomy, depending on age.	Up to £65,000
(b)	Severe abdominal injury causing impairment of function and often necessitating temporary colostomy (leaving disfiguring scars) and/or restriction on employment and on diet.	£21,000 to £32,000
(c)	Penetrating injuries causing some permanent damage but with an eventual return to natural function and control.	£6,000 to £11,500

(H) Bladder

It is perhaps surprising that awards in cases of loss of bladder function have often been higher than awards for injury to the bowels. This is probably because bladder injuries frequently result from carcinogenic exposure (typically to antioxidants such as Nonox S in the rubber industry). The reported decisions are seriously out of date and the indexing-up procedure may be misleading.

(a) Complete loss of function and control. Up to £60,000

(b) Impairment of control with some pain and incontinence. £28,500 to £35,000

(c) Where there has been an almost complete recovery but some fairly long-term interference with natural function. £11,500 to £14,500

The cancer risk cases still occupy a special category and can properly attract awards at the top of the ranges even where natural function continues for the time being. However, these cases will now more appropriately be dealt with by provisional awards of a low level (£5,000) unless the foreseeable prognosis and outcome are clear. Once the prognosis is firm and reliable the award will reflect any loss of life expectancy, the level of continuing pain and suffering and most significantly the extent to which the person injured has to live with the knowledge of the consequences which his death will have for others. The appropriate award for the middle-aged family man or woman whose life expectancy is reduced by 15 or 20 years is £25,000 to £35,000.

(I) Spleen

(a) Loss of spleen where there is continuing risk of internal infection and disorders due to the damage to the immune system. £10,000 to £12,500

(b) Where the above risks are not present or are minimal. £2,000 to £4,000

(J) Hernia

(a)	Continuing pain and/or limitation on physical activities, sport or employment.	£7,000 to £11,500
(b)	Direct (where there was no pre-existing weakness) inguinal hernia, with some risk of recurrence.	£3,250 to £4,250
(c)	Uncomplicated indirect inguinal hernia with no other associated abdominal injury or damage	£1,500 to £3,000

6. Orthopaedic Injuries

(A) Neck Injuries

There is a very wide range of neck injuries. At the highest end of the spectrum is the injury which shatters a life and leaves the person injured very severely disabled. This may have a value of up to £65,000.

At the other end of the spectrum is the minor strain which causes the injured person to be off work for a very short period and to suffer symptoms for only a few weeks. This type of injury would attract an award of between £1,000 and £1,500.

The neck injury giving rise to symptoms for no more than a couple of weeks would attract no more than about £500.

(a) Severe

(i)	Neck injury associated with incomplete paraplegia or resulting in permanent spastic quadriparesis or where the person injured, despite the wearing of a collar 24 hours a day for a period of years, still has little or no movement in the neck and still suffers severe headaches which have proved intractable.	£65,000
(ii)	Injuries which give rise to disabilities which fall short of those in (a) (i) above but which are of considerable severity, *e.g.*, permanent damage to the brachial plexus.	£30,000 to £55,000

(iii) Injuries causing severe damage to soft tissues and/or ruptured tendons. They result in significant disability of a permanent nature. The precise award depends on the length of time during which the most serious symptoms are ameliorated, and on the prognosis. In the region of — £25,000

(iv) Injuries such as fractures or dislocations which cause severe immediate symptoms and which may necessitate spinal fusion. They leave markedly impaired function or vulnerability to further trauma, and some limitation of activities. — £12,000 to £15,500

(b) Moderate

(i) Cases involving whiplash or wrenching type injury and disc lesion of the more severe type resulting in cervical spondylosis, serious limitation of movement, permanent or recurring pain, stiffness or discomfort and the possible need for further surgery or increased vulnerability to further trauma. — £6,500 to £12,000

(ii) Injuries which may have exacerbated or accelerated some pre-existing unrelated condition. There will have been a complete recovery from the effects of the injury within a few years.

This bracket will also apply to moderate whiplash injuries where the period of recovery has been fairly protracted and where there remains an increased vulnerability to further trauma. — £3,500 to £6,500

(c) Minor

Minor soft tissue and whiplash injuries and the like where symptoms are moderate and a full recovery takes place within at most two years.	Up to £3,500

(B) Back Injuries

Relatively few back injuries which do not give rise to paralysis command awards above about £22,500. In those that do there are special features.

(a) Severe

(i) Cases of the most severe injury which do not involve paralysis but where there may be very serious consequences not normally found in cases of back injury, such as impotence or double incontinence.	£45,000 to £70,000
(ii) Cases which have special features taking them outside any lower bracket applicable to orthopaedic injury to the back. Such features include impaired bladder and bowel function, severe sexual difficulties and unsightly scarring and the possibility of future surgery. In the region of	£37,500
(iii) Cases of disc lesions or fractures of discs or of vertebral bodies where, despite treatment, there remain disabilities such as continuing severe pain and discomfort, impaired agility, impaired sexual function, depression, personality change, alcoholism, unemployability and the risk of arthritis.	£18,500 to £30,000

(b) Moderate

(i)	Cases where any residual disability is of less severity than that in (a) (iii) above. The bracket contains a wide variety of injuries. Examples are a case of a crush fracture of the lumbar vertebrae where there is a substantial risk of osteoarthritis and constant pain and discomfort with impairment of sexual function, that of a traumatic spondylolisthesis with continuous pain and a probability that spinal fusion will be necessary, or that of a prolapsed intervertebral disc with substantial acceleration of back degeneration.	£13,250 to £18,500
(ii)	Many frequently encountered injuries to the back, such as disturbance of ligaments and muscles giving rise to backache, soft tissue injuries resulting in exacerbation of an existing back condition or prolapsed discs necessitating laminectomy or resulting in repeated relapses. The precise figure depends upon the severity of the original injury and/or whether there is some permanent or chronic disability.	£6,000 to £13,250

(c) Minor

Strains, sprains, disc prolapses and soft tissue injuries from which a full recovery has been made or which result only in minor continuing disability or as a result of which there has been acceleration or exacerbation of pre-existing unrelated conditions for a fairly brief period of time.	Up to £6,500

(C) Injuries to the Pelvis and Hips

The most serious of injuries to the pelvis and hip can be as devastating as a leg amputation and accordingly will attract a similar award of damages. Such cases apart, the upper limit for these injuries will generally be in the region of £32,500. Cases where there are specific sequelae of exceptional severity would call for a higher award.

(a) Severe

(i) Extensive fractures of the pelvis involving, for example, dislocation of a low back joint and a ruptured bladder or a hip injury resulting in spondylolisthesis of a low back joint with intolerable pain and necessitating spinal fusion. Inevitably there will be substantial residual disabilities, such as a complicated arthrodesis with resulting lack of bladder and bowel control, sexual dysfunction or hip deformity making the use of a caliper essential. £35,000 to £55,000

(ii) Injuries only a little less severe than in (a) (i) above but with particular distinguishing features lifting them above any lower bracket. Examples are (a) fracture dislocation of the pelvis involving both ischial and pubic rami and resulting in impotence, or (b) traumatic myositis ossificans with formation of ectopic bone around the hip. £28,500 to £35,000

(iii) Many injuries fall within this bracket: a fracture of the acetabulum leading to degenerative changes and leg instability requiring an osteotomy and the likelihood of hip replacement surgery in the future, the fracture of an arthritic femur or hip necessitating hip replacement, or a fracture resulting in a hip replacement which is only partially successful so that there is a clear risk of the need for revision surgery. £18,500 to £24,000

(b) Moderate £12,750 to £18,500

Significant injury to the pelvis or hip but where any permanent disability is not major and any future risk not great.

(c) Injuries of Limited Severity £6,000 to £12,750

These cases usually involve hip replacement. Where it has been carried out wholly successfully the award will tend towards the top of the bracket, but the bracket also includes cases where hip replacement is anticipated in the foreseeable future.

(d) Minor Injuries Up to £6,000

These are cases where despite injury there is no residual disability.

(D) Shoulder Injuries

Unless they are associated with severe neck, back or arm injury, shoulder injuries tend to attract modest awards of well under five figures.

(a) Serious £6,000 to £9,000

Dislocation of the shoulder and damage to the lower part of the brachial plexus causing pain in shoulder and neck, aching in elbow, sensory symptoms in the forearm and hand, and weakness of grip.

(b) Moderate £3,750 to £6,000

Frozen shoulder with limitation of movement and discomfort with symptoms persisting for between one and two years.

(c) Minor £2,000 to £3,750

Soft tissue injury to shoulder with considerable pain but almost complete recovery in less than a year.

(d) Fracture of Clavicle £1,500 to £3,250

The level of the award will depend on whether union is anatomically displaced.

(E) Amputation of Arms

(a) Loss of Both Arms £90,000 to £110,000

There is no recent case to offer guidance but the effect of such an injury is to reduce a person with full awareness to a state of considerable helplessness.

(b) Loss of One Arm

The value of such an injury depends upon:

(i) Whether the amputation is above or below the elbow. The loss of the additional joint adds greatly to the disability.

(ii) Whether or not the amputation was of the dominant arm.

(iii) The intensity of any phantom pains.

(1) *Arm amputated at the shoulder* Not less than £60,000

(2) *Above elbow amputation* £47,500 to £55,000

A shorter stump may create difficulties in the use of a prosthesis. This will make the level of the award towards the top end of the bracket. Amputation through the elbow, however, will normally produce an award at the bottom end of the bracket.

(3) *Below elbow amputation* £42,500 to £47,500

Amputation through the forearm with residual severe organic and phantom pains would attract an award at the top end of the bracket.

(F) Other Arm Injuries

(a) Severe Injuries £42,500 to £55,000

Injuries which fall short of amputation but which are extremely serious and leave the person injured little better off than if the arm had been lost: *e.g.*, a serious brachial plexus injury.

(b) Injuries Resulting in Permanent and Substantial Disablement £18,500 to £27,500

Serious fractures of one or both forearms where there is significant permanent residual disability whether functional or cosmetic.

(c) Less Severe Injury £9,000 to £18,500

While there will have been significant disabilities, a substantial degree of recovery will have taken place or will be anticipated.

(d) Simple Fractures of the Forearm £3,000 to £9,000

Uncomplicated fractures of the radius and/or ulna with a complete recovery within a short time would justify an award of £3,000. Injuries resulting in modest residual disability or deformity would merit an award towards the upper end of this bracket.

(G) Injuries to the Elbow

(a) A Severely Disabling Injury £18,250 to £25,000

(b) Less Severe Injuries £7,500 to £15,000

Injuries causing impairment of function but not involving major surgery or significant disability.

(c) Moderate or Minor Injury Up to £6,000

Most elbow injuries fall into this category. They comprise simple fractures, tennis elbow syndrome and lacerations; *i.e.*, those injuries which cause no permanent damage and do not result in any permanent impairment of function.

(H) Wrist Injuries

(a) Injuries Resulting in Complete Loss of Function in the Wrist £22,500 to £27,500

For example, where an arthrodesis has been performed.

(b) Injury Resulting in Significant Permanent Disability, but where Some Useful Movement Remains £11,750 to £18,500

(c) Less Severe Injuries £6,000 to £11,750

These injuries still result in some permanent disability as, for example, a degree of persisting pain and stiffness.

(d) **Where Recovery is Complete the Award will Rarely Exceed** £5,000

(e) **An Uncomplicated Colles Fracture** £3,500

(I) Hand Injuries

The hands are cosmetically and functionally the most important component parts of the upper limbs. The loss of a hand is valued not far short of the amount which would be awarded for the loss of the arm itself. The upper end of any bracket will generally be appropriate where the material injury is to the dominant hand.

(a) **Total Effective Loss of Both Hands** £60,000 to £80,000

Serious injury resulting in extensive damage to both hands such as to render them little more than useless will justify an award of £60,000. The top of the bracket is applicable where no effective prosthesis can be used.

(b) **Serious Damage to Both Hands** £25,000 to £37,500

Such injuries will have given rise to permanent cosmetic disability and significant loss of function.

(c) **Total or Effective Loss of One Hand** £42,500 to £48,750

This bracket will apply to a hand which was crushed and thereafter surgically amputated or where all fingers and most of the palm have been traumatically amputated. The upper end of the bracket is indicated where the hand so damaged was the dominant one.

(d) Amputation of Index, Middle and/or Ring Fingers £28,500 to £40,000

The hand will have been rendered of very little use and such grip as remains will be exceedingly weak.

(e) Serious Hand Injuries Up to £28,500

Such injuries will, for example, have reduced the hand to about 50% capacity. Included would be cases where several fingers have been amputated but rejoined to the hand leaving it clawed, clumsy and unsightly, or amputation of some fingers together with part of the palm resulting in gross diminution of grip and dexterity and gross cosmetic disfigurement.

(f) Severe Fractures to Fingers Up to £17,500

These may lead to partial amputations and result in deformity, impairment of grip, reduced mechanical function and disturbed sensation.

(g) Total Loss of Index Finger £9,000

This is the maximum figure for this injury.

(h) Partial Loss of Index Finger £5,850 to £8,500

This bracket also covers cases of injury to the index finger giving rise to disfigurement and impairment of grip or dexterity.

(i) Fracture of Index Finger £4,250 to £5,850

This level is appropriate where a fracture has mended quickly but grip has remained impaired, there is pain on heavy use and osteoarthritis is likely in due course.

(j)	**Total Loss of Middle Finger**	£7,500
(k)	**Serious Injury to Ring or Middle Fingers**	£7,000 to £7,750
	The top of this bracket is the maximum figure for serious injury involving either of these fingers. Fractures or serious injury to tendons causing stiffness, deformity and permanent loss of grip or dexterity will fall within this bracket.	
(l)	**Loss of the Terminal Phalanx of the Ring or Middle Fingers**	£2,000 to £3,500
(m)	**Amputation of Little Finger**	£4,000 to £5,850
(n)	**Loss of Part of the Little Finger where the Remaining Tip is Sensitive**	£2,000 to £2,750
(o)	**Amputation of Ring and Little Fingers**	£10,500
(p)	**Amputation of the Terminal Phalanges of the Index and Middle Fingers with Further Injury to the Fourth Finger**	£11,750
	Such injury will involve scarring, restriction of movement and impairment of grip and fine handling.	
(q)	**Fracture of One Finger**	£1,000 to £1,750
	There will have been a complete recovery within a few weeks.	
(r)	**Loss of Thumb**	£17,000 to £26,000
(s)	**Very Serious Injury to Thumb**	£9,500 to £17,000

This bracket is appropriate where the thumb has been severed at the base and grafted back leaving a virtually useless and deformed digit, or where the thumb has been amputated through the metacarpo-phalangeal joint.

(t) **Serious Injury to the Thumb** £6,000 to £8,000

Such injuries may involve amputation of the tip, nerve damage or fracture necessitating the insertion of wires as a result of which the thumb is cold and ultra-sensitive and there is impaired grip and loss of manual dexterity.

(u) **Moderate Injuries to the Thumb** £4,500 to £6,000

These are injuries such as those necessitating arthrodesis of the interphalangeal joint or causing damage to tendons or nerves. Such injuries result in impairment of sensation and function and cosmetic deformity.

(v) **Severe Dislocation of the Thumb** £2,000 to £3,000

(w) **Minor Injuries to the Thumb**, in the region of £2,000

Such an injury would be a fracture which has recovered in six months except for residual stiffness and some discomfort.

(x) **Trivial Thumb Injuries** £1,000

These may have caused severe pain for a very short time but will have resolved within a few months.

(y) **Vibration White Finger**

This is a particular form of Reynaud's phenomenon caused by prolonged exposure to vibration. Degrees of severity are measured both on the Taylor Pelmear Scale and on the Stockholm Scale (for the neurological aspects). From the Taylor Pelmear Scale the relevant categories are:

(i) Extensive blanching of most fingers with episodes in summer and winter of such severity as to necessitate changing occupation to avoid exposure to vibration.

(ii) Extensive blanching with episodes in summer and winter resulting in interference at work, at home and with hobbies and social activities.

(iii) Blanching of one or more fingers with numbness, usually occurring only in winter and causing slight interference with home and social activities.

(iv) Blanching of one or more fingertips with or without tingling or numbness.

Note: The top of the bracket (£15,000 plus) would normally represent the most disabled stage 3/4 case on the Taylor Pelmear Scale ((i) to (ii) above). The position within the bracket depends upon:

(a) Length and severity of attacks and symptoms

(b) Extent and/or severity and/or rapidity of deterioration

(c) Age and prognosis

In some cases factors (a), (b) and (c) are more important than the stage the disease has reached.

The brackets can best be defined and valued as follows:

(i)	Most serious	£10,000 to £16,000
(ii)	Serious	£7,500 to £10,000
(iii)	Moderate	£2,500 to £7,500
(iv)	Minor	Up to £2,500

(J) Work-related Upper Limb Disorders

This section covers a range of upper limb injury in the form of the following pathological conditions.

(a) Tenosynovitis. Inflammation of synovial sheaths of tendons usually resolving with rest over a short period. Sometimes this condition leads to continuing symptoms of loss of grip and dexterity.

(b) De Quervain's tenosynovitis. A form of tenosynovitis, rarely bilateral, involving inflammation of the tendons of the thumb.

(c) Tenovaginitis stenovans. Otherwise trigger finger/thumb: thickening of tendons.

(d) Carpal tunnel syndrome. Constriction of the median nerve of the wrist or thickening of surrounding tissue. It is often relieved by a decompression operation.

(e) Epicondylitis. Inflammation in the elbow joint: medial (golfer's elbow), lateral (tennis elbow).

The brackets below apply to all these conditions but the level of the award is affected by the following considerations regardless of the precise condition:

(i) Are the effects bilateral or one-sided?

(ii) The level of symptoms (pain, swelling, tenderness, crepitus)

(iii) The ability to work

(iv) The capacity to avoid the recurrence of symptoms

(v) Surgery

(a)	Continuing bilateral disability with surgery and loss of employment	£10,500 to £11,000
(b)	Continuing symptoms, but fluctuating and unilateral	£7,000 to £7,500
(c)	Symptoms resolving over two years	£4,000 to £4,500
(d)	Complete recovery within a short period	£1,000 to £1,500

(K) Leg Injuries

(a) Amputations

(i) *Total loss of both legs* — £95,000 to £115,000

This is the appropriate award where both legs are lost above the knee and particularly if near to the hip leaving one or both stumps less than adequate to accommodate a useful prosthesis.

(ii) *Below knee amputation of both legs* — £85,000 to £105,000

The top of the bracket is appropriate where both legs are amputated just below the knee.

Amputations lower down result in a lower award.

(iii) *Above knee amputation of one leg* £42,500 to £60,000

The area within the bracket within which the award should fall will depend upon such factors as the level of the amputation, the severity of phantom pains, whether or not there have been any problems with a prosthesis and any side effects, such as depression or backache.

(iv) *Below knee amputation of one leg* £40,000 to £55,000

The straightforward case of a below knee amputation with no complications would justify an award at the bottom of this bracket. At or towards the top of the range would come the traumatic amputation which occurs in a devastating accident, where the injured person remained fully conscious, or cases where attempts to save the leg led to numerous unsuccessful operations so that amputation occurred years after the event.

(b) Severe Leg Injuries

(i) *The most serious injuries short of amputation* £42,500 to £57,500

Some injuries, although not involving amputation, are so severe that the courts have awarded damages at a comparable level. Such injuries would include extensive degloving of the leg, where there is gross shortening of the leg or where fractures have not united and extensive bone grafting has been undertaken.

(ii) *Very serious injuries* £25,000 to £37,500

Injuries leading to permanent problems with mobility, the need for crutches for the remainder of the injured person's life; injuries where multiple fractures have taken years to heal and have led to serious deformity and limitation of movement, or where arthritis has developed in a joint so that further surgical treatment is likely.

(iii) *Serious injuries* £18,250 to £25,000

Serious injuries to joints or ligaments resulting in instability, prolonged treatment or a lengthy period non-weight bearing, the near certainty that arthritis will ensue; injuries involving the hip, requiring arthrodesis or hip replacement, extensive scarring. To justify an award within this bracket a combination of such features will generally be necessary.

(iv) *Moderate injuries* £13,250 to £18,250

This bracket includes severe, complicated or multiple fractures. The level of an award within the bracket will be influenced by the period off work, the presence or risk of degenerative changes, imperfect union of fractures, muscle wasting, limited joint movements, instability in the knee, unsightly scarring or permanently increased vulnerability to future damage.

(c) Less Serious Leg Injuries

(i)	*Fractures from which an incomplete recovery is made*	£8,500 to £13,250
	The person injured will be left with a metal implant and/or defective gait, a limp, impaired mobility, sensory less, discomfort or an exacerbation of a pre-existing disability.	
(ii)	*Simple fracture of a femur with no damage to articular surfaces*	Up to £7,000
(iii)	*Simple fractures and soft tissue injuries*	Up to £4,250
	At the top of the bracket will come simple fractures of the tibia or fibula from which a complete recovery has been made. Below this level fall a wide variety of soft tissue injuries, lacerations, cuts, bruising or contusions, all of which have recovered completely or almost so and any residual disability is cosmetic or of a minor nature.	

(L) Knee Injuries

Knee injuries fall within a bracket extending from a few hundred pounds for a simple twisting injury up to £40,000 or more where there have been considerable problems leading to an arthrodesis.

(a) Severe Injuries

(i)	Serious knee injury where there has been disruption of the joint, gross ligamentous damage, lengthy treatment, considerable pain and loss of function and an arthrodesis has taken place or is inevitable.	£32,000 to £42,500
(ii)	Leg fracture extending into the knee joint causing pain which is constant, permanent, limiting movement or impairing agility and rendering the person injured prone to osteoarthritis and the risk of arthrodesis.	£24,000 to £32,000
(iii)	Less severe injuries than those in (ii) above and/or injuries which result in less severe disability. There may be continuing symptoms by way of pain and discomfort and limitation of movement or instability or deformity with the risk that degenerative changes may occur in the long term as a result of damage to the knee cap, ligamentous or meniscal injury or muscular wasting.	£12,750 to £20,000

(b) Moderate Injuries

(i)	Injuries involving dislocation, torn cartilage or meniscus or which accelerate symptoms from a pre-existing condition but which additionally result in minor instability, wasting, weakness or other mild future disability.	£7,000 to £12,750
(ii)	This bracket includes injuries similar to those in (i) above but	

less serious and also lacerations, twisting or bruising injuries. Where recovery has been complete the award is unlikely to exceed £3,000. Where there is continuous aching or discomfort or occasional pain the award will be towards the upper end of the bracket. Up to £6,500

(M) Ankle Injuries

The vast majority of ankle injuries are worth significantly less than £10,000. The ceiling, however, is about £32,000. This will be appropriate where the degree of disablement is very severe.

(a) Very Severe Injuries £23,500 to £32,000

Examples of injuries falling within this bracket are limited and unusual. They include cases of a transmalleolar fracture of the ankle with extensive soft tissue damage resulting in deformity and the risk that any future injury to the leg might necessitate a below knee amputation or cases of bilateral ankle fractures causing degeneration of the joints at a young age so that arthrodesis is necessary.

(b) Severe Injuries £15,000 to £23,500

Injuries necessitating an extensive period of treatment and/or a lengthy period in plaster or where pins and plates have been inserted and there is significant residual disability in the form of ankle instability, severely limited ability to walk or the like. The level of the award within the bracket will be determined in part by such features as a failed arthrodesis, regular sleep disturbance, unsightly operation scarring and any need to wear special footwear.

(c) **Moderate Injuries** £6,500 to £12,750

Fractures, ligamentous tears and the like which give rise to less serious disabilities such as difficulty in walking on uneven ground, awkwardness on stairs, irritation from metal plates and residual scarring.

(d) **Modest Injuries** Up to £6,500

The less serious, minor or undisplaced fractures, sprains and ligamentous injuries. The level of the award within the bracket will be determined by whether or not a complete recovery has been made and, if recovery is incomplete, whether there is any tendency for the ankle to give way, and whether there is scarring, aching or discomfort or the possibility of later osteoarthritis.

(N) Achilles Tendon

(a) **Most Serious** £17,250 to £19,000

Severance of the tendon and the peroneus longus muscle giving rise to cramp, swelling and restricted ankle movement necessitating the cessation of active sports.

(b) **Serious** £11,750 to £14,500

Where complete division of the tendon has been successfully repaired but there is residual weakness, a limitation of ankle movements, a limp and residual scarring and where further improvement is unlikely.

(c) Moderate £7,000 to £8,500

Complete division of the tendon but where its repair has left no significant functional disability.

(d) Minor £3,500 to £4,750

A turning of the ankle resulting in some damage to the tendon and a feeling of being unsure of ankle support.

(O) Foot Injuries

(a) Amputation of Both Feet £70,000 to £75,000

This injury is treated similarly to below knee amputation of both legs because the common feature is loss of a useful ankle joint.

(b) Amputation of One Foot £37,000 to £48,750

This injury is also treated as similar to a below knee amputation because of the loss of the ankle joint.

(c) Very Severe Injuries £37,000 to £48,750

To fall within this bracket the injury must produce permanent and severe pain or really serious permanent disability. Examples would include the traumatic amputation of the forefoot where there was a significant risk of the need for a full amputation and serious exacerbation of an existing back problem, or cases of the loss of a substantial portion of the heel so that mobility was grossly restricted.

(d) Severe Injuries £21,500 to £31,000

Fractures of *both* heels or feet with a substantial restriction on mobility or considerable or permanent pain. The bracket will also include unusually severe injury to a single foot resulting, for example, in heel fusion, osteoporosis, ulceration or other disability preventing the wearing of ordinary shoes. It will also apply in the case of a drop foot deformity corrected by a brace.

(e) Serious Injuries £12,000 to £18,500

Towards the top end of the bracket fall cases such as those of grievous burns to both feet requiring multiple operations and leaving disfiguring scars and persistent irritation. At the lower end of the bracket would be those injuries less severe than in (d) above but leading to fusion of foot joints, continuing pain from traumatic arthritis, prolonged treatment and the future risk of osteoarthritis.

(f) Moderate Injuries £6,500 to £12,000

Displaced metatarsal fractures resulting in permanent deformity and continuing symptoms.

(g) Modest Injuries Up to £6,500

Simple metatarsal fractures, ruptured ligaments, puncture wounds and the like. Where there are continuing symptoms, such as a permanent limp, pain or aching, awards between £3,250 and £6,500 would be appropriate. Straightforward foot injuries such as fractures, lacerations, contusions, etc., from which complete or near complete recovery is made would justify awards of £3,250 or less.

(P) Toe Injuries

(a) Amputation of All Toes £17,250 to £25,750

The position within the bracket will be determined by, for example, whether or not the amputation was traumatic or surgical and the extent of the loss of the forefoot together with the residual effects on mobility.

(b) **Amputation of the Great Toe**, in the region of — £14,500

(c) **Severe Toe Injuries** — £6,500 to £9,000

This is the appropriate bracket for severe crush injuries, falling short of the need for amputation or necessitating only partial amputation. It also includes bursting wounds and injuries resulting in severe damage and in any event producing significant continuing symptoms.

(d) **Serious Toe Injuries** — £6,500 to £9,000

Such injuries will be serious injuries to the great toe or crush and multiple fractures of two or more toes. There will be some permanent disability by way of discomfort, pain or sensitive scarring to justify an award within this bracket. Where there have been a number of unsuccessful operations or persisting stabbing pains, impaired gait or the like, the award will tend toward the top end of the bracket.

(e) **Moderate Toe Injuries** — Up to £4,500

These injuries include relatively straightforward fractures or the exacerbation of a pre-existing degenerative condition. Only £3,000 or less would be awarded for straightforward fractures of one or more toes with complete resolution within a short period of time and less still for minor injuries involving lacerations, cuts, contusions and bruises, in respect of all of which there would have been a complete or near complete recovery.

7. Facial Injuries

The assessment of general damages for facial injuries is an extremely difficult task, there being two elements which complicate the award.

First, while in most of the cases dealt with below the injuries described are skeletal, many of them will involve an element of disfigurement or at least cosmetic disability.

Secondly, in cases where there is a cosmetic element the courts have invariably drawn a distinction between the awards of damages to males and females, the latter attracting the higher awards.

The subject of burns is not dealt with separately, because burns of any degree of severity tend to be so devastating as to be invariably at the upper ends of the brackets.

In the guidance which follows some effort has been made to distinguish these types of cases but the above considerations must always be borne in mind. Where there is a cosmetic element care must be taken to endeavour to remain broadly within the guidelines which are extracted from reported decisions wherein a subjective element was taken into account.

(A) Skeletal Injuries

(a) Le Fort Fractures of Frontal Facial Bones £11,500 to £17,500

(b) Multiple Fractures of Facial Bones £7,250 to £11,500

Involving some facial deformity of a permanent nature.

(c) Fracture of Nose

(i) Serious fractures requiring a

number of operations and resulting in permanent damage to airways and/or facial deformity. £5,000 to £8,500

(ii) Displaced fracture where recovery complete but only after surgery. £1,850 to £2,250

(iii) Displaced fracture requiring no more than manipulation. £1,250 to £1,500

(iv) Simple undisplaced fracture with full recovery. £750 to £1,000

(d) Fractures of Cheekbones

(i) Serious fractures requiring surgery but with lasting consequences such as paraesthesia in the cheeks or the lips or some element of disfigurement. £4,750 to £7,500

(ii) Simple fracture of cheekbones for which some reconstructive surgery is necessary but from which there is a complete recovery with no or only minimal cosmetic effects. £2,000 to £3,000

(iii) Simple fracture of cheekbones for which no surgery is required and where a complete recovery is effected. £1,150 to £1,450

(e) Fractures of Jaws

(i) Very serious multiple fractures followed by prolonged treatment and permanent consequences, including severe pain, restriction in eating, paraesthesia and/or the risk of arthritis in the joints. £14,250 to £21,250

(ii) Serious fracture with permanent

consequences such as difficulty in opening the mouth or with eating or where there is paraesthesia in the area of the jaw. £8,500 to £14,250

(iii) Simple fracture requiring immobilisation but from which recovery is complete £3,000 to £4,000

(f) Damage to Teeth

In these cases there will generally have been a course of treatment. The amounts awarded will vary as to the extent and/or the degree of discomfort of such treatment. It will often be necessary to award a lump sum in respect of the cost of future dental treatment.

(i) Loss of serious damage to several front teeth. £4,000 to £5,000

(ii) Loss of two front teeth. £2,000 to £2,650

(iii) Loss of one front tooth. £1,000 to £1,700

(iv) Loss of or damage to back teeth: per tooth £500 to £850

(B) Facial Disfigurement

In this class of case the distinction between male and female and the subjective approach are of particular significance.

(a) Females

(i) *Very severe facial scarring*

In a relatively young girl (teens to early thirties) where the cosmetic effect is very disfiguring and the psychological reaction severe. £22,500 to £42,500

(ii) *Less severe scarring*

Where the disfigurement is still substantial and where there is a significant psychological reaction.	£14,500 to £22,500

(iii) *Significant scarring*

Where the worst effects have been or will be reduced by plastic surgery leaving some cosmetic disability and where the psychological reaction is not great or having been considerable at the outset has diminished to relatively minor proportions.	£8,500 to £14,500

(iv) *Less significant scarring*

In these cases there may be but one scar which can be camouflaged or though there are a large number of very small scars the overall effect is to mar but not markedly to affect the appearance and where the reaction is no more than that of an ordinarily sensitive young woman.	£2,000 to £6,500

(b) Males

(i) *Very severe facial scars*

These are to be found especially in males under thirty, where there is permanent disfigurement even after plastic surgery and a considerable element of psychological reaction.	£14,500 to £30,000

(ii) *Severe facial scarring*

This will have left moderate to severe permanent disfigurement.	£8,500 to £14,500

(iii) *Significant but not severe scars*

Such scars will remain visible at conversational distances.	£4,250 to £8,500

(iv) *Relatively minor scarring*

Such scarring is not particularly prominent except on close inspection.	£2,000 to £4,250

(v) *Trivial scarring*

In these cases the effect is minor only.	£850 to £1,600

8. Scarring to Other Parts of the Body

This is an area in which it is not possible to offer much useful guidance. The principles are the same as those applied to cases of facial disfigurement and the brackets are broadly the same. It must be remembered that many of the physical injuries already described involve some element of disfigurement and that element is of course taken into account in suggesting the appropriate bracket. There remain some cases where the element of disfigurement is the predominant one in the assessment of damages. Where the scarring is not to the face or is not usually visible then the awards will tend to be lower than those for facial or readily visible disfigurement.

The effects of burns will normally be regarded as more serious since they tend to cause a greater degree of pain and to lead to greater disfigurement.

There is, however, one area in which an almost "conventional" figure has emerged. In cases where an exploratory laparotomy has been performed but no significant internal injury has been found the award for the operation and the inevitable scar is of the order of £4,000. The situation rarely occurs and when it falls to be valued it is usually by the Criminal Injuries Compensation Board. The suggested figure is based on the effects of inflation on the figure current when these guidelines were first produced.

9. Damage to Hair

(a) Damage to hair in consequence of permanent waving, tinting or the like, where the effects are tingling or "burning" of the scalp causing dry, brittle hair, which breaks off and/or falls out leading to distress, depression, embarrassment and loss of confidence, and inhibiting social life. In the more serious cases thinning continues and the prospects of regrowth are poor or there has been total loss of areas of hair and regrowth is slow. £3,250 to £5,250

(b) Less serious versions of the above where symptoms are fewer or only of a minor character; also, cases where hair has been pulled out leaving bald patches. The level of the award will depend on the length of time taken before regrowth occurs. £1,850 to £3,250

INDEX

ACCELERATION OF PRE-EXISTING DISABILITY OR CONDITION
See **Pre-existing**

ACCIDENT
contingency See **Contingencies**
fatal See **Heads of damage**
insurance
not deducted from loss of earnings, 42
supervening See **Supervening**

ACCOMMODATION
See **Earnings**
Outlays and expenses
Support

ACHILLES TENDON
guidelines for the assessment of general damages for injury to, 394

ACTUARIAL TABLES
court should use in selection of multiplier, 9
Ogden Tables,
use of, 9, 89
PNBA Tables,
use of, 143

AFFINITY
equivalent to consanguinity, 57, 62, 67, 73, 80, 83

AGGRAVATION OF PRE-EXISTING DISABILITY OR CONDITION
See **Pre-existing**

AIDS, APPLIANCES AND EQUIPMENT
See **Outlays and expenses**

ALLOWANCES
See **Benefits**

AMENITIES, LOSS OF
See **Solatium**

AMPUTATION
guidelines for the assessment of general damages for
arms, 379
feet, 395
fingers, 382
legs, 388
toes, 396

ANKLE INJURIES
guidelines for the assessment of general damages for, 393

ANNUITY APPROACH
in practice, 9
purpose of, 7
requirement underlying, 8
See also **Multiplier/multiplicand**

ANTECEDENT AGREEMENT
See **Liability**

ANTENATAL INJURIES
deceased person includes child dying after birth from, 67, 73, 80

ANXIETY
See **Loss of society**
Solatium

APPEAL
court may allow at stage of
additional proof, 4
amendment of pleadings, 4
criteria for, 4

APPLIANCES
See **Outlays and expenses**

ARM INJURIES
guidelines for the assessment of general damages for
amputation, 379
other arm injuries, 380
work-related disorders, 387

ASCENDANT
a relative
of deceased, 73, 80, 83
of injured person, 57,62

ASSESSMENT OF DAMAGES
for loss
postdating trial, 4, 5, 6, 7
preceding trial, 4, 5, 6
is once and for all, 4
object of, 4

ASTHMA
guidelines for the assessment of general damages for, 367

ATTENDANCE
See **Necessary services**
Outlays and expenses

ATTENDANCE ALLOWANCE
as listed benefit, 51
not deducted from damages, 38

AUNT
a relative
of deceased, 73, 80, 83
of injured person, 57, 62

AWARDS OF DAMAGES
comparable
taken into account in assessing solatium, 34
lump sum
final decrees for damages, 3
interim payment of damages, 12
review of See **Appeal**
See also **Awards of provisional damages**
Final decrees for damages
Interest on damages
Interim payment of damages

AWARDS OF PROVISIONAL DAMAGES
application for, 22
conditions precedent for
defender a public authority, public corporation or insured or otherwise indemnified, 22
risk of development of serious disease or suffering of serious deterioration of condition, 22
factors relevant to exercise of court's discretion in making, 24
powers of court in relation to, 23
See also **Further awards of damages**

BACK INJURIES
guidelines for the assessment of general damages for, 375

BALANCE OF PROBABILITY
test for past events, 5
not test for hypothetical state of facts, 5 See **Chances**

BANKRUPTCY
See **Trustee in sequestration**

BENEFITS
contractual See **Loss of earnings**
death See **Loss of support**
family credit See **Earnings**
fringe See **Earnings**
income support
as listed benefit, 38
payable after trial not deducted from loss of earnings, 42
payable before trial deducted from loss of earnings, 40 But see **Benefits, listed**
See also **Earnings**
in kind See **Earnings**
jobseeker's allowance
as listed benefit, 38
payable after trial not deducted from loss of earnings, 42
payable before trial deducted from loss of earnings, 40 But see **Benefits, listed**
listed,
disregarded when assessing

damages, 40 But see **Deductions and set-offs**
interest on damages, 27
recoverable from compensation payment for
cost of care
attendance allowance, 51
care component of disability living allowance, 51
disablement pension increase under ss.104 and 105 of 1992 Act, 51
loss of earnings
disability working allowance, 38
disablement pension under s.103 of 1992 Act, 38
incapacity benefit, 38
income support, 38
invalidity pension and allowance, 38
jobseeker's allowance, 38
reduced earnings allowance, 38
severe disablement allowance, 38
sickness benefit, 38
statutory sick pay for the period ending 6 April 1994, 38
unemployability supplement, 38
unemployment benefit, 38
loss of mobility
mobility allowance, 51
mobility component of disability living allowance, 51
non-recoupable See **Earnings**
recovery of
duty of court to specify amount of compensation payment for
cost of care incurred during the relevant period, 51
loss of earnings during the relevant period, 38
loss of mobility during the relevant period, 51
legislation
Social Security (Recovery of benefits) Act 1997, 317
Social Security (Recovery of benefits) Regulations 1997, 339
relevant period for
in relation to accident or injury, 38, 51
in relation to disease, 38, 51
See also **Interest on damages**
Schedule of damages (Recovery of benefits)

BENEVOLENT PAYMENTS
made in respect of personal injuries
deducted from damages where made directly by wrongdoer, 41
generally not deducted from damages, 42
made in respect of death of relative
not deducted from loss of support, 77

BEREAVEMENT
See **Loss of society**

BLADDER
guidelines for the assessment of general damages for injuries to, 370

BLINDNESS
See **Injuries affecting Sight**

BOWELS
guidelines for the assessment of general damages for injuries to, 370

BRAIN DAMAGE
guidelines for the assessment of general damages for, 353

BROTHER
a relative
of deceased, 73, 80, 83
of injured person, 57, 62

BROTHER-IN-LAW
a relative
of deceased, 73, 80, 83
of injured person, 57, 62

BURIAL
See **Funeral expenses**

CARE
See **Outlays and expenses**
Necessary services

CARE COMPONENT OF DISABILITY LIVING ALLOWANCE
as listed benefit, 51
not deducted from damages, 38

CAREER, LOSS OF
See **Solatium**

CENTRAL HEATING
See **Outlays and expenses**

CHANCES
estimation or evaluation of, 5

CHEEKBONES
See **Facial injuries**

CHEST INJURIES
guidelines for the assessment of general damages for, 364

CHILD
damages payable to or for benefit of
interim payment of damages, 14
final decree for damages, 3
dying from antenatal injuries See **Antenatal injuries**
title to sue of
accepted
as member of deceased's immediately family, 67
as relative of deceased, 73, 80, 83
illegitimate
as member of deceased's immediate family, 67
as relative of deceased, 73, 80, 83
posthumous

as member of deceased's immediate family, 67
as relative of deceased, 73, 80, 83
step
as member of deceased's immediate family, 67
as relative of deceased, 73, 80, 83
See also **Family members**
Loss of earnings

CHILDCARE
See **Deceased person's services**
Personal services

CLEANING
See **Necessary services**
Personal services

CLOTHING AND DRESSING
See **Outlays and expenses**

COHABITANT
a relative
of deceased, 67, 73, 83
of injured person, 57, 62

COMPANY
car See **Earnings**
dividend See **Earnings**
not entitled to recover damages for personal injuries sustained by employee, 37

COMPROMISE
See **Liability**

COMPUTER EQUIPMENT
See **Outlays and expenses**

CONDITION
pre-existing See **Pre-existing**
supervening See **Supervening**

CONGENIAL EMPLOYMENT, LOSS OF
See **Solatium**

CONNECTED PERSON
application to be sisted as additional pursuer by, 70
definition of, 69
dispensation with intimation to, 69
intimation to, 69

CONSANGUINITY
See **Affinity**

CONSECUTIVE ACCIDENTS
See **Supervening**

CONSENT ORDERS FOR PERIODICAL PAYMENTS
nature of, 16

CONTINGENCIES
assessment of, 6
examples of
accident or injury, 7, 46, 79
alternative employment or pension, 46, 48
divorce, 61, 64, 79, 86
illness or disease, 7, 11, 43, 46, 48, 79
mortality, 9
promotion or move to better paid work, 46, 79
uncertainties in medical condition, 55
unemployment or early retirement, 11, 46, 48, 79
variations in amount of earnings, 46, 75
type of
future, 6, 46
hypothetical, 6, 46

CONTRACTUAL PENSION OR BENEFIT
deducted from loss of pension rights, 47
not deducted from loss of earnings, 41

CONTRIBUTION BASED JOBSEEKERS ALLOWANCE
as listed benefit, 38
deducted from loss of earnings, 40 But see **Benefits**

CONTRIBUTIONS
national insurance
hypothetical
deducted from loss of earnings, 40
pension
hypothetical
deducted from loss of earnings, 40
repayment of
deducted from loss of pension rights, 47

CONTRIBUTORY NEGLIGENCE
See **Interim payment of damages**

COOKING
See **Necessary services**
Personal services

COSTS
See **Outlays and expenses**

COUSIN
a relative
of deceased, 73, 80, 83
of injured person, 57, 62

CREMATION
See **Funeral expenses**

CURATORY EXPENSES
See **Outlays and expenses**

DAMAGE
brain See **Brain damage**
hair See **Hair damage**
heads of See **Heads of damage**
psychiatric See **Post traumatic stress disorder**
Psychiatric damage generally
psychological See **Post traumatic stress disorder**
Psychiatric damage generally

DAMAGES
awards of See **Awards of damages**
final decrees for See **Final decrees for damages**
further See **Further awards of damages**
interest on See **Interest on damages**
interim payment of See **Interim payment of damages**
overlapping of See **Overlapping of damages**
provisional See **Provisional awards of damages**

DAUGHTER
a member of deceased's immediately family, 67
a relative
of deceased, 73, 80, 83
of injured person, 57, 62

DAUGHTER-IN-LAW
a member of deceased's immediate family, 67
a relative
of deceased, 73, 80, 83
of injured person, 57, 62

DEAFNESS
guidelines for the assessment of general damages for
partial hearing loss, 361
tinnitus, 362
total deafness, 362
and blindness, 360
and loss of speech, 362
total loss of hearing in one ear, 362

DEATH
See **Executor**
Heads of damage

DECEASED PERSON'S SERVICES
award for loss of
application for
relative, 83-84
relative's executor, 84
See also **Connected person**
title to sue for, 83
See also **Liability**
method of assessment of

factors relevant to
age and expectation of life
of deceased person, 86
of relative, 86
change in nature of services over time, 86
contingencies, such as
divorce, 86
cost of person reasonably employed to perform services, 85
estimated time expended on services, 85
lump sum, 86
multiplier/multiplicand, 86
examples, 311
nature of
childcare, 85, 299, 301
housekeeping and maintenance
car, 306
decorating, 305
furniture repair, 299
gardening, 299, 304, 306
generally, 85, 301, 305, 306
home improvements, 299
See also **Interest on damages**
Personal services

DECORATING
See **Deceased person's services**
Personal services

DEDUCTIONS AND SET-OFFS
against damages for personal injuries generally
benevolent payments
deducted from damages where made directly by wrongdoer, 41
against loss of earnings
contribution based jobseekers allowance, 40 But see **Benefits**
earnings from employment, 40
hypothetical
contributions
national insurance, 40
pension, 40
earnings from employment, 41
income tax, 40
outgoings, 41
income support payable before date of trial, 40 But see **Benefits**
saving attributable to maintenance at public expense in hospital, nursing home or other institution, 41
severance pay, 42
sick pay (occupational), 40
tax rebate, 41
tax saving, 41
against loss of pension rights
contractual (disability or incapacity) pension, 47
hypothetical income tax, 47
lump sum representing commutation of pension payments for retirement period, 47
other occupational pension, 47

repayment of pension contributions, 47
against loss of support
deceased's personal and living expenses, 76
support provided after death by another person, 77
against outlays and expenses
domestic element of cost of care which would have been incurred anyway, 52
enhancement of value of property caused by adaptations, 53
trade-in value of existing property substituted, 53

DELAY
See **Interest on damages**

DESCENDANT
a relative
of deceased, 73, 80, 83
of injured person, 57, 62

DETERIORATION AFTER AWARD
See **Appeal**
Awards of provisional damages
Further awards of damages

DIGESTIVE SYSTEM
guidelines for the assessment of general damages for injuries to, 367

DIMINUTION IN EARNINGS
See **Loss of earnings**

DISABILITY
benefit
contractual
not deducted from loss of earnings, 41
state
disability living allowance, care component of
as listed benefit, 51
not deducted from damages, 38
disability living allowance, mobility component of
as listed benefit, 51
not deducted from damages, 38
disability working allowance
as listed benefit, 38
not deducted from damages, 38
pension
contractual
deducted from loss of pension rights, 47
not deducted from loss of earnings, 41
state
disablement pension
as listed benefit, 38
not deducted from damages, 38
disablement pension increase
as listed benefit, 51
not deducted from damages, 38
pre-existing See **Pre-existing**

DISABLEMENT
pension
as listed benefit, 38
not deducted from damages, 38
pension increase
as listed benefit, 51
not deducted from damages, 38

DISADVANTAGE IN LABOUR MARKET
See **Loss of earnings**

DISASTER FUND
See **Benevolent payments**

DISCHARGE OF LIABILITY
See **Liability**

DISCOUNT
factor, 10
rate, 8

DISEASE
serious See **Awards of provisional damages**
supervening See **Supervening**
See also **Benefits**
Lung disease

DISFIGUREMENT
See **Facial disfigurement**
Scarring to other parts of the body

DISORDER, POST TRAUMATIC STRESS
See **Post traumatic stress disorder**

DISTRESS
See **Loss of society**

DIVIDEND, COMPANY
See **Earnings**

DIVORCE
See **Contingencies**

DIVORCED SPOUSE
See **Spouse, former**

DOMESTIC ASSISTANCE
See **Outlays and expenses**

DOMESTIC TASKS
See **Deceased person's services**
Necessary services
Personal services

DOUBLE RECOVERY
claim for loss of earnings and for services rendered amounts to, 5

DRESSING
See **Necessary services**

DRESSING, CLOTHING AND
See **Outlays and expenses**

DRIVING
See **Necessary services**
Personal services

DUPLICATION OF DAMAGES
See **Overlapping of damages**

EARNINGS
form of,
agreed share of partnership profits, 37
benefits in kind, 37
dividends from limited company, 37
family credit, 37
illegal, 37
income support, 38
non-recoupable benefits, 38
overtime, 37
perquisites, 37
free accommodation, 37
free car, 37
fringe benefits, 37
profits from sole trading, 37
redundancy payment, 38
undeclared earnings, 37
wage or salary from employer, 37
changes in
promoted or otherwise better paid employment, 5, 39, 46
variations prior to date of trial, 43
variations after trial, 46
loss of See **Loss of earnings**

EARNING CAPACITY, LOSS OF
See **Loss of earnings**

ELBOW INJURIES
guidelines for the assessment of general damages for, 381
See also **Arm injuries**

EMPLOYABILITY, LOSS OF
See **Loss of earnings**

EMPLOYEE
no relevant claim for loss of earnings arising out of injuries suffered by, 36

EMPLOYMENT
See **Loss of earnings**

ENGLISH AWARDS OF GENERAL DAMAGES
where comparable should be taken into account in assessing solatium, 34
See also **General damages**

EPILEPSY
guidelines for the assessment of general damages for, 356

EQUIPMENT
See **Outlays and expenses**

EX GRATIA PAYMENTS
See **Benevolent payments**

EXACERBATION OF PRE-EXISTING DISABILITY OR CONDITION
See **Pre-existing**

EXECUTOR
deceased relative's
application by
intimation of action See **Connected person**
nature of claim
funeral expenses, 81
loss of society, 68
loss of support, 74
deceased person's services, 84
title to sue of
funeral expenses, 81
loss of society for the period until relative's death, 68
loss of support for the period until relative's death, 74
deceased person's services for the period until relative's death, 84
injured person's
application by
intimation of action See **Connected person**
nature of claim
loss of earnings, 36
necessary services, 56
outlays and expenses, 49
personal services, 61
solatium, 31
title to sue of
loss of earnings for the period until injured person's death, 36
loss of pension rights for the period until injured person's death, 46
necessary services for the period until injured person's death, 56
outlays and expenses for the period until injured person's death, 49
personal services for the period until injured person's death, 61
solatium for the period until injured person's death, 31
See also **Liability**

EXPECTATION OF LIFE
See **Life**

EXPECTATION OF WORKING LIFE
See **Loss of earnings**

EXPENDITURE
See **Deductions and set-offs**
Outlays and expenses

EXPENSES
See **Funeral expenses**
Necessary services
Outlays and expenses

EYE INJURIES
See **Injuries affecting sight**

FACIAL INJURIES
guidelines for the assessment of general damages for
skeletal injuries to
cheekbones, 400
facial bones, 399
jaw, 400
nose, 399
teeth, 401
facial disfigurement of
females, 401
males, 402

FACULTIES, LOSS OF
See **Loss of faculties**

FAMILY CREDIT
See **Earnings**

FAMILY MEMBERS
no relevant claim arising out of injuries sustained by other
loss of earnings, 36
outlays and expenses, 49
solatium, 31
See also **Relatives**

FATAL ACCIDENTS
See **Heads of damage**

FATHER
a member of deceased's immediate family, 67
a relative
of deceased, 73, 80, 83
of injured person, 57, 62

FATHER-IN-LAW
a member of deceased's immediate family, 67
a relative
of deceased, 73, 80, 83
of injured person, 57, 62

FEAR
See **Solatium**

FEET
See **Foot injuries**

FINAL DECREES FOR DAMAGES
form of, 3
in favour of child, 3
in foreign currency, 3

FINALITY IN LITIGATION, PRINCIPLE OF
consequence of, 4
disapplication of, 4

FINANCIAL LOSS
See **Pecuniary loss**

FINANCIAL OPPORTUNITY, LOSS OF
See **Loss of earnings**

FINGERS
See **Hand injuries**

FLOWERS
See **Funeral expenses**

FOOD
See **Outlays and expenses**

FOOT INJURIES
guidelines for the assessment of general damages for
amputation, 395
other injuries, 395
See also **Toe injuries**

FOREARM
See **Arm injuries**

FOREIGN CURRENCY
decree may be awarded in
for any pecuniary loss, 3
with alternative in sterling, 3

FORMER SPOUSE
a relative
of deceased, 73, 80, 83
of injured person, 57, 62

FRINGE BENEFITS
See **Earnings**

FUNERAL EXPENSES
award of
application for
relative, 80
relative's executor, 81

See also **Connected person**
title to sue for, 80
See also **Liability**
nature of,
flowers, 81
gravediggers' gratuities, 81
headstone, 82
incidental travelling expenses, 82
mourning clothes, 82
transporting of ashes, 82
undertaker's account, 81
See also **Interest on damages**

FURNISHINGS
See **Outlays and expenses**

FURTHER AWARDS OF DAMAGES
application for, 25
criteria for
pursuer has developed the disease or suffered the deterioration, 25
See also **Awards of provisional damages**

GARDENING
See **Deceased person's services**
Necessary services
Personal services

GENERAL DAMAGES
guidelines for the assessment of,
See also **English awards of general damages**

GOODS
See **Outlays and expenses**

GRANDCHILD
a relative
of deceased, 73, 80, 83
of injured person, 57, 62

GRANDPARENT
a relative
of deceased, 73, 80, 83
of injured person, 57, 62

GRATUITY
See **Benevolent payments**

GRAVEDIGGERS
See **Funeral expenses**

GRIEF
See **Loss of society**
Solatium

GUIDELINES
See **Judicial Studies Board Guidelines**

HALF BLOOD
relationship equivalent to full blood, 57, 62, 67, 73, 80, 83

HAIR
guidelines for the assessment of general damages for damage to, 405

HAND INJURIES
guidelines for the assessment of general damages for
amputations, 382
index fingers, 383
ring or middle fingers, 383
thumbs, 384
total effective loss of both hands, 382
total or effective loss of one hand, 382
vibration white finger, 385

HANDICAP IN LABOUR MARKET
See **Loss of earnings**

HEAD INJURIES
See **Brain damage**
Epilepsy
Minor head injury

HEADS OF DAMAGE
for claims for personal injuries
loss of earnings, 36
loss of pension rights, 46
necessary services, 56
outlays and expenses, 49
personal services, 61
solatium, 31
for claims for death of relative
deceased person's services, 83
funeral expenses, 80
loss of society, 67
loss of support, 73

HEADSTONE
See **Funeral expenses**

HEALTH SERVICE, NATIONAL
See **Outlays and expenses**

HEARING, LOSS OF
See **Deafness**

HEATING
See **Outlays and expenses**

HERITABLE PROPERTY
See **Outlays and expenses**

HERNIA
guidelines for the assessment of general damages for, 372

HIPS, INJURIES TO PELVIS AND
See **Injuries to pelvis and hips**

HOBBY, LOSS OF
See **Solatium**

HOLIDAYS AND RECREATION
See **Outlays and expenses**

HOLIDAY, LOSS OF
See **Solatium**

HOME IMPROVEMENTS
See **Deceased person's services**
Personal services

HOSPITAL
See **Deductions and expenses**
Outlays and expenses

HOUSE
See **Earnings**
Outlays and expenses
Support

HOUSEHOLD CHORES
See **Deceased person's services**
Necessary services
Personal services

HOUSEHOLD EXPENSES
See **Outlays and expenses**

HOUSEHOLD REPAIRS
See **Deceased person's services**
Personal services

HOUSEKEEPING
See **Deceased person's services**
Necessary services
Personal services

HOUSEWORK
See **Deceased person's services**
Necessary services
Personal services

HUSBAND
See **Spouse**

HUSBAND, FORMER
See **Former spouse**

ILLEGAL EARNINGS
See **Earnings**

ILLEGITIMATE CHILD
See **Child**

ILLNESS
See **Contingencies**
Supervening

IMPAIRMENT OF TASTE AND SMELL
guidelines for the assessment of general damages for, 363

IMPOTENCE
See **Reproductive system**

INABILITY TO RENDER PERSONAL SERVICES
See **Personal services**

INCAPACITY BENEFIT
as listed benefit, 38
not deducted from damages, 38

INCAPACITY PENSION
See **Disability**

INCOME SUPPORT
as listed benefit, 38
payable after trial not deducted from loss of earnings, 42
payable before trial deducted from loss of earnings, 40 But see **Benefits**

INCOME TAX
hypothetical
deducted from loss of earnings, 40
effect of failure to lead evidence as to net income, 40
tax treatment where partial loss, 40
gross income relevant where damages taxable by foreign government, 40

INCREASES IN EARNINGS
See **Contingencies**
Earnings
Loss of earnings

INDEX FINGER
See **Hand injuries**

INDEX LINKED GOVERNMENT SECURITIES
rate of return for future pecuniary losses based on, 8

INFERTILITY
See **Reproductive system**

INFLATION
taken into account
future loss

pecuniary, 8
past loss
non-pecuniary, 35, 72
pecuniary, 43, 75

INHERITANCE
See **Loss of support**

INJURED PERSON'S SERVICES
See **Necessary services**
Personal services

INJURY
See **Contingencies**
Solatium

INJURIES
See **Ankle injuries**
Antenatal injuries
Arm injuries
Back injuries
Chest Injuries
Elbow injuries
Facial injuries
Foot injuries
Hand injuries
Head injuries
Injuries affecting sight
Injuries affecting the senses
Injuries involving paralysis
Injuries to internal organs
Injuries to pelvis and hips
Knee injuries
Leg injuries
Multiple injuries
Neck injuries
Orthopaedic injuries
Shoulder injuries
Wrist injuries

INJURIES AFFECTING SIGHT
guidelines for the assessment of general damages for
complete loss of sight in one eye, 360
loss of sight in one eye with reduced vision in the remaining eye, 360
minor eye injuries, 361
total blindness, 360
total blindness and deafness, 360
total loss of one eye, 360
transient eye injuries, 361

INJURIES AFFECTING THE SENSES
See **Deafness**
Impairment of taste and smell
Injuries affecting sight

INJURIES INVOLVING PARALYSIS
See **Paraplegia**
Quadriplegia

INJURIES TO INTERNAL ORGANS
See **Asthma**
Bladder
Bowels
Chest injuries
Digestive system
Hernia
Kidney
Lung disease
Reproductive system
Spleen

INJURIES TO PELVIS AND HIPS
guidelines for the assessment of general damages for, 377

INLAND REVENUE
See **Earnings**

IN-LAWS
See **Daughter-in-law**
Father-in-law
Mother-in-law
Son-in-law

INSTITUTION
See **Deductions and set-offs**
Outlays and expenses

INSURANCE
arrangements
injured person's title to sue unaffected by, 31, 36, 46, 49, 56, 61
contributions
hypothetical national insurance
deducted from loss of earnings, 40
money
accident
not deducted from loss of earnings, 42
death
not deducted from loss of support, 77

INSURER
See **Awards of provisional damages**
Interim payment of damages

INTEREST
compound
formula, 8
relevance to annuity approach of, 8
rate of, 8
See also **Interest on damages**

INTEREST ON DAMAGES
application for, 26
duty of court in relation to
allocation of certain heads of damage between past and future
deceased person's services, 85
loss of earnings, 38
loss of society, 71
loss of support, 75
necessary services, 58
personal services, 63
outlays and expenses, 52
solatium, 32
exercise of the power to award interest unless reasons special to the case why not, 26
having regard to the legal rate of interest from time to time prevailing, 27
powers of court in relation to
delay in
pursuing claim for past non-pecuniary loss, 27
pursuing claim for past pecuniary loss, 27
interim payment, 28
past loss
cumulative and continuing, 28
cumulative but ceased, 28
not cumulative, 27
tender, 28
review of award of , 26

INTERIM PAYMENT OF DAMAGES
application for, 12
conditions precedent for
defender insured, a public authority or a person whose means and resources such as to enable him to make the interim payment, 12
defender has admitted liability or pursuer would succeed on question of liability without any substantial finding of contributory negligence on his part, 13
factors relevant to exercise of court's discretion in making
effect on pursuer of delay in payment of his damages, 13
occurrence or otherwise to date of losses, 13
proximity to trial, 13
method of assessment of damages, 13
powers of court in relation to
for child, 14
in one lump sum or otherwise, 14
payment to defender by other defender or third party, 15
periodical payments with parties' consent, 15
repayment of interim payment, 15
where change of circumstances, 15

INTERNAL ORGANS, INJURIES TO
See **Injuries to internal organs**

INTIMATION OF ACTION
See **Connected person**

INVALIDITY PENSION AND ALLOWANCE
as listed benefit, 38
not deducted from damages, 38

JAW
See **Facial injuries**

JOBSEEKER'S ALLOWANCE
as listed benefit, 38
payable after trial not deducted from loss of earnings, 42
payable before trial deducted from loss of earnings, 40 But see **Benefits**

JUDICIAL STUDIES BOARD GUIDELINES
details of, 349-405
use of, 34

JURY
award by
solatium, 33

KIDNEY
guidelines for the assessment of general damages for injuries to, 370

KNEE INJURIES
guidelines for the assessment of general damages for, 391

LAUNDRY
See **Outlays and expenses**
Necessary services
Personal services

LEG INJURIES
guidelines for the assessment of general damages for
amputations, 388
other leg injuries, 389
See also **Achilles tendon**
Ankle injuries
Foot injuries
Knee injuries
Toe injuries

LEISURE TIME. LOSS OF
See **Solatium**

LIABILITY
discharge by antecedent agreement or otherwise of
to relative, 68, 74, 81, 84
limitation by antecedent agreement or compromise or otherwise of
to deceased's executor, 36, 49, 56, 62
to relative, 68, 74, 81, 84

LIFE
expectation of
shortening of life irrelevant
loss of earnings, 45
solatium, 32 But see **Suffering**
taken into consideration
deceased person's services, 86
loss of earnings, 45

loss of pension rights, 48
loss of support, 78
necessary services, 61
outlays and expenses, 54
personal services, 64
tables, 163

LIMITATION OF LIABILITY
See **Liability**

LOSS
future, 6
negative See **Deceased person's services**
Loss of earnings
Loss of pension rights
Loss of society
Loss of support
Necessary services
Personal services
Solatium
non-pecuniary See **Deceased person's services**
Loss of society
Necessary services
Personal services
Solatium
past, 4, 5
pecuniary See **Funeral expenses**
Loss of earnings
Loss of pension rights
Necessary services
Loss of support
Outlays and expenses
positive See **Funeral expenses**
Necessary services
Outlays and expenses
Solatium

LOSS OF AMENITIES
See **Solatium**

LOSS OF EARNING CAPACITY
See **Loss of earnings**

LOSS OF EARNINGS
award for
application for
injured person, 36
injured person's executor, 36 See also **Connected person**
Liability
injured person's trustee in sequestration, 37
See also **Employee**
Family members
factors relevant to assessment of
failure to mitigate loss, 41, 177, 178, 179, 180, 184, 195, 199, 200, 204, 206, 208, 214, 215, 218, 226, 230, 251, 271, 272

pre-existing disability or condition, 6, 174, 177, 182, 183, 184, 185, 192, 193, 197, 198, 199, 202, 203, 207, 209, 213, 217, 222, 228, 236, 242, 245, 249, 255, 258, 259, 263, 266, 277, 279

pre-existing weakness or vulnerability, 6, 221, 265, 267, 277

supervening events, such as

accident, 6

illness or disease, 6, 43, 196, 199, 217, 234

promotion, 191, 247

redundancy, 11, 43, 173, 176, 179, 180, 185, 192, 196, 198, 199, 202, 203, 204, 211, 214, 219, 226, 271, 272, 279

See also **Deductions and set-offs**

factors not relevant to assessment of

benevolent payments (unless made directly by wrongdoer), 41

contractual pensions or benefits (including any payment by friendly society or trade union), 41

accident insurance, 42

disability scheme payments, 42

income support payable after date of trial, 42

payments made by employer subject to obligation to reimburse, 42

redundancy payments, 42

shortening of injured person's life, 45

state pensions or retirement benefits, 42

travel expenses generally, 40

method of assessment of

future loss

factors relevant to

age of injured person, 45

contingencies, such as

accident, 46, 197

alternative employment, 46, 181, 182, 187, 188, 190, 191, 192, 193, 194, 195, 196, 197, 203, 206, 209, 211, 212, 213, 214, 215, 220, 221, 223, 225, 228, 232, 233, 236, 238, 239, 240, 245, 246, 248, 250, 256, 257, 266, 267, 271, 273, 274, 277, 279, 281, 283

deferment of commencement of period of loss, 46, 221

deterioration in medical condition, 221, 225, 251, 252, 266, 270

early retirement, 198, 202, 203, 223, 235, 281

illness, 46, 183, 207, 281

improvement in medical condition, 187, 195

promotion, 46, 175, 186, 191, 239

redundancy, 46, 183, 187, 191, 201, 203, 208, 229, 232, 245, 252

uncertainties in employment prospects, 216, 227, 229, 230, 233, 234, 240, 255, 257, 262, 263, 266, 268, 275

variations in amount of earnings, 46, 208, 238, 246

normal retirement age applicable to injured person's employment, 46

lump sum, 43, 312

child, 44

examples, 312

loss of opportunity (or loss of earning capacity or of employability or handicap or disadvantage on the labour market), 39, 44

multiplier/multiplicand, 43

examples, 308

past loss, 43

loss of opportunity, 39, 44

nature of See **Earnings**

See also **Interest on damages**

LOSS OF EMPLOYABILITY
See **Loss of earnings**

LOSS OF FACULTIES
See **Solatium**

LOSS OF FINANCIAL OPPORTUNITY
See **Loss of earnings**

LOSS OF OPPORTUNITY
See **Loss of earnings**

LOSS OF PENSION RIGHTS
award for
application for
injured person, 46
injured person's executor, 46 See also **Connected person**
Liability
injured person's trustee in sequestration, 46
factors relevant to assessment of
See **Deductions and set-offs**
method of assessment of
factors relevant to
age of injured person, 48
contingencies, such as
another pension, 48
dismissal, 48
illness, 48
redundancy, 48
deferment of commencement of period of loss, 48
expectation of life at commencement of loss, 48
value of any lump sum benefit, 48
lump sum, 47
multiplier/multiplicand, 47
examples, 309
See also **Pension**

LOSS OF SERVICES
See **Deceased person's services**
Necessary services
Personal services

LOSS OF SOCIETY
award for
application for
relative, 68
relative's executor, 68
See also **Connected person**
title to sue for, 67
See also **Liability**
components of,
distress and anxiety endured in contemplation of deceased's suffering, 71
grief and sorrow, 71
loss of non-patrimonial benefit from deceased's society and guidance, 71
factors relevant to assessment of

age and expectation of life
of deceased, 71, 72
of relative, 71, 72
circumstances of joint life, 71
conduct of deceased
towards others, 71
towards relative, 71
contact between deceased and relative, 71
death of surviving spouse, 72
factors not relevant to assessment of
widow's
prospects of remarriage, 72
remarriage, 72
method of assessment of
comparable awards
previous awards updated, 72
judicial experience, 72
facts of case, 72
See also **Interest on damages**

LOSS OF SUPPORT
award for
application for
relative, 74
relative's executor, 74
See also **Connected person**
apportionment of, 78
title to sue for, 73
See also **Liability**
factors relevant to assessment of
award of provisional damages for loss of future earnings, 76
relative working and pooling resources with deceased, 76
See also **Deductions and set-offs**
factors not relevant to assessment of
patrimonial gain or advantage accruing to relative from deceased or any other person by way of
settlement, 77
succession, 77
payments made as a result of the deceased's death by way of
benefit, 77
gratuity, 77
insurance money, 77
pension, 77
surviving spouse's private means, 77
widow's
prospects of remarriage, 77
remarriage, 72
method of assessment of
factors relevant to
age and expectation of life
of deceased, 78
of relative, 78, 292
contingencies, such as
divorce, 79, 292
early retirement, 79, 286, 291

generally, 79
illness, 79
promotion, 285
uncertainties in employment prospects, 300
unemployment, 79, 294
variations in amount of earnings, 79, 289, 291
expectation of working life of deceased, 78, 296
lump sum, 284, 285, 286, 287, 291, 296, 304
multiplier/multiplicand, 77
examples, 310
nature of See **Support**
See also **Interest on damages**

LUMP SUM, PENSION
See **Deductions and set-offs**
Loss of pension rights

LUMP SUM AWARDS
See **Awards of damages**
Loss of earnings

LUNG DISEASE
guidelines for the assessment of general damages for, 365
See also **Asthma**

MAINTENANCE
See **Deceased person's services**
Personal services

MARRIAGE
See **Loss of society**
Loss of support

MARRIAGE PROSPECTS
See **Loss of society**
Loss of support

MARRIAGE PROSPECTS, LOSS OF
See **Solatium**

MEDICAL SUPPLIES
See **Outlays and expenses**

MEDICAL TREATMENT
See **Outlays and expenses**

MIDDLE FINGER
See **Hand injuries**

MINOR HEAD INJURY
See **Head injuries**

MOBILITY ALLOWANCE
as listed benefit, 51
not deducted from damages, 38

MOBILITY COMPONENT OF DISABILITY LIVING ALLOWANCE
as listed benefit, 51
not deducted from damages, 38

MONEY
See **Foreign Currency**
Inflation

MORTALITY
multipliers calculated with allowance for, 9
See also **Ogden Tables, Tables 1-20**
multipliers calculated without allowance for, 10, 12
See also **Contingencies**
Ogden Tables, Tables 21 and 22
PNBA Tables

MOTHER
a member of deceased's immediate family, 67
a relative
of deceased, 73, 80, 83
of injured person, 57, 62

MOTHER IN LAW
a member of deceased's immediate family, 67
a relative
of deceased, 73, 80, 82
of injured person, 57, 62

MOTOR VEHICLE
See **Outlays and expenses**

MOTOR INSURERS' BUREAU
See **Interim payment of damages**

MULTIPLE INJURIES
See **Solatium**

MUSICAL ACTIVITY OR HOBBY, LOSS OF
See **Outlays and expenses**

MULTIPLICAND
See **Multiplier/multiplicand**

MULTIPLIERS
tables of
with allowance for male mortality
loss of earnings or support
to age 60
historic mortality, 114
projected mortality, 130
to age 65
historic mortality, 112
projected mortality, 128
loss of pension
from age 60

historic mortality, 120
projected mortality, 136
from age 65
historic mortality, 116
projected mortality, 132
pecuniary loss for life
historic mortality, 108
projected mortality, 124
with allowance for female mortality
loss of earnings or support
to age 60
historic mortality, 115
projected mortality, 131
to age 65
historic mortality, 113
projected mortality, 129
loss of pension
from age 60
historic mortality, 122
projected mortality, 138
from age 65
historic mortality, 118
projected mortality, 134
pecuniary loss for life
historic mortality, 110
projected mortality, 126
with no allowance for mortality
annual payments for fixed periods, 141, 147
future single payments, 140, 145
periodic multipliers, 149
selected
future inability to render personal services, 310
future outlays and expenses, 310
loss of deceased's services, 311
loss of future earnings, 308
loss of pension rights, 309
loss of support, 310
See also **Actuarial tables**

MULTIPLIER/MULTIPLICAND
multiplicand
represents annual loss or expense, 9
selection may reflect contingencies or imponderables, 9
multiplier
represents an appropriate number of years' purchase, 9
selection may reflect contingencies and other adjusting factors, 9
See also **Actuarial tables**
Annuity approach
Discount
Multipliers

NATIONAL HEALTH SERVICE
See **Deductions and set-offs**
Outlays and expenses

NATIONAL INSURANCE CONTRIBUTIONS
- hypothetical
  - deducted from loss of earnings, 40

NECESSARY SERVICES
- award for
  - application for
    - injured person, 56
    - injured person's executor, 56 See **Connected person** **Liability**
    - injured person's trustee in sequestration, 57
  - components of
    - reasonable remuneration for the necessary services, 59, 60
    - repayment of reasonable expenses incurred in connection therewith, 59, 60
  - requirement to separate from any other award for services, 58
  - title to sue for, 57
- factors relevant to assessment of
  - kinds of charges made for the kinds of services performed, 59
  - nature, quality and extent of services, 59
  - relative's lack of qualifications, 60
  - relative's prior earnings, 59
- method of assessment of
  - examples, 314
  - future services
    - factors relevant to
      - age and expectation of life
        - of injured person, 61
        - of relative, 61
      - contingencies, such as
        - divorce, 61
    - lump sum, 61
    - multiplier/multiplicand, 60
      - examples, 310
  - past services, 59
- nature of
  - household chores
    - bagging domestic coal, 275
    - changing bed linen, 59, 237, 249
    - chopping sticks, 242
    - cleaning, 59, 247
    - cooking, 59, 229, 237, 240, 245, 247, 251, 254, 275
    - driving, 217
    - gardening, 234, 255, 256, 257, 263, 279
    - grass-cutting, 59, 250, 251
    - hanging curtains, 283
    - hanging out the washing, 283
    - heavy lifting, 251, 267
    - hoovering, 225, 233, 275
    - housekeeping, 232, 237, 257
    - housework, 212, 219, 240, 245, 249, 251, 255, 273, 276, 277
    - ironing, 233, 237, 258
    - laundry, 237, 247
    - lifting the children, 225
    - lighting fires, 242, 275
    - making beds, 233

moving furniture, 225, 281
shopping, 219, 233, 245, 250, 251, 254, 255, 258, 267, 277
taking on visits, 250
walking the dog, 217
window-cleaning, 59, 233, 250, 277, 283
nursing and attendance
accompanying out of doors, 58, 204
applying lotion, 242
attending to shoes, 242
bathing, 58, 204, 217, 230, 242, 254, 264, 272, 274, 277, 280
care generally, 222, 254, 260
changing dressing, 257, 275
cleaning the mouth, 254
cutting up food, 58, 204, 281
disposing of urine, 272
dressing, 207, 217, 227, 230, 251, 272, 274, 275, 277, 280, 281
driving, 250, 254, 256, 274, 282
drying, 242, 245
feeding, 59, 207, 249, 264, 272, 274, 275, 280, 283
giving medication, 223
helping in and out of bath, 59, 227, 246, 250, 272
helping out of bed, 281
helping to avoid fall, 59
helping to move around the house, 217, 257
helping to rise after fall, 58
helping with personal toilet and hygiene, 207, 280, 281, 283
helping with shower, 245
helping with stairs, 59, 250, 272, 280
nursing generally, 223, 226, 230, 241, 254, 261
shaving, 58, 230, 274
sponging down, 254
washing hair, 254, 281
support
emotional, 59, 223, 259, 272, 275
psychological, 59, 223, 253, 273

NECK INJURIES
guidelines for the assessment of general damages for, 373

NEGATIVE LOSS
See **Loss**

NEPHEW
a relative
of deceased, 73, 80, 83
of injured person, 57, 62

NIECE
a relative
of deceased, 73, 80, 83
of injured person, 57, 62

NON-PECUNIARY LOSS
See **Loss**

NON-RECOUPABLE BENEFITS
See **Benefits**
Earnings

NOSE
See **Facial injuries**

NUMBER OF YEARS' PURCHASE
See **Multiplier/multiplicand**

NURSING
See **Outlays and expenses**
Necessary services

NURSING HOME
See **Deductions and expenses**
Outlays and expenses

OCCUPATIONAL SICK PAY
deducted from loss of earnings, 40

OGDEN TABLES
See **Actuarial tables**

OPPORTUNITY, LOSS OF
See **Loss of earnings**

ORTHOPAEDIC INJURIES
See **Achilles Tendon**
Ankle injuries
Arm injuries
Back injuries
Elbow injuries
Foot injuries
Hand injuries
Injuries to pelvis and hips
Knee injuries
Leg injuries
Neck injuries
Shoulder injuries
Toe injuries
Work related upper limb disorders
Wrist injuries

OUTLAYS AND EXPENSES
award for
application for, 49
injured person, 49
injured person's executor, 49 See also **Connected person**
Liability
injured person's trustee in sequestration, 50
See also **Family members**
factors relevant to assessment of
whether costs in fact incurred or likely to be incurred for medical treatment, 52
whether costs reasonably incurred

may be reasonable notwithstanding that treatment turns out to be unnecessary and useless, 52
may be reasonable for injured person to insist on being treated at home, 52
See also **Deductions and set-offs**
factors not relevant to assessment of
possibility of avoiding expenses by taking advantage of NHS facilities, 52
method of assessment of
future loss
factors relevant to
age and expectation of life of injured person, 54
contingencies, such as
uncertainties in respect of injured person's future medical condition, 55

goods and items, 54
heritable property, 53
services
examples, 314
lump sum, 54
multiplier/multiplicand, 54
examples, 310
past loss, 53
nature of
goods and items
aids, appliances and equipment, 50, 191, 238, 248, 269
central heating, 50, 248
clothing and dressing, 50, 191, 238, 269
computer equipment, 269
food, 50, 261
furnishings, 50, 248
heating, 50, 269
holidays and recreation, 50, 239
laundry, 50, 269
medical supplies, 50, 271
motor vehicle, 50, 191
running costs of home generally, 191, 239, 261
telephone, 50
transport, 50, 191, 231, 247, 248, 269, 280
wheelchair, 54
heritable property
adaptations, 50, 191, 239, 250, 269, 280
construction, 51
purchase, 51, 231
services
curatory, 50, 205, 210, 262
domestic assistance, 50, 189
medical treatment, 52, 231, 233
nursing (care and attendance), 50, 177, 182, 191, 205, 222, 231, 231, 239, 261, 269
residential care, 50, 210
See also **Interest on damages**

OVERLAPPING OF DAMAGES
avoidance of, 5
risk of, 5

OVERTIME
See **Earnings**

PAIN AND SUFFERING
See **Solatium**

PARALYSIS, INJURIES INVOLVING
See **Injuries involving paralysis**
See also **Back injuries**
Neck injuries

PARENT
See **Father**
Mother

PARENT-IN-LAW
See **Father-in-law**
Mother-in-law

PARTNER
no relevant claim for loss of earnings out of injuries suffered by, 37
See also **Earnings**

PAST LOSS
See **Loss**

PATRIMONIAL GAIN OR ADVANTAGE
See **Succession**

PAY
See **Earnings**
Severance pay
Sick pay

PAYMENTS
See **Benefits**
Benevolent payments
Consent orders for periodical payments
Deductions and set-offs
Earnings
Interim payment of damages
Support

PECUNIARY LOSS
See **Funeral expenses**
Loss of earnings
Loss of pension rights
Loss of support
Necessary services
Outlays and expenses

PELVIS, INJURIES TO HIPS AND
See **Injuries to pelvis and hips**

PENSION
contributions
hypothetical
deducted from loss of earnings, 40
repayment of
deducted from loss of pension rights, 47
nature of
not strictly speaking earnings but earned income, 46
type of
contractual (disability or incapacity)
deducted from loss of pension rights, 47
not deducted from loss of earnings, 41
death
not deducted from loss of support, 77
disablement
disablement pension
not deducted from damages, 38
disablement pension increase
not deducted from damages, 38
occupational
deducted from loss of pension rights, 47
state
not deducted from loss of earnings, 42
See also **Benefits**
Loss of pension rights

PERQUISITES
See **Earnings**

PERSONAL EXPENDITURE
See **Deductions and set-offs**

PERSONAL INJURIES
See **Executor**
Heads of damage

PERSONAL SERVICES
award for loss of injured person's
application for
injured person, 61
injured person's executor, 61 See also **Connected person**
Liability
injured person's trustee in sequestration, 62
requirement to separate from any other award for services, 63
title to sue for, 62
factors relevant to assessment of
cost of person reasonably employed to perform services, 64
estimated time expended on services, 64
method of assessment of
examples, 314
future services
factors relevant to assessment of
age and expectation of life
of injured person, 64
of relative, 64

change in nature of services over time, such as
childcare, 64
contingencies, such as
divorce, 64
lump sum, 64
multiplier/multiplicand, 64
examples, 310
past services, 64
nature of
childcare, 63, 237
housekeeping and maintenance
cleaning, 228, 262
cooking, 262
decorating, 280
gardening, 230, 254, 260, 267, 272, 274, 280, 281, 282
getting in the coal, 282
hanging out the washing, 228
household repairs, 280
housework, 219, 276, 277
laundry, 262
shopping, 219, 257, 277
window-cleaning, 228, 277, 280, 283

PNBA TABLES
See **Actuarial tables**

POSITIVE LOSS
See **Loss**

POST TRAUMATIC STRESS DISORDER
guidelines for the assessment of general damages for, 358

POSTHUMOUS CHILD
See **Child**

PRECEDENT
See **Comparable awards**

PRE-EXISTING
disability or condition, 6
weakness or vulnerability, 6
See also **Loss of earnings**

PREGNANCY
See **Reproductive system**

PRIVATE MEANS
See **Loss of support**
Solatium

PROBABILITY
See **Chances**
See also **Balance of probability**

PROFITS
See **Earnings**

PROMOTION
See **Contingencies**
Earnings
Loss of earnings
Loss of support
Support

PROVISIONAL DAMAGES
See **Awards of provisional damages**

PSYCHIATRIC DAMAGE GENERALLY
guidelines for the assessment of general damages for, 357
See also **Post traumatic stress disorder**

PSYCHOLOGICAL DAMAGE
See **Damage, Psychiatric**

PUBLIC AUTHORITY
See **Awards of provisional damages**
Interim payment of damages

PUBLIC CORPORATION
See **Awards of provisional damages**

PUBLIC EXPENSE
See **Deductions and set-offs**
Outlays and expenses

PUBLIC SECTOR SETTLEMENT
advantages and disadvantages, 19
definition, 17
guarantee by Minister of Crown, 18
incidence of tax, 18
See also **Structured settlement**

QUADRIPLEGIA
See **Injuries involving paralysis**

REBATE, TAX
deducted from loss of earnings, 41

RECOVERY OF BENEFITS
See **Benefits**

RECREATION
See **Outlays and expenses**

REDUCED EARNINGS ALLOWANCE
as listed benefit, 38
not deducted from damages, 38

REDUNDANCY
See **Earnings**
Loss of earnings
Supervening

RELATIVES
See **Aunt**
Brother
Cohabitant
Cousin
Daughter
Daughter-in-law
Father
Father-in-law
Former spouse
Grandchild
Grandparent
Mother
Mother-in-law
Nephew
Niece
Sister
Son
Son-in-law
Spouse
Uncle
See also **Executor**
Family members
Liability

REMUNERATION
from employment deducted from loss of earnings, 40
See also **Earnings**
Support

REPRODUCTIVE SYSTEM
guidelines for the assessment of general damages for injuries to
male
impotence, 368
infertility, 368
female
failed sterilisation leading to unwanted pregnancy, 369
infertility, 369

RESIDENTIAL CARE
See **Outlays and expenses**

RETIREMENT
age See **Loss of earnings**
benefit or pension
occupational
deducted from loss of pension rights, 47
state
not deducted from loss of earnings, 42
early See **Contingencies**

REVIEW OF AWARDS OF DAMAGES
See **Appeal**

RING FINGERS
See **Hand injuries**

RUNNING COSTS OF HOME
See **Outlays and expenses**

SALARY
See **Earnings**

SAVINGS
attributable to maintenance at public expense in hospital, nursing home or other institution deducted from loss of earnings, 41

SCARRING
See **Facial disfigurement**
Scarring to other parts of the body

SCARRING TO OTHER PARTS OF THE BODY
guidelines for the assessment of general damages for, 404

SCHEDULE OF DAMAGES (RECOVERY OF BENEFITS)
form of, 171
requirement to lodge in court
cost of care claim, 51
loss of earnings claim, 38
loss of mobility claim, 51

SELF-EMPLOYED
See **Earnings**

SENSES, INJURIES AFFECTING THE
See **Injuries affecting the senses**

SEQUESTRATION, TRUSTEE IN
See **Trustee in sequestration**

SERVICES
See **Deceased person's services**
Necessary services
Outlays and expenses
Personal services

SET-OFFS
See **Deductions and set-offs**

SETTLEMENT
See **Loss of support**

SETTLEMENT, PUBLIC SECTOR
See **Public sector settlement**

SETTLEMENT, STRUCTURED
See **Structured settlement**

SEVERANCE PAY
deducted from damages, 42

SEVERE DISABLEMENT ALLOWANCE
as listed benefit, 38
not deducted from damages, 38

SEXUAL ORGANS
See **Reproductive system**

SEXUAL POTENCY. LOSS OF
See **Solatium**

SHOCK, TRANSIENT
See **Solatium**

SHOPPING
See **Necessary services**
Personal services

SHOULDER INJURIES
guidelines for the assessment of general damages for, 378

SICK PAY
occupational
deducted from loss of earnings, 40
statutory
as listed benefit (for period ending 6 April 1994), 38
not deducted from damages, 38

SICKNESS BENEFIT
as listed benefit, 38
not deducted from damages, 38

SIGHT
See **Injuries affecting sight**

SMELL, LOSS OF
See **Impairment of taste and smell**

SOCIAL SECURITY BENEFITS
See **Benefits**

SOCIETY, LOSS OF
See **Loss of society**

SOLATIUM
assessment of,
generally as a single entity, 32
award of
application for
injured person, 31

injured person's executor, 31 See also **Connected person Liability**
injured person's trustee in sequestration, 32
See also **Family members**
components of
loss of amenities, such as
loss of career, 33
loss of congenial employment, 33
loss of holiday, 33
loss of leisure time, 33
loss of marriage prospects, 33
loss of musical activity or hobby, 33
loss of sexual potency, 33
loss of sporting activity or hobby, 33
loss of faculties, 32, 33
pain and suffering, 32, 33
from awareness of reduced expectation of life, 32
factors relevant to assessment of
age of injured person and period of life involved, 32, 33
failure to mitigate loss, 33
nature and consequences of injuries, 32, 33
absence of consequences not a bar to recovery, 33
anxiety, fear, grief or transient shock not personal injuries, 33
unaware pursuer may still recover, 33
pre-existing disability or condition, 6
pre-existing weakness or vulnerability, 6
supervening events, such as
accident, 6
illness or disease, 6
factors not relevant to assessment of
injured person's economic and social position, 33
method of assessment of
comparable awards
neighbouring jurisdiction's, 34
previous awards updated, 34
facts of case, 33, 34
judicial experience, 33, 34
number of injuries
multiple injuries, 34
single injuries, 34
See also **Interest on damages**

SOLE TRADER
See **Earnings**

SON
a member of deceased's immediate family, 67
a relative
of deceased, 73, 80, 83
of injured person, 57, 62

SON IN LAW
a member of deceased's immediate family, 67
a relative
of deceased, 73, 80, 83

of injured person, 57, 62

SORROW, GRIEF AND
See **Loss of society**

SPEECH, LOSS OF
See **Deafness**

SPLEEN
guidelines for the assessment of general damages for injuries to, 371

SPORTING ACTIVITY OR HOBBY, LOSS OF
See **Solatium**

SPOUSE
a member of deceased's immediate family, 67
a relative
of deceased, 73, 80, 83
of injured person, 57, 62
See also **Family members**

SPOUSE, FORMER
See **Former Spouse**

STATUTORY SICK PAY
See **Sick pay**

STEPCHILD
See **Child**

STERILISATION
See **Reproductive system**

STERILITY
See **Reproductive system**

STRUCTURED SETTLEMENT
advantages and disadvantages, 19
definition, 16
incidence of tax, 18
model, 166
See also **Public sector settlement**

SUCCESSION
See **Loss of support**

SUFFERING
See **Solatium**

SUPERANNUATION
See **Pension**

SUPERVENING
events, such as
accident, 6, 7, 46

illness or disease, 6, 7, 11, 43, 46
redundancy, 11, 43, 46
See also **Loss of earnings**

SUPPORT
form of
by deceased
money, 75
fluctuations in pay, 75
inflation, 75
increases in rate of pay, 75, 79
move to better paid job, 79
promotion, 79
nominal employment of relative, 75
other emolument, such as
tied cottage, 75
to injured person
emotional See **Necessary services**
psychological See **Personal services**
loss of See **Loss of support**
See also **Benefits**

TABLES
See **Actuarial tables**
Life tables

TASTE, LOSS OF
See **Impairment of taste and smell**

TAX
See **Deductions and set-offs**

TEETH
See **Facial injuries**

TELEPHONE
See **Outlays and expenses**

THUMB
See **Hand injuries**

TIED COTTAGE
See **Support**

TINNITUS
See **Deafness**

TOE INJURIES
guidelines for the assessment of general damages for
amputation, 396
other injuries, 397

TRANSPORT
See **Outlays and expenses**

TRAVEL EXPENSES
See **Loss of earnings**
Necessary services

TREATMENT, MEDICAL
See **Outlays and expenses**

TRUST FUND
See **Benevolent payments**

TRUSTEE IN SEQUESTRATION
title to sue of
for debtor's
solatium (in depending action), 32
loss of earnings, 37
loss of pension rights, 46
necessary services, 57
outlays and expenses, 50
personal services, 62

UNAWARE PURSUER
See **Solatium**

UNCLE
a relative
of deceased, 73, 80, 83
of injured person, 57, 62

UNDERTAKER'S ACCOUNT
See **Funeral expenses**

UNEMPLOYABILITY SUPPLEMENT
as listed benefit, 38
not deducted from damages, 38

UNEMPLOYMENT
See **Loss of earnings**

UNEMPLOYMENT BENEFIT
as listed benefit, 38
not deducted from damages, 38

UPPER LIMB DISORDERS, WORK-RELATED
See **Arm injuries**

VIBRATION WHITE FINGER
See **Hand injuries**

VULNERABILITY, PRE-EXISTING
See **Pre-existing**

WAGES, LOSS OF
See **Loss of earnings**

WASHING
See **Necessary services**
Personal services

WEAKNESS, PRE-EXISTING
See **Pre-existing**

WHITE FINGER
See **Hand injuries**

WIDOW
See **Spouse**

WIDOWER
See **Spouse**

WIFE
See **Spouse**

WIFE, FORMER
See **Former spouse**

WINDOW-CLEANING
See **Necessary services**
Personal services

WORK
See **Loss of earnings**

WORK-RELATED UPPER LIMB DISORDERS
See **Arm injuries**

WORKING LIFE
See **Loss of earnings**

WRIST INJURIES
guidelines for the assessment of general damages for, 381
See also **Arm injuries**